Engaging the
Doctrine
of Revelation

ENGAGING THE
DOCTRINE
OF REVELATION

*The Mediation of the Gospel
through Church and Scripture*

MATTHEW LEVERING

Baker Academic

a division of Baker Publishing Group
Grand Rapids, Michigan

Published by Baker Academic
a division of Baker Publishing Group
P.O. Box 6287, Grand Rapids, MI 49516-6287
www.bakeracademic.com

Printed in the United States of America

Library of Congress Cataloging-in-Publication Data is on file at the Library of Congress, Washington, DC.

ISBN 978-0-8010-4924-8

Scripture quotations are from the Catholic Edition of the Revised Standard Version of the Bible, copyright © 1965, 1966 National Council of the Churches of Christ in the United States of America. Used by permission. All rights reserved.

14 15 16 17 18 19 20   7 6 5 4 3 2 1

To Guy Mansini, OSB

Contents

Acknowledgments

This book is dedicated to Guy Mansini, in gratitude for all the help he has given me over the years and for the help he gave me on this book. Driven by love for Jesus Christ and blessed with extraordinary intellectual gifts, Guy shares his theological wisdom with generosity and humility. Monk, parish priest, teacher, and forester, Guy is above all a theological master.

In writing this book I have incurred many debts. Peter Bellini of United Theological Seminary gave me the basic idea for chapter 1 during a lunch that we shared. At a conference on "Reading God's Word: Ratzinger's Erasmus Lecture a Generation Later" at Ave Maria University I gave a portion of chapter 2; many thanks to Gregory Vall, Michael Dauphinais, and Fr. Matthew Lamb for the invitation to speak. An earlier version of chapter 3 was delivered as "Priesthood and Revelation: Addressing the Problem of Priestly Rivalry," the 2013 Thomas Lecture at Saint Meinrad Seminary and School of Theology. Thanks to Denis Robinson, OSB, Keith Lemna, Guy Mansini, Kyle Rodden, and others for their hospitality and the fruitful discussion that helped to clarify my thoughts. Chapter 4 will appear in a Festschrift for John Webster, who has done me many kindnesses over the years. Part of this chapter was delivered as the Aquinas Lecture at Blackfriars, Oxford, in January 2013; thanks to Simon Gaine, OP, to his Dominican brethren, and to William Carroll for the invitation and hospitality.

Chapter 5 was prepared for the Tradition Conference in July 2013 at the University of Notre Dame Australia; many thanks to my Australian friends (new and old), including Bishop Anthony Fisher, OP, Hayden Ramsey, Paul Morrissey, Robert Tilley, Nigel Zimmermann, and Tracey Rowland. Bishop Fisher generously shared with me his keynote lecture, "Catholic Moral Tradition," from which I benefited in chapters 5 and 6. William Portier helped me with sources for chapter 5. I delivered part of chapter 6 at the Christian Systematic Theology Section at the 2012 meeting of the American Academy of Religion. Thanks to James Ernest and David Stubbs for the invitation and to Khaled Anatolios, my teacher and a mentor since my graduate student days, for his helpful comments.

An earlier version of chapter 8 was presented as "God and Greek Philosophy in Contemporary Biblical Scholarship" to the Development of Early Trinitarian Theology Session convened by Mark Weedman at the Society of Biblical Literature's 2009 meeting and later published under the same title in *Journal of Theological Interpretation* 4 (2010): 169–85; thanks to Joel B. Green, editor of the *Journal of Theological Interpretation*. I presented a different version of chapter 8 to a group of faculty and students at Keble College, Oxford, in January 2013, at the kind invitation of Markus Bockmuehl, and I benefited greatly from the vigorous discussion.

As the manuscript began to take shape, Peter Bellini offered valuable comments on chapter 1; Darren Sarisky provided keen insight into chapters 2 and 4; Andrew Meszaros corrected chapters 5 and 6; Aaron Pidel, SJ, offered suggestions for chapter 7; and Michael Allen and Scott Swain helped with chapter 8. The help from these friends and scholars made the end result much better. Guy Mansini and Stewart Clem read and critiqued the entire manuscript, and I owe them gratitude for their generous and helpful criticisms. Dave Nelson, in his editorial role at Baker Academic, expressed interest in the book at an early stage and was tremendously encouraging and helpful—including reading and commenting on a full draft—as the book moved toward publication.

Elizabeth Farnsworth, a talented doctoral student at the University of Dayton, did the bibliography and helped me acquire books and articles during the writing of this book. She also spearheaded the arrangements for the two conferences hosted by my Center for Scriptural Exegesis, Philosophy, and Doctrine at the University of Dayton, one of which, "*Dei Verbum* at 50: Toward a Clarification of the Inspiration of Scripture," was greatly helpful for chapter 7.

Let me specially thank Fr. Robert Barron, rector of Mundelein Seminary, for bringing me to Mundelein Seminary as the Perry Family Foundation Professor of Theology, through the wonderful generosity of Jim and Molly Perry. Mundelein Seminary is an extraordinary place to work and worship.

To my wife, Joy, how blessed I am to be your husband. Surely moving our whole family to Mundelein less than two weeks after we accepted the job was one of your greatest feats. God be praised for you, for our marriage, and for our children. To our Levering and Moretz extended families, deep gratitude.

Sadly, my beloved mother-in-law, Ann Moretz, died on October 17, 2013. Dear God, we commend Ann to you, and we rejoice in her lifelong witness to Jesus Christ.

This book has its source in my urgent desire to know our Creator, infinite life and love, the one who sustains us and gives us eternal life with him, for which I am eager. "O God, thou art my God, I seek thee, my soul thirsts for thee; my flesh faints for thee, as in a dry and weary land where no water is. So I have looked upon thee in the sanctuary, beholding thy power and glory. Because thy steadfast love is better than life, my lips will praise thee. So I will bless thee as long as I live; I will lift up my hands and call on thy name" (Ps. 63:1–4).

Introduction

The Letter to the Hebrews proclaims, "God spoke of old to our fathers by the prophets," and, "In these last days he has spoken to us by a Son" (Heb. 1:1–2).[1] How, then, do human beings today ("in these last days") truly receive this merciful revelation? Since "God spoke of old to our fathers by the prophets" and "has spoken to us by a Son," God evidently intended for his revelatory words and deeds to be mediated by the people formed by his covenantal love. Where and in what ways does this mediation take place so that humans in all generations can receive the fullness of the gospel?

The evident answers are the Church and Scripture, or Scripture and the Church. The Letter to the Hebrews itself mediates to us God's revelation, as does Scripture as a whole. But it is not possible to conceive of Scripture, at any stage of its composition and collection into a canonical unity, outside of the liturgical community of the people of God. The Lutheran theologian Carl Braaten rightly points out that "there is no gospel apart from the church and its sacramental life. . . . There is no such thing as churchless Christianity, for that would posit the possibility of relating personally to Christ without

---

1. See the commentary on Heb. 1:1–2, paired with 2 Pet. 1:19–21 and 1 Cor. 2:11–13, in Edith Humphrey, *Scripture and Tradition*, 70–73. Humphrey argues that

> we should understand the "we" and "us" of 2 Peter 1, Hebrews 1, and 1 Corinthians 2 as the communal "we"—apostolic insights that have been clarified and passed on in the Christian community. In all this, the verbal word, the written word, and Jesus the Word come together, imparted internally among and within the community. To understand the revelation of God involves the vivifying power of the Holy Spirit within those who are teaching such mysteries and within those who are receiving them. Reception is not a private matter, but it is at once personal and communal, pertaining to the "spirit" in each person and pertaining also to the "Spirit" who has been imparted to each as well as to the body of believers. (73)

being a member of his body, the Church."[2] Just as Israel's Scriptures cannot be conceived outside of the worshiping community, so also the New Testament writings make sense only in light of Jesus's eschatological reordering of Israel around himself (the messianic King and new Temple) by calling the Twelve and giving them the mission of making "disciples of all nations" (Matt. 28:19). It is in this community of believers that divine revelation has been received, enacted, and handed down.

Yet, is this mediation a faithful one, so that believers are now able to "worship the Father in spirit and truth" (John 4:23)? Indeed, James Dunn draws attention to the fact that the New Testament is already "tradition," and he invites us to consider "what the tradition process has involved and still involves."[3] He finds that "while the core and substance of the tradition remains stable through time and multiple retellings, the forms it takes are diverse and variable."[4] In Dunn's view the tradition process that we find in the New Testament continues throughout the history of the Church. Along similar lines, Francis Watson has identified a "precanonical phase" in which "gospels proliferate unchecked," with each adding "its own distinctive material while selecting, interpreting, and reinterpreting material derived directly from its predecessors."[5] Indeed, for Watson, cognizant of the early Church's privileging of quite different texts in different local churches, "The fourfold gospel represents a decision about community order and organization rather than a historical, literary, or theological judgement about the nature of earlier gospel literature."[6] But for

2. Braaten, "Problem of Authority in the Church," 55; see also Robert Jenson's *Canon and Creed*. As Jenson states, "In some academic and ecclesial circles, canon and creed are even assumed to be in competition for our loyalty. The Scripture is regarded as a deposit of ancient Israelite and early Christian 'religion'; and the creeds are thought to be the result of later and alienating 'philosophical' influences. . . . Thus it is widely supposed that we can cling to Scripture or cling to church doctrine, or possibly to both in different contexts, but cannot cling to both with the same grasp" (2). For a particularly rich meditation on the church, tradition, and Scripture, see Dumitru Staniloae, *Experience of God*, chap. 4: "The Church as the Instrument for Preserving Revelation."

3. Dunn, *The Oral Gospel Tradition*, 353. See the valuable discussion provided by D. H. Williams, *Retrieving the Tradition and Renewing Evangelicalism*, chaps. 2 and 3.

4. Dunn, *The Oral Gospel Tradition*, 360. Admittedly, Dunn thinks that this stable core allows for profound error in the retellings, so that the doctrinal traditions of the Christian churches are not of much value, in terms of referring to realities, except insofar as they contain the stable core. For Dunn, the content of this stable core does not include the worship of Christ (or Christ's divinity): see Dunn, *Did the First Christians Worship Jesus?* The Church's doctrinal tradition, like canonical Scripture itself, does not do away with theological diversity, but it does make judgments that establish boundaries and paths for Christian reflection on faith and morals (much like the canonization of Scripture does). At stake is the intelligibility of the stable core as divine revelation.

5. Watson, *Gospel Writing*, 413.

6. Ibid., 407. Watson might better have said "as well as" instead of "rather than." For the significance of eyewitness testimony, see Bauckham, *Jesus and the Eyewitnesses*; Bauckham,

my purposes Dunn's insight suffices to frame the issue; namely, our ability to hear and participate in divine revelation ("the core and substance of the tradition") is inseparable from the covenantal community's "tradition process."[7]

The New Testament itself recognizes this. After Jesus's ascension, the community of disciples, gathered in the upper room in Jerusalem, takes center stage. After Pentecost, the community spends its days "attending the temple together" and liturgically "breaking bread" (Acts 2:46) as commanded by Jesus. Paul receives "a revelation of Jesus Christ" (Gal. 1:12), but he also takes care to confer with Peter, James, and John. The community transmits its faith under the leadership of bishops and elders commissioned by the apostles to "care for God's church" (1 Tim. 3:5) and to "attend to the public reading of scripture, to preaching, to teaching" (1 Tim. 4:13). They are to "maintain the traditions" (1 Cor. 11:2), not least by celebrating the Eucharist as a communion in Christ's body and blood (1 Cor. 10–11), a communion that makes the Church into "one body" (1 Cor. 10:17), the "body of Christ" (1 Cor. 12:27). Jesus promises to be with the community of believers "to the close of the age" (Matt. 28:20) and to guide them by his Spirit "into all truth" (John 16:13).

Put simply, we do not have divine revelation without faithful mediation—and the mediation of God's words and deeds that we find in canonical Scripture is inseparable from the mediation of the covenantal community. The purpose of this book, then, is to explore the missional, liturgical, and doctrinal forms of the Church's mediation of divine revelation and to appreciate Scripture's inspiration and truth in this context. The first chapter examines the Church as a missional community formed by the revelatory missions of the Son and Holy Spirit. The second chapter argues that the liturgy is the primary context for the proclamation, interpretation, and enactment of God's revelation. The third chapter explores the hierarchical priesthood as an instrument of unity in the mediation of divine revelation. The fourth chapter underscores that the

---

Testimony of the Beloved Disciple. See also Byrskog, "A 'Truer' History: Reflections on Richard Bauckham, *Jesus and the Eyewitnesses: The Gospels as Eyewitness Testimony*"; Matera, "The Jesus of Testimony"; Seitz, "Accordance: The Scriptures of Israel as Eyewitness."

7. Robert Jenson points out that in the second century AD, "the telephone-game problem became apparent. A living memory of the Lord could no longer be so immediately dispositive. How do we know what does or does not belong to the message? How do we know if we heard rightly from our predecessors? How do we find the direction and limits of newly possible or demanded interpretation?" (*Canon and Creed*, 4). Indeed, this problem was already present in Israel prior to Christ. For Jenson, it was in the second century that "the Spirit—or so again most of the ecumene has believed—granted touchstones of the true gospel and just so institutions of the community's historical self-identity. Three linked developments are commonly noted: the formation of a specifically Christian scriptural canon of Old and New Testaments, increased attention to explicit statements of the faith, and the appearance of a sacramentally ordered church governance with special responsibility for continuity of teaching and life: the episcopate" (5).

gospel cannot be separated from the Church's councils and creeds. The fifth chapter engages the Church's handing on of divine revelation in Tradition. The sixth chapter focuses on the development of doctrine that occurs as the Church's understanding of divine revelation deepens under the guidance of the Holy Spirit. The seventh chapter discusses the truth of inspired Scripture, with a focus on the question of historical reference. The eighth and final chapter examines the contributions of Hellenistic philosophical culture to the communication of divine revelation in Scripture's portrait of the living God.

In my view, these eight chapters comprise the foundational elements of the mediation of divine revelation in the Church and in Scripture. Each chapter, however, treats an area of intense debate, not only between Protestants and Catholics but also among Catholics themselves. In dialogue with opposing views, each chapter argues that the Church (and/or Scripture) effectively mediates divine revelation under the guidance of Christ and his Spirit. In making my case, I draw extensively upon Scripture, as well as upon theologians such as Origen, Augustine, Thomas Aquinas, John Henry Newman, Alexander Schmemann, Hans Urs von Balthasar, and Joseph Ratzinger. I should note that none of the chapters is comprehensive in the sense of a synthetic survey. Instead, guided by the Second Vatican Council's Dogmatic Constitution on Divine Revelation, *Dei Verbum*,[8] each chapter engages a portion of the ongoing debate.

This book stands against "ecclesiastical fall narratives," which call into question the very possibility of truthful mediation of divine revelation. We cannot cordon off the truth of the gospel (let alone Scripture or its interpretation) from the truthfulness of the Church, both because Scripture identifies the Church as the Spirit-filled interpreter of revelation and because historical study shows that scriptural texts and canonical Scripture itself are inextricably

---

8. The First Vatican Council's Dogmatic Constitution on the Catholic Faith, *Dei Filius*, complements the emphases of *Dei Verbum* by focusing on the relationship between supernatural revelation, faith, and reason. *Dei Filius* also reaffirms the teachings of the Council of Trent regarding Scripture and Tradition:

> This supernatural revelation, according to the belief of the universal church, as declared by the sacred council of Trent, is contained in written books and unwritten traditions, which were received by the apostles from the lips of Christ himself, or came to the apostles by the dictation of the holy Spirit, and were passed on as it were from hand to hand until they reached us. . . . Now since the decree on the interpretation of holy scripture, profitably made by the council of Trent, with the intention of constraining rash speculation, has been wrongly interpreted by some, we renew that decree and declare its meaning to be as follows: that in matters of faith and morals, belonging as they do to the establishing of christian doctrine, that meaning of holy scripture must be held to be the true one, which holy mother church held and holds, since it is her right to judge of the true meaning and interpretation of holy scripture. (*Dei Filius*, chap. 3, 806)

With respect to our reception of revelation, *Dei Filius* emphasizes that the Holy Spirit's gift of supernatural faith enables us to believe.

embedded in the covenantal community. As a theological study of the mediation of divine revelation, the book complements other studies of revelation that focus on topics such as faith, prophecy, miracles, the perception of revelation, the development of the biblical canon, and so forth.[9]

Catholic Theology of Revelation since Vatican II: A Brief Sketch

Before proceeding, however, let me situate my approach on the broader map of contemporary discussions of the doctrine of revelation. Contemporary Catholic theology of revelation enjoys the Second Vatican Council (1962–1965) as its touchstone.[10] As a youthful theological advisor to Cardinal Josef Frings of Cologne, Joseph Ratzinger played a major role in formulating the majority response to the preparatory Theological Commission's *Schema Constitutionis dogmaticae de fontibus Revelationis*.[11] Ratzinger later described this *Schema* as "a canonization of Roman school theology," and his summary of its contents identifies the central challenges facing the doctrine of revelation today. "All the relevant questions were decided in a purely defensive spirit: the greater extent of tradition in comparison with Scripture, a largely verbalistic conception of the idea of inspiration, the narrowest interpretation of inerrancy ('in qualibet re religiose vel profana'), a conception of the historicity of the Gospels that suggested that there were no problems etc."[12] In the view of Ratzinger and

9. On the perception of revelation, see especially Hans Urs von Balthasar, *Glory of the Lord*, especially vol. 1, *Seeing the Form*, as well as his *Theo-Drama*, especially vol. 1, *Prolegomena*. For a succinct discussion of Balthasar's theology of revelation as the dramatic manifestation of God's glory in the kenotic form of Jesus Christ, see Chapp, "Revelation."

10. On *Dei Verbum* and its reception, from the perspective of scholars who came of age in the 1960s and who were significantly influenced by the *nouvelle théologie*, see Daley, "Knowing God in History and in the Church"; F. Martin, "Some Aspects of Biblical Studies since Vatican II"; F. Martin, "Revelation and Its Transmission"; Farkasfalvy, "Inspiration and Interpretation"; Scheffczyk, "Sacred Scripture"; Vanhoye, "Reception in the Church."

11. See especially Wicks, "Six Texts by Prof. Joseph Ratzinger"; Wicks, "Vatican II on Revelation." For the *Schema* and the response to it, see also Daley, "Knowing God in History and in the Church," 344–47; Dulles, "Revelation, Scripture, and Tradition"; Farkasfalvy, *Inspiration and Interpretation*, 168–71; O'Malley, *What Happened at Vatican II*, 141–52.

12. Ratzinger, "Dogmatic Constitution on Divine Revelation," 159. For the "Roman school" on inspiration, see, for example, Billot, *De Inspiratione*; Bea, *De Inspiratione*; Höpfl and Gut, *Introductio Generalis*. Ratzinger's essay avoids the exaggerations that one finds in more triumphalistic accounts of the Second Vatican Council, such as Enzo Bianchi's claim that "after centuries in exile the word of God once more occupies its central place in the life of the Catholic Church" ("Centrality of the Word of God," 115). Bianchi goes on to say, more soberly but still without documentation regarding actual lay piety and with a seeming animus toward doctrine, that "it is true, of course, that the Catholic Church had always lived by the word of God. But inasmuch as habitual familiarity with the scriptures was reserved to clerics and specialists, the general situation was in fact one in which the centrality of the word was eclipsed, dimmed, as

others, the *Schema*'s approach largely ignored the crucial historical questions that needed answering. Ratzinger thought that had the Council Fathers accepted the *Schema*, they would have been shutting down the effort to address the Enlightenment's historical challenges.[13]

What were these historical challenges? As Ratzinger says, the main one was that "the sacred books, believed to be the work of a very few authors to whom God had directly dictated his words, suddenly appeared as a work expressive of an entire human history, which had grown layer by layer throughout millennia, a history deeply interwoven with the religious history of surrounding peoples."[14] A similar situation held for the Church's tradition and development of doctrine: "Liturgical forms and customs, dogmatic formulations thought to have arisen with the apostles, now appeared as products of complicated processes of growth within the womb of history. And the very human factors in this growth were becoming increasingly evident."[15]

---

it were, by ecclesiastical traditions and a system of doctrinal and disciplinary mediations that intervened between the consciousness of the faithful and the sacred scriptures, which served only in a formal sense as the criterion for the validity or invalidity of the life of the Church" (115). Bianchi's article includes valuable insights nonetheless, including his warning against "a neo-Marcionist choice of some biblical texts and rejection of others" and his insistence on "the fact that the liturgy and prayer are the authentic and truly fruitful context for the word and that only in union with the Church as a whole can a full understanding of the scriptures be achieved" (135).

13. Thus Komonchak comments, "The Council can be read as an acceptance by the Church of the challenges of historical consciousness: acceptance of the need and role of critical history; a new awareness of and appreciation for cultural and historical diversity; a greater sense of individual and collective responsibility for the future of humanity. Catholic theology could not but be affected at its roots. The reign of neo-scholasticism ended with astonishing speed. History, social science, and hermeneutics became integral dimensions of the theological enterprise" ("Local Realization of the Church," 87). See also de la Potterie, "History and Truth," for a position on "truth-as-revelation" (98) sensitive to the twin problems of historicist and Hegelian understandings of history; and, for the way in which the Church's acceptance "of the challenges of historical consciousness" was molded by desire for a restored unity of Christ and culture, Reno's "Rahner the Restorationist."

14. Ratzinger, *Theological Highlights of Vatican II*, 148. For background to this development, see Legaspi, *Death of Scripture and the Rise of Biblical Studies*. Legaspi focuses on the contributions made by the German scholar Johann David Michaelis (1717–1791), although historical-critical work has been ongoing at least since the Renaissance. Legaspi helpfully points us to the critique of Michaelis's approach offered by Johann Georg Hamann (1730–1788), who questioned "the internal coherence of a method that contextualized the Bible in purely human terms" (Legaspi, *Death of Scripture and the Rise of Biblical Studies*, 161). At stake is what notion of "history" we bring to our biblical exegesis: Is it the providential and Christological-pneumatological view of "history" taught by the Bible, or is it a notion of "history" shorn of God? See also along these lines Ratzinger, *Jesus of Nazareth: From the Baptism*, xi–xxiv; Ratzinger, "Biblical Interpretation in Conflict."

15. Ratzinger, *Theological Highlights of Vatican II*, 148. See also Ratzinger's "On the Status of the Church and Theology Today," 379–82, where he describes the background to *Gaudium et Spes*.

Thus Ratzinger and many others rejoiced when in fall 1962 Pope Paul VI removed the *Schema* from the Council's agenda and instead created a "Mixed Commission," which included Cardinal Frings, to oversee the revision of the *Schema*. When in 1964 serious work began on the text that was to become *Dei Verbum*, a subcommission was appointed that included Ratzinger, Yves Congar, Alois Grillmeier, Karl Rahner, and others of generally like mind.[16]

The approach to divine revelation that informs *Dei Verbum* can be seen in the work of the Jesuit theologian René Latourelle. Born nine years before Ratzinger, Latourelle published his *Théologie de la Révélation* in 1963, and in 1966 an expanded edition appeared in English.[17] Latourelle recognizes that revelation "is closely bound up with many other realities, such as history, Incarnation, Church, light of faith, the economy of signs (miracles) which accompany or constitute revelation."[18] He focuses on Jesus Christ, who is the incarnate Son of God, and on the faith-filled Church that lives in history. Along these lines, Latourelle states that "we can say that history is revelation, that Christ is revelation in person, that the light of faith is inner revelation, that the Church is concrete revelation, that miracles are a revelation of accomplished salvation."[19] He emphasizes three categories for understanding revelation: word, testimony, and encounter. These three are joined intimately together; for example, a "word"

16. For further historical background to *Dei Verbum*, see Wicks, "*Dei Verbum* Developing"; Wicks, "*Dei Verbum* under Revision"; as well as more specialized articles by Wicks cited in these two pieces. Wicks makes use of diaries and recollections of the Council by notable *periti* including Yves Congar, Henri de Lubac, Umberto Betti, and Gérard Philips. See Congar, *My Journal of the Council*; de Lubac, *Carnets du concile*; Betti, *Diario del concilio*; Betti, *La dottrina del Concilio Vaticano*; Philips, *Carnets conciliaires de Mgr. Gérard Philips*.

17. See Latourelle, *Theology of Revelation*. The English edition has a final chapter on *Dei Verbum*. From the same time period, see also Moran, *Theology of Revelation*; Rahner and Ratzinger, *Revelation and Tradition*. Ratzinger's essay in *Revelation and Tradition* has been reprinted as "Question of the Concept of Tradition." See also Ratzinger, *Theology of History in St. Bonaventure*, 64–69. Discussing Ratzinger's perspective, W. Wright observes:

Revelation, then, involves both the objective content of the Word of God and its subjective reception in believers. . . . The ecclesial reception and interpretation of the realities of Jesus's life can be regarded as essential to revelation because of the presence of the Word both in the life of Jesus and in the Church and believers by faith. The process of ecclesial reception and interpretation in faith of biblical realities, evident in the New Testament traditions of the institution of the Eucharist, can be extended analogously to the post-biblical Church. The non-identity of revelation and Scripture, the fact that the reality of revelation is more than Scripture, and the presence of the indwelling Word in the Church and believers by faith all create the space for the post-biblical articulation of revelation's contents in the Church's dogmatic formulae. ("Pre-Gospel Traditions and Post-critical Interpretation," 1025–26)

See also Canty, "Bonaventurian Resonances"; F. Martin, "Joseph Ratzinger"; Bellandi, *Fede cristiana*.

18. Latourelle, *Theology of Revelation*, 313.

19. Ibid.

in this sense has a specific content, addresses or calls another person, and un-veils something of the interiority of the speaker. As Latourelle says, "Word is primarily an *interpersonal* encounter."[20] As revealed by his word, God "wants to be a *Me* addressing *You*, in an interpersonal and living relationship, with a view towards communication, dialogue, sharing."[21] God's word reveals that he is love; his word is love. God's love appears especially in God's sharing knowledge about himself with us. Thus Latourelle states, "The mystery of the Trinity, primarily, is the divine secret par excellence, the secret of divine intimacy, known only to the three Divine Persons, for only they make up this secret. . . . In revealing this secret, God initiates man into what is most intimate in God: the mystery of his own life, the heart of his personal subsistence."[22] In teaching us about his triune life, God invites us to share in his life as friends.

In the history of salvation, prophets and apostles give testimony to God's word; and Christ preeminently gives testimony. Latourelle remarks, "This testimony the Church receives, preserves, and protects, but also proposes, explains, interprets, assimilates, and grows to *understand* more and more."[23] Even the revelatory activity of the holy Trinity can be conceived in terms of testimony. The Son gives testimony to the Father, but the Father too testifies to the Son in many ways—by testifying at Christ's baptism, by raising Christ, and by drawing people to faith in Christ. Similarly the Son gives testimony to the Holy Spirit, and the Spirit comes to testify to the Son. Latourelle observes, "There are three who reveal or give testimony and these three are one. The testimony is a secret bond between eternity and time, between heaven and earth."[24] The testimony of the apostles to their intimacy with Christ shows that the Church is established upon "an initiation to the personal mystery which is he himself [Christ]."[25] Latourelle emphasizes that revelation must be understood as a communication between persons: "Persons are not problems which can be enclosed within a formula and solved in an equation. Persons can be known only by revelation. We have access to personal intimacy only through the free testimony of the person. And persons testify to themselves only under the inspiration of love."[26] Divine revelation abounds in truth content,

---

20. Ibid., 316. Along similar lines, see Kuntz's study of Old Testament theophanies, *Self-Revelation of God*.

21. Latourelle, *Theology of Revelation*, 318. For a similar perspective on revelation and faith, see Ratzinger, *Offenbarungsverständnis*, especially 88–102.

22. Latourelle, *Theology of Revelation*, 319.

23. Ibid., 320.

24. Ibid., 321.

25. Ibid., 323.

26. Ibid. It would be a mistake to follow this path to the exclusion of human knowledge of God by natural reason. On this point see, for example, White, "Toward a Post-Secular, Post-Conciliar

but this content is not merely impersonal facts about God known outside the realm of living faith, hope, and love.

In comparison to Latourelle's book, as well as to comparable Eastern Orthodox approaches such as that of Dumitru Staniloae's *Revelation and the Knowledge of God* (published in 1978 as the first volume of his *Dogmatic Theology*), the leading Catholic treatments of divine revelation in the decade following the Council sound a different and, all too frequently, a discordant note. [27] In *God the Future of Man* (1968) and *The Understanding of Faith* (1974), for example, Edward Schillebeeckx describes his decision to do theology hermeneutically and critically by reconceiving all doctrine on the basis of a new liberative praxis (broadly modeled by Jesus) that anticipates the One who is coming. Schillebeeckx breaks decisively with the approach of his earlier two-volume collection of essays, *Revelation and Theology*, essays that had been

---

Thomistic Philosophy"; Clarke, "Is a Natural Theology Still Viable?" Quoting Vatican I's *Dei Filius*, *Dei Verbum* affirms, "The sacred Synod professes that 'God, the first principle and last end of all things, can be known with certainty from the created world, by the natural light of human reason' (cf. Rom. 1:20). It teaches that it is to his revelation that we must attribute the fact 'that those things, which in themselves are not beyond the grasp of human reason, can, in the present condition of the human race, be known by all men with ease, with firm certainty, and without the contamination of error'" (*Dei Verbum*, §6, 752–53).

27. Staniloae's book appeared in English as *The Experience of God*. In this book, Staniloae first treats natural revelation of "the supreme Personal reality" (9) and then explores how "in supernatural revelation, God makes himself known clearly as person, inasmuch as he calls and sends out a particular person to a particular human community" (24). He succinctly treats God's supernatural acts in salvation history, and he observes that "the truly new and final period is inaugurated by the extraordinary supernatural acts of Jesus Christ" (26). Regarding Scripture and tradition, Staniloae observes insightfully:

> The Church is the milieu in which the content of Scripture or of revelation is imparted through tradition. Scripture or revelation needs tradition as a means of activating their content, and they need the Church as the practicing subject of tradition and the milieu where the content of Scripture or of revelation is imparted. But the Church also needs Scripture in order to be quickened through it and grow in the knowledge and experience of Christ, and to apply the Scripture more and more richly in her own life through tradition. (54)

Regarding the Church, Staniloae comments further:

> As revelation incorporated and lived out by a human community, the Church herself is a part of revelation, namely, the point where revelation has its final end and begins to bear fruit. In his resurrection and ascension as man, the Son of God had to reach the endpoint of his work of salvation and revelation so that he might send his Spirit through whom he imparts to men his own final state or revelation and might, thus, found the Church simultaneously with the descent of the Spirit into men. . . . Revelation gives birth to the Church as the concrete and continuing means through which the humanity saved in Christ extends outwards in time and space. With this in view, the Church gives rise to the full organizing of her own essential structures, a work carried out and put into practice by tradition at its beginning, but described afterwards only in part within the Scripture of the New Testament. By preserving apostolic tradition in this way, the Church has thereby also preserved the integrity of revelation, even though, on the other hand, she is herself the work of revelation. (56)

at the cutting edge of Catholic theological discourse during the two decades over which they were written. Somewhat similarly, James Burtchaell's *Catholic Theories of Biblical Inspiration Since 1810: A Review and Critique* (1969) concludes with respect to the inspiration of Scripture that "this has been an unhappy controversy" and that "too many men struggled for too many years to such meagre advantage." Another representative work, Nicholas Lash's *Change in Focus: A Study of Doctrinal Change and Continuity* (1973), argues that new creeds will be needed to update and reenvision dogmatic formulae.

In 1983 Avery Dulles's *Models of Revelation* appeared, rooted in research undertaken in the 1970s and demonstrating a keen awareness of current trends. The first part of Dulles's book divides theories of revelation into five "models": propositional doctrine (the neoscholastics, Carl F. H. Henry), salvation history (Oscar Cullmann, Jean Daniélou, Wolfhart Pannenberg), inner experience (Friedrich Schleiermacher, George Tyrrell, William James), dialectical presence (Karl Barth, Rudolf Bultmann), and new awareness or transformed consciousness (Pierre Teilhard de Chardin, Karl Rahner, Paul Tillich).[28] Dulles indicates the strengths and weaknesses of each approach without fully agreeing with any of them.

In his constructive theological section (part 2 of the book), Dulles develops a "symbolic approach" to revelation, indebted to Karl Rahner's theology of symbol. Dulles explains that "revelation precedes faith inasmuch as, before anyone can believe, there must be symbols wherein God expresses what he is, and wills to be, for the world. These symbols, before their meaning is understood and accepted, are virtual revelation."[29] In this sense, revelation has priority, but

---

28. See also H. Richard Niebuhr, *Meaning of Revelation*, especially his nuanced account of the anthropocentrism of Schleiermacher and Ritschl. For Niebuhr, "because God and faith belong together the standpoint of the Christian theologian must be in the faith of the Christian community, directed toward the God of Jesus Christ. Otherwise his standpoint will be that of some other community with another faith and another god. There is no neutral standpoint and no faithless situation from which approach can be made to that which is inseparable from faith" (37). Niebuhr seeks to highlight the experiential and personal dimension of revelation, its existential immediacy (thereby downgrading the historical mediation of revelation), without falling into anthropocentrism or neglecting the centrality of Jesus Christ:
> Revelation means the moment in our history through which we know ourselves to be known from beginning to end, in which we are apprehended by the knower; it means the self-disclosing of that eternal knower. . . . What this means for us cannot be expressed in the impersonal ways of creeds or other propositions but only in responsive acts of a personal character. We acknowledge revelation by no third person proposition, such as that there is a God, but only in the direct confession of the heart, "Thou art my God." (152–54)

Why "responsive acts of a personal character" should exclude "creeds or other propositions," however, is unclear.

29. Dulles, *Models of Revelation*, 279. See also his *Revelation Theology*. It is difficult to understand exactly what Dulles means by invoking "symbols wherein God expresses what he

in another sense, says Dulles, faith has priority because the symbols provided by God yield their meaning only to seekers who possess "a kind of implicit faith."[30] In my view the category of "symbol" is insufficient when it comes to the cognitive dimension of divine revelation, which includes what Nicholas Wolterstorff terms "divine discourse."[31] Yet Dulles, as one would expect, provides an excellent account of what the doctrine of revelation is about:

> Christian faith and theology, for nearly two thousand years, have been predicated on the conviction that God gave a permanently valid revelation concerning himself in biblical times—a revelation that deepened progressively with the patriarchs, Moses, and the prophets, until it reached an unsurpassable climax in Jesus Christ. The Christian Church down through the centuries has been committed to this revelation and has sought to propagate it, defend it, and explain its implications.[32]

Although Dulles's book remains the best-known Catholic study in English of the doctrine of revelation, two further works deserve our attention. The first is John F. Haught's *The Revelation of God in History* (1988). Haught's book

---

is, and wills to be, for the world" that are already such "before their meaning is understood and accepted," especially since Dulles himself considers the cognitive dimension to belong intrinsically to a "symbol."

30. Dulles, *Models of Revelation*, 279.

31. See Wolterstorff, *Divine Discourse*. For an account of "symbol" that explicitly discounts the role of propositional knowledge in theology, see Haight, *Jesus Symbol of God*, 9. For his part, Dulles carefully argues that

> the symbolic approach does not require a wedge to be driven between symbol and doctrine, as though anything conceded to doctrine had to be subtracted from symbol. In the theory of symbol set forth in the last chapter, symbol has been presented as cognitive. Not only does it give rise to thought, it is reflected and prolonged in thought. As a very dense and vivid form of communication, symbol can be diffracted and analyzed in propositional statements. The Christological doctrines of the Bible and of the Church have emerged, in great part, through meditation on the Christian symbols. From the beginnings of Christianity, the symbols of faith were understood within a doctrinal context that included the teaching of the Hebrew Scriptures and that of Jesus himself. (*Models of Revelation*, 161)

He recognizes that Jesus's words "were no doubt revelatory," although "Jesus taught by preference through parable and paradox" (ibid.). But Dulles insists that "the symbolic realities of Christ's life and the metaphorical language of the early confessions" are "paradoxical and evocative rather than propositional" (161–62). I find that the category of "symbol," at least when it is the primary category, downplays propositional knowledge in a manner that is unhelpful. For comparison of Haight and Dulles (and Karl Rahner) on "symbol," see Ronnie Rombs, "Augustine on Christ," 48–53. Among evangelical scholars, the effort to avoid propositionalism often takes the form of focusing on the category of "narrative": see, for example, the account of doctrine offered by N. T. Wright in his "Reading Paul, Thinking Scripture," 59–71. As Wright observes, doctrines (and creeds or "symbols") belong to the "packing and unpacking, compressing and expanding" that the scriptural authors themselves do with respect to the "entire story" (64).

32. Dulles, *Models of Revelation*, 3.

exemplifies the impact of the antipropositional shift in Catholic theology. He emphasizes that "revelation is not primarily the uncovering of information that is otherwise inaccessible to reason and ordinary experience. Such a 'gnostic' idea, tempting though it has been since very early in the history of Christianity, trivializes the idea of revelation, making it appeal more to our sense of curiosity than to our need for transformation and hope."[33] In personalist terms, Haught argues that revelation is simply "God's gift of self," which comes to us "not as a proposition or doctrine but as a *promise* of ultimate fulfillment."[34] Put another way, revelation consists in "the revelation of our relationship to an ultimate environment of unconditional love."[35] From this perspective, Haught suggests that we should interpret Christ primarily in universal terms rather than in the context of Israel and the Church. In this way, Haught thinks, "belief in the universal significance of Christ can actually open up areas that would otherwise be overlooked. For if the name 'Christ' stands for anything, it means openness, compassion, understanding, acceptance, tolerance, justice and freedom."[36] The key point is that faith in Christ "allows no construal of revelation as a restrictive body of truths that prohibits us in any way from exploring the vast universe of nature, culture and religion."[37]

33. Haught, *Revelation of God in History*, 14.
34. Ibid. Along the same lines, Haught remarks that
> revelation is not informative in the sense of adding horizontally to the list of "facts" in the content of our consciousness. Revelation is the unfolding of a relationship between God and the world. . . . Revelation does not give us information that may be placed side by side with scientific knowledge. Instead revelation mediates to us the mystery of God's boundlessly loving relationship to the universe, society, history and personality. . . . Science and history can provide helpful assistance in understanding the circumstances within which the mystery of God is disclosed. But it would be a misunderstanding of revelation to place its content in the same realm of ideas as those discussed by cosmologists, scientists or historians. Revelation, as the uncovering of God's relation to the world, offers us a content that is much more pervasive and foundational than what we can receive through ordinary ways of gathering information. It will appear as unrealistic only if we try to transform this content into the relatively trivial mode of competing information about the world or history. (90–91)

But if revelation unfolds a relationship in history between God and humans, it is unclear how such a relationship could unfold without adding to our propositional judgments of truth (including truth about history), given that our mode of knowing is inescapably propositional.
35. Ibid., 93. Here Haught rightly emphasizes that faith in divine revelation enables us to avoid placing our hope and trust in such things as our status among our peers or our human friendships, which cannot bear the weight of our desire for an unconditional and enduring love. As he says, "Instead we can see others' love and fidelity as symbols or sacraments of an ultimate fidelity to promise. And when the others fail us, their weaknesses need not be taken as a major threat to our own sense of significance" (ibid).
36. Ibid., 68.
37. Ibid., 68–69. Haught prefaces these remarks by noting:
> In the writings of the New Testament and in Christian tradition we are told, often in so many words, that the fullness of revelation occurs in Jesus the Christ. Can a Christian

Haught does not think that he has thereby devalued the particularity of Christ. He suggests that the role of this particularity, as found in Scripture, is to "provide the liberating images in which our consciousness dwells so that it may *break out* into an exploration of the inexhaustible mystery that manifests itself everywhere and especially in the world's religious traditions."[38] The particularity of Jesus Christ provides "liberating images" that propel us into the "inexhaustible mystery" that is always revealing itself, both in the wonder of the universe and in the profound symbols of all the world's religions. For Haught, the most important way in which Christ orients us in hope toward transcendent mystery is by his "reference to God as 'Abba.'"[39] Here Haught himself seems to introduce something of a propositional element into revelation: "The term 'Abba' already signifies that each person is cared for in a way that should evoke a child-like sense of trust, as well as an awareness of the futility of our attempts to secure our existence by way of heroics. Jesus's parables all unfold this central idea."[40]

In my view, Haught's critique of propositional revelation makes God's revelation much less personal, as well as much less rich in its content. Thus Haught can say only that the Church is "founded by the revelatory promise and is itself a sign or 'sacrament' of God's fidelity to the promise of an ultimately fulfilling future for the world and history," rather than saying that Jesus Christ established his Church out of love for us.[41] Haught provides a sense of the multitude of images that point humans toward the ineffable transcendent, and he underscores God's unconditional love. But he does not give a real sense of the ways in which God's revelation transforms not only our hearts but also

---

honestly engage other religions while clinging to this particularity of belief? Avery Dulles quite correctly says: "Without repudiating its own foundations Christianity cannot deny the permanent and universal significance of Jesus Christ as the preeminent 'real symbol' of God's turning to the world in merciful love." But, as Dulles and other theologians also insist, such a confessional statement does not preclude the possibility of open dialogue and genuine willingness to learn new things about mystery from other positions. (67–68) Haught goes on to say that Christians "can respect the fact that there are many other pathways to mystery without denying that they belong to a special story of their own" (96). The problem here consists in Haught's description of Christianity as a "pathway to mystery," and his corresponding reduction of the grace of the Holy Spirit to "the graciousness of mystery" (97). Christianity is much more than this.

38. Ibid., 69.
39. Ibid., 78.
40. Ibid. At the end of his book, Haught approves "the existence of a Church and a teaching tradition" as made necessary "by the intrinsically social, narrative and historical character of revelation" (97), but it is unclear what propositional knowledge could be rightly taught by the Church, within the limits of Haught's approach (other than the unconditional love that "God" offers us).
41. Ibid., 98.

our minds through cognitive content (as, for instance, in Paul's affirmation that "if you confess with your lips that Jesus is Lord and believe in your heart that God raised him from the dead, you will be saved" [Rom. 10:9]). The result is a reductive vision of the Christian life, a restriction on the divine teaching that pertains to "our abiding within a community founded on hope in God's promise" and to our "actively shaping history through the practice of justice and liberation."[42]

Much more fruitful is Gerald O'Collins's *Rethinking Fundamental Theology* (2011), which builds upon various earlier books by O'Collins, including his *Theology and Revelation* (1968), *Fundamental Theology* (1981), and *Retrieving Fundamental Theology* (1993).[43] O'Collins's *Rethinking Fundamental Theology* takes up a wide range of themes, as befits his understanding of "fundamental theology." For example, he has chapters on the existence and

42. Ibid., 88. Haught reduces ecclesiology to anthropology:

It is the nature of our human existence that we come to understand ourselves only in community with others. Existence in community is not just accidental to our being as humans. It is constitutive of our existence to be in relation to others. Moreover, it is natural to any community that it base its very existence and identity on the great myths or stories that narrate how it came into being and what makes it specially significant. Such stories give the members of the community a sense of their origins and destiny, a sense of what is important, a sense of common purpose. It is impossible to live meaningfully except in relation to such communally shared stories. The particular face that mystery will take for us is inevitably shaped by the narrative traditions that mold the character of the community in which we reside. It is these narrative traditions that provide the material for the symbolic and mythic expressions through which we as individuals come face to face with mystery. (96)

By prefacing his comments on Scripture and Tradition in this way, he turns them into anthropocentric realities, true because we find them meaningful for community building: "So meaningful are the stories of God's fidelity recounted in the Scriptures that members of the community spontaneously seek to retell them to their children and to others so that they also might indwell the healing images imprinted in the biblical material" (ibid.). "Tradition" becomes simply the result of the accumulated retellings, leaving us with the difficulty of distinguishing between true and false traditions: "The deposit of this continual retelling throughout the centuries is known as *Tradition*, and together with Scripture it provides a normative basis for the community's relating to the revelatory promise out of which it has its being" (ibid.).

43. See O'Collins, *Rethinking Fundamental Theology*; O'Collins, *Theology and Revelation*; O'Collins, *Fundamental Theology*; O'Collins, *Retrieving Fundamental Theology*. It is instructive to compare O'Collins's 2011 book especially to *Retrieving Fundamental Theology*, from which his 2011 book draws some material (even occasionally verbatim). The way that O'Collins reworks his 1993 book's two chapters on "symbol" into a much more nuanced and wider-ranging chapter in the 2011 book is notable. In the 1993 book, whose quality is much inferior to the 2011 book, he sums up his position by stating, "God's 'symbolic self-communication' describes the 'how' or the route of divine revelation. 'Love' catches up its essential content" (*Retrieving Fundamental Theology*, 120). This emphasis on a "symbolic" self-communication and on revelation's "essential content" differs from the 2011 book. His very short *Theology and Revelation* (1968), especially because of its biblical concreteness, offers much excellent material that the 2011 book redeploys.

attributes of God, Jesus Christ's preaching and miracles, Jesus's paschal mystery, and Jesus's founding of the hierarchical Church. In each of these chapters he devotes extensive labor to showing the plausibility of central Christian claims, such as God's existence, the reliability of the Gospels, the truth of Jesus's resurrection, and Jesus's preparation for a hierarchical Church that would last for some time (rather than supposing that Jesus expected the eschatological end to come immediately). An apologetic focus also colors his chapters on themes that pertain more explicitly to the doctrine of revelation: for example, his chapters on "general and special revelation," on faith as the response to revelation, on Tradition, on Scripture's inspiration and truth, and on the universal presence of Christ and the Holy Spirit and thus the relationship of Christian revelation to other religions.

With respect to the themes that I treat in the present book, O'Collins's *Rethinking Fundamental Theology* provides a valuable introduction, marked by clear and accessible synthesis. With Latourelle and *Dei Verbum*, O'Collins holds that "revelation is primarily a personal encounter with God (who is the Truth) rather than the communication of a body of truths."[44] Yet he also makes clear that the personal model and the propositional model of revelation need not be in conflict. After all, in human knowing, "experience, thought, and language form a distinguishable but inseparable unity. . . . It is impossible for us as thinking and speaking beings to have non-interpreted experiences."[45] Far from excluding the propositional model, the personal model of revelation implies propositional content. As O'Collins says, "The experience of a revealing and redemptive dialogue with God does not remain private, incommunicable, and locked away within an inarticulate subjectivity. . . . In addressing human beings, God says something that they can formulate and pass on."[46] Nor are these propositions simply a second-order articulation of a primal experience. Within the revelatory experience itself, there is cognitive content.

O'Collins also carefully argues that "at the heart of the biblical history of revelation and salvation lies a set of events which certainly occurred—to be experienced then by believers and non-believers alike and accessible now to common historical investigation."[47] In these events, God does not act in a way that would force people to believe; instead, God ensures that "we have enough light to make us responsible but not enough to take away our freedom."[48] O'Collins speaks of a "foundational" revelation in Israel and Christ Jesus (as

44. O'Collins, *Rethinking Fundamental Theology*, 204.
45. Ibid., 48–49.
46. Ibid., 67.
47. Ibid., 81.
48. Ibid., 83.

interpreted by his apostles). This foundational revelation gives rise to an ongo-ing "dependent" revelation, since the foundational revelation "continues and calls people to faith in a living encounter with God."[49] Both the foundational and the "dependent" revelation are ordered to a future or "eschatological" revelation in which God's saving work is entirely complete.[50] Lest there be any misunderstanding, O'Collins makes clear that the "dependent" or "ongoing revelation does *not add* to the essential 'content' of what was fully revealed through Christ's life, death, resurrection, and the sending of the Holy Spirit."[51]

When he turns to the Church's mediation of divine revelation, O'Collins points out that "the first Christians and their leaders, the original recipients and bearers of the normative revelation in Christ, will play for all time an indispensable role in understanding and interpreting Jesus, his teaching, and all the events in which he was involved."[52] The Gospels show that Jesus chose twelve disciples from his wider group of followers and "gave them some kind of authoritative office and leadership role."[53] Even though the New Testa-ment is not entirely clear with respect to the various offices it describes (for example, *episcopoi*, presbyters, deacons), the New Testament bears witness that the early Christian communities were ordered in a hierarchical rather than egalitarian fashion. If we believe that the Holy Spirit was powerfully at work among the early Christians, then it makes sense "to recognize that the same Spirit guided Christians in the foundational period to develop certain forms of leadership and, later, to collect into a canon the Scriptures which reflect that development (in particular, Acts and the Pastoral Epistles)."[54] The Church is apostolic not least, then, in its ordered episcopal structure.

Regarding Tradition, O'Collins first shows that its practical necessity has been ecumenically accepted, and so the question now is how to distinguish authoritative Tradition. With respect to the relationship between Scripture and Tradition, he points out that "if the community's tradition, along with the inspiration of the Holy Spirit, led to the formation of the Scriptures, one would

49. Ibid., 131. Mistakenly, in my view, O'Collins criticizes John Henry Newman's position that the development of doctrine does not constitute "new" revelation. O'Collins wants to emphasize the ongoing character of revelation, the living encounter with Christ in the Spirit that is still happening today.

50. Ibid.

51. Ibid. O'Collins goes on to say that our "'believing in' and 'believing that' also involve accepting the foundational witness to the experience of God coming from the Old Testament and the New Testament. When experiencing in faith who God is and what God is like, believers today depend on the prophetic and apostolic witness" (167).

52. Ibid.

53. Ibid., 277.

54. Ibid., 287.

expect tradition to remain active in interpreting and applying the Scriptures."[55] The Bible in this sense cannot be separated from the Church, even though, as *Dei Verbum* affirms, the Church's magisterium serves the scriptural word of God rather than the other way around. The Holy Spirit's guidance of the Church includes working through the bishops (including—uniquely—the bishop of Rome), rather than simply working through "individual believers reading the Scriptures, preachers expounding the Scriptures, and ministers using the Scriptures in administering the sacraments."[56] It is the Holy Spirit that enables the Church to hand on Tradition—that is, to hand on the entirety of what has been revealed in Jesus Christ. O'Collins discusses eight elements that guide the Church and individual believers in discerning the true content of this Tradition: the magisterium, the Vincentian canon, the "sensus fidei," continuity with the apostolic Church, the Nicene and Apostles' Creeds, apostolicity, Scripture, and the risen Lord. He remarks that the Church of each generation inevitably hands on Tradition in a somewhat different form from that in which it had been received, although "an essential continuity is maintained."[57]

O'Collins differentiates Scripture from revelation per se, since the written words record the interpersonal events that constitute divine revelation. Scripture also includes much material that God inspired to be present but that does not directly record events or words in which God was explicitly making himself known. O'Collins defines biblical inspiration as "a special impulse from the Holy Spirit to set certain things down in writing," and thus all who were involved in the writing and editing of scriptural texts were inspired by the Holy Spirit.[58] In this way God is the "author" of Scripture. O'Collins argues that the whole of Scripture was written and edited under the inspiration of the Holy Spirit but that, nonetheless, not all biblical texts possess the same degree of inspiration. The charism of inspiration ended after the last biblical text was written, since it "belonged to the divine activity of establishing the Church."[59] The entire inspired Bible is inerrant, but only in a certain sense, since the Bible does contain errors that arise from the specific intentions of the biblical authors (for example, they did not intend to write natural science), as well as from their cultural presuppositions and the genres in which they wrote. Rather than being a string of true propositions, Scripture exhibits progress in truth—for example, in its understanding of God. The whole Bible

55. Ibid., 198.
56. Ibid.
57. Ibid., 215.
58. Ibid., 224.
59. Ibid., 232.

is nonetheless inerrant because the Bible, as a canonical whole, is about Christ and about life in Christ.[60]

This above brief summary indicates three postconciliar paths in Catholic theology of divine revelation. The first (Dulles) focuses on the category of "symbol" so as to express the richness of revelation, with its interplay of event and word, and to get beyond propositionalist accounts of revelation—without denying the role of propositions. The second (Haught) leaves propositional revelation almost entirely behind and argues that "revelation" simply consists in human images that express God's love for us and that orient us trustingly toward transcendent mystery. The third (O'Collins 2011) securely retrieves propositional revelation, but in a manner that prioritizes the personal dimension of revelation that the advocates of "symbol" highlighted. For readers looking for a synthetic introduction, O'Collins's book is the one to read.[61]

Recent Protestant Approaches: Paul Ricoeur, Richard Swinburne, and Colin Gunton

Three recent Protestant approaches to the doctrine of revelation also merit attention. First, in his short but widely read essay "Toward a Hermeneutic of the Idea of Revelation" (1977), Paul Ricoeur emphasizes that revelation is not "the body of doctrines imposed by the magisterium as the rule of orthodoxy."[62]

60. See ibid., 242–43. Earlier, O'Collins states, "The series of collective experiences, in which God acts and which together make up the history of revelation and salvation, include events that undoubtedly took place (like the reign of King David, deportation to Babylon, the preaching of John the Baptist, the ministry of Jesus, and the fall of Jerusalem) and things like the creation and fall of Adam and Eve that have a mythical rather than an historical character" (80). In his section on biblical inerrancy, he remarks that the early chapters of Genesis aim to

> reflect on the nature of God and human beings, and in no sense give even an incomplete account of the "pre-historical" origins of the human race. If we ignore that fact, hopeless puzzles turn up. When, for instance, Cain murdered Abel and was about to be sent away as "a fugitive and wanderer upon the earth," God "put a mark on Cain, lest any who came upon him should kill him." So Cain left Eden for the land of Nod, "knew his wife, and she conceived Enoch" (Gen. 4:15–17). We would mistreat the story if we were to start asking: where did the others come from who might have threatened Cain's life? For that matter, where did his wife come from, if Adam and Eve were the parents of all human beings? Genesis is not a book about human origins that answers such questions. (238–39)

I agree that Genesis does not answer such questions, but it seems that we do need to defend the unity of the human race and a historical fall. For recent, divergent perspectives on this topic, see Kemp, "Science, Theology, and Monogenesis"; Enns, *Evolution of Adam*.

61. Mention should also be made of Grant Kaplan's *Answering the Enlightenment*, a historical study of the nineteenth-century Tübingen theologian Johannes Kuhn. This book has valuable overviews of the reductive accounts of revelation offered by Gotthold Lessing, Immanuel Kant, and Johann Gottlieb Fichte. See also Kaplan's edition of Kuhn's writings, *Faithfully Seeking Understanding*.

62. Ricoeur, "Toward a Hermeneutic of the Idea of Revelation," 74.

Nor should revelation, in his view, be understood as divine speech, let alone as divine authorship of biblical texts or as the making known of the goal of history. Instead, Ricoeur suggests that revelation is rooted in certain founding events marked by "God's trace," as refracted in the poetics of narrative/prophecy/law/wisdom/psalm.[63] The resulting "revelation" consists in the *manifestation* of a new world or new being. Indebted to Jean Nabert's *Désir de Dieu*, Ricoeur also highlights the category of "testimony." The main thing for Ricoeur, advocating a strongly antipropositional view, is that "in none of its modalities may revelation be included in and dominated by knowledge," because "the God who reveals himself is a hidden God and hidden things belong to him."[64]

In Richard Swinburne's *Revelation: From Metaphor to Analogy* (1992), by contrast, we find a strong defense of propositional revelation linked to an emphasis on revelation's credibility. Swinburne first provides an analysis of terms that have to do with propositional and symbolic communication, including an account of analogy and metaphor rooted in analytic philosophy, as well as a survey of various genres such as typology and allegory. He then offers some preambles to the plausibility of revelation: an all-powerful and all-good God exists, humans have free will and can shape their character in ways that fit them for heaven, humans need instruction about how to live and

---

63. Ibid., 80–81.
64. Ibid., 93. Nicholas Wolterstorff comments insightfully on Ricoeur's position:
   At the end of the discussion, God's speech has entirely disappeared from view, completely absorbed by manifestation; and it is not even clear that the manifestation brought to speech in biblical discourse is God's self-manifestation, as opposed to agentless manifestation. . . . A striking feature of Ricoeur's discussion is his complete neglect of the fact that attributions of speech to God pervade all the discourse-genres of the Bible. . . . To use Ricoeur's conceptuality: an aspect of the world projected by all these texts is that of God speaking. Ricoeur has resisted the "imprisonment" (76) of revelation within the divine-speech model in such a way as to imprison divine speech within the manifestation model. (*Divine Discourse*, 62)
Wolterstorff insists upon the importance, in Scripture and theology, of the claim that God speaks (though not through a vocal apparatus, of course), so that revelation is not limited only to "manifestational" revelation but also includes propositional revelation of various kinds. But he also carefully distinguishes between divine speech (deputized and appropriated) and "revelation," even though, as he says, "divine assertion is one of the media of divine revelation" (35). For Wolterstorff's helpful account of biblical prophecy and apostolic teaching, see *Divine Discourse*, 45–51. Rowan Williams too interacts at some length with Ricoeur's proposal, which provides the building blocks of Williams's own approach, but Williams's focus is on how Christians "develop meaningful constructs out of historical process and decision" ("Trinity and Revelation," 132). Thus, in his view, "revelation" as revolving around Jesus is grounded in Jesus's power to generate a new community. Williams is trying to grapple, in a nonmetaphysical and community-focused fashion, with how the first followers of Jesus ended up associating him so closely with the "decisive generative quality" (broadly understood) of the Creator God (143). F. Martin engages more fruitfully with Ricoeur's theory of revelation in "Literary Theory, Philosophy of History, and Exegesis."

about what God has done to rescue them from sinful alienation and to make them fit for heaven, humans become good by making an effort to learn about God and by helping each other to learn about and obey God. To be plausible, revelation needs to be true, but it does not have to be true in all ways, since God can allow for the presence of some culture-relative concepts. For Swinburne too, "An effective revelation cannot consist solely of original documents or other proclamations; *continuing* guidance is required, a mechanism which helps translators of the original revelation to get their translation right."[65] This mechanism could be some kind of infallibility, or it could be simply God's ensuring that the Church will never get the crucial things permanently wrong. A true revelation cannot be something that can be empirically proven to be false. Miracles, and resurrection above all, count as significant evidence in favor of the veracity of a revelation, but these miracles should not be so evident as to undermine the arduous and meritorious striving for God that belongs to the purpose of revelation.[66]

On the basis of this reflection on the possibility of revelation and on how we might recognize a true revelation, Swinburne turns to God's actual revelation, which he describes as follows: "The original propositional revelation was the teaching of God to the Israelites of the centuries BC about himself and his dealings with them and other nations, culminating in the teaching of Jesus Christ, including his teaching about the significance of his actions, and the teaching of the first apostles about the significance of those actions."[67] Without downgrading Jesus's deeds (or other revelatory events), Swinburne focuses on "propositional revelation"—that is, on the communication of truths, including, of course, truths about Jesus's deeds. He holds that such revelation came definitively to an end at the death of the last apostle, and he notes that this revelation existed prior to canonical Scripture.[68] He pays careful attention

65. Swinburne, *Revelation*, 81.

66. William Abraham, in a study that focuses on how revelation can be said to count as "knowledge," argues that the believer who recognizes faith as enabling a real knowledge of God's revelation can justify this knowledge on the basis not of a general theory of epistemology (let alone simply on the basis of entering into the world of the biblical narratives) but on the basis of all the public resources for communal and personal knowing that the canonical heritage provides. See Abraham, *Crossing the Threshold of Divine Revelation*. This emphasis on the canonical heritage seems appropriate, but I do not think that realist epistemology needs to be discarded.

67. Swinburne, *Revelation*, 101.

68. For a quite different approach, see Thiemann, *Revelation and Theology*, indebted especially to Barth's *Church Dogmatics*, I.1, *The Doctrine of the Word of God*, and III.2, *The Doctrine of Creation*, as well as to the work of George Lindbeck, Hans Frei, and Stanley Hauerwas. Thiemann is particularly interested in the possibility and actuality of divine revelation given the structures of human cognition and faith. Thiemann emphasizes, however, that the only basis for answering such questions consists in Scripture's "narrated promise addressed to the reader" (*Revelation*

to the genres of New Testament writings and recognizes that sometimes it is difficult to be certain whether the New Testament authors (or for that matter the Old Testament authors) intended to be speaking literally or metaphorically. Three groups of Jesus's actions strike him as clearly attested by the New Testament: founding a Church, dying on the cross, and rising from the dead. The resurrection of Jesus has the preeminent role in historical arguments for the truthfulness of Christian revelation. In Swinburne's view, having given a revelation open to interpretation, God had also to "provide a Church in which such interpretations have some chance of being correct."[69] This means that today we face the problem of discerning which Christian community is the Church that Christ founded.

Much depends for Swinburne on this insistence that there needs to be a (generally) doctrinally faithful Church as a "vehicle of revelation."[70] Yet he is well aware of the major differences between Eastern Orthodoxy, Roman Catholicism, Anglicanism, and Protestantism. He traces out views of doctrinal development—which, as he makes clear, long precede Newman—and of the authority of Scripture and of the Church (including councils and the pope). On this basis, he concludes that "we need an external criterion for a true development, that is, that it is developed in a Church which is the 'closest continuer' of the Church of the apostles."[71] Here he favors the view of dogma and Church structure that he associates with the Anglican and Eastern Orthodox churches. He also devotes a chapter to creeds, focusing on how the creeds use words—for instance, the attribution of "omnipotent" to God (Swinburne accepts a Scotist view of univocity) and the metaphorical description of Jesus Christ as being at the right hand of the Father.

Swinburne's final chapter treats the Bible, beginning with some comments on the various biblical genres. He allows for "false scientific or historical presuppositions" in Scripture, as well as for broadly historical writings that include

---

and Theology, 25). For Thiemann, to encounter God's revelation is to be drawn into the biblical text and to accept the text's promise as true. See also the narrative theology of Surin, *Turnings of Darkness and Light*. For a critique of such approaches, see Murphy, *God Is Not a Story*.

69. Swinburne, *Revelation*, 119. For criticism of this position as a circular argument, see Ward, *Religion and Revelation*, 245–47. Ward concludes that "Swinburne is not wrong to think the Church is important in establishing historical credibility, as are the resurrection and background belief in God. What is wrong is the attempt to find one independent guarantee of biblical credibility. There are in fact many reasons inclining one to accept the New Testament as basically reliable" (246). I think that Swinburne would agree that there are many reasons, while continuing to insist on the necessity of the existence of an authoritative Church. Swinburne and Ward at least agree that Christian theology cannot do without plausible historical claims about Jesus Christ; see Ward's criticisms of the position of Harvey, *The Historian and the Believer*.

70. Swinburne, *Revelation*, 124.

71. Ibid., 141.

material that the author did not intend to be taken as literal historical exposition, and he notes that the redaction of biblical books sometimes significantly altered their meaning.[72] He evaluates issues such as pseudepigraphy with an eye to whether it affects biblical truth. He emphasizes the unity of the Bible, with God as its author, and he explores how this should affect our reading of the various biblical texts. In his view, Scripture cannot simply be interpreted by Scripture but instead requires, if it is to be read as communicating revelation, that it be read through "the Church's creeds and other tradition of public teaching of items treated as central to the Gospel message."[73] In this way, the New Testament governs the reading of the Old and in some cases requires metaphorical reading of Old Testament passages.

In short, Swinburne's approach is couched as a philosophical study of what would be necessary for a divine revelation (with cognitive content, and thus propositional) to be truly given, and of whether Christian claims to have received divine revelation are plausible and, if so, how. He focuses in particular on the Church and the Bible, which lead him into topics such as the Church's authority and creeds (doctrinal development) and the Bible's unity, genres, and truth. He gives significant weight to the resurrection of Jesus as the guarantee of the truthfulness of the gospel. I find his account of the Church, gospel, and Scripture to be nuanced and balanced, even if I occasionally disagree with him. Some will be put off by his evident debt to John Locke and by his efforts to sift the "evidence for the truth of revelation," given that he does not highlight the role of the Holy Spirit and the eyes of faith (as I think he should do).[74] But to my mind, he has offered a valuable exposition of the basic issues that are in play in any defense of the doctrine of revelation.[75]

72. Ibid., 161.
73. Ibid., 177.
74. Ibid., 217. Swinburne complains about "those writers of the last two centuries whose theological thinking derives from the philosophies of Kant and Kierkegaard and who seem to hold that faith in the Christian Revelation can in some sense be 'rational' without there being any evidence for it" (ibid.). For discussion of Locke on the knowledge of God and on revelation, see Wolterstorff, *Divine Discourse*, 261–69, 278–79. For evaluation and critique of certain aspects of Swinburne's project, see, for example, Crisp, "On Believing That the Scriptures Are Divinely Inspired"; Plantinga, *Warranted Christian Belief*. Crisp, like Swinburne, emphasizes the significance of an authoritative Church. See also Lackey, *Learning from Words*.
75. For an alternative to Swinburne's project, offering sustained attention to other religions' claims to revelation and consideration of cultural-anthropological factors from a liberal Anglican perspective, see Ward's *Religion and Revelation*. In Ward's account, Karl Barth's (and Emil Brunner's) account of divine revelation comes in for particularly stern critique:

> The difficulty for this view is that once one has characterized all religions, including one's own, as products of pride and stupidity, how is one ever to attain to truth about God? Barth's answer is hardly satisfactory. He simply asserts that "Scripture is the only valid testimony to revelation." But how can anyone know this, if every human judgement

Lastly, Colin Gunton's *A Brief Theology of Revelation* (1995), a more explicitly theological work than Swinburne's, opens with a vigorous defense of propositional truth in the mediation of divine revelation. As Gunton frames the question of epistemological realism, "Does our language or does it not refer, or affect to refer, to realities which lie beyond it, however elusively? Does it or does it not affect to describe, albeit partially, obliquely and inadequately, those things which truly are?"[76] He points out that revelation could not be handed down from generation to generation, as is commanded in Deuteronomy 6:4–7, without employing true propositions.[77] While granting

---

is sinful, *including this one*? Indeed, one can very easily turn the tables on Barth and insist (as it seems very plausible to do) that the belief that everyone else's revelation is incorrect and only one's own is true, is a particularly clear example of human pride and self-interest. . . . One may claim that this possession is by the grace of God alone—but this only makes the element of human pride more pronounced, since one is now asserting that grace is only truly possessed by oneself. One can hardly get more proud, more self-righteous, and more short-sighted than that. (17)

Ward agrees with Barth and Brunner against the Enlightenment project of reducing divine revelation to what can be known by human reason alone, but he insists that reason nonetheless has a role, limited but not insignificant, in evaluating purported claims to revelation. I share Ward's concerns here, but find him to be somewhat overconfident in his effort to transpose Christian categories for divine revelation to revelations present in Buddhism and Hinduism, for example. Further, I differ from Ward's anthropocentric view of theology's sources, which strikes me as underestimating (due to his sensitivity to modern research into historical context) the ability of the Holy Spirit to guide the communication of the gospel in Scripture and Tradition. Ward rejects the notion of theology as faith seeking understanding, and he denies that "theology" can take certain cognitive contents of revelation "as a given, as something settled, definitive, and complete" (39).

76. Gunton, *Brief Theology of Revelation*, 9.

77. In this regard Gunton remarks:

George Lindbeck's critique of what he calls the cognitive-propositional conception of theology is in effect an attack on the notion of revealed religion. As has been pointed out often enough, he gains his point only by a very tendentious account of the cognitive approach. . . . Against the implicit suggestion that propositionalism is a kind of optional and vaguely reactionary or disreputable position, it must be protested in the name of logic that it is as a matter of fact the case that once something is true it is always true. That is not, however, the same as believing . . . that doctrines, once formulated, must always be expressed in the same precise form of words. (ibid., 7–8)

For a stronger rejection of propositions, Gunton cites Downing, *Has Christianity a Revelation?* Paul Helm likewise criticizes antipropositionalist views, which he describes as the position that "God does not tell us about himself in letters, he reveals *himself*. The letters are only a token for the man himself" (*Divine Revelation*, 40). In response to such views, Helm observes that

if there is no experience of seeing God or of otherwise experiencing him in a direct, proposition-less way, then the contrast between God revealing *himself* and only revealing propositions about himself is a misleading one. Someone may say that people have experienced God in mystical vision, but if so the point about mystical experience is that in it God is experienced as the inexpressible. In mystical experience no one can give an account of a mystical experience in his own or any other language, not because he does

that propositional judgments are secondary to God's revelatory presence, he notes that they are nonetheless "in intrinsic relation to that which they articulate."[78] Attempting to delimit the particular bounds of the doctrine of revelation, as distinct from the related doctrines of creation, salvation, and so forth, Gunton suggests that the doctrine of revelation specifically depends upon five elements that have been called into question in the modern period: Bible, creed, Church, tradition, and authority.[79] His five chapters therefore explore the creedal confession of faith, the scriptural doctrine of creation as upholding the possibility of universal truth, biblical inspiration and the fixed canon of Scripture, tradition as the doctrine and practices that pertain to a proper handing down of authoritative apostolic teaching, and the eschatological character of the Church's knowledge and its dependence on the Holy Spirit.

---

not have the words available to do full justice to his experience but because no words *could* express what has taken place" (ibid.).

It seems to me that God could indeed inspire the appropriate words, even if no words could be fully adequate. I agree with Helm, however, that we need to be careful not to separate revelation from propositions (especially because Jesus often taught in propositions), even if in my view we should distinguish the two. See also the valuable response of Colman O'Neill, OP, to Lindbeck, "Rule Theory of Doctrine and Propositional Truth."

78. Gunton, *Brief Theology of Revelation*, 101. For his part, René Latourelle observes, "If revelation comes to us through the vehicle of human notions and human propositions, how can these notions and propositions give us access to the divine mystery?" (*Theology of Revelation*, 324). Latourelle argues that the answer consists in the ability of human words to speak analogously about divine realities.

79. Gunton rightly insists that "revelation is a secondary doctrine, in that its function is to preserve and explain the character of that which is revealed. . . . A similar point would be to say that revelation is largely to do with the epistemic, not the soteriological or experiential dimension of the Christian faith" (*Brief Theology of Revelation*, 110). By comparison, see Gabriel Fackre's *The Doctrine of Revelation: A Narrative Interpretation*. For Fackre, divine revelation is "the pattern of God's decisive actions among us" as found in the whole story of salvation in its canonical shape, from Genesis to Revelation, with the divine "disclosures" that are intrinsic to God's saving actions (5, 7). Divine revelation cannot be limited to any one element of the whole story, since revelation is an active historical reality whose origin and goal is trinitarian communion. After a first chapter titled "The Trinitarian Source of Disclosure," Fackre therefore divides his book into three parts, covering "general revelation," "special revelation," and "revelation as reception," respectively. Insightfully responding to Tillich's treatment of revelation, Fackre asks, "When the 'medium' as interpreted by cultural and philosophical frameworks plays such a key role in the formulation of the message itself, what happens to the *critical* function of the Christian message? How is 'revelation' whose content has been described in terms provided by 'reason' free to answer the questions posed by reason?" (84). Fackre goes on to offer accurate critiques of the positions of theologians who are largely indebted to Tillich, such as David Tracy, Rosemary Radford Ruether, and John Cobb. For Fackre, the doctrine of revelation can be understood only by narrating the entirety of the creative and redemptive work of the Father, Son, and Holy Spirit. I appreciate the strengths of this approach, but like Gunton I think that the *doctrine* of revelation has a smaller scope. See also Pannenberg et al., *Revelation as History*.

Gunton fears that *Dei Verbum*'s affirmation that "Tradition transmits in its entirety the word of God which has been entrusted to the apostles by Christ the Lord and the Holy Spirit" exaggerates the Church's capacities.[80] After all, the "word of God," divine revelation, is inexhaustibly rich. As Gunton observes, "Does the tradition—*can* the tradition—transmit the word of God 'in its entirety'? There seems to be reason to believe that the content is more elusive than that, and that is why some doubt should be expressed about the Council's confidence in the Magisterium's capacity to speak the final word on the interpretation of revelation."[81] But I would point out that the "word of God" to which *Dei Verbum* is here referring is, according to *Dei Verbum*, "the full and living gospel" consisting in "divinely revealed realities."[82] Well aware that such realities cannot be exhausted by the Church, *Dei Verbum* states that "the Church is always advancing toward the plenitude of divine truth"—advancing toward it eschatologically, even while "possessing" it in the revealed realities.[83]

From Gunton's perspective, *Dei Verbum*'s ecclesiology (like overconfident liberal theology, a parallel that Gunton draws from Barth) "fails to allow truth to be the daughter of time and rather represents attempts to anticipate too confidently the judgement of God."[84] This overconfidence, in Gunton's view, leads the Church to place itself and its tradition over the gospel of the risen and exalted Christ. Without denying the role of tradition—indeed, Gunton argues for John Calvin's broad acceptance of tradition—Gunton thinks that Catholics have fallen into a "premature confidence" in the Church's authority, which has too often led to the Church embodying "coercive power" rather than love.[85] For Gunton, then, "the greater weight one can throw

---

80. *Dei Verbum*, §9, 755.

81. Gunton, *Brief Theology of Revelation*, 96.

82. *Dei Verbum*, §§7, 11, 753, 756.

83. Ibid., §8, 754.

84. Gunton, *Brief Theology of Revelation*, 96n19. See also Maartin Wisse's similar view that the old controversy between Protestants and Roman Catholics over the question of whether the anchor point of orthodoxy should be Scripture alone or Scripture and tradition, from Augustine's point of view, is a meaningless question. Of course it should be more than Scripture alone, as, for truth to be found, a community of faith and justice is the absolute requirement for a faithful reading practice of this text to take place. But, of course, at the same time, it cannot be that truth consists in some fixed institutional context either, as the community of justice finds its fulfilment in the creative presence of God rather than the fixed pinning down of God's presence in some earthly phenomenon. (*Trinitarian Theology beyond Participation*, 246–47)

No one, however, is advocating a "fixed pinning down of God's presence in some earthly phenomenon." True Scripture and true creeds mediate divine revelation in a manner that is enduringly true, but they do not thereby restrictively fix or pin down the Triune God's presence to his Church (unless truth pins God down).

85. Gunton, *Brief Theology of Revelation*, 97, 103.

upon the faith once for all delivered to the saints, by which is meant the confession of Jesus and his meaning as the revelation of God, found alike in the apostolic preaching and the rule of faith, the less we have to trust in the judgement of offices, whether Holy [i.e., Catholic or Orthodox] or Protestant administrative."[86]

While affirming that tradition needed the pruning that the Reformers undertook, Gunton grants that "without certain beliefs, about God, Christ, salvation, the church and the work of the Spirit, Christianity would not be recognisably continuous with what it once was."[87] He argues that attention to the apostolic preaching and the rule of faith ensures that the Church avoids rupture of this kind. He urges too that we "give due place and function to the Holy Spirit."[88] The Spirit's revelatory action points to the Son Jesus Christ, who reveals the Father. In this regard, the Spirit's work of mediating revelation is eschatological, always pointing us to the fullness that is to come with Jesus's return in glory, but that is not present yet.

Gunton's insistence on the eschatological character of the Church's knowledge attempts to hold together three elements. First, there is a core body of revelation about God, Jesus, the Holy Spirit, the Church, and so forth. Gunton does not find any "rupture" in this core body of revelation; in his view, it has been mediated to us effectively so that we can truly know the realities of faith today. Second, the apostolic preaching and prophetic testimony that formed the Bible are unique. Although biblical inspiration does not mean freedom from all error, it does mean that Scripture inerrantly communicates to all generations the saving action of God in Jesus Christ and the Holy Spirit. Third, believers require the Church's mediation of the apostolic teaching and practice ("tradition"). Yet tradition is often erroneous and overreaching, and it must frequently be pruned of elements that would lead people away from Jesus Christ.

As I explain more fully in the chapters that follow, I agree with Gunton's view that Scripture's truthfulness does not depend on an absolute lack of any kind of error, just as I agree with his insistence that there has been no rupture in the mediation of "certain beliefs, about God, Christ, salvation, the church and the work of the Spirit." Given his view that certain beliefs must be sustained throughout history in order for Christianity to be Christianity, however, why not suppose that the Church's truthfulness is, under the direction of the Church's exalted Head and by the power of the Spirit, broadly similar

86. Ibid., 103–4.
87. Ibid., 87.
88. Ibid., 119.

to Scripture's truthfulness? Gunton emphasizes, "Whatever it may mean to say that the church or her representatives are apostolic, it cannot mean that she is in the same relation to revelation as the apostles."[89] This strikes me as right, even if in need of unpacking, not least by the qualification that he immediately adds: "But that need not exclude an intrinsic relationship, too, because without our predecessors in the tradition we should be unable to appropriate that which the prophets and apostles mediate."[90]

In my view, we need not claim for the later Church the *same* "relation to revelation" as the apostles, but we can still argue that the Church, like the prophets and apostles, mediates divine revelation in the process of appropriating it under the guidance of the Holy Spirit. Without placing the Church over revelation, the Spirit can guarantee the Church's preservation from error in its definitive interpretations of revelation—which differs from guaranteeing the truthfulness of everything the Church says and does. This perspective enables us to give due weight to "the church of the living God, the pillar and bulwark of the truth" (1 Tim. 3:15). In short, we can accept the existence of errors within the Church's works and teachings over the centuries, so long as we do not suppose that these (reformable) errors produced a rupture, that is to say a false definitive doctrine about faith or morals in the heart of the transmission of revelation.

As we have seen, for Gunton the Church generally tends to become a problem, one that must be constantly monitored and pruned lest it proceed to exclude Jesus Christ. At the same time, in Gunton's view, the Church manages to keep handing down the basic Christian message, so that Christianity remains Christianity rather than corrupting into something quite different. Gunton grants that Scripture alone cannot ensure this continuity, as the Nicene debates (among many others) show. As he says, "Without our predecessors in the tradition we should be unable to appropriate that which the prophets and apostles mediate." The Church necessarily has a mediatorial role. If so, then the doctrine of revelation requires an account of the Holy Spirit's work in the Church (under the headship of the exalted Christ) that ensures, more fully than Gunton seems willing to admit, the Church's truthful transmission of the realities of faith. Certainly the eschatological consummation far outpaces the Church as we experience it now. Pruning is inevitably necessary, but not the pruning of truths that have been taught definitively by Christ's Church, for the sake of the salvation of the world, in its communication of divine revelation under the guidance of the Holy Spirit.

89. Ibid., 101.
90. Ibid.

The Plan of the Work

My book focuses on the mediation of divine revelation, or specifically on how the Triune God, ever present and active, sustains the handing on of revelation by "the Israel of God" (Gal. 6:16), the community that Peter describes as "a chosen race, a royal priesthood, a holy nation, God's own people," whose mission is to "declare the wonderful deeds of him who called [believers] out of darkness into his marvelous light" (1 Pet. 2:9). As a final step in this introduction, therefore, let me review the chapters of the book in a bit more detail.

Chapter 1 argues that the intrinsic place of the Church within divine revelation can best be seen through the theology of "mission." I begin with Thomas Aquinas's doctrine of the missions of the Son and Holy Spirit. These missions unite Christ Jesus, the Church, and all believers: the visible missions are found in Jesus Christ and at Pentecost, and by grace we receive the invisible missions of the Son and Spirit illuminating our minds and hearts. I extend this insight by means of Hans Urs von Balthasar's writings on Christ's mission and our sharing in it. For Balthasar, Christ simply is his mission, and all other persons have a mission by participating in some way in Christ's mission. The connection between Christ and the Church is made in terms of mission, and this connection shows how the Church's mission shares intimately in Christ's revelatory mission of kenotic love. I then take up the more standard meaning of mission—namely, evangelization and God's plan for the salvation of all nations—via the work of Christopher Wright. The goal of this first chapter is to underscore the intimate connection between divine revelation and the Church, in a manner that does not undermine the Triune God's priority.

Chapter 2 discusses revelation with a focus on the liturgical context of its actualization: we preeminently share in the revelatory missions of the Son and Holy Spirit in and through the liturgy, which builds up the Church in charity and illumines the Church with the wisdom of the gospel. My approach again involves drawing together significant voices for the purpose of evaluating and further developing their insights. I begin with the Reformed theologian John Webster's *Holy Scripture*, a book that offers a rich account of divine revelation and biblical inspiration but downplays the liturgical context of scriptural interpretation. Examining Scripture's testimony regarding itself, I suggest that Scripture conceives of itself as primarily proclaimed and interpreted in a liturgical context. I then argue that Alexander Schmemann's and Joseph Ratzinger's portraits of Scripture and the eucharistic liturgy fill the lacuna we find in Webster. Schmemann and Ratzinger rightly identify the liturgy as the primary place in which divine revelation is received, proclaimed, and interpreted.[91]

The third chapter treats revelation and the hierarchical priesthood. Is the priestly mediation of revelation, a mediation that has occurred for millennia, a good thing? The chapter begins with the criticisms of priestly mediation put forward by John Calvin and Thomas Hobbes. These criticisms drew upon Renaissance reconstructions of early Christianity and were located within a context of severe ecclesiastical corruption and strife among Christians. Calvin and Hobbes argue that after an original period of innocence, during which Christians were in harmony with each other, the bishops of Rome seized power and destroyed the Church by departing entirely from the New Testament model of the Christian pastorate. In response, I examine what Jesus and the apostles have to say about "priestly" rivalries. I suggest that Jesus, in establishing a hierarchical order among his followers, was fully aware of such tensions and that he gifted the Church with the Petrine ministry in order to ensure the fruitfulness of such tensions within the mediation of divine revelation. Rather than looking back to an idealized epoch or excoriating the failings of the hierarchical priesthood, we can affirm that Jesus intended a hierarchical priesthood for his Church, founded upon the apostles, as part of the faithful handing on of revelation.

The first three chapters, then, examine the Church's mediation of divine revelation by reflecting on "mission," the liturgy, and the hierarchical priesthood. The priority of the work of the Father, Son, and Holy Spirit is emphasized throughout. Chapter 4 discusses revelation and the gospel. Its starting point is the biblical scholar Scot McKnight's recent book *The King Jesus Gospel*. McKnight presents the gospel as the story of Jesus, the Messiah of Israel and Son of God who comes to restore and redeem Israel and to bring to fulfillment God's plan of salvation for the whole world. He contrasts this understanding of the gospel—inclusive of the whole story of salvation—with an understanding

---

91. See Pope Benedict XVI's *Verbum Domini*, § 52: "In considering the Church as 'the home of the word', attention must first be given to the sacred liturgy, for the liturgy is the privileged setting in which God speaks to us in the midst of our lives; he speaks today to his people, who hear and respond. Every liturgical action is by its very nature steeped in sacred Scripture. . . . *A faith-filled understanding of Scripture must always refer back to the liturgy*, in which the word of God is celebrated as a timely and living word." In the liturgy, Christ speaks to the Church and opens the Scriptures to the Church, and "in the liturgical action the word of God is accompanied by the interior working of the Holy Spirit who makes it effective in the hearts of the faithful" (ibid.). Pope Benedict goes on to underscore "the *performative* character of the word itself. In salvation history there is no separation between what God *says* and what he *does*. His word appears as alive and active (cf. Heb 4:12), as the Hebrew term *dabar* itself makes clear. In the liturgical action, too, we encounter his word which accomplishes what it says" (§ 53).

of the gospel that reduces it to justification by faith. Throughout his book, he calls for a "gospel culture" whose lineaments he finds in 1 Corinthians 15 and in the early creeds of the Church. I suggest that this culture can be enriched today by the insights of Thomas Aquinas in commenting upon Paul's use of the term "gospel" in Romans and Galatians. For Aquinas, as for McKnight, the gospel is Jesus Christ, and Aquinas helps us to see even more clearly how the creeds and the councils of the Church build up the Church's "gospel culture" by expositing Christ in his fullness.

Chapter 5 underscores that the transmission of the gospel entails Tradition, by which the Church hands on the whole of divine revelation. Not only Protestants but also some Catholics argue that the Church's Tradition is marked by errors, accretions, and ruptures. As an example, I engage Terrence Tilley's *Inventing Catholic Tradition*. His viewpoint strips Tradition of its propositional, doctrinal content and understands its "fidelity" in terms of an ever-changing, amorphous adaptability. By contrast, I find that Scripture presents a quite different understanding of Tradition. Focusing on the New Testament's references to "tradition" (παράδοσις), I show that the New Testament rejects the kind of tradition that Tilley proposes and instead affirms that divine revelation has a specific cognitive content that must be transmitted. Tradition cannot be less than this.

Chapter 6 examines revelation and development of doctrine. The chapter begins with *Dei Verbum*'s account of doctrinal development, which holds that although divine revelation is complete in Jesus Christ, the Church's understanding of this revelation grows and progresses over the centuries under the guidance of the Holy Spirit. In support of *Dei Verbum*'s position, I explore John Henry Newman's portrait of true development of doctrine, as distinct from corruption. John T. Noonan's *A Church That Can and Cannot Change*, however, suggests that Newman's concern to avoid positing a doctrinal corruption is misplaced because (in Noonan's view) the history of moral doctrine shows that the Church blatantly contradicts itself. I devote significant space to Noonan's critique in order to ask whether we can still hold, with Newman, to the contrast between "development" and "corruption" of doctrine. In order to highlight the ability of true doctrinal development to allow for breaks and changes, so long as these breaks or changes do not negate definitive doctrine, I employ Lewis Ayres's and Khaled Anatolios's helpful recent studies of doctrinal development in the Nicene period.

Chapter 7 discusses revelation and biblical inspiration, with a focus on the historical reference of inspired Scripture. The claim that Scripture is inspired by God and mediates divine revelation might seem to be undermined if Scripture's historical narratives communicate some events that did not actually happen.

Yet it also seems clear that Scripture's historical narratives are highly diverse in their approaches to the past. Even those narratives that approach the past in a manner closest to modern historiography deviate significantly from the practice of modern historiography. I begin by investigating Scripture's approach to its own historical reference. On the one hand, at times biblical authors explicitly insist that they are recounting an event that happened—for example, in 1 Corinthians 15 with regard to Christ's resurrection. On the other hand, sometimes the question of historical reference simply does not come up or is presumed. When the New Testament authors interpret Scripture (the Old Testament),[92] they show little interest in determining questions of historical reference. Turning to the patristic period, I examine Origen's and Augustine's ways of answering the question of historical reference. Both Origen and Augustine have a richer view of history than do modern historians, since both Origen and Augustine consider history (and historical texts) to be filled with providentially ordained typological resonances. This richer view of history offers, in my view, a way of handling scriptural texts that describe figures or events that did not exist. Such texts do not thereby lose all historical reference. We can affirm this without undermining the historical actuality of the central elements of the gospel.

Lastly, chapter 8 explores divine revelation and Hellenistic philosophical culture, or more specifically the presence within Scripture of Hellenistic philosophical insights that, in a partial and limited way, succeed in referring to the living God. Can a pagan culture, despite its grave errors about God, formulate some judgments about God that in fact are true? I first present the views of Daniel Kirk and Kavin Rowe, who in different ways emphasize the incommensurability of Hellenistic concepts of divinity with the Creator God of Israel. I then examine the portraits of God offered in Acts 17 and 19 in order to argue that Acts envisions some true pagan insight into God. Along these lines, I investigate the relationship between Wisdom of Solomon and Romans 1, each of which attributes both idolatry and insight to the Hellenistic philosophers. Lastly, inquiring into historical reconstructions of the development of the doctrine of God in Israel, I argue that Hellenistic philosophical insights helped to clarify certain ambiguities in the Old Testament's expression of revelation. My conclusion is that we should view Hellenistic philosophical culture as providentially providing the scriptural communication of divine revelation with some important and true insights about God.

92. Although most New Testament references to "Scripture" clearly mean the Old Testament, some New Testament texts may show awareness of their status as Scripture: see D. Moody Smith, "When Did the Gospels Become Scripture?"; Moloney, "Gospel of John as Scripture."

Colin Gunton has pointed out that "the mediatedness of revelation" needs to be reclaimed today.[93] As Gunton observes, there are a number of ways of denying the centrality of mediation, including the liberal quest for the "essence of Christianity," a wooden biblical fundamentalism, and an insistence upon "revelational immediacy."[94] There are also a number of ways of denying the efficacy of mediation—for example, by denigrating propositional truth, historicizing the gospel, or holding that the Church constantly reinvents rather than transmits revelation. The doctrine of revelation, as distinct from other Christian doctrines, largely has to do with the ecclesial and scriptural mediation of "Jesus Christ and him crucified" (1 Cor. 2:2), the mediation of "the word of truth, the gospel of your salvation" (Eph. 1:13). In Christ Jesus, says Paul to the Ephesians, "you also, who have heard the word of truth, the gospel of your salvation, and have believed him, were sealed with the promised Holy Spirit, which is the guarantee of our inheritance until we acquire possession of it, to the praise of his glory" (Eph. 1:13–14). How does this "word of truth"

93. Gunton, *Brief Theology of Revelation*, 5.

94. Ibid., 3. The phrase "revelational immediacy" is Gunton's, and he has in mind Karl Barth's position in this regard. See especially Barth, *Church Dogmatics*, I.1, *The Doctrine of the Word of God*; for further critical discussion of Barth's view, see Wolterstorff, *Divine Discourse*, 63–74. Wolterstorff notes that Barth considers "revelation" in the strict sense to be solely "God's speaking by way of the dwelling among us of the person, Jesus Christ" (*Divine Discourse*, 63). Scripture and proclamation mediate this revelation to us, in such a way that God can make these words his speech for us (though not his speech per se). Wolterstorff explains that for Barth,

> just as it is only through the witnesses that you and I today have access to God's revelatory word consisting in Jesus Christ dwelling among us, so also it is only through Scripture that we have access to those witnesses. Revelation is mediated by the witnesses and the witnesses are mediated by Scripture. . . . Though the witnesses' acts of witnessing-of and witnessing-to revelation occur under the superintendence of the Spirit, the speech of the witness remains purely human speech. So also, though contemporary proclamation concerning revelation is under the guidance of the witnesses, the speech of the preacher remains purely human speech. . . . Nonetheless, Scripture and contemporary proclamation do become the instrument of God's speaking to particular persons—always to particular persons—on specific occasions. (69–70)

Wolterstorff terms this position "eventism" (71). Along similar lines, see the nuanced engagement with Barth's position in McCall, "On Understanding Scripture as the Word of God." For positive views of Barth's position, see Vanhoozer, "A Person of the Book?"; McCormack, "Being of Holy Scripture"; and T. Hart, "Revelation." Hart remarks,

> Information about Jesus's life, character, actions, death and resurrection is not knowledge of God in the sense that Barth intends it and in the event of revelation it is precisely *God himself* who is known. For this to happen, the particular form of Jesus's humanity is necessary but not sufficient. The veil must become transparent. Faith must be called into being, faith which travels through and transcends the veil of the flesh to a depth of reality to which the created form now points and corresponds, not in and of itself, but as God takes it up into his dynamic revealing activity. (52–53)

come to us today? The answer, rooted in the active presence of Christ and the Holy Spirit, includes the canon of Scripture and "the church, which is his body, the fulness of him who fills all in all" (Eph. 1:22–23).

The conviction that "in many and various ways God spoke of old to our fathers by the prophets; but in these last days he has spoken to us by a Son, whom he appointed the heir of all things, through whom also he created the world" (Heb. 1:1–2), and that this gospel has been faithfully received and handed down by the Church even unto us today, is a cause for joy and hope, as well as salutary repentance. Despite our failings, God has ensured the faithful mediation of his revelation within the liturgical community that participates in these revealed realities. With Moses, then, let us beseech the living God, our Creator and Redeemer, "If now I have found favor in thy sight, O Lord, let the Lord, I pray thee, go in the midst of us . . . and pardon our iniquity and our sin, and take us for thy inheritance" (Exod. 34:9).

ONE

Church

Dei Verbum anchors its treatment of divine revelation in the Father's sending (*missio*) of the Son: "For he sent his Son, the eternal Word who enlightens all men, to dwell among men and to tell them about the inner life of God. Hence, Jesus Christ, sent as 'a man among men,' 'speaks the words of God' (John 3:34), and accomplishes the saving work which the Father gave him to do."[1] *Dei Verbum* specifies that the mission of the Son "completed and perfected revelation," not only by his words and deeds but also by his "sending the Spirit of truth."[2] According to *Dei Verbum*, then, the theology of the divine missions provides the basis for all reflection on divine revelation and its human mediation.[3] As a theological term, however, "mission" can mean various things. First, it can signify the Father's sending of the Son and the Holy Spirit for the salvation of the world, as in the above passage from *Dei Verbum*. In this

1. *Dei Verbum*, §4, 751.
2. Ibid., 752.
3. See Newbigin, *Open Secret*, which begins with the opening sentence of *Lumen Gentium*. Newbigin remarks:

> Fundamental to everything else that came forth from the council were the reaffirmation of the missionary character of the church, the recognition of the unfinished task which that implies, the confession that the church is a pilgrim people on its way to the ends of the earth and the end of time, and the acknowledgment of the need for a new openness to the world into which the church is sent. This new readiness to acknowledge the missionary character of the church, to confess that "there is no participation in Christ without participation in his mission to the world," is not confined to the Roman Catholic church. All the old established churches of the Western world have been brought to a new recognition that mission belongs to the very being of the church. (1)

sense, "mission" describes the salvific activity of the Son and the Spirit, and
includes not only their visible missions in the incarnation and Pentecost but
also their invisible missions in human souls at all places and times. Second,
"mission" can signify a particular "vocation" in God's economy of salvation.
Jesus Christ preeminently receives a mission, the mission of the Messiah. But
the patriarchs, prophets, and leaders of Israel, as well as the whole people
of God, also receive a mission, as do the apostles and indeed each and every
Christian. All human beings are called to a "mission" inscribed within the
salvific mission of Christ.[4]

Third, "mission" can be taken in the sense of the Church's evangelizing
mission, rooted not least in the risen Jesus's command, "Go therefore and
make disciples of all nations" (Matt. 28:19), and embodied by Paul's remark
to the Corinthians, "Woe to me if I do not preach the gospel!" (1 Cor. 9:16).
It is in this sense that the Second Vatican Council's Decree on the Church's
Missionary Activity, *Ad Gentes*, proclaims, "The Church on earth is by its
very nature missionary since, according to the plan of the Father, it has its
origin in the mission of the Son and the Holy Spirit."[5] As *Ad Gentes* says,
the Church's missionary task "unfolds the mission of Christ, who was sent
to evangelize the poor."[6]

The task of this chapter is to elucidate these three senses of "mission" and
to show how they illumine the Church's mediation of divine revelation. For
each of the three senses of "mission"—the missions of the Son and the Spirit,
Christ's mission and ours, and evangelization—I concentrate upon the work
of one theologian for whom the particular sense of "mission" has an especially central role. With respect to the trinitarian missions, I focus upon the
theology of Thomas Aquinas. As Gilles Emery observes, the doctrine of the
trinitarian missions is "the pivot, indeed a real key, of St. Thomas's Trinitarian theology: *the revelation of the Trinity and the gift of salvation consist in
the missions of the divine persons*."[7] Regarding Christ's mission and ours,

---

As Newbigin goes on to say, "A church that is not 'the church in mission' is no church at all"
(2). Along similar lines, see more recently Bellini, *Participation*, which grounds epistemology in
the reality of creatures' participation in God and ties both to the theology of mission.

4. See chap. 5 of *Lumen Gentium* (396–402) on the universal call to holiness. See also Congar,
Lay People in the Church.

5. *Ad Gentes*, §2, 814.

6. Ibid., §5, 818. See also Newbigin, *Open Secret*, 16–17; Bevans and Schroeder, *Constants
in Context*; R. Martin, *Will Many Be Saved?*

7. See Emery, "*Theologia* and *Dispensatio*," 560; cf. 515–16. By contrast, Nicholas J. Healy
states that "Thomas's account of the relation between mission and procession does not figure
prominently in his discussion of the nature of the trinitarian processions. The question on
the divine missions appears at the very end of the treatise on the Trinity in the *Summa*, after
Thomas has already treated the identity of the persons and their mutual relations." See N. Healy,

I examine Hans Urs von Balthasar's theology of Christ's supreme mission-consciousness (kenotic love) and our participation in Christ by embracing our missions of love. I then move on to the biblical scholar Christopher Wright, who emphasizes God's saving mission of mercy with a particular reference to the evangelizing mission to the nations. He interprets God's revelation to Israel as already including *in nuce* the Church's mission as a light to all nations, to proclaim and imitate Christ.

The distinctive perspectives of Aquinas, Balthasar, and Wright agree on this: through the missions of the Son and Spirit, the Church is enabled to share in and make present for the whole world the salvific, revelatory mission of Jesus Christ, both as regards its content and as regards its kenotic form (charity). In this way, divine revelation can be said to include the active participation of the Church, without imagining that the Church gives to itself the revelation that God, in Christ and the Spirit, has given to the Church once and for all.[8]

Thomas Aquinas: Revelation and the Missions of the Son and Holy Spirit

Does "mission" name something in God? It might seem that even granting the reality of processions in God, "mission" would be an inappropriate word to denote the salvific activity of the Son and Holy Spirit in the world. "Mission" seems to describe moving from one place/condition to another place/condition, as if the Son and the Holy Spirit, leaving behind their eternal existence with the Father, parachuted into the world. "Mission" also seems to suggest that the Son and Holy Spirit are distinct from the Father and from each other not solely in terms of their eternal relations but also on the basis of distinct missions. If this were so, then the distinction of missions would produce new real "relations" in God, thereby producing new divine Persons. Mission might also seem unreal when applied to the Son and Holy Spirit. If the Triune God had not freely created the world, then there would have been no missions, but there would still have been eternal divine Persons. These eternal divine Persons—the Son and Holy Spirit—are supremely who they are, and they cannot be changed by anything. If the historical missions do not change the Son

---

Eschatology of Hans Urs von Balthasar, 124–25. For much stronger concerns regarding a supposed separation of "theologia" and "oikonomia" in Aquinas, see LaCugna, *God for Us*. LaCugna's view has been widely critiqued, including by Emery.

8. On the latter point see the Dogmatic Constitution on Divine Revelation, *Dei Verbum*, §4, 752: "The Christian economy, therefore, since it is the new and definitive covenant, will never pass away; and no new public revelation is to be expected before the glorious manifestation of our Lord, Jesus Christ" (cf. 1 Tim. 6:14 and Titus 2:13).

and Spirit, then it appears that the missions are simply metaphorical, naming something that does not really involve the actual divine Persons.

By Thomas Aquinas's time, of course, the theology of divine missions was part of the Church's heritage.[9] But he presents this theology in a way that is particularly helpful for understanding the relationship between divine revelation and the Church. He builds his case for the missions of the Son and Holy Spirit on the basis of biblical texts from the Gospels and Paul, with Isaiah and the Wisdom of Solomon in the background. Specifically, in the eight articles of *Summa theologiae* I, question 43, he cites the following passages of Scripture to elucidate the missions:

> Matthew 3:16–17: "When Jesus was baptized, he went up immediately from the water, and behold, the heavens were opened and he saw the Spirit of God descending like a dove, and alighting on him; and lo, a voice from heaven, saying, 'This is my beloved Son, with whom I am well pleased.'"

> Matthew 17:5: "A bright cloud overshadowed them, and a voice from the cloud said, 'This is my beloved Son, with whom I am well pleased; listen to him.'"

> John 1:10: "He was in the world, and the world was made through him, yet the world knew him not."

> John 7:39: "Now this he said about the Spirit, which those who believed in him were to receive; for as yet the Spirit had not been given, because Jesus was not yet glorified."

> John 8:16: "My judgment is true, for it is not I alone that judge, but I and he who sent me."

> John 14:23: "If a man loves me, he will keep my word, and my Father will love him, and we will come to him and make our home with him."

> Acts 2:4: "They were all filled with the Holy Spirit and began to speak in other tongues, as the Spirit gave them utterance."

> Romans 5:5: "Hope does not disappoint us, because God's love has been poured into our hearts through the Holy Spirit which has been given to us."

---

9. See Ayres, *Augustine and the Trinity*, 181–88; Maier, *Les Missions divines selon saint Augustin*; Gioia, *Theological Epistemology of Augustine's "De Trinitate,"* 28, 78–81. See also, for example, Richard of St. Victor's *On the Trinity* 6.14. On Thomas Aquinas's theology of the trinitarian missions, see Emery, "*Theologia* and *Dispensatio*"; Emery, "Missions invisibles et missions visibles"; Levering, "Christ, the Trinity, and Predestination." For an ecclesiology rooted in Aquinas's theology of the missions of the Son and Holy Spirit—which is our focus here—see Journet, *L'Église du Verbe Incarné*. See also Saward, "*L'Église a ravi son coeur*," particularly 131–33.

Galatians 4:4–5: "When the time had fully come, God sent forth his Son, born of woman, born under the law, to redeem those who were under the law, so that we might receive adoption as sons."

Hebrews 2:3: "How shall we escape if we neglect such a great salvation? It was declared at first by the Lord, and it was attested to us by those who heard him."

Isaiah 48:16: "And now the Lord God has sent me and his Spirit."

Wisdom 9:10: "Send her forth from the holy heavens, and from the throne of your glory send her, that she may be with me and toil, and that I may learn what is pleasing to you."

Aquinas presents these biblical texts within an interpretative context shaped by Augustine's *On the Trinity*.[10] He quotes from books 2, 3, 4, 9, and 15 of *On the Trinity*, with book 4 being the most frequently cited. In book 4 Augustine carefully defends the claim that the Father is not superior to the Son or Holy Spirit even though the Father is not sent. Augustine has in view both the visible missions of the Son and Spirit (the incarnation and Pentecost) and their invisible missions in the souls of believers. Aquinas makes much of Augustine's statement that the Son is "sent to anyone when he is known and perceived by him, as far as he can be perceived and known according to the capacity of a rational soul either making progress toward God or already made perfect in God."[11] Aquinas also quotes more than once Augustine's assertion that the Father is not sent. Among the texts quoted by Aquinas in question 43, Augustine in book 4 cites John 7:39; Galatians 4:4; and Wisdom 9:10. In the same book, Augustine also cites cognate passages such as Wisdom 7:25–27 and John 14:26; 15:26; and 16:28.

When one canvasses the other books of Augustine's *On the Trinity* from which Aquinas quotes in question 43, it becomes clear that rather than trying to break new ground in the biblical passages that he cites, Aquinas is selecting certain texts that already enjoy a central place in Augustine and in the theological tradition. In the objections of the first two articles of question 43, Aquinas also quotes Jerome, Hilary of Poitiers, and Gregory the Great, but he quotes these fathers in order to rule out potential misunderstandings, not

---

10. Bruce Marshall observes that without following Augustine slavishly, "Aquinas, like virtually every scholastic writer on the Trinity in the Middle Ages, is more deeply engaged with Augustine than with any other patristic figure. No text of Augustine gets more attention from Thomas than the *De Trinitate*, and very many of the topics and formulas that preoccupy Aquinas and other medieval Trinitarian theologians can be traced to their involvement with this work" ("Aquinas the Augustinian?," 45). See also in the same volume Emery, "Trinitarian Theology as Spiritual Exercise," 1–40, and Goris, "Theology and Theory," 62–78.

11. See Augustine, *The Trinity*, 4.5.28, 173.

in order to ground or advance his own arguments. This is a sharp contrast to his use of Augustine in question 43: quotations of Augustine appear in the objections, *sed contra*, *respondeo*, and answers to the objections, and these quotations of Augustine play a major role in determining Aquinas's own position. This is so especially in four respects: the Father is not sent; the Son and Holy Spirit are invisibly sent when a person is enlightened by faith and is sanctified; the purpose of the Spirit's mission is our sanctification in charity, a purpose that involves and presumes the Son's mission, which vivifies our faith; and the visible mission of the incarnate Son differs in kind from the visible mission of the Spirit at Christ's baptism and at Pentecost.

Rooted in Scripture as interpreted by Augustine, Aquinas's theology of the missions of the Son and Holy Spirit emphasizes that the revelation of God in the mission of the Son is inseparable from the mission of the Holy Spirit. It is in the visible mission of the incarnate Word that God fully reveals the truth of salvation, the truth about himself and about us. This visible mission is received as revelation through the visible mission of the Holy Spirit at Pentecost, and through the invisible missions of the Word inspiring faith and of the Holy Spirit healing and sanctifying us in charity.[12]

Against misconceptions of these missions, Aquinas observes that the change is in the creature rather than in the divine Person to whom the creature is united. In technical language, Aquinas explains that "mission not only signifies procession from the principle [the Father], but also determines the temporal term of the procession. . . . Hence the procession may be called a twin procession, eternal and temporal, not that there is a double relation to the principle, but a double term, temporal and eternal."[13] The procession of the Son coming forth from the Father is not combined with a second procession in which the Father sends the Son into the world. Rather, there is only one procession constitutive of the Son, but the Son is nevertheless rightly said to be "sent" into the world because the procession has two terms: the Son's eternal subsistence and his temporal subsistence as Jesus Christ. The visible mission of the Son is not a

---

12. Gilles Emery notes that in the *respondeo* of question 43, article 7,

St. Thomas emphasizes two functions of the visible missions: (1) revelation (*demonstrare*, *manifestare*) and (2) sanctification (*sanctificatio*). Regarding the first aspect (revelation), the visible missions of the Son and Spirit manifest their invisible missions. This means that the visible missions involve a dual disclosure: they manifest the eternal procession of the Son and Spirit (they reveal the persons themselves in their eternal origin), and they manifest the donation of these persons in grace. A similar connection between the visible and the invisible is found in St. Thomas's teaching on Christ's miracles. ("*Theologia* and *Dispensatio*," 529)

13. *Summa theologiae* I, q. 43, a. 2, ad 3. For the Johannine basis of this theology of divine procession/mission, see also Sokolowski, *Eucharistic Presence*, 157–58.

change in the Son, but a change that occurs on the side of the creature that is united to the Son in the incarnation.[14] Likewise, the mission of the Holy Spirit is not a second procession of the Holy Spirit but a temporal "term" whereby creatures are sanctified by the Holy Spirit. Sanctifying grace makes the Holy Spirit present to creatures in this way.

Among the biblical verses quoted by Aquinas in question 43, perhaps the most illuminating are John 7:39 and 14:23 and Galatians 4:4. Especially in John 7:39, one can see how divine revelation requires the unity of the visible mission of the Son and the invisible mission of the Spirit. The context is Jesus's proclamation at the Feast of Tabernacles, "If any one thirst, let him come to me and drink. He who believes in me, as the scripture has said, 'Out of his heart shall flow rivers of living water'" (John 7:37–38). The evangelist John explains, "Now this he said about the Spirit, which those who believed in him were to receive; for as yet the Spirit had not been given, because Jesus was not yet glorified" (John 7:39).[15] At this time his disciples and the Jewish people did not understand Jesus's words; he was revealing the mystery of God, but they did not yet understand the revelation in faith. They needed the Spirit in order to fully receive his words and deeds as divine revelation. The visible mission of the Son requires to be united, in the revelatory drama, with the invisible missions of the Son and Holy Spirit illuminating and sanctifying the people of God so that we can perceive and perform revelation.

One can see the same thing in John 14:23, especially when this verse is read in its context. The evangelist notes that in the midst of Jesus's farewell discourse, the disciple Judas (not Judas Iscariot) asks Jesus, "Lord, how is it that you will manifest yourself to us, and not to the world?" (John 14:22). Jesus has promised to make himself known to the disciples even after his Pasch, and Judas asks how this will be possible. The answer is that the visible mission of the Son in Jesus Christ is manifested to us interiorly by a corresponding invisible mission of the Son and Spirit, an invisible mission that draws the believer into the life of the Father. Thus in John 14:23 Jesus states, "If a man loves me, he will keep my word, and my Father will love him, and we will come to him and make our home with him"—a promise that becomes manifestly trinitarian in verse 26, where Jesus promises, "The Counselor, the Holy Spirit, whom the Father will send in my name, he will teach you all things, and bring to your remembrance all that I have said to you." Regarding the invisible missions of the Son and Spirit, Aquinas explains that "the two missions are united in the root, which is grace, but are distinguished

14. See Weinandy, "Aquinas: God *IS* Man," 67–89.
15. See Morris, *Gospel according to John*, 378–79.

in the effects of grace, which consist in the illumination of the intellect and the kindling of the affection. Thus it is manifest that one mission cannot be without the other, because neither takes place without sanctifying grace, nor is one person separated from the other."[16]

To show that mission is temporal rather than eternal, Aquinas quotes Galatians 4:4 in the *sed contra* of question 43, article 1. Paul teaches that "God sent forth his Son, born of woman, born under the law, to redeem those who were under the law, so that we might receive adoption as sons" (Gal. 4:4–5). This adoption, Paul goes on to say, involves the indwelling Spirit: "And because you are sons, God has sent the Spirit of his Son into our hearts, crying, 'Abba! Father!'" (Gal. 4:6).[17] The invisible mission of the Holy Spirit belongs to the dynamism of divine revelation, in which God sends into the world both his Son and his Spirit so as to make us adopted children of God, sharers in the divine life. It follows that although divine revelation does not in any way originate with the Church, the Church is not merely an inert receptacle of divine revelation, because revelation always involves the united missions of the Son and Holy Spirit.[18] The community is interiorly and not simply exteriorly united by the revelatory missions, visible and invisible, of the Son and Spirit.

The faith and charity of believers, by which we are configured to Christ and by which we are enabled to bear witness to Christ in the world, come from the missions of the Son and Holy Spirit. Aquinas explains that "for a divine person to be sent to anyone by grace, there must be a likening of the soul to the divine person who is sent, by some gift of grace."[19] The invisible mission of the Holy Spirit occurs "by the gift of charity," because the Holy Spirit proceeds as Love.[20] The invisible mission of the Son, who is the Word "who breathes forth Love," occurs "not in accordance with every and any kind of intellectual perfection, but according to the intellectual illumination, which breaks forth into the affection of love."[21] These invisible missions are inseparable from the revelation of God in the visible mission of the Son and in the visible mission of the Spirit at Christ's baptism and Pentecost. In short, the Church's participation in divine revelation comes about through the missions

16. *Summa theologiae* I, q. 43, a. 5, ad 3. See also Emery, "Holy Spirit," 127–62; B. Marshall, "What Does the Spirit Have to Do?," 62–77.

17. For discussion see Witherington, *Grace in Galatia*, 287–91.

18. Clarifying John 7:39's statement that the Holy Spirit had not yet been sent, Aquinas states, "The invisible mission was directed to the Old Testament Fathers, as appears from what Augustine says (*De Trin.* iv.20), that the invisible mission of the Son 'is in man and with men. This was done in former times with the Fathers and Prophets'" (*Summa theologiae* I, q. 43, a. 6, ad 1).

19. *Summa theologiae* I, q. 43, a. 5, ad 2.

20. Ibid.

21. Ibid.

of the Son and Spirit that enable us to believe, obey, and imitate Christ's revelatory words and deeds.[22]

Hans Urs von Balthasar: Revelation and Jesus's Universal Mission-Consciousness

Hans Urs von Balthasar offers an existential deepening of our theme. I will
present his approach and remark upon its strengths, while at the same time
indicating where I think it needs adjustment.

In the third volume of his *Theo-Drama*, with reference to Aquinas's theology
of mission, Balthasar depicts Jesus Christ as most perfectly "sent."[23] Balthasar

22. Aquinas's discussion grounds the unity of the "Church" across time and space, a unity
that Aquinas also takes as a dogmatic given. Here, therefore, might be the place to note
Markus Bockmuehl's emphasis on the early Christians' understanding of themselves as "in
communion with the church of the great apostolic foundations" ("Doctrine of the Church,"
42). Admittedly, Bockmuehl also points out, "Historically, of course, Christian communities
of all denominational and creedal stripes have always tended to claim for their own particular ecclesial order the imprimatur of none other than Christ himself and his apostles. The
reality is that there was never a time when diversity was not part of the very fabric of the
Jesus movement; even Luke's harmonic account of the church in Jerusalem makes that clear"
(43). Unity-in-diversity (or diversity-in-unity) certainly belongs to the Catholic Church in all
ages. Yet the human mediation of divine revelation (including the unique scriptural mediation) relies on the fact that Jesus founded a visible Church and sent the Holy Spirit upon it
at Pentecost, and that Jesus governs his Church at the right hand of the Father. This claim
does not imply ecclesial triumphalism, which would be absurd, but it does involve a visible
and liturgically identifiable Catholic Church through the centuries (just as God formed the
people of Israel as a visible and identifiable people). Bockmuehl strongly affirms that Jesus
intended to form an eschatological, missional community (Church) in which Israel would be
reconfigured around himself:

> We can say with some confidence that Jesus's calling and commissioning of groups such
> as the Twelve and the Seventy was deliberately symbolic of an eschatological renewal of
> Sinaitic Israel gathered around twelve tribal princes and seventy elders—what Stephen
> in Acts 7 calls "the *ekklēsia* in the wilderness" (Acts 7:38). All four Gospels affirm that
> Jesus singled out twelve men as an inner core of the larger group of disciples, although
> relatively less is made of this in John. New Testament scholarship generally regards their
> appointment as authentic, and their symbolism too is not in serious doubt. In its biblical
> and Jewish setting this eschatological institution of the Twelve conveys a theocentric and
> specifically messianic reconstitution of the entire biblical Israel under the leadership of
> tribal judges and their king. This restoration of biblical Israel's twelve tribes was a mes-
> sage deeply rooted in the Old Testament and of some continuing interest in the early
> church, even after the demise of the Twelve. (ibid.)

23. Donald MacKinnon insightfully remarks regarding Balthasar's Christology in the *Theo-
Drama*, "The focal point of Balthasar's whole exposition is found in the concept of *Sendung* or
mission. Like *doxa* in the fourth Gospel it is a focus of conceptual interpenetration. . . . Certainly
kenosis remains profoundly significant for Balthasar; indeed it dominates his imagination in the
many passages in which he gives free rein to his mastery of his own language and recaptures the
emphases of the earlier monograph on the Paschal mystery. Yet in the present work, mission is a

points not only to the repeated Johannine testimony to the one "whom God has sent" (John 3:34) but also to such Synoptic texts as Matthew 10:40: "He who receives you receives me, and he who receives me receives him who sent me" (see also Luke 9:48; Mark 9:37). The question regarding the identity of Jesus must receive the answer that Jesus is supremely and without remainder the one who is sent. The "personhood" of Jesus, therefore, is identical with mission: he is his (relational) mission, to a complete degree that cannot be claimed for any other human being. Balthasar argues that this unity of person and mission in Jesus reveals Jesus's divinity, since only in the holy Trinity can person and mission be the same.[24] Jesus's very personhood consists in being sent, just as the Son comes entirely from the Father who begets and sends him. Indeed, Jesus's whole self-understanding consists in his awareness that he has been sent, and this self-understanding perfectly corresponds with who Jesus is. Jesus has an "absolute sense of mission."[25]

Jesus's perfect mission-consciousness ensures that he is utterly abandoned to and indistinguishable from his filial mission. It follows, says Balthasar, that

---

more inclusive concept than self-emptying and demands in its use a more searching discipline" (MacKinnon, "Some Reflections," 168).

24. As Balthasar states, "Here, indeed, in the mission of Jesus, where an exact definition of personal uniqueness coincides with its universal significance, we have the irrefutable expression of his divinity" (*Dramatis Personae*, 207). To conclude that the Gospels' narration of Jesus's mission provides us with "the irrefutable expression of his divinity" seems a stretch, but certainly it is true that no merely human person can be absolutely identical with his or her mission. For appropriate cautions see Kilby, *Balthasar*, 95–98.

25. Balthasar, *Dramatis Personae*, 160; cf. 224: "Jesus experiences his human consciousness entirely in terms of mission." As Aidan Nichols, OP, comments:

The idea of mission, of being "sent" or of having (in some heightened solemn sense) "come," "come out" or "forth," is not only Johannine but also Synoptic. In the Parable of the Wicked Husbandmen, moreover, all three Synoptic evangelists agree in distinguishing between the earlier sending of "servants," and the final sending of the "son." But it is in John above all that Jesus's knowledge of himself coincides with his knowledge of being sent. He does not do the Father's will incidentally but lives from it, for apart from it he can do nothing. The One who sends is seen to be present in the One who is sent. The latter is so dependent on the One who sends him that his entire being is in motion towards him: he is returning to him. (*No Bloodless Myth*, 101)

Nichols goes on to explain:

Using this concept of mission as a key term, Balthasar can put forward what he calls a Christology of consciousness and, on that basis, a Christology of being, two ways, the second deeper than the first, of looking at the work and person of Christ. The Christology of consciousness explores the coincidence of Jesus's mission-consciousness with his person. This mission, itself more than human, for to reconcile the whole world with God is not a simply human undertaking, is in no way heteronomous *vis-à-vis* the person of Jesus. . . . "Who he is" is exhaustively expressed in his being from the One who addresses him as "My beloved Son." (101–2)

See also N. Healy, *Eschatology of Hans Urs von Balthasar*, 121–22; Waldstein, "Mission"; Schwager, *Jesus of Nazareth*; Schönborn, *God Sent His Son*, 187–88.

Jesus must thereby reveal his divine Father "in every situation of his life—even if part of his task, in the long years of his hidden life and ultimately on the Cross, was to manifest God's hiddenness."[26] Revelation of the Father is Jesus's mission, and Jesus is identical with his mission. Revelation and mission are thus two sides of the same coin, so that as Jesus increased in age he also increased in the depth of his revelatory mission-consciousness. At every stage of his life, guided by the Holy Spirit, he was completely immersed in the revelatory mission-consciousness suitable for precisely that stage. Balthasar emphasizes that "the Son's *missio* is the economic form of his eternal *processio* from the Father. This mission of the Son draws the mission of the Spirit in its wake, in a twofold form: first the Spirit is sent from the Father upon the incarnate Son, and then the Spirit is sent from the Father and the exalted Son upon the Church and the world."[27] Although Balthasar's presentation of the cross as the "economic form" of the Son's eternal procession mistakenly imports alienation into the relation of Father and Son,[28] Balthasar is right to observe that the theology of the missions of the Son and Spirit "opens up the triune God's involvement in the whole world drama, which Irenaeus calls God's 'becoming accustomed' to dwelling with man and which Thomas designates as the invisible 'missions' of Son and Spirit into the whole of history—before and after Christ."[29]

For Balthasar, *only* Jesus is a "person" in a strict sense. It follows that "others can claim to be persons only in virtue of a relationship with him and in dependence on him."[30] Regarding other "persons," Balthasar affirms

26. Balthasar, *Dramatis Personae*, 173.

27. Ibid., 201. In confirmation of the point that "the Son's *missio* is the economic form of his eternal *processio* from the Father," Balthasar cites Thomas Aquinas, *Summa theologiae* I, q. 43, a. 1. See Nichols, *No Bloodless Myth*, 103; N. Healy, *Eschatology of Hans Urs von Balthasar*, 115–18. In thinking about this "economic form," the created humanity of Jesus needs to be kept at the forefront, so that the temporal createdness of the Son's mission, as distinct from the eternality of the Person of the Son, remains clear. The Person and mission of the Son should neither be separated nor simply equated without further explication.

28. On this topic see chap. 4 of my *Scripture and Metaphysics* and chap. 5 of my *Predestination*. For similar concerns, see Kilby, *Balthasar*, 99–122. See also Schenk, "What Does the Trinity 'Add'?," 111:

> If Balthasar has replaced suffering's toleration by the Trinity or by the humanity of Christ (*voluntas in obliquo, voluntas rationis*) with an absolute and antecedent will of it (*in recto*), if he has heeded the unseparated character of Christ's natures in the hypostatic union at the price of their unmixed duality, if he has made kenotic suffering normative by deifying it, then it needs to be asked whether the retrieval of the Trinity as beyond suffering—precisely as a gospel of human hope—might not allow us to embrace with the living Jewish community their more genuine understanding of the Old Testament as a covenant of hope for salvation from suffering.

29. Balthasar, *Dramatis Personae*, 201; he cites *Summa theologiae* I, q. 43, aa. 5, 7.

30. Balthasar, *Dramatis Personae*, 207.

that "we can say that their conscious subjects are endowed with a part or aspect of his universal mission."[31] Before specifying how this is so, Balthasar remarks that "the important thing here is to realize that this participation [in Christ's mission] is what makes conscious subjects into persons in the Christian sense. Accordingly, the greater the participation, the greater the subject's personal definition will be and the more universal (and ecclesial) his mission."[32] Since Christ's mission is kenotic love and obedience to the point of abandonment, those who love more will be more fully "persons" and will share more deeply in Christ's mission. This way of defining personhood, based on grace and charity, differs from definitions of human personhood that are based upon the incommunicable uniqueness of individuals who share human nature, as well as from definitions of human personhood based upon the "image of God" as a gift of creation rather than of grace. In my view, Balthasar should have retained the rootedness of "personhood" in human nature and emphasized that grace and charity—that is to say, participation in Christ's mission of supreme charity—perfect, elevate, and fulfill our personhood. In this way, his key point about sharing in Christ's personhood or mission could be retained without calling into doubt the "personhood" of those who consciously reject Christ.[33]

Regarding our missions (or our participation in Christ's mission), Balthasar rightly notes that these are not natural to us, let alone identical with us. As he explains, "These missions do not, as in Christ's case, constitute an *a priori synthesis* with his person, but are synthesized *a posteriori* along with the created, chosen persons [*Geistpersonen*]."[34] Since this is so, we as sinners can fail—or at least try to fail—to be persons. Balthasar comments that "sinners only partially accept and fulfill their missions and can even reject them entirely."[35] It would seem that those sinners who entirely rejected their missions would cease to be "persons," although what Balthasar means by this is simply the deprivation of charity, of the graced life that God calls each human

---

31. Ibid. See Nichols, *No Bloodless Myth*, 104–5.

32. Balthasar, *Dramatis Personae*, 207. See McIntosh, "Christology," 32–35. McIntosh argues: The key for Balthasar is Ignatius' clarity about opening oneself to the call of Christ and the discovery that this call, while unique for each person, always leads to an inner participation in Jesus's mission from the Father, and that it is precisely the following of the call and the sharing in this mission that brings about the fulfilment of personal identity. Mission is constitutive of personhood because mission is the concrete form by which God turns to each being, drawing it out from the potentiality of its nature, into relational converse, and so onwards into the risk of free personal existence. (32–33)

33. In short, to be a "person" does not require being a fully fulfilled person. On the *imago dei*, see my *Jewish-Christian Dialogue*, chap. 3.

34. Balthasar, *Dramatis Personae*, 207–8.

35. Ibid., 208.

to attain. As Balthasar observes, "In the plan of God, each conscious subject is created for the sake of his mission—a mission that makes him a person."[36] I agree that each human "is created for the sake of his mission"—namely, a particular work of love—but I do not think that it is solely this graced mission that makes the human being a "person."[37]

Balthasar goes on to make more adequate distinctions, even if he still does not affirm that "personhood" belongs to all individuals of human nature. For instance, Balthasar states, "In Christ it has been made possible for a conscious subject to rise above his natural level to that of the ('super-natural') person. In positive terms, this presupposes that the created spirit, man, can be an image (*imago*) of God; negatively, it implies that he is deficient and needs to be perfected and given a 'likeness' (*similitudo*) to God; such a likeness can only be imparted by God, in Christ."[38] At various points in his corpus, Balthasar also argues that we can hope that the movement to personhood from nonpersonhood will occur even for unrepentant sinners who have entered (along with Christ) into "hell" itself. As Balthasar puts it, "*In Christo* . . . every man can cherish the hope of not remaining a merely individual conscious subject but of receiving personhood from God, becoming a person, with a mission that is likewise defined *in Christo*."[39]

Balthasar's approach helps us to see clearly where the Church fits into revelation: Christ is revelation (in his mission), and the Church is constituted by participation in Christ's revelatory mission through diverse forms of kenotic love under the guidance of the Holy Spirit. Since Christ's mission is universal, it "extends to the sphere of all (human) conscious subjects, and so they are drawn into the 'area' of the unique Person of the God-man."[40] The Eucharist has a particularly central role. As Roch Kereszty observes in an essay on Balthasar's theology:

36. Ibid.

37. Again, a better way of putting it is that by participating in Christ's mission through the grace of the Holy Spirit, we become the persons that God wishes us to be, so that our personhood is perfected and elevated.

38. Balthasar, *Dramatis Personae*, 208.

39. Ibid., 220. See also John Webster's helpful way of phrasing our mission in Christ:
Human work is the work of beings whose self-definition is not their own project but a responsible endeavour truthfully and faithfully to live out the calling of the Holy One. Responsibility does not mean the end of all human mobility or plasticity, for it is characteristic of the kind of creature that we are that we discover our identity by fulfilling a vocation through time; we *become* holy. But the becoming is, precisely, discovery, not invention; it is not our generation of a self-narrative, not life politics or an ascetics (aesthetics) of the self, but the enactment of an office: "You shall be holy, for I, the Lord your God, am holy." (*Holiness*, 104)

40. Balthasar, *Dramatis Personae*, 231.

Against this background we understand better why the Eucharist so eminently embodies the mission of the Church. As we are drawn into the unfathomable depths of Christ's love, we become conformed to Him so that we can empty ourselves of our own self-centered existence and learn to love our fellow human beings with the very love of Christ. In this way we share in the life-giving and life-nourishing mission of the Word made flesh. The common mission of the ecclesial Body of Christ includes every member's unique mission, which participates in the universal redemptive mission of the Son.[41]

Christ's mission grounds all other missions in such a way that all revelation, the entire history of God with his people, relates to Christ's mission.[42] The whole of history, then, is a drama of decision—for or against the living God—with Christ at the center. Balthasar points out that Christ's mission reveals both God's taking the part of sinners and God's sorrowful forsakenness vis-à-vis sinners.[43]

41. Kereszty, "Eucharist and Mission," 9. The background that Kereszty has in view is Mary's *fiat* prayer ("Let it be to me according to your word" [Luke 1:38]). For further discussion see especially Healy and Schindler, "For the Life of the World," 51–63. As Healy and Schindler remark, "For in the gift of the Eucharist, Christ endows the Church with the 'real presence' of his body and blood together with an inner participation in his mission to the world" (51). See also Kimberly Hope Belcher's reflections on Balthasar in her constructive theology of baptism: "It is the human enacting of Christ's obediential kenosis (for which liturgy is identity-forming 'practice'—efficacious engagement) that allows the drama of human existence to retain its theological character. It is by the church's ethical life in the world that the world continues to be the manifestation of the absolute self-giving of Father and Son in the Spirit" (*Efficacious Engagement*, 132).

42. As Larry Chapp astutely puts it, "For Balthasar, the 'what' of revelation is more appropriately referred to as the Who: revelation is given once and for all in a definitive manner in Jesus, but *what* is given is nothing less than the offer for historical humanity to participate in trinitarian eternity. In the 'concrete universal' that is the prototypical hypostatic humanity of Jesus, an 'opening' is revealed which can only be entered into by way of engraced participation" ("Revelation," 22). Chapp notes that Balthasar is well aware that the Church can render Christ's mission "opaque through the sinfulness of her members" (23). The point, however, is that "by rendering revelation contemporaneous to all generations," the Church and Scripture "are themselves to be viewed historically, that is to say, 'personologically,' as living manifestations of the Christ-event that call forth a response in the form of a decision" (ibid.). See also Mongrain, *Systematic Thought*, 109–13.

43. Balthasar embeds this forsakenness in the immanent life of the Son and Father. Too loosely in my view, he argues:

> If we are to follow biblical revelation, we must not split the Son of God in the exercise of his mission into the one who carries out his mission on earth and the one who remains unaffected in heaven, looking down at the "sent" Son. For he is One: he is the eternal Son dwelling in time. The event by which he consents to be transferred from the form of God into the "form of a servant" and the "likeness of men" (Phil. 2:6f.) affects him as the eternal Son. . . . This "infinite distance," which recapitulates the sinner's mode of alienation from God, will remain forever the highest revelation known to the world

Does revelation also take place before Christ? Balthasar argues that Jesus "sees himself as the climax, fulfilling and transcending a whole series of (prophetic) missions, fulfilling and surpassing the divine giving of the Law in Moses and, finally, fulfilling a divine world order that existed 'from the beginning'" (Matt. 19:8).[44] On this view, the relationship of Jesus's mission to the missions/revelation that we find in Israel's Scriptures is one of the former fulfilling the latter, which participate in and prepare for the former. Jesus reveals God to us in a way that both fulfills the revelation mediated by the Old Testament and goes beyond it.[45]

In short, the existential concentration of mission in the person of Christ Jesus, and its relation to kenotic obedience, stands out in Balthasar's portrait. Because Christ invites our participation in his salvific and revelatory mission, divine revelation in Christ intrinsically involves the missions of all who belong to the people of God.[46]

Christopher Wright: Revelation and the Mission to the Gentiles

The broad sweep of God's mission of mercy in human history, and the call to an evangelizing mission, take center stage in Christopher Wright's *The Mission of God*. Wright's focus on the whole of history and on concrete evangelization adds a significant element to our portrait of the relationship of divine revelation and the Church. Wright seeks "to demonstrate that a strong theology of the mission of God provides a fruitful hermeneutical framework within which to read the whole Bible."[47]

---

of the diastasis (within the eternal being of God) between Father and Son in the Holy Spirit. (*Dramatis Personae*, 228)

For critical discussion see B. Marshall, "Unity of the Triune God," 1–32; White, "Intra-trinitarian Obedience," 377–402; White, "Kenoticism," 1–41; White, "Crucified Lord," 157–89; Mansini, "Can Humility and Obedience Be Trinitarian Realities?," 71–98; Emery, "*Theologia* and *Dispensatio*." Balthasar's position, of course, requires him to accept substitution rather than satisfaction as his model for the cross: "It is on the Cross that the sinner changes place with the only Son" (*Dramatis Personae*, 239). See also N. Healy, *Eschatology of Hans Urs von Balthasar*, 105–7, 126–27.

44. Balthasar, *Dramatis Personae*, 250.

45. See also Balthasar's *Theology: The Old Covenant*, vol. 6 of *The Glory of the Lord*. For further discussion see Walatka, "Theological Exegesis," 300–317; Riches, "Biblical Basis of Glory," 61–63; Dickens, *Hans Urs von Balthasar's Theological Aesthetics*; Dickens, "Balthasar's Biblical Hermeneutics," 175–86.

46. Thus Mark McIntosh notes that for Balthasar "a saintly life of sharing in Christ's mission opens one to the grace of contemporaneity with the gospel. . . . The Spirit not only leads the disciples 'into the truth of what has taken place—but, in the same Spirit, they are given a participation in Jesus's own existence' (*TD3*, 131)" ("Christology," 29).

47. C. Wright, *Mission of God*, 26. For recent evangelical Protestant theologies of mission, see also Köstenberger and O'Brien, *Salvation to the Ends of the Earth*; Bauckham, *Bible and*

He first warns against resting Christian mission entirely on Matthew 28:19–20, "Go therefore and make disciples of all nations, baptizing them in the name of the Father and of the Son and of the Holy Spirit, teaching them to observe all that I have commanded you." Contrary to some interpretations, this text does not provide an eschatological timetable, as though when all nations have heard the gospel then Christ will return. In every generation, after all, the people even of previously evangelized nations need to hear the gospel anew. Those who downplay Matthew 28:19–20, however, can fall into the opposite extreme of neglecting the necessity of mission. Wright also observes that the trinitarian processions and missions are the source of the Church's mission. Mission in the Church arises in joyful and prayerful response to the missions of Christ and the Holy Spirit. The center of mission is the Triune God, not human actions.[48]

Turning to the story of the Old Testament, Wright summarizes it as being about the identity of YHWH, the identity of human beings, the reasons for our corruption and alienation, and the way in which this situation is going to be restored for all nations through YHWH's election of Israel. YHWH's mission of covenantally electing and acting on behalf of Israel establishes Israel's mission of holiness for the world. For Wright, it is particularly important to perceive that YHWH's election of Israel always had the blessing of all nations in view (see Gen. 12:3).[49] As the prophesied Messiah, Jesus acts on behalf of YHWH and indeed shares in his identity, and Jesus's restoration of Israel

---

Mission. As Carl E. Braaten observes, "Christ is Lord of the church and the world, inasmuch as his universal Lordship possesses eschatological finality with respect to the totality of the created world. There is no way that the church can claim to possess a private relation to Jesus Christ that does not involve her in an outward thrust of mission to the world" (*Mother Church*, 54).

48. Pope John Paul II's encyclical *Redemptoris Missio* similarly emphasizes our sharing in the incarnate Son's mission through the work of evangelization: "The mission of Christ the Redeemer, which he entrusted to the Church, is still very far from completion. As the second millennium after Christ's coming draws to an end, an overall view of the human race shows that this mission is still only beginning and that we must commit ourselves wholeheartedly to its service." See John Paul II, *Redemptoris Missio*, §1, 436; cf. Pope John Paul II's apostolic letter *Novo Millennio Ineunte*. For an Orthodox treatment of the same themes, see Archbishop Anastasios Yannoulatos, *Mission in Christ's Way*, which collects his essays on mission from 1964 to 2003.

49. See the concerns raised by Moberly, "Genesis 12:1–3," 141–61. However, as the next chapter of his book makes clear, Moberly is particularly concerned to challenge the views of Christian Zionists such as Jerry Falwell, whose arguments are quite different from those of Wright. Even if, as Moberly thinks, "the culminating promise to Abraham is restricted in its concern to Abraham" in its original context, Moberly also recognizes that "the wider context of scripture and Jewish tradition" (161) leads not only Christian commentators but also Jewish ones to read Genesis 12:1–3 not least as signaling the blessing of all nations: "A construal of Abraham as mediator of divine blessing to the nations is in fact also attested in Jewish interpretation down the ages" (159–60). In the course of a broader argument with Jon D. Levenson (with whom I largely agree), Walter Brueggemann rightly observes that in the Hebrew Bible/Old Testament

encompasses the blessing of all nations.[50] According to Wright, Jesus does not reveal a new divine identity or a new mission but rather confirms and fulfills the identity and mission that the Old Testament story has already led us to expect. The commandment of love fulfills the commandments given to Israel. A "missional hermeneutic" is therefore based not simply on the Great Commission or the New Commandment to love one another (John 13:34) but on the entirety of Scripture's "Great *Communication*—the revelation of the identity of God, of God's action in the world and God's saving purpose for all creation."[51] This vision of mission includes a wide variety of elements, including preaching the gospel, social justice, Church order, and so forth. It also underscores our participation as Christians in the trinitarian life, a participation engendered by the missions of the Son and Holy Spirit.[52]

To sketch the basic story of Scripture—the mission of God, Israel, Jesus, and the Church—Wright highlights a variety of biblical texts, including Genesis 3–11; Isaiah 42, 43, and 49; Psalm 2; 2 Corinthians 5; Luke 24; and Acts 1 and 13. As he makes clear, the Church's mission is "the committed *participation* of God's people in the purposes of God for the redemption of the whole creation."[53] Indeed, I would add that if this is the Church's mission, then it can be seen from another angle that mission *is* the Church. The Church is the missions that God gives human beings so that we might share in God's redemptive mission. Wright ensures that the Church's mission is never viewed in isolation from the whole story. God's identity too is not known outside of his mission to Israel and ultimately to the whole world in Christ Jesus. Wright cautions that this approach to the Bible's story does not claim that every detail fits easily into the framework of mission but rather claims simply that the Bible tells a broadly unified story.[54]

Commenting on Deuteronomy 27–32, Wright finds God will reveal his name to the nations even through Israel's disobedience, in a manner that not only judges Israel but also restores, vindicates, and includes Israel. He observes that

"there is a recurring restlessness about a Jewish reading and a push beyond that to a reading as large as the nations and as comprehensive as creation" (*Theology of the Old Testament*, 95).

50. For exegetical studies supportive of this view, see especially N. T. Wright, *New Testament and the People of God*; N. T. Wright, *Jesus and the Victory of God*; C. Rowe, *Early Narrative Christology*; Gathercole, *Pre-existent Son*; Hurtado, *Lord Jesus Christ*; McDonough, *Christ as Creator*.

51. C. Wright, *Mission of God*, 60.

52. Among Protestant works that connect the Church's mission to the theology of the Trinity, Wright references Vicedom, *Mission of God*; Newbigin, *Trinitarian Doctrine for Today's Mission*. See also Wainwright, *Lesslie Newbigin*.

53. C. Wright, *Mission of God*, 67.

54. See ibid., 68–69. For accessible presentations of the Bible as a unified whole, see also Dauphinais and Levering, *Holy People, Holy Land*; Bartholomew and Goheen, *Drama of Scripture*.

"the history that will see the judgment and restoration of *Israel* will also see the judgment and blessing of the *nations*. Each sequence will be intertwined with the other."[55] Similarly, he emphasizes the way in which certain psalms and prophetic texts universalize the Davidic kingship by linking it with the kingship of God: God will reveal himself and reign over the entire world through the Davidic king.[56] Again, tracking the theme of a new covenant through various prophetic texts, Wright shows that "in its Old Testament development, the anticipated new covenant picks up themes from all of the preceding covenants—Noah, Abraham, Sinai and David, and in several places expands them to include the nations within the ultimate scope of God's saving covenantal mission."[57] In the New Testament fulfillment of this covenantal mission, God reveals himself even more fully through the sacrificial love enacted by Jesus at his final Passover meal, when "he took a cup, and when he had given thanks he gave it to them, saying, 'Drink of it, all of you; for this is my blood of the covenant, which is poured out for many for the forgiveness of sins'" (Matt. 26:27–28).[58]

Revelation, then, occurs in the very texture of God's mission in Israel and in Jesus Christ. As Wright puts it, binding together all the biblical texts "is the grand narrative of God's mission, ever since Abraham, to bring blessing to the nations through this people whom he has called to be his special possession."[59] Paul's preaching to the gentiles and their entrance into the covenant community, which we see in Paul's letters and in Acts, confirms a narrative already in place, but does so now on the basis of God's mission in Jesus. Commenting

55. C. Wright, *Mission of God*, 342. For discussion of the judgment and restoration of Israel and the blessing of the nations, see, for example, Bryan, *Jesus and Israel's Traditions*; Pao, *Acts and the Isaianic New Exodus*.

56. See N. T. Wright, *Jesus and the Victory of God*, 489–509; Bird, *Are You the One Who Is to Come?*, especially 31–40.

57. C. Wright, *Mission of God*, 352. With respect to Isaiah, see Pao, *Acts and the Isaianic New Exodus*, 218–27.

58. See C. Wright, *Mission of God*, 353. For further reflection see McKnight, *Jesus and His Death*, 259–374; Perrin, *Jesus the Temple*, 177–79; Koenig, *Feast of the World's Redemption*. For the view that "Jesus's eucharistic words and deeds find a likely context in the multifarious and well-attested ancient Jewish efforts to channel the temple's sanctity into various other ritual activities," see Klawans, *Purity, Sacrifice, and the Temple*, 244. Even if more should be said, McKnight seems right to point out that although Jesus does not reject the temple outright, "when, however, we take into consideration the prediction of the temple's destruction and his anti-establishment words (Mark 11–13), we can safely argue that Jesus's last supper is a fundamental reorientation of the temple order. The scholars, wide-ranging as they are, who connect these three dots (entry, temple incident, and last supper) have offered a potent hypothesis that helps explain how Jesus understood his death. The temple, standing for the nation, is about to be destroyed; God has appointed Jesus's death as the means of escape; those who eat his body and drink his blood will be passed over" (*Jesus and His Death*, 326).

59. C. Wright, *Mission of God*, 353.

on Matthew 28:20, where the risen Jesus says "I am with you always, to the close of the age," Wright adds that "the covenant presence of God among his people in the Old Testament becomes the promised presence of Jesus among his disciples as they carry out the mission he lays on them."[60]

When Wright turns to "the life of God's missional people," he focuses first on ethics.[61] The holiness of the people of God has as its ultimate purpose the fostering of God's mission to bless all nations. In this vein, Wright speaks of "the missional reason for the very existence of the church as the people of God."[62] By obediently reflecting God's righteousness and justice in the world, the people of God help to reveal God to the world. The people of God are a "kingdom of priests" (Exod. 19:6) that has the goal of "bringing the knowledge and law of God to the nations and bringing the nations to God in covenant inclusion and blessing."[63] The holiness of God's people is the way that God intends them to fulfill their mission, the mission for which he has elected them. Wright adds that holiness, for Israel and for the Church, has not only an ethical dimension but also a symbolic/sacramental one. His list of the requirements for Israel's holiness (rooted in Lev. 19), however,

60. Ibid., 355. For theological discussion of Christ's ongoing presence to the Church, see Farrow, *Ascension and Ecclesia*; Farrow, *Ascension Theology*.

61. C. Wright, *Mission of God*, 357. On this topic, one might see especially Newbigin, *Open Secret*, chap. 8, "Mission as Action for God's Justice." See also such works as Witherington, *Indelible Image*, 2:421–748; Matera, *New Testament Ethics*; Verhey, *Remembering Jesus*.

62. Wright, *Mission of God*, 369.

63. Ibid., 370. From a different angle, but also with regard to Christ's kingdom, Archbishop Anastasios reminds us that "the Father's will is *already a reality*. Myriads of other beings, the angels and saints, are already in harmony with it. The realization of God's will is not simply a desire; it is *an event* that illuminates everything else. The center of reality is God and His Kingdom. On this, the realism of faith is grounded. On this ontology is based every Christian effort on earth" (Yannoulatos, *Mission in Christ's Way*, 4). This theocentric understanding of Christ's kingdom helps to avoid the triumphalism that Lesslie Newbigin fears. Newbigin observes, "The church misunderstands itself if it thinks that it is itself the place where the truth and righteousness of the reign of God are embodied as against the reign of evil in the world. This ancient temptation to identify the church with the kingdom of God seems to be present again in some manifestations of the theology of liberation. The relation of the church to the kingdom is a more complex one and, I am convinced, can be truly grasped only by means of the trinitarian model" (*Open Secret*, 139). For Newbigin, however, the Holy Spirit's sovereignty over the Church is such that the Church "cannot impose its own ethical insights at any one time and place upon those whom the Spirit calls into its company" (140). No doubt Newbigin here has in view a certain overreaching among missionaries in non-Christian cultures, as well as the human (and thus fallen) dimension of the Church's life and teaching. Yet Newbigin's claim goes too far, since Christian faith includes and mandates a way of life whose basic components are taught in Scripture and whose bounds are identifiable by the Church in its formal teaching under the guidance of the Holy Spirit. For further theological perspectives on God's priestly people, see Congar, *Lay People in the Church*, chap. 4; Leithart, *Priesthood of the Plebs*; Schnackenburg, *God's Rule and Kingdom*, 215–317.

strongly privileges the ethical dimension.[64] The people of God have the mission of "being God's visible model to the nations," through their witness (obedience, loyalty) to God's covenant and through their coming to know the living God.[65]

The goal of this mission is the full accomplishment of "the redemption of the nations and the restoration of creation."[66] Since Israel could not accomplish this mission (given human fallenness), God took flesh as Israel's Messiah, Jesus Christ, and fulfilled the mission on behalf of Israel, for the reconciliation of the whole world. The Church is the people of God ordered around Jesus Christ, the elect covenantal community of Jews and gentiles, which carries on Israel's mission to manifest God's blessing to the world and to bring the nations to glorify the living God. Wright finds this point in various New Testament texts, including Matthew 28:18–20 (quoted above); 1 Peter 2:9, "You are a chosen race, a royal priesthood, a holy nation, God's own people, that you may declare the wonderful deeds of him who called you out of darkness into his marvelous light"; and John 13:35, "By this all men will know that you are my disciples, if you have love for one another."

The scope of the Church's mission, says Wright, is the whole creation, which has an eschatological goal that God is bringing about: the new creation, a transformed world in which evil, sin, and death will be no more. When he discusses our mission to our fellow humans, he grounds his ethical principles in the doctrine that we are all made in the image of God (Gen. 1).[67] Since we are in God's image, God gave us the mission of exercising holy dominion over the earth. We are relational creatures, made for marriage, family, and social life. Sin, however, not only delivers us to death and alienates us from

64. For a corrective that integrates worship and ethics from a Protestant perspective, with a focus on the kind of political society the worshiping Church is called to be, see Wannenwetsch, *Political Worship*. Wannenwetsch's book would have benefited from engaging Catholic and Orthodox theology. The connection that Brian Brock draws between ethics and Augustine's reading of the Psalms is fruitful in this regard: see Brock, *Singing the Ethos of God*, 132–64. See also Archbishop Anastasios's reflections on the communion of love—with emphasis on care for the poor and the oppressed, on care for the health of the earth's ecosystems, and on the need for continual repentance and the eucharistic liturgy—in Yannoulatos, *Mission in Christ's Way*, 9–22.

65. Wright, *Mission of God*, 380.

66. Ibid., 382.

67. For further ethical reflection (from diverse perspectives) highlighting the image of God, see N. Harrison, *God's Many-Splendored Image*; Pinckaers, "Ethics and the Image of God"; Middleton, *Liberating Image*. In light of the transformation/deification of the image of God, Archbishop Anastasios is right to say that "mission is not a question of proclaiming some ethical truths or principles, but the beginning of the transfiguration inaugurated by the 'light of the gospel of the glory of Christ' (2 Cor. 4:4; cf. 4:6), through which we are called 'so that [we] may obtain the glory of our Lord Jesus Christ' (2 Thess. 2:14)" (Yannoulatos, *Mission in Christ's Way*, 50–51).

God but also mars our actions and the societal structures in which we live. Wright deems HIV/AIDS to be the greatest emergency of our time (especially in Africa), and he tests Christian mission by the standard of how Christians have responded to this crisis—keeping in view the centrality of the Christian proclamation of Jesus's resurrection and ours.

Wright concludes with a chapter on Israel and the nations, examining the complex relationships of God's justice, mercy, and election. God is consistently concerned not only for Israel but also for the nations. What God does for Israel, therefore, is also a sign to the nations: "May God be gracious to us and bless us and make his face to shine upon us, that thy way may be known upon earth, thy saving power among all nations. Let the peoples praise thee, O God; let all the peoples praise thee! Let the nations be glad and sing for joy, for thou dost judge the peoples with equity and guide the nations upon earth" (Ps. 67:1–4; cf. Pss. 86; 102; and others). Prophetic texts, especially in Isaiah but in numerous other prophets as well, also look forward to the nations' joining in the worship of Israel's God. Consider Isaiah 19:24–25, "In that day Israel will be the third with Egypt and Assyria, a blessing in the midst of the earth, whom the Lord of hosts has blessed, saying, 'Blessed be Egypt my people, and Assyria the work of my hands, and Israel my heritage.'" For his part, Jesus commands that the gospel be preached to the nations, and the book of Acts (and Pauline letters) shows the success of this mission—even if these biblical texts also exhibit controversies that arose regarding what to require of the converted gentiles.

In short, for Wright revelation and the Church are intrinsically connected through the mission of God.[68] Although divine revelation is completed at the end of the apostolic age, divine revelation's dramatic character means that in a real sense revelation is ongoing until every last human being has determined, by God's grace, his or her relation to Christ's mission.

Conclusion: Revelation and the Church

Aquinas, Balthasar, and Wright help us to see why divine revelation and the Church are intrinsically bound together; the Church is no mere receptacle. As Aquinas makes clear, the revelation of God takes place through the visible and invisible missions of the Son and Spirit. Absent the vibrant theology of the trinitarian missions that we find in Aquinas (and in Scripture), the theocentric character of revelation would seem to exclude the active role of

---

68. See also Yannoulatos, *Mission in Christ's Way*, 42, 44–45.

the Church, lest mere humans be situated in the place of God or lest revelation be imagined as the Church's work over the centuries rather than as
God's work in Christ and the Spirit. The way to understand the active place
of the Church in divine revelation is to reflect upon the missions of the Son
and Spirit.

Balthasar identifies Christ's kenotic love and obedience as the center of
revelation, so that revelation is in a certain sense coextensive with Christ's
"person," Christ's supreme mission-consciousness. The Church is the community of human subjects who become persons by embracing their missions
in Christ.[69] As a community of persons in Christ, built up by the Eucharist,
the Church mediates and participates in his salvific mission by the power of
the Holy Spirit.

Wright envisions this mediation primarily in terms of the ongoing historical extension of God's mission of mercy to all peoples. By proclaiming and
witnessing to the gospel, the Church extends to the nations the good news
of divine revelation. The movement envisioned by Wright is one of going out
into the world to proclaim the gospel.

These three senses of "mission" are clearly complementary. The horizontal
axis—the extension of revelation to the nations over the course of history—
and the vertical axis of participation in Christ's mission require each other.
Both the horizontal and the vertical axis depend entirely on the united missions (visible and invisible) of the Son and Holy Spirit. Reflection on mission
enables us to see that revelation, while being the action of the Triune God,
cannot be understood outside the participation and mediation of the Church.
Preeminently in the eucharistic liturgy, which builds the Church in charity, the
Church even now shares in and communicates the revelatory mission of Christ.
Anticipating the next chapter, therefore, we may allow Joseph Ratzinger the
last word, from his *Spirit of the Liturgy*: "Ultimately, the difference between
the *actio Christi* and our own action is done away with. There is only *one*

69. Again we might quote Archbishop Anastasios:
   It is not quite correct to say that "the mission is not ours, but Christ's." It is also ours,
   inasmuch as we are incorporated into Christ: "All things are yours," St. Paul would say
   again in this case, "and you are Christ's; and Christ is God's" (1 Cor. 3:22–23). Since
   the Christian mission is incorporated into God's mission, the final goal of our mission
   surely cannot be different from His. . . . Our participation in this glory has already begun
   with our incorporation into Christ. "The glory which thou hast given me I have given
   to them" (John 17:22; cf. 1:14)—that is, the glory of the Sonship—and "those whom he
   justified he also glorified" (Rom. 8:30; cf. 2 Cor. 4:6)." (45–47)
   Archbishop Anastasios, like Balthasar, connects "glory" with kenotic love. The phrase "the
mission is not ours, but Christ's," with which Archbishop Anastasios disagrees, comes from
Newbigin, *One Body, One Gospel, One World*, 28.

action, which is at the same time his and ours—ours because we have become 'one body and one spirit' with him. The uniqueness of the Eucharistic liturgy lies precisely in the fact that God himself is acting and that we are drawn into that action of God."[70]

70. Ratzinger, *Spirit of the Liturgy*, 174. Ratzinger prefaces this remark by stating:
The real "action" in the liturgy in which we are all supposed to participate is the action of God himself. . . . But how can we part-icipate, have a part, in this action? Are not God and man completely incommensurable? Can man, the finite and sinful one, cooperate with God, the Infinite and Holy One? Yes, he can, precisely because God himself has become man, become body, and here, again and again, he comes through his body to us who live in the body. The whole event of the Incarnation, Cross, Resurrection, and Second Coming is present as the way by which God draws man into cooperation with himself. As we have seen, this is expressed in the liturgy in the fact that the petition for acceptance is part of the *oratio*. True, the Sacrifice of the Logos is accepted already and forever. But we must still pray for it to become *our* sacrifice, that we ourselves, as we said, may be transformed into the Logos (*logosiert*), conformed to the Logos, and so be made the true Body of Christ. (173)
On the sacraments as the work of the ascended Christ, see O'Neill, *Sacramental Realism*, 62, 72, 120–28, 215; Weinandy, "Human Acts," 150–68.

T W O

Liturgy

Dei Verbum observes, "The Church has always venerated the divine Scriptures as she venerated the body of the Lord, in so far as she never ceases, particularly in the sacred liturgy, to partake of the bread of life and to offer it to the faithful from the one table of the word of God and the body of Christ."[1] In the first chapter, I showed that the missions of the Son and Holy Spirit imply that the Church's mediation is not extrinsic to revelation. This second chapter focuses on the eucharistic liturgy, in which Christ and the Holy Spirit enable us to share in Christ's self-offering to the Father. The liturgy is the primary place in which the Church participates in and interprets the revelation of God.[2] Both chapters have to do with the trinitarian foundations of the Church's faithful mediation of revelation.

In Protestant ecclesiology, however, the Church's mediation is inevitably a creaturely and fallen work that stands in need of scriptural correction in light of God's sovereignty over the Church. Since among contemporary theologians John Webster has best articulated this concern, this chapter first examines Webster's theology.[3] I then explore Scripture's own testimony to its properly

---

1. *Dei Verbum*, §21, 763.

2. This perspective has been well argued by F. Martin, "Reading Scripture in the Catholic Tradition." See also James Barr's point that "within the Bible itself religion was not a scriptural religion in the sense that it later, and especially after the Reformation, became normal to suppose" (*Holy Scripture*, 4; cf. 11–13), although Barr does not pay attention to liturgy.

3. See also Billings, *Word of God for the People of God*. Billings, however, gives more attention to the liturgy than does Webster, as, for example, in his treatment of a hymn of Bernard of Clairvaux's, see ibid., 64–67. See also 220–24, especially Billings's conclusion that "at the heart

liturgical context as preparation for a detailed engagement with the liturgical context and goal of divine revelation according to Alexander Schmemann and Joseph Ratzinger. On this basis, I propose that deeper engagement with the liturgical mediation of divine revelation would enrich Webster's effort to provide "an account of what Holy Scripture *is* in the saving economy of God's loving and regenerative self-communication."[4]

John Webster on Holy Scripture

At the outset of his *Holy Scripture*, Webster observes that the term "Scripture" refers primarily to a particular collection of texts, while also referring both to God as the origin of Scripture and to the Church as the community that uses Scripture. How are these three realities (God, Scripture, Church) related? Webster explains that the texts of Scripture have an "origin, function, and end in divine self-communication," and as such they require our obedient response in faith.[5] The texts serve God's self-communication, and to read them as though they were independent of God's self-communication (or as though they could be interpreted by bracketing this divine self-communication) is an error. The Church's response is important and indeed always present—otherwise there would not be communication—but the Church's response is caused by God's "communicative grace" in the scriptural economy.[6] God, not the Church, is the key referent of the collection of texts that is Scripture. Thus far Webster and I agree.

Theologies of Scripture that highlight the Church, generally by highlighting the liturgical proclamation/actualization of Scripture, strike Webster as mistaken. As an example of the problem, he points to Wilfred Cantwell Smith's view that Scripture refers not to texts per se but to the community's practices in relation to certain texts. Smith holds that one cannot claim that Scripture "is" anything because what "Scripture" signifies is an ongoing, ever-changing community practice. This account of Scripture is completely human-centered and, in Webster's view and my own, erroneous. A more moderate position

---

of this journey and transformation—not on the periphery—is the communal act of worship, centered in the act of discerning, celebrating, and tasting the Word together through God's word in Scripture" (223). Here Billings cites Simon Chan, *Liturgical Theology*, 21–61; see also Vanhoozer, *Drama of Doctrine*, 410.

4. Webster, *Holy Scripture*, 2. Webster's insistence on theology's "pursuing its proper end in fellowship with God" ("Domain of the Word," 4) is one of the things that make his work so rich and valuable. See also Webster's "Theological Theology," 11–31. For a related engagement with Webster's book, see Ayres, "'There's Fire in That Rain,'" 624–27. Ayres draws upon Ratzinger, "Question of the Concept of Tradition."

5. Webster, *Holy Scripture*, 5.

6. Ibid., 6.

is offered by Ingolf Dalferth, who considers "Scripture" to be such when it is actualized by the Church's liturgical proclamation of scriptural texts. Webster states, "Dalforth's concern is, clearly, a legitimate Reformation point of conscience: the desire to avoid any account of the nature of Scripture *extra usum*. . . . The problem arises when use and action are identified too closely with 'kerygmatic-doxological use' of Scripture by the Church."[7] Liturgy-centered accounts of Scripture, Webster fears, lead to the view that Scripture is "Scripture" only when the Church is actively using the biblical texts in proclamation and worship. In fact, Scripture is "Scripture" because God makes it so, not because humans make it so.[8]

Having established his theocentric approach to the theology of Scripture, Webster turns in his first chapter to the nature of revelation, sanctification, and inspiration. Regarding the doctrine of revelation, he emphasizes that it must be seen not as an epistemological doctrine that has to do with the warrants for Christianity but as the action of the Triune God. Revelation "denotes the communicative, fellowship-establishing trajectory of the acts of God in the election, creation, providential ordering, reconciliation, judgement and glorification of God's creatures."[9] Webster defines "sanctification" in this context as "the act of God the Holy Spirit in hallowing creaturely processes, employing them in the service of the taking form of revelation within the history of the creation."[10] God sanctifies the fully human historical production of the texts so

7. Ibid., 7–8. See Ingolf U. Dalferth, "Die Mitte ist außen," 183. See also W. Smith, *What Is Scripture?*

8. See also Webster's "On Evangelical Ecclesiology." Webster argues, "The Word is not *in* the church but announced *to* the church through Holy Scripture. The church is therefore not first and foremost a speaking but a hearing community" (190). See also Webster's "Illumination" and his "Self-Organizing Power of the Gospel of Christ." In the latter essay, which defends ministerial order (episcopacy), Webster states:

> Order does not constitute the church apart from the vivifying and sanctifying grace of the Spirit; but the life and holiness which the Spirit bestows are ordered because human, social and continuous. The danger of collapsing Spirit into structure ought not to frighten us into the equal danger of a purely punctiliar or actualistic ecclesiology. Church order is the social shape of the converting power and activity of Christ present as Spirit. This is not to claim that the Spirit can be formalized, or reduced to a calculable and manipulable element in what is envisaged as an immanent social process. (197–98)

Yet Webster still thinks that in order to "maximize Christology and pneumatology," he must "relativize (but not minimize or abolish) ecclesial action and its ordered forms" (198).

9. Webster, *Holy Scripture*, 17. See also the eloquent portrait of revelation given in Webster's *Holiness*: "As the gracious presence of God, revelation is itself the establishment of fellowship. It is not so much an action in which God informs us of other acts of his through which we are reconciled to him; rather, talk about revelation is a way of indicating the communicative force of God's saving, fellowship-creating presence. . . . The idiom of revelation is as much moral and relational as it is cognitional" (14).

10. Webster, *Holy Scripture*, 17–18. See also Webster, "Domain of the Word," 14–16.

as to make them part of the economy of divine self-communication. Webster contests the modern insistence that history can exhibit the divine presence only either extrinsically or through a rarefied form of human experience. In this regard he cautions that some theologians mistakenly "leapt to the defence of Scripture by espousing a strident supernaturalism, defending the relation of the Bible to divine revelation by almost entirely removing it from the sphere of historical contingency, through the elaboration of an increasingly formalised and doctrinally isolated theory of inspiration."[11]

In accounting for the creaturely history of the biblical texts, Webster eschews the notions of divine "accommodation" or "condescension."[12] In the modern context, he points out, these terms tend to suggest that the creaturely history is the human element and the core teaching the divine element. This once more separates the divine action from the historical, creaturely reality, as though God were extrinsic to human history except for certain purely "supernatural" moments. Webster also avoids the analogy of the hypostatic union, which presents Scripture as both "fully human" and "fully divine." In addition to the fact that there is only one incarnation, that of the Son, this analogy divinizes Scripture "by claiming some sort of ontological identity between the biblical texts and the self-communication of God."[13] Indebted to Karl Barth, Webster prefers to understand Scripture as prophetic and apostolic "testimony," since this allows for the creaturely history of the biblical texts without divinizing Scripture, and at the same time preserves the focus on the self-revealing God.[14] Yet he recognizes that

11. Webster, *Holy Scripture*, 20. Along these lines, see some of the approaches that I describe in my "Inspiration of Scripture." For a further instance, see B. Harrison, "Restricted Inerrancy," which rightly rejects the notion that only parts of Scripture are inspired and inerrant, but goes too far by claiming that the affirmations made in the writings of Scripture contain no error of any kind. For a better path, see Betz, "Glory(ing) in the Humility of the Word"; Farrow, *Word of Truth*; Work, *Living and Active*.

12. For discussion of "accommodation," including its role in the fathers, see Sparks, *God's Word in Human Words*, 229–59. See also Wolterstorff, *Divine Discourse*, 206–12; Betz, "Glory(ing) in the Humility of the Word," 163.

13. Webster, *Holy Scripture*, 23; in the same vein see his "Domain of the Word," 13. For further concerns about this analogy, see also Ayres and Fowl, "(Mis)reading the Face of God." The analogy is defended by Enns, *Inspiration and Incarnation*, 17; and for extensive use of the analogy see Work, *Living and Active*. Paragraph 13 of *Dei Verbum* contains a version of the analogy: "Indeed the words of God, expressed in the words of men, are in every way like human language, just as the Word of the eternal Father, when he took on himself the flesh of human weakness, became like men" (758).

14. In "Domain of the Word," Webster remarks regarding the "prophets and apostles" (authors and redactors of Scripture), "Their speech is a creaturely accompaniment of and accessory to the divine Word, integrated into a divine movement. . . . In this—in the fact that the Word accomplishes his act of self-utterance through these human auxiliaries—lies the basic *mystery* of Scripture" (8). This claim that human words are "integrated into a divine movement" suggests

when one emphasizes the creatureliness of the texts (in order to highlight the transcendence and perfection of the Word), then "the annexation of the Bible to revelation can appear almost arbitrary: the text is considered a complete and purely natural entity taken up into the self-communication of God."[15] The answer to this problem consists in underscoring the sanctifying work of the Holy Spirit within "all the processes of the text's production, preservation and interpretation."[16]

Webster briefly reviews two possible alternatives to his approach: Scripture as a "means of grace" (William Abraham), and Scripture's "servant form" (G. C. Berkouwer and Herman Bavinck).[17] Although he appreciates these concepts in certain ways, he expresses reservations. If Scripture is a "means of grace," then it mediates God's self-communication. Webster worries that what mediates takes priority over what is mediated, so that what is mediated (God's self-communication) would be passive until Scripture mediates it.[18] By contrast, the concept of "testimony" puts the emphasis on God revealing, and thereby undercuts our fallen tendency to put creaturely things first.[19] Webster recognizes that the concept of "servant form" helpfully emphasizes that "the creatureliness of the text is not an inhibition of its role in the communicative self-presentation of God; and so the text does not have to assume

---

participation, although Webster prefers to say solely that "the instrumentality of human words and texts in revelation emerges from God's consecration of a certain history to serve in the publication of his own Word. By the Spirit God raises up living instruments, *instrumenta animata*" (16). In this regard Webster cites Stephen Holmes, "Christology, Scripture."

15. Webster, *Holy Scripture*, 24.

16. Ibid. See also Daley, "'In Many and Various Ways,'" 601.

17. See Abraham, *Canon and Criterion in Christian Theology*; Abraham, *Divine Inspiration of Scripture*; Bavinck, *Our Reasonable Faith*; Bavinck, *Reformed Dogmatics*, vol. 1, *Prolegomena*; Berkouwer, *Holy Scripture*.

18. Along similar lines, Webster cautions against describing the Church's acts as "mediation of the acts of God" ("On Evangelical Ecclesiology," 185). He explains:

Such language certainly has a long tradition of usage across the confessions, and ought not to be discarded lightly. And it is genuinely theological, far from the easy pragmatic immanentism which can afflict some theologies of the visible church. But nevertheless it can unravel rather quickly (this often happens when it is used in the context of sacramental theology or the theology of ministerial order). Only with some real vigilance can it be used without some damage to the proper distinction between *opus Dei* and *opus hominum*. Otherwise, the purity and sufficiency of the work of God is in some measure broken down; divine agency, if not suspended, is at least relegated to background status and so in some measure inhibited. (ibid.)

19. In "On Evangelical Ecclesiology," Webster argues in favor of "testimony" or "attestation" as descriptions of the work of the Church. He states, "Testimony is astonished indication. Arrested by the wholly disorienting grace of God in Christ and the Spirit, the church simply *points*. . . . Strictly subordinate to that which it is appointed and empowered to indicate, raised up not to participate in, extend or realize a reality which lies quite outside itself, the church lifts up its voice and says: Behold the Lamb of God who takes away the sin of the world" (185).

divine properties as a protection against contingency."[20] But Webster prefers the notion of active and nonextrinsic "sanctification" because it applies not only to the finished form of the Bible but also to all the historical processes by which the Bible came to be. God governs the "entire historical course of the creaturely reality so that it becomes a creature which may serve the purposes of God."[21] Thus the biblical texts have a being or ontology that is given them by God, not by us; they are "sanctified, that is, Spirit-generated and preserved" in "the communicative economy of God's merciful friendship with his lost creatures."[22]

Regarding inspiration, Webster emphasizes that it must not be viewed as if it were the reason why Scripture is revelatory. Rather, the opposite is the case: because Scripture communicates God's self-revelation, Scripture is inspired. Put another way, inspiration is "a corollary of the self-presence of God which takes form through the providential ordering and sanctification of creaturely auxiliaries."[23] While affirming that Scripture "is the instrument of divine teaching which proceeds from God," we must not ground faith's certitude on anything but God, and we must not objectify God's presence in Scripture so as to deprive God of his ineffable mystery or to replace his free activity with something that is not God.[24] Webster states that "inspiration does not mean that the truth of the gospel which Scripture sets before us becomes

20. Webster, *Holy Scripture*, 25.
21. Ibid., 26.
22. Ibid., 29. Webster is here responding especially to Jeanrond, *Text and Interpretation*. Webster puts the central point particularly well in the preface to his *Domain of the Word*:

> In a well-ordered Christian theology, the divine movements of revelation, inspiration and illumination do not compromise the human movements of authorship and interpretation. Showing that this is so, however, obliges theology to attend to doctrinal work on creation, providence and the Holy Spirit, in order to demonstrate that divine revelation is not a unilateral cognitive force but a compound act in which the creator and reconciler takes creatures and their powers, acts and products into his service. God speaks from his human temple. (ix)

This sense of "a compound act" and of God speaking "from his human temple" seems to allow for a participatory mediation of divine revelation, but in the first essay of this collection Webster reiterates that he remains "unconvinced by the necessity and usefulness of the theology of participation" ("Domain of the Word," 14n27; cf. likewise his "Biblical Reasoning," 126–27). Insofar as Webster's concerns about participation flow from a concern to avoid conceiving of the Church's agency as autonomous, I am sympathetic to them. Thus I fully agree when he says, "Revelation is not merely an offer or initial manifestation which requires completion by a self-originating human act; rather, the scope of revelation includes the generation of acts of intelligence, the moving of creatures to the operation of their given powers" (*Domain of the Word*, ix).

23. Webster, *Holy Scripture*, 32. He is responding to (among others) David Law's *Inspiration*. See also Webster, "Domain of the Word," 16–17.
24. Webster, *Holy Scripture*, 32.

something to hand, constantly available independent of the Word and work of God, an entity which *embodies* rather than *serves* the presence of God."[25] The inspiration of Scripture is an aspect of God's revelatory and sanctifying activity, not an epistemological foundation for Scripture that makes Scripture's truth accessible outside the work of Christ and the Holy Spirit. Webster also comments on efforts to locate inspiration outside the biblical text, or in the texts only insofar as they are being read and proclaimed by the Church (such as in the liturgy). The problem with these approaches is that the Spirit no longer seems to be working in the production of the texts themselves, and also that the central focus moves from God's activity and purposes to the activity and purposes of the human authors or human community.[26] The biblical texts are not revelation reified or objectified (as if the texts could now replace God's revelatory and sanctifying activity), but neither are the biblical texts separable from God's revelation of his active presence and saving mercy.

In short, Webster's treatment of revelation, sanctification, and inspiration deftly transcends both literalist and liberal perspectives on Scripture. In his second chapter, Webster again warns against focusing on human activity rather than on the Triune God's activity. Scripture is God's word, and Scripture serves the divine Word who establishes the Church. The Church is always "the *hearing* church."[27] Webster insists that far from being one of the Church's possessions, subservient to the Church, Scripture renders the Church "ecstatic" or opened up to the Word in "humble listening."[28] Likewise, the Church's apostolicity is properly its stance toward the One who commissions and sends, not primarily

---

25. Ibid., 33. From a complementary perspective, see Kevin Vanhoozer's gentle critique of "propositionalism" in his *Drama of Doctrine*, 266–78.

26. Webster defends verbal inspiration: like the sacrament of the Eucharist, "inspiration concerns the relation of God's communication and specific creaturely forms; inspiration, that is, involves *words*" (*Holy Scripture*, 38). For a similar insistence on the value of the words themselves, see Leithart, *Deep Exegesis*.

27. Webster, *Holy Scripture*, 46. Here Webster cites Jüngel, "Church as Sacrament?," 205. I agree that the Church must always be "the *hearing* Church," so long as this "hearing" is not separated from a proper understanding of the Church's christological-pneumatological (and thus eucharistic) constitution. Interpreting my *Participatory Biblical Exegesis*, 139–40, Webster suggests that I envision the "Christological and pneumatological authority of the Church" to belong to the Church in an autonomous manner, as though the Church had subsumed the Word and Spirit into its own authoritative functions. If this were my meaning, then Webster would be right to respond, as he does, that "the teaching church is first and foremost the hearing church, a domain of receiving before one of teaching and proclamation; in a real sense, the Word is and must remain alien if it is to communicate its benefits" ("Domain of the Word," 25). But Webster has misunderstood my meaning, since I too place the activity of Christ and the Holy Spirit at the center of the Church's ontology.

28. Webster, *Holy Scripture*, 47. In this chapter, Webster has in view the position of George Lindbeck and those influenced by him; see also Webster's "On Evangelical Ecclesiology."

something inward-looking.[29] Through Scripture, the Word challenges and reforms the Church: "Scripture is not the domestic talk of the Christian faith, or simply its familiar semiotic system. It is the sword of God, issuing from the mouth of the risen one."[30] Although we encounter God's saving presence in the Church (and thus Scripture's authority cannot be separated from its ecclesial context), the Church acknowledges Scripture's authority rather than conferring authority on Scripture, even in the act of canonization.[31] Webster describes biblical authority not as rooted in inspiration in a formal or foundational sense, but as rooted in "God as sanctifying, inspiring and authorizing presence; the Spirit as the one who enables recognition of, trust in and glad submission to the claim of Scripture's gospel content; the church as faithful, self-renouncing and confessing assembly around the lively Word of God."[32] Scripture's authority consists in testifying to God's authority as judge over the Church and in opening up the Church to God's authoritative presence.

For Webster, when the Church speaks its canonizing word, we should recognize the priority and governance of "Christ's self-utterance" and of "the Holy Spirit who animates the church and enables its perception of the truth."[33]

29. For a Catholic perspective on the apostolicity and catholicity of the Church, see, for example, Ratzinger, "Primacy, Episcopacy, and *Successio Apostolica*"; Ratzinger, "Key Question."

30. Webster, *Holy Scripture*, 52. In "On Evangelical Ecclesiology" Webster makes this same point (188), and he adds, "Consecrated by God for the purpose of Christ's self-manifestation, Holy Scripture is always intrusive, in a deep sense *alien*, to the life of the Church" (189). On this view, the Church must continually place "itself beneath Holy Scripture as the law by which its mind and actions are ruled" (191). Scripture is "*alien*" because it comes from God; on this point Webster draws attention to Armin Wenz's *Das Wort Gottes*.

31. See also Webster, "Domain of the Word," 18, where Webster denies that Scripture's unity is in any sense "a function of canonization, as if the church's establishment of a list of authorized texts created (rather than recognized) the unity of these texts," and he affirms instead that Scripture's unity comes from "the fact that these texts, in all their incontrovertible diversity of origin and composition and matter, are gathered and formed into a unity by Christ." Webster nonetheless observes that "the church's acts of judgment (its 'decisions') are governed by the Holy Spirit who animates the church and enables its perception of the truth" (36). But for Webster, any emphasis on the canonizing Church undermines the "freedom of God," turns "the canon into an inviolable possession" of the Church, gives prideful "material form to the sanctity and safety of the church's mind," "lifts the church's life out of temporality," and "makes indefectibility into something other than a *promise*" (46). For other views of the canon's relation to the Church, making clear that our choices are not limited to either an autonomous Church or a free God, see Ratzinger, "Formal Principles of Catholicism," 148–51; Allert, *High View of Scripture?*; Wolterstorff, *Divine Discourse*, 54–56, 294–95. The anthropocentrism that concerns Webster can be seen, I would add, in Helmer and Landmesser's introduction to their edited volume *One Scripture or Many?*

32. Webster, *Holy Scripture*, 55–56.

33. Ibid., 60. Webster thinks that Catholic (and Orthodox) ecclesiology places the Church in a sovereign position, as he points out in his "On Evangelical Ecclesiology" by reference to de Lubac's *Catholicism*. He cautions against "the negative effects upon Christology of an

What seems to be a judgment on the part of the Church is in fact an assent and submission to Christ's authority. The Church thereby commits itself to passivity in the sense of allowing "all the activities of the church (most of all, its acts of worship, proclamation and ruling) to be as it were enclosed by the canon," so as to be obedient to God.[34] The question of which canon we should be obedient to, and of the Protestant rejection of the Catholic canon, does not occupy Webster, no doubt because his central concern is to underscore God's absolute priority.

In chapter 3, "Reading in the Economy of Grace," Webster addresses crucial debates in Reformed theology, such as the meaning of the "perspicuity" and "clarity" of Scripture.[35] He is concerned to delineate what constitutes "faithful reading in the economy of grace."[36] His emphasis is that reading Scripture involves hearing God's challenging, judging, and reconciling word. As he says, therefore, "The creaturely act of reading Holy Scripture is an event in the history of God's revelatory self-giving to humankind (in this respect it is analogous to the action of 'receiving' the sacraments)."[37] Our response to this revelatory self-giving is less "understanding" than it is repentance: because we are sinners, true scriptural "reading can only occur as a kind of brokenness, a relinquishment of willed mastery of the text."[38] In this "mortification and vivification of the reader," furthermore, the scriptural reader must adopt

over-elaborated theology of the spousal union between Christ and the church; the elevation of the church beyond creaturely status; an apparent transference of agency from Christ to the church" (165). Against communion ecclesiology, Webster wishes to speak of a "fellowship" between God and humans in Christ, but not a "mutual participation" (171). The key for Webster is that the risen and ascended Christ remain utterly sovereign, so that "he transcends the church even as he enters into intimate fellowship with it" (174). He notes in a more recent essay, "I remain uneasy with at least some uses of the idiom of participation in the theology of creation and salvation, chiefly because of its slender exegetical foundation, but also because of its sometimes hectoring and often drastically schematic history of Christian thought, and its apparent lack of concern with the hypertrophy or atrophy of some tracts of Christian teaching" ("Perfection and Participation," 380; cf. 386–87 for evidence that Webster knows well the standard objections to traditional Reformed concerns about participation). Further insight into Webster's view in this regard is found in his "Purity and Plenitude," especially 57–64. For exegetical insights into the theological significance of the doctrine of participation, see Hays, "What Is 'Real Participation in Christ'?"

34. Webster, *Holy Scripture*, 65.

35. In this regard Webster offers a strong critique of J. K. A. Smith, *Fall of Interpretation*. He also engages critically and constructively with such works as Jeanrond's *Text and Interpretation*. For further discussion see Webster's "On the Clarity of Holy Scripture"; Webster, "On Evangelical Ecclesiology," 190.

36. Webster, *Holy Scripture*, 86.

37. Ibid., 87.

38. Ibid., 88. The eschatological stance is equally emphasized by Wenz, in his *Das Wort Gottes*, cited by Webster.

certain reading practices such as attentiveness, rejection of idle curiosity, and confidence that the Holy Spirit will free the reader to read well.[39] Webster's focus throughout chapter 3 is on the individual reader, and although Webster steers clear of individualism, I note that he does not give significant attention to the "reading" or proclamation of Scripture that the Church does in the liturgy.[40]

In Webster's fourth and final chapter, he commendably sets theological reason "under the sign of baptism."[41] He focuses here on the office of theology, which serves "the edification of the church by guiding the church's reading of Holy Scripture."[42] Contrasting Zacharius Ursinus's "Hortatory Oration to the Study of Divinity" (1558) with G. W. F. Hegel's *Lectures on the Philosophy of Religion*, he comments on theology's contemporary fragmentation and on the necessity of theology "being centered on Scripture as the revelatory and pastoral heart of the entire theological enterprise."[43] He argues for the importance of theological study so long as its modest role is kept in view. He explains that theology is first and foremost "an exercise of the church's *hearing* of the gospel in Scripture," and that theology must not allow its dogmatic exposition to domesticate, control, or "de-eschatologise the church's apprehension of the gospel."[44]

39. Webster, *Holy Scripture*, 90.

40. In "On the Clarity of Holy Scripture" Webster states that the setting of biblical interpretation

> is best described by use of soteriological, ecclesiological and pneumatological teaching: the Christian interpreter is *reconciled to God, drawn into the fellowship of the saints and illuminated by the Holy Spirit.* . . . The Christian interpreter is one who has been extracted from the darkness of sin by the judgement and mercy of God, and set in the sphere of the church, the chosen race, the royal priesthood, the holy nation which is what it is by virtue of the divine call out of darkness into light. Christian interpretation of Holy Scripture is determined by this setting; the 'hermeneutical situation' (that is, the constitutive elements of the business of scriptural interpretation—God, text and readers, and the field of their interactions) is not an instance of something more basic but an episode in the history of salvation. At every point it is defined by the fact that it involves this God (the one who is light and who in Jesus Christ and the Holy Spirit is luminously present), this text (Holy Scripture as the assistant to that presence), and therefore this reader (the faithful hearer of this God in and through this text). Pneumatology has an especially important role in achieving the right kind of theological determinacy in an account of the anthropological, readerly element. (63)

Here again, however, Webster has the individual reader, rather than liturgical reading, in mind. This is less true in his "Domain of the Word," which treats "the accumulated reading acts of the church—its exegetical traditions" and its preaching ministry ("Domain of the Word," 24).

41. Webster, *Holy Scripture*, 134.

42. Ibid., 128.

43. Ibid., 121. See Ursinus, "Ursine's Hortatory Oration"; Hegel, *Lectures on the Philosophy of Religion*. For crucial background to Webster's perspective, see also Karl Barth's *Evangelical Theology*.

44. Webster, *Holy Scripture*, 129–30.

In these chapters and in his other writings, Webster highlights the need to keep God at the center.[45] In part, I think, Webster's concerns about anthropocentric theology can be addressed by attention to the ongoing missions of the Son and the Spirit, the missions that constitute the Church as Christ's body and that sustain the modes of the Church's mission.[46] It is also worth emphasizing that the Church of the liturgy is always the hearing and receptive Bride.[47] Webster does not, of course, entirely neglect the role of the liturgy. In his book *Holiness*, published in the same year as his *Holy Scripture*, he affirms that "to participate in that common human life [of the Church], hearing the gospel in fellowship under the word of God and living together under the signs of baptism and the Lord's supper, is to exist in a sphere in which God's

45. It seems that the point Webster wishes to uphold—the active sovereignty and lordship of Christ and the Holy Spirit—could be upheld while avoiding the severe tension found in Webster's claim that "although the acts of Christ are incommunicable, non-representable, Christ himself freely chooses to represent himself through human ministry" ("Self-Organizing Power of the Gospel of Christ," 200). Affirming Christ's lordship does not require refusing, as Webster does, "to see the church's ministry as a co-ordination or co-operation between divine and human agents" (201), unless this cooperative agency is presumed to be a competitive one in which the parties are equal. See also Webster's *Holiness*, 55, where he distinguishes sharply between seeing "the work of the Church as an actualization of or sharing in the divine presence and action" and seeing the work of the Church as "a testimony to that presence and action." But graced participation in God does not mean that all is not grace.

46. For Webster, the Church should be conceived as constantly and freely actualized anew by the Holy Spirit. Webster states that

> the church's visibility has its centre outside itself, in the ever-fresh coming of the Spirit. The "phenomenal" form of the church is therefore the phenomenal form of the *church* only in reference to the Spirit's self-gift. The phenomena of church life—words, rites, orders, history and the rest—do not automatically, as it were *ex opere operato*, constitute the communion of saints; rather, the church becomes what it is as the Spirit animates the forms so that they indicate the presence of God. . . . Only through the Spirit's agency are the phenomena to be grasped as phenomena of the *church*. ("On Evangelical Ecclesiology," 181–82)

47. Properly understood, the liturgy underscores Webster's oft-repeated point that faithful reading is not so much constructive or constitutive of what is heard, but *consent*. . . . Reading is an exercise in *conscientia*, not in the modern sense of reflexive moral awareness, but in the much larger sense of "the response of the human consciousness to the divine judgment," in which we are stripped of our efforts to impose a shape on the text and made capable of free and attentive listening. . . . A Christian anthropology of reading will need to emphasize both the overruling and redirecting activity of the Spirit in the reader (what Calvin calls the "bidding of God's Spirit"), and also the reader's own invocation of the Spirit, which is the basic act of existence in Christ. Christian reading is thus, very simply, a *prayerful* activity. ("Hermeneutics in Modern Theology," 82)

In "Hermeneutics in Modern Theology," without explicitly mentioning the liturgy, Webster notes that "Christian readers read as part of the company of God's people, who assemble to hear God speak" (84). But in this essay too his focus remains centered upon individual reading—even if individual Christians, as he recognizes, cannot be separated from the whole church.

limitless power is unleashed and extends into the entirety of human life."[48] But the question is whether the liturgy is or should be the preeminent place in which God's scriptural word speaks to his people. If so, then the Church's liturgical mediation of revelation, by the power of Christ and the Holy Spirit, has a much more significant place than Webster allows in *Holy Scripture*. One way to address this question may be to ask how Scripture itself envisions the contexts in which Scripture is read and proclaimed.

Scripture on Scripture: God's Word in Liturgical and Sanctifying Context

When Scripture talks about Scripture, it does so most frequently within liturgical and sanctifying contexts.[49] According to Scripture, the beginning of God's word as written took place at Mount Sinai, when God calls Moses (and perhaps Aaron as well) to come up Mount Sinai to hear the Ten Commandments. When Moses draws near to "the thick darkness where God was" (Exod. 20:21), God communicates his ordinances to Moses. Moses then speaks God's words to the whole people, who promise to obey God's words. At this stage Scripture comes to be: "And Moses wrote all the words of the LORD" (Exod. 24:4). After writing the words, Moses builds an altar, offers sacrifice, sprinkles half of the sacrificial blood upon the altar, reads the "book of the covenant" (Exod. 24:7) aloud to the assembled people, obtains their oath of obedience to God's words, and sprinkles the other half of the blood upon the people. The reading of the "book of the covenant" (Scripture) and the sacrificial renewal of the covenant belong together. The first liturgical reading of Scripture ends with an experience of intimate, indeed eucharistic, communion with God: "Then Moses and Aaron, Nadab, and Abihu, and seventy of the elders of Israel went up, and they saw the God of Israel; and there was under his feet as it were a pavement of sapphire stone, like the very heaven for clearness. And he did not lay his hand on the chief men of the people of Israel; they beheld God, and ate and drank" (Exod. 24:9–11).[50]

48. Webster, *Holiness*, 2. Webster recognizes that the theological task requires prayer and "fellowship under the Word—that is, common life led by delight in the common reality of the communicative presence of God" (*Holy Scripture*, 135).

49. Thus Markus Bockmuehl, himself an expert in historical-critical scholarly methods, urges that we seek (beyond the standard confines of historical-critical, nonecclesial biblical scholarship) "a 'thick' historical reading of the biblical texts that accounts for the ecclesial dynamic of life and worship in which they have in fact had their existence" (*Seeing the Word*, 77; cf. 47).

50. For historical-critical background, see Childs, *Book of Exodus*, 497–511. Childs observes:

Commentators are generally agreed that the difficulties of the chapter lie on both the literary and the pre-literary level. On the literary level, vv. 1, 2, 9–11 attach to vv. 3–8

In the book of Exodus, of course, Moses does not do all the writing; God also writes. God calls him to ascend Mount Sinai and receive "the tables of stone, with the law and the commandment," which God has "written for their instruction" (Exod. 24:12). When Moses goes up the mountain, God's glory covers it for six days, and on the seventh day, God calls Moses into his Sabbath. The first thing that God teaches Moses is how the people are to worship. He commands Moses to build a tabernacle in accord with the pattern that he shows him. After a lengthy discourse on the tabernacle, the priestly vestments, the sacrifices, and the Sabbath, God hands Moses "the two tables of testimony, tables of stone, written with the finger of God" (Exod. 31:18; cf. Exod. 32:16).[51] But those who worship the golden calf are given no access to God's writing, whether that writing is graven in the two stone tablets or, as Moses says to God, in "thy book which thou have written" (Exod. 32:32).

The ensuing account of God showing Moses his glory is linked with God rewriting the Decalogue on two stone tablets. God commands Moses, "Cut two tables of stone like the first; and I will write upon the tables the words that were on the first tables, which you broke. Be ready in the morning, and come up in the morning to Mount Sinai, and present yourself there to me on the top of the mountain" (Exod. 34:1–2). There God reveals his glory to Moses, who is holding in his hand the two tablets for God's use. Moses then comes down the mountain with his face shining and with "the two tables of the testimony in his hand" (Exod. 34:29).[52] Just as Moses the mediator reflects God's glory, so also, in its own way, does God's writing. Scripture reflects God's glory and his eternal "book" of life (Exod. 32:32).

The liturgical place of Scripture is emphasized by the construction, parallel with the giving of the tablets of the law, of the "ark of the testimony" (Exod. 39:35) to be kept in the "tabernacle of the testimony" (Exod. 38:21). When the Israelites complete the building of the tabernacle, God's glory fills it (Exod. 40:34–35), just as Moses saw God's glory when he approached God on Mount Sinai. The testimony of God (Scripture) finds its meaning within the context

---

in a way which suggests the joining of written sources, rather than the fusion of oral tradition. On the oral level, both these sections of the chapter appear to reflect old oral tradition which once functioned independently of their present narrative context. If we begin with the oral tradition, there is a fairly wide consensus that vv. 3–8 reflect both in form and content a covenant renewal ceremony. The stereotyped pattern of the reading of the law, acknowledgment by the people, sacrifice with blood manipulation, would seem to indicate a ritual pattern with its roots in the institutional life of Ancient Israel. (501)

51. Childs provides an extensive historical-critical discussion that concentrates on the tabernacle (and that comments also on the connection to the Epistle to the Hebrews): see ibid., 523–52.

52. For historical-critical discussion and connections with the New Testament, see ibid., 601–24.

of the tabernacle and the priestly service of Aaron and his sons. Moses in the book of Deuteronomy instructs the people to teach these words of God to their children and to meditate on them continually. He urges the people, "Bind them as a sign upon your hand," and, "Write them on the doorposts of your house and on your gates" (Deut. 6:8–9; cf. Deut. 11:18–20). The king himself must be guided by God's words: "When he sits on the throne of his kingdom, he shall write for himself in a book a copy of this law, from that which is in charge of the Levitical priests; . . . and he shall read in it all the days of his life" (Deut. 17:18–19).[53] The book of the law, kept by the priests, will prevent the king from becoming proud and will enable the king to follow God's commandments so that both the king and the whole people will flourish. Moses writes the words of the law "in a book" (Deut. 31:24) and hands it to the Levitical priests for liturgical safekeeping in the ark.

But although the ark of the covenant remains a significant protagonist for some time, the sacred writings fall out of sight—so much so that when King Josiah undertakes to repair the temple, his high priest, Hilkiah, discovers "the book of the law in the house of the LORD" (2 Kings 22:8). Rather than reading the book himself, Hilkiah gives it to the scribe Shaphan, who reads the book and finds it important enough to read it aloud to Josiah.[54]

The liturgical place of Scripture stands out once again in Josiah's reaction to the discovery of the book of the law in the recesses of the temple. As with Moses descending from Mount Sinai to discover the golden calf, Josiah has discovered a liturgical failure of Israel far greater than he could have imagined when he began his efforts to renovate the temple. Not only have the sacred writings apparently been lost for generations, but also the Passover of the Lord—the central liturgical feast—has not "been kept since the days of the judges who judged Israel, or during all the days of the kings of Israel or of the kings of Judah" (2 Kings 23:22). Liturgical forgetfulness means scriptural ignorance and vice versa. Josiah implements a set of liturgical reforms aimed primarily at rooting out idolatry, and he renews the covenant with all Judah by reading the Scripture aloud to the whole people and leading the people in a covenantal oath "to perform the words of this covenant that were written in this book" (2 Kings 23:3).

After the destruction of the temple and the Babylonian exile, the returned exiles rebuild the temple and keep the Feast of Booths and Passover. In this liturgical context, Ezra and the sacred writings enter into the story. Descended

53. On the place of this law within the unenforceable "reward type" of Deuteronomistic laws, see Carmichael, *Laws of Deuteronomy*, 39.

54. See the succinct summary in Leithart, *1 & 2 Kings*, 266–67. For historical-critical reconstruction, see van der Toorn, *Scribal Culture*, 87.

from Aaron, Ezra "set his heart to study the law of the LORD, and to do it, and to teach his statutes and ordinances in Israel" (Ezra 7:10). Ezra leads a large group of returning exiles, among whom are a number of priests bearing gifts for the temple. When he arrives in Jerusalem, he finds that the exiles who returned earlier have assimilated, largely through intermarriage, with the surrounding peoples and their idolatrous cults. The sacred writings serve here to ensure that the rebuilding of the temple and the liturgical celebrations are not for naught. After Nehemiah rebuilds the walls of Jerusalem, Ezra reads "the book of the law of Moses which the LORD had given to Israel" (Neh. 8:1) to the whole people.[55] His assistants help the people understand the words of the law by giving "the sense, so that the people understood the reading" (Neh. 8:8). On each day of the Feast of Booths, Ezra reads "from the book of the law of God" (Neh. 8:18). Ezra then leads the people in a renewal of covenant in which the people swear to obey God's law and worship him faithfully in the temple.[56] The psalmist declares, "How sweet are thy words to my taste, sweeter than honey to my mouth" (Ps. 119:103). "One thing have I asked of the LORD, that will I seek after; that I may dwell in the house of the LORD all the days of my life, to behold the beauty of the LORD, and to inquire in his temple" (Ps. 27:4).

At age twelve, Jesus already understands the law with a profundity that astounds the elders in the temple (Luke 2:46–47). At the outset of his ministry, Jesus proclaims the Scripture and applies it to himself. Having read aloud Isaiah 61:1–2 in the synagogue at Nazareth, he tells the congregation, "Today this scripture has been fulfilled in your hearing" (Luke 4:21). At the Feast of Tabernacles, Jesus presents himself as the fulfillment of Scripture's promise of salvation: "If any one thirst, let him come to me and drink. He who believes in me, as the scripture has said, 'Out of his heart shall flow rivers of living water'" (John 7:37–38). After his resurrection, he shows the two disciples on the road to Emmaus that Scripture foretold the death and resurrection of the Messiah: "Beginning with Moses and all the prophets, he interpreted to them in all the scriptures the things concerning himself" (Luke 24:27). The two disciples are able to recognize him only when he liturgically breaks bread with them. The full meaning of the Scripture then becomes clear to them. Soon afterward, the risen Jesus appears to the eleven disciples, and in a similar way he "opened their minds to understand the scriptures" (Luke 24:45).[57]

55. For historical-critical background, see, for example, the essays in van der Toorn, *The Image and the Book*.

56. For historical-critical discussion of the figures of Ezra and Nehemiah, see Blenkinsopp, *Ezra-Nehemiah*.

57. For historical-critical analysis of these texts from Luke, see Fitzmyer, *Gospel according to Luke*. Historical-critical reconstructions would not affect my argument here, however.

The relationship of the sacred writings of Israel to Jesus thus has various dimensions. According to the Gospel of Luke, Jesus liturgically read God's words and proclaimed himself to be their fulfillment. The Gospels show Jesus using Scripture for the purpose of worshiping God and avoiding temptation. By the authority of his teaching, furthermore, Jesus generated more Scripture. His "blood of the covenant," which was "poured out for many" (Mark 14:24), revealed the Messiah to be the liturgical site where Israel's relationship to God was consummated (see John 19:30).[58] His body is the true temple (John 2:19–22). As the evangelist John teaches: "He spoke of the temple of his body. When therefore he was raised from the dead, his disciples remembered that he had said this; and they believed the scripture and the word which Jesus had spoken" (John 2:21–22).[59]

In this fulfillment, the Scripture now becomes twofold: "the scripture and the word which Jesus had spoken" (John 2:22). Worship in the body of Christ is nourished by the whole of Scripture and has its eschatological consummation in view. Even now, as Jesus promises, "If a man loves me, he will keep my word, and my Father will love him, and we will come to him and make our home with him" (John 14:23).

Writing to Timothy, Paul warns against "myths and endless genealogies which promote speculations rather than the divine training that is in faith" (1 Tim. 1:4; cf. 1 Tim. 4:7), and he urges Timothy to "attend to the public reading of scripture, to preaching, to teaching" (1 Tim. 4:13).[60] Paul reminds Timothy, "From childhood you have been acquainted with the sacred writings which are able to instruct you for salvation through faith in Christ Jesus" (2 Tim. 3:15). These sacred writings have as their purpose our salvation. Paul attaches our "desire to live a godly life in Christ Jesus" (2 Tim. 3:12) to the use that Timothy, and the community of believers, make of Scripture. Paul states, "All scripture is inspired by God and profitable for teaching, for reproof, for correction, and for training in righteousness, that the man of God may be complete, equipped for every good work" (2 Tim. 3:16–17). While this passage can be read in an individualistic manner, Paul likely has in view primarily the liturgical "public reading," overseen by Timothy, in which our "training for righteousness" fully takes place.

58. For discussion of John 19:30, where Jesus is said to have given up or "traditioned" his spirit, see Humphrey, *Scripture and Tradition*, 121.

59. On John 2:21–22 see Richard Bauckham's *Testimony of the Beloved Disciple*, 120–21. Among other things, Bauckham's work challenges Bultmannian approaches to the Gospel of John such as John Ashton's *Understanding the Fourth Gospel*. See also Hengel, *Johannine Question*, 94–135.

60. For the debate about Pauline authorship of 2 Timothy (a debate whose outcome would not affect my argument here), see, for example, Johnson, *Writings of the New Testament*, 255–57; Montague, *First and Second Timothy, Titus*, 16–24.

Alexander Schmemann and Joseph Ratzinger: The Bible and the Liturgy

Arguably, then, Scripture envisions itself as primarily being read and interpreted liturgically.[61] Biblical scholars such as Oscar Cullmann, Denis Farkasfalvy, John Paul Heil, and Donald Senior have likewise emphasized that the biblical texts were written and edited within liturgical contexts.[62] But if so, how might theologians address Webster's concern that emphasizing the Church's liturgical mediation risks adopting a human-centered stance? I suggest that we look for guidance here to Alexander Schmemann and Joseph Ratzinger. Both are profoundly aware that in the early Church, as Ratzinger observes, "the reading of Scripture and the confession of faith were primarily liturgical acts of the whole assembly gathered around the Risen Lord."[63]

Alexander Schmemann: Theology, Life, and Liturgy

In *For the Life of the World*, Schmemann sets forth his "different approach to sacrament" and its significance for Christian mission/witness in the world.[64] Theology, he argues, must begin with our encounter with the risen Christ in the Eucharist: "For the basic question is: *of what are we witnesses*? What have we seen and touched with our hands? Of what have we partaken and been made communicants? Where do we call men? What can we offer them?"[65] A

61. See also Pope Benedict XVI, *Verbum Domini*, §§52–56. After noting that "every liturgical action is by its very nature steeped in sacred Scripture" (§ 52), he underscores "the *sacramentality* of the word. . . . The Word of God can be perceived by faith through the 'sign' of human words and actions. Faith acknowledges God's Word by accepting the words and actions by which he makes himself known to us. The sacramental character of revelation points in turn to the history of salvation, to the way that word of God enters time and space, and speaks to men and women, who are called to accept his gift in faith" (§56).

62. Cullmann, *Early Christian Worship*; Farkasfalvy, *Inspiration and Interpretation*; Heil, "Paul and the Believers of Western Asia"; Senior, "Gospels and the Eucharist." Similarly, see also the eschatological emphasis of Séamus Tuohy, "Communion in the Supper of the Lamb." See also the emphasis on priestly scribes and on the temple context found in such works as van der Toorn, *Scribal Culture*.

63. Ratzinger, "Formal Principles of Catholicism," 150.

64. Schmemann, *For the Life of the World*, 21. For background and programmatic insights, see Fagerberg, "Cost of Understanding Schmemann"; Mills, *Church, World, and Kingdom*; Fisch, "Schmemann's Theological Contribution." Admittedly, Schmemann at times blames the West in a rather undifferentiated fashion; for a helpful corrective, see Marcus Plested's *Orthodox Readings of Aquinas*. Schmemann's approach bears similarities with Louis Bouyer's *Liturgical Piety*.

65. Schmemann, *For the Life of the World*, 21. See also his essay "Liturgy and Theology," where Schmemann warns against a theology that "is viewed as an intellectual abstraction nowhere to be really applied; as an intellectual game which the people of God—clergy and laity—simply ignore. In our Church today, professional theologians constitute a kind of *Lumpenproletariat* and, what is even more tragic, seem to be reconciled to this status" ("Liturgy and Theology," 50).

theology that is "liturgical" in Schmemann's sense must offer to the world
Christ's gift of eternal life, made present in the communion of the eucharistic
liturgy. The life that Christ offers is something infinitely more than can be
imagined in this-worldly terms.[66] Schmemann, therefore, focuses his theological attention on Christ's eschatological conquest of death, in which we
participate liturgically: "I know that in Christ this great Passage, the *Pascha*
of the world has begun, that the light of the 'world to come' comes to us in
the joy and peace of the Holy Spirit, for *Christ is risen and Life reigneth*."[67]
It is this insight—that the eschatological Passage has begun in Christ—that
fuels a theology that is "liturgical."

For Schmemann "eternity has entered into our life already here and now,"
insofar as we know and love God through Christ.[68] To love God and each
other is to experience the fullness of life, and so "the name of this eternity is
'peace and joy in the holy Spirit' (Rom. 14:17), and of this joy Christ says, 'no
one will take your joy from you' (John 16:22)."[69] Our sharing in eternal life,
God's life, in the eucharistic liturgy is not a flight from this world. Rather,
our eucharistic sharing in eternal life—the purpose of revelation—enables us
to act in this world with a joyful love that otherwise would not be possible,
given the "sadness and suffering," the "fear and darkness," that characterize
human life.[70]

In his *Introduction to Liturgical Theology*, Schmemann begins with the fact
that the Church can become privatized, so that the liturgy seems to exist for
an inner circle. The purpose of the Church, however, is not solely to perform

---

66. Thus the purpose of Christianity is not to help ourselves and others to avoid suffering
and death. For Schmemann "the heart of the matter" is that

> for Christianity *help* is not the criterion. Truth is the criterion. The purpose of Chris-
> tianity is not to help people by reconciling them with death, but to reveal the Truth about
> life and death in order that people may be saved by this Truth. . . . Christianity is not
> reconciliation with death. It is the revelation of death, and it reveals death because it is
> the revelation of Life. Christ is this Life. And only if Christ is Life is death what Chris-
> tianity proclaims it to be, namely the enemy to be destroyed, and not a "mystery" to be
> explained. (ibid., 99–100)

67. Ibid., 106.

68. Schmemann, *O Death, Where Is Thy Sting?*, 86.

69. Ibid., 87.

70. Ibid., 86. On the relationship of theology and the world, see also Schmemann's search for
a "third way" between worldly and world-denying theologies in his "Liturgy and Eschatology,"
89–100; he argues that we need to recover "the reality that the whole of Christian theology is
eschatological, and the entire experience of life likewise. It is the very essence of Christian faith
that we live in a kind of rhythm—leaving, abandoning, denying the world, and yet at the same
time always returning to it; living in time by that which is beyond time; living by that which is
not yet come, but which we already know and possess" ("Liturgy and Eschatology," 95). See
also Kadavil, *World as Sacrament*.

the liturgy for its members; rather, the purpose of the Church is to proclaim, embody, and manifest the gospel. As Schmemann states, "Christian worship, by its nature, structure and content, is the revelation and realization by the Church of her own real nature. And this nature is the new life in Christ—union in Christ with God the Holy Spirit, knowledge of the Truth, unity, love, grace, peace, salvation."[71] In other words, the Church "realizes" and "reveals" in the liturgy what God is enabling her to be through Christ's Pasch and in the Holy Spirit. The holy Trinity operates in Christ's Pasch and in the liturgy that is the Church's participation in Christ's Pasch. Elsewhere, Schmemann describes the Eucharist as "the very *act of passage* in which the Church fulfills herself as a new creation. . . . It is the '*Eschaton*' of the Church, her manifestation as the world to come."[72] It is so not because of any power of the Church, but because of Jesus Christ, who in the liturgy takes the Church "into His Ascension, His *passage* to His Father."[73]

Why, however, is the liturgy needed for revealing and realizing the Church's "new life in Christ"? Is not this new life revealed by God through Scripture and received in faith? Schmemann answers first by pointing out that worship is not

71. Schmemann, *Introduction to Liturgical Theology*, 29. Along these lines, and with emphasis that the Church always has "new life" in Christ and the Holy Spirit (rather than autonomously), see Schmemann, "Theology and Eucharist," 78:

> The descent of the Holy Spirit at Pentecost, by inaugurating a new *aeon*, announced the *end* of this world, for as no one can partake of the "new life" without dying in the baptismal death, no one can have Christ as his *life* unless he has died and is constantly dying to this world: "For you have died, and your life is hid with Christ in God" (Col. 3:3). But then nothing which is of this world—no institution, no society, no church—can be identified with the new *aeon*, the new being. The most perfect Christian community—be it completely separated from the evils of the world—as a community is still *of* this world, living its life, depending on it. It is only by *passing* into the new *aeon*, by an anticipation—in faith, hope and love—of the world to come, that a community can partake of the Body of Christ, and indeed manifest itself as the Body of Christ.

72. Schmemann, "Theology and Eucharist," 78; cf. 82–83, where Schmemann argues that "Eucharist—'thanksgiving'—is indeed the very content of the redeemed life, the very *reality* of the Kingdom as 'joy and peace in the Holy Spirit,' the end and the fulfillment of our ascension into heaven" (83).

73. Schmemann, "Liturgical Revival and the Orthodox Church," 112. Schmemann adds that "in the Eucharist, which is the Sacrament of the Church, the *Epiclesis* means that the ultimate transformation has become possible only because of our entrance into heaven, our being in the *Eschaton*, in the day of Pentecost which is the day after and beyond the seventh day, the day which is beyond time, the day of the Spirit" (113). See also in the same volume Schmemann's "Symbols and Symbolism in the Byzantine Liturgy," where he sets forth Maximus's theology of *mysterion* and symbol (in preparation for his own view of "eschatological symbolism"). For a related insistence, from a different angle, that in the liturgy "we are raised to the point where eternity and time meet, and at this point we become real *contemporaries* of the biblical events from Genesis up to the Parousia, experiencing them here and now as eye-witnesses," see Paul Evdokimov, *Orthodoxy*, 247.

"secondary to the Church."[74] The Church is unimaginable without worship. Without worship, "there is no Church."[75] But worship is not for its own sake, as if it were a private aesthetic experience. In and through the liturgy, Christ and the Holy Spirit actively direct us to God the Father. By the grace of the Holy Spirit, we are united to Christ's Pasch and become his Body, sharing in his self-offering to the Father. Because God the Trinity is at work in the liturgy, the liturgy is "the source of that grace which always makes the Church the Church, the people of God, the Body of Christ, 'a chosen race and a royal priesthood' (1 Pet. 2:9)."[76] The Church at worship already manifests something of the eschaton. The importance of the liturgy goes far beyond the satisfying of individual needs or the carrying out of parish duties; rather, the Church as the bearer of the Triune God's activity (in the liturgy) has the mission of evangelizing the world, and everything about the Church reflects this liturgical operation of the holy Trinity.

On this basis, Schmemann explores the meaning of the "Ordo" or liturgical rite, inclusive of the liturgy of the Eucharist, of the daily office, and of the liturgical year. The Church has failed in its duty if it treats the fulfillment of the Ordo along the lines of a rote fulfillment of a mere custom or duty. Rather, the Church must understand the Ordo as centered upon the constant actualization of Christ's unrepeatable Pasch, an actualization that manifests and realizes a unique "past event in all its supra-temporal, eternal reality and effectiveness."[77] The whole Ordo of the Church's worship should be understood in relation to the Eucharist, although it would be a mistake to reduce the content of the Ordo to the Eucharist alone. With regard to the eucharistic liturgy, Schmemann notes the connection of the liturgical patterns of the early Christians with those of the synagogue. The earliest Christian worship did not reject the temple cult but did have its own distinctive elements, including baptism, the Eucharist, and specifically Christian prayers. He states, "The modern Christian accepts the Old Testament because he believes in the New. But they believed in the New because they had seen, experienced and perceived the fulfillment of the Old. Jesus was the Christ."[78]

74. Schmemann, *Introduction to Liturgical Theology*, 29.
75. Ibid.
76. Ibid. Thus John Meyendorff, drawing on Irenaeus and John Zizioulas, states that "this new 'insufflation' of the Spirit does not occur in the human individual, but happens within the total 'recapitulation' of humanity, of which *the eucharistic assembly of the local church* is the concrete realization" (Meyendorff, *Catholicity and the Church*, 26). Elsewhere Schmemann points out, "In the patristic perspective, the Church is primarily the gift of new life, but this life is not that *of the Church*, but the life of Christ in us, our life in Him" (Schmemann, "Theology and Eucharist," 76).
77. Schmemann, *Introduction to Liturgical Theology*, 43.
78. Ibid., 59.

Although Schmemann does not say this explicitly, then, the orientation of the liturgy and the orientation of Scripture are one and the same. Both turn us away from our own sufficiency and lead us into the sufficiency of God, whose path for our salvation takes form in Israel and preeminently in Jesus Christ. As Schmemann observes, the earliest Jewish Christians understood Christianity as "the fulfilment and ultimate perfection of the one true religion, of that one sacred history of the Covenant between God and his people."[79] This fulfillment of Israel's worship in the Messiah does not mandate a "harsh" supersessionism, but it does hold that divine revelation to Israel, and Israel's corresponding worship, find their fulfillment in the Ordo at whose center is the eucharistic remembrance of Jesus's Pasch.[80] Rooted in the synagogue's pattern of liturgical reading of Scripture followed by *kiddush*, the eucharistic liturgy is a God-centered ordering because, like the Scripture it proclaims, it draws us into the new, eschatological life in Christ and the Spirit.

Schmemann shows this as well with regard to the "liturgy of time," the daily office and liturgical year. He states with regard to the Jewish cult, "It is not only divided up into hours, days, weeks, and months, a great part of it is also devoted to prescriptions connected with time, and its very content can be defined as a kind of liturgical expression and sanctification of time."[81] The earliest Christian Ordo adopted from Israel this "liturgy of time," now reordered around the Messiah. There is no opposition, then, between the liturgy of time and "the eschatological nature of the Eucharist."[82] The liturgy of time is entirely directed, in the Jewish liturgy as well as the Christian, toward the Lord and his kingdom; it has its roots in God's action, not ours. Time is redefined as belonging radically to God and as moving toward the fulfillment that God will accomplish (the messianic kingdom of God), and thus as "eschatologically transparent" to God's presence and action.[83] In the Christian liturgy, then, we find that Christ's "Kingdom has entered into the world, becoming the new life in the Spirit given by him as life within himself. This messianic Kingdom or life in the aeon is 'actualized'—becomes real—in the assembly of the Church . . . when believers come together to have communion

---

79. Ibid., 59–60.

80. On the difference between "harsh" and "mild" supersessionism, see my *Jewish-Christian Dialogue*, chap. 1.

81. Schmemann, *Introduction to Liturgical Theology*, 68–69. For further insights along these lines, see Franz Rosenzweig, *Star of Redemption*, especially part 3; Heschel, *Sabbath*.

82. Schmemann, *Introduction to Liturgical Theology*, 69. This opposition, Schmemann says, is a thesis advocated by Gregory Dix; see Dix, *The Jew and the Greek*.

83. Schmemann, *Introduction to Liturgical Theology*, 71. Schmemann is engaging here with Oscar Cullmann's *Christ and Time*.

in the Lord's body."[84] The key point for our purposes is that the liturgy is
fully theocentric: it is the work of Christ and the Holy Spirit, who enable
our participation in their life. The liturgy is the true home for the reading
of Scripture that Webster enjoins; it is in and through the liturgy that revelation is truly proclaimed, interpreted, and enacted for the life of the world.

Joseph Ratzinger: Scripture, History, Liturgy

Schmemann shows how everything Christian, including Scripture, finds
its center in the Church's liturgical life, which by the Holy Spirit actualizes
Christ's gift to us of eternal life or the kingdom of God. The liturgy—the whole
Ordo with the eucharistic liturgy at the center—thereby fulfills the covenantal
promises of the Old Testament and makes present the covenantal promises
of the New. Indeed, for Schmemann it would be impossible for Christians to
read Scripture outside the context of the liturgy. Joseph Ratzinger advocates
a similar perspective, and he applies it specifically to the nature of biblical
exegesis today.

Agreeing with *Dei Verbum* §12, Ratzinger argues in the first volume of his
Jesus of Nazareth for the necessity of the historical-critical method, especially
since the historicity of God's saving work is a central claim of Christian
faith. At the same time, he notes that the historical-critical method, given
its understanding of "history" as a succession of temporal moments with
no metaphysical or providential relationship to God, must leave strictly in
the past the history that it seeks to reconstruct. Although it can demonstrate
the intrabiblical exegesis that relates the texts to each other, the historical-
critical method cannot defend the unity of the diverse texts as one "Bible."

---

84. Schmemann, *Introduction to Liturgical Theology*, 72. It will be clear that Schmemann's
perspective is quite different from that of Paul F. Bradshaw, who argues that

> in the second half of the first century there were Christian communities that still did not
> connect the tradition of the sayings of Jesus about his body and blood over bread and cup
> directly with a Passover meal at which he made an eschatological statement but at most
> only with "the night when he was handed over," just as St. Paul—and presumably the
> community from which he inherited his tradition—did. It is equally probable that there
> were other Christian communities that knew nothing of that particular tradition but may
> have been aware only of stories that Jesus celebrated the Passover with his disciples and
> engaged in discourse with them, including making eschatological statements, all of which
> had no direct effect in shaping the pattern of their regular ritual meals together beyond a
> heightened expectation of his imminent return. (*Eucharistic Origins*, 10)

Bradshaw's reconstruction relies particularly upon Léon-Dufour, *Sharing the Eucharistic
Bread*: see Bradshaw, *Eucharistic Origins*, 6–7. In my view, Bradshaw's hypothesis should be
revised—and indeed reversed—in light of the more global approach of scholars such as N. T.
Wright, Nicholas Perrin, Scot McKnight, and others. See Wright, *Jesus and the Victory of God*,
554–63; Perrin, *Jesus the Temple*; McKnight, *Jesus and His Death*, 259–374.

In the ability of biblical words to be appropriated by later biblical authors, however, Ratzinger identifies an openness of the words themselves to a fulfillment or deeper value unknown to the original authors. This openness of the words corresponds to the openness of the community in which they were written: the people of God journey forward in faith, and the sacred writings live within this community of believers.[85] The words have their full, transhistorical meaning within the presence of God to his people and of his people to God.[86]

This theocentric account of Scripture and its interpretation in the people of God receives confirmation and enhancement in Ratzinger's *The Spirit of the Liturgy*. Examining the nature of the liturgy, he argues that it cannot simply be conceived as sacred "play," since this leaves the reference to God overly indeterminate. Our understanding of the liturgy should instead begin with Scripture, specifically Moses's request to Pharaoh to let the people of Israel go three days' journey into the wilderness to worship God. God sets the terms, not Pharaoh. Pharaoh offers various compromise proposals, but Moses cannot accept them because God has commanded that God be served in a particular way. Moses is not merely using the worship of God as a cover for his desire to gain land for the Israelites: the purpose of the Promised Land itself, which God wills to give Israel, is "to be a place for the worship of the true God."[87] Israel's possession of the land depends on Israel's holiness, its obedience to God's commandments, and its submission to the reign of God. At Mount Sinai, then, Israel receives God's commandments and covenant, "concretized in a minutely regulated form of worship."[88] Liturgy, law, and life are united, since it is a holy life that is our true offering to God, and since we live rightly only when we look toward God in prayer and praise. But this requires knowing God and entering into covenant with him, something that cannot happen without God's self-communication. As Ratzinger puts it, "Man himself cannot simply 'make' worship. If God does not reveal himself, man is

85. Thus Ratzinger remarks, "in opposition to any mere biblicism," that "the text has a reality capable of shaping history only because of its own history, because of its acceptance into the faith, life, prayer and reflection of the Church; we cannot properly understand it without this history that depicts its course" (Ratzinger, "Key Question," 272).

86. See Ratzinger, *Jesus of Nazareth: From the Baptism*, xi–xxiv. See also Ratzinger, "Biblical Interpretation in Conflict," 23–24. On Ratzinger's project in his two-volume *Jesus of Nazareth*, see especially W. Wright, "A 'New Synthesis'"; W. Wright, "Pre-Gospel Traditions and Post-Critical Interpretation."

87. Ratzinger, *Spirit of the Liturgy*, 17. For discussion of Ratzinger on the liturgy, see Wainwright, "Remedy for Relativisim"; Heim, *Joseph Ratzinger*, 517–22; Nichols, *Thought of Pope Benedict XVI*.

88. Ratzinger, *Spirit of the Liturgy*, 17.

clutching empty space. Moses says to Pharaoh: 'We do not know with what
we must serve the Lord.'"[89]

Ratzinger recognizes, of course, that humans can and do invent liturgical
forms. Even after the fall, humans have some kind of awareness that "God"
exists, and humans strive in various ways to relate to God. But liturgy, as a
personal communion, requires "a real relationship with Another."[90] Only
God can give us this relationship, and on top of this, only God can thwart
our fallen desire to manipulate him and to be like gods ourselves. Ratzinger
notes, "The dance around the golden calf is an image of this self-seeking
worship."[91] In order to worship truly, we must be turned outward by the living God's commandments, including his liturgical commandments. Yet this
dependence on God is not something that fallen humans desire. The liturgy
must therefore be rooted in redemption, in "deliverance from estrangement."[92]
We need a Redeemer to take us back to God. Ratzinger concludes that for
this reason, "All worship is now a participation in this 'Pasch' of Christ, in
his 'passing over' from divine to human, from death to life, to the unity of
God and man."[93]

At this point Ratzinger returns to Israel's liturgy, specifically the sacrificial
cult set forth in Leviticus. He argues that Leviticus's impression of providing
an unchanging cult is undermined by Leviticus 26, with its warning of exile
and its promise of mercy. Leviticus's sacrificial cult should also be read in light
of Genesis 22, where God provides the sacrificial ram rather than requiring
Abraham to sacrifice his son Isaac: "Representative sacrifice is established by
divine command. God gives the lamb, which Abraham then offers back to
him."[94] In Exodus 12–13 too, God connects the rules for the Passover lamb with
God's claim upon the firstborn of Israel; the firstborn (and thus by extension all
creation) belong to God and should be offered to God. The inner insufficiency
of the temple's cult of animal sacrifice was recognized by the prophets and
psalmists. Similarly, the tent of meeting and temple are only images or replicas
of the pattern that Moses saw on Mount Sinai (Exod. 25:40). In his speech
in the book of Acts before his martyrdom, Stephen emphasizes that Israel's
cult and indeed all the central institutions of Israel point beyond themselves
to something greater, including to a new prophet whom God will raise up
(Deut. 18:15) and who "will lead the people out of the age of the tabernacle

89. Ibid., 21.
90. Ibid., 22.
91. Ibid., 23.
92. Ibid., 33.
93. Ibid., 34.
94. Ibid., 38.

and its impermanence, out of all the inadequacy of sacrificial animals."[95] In Jesus Christ, crucified and risen, the new temple has appeared; in and through him we are enabled to worship God. This is not only Stephen's perspective but also the prophecy of Jesus himself prior to his crucifixion.

For our purposes, the key point here is the theocentric character of the liturgy. The Church's liturgy, whose development correlates with the development of the Scriptures in the economy of salvation, is God's work for us, even though it is also our sharing in this work. Ratzinger states, "The prayer of the man Jesus is now united with the dialogue of eternal love within the Trinity. Jesus draws men into this prayer through the Eucharist, which is thus the ever-open door of adoration and the true Sacrifice."[96] Jesus's widespread arms on the cross indicate the full scope of his call to all people to worship the Father through him in the Holy Spirit. The eucharistic liturgy places us directly within this eschatological dynamism.

Earlier in this chapter, we focused on the point that according to Scripture the standard place for Scripture to be proclaimed and interpreted is liturgical; Scripture is meant to have a liturgical context and to nourish the liturgical dynamism of our movement toward God. Ratzinger shows more concretely how the liturgy develops in Scripture. The sacrificial laws of Leviticus should be read in light of God's provision of the ram (Gen. 22), of the Passover lamb and the consecration of the firstborn (Exod. 13), of the prophetic critique of animal sacrifice, of the eschatological orientation of the temple, and of the promise of a new prophet like Moses. The scriptural testimony to God's revelation regarding worship, in other words, shows already that the animal cult and temple are provisional. Ratzinger highlights the way in which Jesus Christ fulfills Israel's cult and extends it to all nations by incorporating all people into his self-offering.

When read according to Ratzinger's exegetical principles, therefore, Scripture shows that the liturgy—and preeminently the eucharistic liturgy—comes to us from God and inscribes us within the salvation history that Scripture describes. Just as the liturgy is something that only God can give us, so also God's word in Scripture possesses (as Ratzinger says in his commentary on

---

95. Ibid., 41–42. For further reflection on sacrifice—from a Jewish perspective—see Moshe Halbertal, *On Sacrifice*. Halbertal's view of Christian doctrine regarding Jesus's sacrificial death, however, is incomplete because it lacks a strong sense of Jesus's charity as the cause of his sacrificial death. On the centrality of Jesus's charity in his free self-offering, see Cessario, "Aquinas on Christian Salvation"; see also Thomas Aquinas's discussion of this point, indebted to Augustine and John Chrysostom, in *Summa theologiae* III, q. 47, aa. 1–3. Yet Halbertal is surely right to diagnose some Christian anti-Semitism as rooted in the desire of some Christians to blame others for Jesus's death: see Halbertal, *On Sacrifice*, 35–36. See also Huizenga, *New Isaac*.

96. Ratzinger, *Spirit of the Liturgy*, 49.

Dei Verbum) "sovereign supremacy above all human eloquence and activity of the Church."[97] It is the liturgy that best ensures the theocentric account of Scripture that Webster advocates. As Ratzinger says, "The reading of Scripture . . . reaches its highest point when the Church listens to the word of God in common in the sacred liturgy and within this framework itself experiences the active presence of the Logos, the Word in the words."[98] In the Spirit, the Church actualizes divine revelation liturgically; through the Church's mediation, the Word speaks and is spoken truthfully.

Conclusion: Revelation and Liturgical Mediation

I began this chapter with John Webster's *Holy Scripture*, which eschews liturgical emphases due to fear of placing the focus on humans and depriving God's word of its proper voice. Against this caution, I argued that Scripture bears

97. Ratzinger, preface to *Commentary on the Documents of Vatican II*, 3:167. The sovereignty of God's word in Scripture above any of the words or deeds of the Church does not, however, require imagining the Scriptures outside their ecclesial subject. As Ratzinger observes elsewhere, "We owe to the Church of the Fathers the canon of Scripture, the *symbola* and the basic forms of liturgical worship" ("Formal Principles of Catholicism," 151). In this regard Ratzinger warns against neglecting the ecclesial subject in and through which the Scriptures were written: in his view, it is a mistake "to define the Fathers no longer—in the manner of Catholic theology—as ecclesial, because of their significance for the Church, but rather as scriptural, because of their position with regard to Scripture. . . . For the Fathers themselves, their scriptural way was not distinguishable from their ecclesial way, and to separate them is to open an unhistorical perspective" (141). In the foreword to his *Jesus of Nazareth*, Ratzinger emphasizes that the Scriptures arise from within God's encounter with his people:

> Neither the individual books of Holy Scripture nor the Scripture as a whole are simply a piece of literature. The Scripture emerged from within the heart of a living subject—the pilgrim People of God—and lives within this same subject. . . . The connection with the subject we call "People of God" is vital for Scripture. On one hand, this book—Scripture—is the measure that comes from God, the power directing the people. On the other hand, though, Scripture lives precisely within this people, even as this people transcends itself in Scripture. . . . The People of God—the Church—is the living subject of Scripture; it is in the Church that the words of the Bible are always in the present. This also means, of course, that the People has to receive its very self from God, ultimately from the incarnate Christ; it has to let itself be ordered, guided, and led by him. (xx–xxii)

98. Ratzinger, chap. 6 in *Commentary on the Documents of Vatican II*, 3:271. Ratzinger adds, "The private reading of Scripture points ultimately towards this reading of the Bible that is in the fullest sense 'ecclesial,' but this ecclesial reading would lose its soul, were it not constantly nourished by total personal immersion in the word of God. In the daily enthronement of the Gospel the Council gave to the liturgy of the word a particularly solemn quality and thus endeavoured to place itself, as the 'listening Church' (which it wanted, and had to be, precisely as the 'teaching Church': cf. Article 10), entirely under the dominion of the Gospel" (ibid.). He makes clear that this dominion needs to increase: "This dominion of the Gospel should last beyond the Council and can do so only if the Church lets itself be increasingly penetrated by the word of Scripture" (ibid.).

witness to the liturgical context in which it is to be proclaimed, interpreted, and enacted. But the question then is whether Scripture becomes domesticated in the liturgy, so that God's word can no longer renew and transform the Church.

To address this concern, I examined the writings of one Orthodox and one Catholic theologian. Alexander Schmemann's primary worry is that the Church (the Orthodox Church) has grown overly accustomed to the eucharistic liturgy, so that the liturgy as a world-changing reality is no longer apparent to believers. For Schmemann, revelation communicates to us Christ's life in glory and draws us into the eschatological kingdom of God. The Christian liturgy—preeminently but not exclusively that of the Eucharist—is God's action of drawing time into eternity through Christ and the Spirit, thereby accomplishing the purpose of revelation. In the liturgy, the Church shares in Christ's passage, his overcoming of death for the life of the world.

For his part, Ratzinger suggests that the book of Exodus can serve as an extended commentary on liturgical worship. The people seek to make worship for themselves (the golden calf), but in fact only the worship that God gives them provides life-giving communion. Israel's sacrificial worship also points continually beyond itself to Jesus Christ, crucified and risen. The liturgy of the Eucharist, then, enables us to hear God's life-giving word in the midst of its enactment: the temporal barriers fall away, and God speaks to us his sacrificial and transformative Word, in whom we have eternal life through his Holy Spirit. Scripture is most itself when proclaimed in the eucharistic liturgy, because in the liturgy God is drawing us into the realities that Scripture describes.

Schmemann and Ratzinger shed light on why Scripture emphasizes its liturgical context and purpose. They show us that it is the liturgy that trains us in eschatological desire and opens us anew to the salvific agency of Christ and the Holy Spirit for our deification. Indeed, God reveals himself to us so that we "may have life" through the "name" of Jesus Christ (John 20:31), and this "life" consists ultimately in worship. Thus, in the book of Revelation, the new Jerusalem (the glorified Church) is known by its worship: "There shall no more be anything accursed, but the throne of God and of the Lamb shall be in it, and his servants shall worship him; they shall see his face, and his name shall be on their foreheads" (Rev. 22:3–4). It can be no surprise, then, that it is preeminently in the eucharistic liturgy, where the Church shares in Christ's gift of himself, that we hear Scripture as it is truly meant by God to be heard.

THREE

Priesthood

Dei Verbum describes the beginnings of the Christian priesthood, rooted in Jesus's commissioning of the apostles and their appointment of successors by the laying on of hands (see 2 Tim. 1:6): "In order that the full and living gospel might always be preserved in the Church the apostles left bishops as their successors. They gave them 'their own position of teaching authority.'"[1] The question is not only whether the apostles actually did this, but also—and perhaps even more importantly—whether it was a good idea. Given the inevitable strife among the leaders of the covenantal community, why should the mediation of divine revelation rely upon them? Even if my first two chapters are correct about the Church and the liturgy, it may seem that the hierarchical priesthood, inclusive of the papacy, has undercut the mission of Christ's entire priestly people and, through centralization of power, has failed to mediate divine revelation faithfully.[2] Would Christians be better served by

---

1. *Dei Verbum*, §7, 753–54. The interior quotation is from Irenaeus of Lyons's *Against the Heresies* 3.3.1 (PG 7:848).

2. See Uche Anizor's discussion of Martin Luther's critique of the sacramental (hierarchical) priesthood, which for Luther inevitably undermines the common priesthood: Anizor, *Kings and Priests*, chap. 6. See also the similar perspective of Leithart, *Priesthood of the Plebs*. For an exposition of the relationship of the common priesthood of all believers and the hierarchical priesthood, showing the biblical roots of this distinction, see Torrell, *Priestly People*; Congar, *Lay People in the Church*. For the argument that Jesus Christ instituted a hierarchical priesthood, thereby ensuring the formation of his priestly people in eucharistic receptivity and obedience, see my *Christ and the Catholic Priesthood* (R. Brown argues the opposite in *Priest and Bishop*). In the present chapter, rather than reprising *Christ and the Catholic Priesthood*, I approach the issue from another angle, in light of the first two chapters' accounts of the Church's missional

doing everything possible to minimize priestly hierarchy and power—for instance, by adopting more democratic (and less liturgical) modes such as popularly elected pastors/elders and itinerant preaching unimpeded by centralized bureaucracies?[3]

The dangers of priestly power are keenly depicted in Desiderius Erasmus's *The Praise of Folly*. Erasmus's narrator, "Folly," proclaims that "the life-style of princes has long since been diligently imitated, and almost surpassed, by popes, cardinals, and bishops."[4] "Folly" points out that the bishops and pope no longer lead lives of self-sacrifice and of administering spiritual gifts. Instead, they seek wealth, prestige, and power. As "Folly" puts it, "They think they have done quite well by Christ if they play a bishop's role with mystical and almost theatrical pomp, with ceremonies, with titles like 'your Beatitude,' 'your Reverence,' 'your Holiness,' with blessings and anathemas."[5] Rather than teaching, preaching, praying, and sharing in the suffering of their flock, they live a life of ease and devote themselves to severely punishing those who step out of line and to attacking those who threaten their "fields, towns, taxes, imposts, dominions."[6] Fifteenth-century popes did indeed wage war for petty gain and live in a corrupt manner, unbefitting of the mediation of divine revelation.[7] Over the centuries, many members of the Church's hierarchy (like many lay Christians in worldly domains) have abused their power. Is the answer to this problem to get rid of priestly hierarchy?

---

participation in Christ (the common priesthood) and of the liturgical proclamation, enactment, and handing on of divine revelation (which involves the eucharistic role of the hierarchical priesthood). The present chapter focuses on the point that the gospel inevitably is interpreted and handed down by the leaders of the Church. I should note that in general I find Anizor's emphasis on the priestly mediation of divine revelation to be quite helpful. See also my *Betrayal of Charity*, chaps. 5–6.

3. For the empirical efficacy of such modes (especially early Methodist itinerant preaching and church building), see Hatch, *Democratization of American Christianity*; Butler, *Awash in a Sea of Faith*. For a more recent evangelizing movement, see Kimball, *Emerging Church*. Important recent evangelical ecclesiologies include Volf, *After Our Likeness*; Harper and Metzger, *Exploring Ecclesiology*; Husbands and Treier, *Community of the Word*. Volf (who has since become an Episcopalian) argues that "all the members of a church have the right to act with regard to spiritual matters in the church or to elect the 'officers,' for, as John Smyth wrote, 'the brethren joyntly have *all* powre both of the Kingdom & priesthood *immediately* from Christ.' From the Free Church perspective, the catholicity of charismata thus means that each congregation contains *all* ministries within itself necessary to mediate salvation, and that the totality of its members is the bearer of these ministries. Here catholicity means *the fullness of spiritual gifts allotted to the local church*" (*After Our Likeness*, 273). For discussion see my *Christ and the Catholic Priesthood*, chap. 1.

4. Erasmus, *Praise of Folly*, 110.

5. Ibid., 112.

6. Ibid., 113.

7. For the time period see, for example, Ross King's *Machiavelli*.

In evaluating the place of hierarchical priesthood in the mediation of divine revelation, much depends on how one envisions the earliest Church. I therefore begin the chapter with two influential accounts of Church history—by John Calvin and Thomas Hobbes, respectively—that hold that the earliest Christian community was marked by a serene lack of priestly rivalry, but that this original peace was undermined by the powermongering of the bishops and pope, leading to the need to establish Christian unity through different means. In response to views of this kind, I argue that in the New Testament we already find significant priestly rivalry as well as crucial ways that Jesus and/or the first Christians provide for resolving such conflicts.[8] In the Gospels, Jesus offers both spiritual and structural solutions to conflicts among his disciples. I concentrate first upon the spiritual solutions, which are ultimately rooted in the reconciling power of Jesus's cross. I then examine the structural solutions that Jesus provides. As a means of resolving conflicts while allowing for fruitful tensions, Jesus distinguished the Twelve from among his broader group of disciples and commissioned Peter as leader of the Twelve.[9] I conclude that in the mediation of divine revelation, the hierarchical priesthood has an irreplaceable role.[10]

8. In what follows, I use the term "rivalry" in a broad sense that includes, without being limited to, the "mimetic rivalries" to which René Girard has drawn attention: see, for example, Girard, *I See Satan Fall Like Lightning*, 10–11. For Girard, mimetic rivalries build until the community claims a "scapegoat," an innocent target "of a senseless collective transference that is mimetic and mechanical" (1). Myths approve this scapegoating, but the Bible emphatically rejects it, as we can see in the narratives of Jesus's passion and resurrection. Jesus, says Girard, "is an unsuccessful scapegoat whose heroic willingness to die for the truth will ultimately make the entire cycle of satanic violence visible to all people and therefore inoperative" (2). The paschal mystery, on this view, unmasks rivalrous conflict for what it really is and reveals the full ugliness of those who partake in it, thereby prompting people to ask for the forgiveness that the paschal mystery accomplishes and bestows. For discussion and critique of some aspects of Girard's theory, see my *Betrayal of Charity*, chap. 8. For a creative use of Girard's theory in application to conflicts among the first Christians, see Astell, "'Exilic' Identities."

9. For historical-critical reconstructions of apparent conflicts among the priestly families that were responsible for the mediation of divine revelation in Israel, see, for example, Friedman, *Who Wrote the Bible?*; Nasuti, *Tradition History and the Psalms of Asaph*; Schley, *Shiloh*; Blenkinsopp, *Judaism: The First Phase.*

10. For the distinct, related ways in which the common/baptismal priesthood and the ministerial/hierarchical priesthood participate in Christ's threefold office of Priest, Prophet, and King, see the Second Vatican Council's Dogmatic Constitution on the Church, *Lumen Gentium*, §§9–13, 359–65. See also Congar, "Different Priesthoods." Congar shows that "while the ministerial or hierarchical priesthood of the body of Christ is essentially a ministry of living faith, that is, a spiritual sacrifice of the faithful, it is also, essentially and decisively, a ministry of the eucharistic celebration. It is only by my communion in the eucharist that I can offer that spiritual sacrifice, in spirit and in truth, which God seeks from his people, now become the body of Christ. That celebration is sacramental and liturgical" ("Different Priesthoods," 78).

John Calvin and Thomas Hobbes on Priestly Rivalry

John Calvin

In book 4 of the *Institutes of the Christian Religion*, John Calvin gives a history of the priestly office in the Church. He begins by noting that even though Christ alone governs the Church by his word, Christ freely "uses the ministry of men, by making them, as it were, his substitutes [vicars (Latin), lieutenants (French)], not by transferring his right and honour to them, but only doing his own work by their lips, just as an artificer uses a tool for any purpose."[11] Quoting Ephesians 4:4–16, he shows that Christ intends believers to be united in his Body through the "ministry of men," to whom Christ gives the necessary grace, and through whom Christ "dispenses and distributes his gifts to the Church, and thus exhibits himself as in a manner actually present by exerting the energy of his Spirit in this his institution."[12] Without question, then, a priestly ministry is needed and willed by Christ in the Church. Paul identifies these ministers as apostles, prophets, evangelists, pastors, and teachers; and, of these, Calvin observes, only pastors and teachers have "an ordinary office in the Church."[13] Teachers help in the interpretation of Scripture, whereas pastors are charged with governance, exhortation, and administration of the sacraments.

In Acts and the Epistles of Paul, Calvin goes on to say, pastors are identified by three terms that are used synonymously: bishops, presbyters, and elders. Each church too had a senate or council of venerable men whose task was to undertake fraternal correction so that the religious and moral standards of the church remained high.[14] To be a pastor of a church required an interior

---

11. Calvin, *Institutes*, 2:316. J. Todd Billings comments that for Calvin,
    no Christian is head of the church. Christ alone is the head, and dependence upon Christ leads to greater dependence upon one another. The Spirit, binding together believers, also distributes gifts for the function of building up Christ's Body. As Calvin discusses the offices of the church in book 4 of the *Institutes*, he avoids reference to rank, but turns instead to function: rather than emphasizing a chain of command in the church from the top down, Calvin claims that Paul "assigns [to believers] nothing but the common ministry, and a particular mode to each." While some are given authority for leadership in the church, Calvin seeks to emphasize how the different roles in the church are constituted by their functions in the service of Christ and his Body. (*Calvin, Participation, and the Gift*, 172–73)
    For a historical reconstruction of the emergence of bishops and of the papacy, see Rist, "Origin and Early Development of Episcopacy at Rome," as well as the sources Rist cites in his essay.
    12. Calvin, *Institutes*, 2:317.
    13. Ibid., 318.
    14. For Calvin's efforts to implement this in Geneva, see Bruce Gordon's biography *Calvin*; but for a warning against associating Calvin too closely with Geneva, see Oberman, "Toward the Recovery of the Historical Calvin," 100–101. Even so, Oberman grants Calvin's heavy

call and an exterior call. The exterior call took place by means of a popular election involving all the members of the church. After this election, the consecration of the new pastor would occur through the laying on of hands. The pastors or teachers of the churches in a particular city "selected one of their number to whom they gave the special title of bishop, lest, as usually happens, from equality dissension should arise."[15] The bishop, however, did not "have dominion over his colleagues," but instead the bishop's role was to consult, to bring forward matters for discussion, and to implement what the meeting of pastors (or presbyters) decided upon.[16] In this regard, Calvin quotes from Jerome's commentary on Titus 1, where Jerome states that originally a bishop and a presbyter were the same, and churches were governed by a council of presbyters. This original arrangement, which Calvin thinks lasted until dissensions arose, should squelch the pride of bishops and remind them that their preeminence is due to custom rather than to Jesus Christ.

In this imagined original priestly harmony, the bishop was required to be preeminent in holiness and to be subject to the will of the meeting of all the presbyters of the city. In the same way, each province had an archbishop appointed by the bishops of the province's cities. When a crisis required that the bishops meet to decide upon a matter of faith or practice, the archbishop oversaw the synod of bishops. Calvin supposes that there could also, in rare cases, be a patriarch appointed "to be superior to archbishops."[17] Unfortunately, says Calvin, this structure eventually received from some persons the unbiblical name "hierarchy," but far from desiring dominance or primacy, "the ancient bishops had no wish to frame a form of church government different from that which God has prescribed in his word."[18] Rather than accumulating riches or unnecessarily adorning church buildings, the churches had deacons (and later had more complicated rules) to distribute the church's wealth to those in need.

ecclesiological debt to his Genevan context: see Oberman, "Calvin's Legacy," 142–45, 153–54. Oberman observes that "Calvin described the Scriptural data concerning the diaconate as though he were reading them from the Bible, but in a number of specific instances he lifted them straight from the practice of Geneva" (142).

15. Calvin, *Institutes*, 2:328.

16. Ibid. See Billings, *Calvin, Participation, and the Gift*, 173: "It is important that the free, active will of believers participate in the process of choosing church officers. . . . The church, as a place that seeks to fulfil God's law through the administration of the Spirit, should display a type of 'participatory equity.' It should function through the organic coordination of complementary gifts of the Spirit. This does not eliminate the notion of authority within the church, but it functionalizes that authority, giving it participatory checks and balances."

17. Calvin, *Institutes*, 2:330.

18. Ibid.

In Calvin's view, this harmonious structure lasted for a relatively long time, not least because "in electing bishops, the people long retained their right of preventing any one from being intruded who was not acceptable to all."[19] Calvin notes that even in the time of Gregory the Great, elections of bishops still required the consent of the clergy of the city, as well as the consent of the people (or at least the leading persons in the city). Indeed, elections of the bishop of Rome proceeded in this way as late as the eleventh century. In the laying on of hands required for a new presbyter or pastor, the bishop presided and was joined by the presbyters of the city, all of whom laid on hands.

Calvin argues that a terrible rivalry eventually distorted the harmonious arrangement of the "primitive and early Church."[20] The blame for this power struggle largely rests with the papacy. Calvin explains that the popes came to control the appointment of bishops and negated the role of the consent of the pastors and of the people. Ambitious, shameless, and corrupt bishops were appointed. Bishops claimed the right to appoint the presbyters and to dominate them. As Calvin says, "In the courts of princes in the present day, you may see youths who are thrice abbots, twice bishops, once archbishops."[21] Such bishops appoint presbyters who live far away and do nothing but draw a salary. All sorts of nonbiblical offices emerged by which unholy persons could fatten their salaries without preaching or performing the sacraments, including "canons, deans, chaplains, provosts, and all who are maintained in idle offices of priesthood."[22] The reign of the papacy, Calvin observes, has stooped to lows known only to lawless robbers. In light of this corruption, rooted in overwhelming greed and lust for power, Calvin says of the pope and his bishops

19. Ibid., 2:335.
20. Ibid., 2:340. Heiko Oberman notes that for Calvin, the medieval Catholic Church had in fact seceded from the true Church. In response to Cardinal Sadoleto's accusation that Calvin had apostatized by seceding from the Church, says Oberman:

> Calvin does not argue against or reject this equation [secession = apostasy]: for him also secession was apostasy or, in any case, decline, *ruina ecclesiae*, the collapse of the church. However, with these words he [Calvin] was describing the medieval church which had increasingly become the papal church, an instrument of power in which the real marks of the real church were obscured and suppressed. The true Church of Christ, the Catholic Church, though it can be found in the medieval church, is no longer identical with it. . . . The church is not constituted by individual believers but by the office which represents Christ, whether that be the consistory, or in later times the synod or even a bishop, a possibility for which Calvin expressly leaves room. It is the Christ-representing office which works through preaching and the ministry of the Word in baptism and the Lord's Supper. The church Calvin discovered is not the invisible church but the visible church of all times and all places which begins its pilgrimage through history in God's election and ends it in the feast around the throne of the Lamb. ("Calvin's Legacy," 128–29)

21. Calvin, *Institutes*, 2:344.
22. Ibid., 2:346.

that "their kingdom is the tyranny of Antichrist."[23] The offices of the early church have been thoroughly corrupted, and what remains are "mere masks."[24]

With regard to the papacy, Calvin asks the following question: "Is it necessary for the true order of the hierarchy (as they term it), or of ecclesiastical order, that one See should surpass the others in dignity and power, so as to be the head of the whole body?"[25] Among the Jewish people, he notes, the rightful seat of priestly authority was Jerusalem. This was because of the idolatry of the nations. Now that the Church has spread around the world, however, "it is altogether absurd to give the government of East and West to one individual."[26] The transfer of priesthood due to change from the Old to the New Covenant, as described by Hebrews, does not entail a transference to the papacy; rather, the only high priest whom we now need is Jesus Christ. Calvin treats Matthew 16:18–19 and John 21:15 in light of other texts such as 1 Peter 5:2 and 2 Corinthians 5:18, so as to show that Peter did not receive anything that he did not communicate equally to others. Quoting Augustine's *Homilies on John*, he observes that Peter simply received the keys on behalf of the whole Church, rather than as his exclusive power. Peter had a preeminent role among the apostles, but it was not a preeminence of power. Furthermore, the preeminence of Peter does not mean that the bishop of Rome (or anyone else) should be preeminent. To those who argue that the best form of government for the Church is a monarchy, Calvin replies that the Church's one head is Christ. He grants that early Christians gave special honor to the church in Rome, but he notes that this was because of its relative calmness and because the seat of empire was there, in addition to its association with Peter. He quotes Jerome's letter to Nepotian as well as a treatise of Cyprian in order to show that all the bishops were intended to be equal.

Continuing his historical exposition, he notes that the bishop of Rome received a special place at the Councils of Nicea and Chalcedon, but he emphasizes that this did not mean that the bishop of Rome presided over each of the early councils. Indeed, Pope Gregory the Great strongly rejected "the title of universal bishop" as unworthy of the Christian faith, when John of Constantinople sought to claim this title.[27] Calvin argues that Gregory was mistaken in thinking that this title had been offered to Pope Leo the Great at Chalcedon, but in any case Gregory rightly rejected it. The bishop of Rome had a strictly limited role in the early church. Other bishops felt free to correct

23. Ibid., 2:348.
24. Ibid., 2:353.
25. Ibid., 2:354.
26. Ibid.
27. Ibid., 2:368.

him, and he could not meddle in ecclesiastical elections outside his patriarchate. He did not have jurisdiction to call a universal council (only the emperor had such power). In the Donatist controversy, Constantine actually relied more on the bishop of Arles than on the bishop of Rome. Pope Leo the Great, Calvin observes, did make some overly ambitious claims, but even he recognized his jurisdictional limits. But, toward the time of Charlemagne, things began to get a great deal worse. By the time of Bernard of Clairvaux in the twelfth century, the bishop of Rome and indeed the entire ecclesiastical structure in Rome had become completely corrupt. The bishop of Rome began to claim absolute power and to defend his authority even by means of fabrications. Calvin states, "When the Pope extends his jurisdiction without limit, he does great and atrocious injustice not only to other bishops, but to each single church, tearing and dismembering them, that he may build his see upon their ruins."[28]

Concluding his critique, Calvin observes that the task of a bishop is to teach the gospel, to administer the sacraments, and to maintain holy discipline in the church. In all three areas, the bishop of Rome (that is, the papacy) has utterly failed. Instead of teaching the gospel, the papacy has asserted and confirmed numerous "perverse and impious doctrines, so full of all kinds of superstition, so blinded by error and sunk in idolatry."[29] By persecuting the gospel, the papacy reveals itself to be Antichrist. Calvin grants that it may seem "slanderous and petulant" to call the papacy Antichrist.[30] It is the papacy, however, that "uses the name of Christ as a pretext, and lurks under the name of Church as under a mask."[31] Citing various biblical passages, he connects the Antichrist with the papacy's claims to a Christ-like and God-like power. The pope, who claims to unify the Church, in fact devastates and corrupts the Church. The religion professed in Rome, he says, goes so far as to reject the existence of God, to argue that the New Testament is based on lies and myths, and to deny the resurrection of the dead and the life to come. In addition to the impiety of recent popes, he mentions Pope John XXII's denial of the immortality of the soul. The point is this: "For a long period, the Roman Pontiffs have either been altogether devoid of religion, or been its greatest enemies. The see which they occupy, therefore, no more makes them the vicars of Christ, than it makes an idol to become God, when it is placed in the temple of God."[32] They have claimed power over the word of God without being obedient to the word of

---

28. Ibid., 2:381. For a similar historical narrative from a twentieth-century Catholic theologian, focusing largely on the period after the Reformation, see Schillebeeckx, *Church*, 198–228.

29. Calvin, *Institutes*, 2:383.

30. Ibid., 2:384.

31. Ibid.

32. Ibid., 2:386.

God; their claim to power has been based on an utter illusion, because it is only the word of God that has true power, and those who rebel against it can have no authority in the Church.[33]

For Calvin, then, the history of the priesthood runs downhill. It had a good beginning that lasted for a few centuries, in which priests and bishops were elected by the people and none thought themselves to have hierarchical power. This was followed by the compression of power into the hands of the papacy and the near-destruction of Christian faith. The diversity of voices at the beginning preserved the harmony of the gospel, whereas the power of the papacy, despite claiming to unify the Church, turned everything into disharmony. Calvin admits that there were rivalries in the early Church, but these rivalries did not endanger the Church until the bishop of Rome claimed to have the power to unite the diverse voices as he saw fit.

Thomas Hobbes

Writing a century after Calvin, Thomas Hobbes seeks to reintroduce an embodied principle of theological and exegetical unity, now located in the king.[34] In his *Leviathan* (1651), he does this in critical dialogue with Robert Bellarmine's *On the Supreme Pontiff*, which was published in the late sixteenth century.[35] Against Bellarmine, Hobbes holds that Christ gave his

33. See ibid., 2:390. In his discussion of the first edition (1536) of Calvin's *Institutes*, Karl Barth puts it this way: "When people do not bow before the Word of God but before something human, then ecclesiastical authority is a deception and illusion, contrary to Christian freedom and indeed to God himself. Nowhere does God recognize anything as his except where his Word is heard and very carefully (*religiose*) obeyed. . . . Hence there can be no appeal to the authority and tradition of the church" (Barth, *Theology of John Calvin*, 198–99). As Barth says, for Calvin the Church "is the company of those who are united in Christ and it dare speak only out of God's Word. This company is to be heard, and no other church. . . . A pastorate that is not based on obedience to God is a matter of caprice (*licentia*). Against it may be brought all that Jeremiah and his like had to say against the priests and prophets. But that is how it is with the pope and bishops and councils. The royal rule of Christ puts an end to all human dominion" (199). Church order "can be justified only if we see its totally human and temporal and earthly character and divest it of any religious character" (ibid.).

34. Hobbes may once have been secretary to Francis Bacon. It may be worth noting here Bacon's short essay "Of Unity in Religion," in Bacon, *Essays*, a work that first appeared in 1597 and was published in its final form in 1625. Writing in the context of Catholic and Puritan attempts to undo the Elizabethan Settlement, Bacon describes religion as "the chief band of human society" and claims that "quarrels and divisions about religion were evils unknown to the heathen. The reason was, because the religion of the heathen consisted rather in rites and ceremonies than in any constant belief. For you may imagine what kind of faith theirs was, when the chief Doctors and Fathers of their church were the poets" (67).

35. For background see Springborg, "Thomas Hobbes and Cardinal Bellarmine"; Martinich, "Bible and Protestantism in *Leviathan*"; Martinich, *Two Gods of Leviathan*. For background on the religious conflict (not simply Catholic-Protestant, but also intra-Protestant) in which

apostles no power other than the "power to proclaim the kingdom of Christ, and to persuade men to submit themselves thereunto, and by precepts and good counsel to teach them that have submitted what they are to do, that they may be received into the kingdom of God when it comes."[36] Christ's ministers receive the power to teach and administer sacraments, but no other power. Unlike kings or parents, they have "no right of commanding."[37] Hobbes adds that since no external coercion can affect our internal faith, which is God's gift to us, religious faith cannot be affected even by bad kings who forbid us to believe in Christ. When we are baptized, we become a loyal subject of God and Christ, but by Christ's own decree his kingdom does not begin until the next life and so here on earth we remain subject to the king of our country.

Moreover, Hobbes points out that in the Old Testament "the canonizing, or making of the Scripture law, belonged to the civil sovereign"—namely, Moses (and later Ezra).[38] Likewise, it was Constantine who authorized Christianity and made its books canonical; the apostles did not have the authority to canonize their own writings. The New Testament is "canonical," in the sense of being a law to be obeyed, only where the sovereign authority has made it so. Since Christ's kingdom is not of this world, he subjects all those who believe in him to the authority of the laws of the commonwealth in which they live and thus to the authority of the sovereign lawgiver. The New Testament exhorts but does not command; it relies on persuasion rather than power. The same is true for the councils of the Church, which take on the status of obligatory law only when the sovereign makes it so in his domain. The term "bishop," furthermore, is synonymous with "pastor," "elder," and "teacher." It denotes no coercive power, even in the Church. Like Calvin, Hobbes holds that among the early Christians, each congregation elected its own bishop (or elders or pastors), and he notes that this procedure still holds sway in the election of the bishop of Rome.[39]

For Hobbes, it is crucial that "the right of judging what doctrines are fit for peace, and to be taught the subjects, is in all commonwealths inseparably annexed . . . to the sovereign power civil, whether it be in one man or in one

Hobbes lived, see R. Harrison, *Hobbes, Locke, and Confusion's Masterpiece*, 8–26. Harrison notes that for Richard Hooker, the sixteenth-century Anglican theologian, "the commonwealth of England and the church of England is the same thing, a thing with one head" (*Hobbes, Locke, and Confusion's Masterpiece*, 18). For further context see Chung-Kim, *Inventing Authority*; Payton, *Getting the Reformation Wrong*.

36. Hobbes, *Leviathan*, 336.
37. Ibid., 337.
38. Ibid., 352.
39. See ibid., 361.

assembly of men."[40] When pagan kings converted to Christianity, they did not lose this power. The sovereign is, in his country, "the Church by representation" and "the supreme pastor," which means that when bishops are elected by the people, the people do so on behalf of the sovereign.[41] It is for the king, due to his paternal power over the commonwealth (which is coextensive with the Church in his realm), to decide what is suitable for his subjects to learn. All other pastors in a commonwealth act on the authority of the supreme pastor of the commonwealth—namely, the king or queen.[42] It is entirely up to the sovereign to grant ecclesiastical power, under the sovereign, to the pope or to other bishops; and it is also the sovereign who "is to appoint judges and interpreters of the canonical Scriptures; for it is he that maketh them laws."[43]

At this stage, Hobbes undertakes an extensive rebuttal of the conclusions of Bellarmine's *De Summo Pontifice*. In the pope's own lands, says Hobbes, the pope has dominion; in all other lands the pope is nothing more than a teacher, who teaches at the permission of the master of the "family" or commonwealth. Regarding Matthew 16:18, Hobbes holds that Christian faith requires simply acknowledging that Jesus is the Christ, not acknowledging a Petrine office in the Church. He emphasizes that Emperor Constantine, not the bishop of Rome, had sovereign power over the Church in the Roman Empire. Since Scripture contains no command to obey Peter, Christians cannot be justified in obeying the pope rather than their lawful sovereign. Christ taught us to obey the lawful sovereign, not to disobey. Along these lines, Hobbes repeats that the canons of councils are not laws but counsels aimed at furthering our salvation. The key point in response to Bellarmine is that "all bishops receive jurisdiction, when they have it, from their civil sovereigns."[44]

Hobbes too tells a history of priestly rivalry. Like that of Calvin, it begins with peace. The apostles were obeyed solely because of their "wisdom, humility, sincerity, and other virtues."[45] Their converts enjoyed freedom of conscience and owed obedience to none but the civil authorities. But later councils of presbyters claimed the authority to compel believers to believe what the councils taught. Soon it happened that "the presbyters of the chief

---

40. Ibid., 366.
41. Ibid., 367.
42. Hobbes discusses in some detail Queen Elizabeth's supremacy over the Church of England.
43. Ibid., 373.
44. Ibid., 388. Hobbes dismisses the notion that the pope is the Antichrist, since the pope does not claim to be the Christ, as the prophesied Antichrist will do.
45. Ibid., 481.

city or province got themselves an authority over the parochial presbyters, and appropriated to themselves the names of bishops."[46] Once this had occurred, it was but a short step to the bishop of the imperial capital city, Rome, claiming for himself power over all other bishops and thus over all Christians. The Church moved from the peaceful pastors of the apostolic age, to the power-hungry bishops of later ages, to the centralization of power in the bishop of Rome. In Hobbes's view, the reversal of this priestly distortion was accomplished in England. First, Queen Elizabeth rejected the power of the pope and gained power over the Church in England. The "presbyterians" then put down the bishops. As a result, English people are back to the apostolic condition, free to follow the apostolic teaching without giving obedience to any but the civil sovereign.

For Calvin, the answer to the spread of rivalrous priesthoods is to restore elections and popular determination of church order at a local level, doing away with the pope as a unifying principle so as to lift up the Word of God. For Hobbes, the spread of rivalrous priesthoods also requires removing the pope and bishops from their pedestals, but he asserts an earthly unifying principle—namely, the civil sovereign. To do without an embodied unifying principle is impossible, in Hobbes's view, because people need unity in order to save themselves from their lust for power. He compares the Catholic Church to the fairy kingdom: all fairies have one king (Oberon), and fairies thrive upon obscurity, enchanted buildings, and the abhorrence of rationality. Now that the Catholic priesthood (with the pope at its head) has been swept away, we can see once again that the only workable visible principle of unity in a commonwealth is the civil sovereign. Such unity is absolutely necessary because every human possesses "a perpetual and restless desire of power after power, that ceaseth only in death."[47] The solution to this endemic "war of every man against every man" is the unity provided by a commonwealth in which the people "confer all their power and strength upon one man, or upon one assembly of men, that may reduce all their wills, by plurality of voices, unto one will. . . . This is the generation of that great LEVIATHAN, or rather (to speak more reverently) of that *Mortal God* to which we owe, under the *Immortal God*, our peace and defence."[48] The resulting unity is sustained by the distinction between the sovereign who rules and all others who are subjects of the sovereign alone. Without this visible principle of unity, unchecked power-mongering—the war of all against all—would reign supreme.

46. Ibid.
47. Ibid., 58.
48. Ibid., 78, 109.

An Alternative Portrayal

But is there another way to address the problem of priestly power conflicts, an obvious problem even if we do not accept the historical narratives of Calvin or Hobbes? In what follows, I will look for evidence of "priestly" rivalry in the New Testament and ask how Jesus and/or his apostles resolve this rivalry. Although I do not here discuss Jesus's Pasch at any length, my discussion takes place under its light, since it is the fundamental cause of our entering into the life of self-giving love as members of one Body in the Holy Spirit.

Let me begin with Mark 10.[49] Here Jesus warns his disciples against trusting in riches, in light of the rich man who "went away sorrowful" (Mark 10:22) because he could not accept Jesus's invitation to sell all he has and follow Jesus. Peter, speaking on behalf of the other disciples, says to Jesus, "Lo, we have left everything and followed you" (Mark 10:28). In reply, Jesus promises them that their self-sacrifice will receive an abundant reward in the life to come. But in the same chapter of Mark's Gospel, while they are on the road to Jerusalem and to Jesus's death, James and John ask Jesus to give them the most exalted places in his kingdom. Hearing of the request of James and John, the other disciples are very upset. This seems already to be a priestly rivalry or power struggle that has the potential to divide the Church.

In response, Jesus presents his disciples with a model of nonrivalrous leadership, whose supreme instance is his cross, which Jesus prophetically calls "the baptism with which I am baptized" (Mark 10:38). Jesus tells his indignant disciples, "You know that those who are supposed to rule over the Gentiles lord it over them, and their great men exercise authority over them. But it shall not be so among you; but . . . whoever would be first among you must be slave of all" (Mark 10:42–43; see also Luke 22:24–26, which places this scene right after the Last Supper). The very next scene in the Gospel of Mark depicts Jesus leaving Jericho with his disciples, and the blind beggar, Bartimaeus, sitting by the roadside calling out as Jesus passes by, "Jesus, Son

49. See also the discussion in M. Healy, *Gospel of Mark*, 207–15. Healy states:
   In the ancient world, as today, authority is naturally assumed to entail perks and benefits for those who wield it, and the powerful often enjoy throwing their weight around. But Jesus's command is stark: "It shall not be so among you." His disciples are to display a radical and countercultural attitude toward leadership. There is no place for self-promotion, rivalry, or domineering conduct among them. Jesus does not deny that there will be offices of authority in the community he is establishing, the Church. Nor does he reject the aspiration to greatness that lies deep in the human heart. Rather, he reveals that the only way to greatness, paradoxically, is by imitating him in his humble, self-emptying love. The whole mentality on which Church leadership is exercised must be that of service (*diakonia*), acting entirely for the benefit of others, putting oneself at their disposal, caring for their humblest needs (see John 13:14; Phil. 2:3–4). (214)

of David, have mercy on me!" (Mark 10:47). The crowd tries to silence him, but Jesus calls him to himself and grants him his sight. Without denying the miraculous character of the event, we can say that its purpose may well be to show that being a leader among Christians (and thus being the "slave of all") requires begging for and relying entirely on Jesus's merciful cross, a reliance that gives us true "sight" (faith).

A similar event is recorded in the Gospel of Luke. After the transfiguration, when Jesus's glory is revealed to Peter, James, and John, Jesus shows his power over unclean spirits by casting out a demon that his disciples have been unable to cast out. As they marvel at his power, he tells them that he will "be delivered into the hands of men" (Luke 9:44), a prophetic reference to the cross. They do not understand what he is saying. Instead, they begin to argue with each other about their own status: "An argument arose among them as to which of them was the greatest" (Luke 9:46).[50] There seems to be a good deal of irony here, because they had all just failed to cast out the unclean spirit. Surely this moment was hardly opportune for rivalry about which one of them was greatest! Especially given the connection between glory and humility that Jesus has recently made through his transfiguration and his prophetic words about his coming death, we can see how distorted their desires for power are. When Jesus perceives what they are thinking, he instructs them again about true greatness. Placing a child by his side, he says to them, "Whoever receives this child in my name receives me, and whoever receives me receives him who sent me; for he who is least among you all is the one who is great" (Luke 9:48). In light of Jesus's glory and humility, manifested in his transfiguration and cross, the solution to priestly rivalry is to be the servant of all ("least among you all") by devoting oneself to the mission of welcoming adopted children of God in Christ's name. This mission can be accomplished only when one is configured to Jesus's humility, since otherwise one either will not seek to receive God's adopted children or will attempt to receive them in one's own name. We attain true greatness when our desires are configured to Jesus's desire—namely, his goal of drawing us into the glorious life of love that belongs to him as the Son of the Father.

Another case of rivalry occurs when Judas Iscariot is angered by Jesus's permitting Mary of Bethany to anoint Jesus with "a pound of costly ointment of pure nard" (John 12:3). Judas is dismayed, or at least claims to be dismayed, on the grounds that such expensive ointment is a luxury and the money spent

50. See J. Green, *Gospel of Luke*, 385–93. For Green the key point is that Jesus "calls upon his followers to welcome those of the lowest status, the poor (see above on 4:18–19), even this child, 'in my name' (see above on v. 24); that is, to act in this way is to perform in a way consistent with Jesus's own commitments and commission" (392).

on it could have been used to feed the poor. Although we learn from the evangelist that Judas's disappointment is a mask for his greed, nonetheless Jesus's response to him is significant: "Let her alone, let her keep it for the day of my burial. The poor you always have with you, but you do not always have me" (John 12:7–8). In this case of contention between Judas Iscariot and Mary of Bethany, Jesus resolves the dispute by making clear that their primary focus should be on him and on his Pasch. From that focus will flow acts of almsgiving in their proper order, since the cross heals our alienation and enables us, in the Holy Spirit, to love God and neighbor as we should, without rivalry and envy.

Consider too the conflict between the sisters Mary and Martha of Bethany. Martha wears herself out serving Jesus and making him comfortable in their home. Mary does not help with this work but instead sits at Jesus's feet and learns from him. It would seem that Jesus, with his emphasis on service, should defend Martha when she complains that Mary is not helping her. But Jesus does not take Martha's side and rebuke Mary. Instead he responds to Martha's complaint by correcting Martha, even if he does so in a relatively gentle fashion: "Martha, Martha, you are anxious and troubled about many things; one thing is needful. Mary has chosen the good portion, which shall not be taken away from her" (Luke 10:41–42). Has Jesus thereby shamed Martha, despite all her service to him? It would seem that at least he could have asked Mary to split the work with Martha or could have volunteered to do a portion of the work himself. Jesus, however, rejects the very terms of the rivalry. Simply listening to Jesus is a vocation and a work in itself. This does not devalue Martha's work of service to Jesus. But hearing Jesus's word has priority over service; indeed, the latter ultimately flows from the former.

This very point is underscored by Jesus's teachings just prior to entering the village and home of Martha and Mary. First, a teacher of the Torah asks Jesus, "Teacher, what shall I do to inherit eternal life?" (Luke 10:25). Jesus directs the question back to the questioner by asking him what the Torah teaches on this matter. When the questioner replies that the Torah teaches that "you shall love the Lord your God with all your heart, and with all your soul, and with all your strength, and with all your mind; and your neighbor as yourself" (Luke 10:27), Jesus confirms that doing so will lead to eternal life. The teacher of the law then asks who counts as a "neighbor." In reply, Jesus tells the parable of the good Samaritan. The whole point of this parable is that those who pass by the oppressed and afflicted do not in fact love their neighbors; no matter what their position in the community, they have failed and will be held accountable. The seeming outsider—the Samaritan—turns out to be the true insider, since "he had compassion" (Luke 10:33). The teaching to which Mary "listened" (Luke 10:39), in short, would have instructed her in the compassionate path of Martha. This teaching, in which the place of Jesus turns out—on the cross—to be the place of the innocent victim in the parable, has a crucial role in unmasking the self-serving motives that produce rivalry.

We might also think of the rivalry found in Jesus's parable of the laborers in the vineyard. Some are hired at the beginning of the day, while others are hired only toward the very end of the day. The former complain when the owner of the vineyard rewards the later workers in exactly the same way as he rewards the workers who bore "the burden of the day and the scorching heat" (Matt. 20:12). The parable requires us to recognize that everything proceeds from God's sheer generosity. In the Gospel of Matthew, this parable directly precedes both Jesus's prophetic foretelling to his disciples of his cross and resurrection (Matt. 20:18–19) and the sons of Zebedee's rivalrous request to be placed at the side of Jesus in his kingdom. According to this Gospel, it was their mother who made the request on their behalf; but the other disciples react with the same indignation that we saw above. In response, Jesus warns them not to act like gentile rulers and "great men" (Matt. 20:25) but instead to recognize that whoever would be great among them must be their servant, and whoever would be first among them must be their slave, "even as the Son of man came not to be served but to serve, and to give his life as a ransom for many" (Matt. 20:26–28). The connection with the cross, which shows the evil of rivalry and overcomes rivalry, is explicit here.

Perhaps the prime example of priestly rivalry occurs in the narratives of the Last Supper, and particularly in Luke's Gospel. At the very outset of Luke's narrative of the Last Supper, he writes that as the Feast of Passover was approaching, "Satan entered into Judas called Iscariot, who was of the number of the twelve; he went away and conferred with the chief priests and officers how he might betray him to them" (Luke 22:3–4). This is rivalry in its starkest form: rebellion not simply against the status of another disciple but against Jesus himself. But Judas's rivalrous rebellion is not the only instance of rivalry that Luke associates with the Last Supper. On the contrary, when Jesus finishes the Passover meal at which he instituted the Eucharist, the disciples do the very opposite of the "remembrance" of Jesus (Luke 22:19) that Jesus has commanded. When he tells them that one of them would betray him, they begin "to question one another, which of them it was that would do this" (Luke 22:23). The rivalrous implications of the pointed questions that they pose to each other lead directly, according to Luke, into their dispute over "which of them was to be regarded as the greatest" (Luke 22:24). Jesus has to remind them that he himself is among them "as one who serves," so that the greatest would be the "one who serves" (Luke 22:27). Jesus also has to encourage Peter, who Jesus knows will deny him. Jesus exhorts Peter, "When you have turned again, strengthen your brethren" (Luke 22:32). But Peter proudly insists that he will not fail: "Lord, I am ready to go with you to prison and to death" (Luke 22:33).

What, then, is the solution to this rivalrous pride, which appears to be endemic among Jesus's disciples, and not only Judas? Luke's narrative indicates that the solution is the Eucharist, in which we liturgically "remember" or participate in Jesus's sacrificial love on the cross: "This is my body which is given for you. Do this in remembrance of me" (Luke 22:19). The Eucharist is here connected with imitating Jesus's kenotic love as "one who serves." The Eucharist also provides a foretaste of the heavenly banquet of the consummated kingdom of God (see Luke 22:30). It is in celebrating the Eucharist—in participating in Jesus's Pasch, which exposes and overcomes all rivalry—that the disciples will be able to "remember" Jesus in kenotic love rather than rivalry.[51]

As a last example from the Gospels, it may be that Peter and the beloved disciple in John's Gospel instruct us about rivalry. In a reversal of Peter's denial of Jesus after Jesus's arrest, the risen Jesus three times asks Peter if Peter loves him. When Peter responds yes, Jesus tells Peter, "Feed my lambs" (John 21:15). Jesus also here prophesies that Peter will be martyred. Jesus concludes this talk with Peter by urging him, "Follow me" (John 21:19). At this point, however, Peter sees the beloved disciple and asks Jesus, "Lord, what about this man?" (John 21:21). In asking about Jesus's plans for another disciple, Peter seems to have made an error, perhaps even a rivalrous error. In response, Jesus again commands Peter to direct his attention strictly to following Jesus, rather than worrying about the vocations that Jesus gives to other disciples. Jesus tells Peter, "If it is my will that he remain until I come, what is that to you? Follow me!" (John 21:22).[52] To avoid rivalry, each disciple of Jesus must concentrate upon his or her own mission of following Jesus by carrying his or

---

51. For a Baptist perspective that emphasizes liturgical (eucharistic) worship as formative of Christian character, see E. Newman, *Untamed Hospitality*.

52. The conclusion drawn by Richard Bauckham is that since the Gospel of John gives Peter "primarily the role of shepherd," the beloved disciple, with his much different role,

> becomes at the end irrelevant to Peter's own call to discipleship (21:20–22). . . . The different, complementary roles of the two disciples show that it is not rivalry between different branches of early Christianity (the so-called great church and the Johannine churches) that is at stake in their relationship. The Gospel acknowledges Peter's leading role in the whole church, to which its own community belongs, while claiming for the beloved disciple a role of witnessing to the truth of Jesus that is equally significant for the whole church. . . . Just as Peter's role in the story enables him to become the chief under-shepherd of Jesus's sheep not within the narrative but later, so the beloved disciple's role in the story enables him to witness to others not within the narrative but later. (*Testimony of the Beloved Disciple*, 85, 87)

her cross in self-sacrificial love. In Peter's case, Jesus prophetically describes Peter's eventual martyrdom: "Truly, truly, I say to you, when you were young, you girded yourself and walked where you would; but when you are old, you will stretch out your hands, and another will gird you and carry you where you do not wish to go" (John 21:18).

The book of Acts depicts a variety of conflicts within the nascent Church, as Jesus's followers "devoted themselves to the apostles' teaching and fellowship, to the breaking of bread and the prayers" (Acts 2:42). These conflicts should not lead us to deny the power of Pentecost, when the Holy Spirit comes upon the apostles and equips them for bravely and boldly proclaiming the gospel of Jesus Christ. The Pentecostal descent of the Holy Spirit unifies the multitude gathered in Jerusalem, as Jews from all nations hear the gospel proclaimed in their own language (see Acts 2:4–11). Peter bears witness to the multitude that Jesus, who was crucified, is the living "Lord and Christ" (Acts 2:36) of Israel: "This Jesus God raised up, and of that we all are witnesses. Being therefore exalted at the right hand of God, and having received from the Father the promise of the Holy Spirit, he has poured out this which you see and hear" (Acts 2:32–33). Peter and John are arrested for their preaching, but they refuse to stop; and the martyrdom of Stephen, in which Saul/Paul is involved, leads to the further spread of the gospel. The book of Acts shows the Christian movement triumphing over rivalry and spreading the gospel of self-sacrificial love through the Roman empire—a development that Kavin Rowe evocatively describes as "world upside down."[53]

Yet, it would obviously be a mistake to think of the early Christian community, filled with the Holy Spirit and ordered around "the apostles' teaching and fellowship" and "the breaking of bread and the prayers" (Acts 2:42), as without rivalry. For example, Acts reports that "when the disciples were increasing in number, the Hellenists murmured against the Hebrews because their widows were neglected in the daily distribution" (Acts 6:1). This conflict is resolved by the establishment of deacons to take charge of matters that the apostles lack time to handle well. The apostles then concentrate upon "preaching the word of God" (Acts 6:2).[54] The rivalry that could have emerged does not do

53. See C. Rowe, *World Upside Down*.

54. For historical-critical discussion, see Johnson, *Acts of the Apostles*, 106, where Johnson argues that Luke is here distinguishing between Jews who primarily spoke Aramaic ("Hebrews") and Jews who primarily spoke Greek ("Hellenists"). He adds that "the allusion to the 'daily distribution' corresponds with what we know of organized Jewish charity in local communities. Each community would offer a daily 'soup kitchen' for transients and the destitute, and a 'chest' for meeting long-term needs" (ibid.). See also Dunn, *Christianity in the Making*, 2:246–54. In Dunn's view, "The Hellenists more than likely looked down on the Hebrews as parochial and traditionalist. Equally, the Hebrews probably regarded the Hellenists as those who were diluting

so, or at least is diffused, when the apostles find a way of focusing on their particular mission.

Another conflict involves disagreement about the mission to the gentiles. Given the intensity of the disagreement, Paul and Barnabas are summoned to Jerusalem to discuss the matter with "the apostles and the elders" in Jerusalem (Acts 15:2).[55] The matter is resolved by means of a council at which the apostles Peter and James speak authoritatively. A later conflict involves Paul and Barnabas, who disagree with each other about the wisdom of taking Mark with them on their missionary tour, since Mark abandoned them once before. The "sharp contention" (Acts 15:39) between Paul and Barnabas is resolved by separation. Barnabas and Mark go to Cyprus, while Paul and Silas go to Syria and Cilicia.[56]

Even more potentially serious than any conflict recorded in Acts is the conflict between Paul and Peter that we find mentioned in Paul's Epistle to the Galatians. In this epistle, Paul is striving to persuade the Galatian Christians not to obligate themselves to the observance of the Mosaic law. Paul recounts his trip to Jerusalem with Barnabas, when he and Barnabas were called upon to defend their preaching of the gospel. He reports that from "James and Cephas [Peter] and John, who were reputed to be pillars," Paul and Barnabas received "the right hand of fellowship," that they "should go to the Gentiles," and the other three "to the circumcised" (Gal. 2:9). But Paul goes on to say that he was later compelled to publicly rebuke Peter at Antioch. According to

---

and compromising key traditions of their shared faith and praxis as Jews" (251). For an earlier discussion, identifying four groups of conflicting positions among the first Christians with respect to "what faith in Jesus implied by way of Jewish observances" (2) and sifting through the diversity and conflict that this implied for the earliest Christian communities in Antioch and Rome, see Brown and Meier, *Antioch and Rome*.

55. See the historical-critical reconstruction in Hengel, *Acts and the History of Earliest Christianity*, 116.

56. As James Dunn reconstructs the conflict:

> In the circumstances reported in Galatians 2:11–14, and even more if Paul had failed to persuade Peter of the error of his ways, Paul must have felt abandoned by his erstwhile closest colleague, Barnabas. . . . Luke indeed confirms that such a breach occurred: Paul and Barnabas parted company and engaged in quite separate missions—Barnabas back to Cyprus, and Paul to the churches of Syria and Cilicia (Acts 15:39–41). But the reason Luke gives is entirely different. In Acts the breach occurs because of "a sharp disagreement (*paroxysmos*)" between Paul and Barnabas over Barnabas's proposal to take John Mark with them on their return (pastoral) visit to the churches they had established (Acts 15:36–39). It may not be necessary to choose between the two reasons for the breach—the one indicated in Luke's account and the other suggested by Paul's account. But here again it is unlikely that Luke has told the whole story. (*Christianity in the Making*, 2:492)

Like other scholars, Dunn envisions a lasting breach between Paul and the churches of Antioch, Syria, and Cilicia.

Paul, Peter had eaten with the gentiles (thereby breaking Jewish law) before the arrival of Jewish Christians who "came from James" (Gal. 2:12). When these men arrived, Peter switched sides and no longer ate with gentiles. Mortified by Peter's failure to defend "the truth of the gospel," Paul recalls, "I said to Cephas before them all, 'If you, though a Jew, live like a Gentile and not like a Jew, how can you compel the Gentiles to live like Jews?'" (Gal. 2:14). Paul does not say how Peter responded, but the fact that Paul tells the story and nonetheless retains his overall positive view of Peter indicates that his intervention must have in some fashion been successful.[57]

What can we learn from these conflicts over precedence, vocation, and fidelity? They generate the following insights and practices for overcoming rivalry: to be great is to be servant of all and to rely on the merciful power of Jesus's cross; to be great is to build up God's family of adopted children in Christ; we should focus on our own vocation rather than that of others; hearing Jesus's word is the source of compassionate action; any reward that we receive is God's gift; and we overcome rivalry when we "remember" Jesus by celebrating the Eucharist. But they also suggest that the Church has a hierarchical structure willed by Jesus and that a council of the Church has authority in the Holy Spirit to resolve conflicts. At the same time, members of the hierarchical priesthood can be publicly rebuked for hypocrisy.

What about the role of Peter, who receives from Jesus "the keys of the kingdom of heaven" (Matt. 16:19)?[58] The Petrine office cannot, of course, take the

---

57. For discussion see Humphrey, *Scripture and Tradition*, 82–84; Bockmuehl, *Simon Peter*, 28–29, 92–95; Hengel, *Saint Peter*, 57–65; Dunn, *Christianity in the Making*, 2:470–94. Hengel underscores the seriousness of the division: "The deep divide that was signified by the dramatic, public, drawn-out dispute between Peter and Paul is something we cannot portray deeply enough" (*Saint Peter*, 63). Without dismissing the importance of the divide, Bockmuehl notes that

> within five years or so of Galatians, Paul sounds much more positive about the role of Peter. For instance, 1 Cor. 1:12 reports what seems to be a Cephas party in Corinth, but far from treating either this party or that of Apollos as rival factions to be defeated, Paul seeks to unite them. Paul here speaks quite deliberately of Peter and Apollos in positive terms as his fellow "servants of Christ and stewards of the mysteries of God" (1 Cor. 4:1–2 ESV). So also in 1 Cor. 9:5, Cephas is the only figure named among the apostles and siblings of the Lord who are traveling missionaries accompanied by their wives. In chap. 15, Peter is again singled out as the first apostolic resurrection witness (note Mark 16:7; Luke 24:34) and is clearly regarded as something of a key figure. That appraisal is quite in keeping with Galatians 1:18. It is the Antioch incident that constitutes an evidently temporary exception to what appears to be a relationship of friendly respect, if not necessarily of cordiality. (*Simon Peter*, 29)

For her part, Humphrey ably critiques the schema of "Pauline libertarians opposed by rigid Jewish Christians, and then the emergence of a compromise, 'early Catholicism'" (*Scripture and Tradition*, 82).

58. For historical-critical analysis, see Davies and Allison, *Gospel according to Saint Matthew*, 2:602–52. They conclude, "One should seriously entertain the notion that Matthew

place of the spiritual transformation that Jesus insists upon; this is shown not least by Jesus's warning to Peter, "Get behind me, Satan! You are a hindrance to me; for you are not on the side of God, but of men" (Matt. 16:23). Absent interior renewal, Peter will falter in many ways and will need rebuking for his hypocrisy. Yet Peter's mission remains one of the instruments by which the risen Jesus works to ensure "that they may be one" just as he and the Father are one (John 17:22). In light of the eucharistic form of the Church's sharing in divine revelation, Jesus's unique commission of the repentant Peter, "Feed my lambs" (John 21:15), takes on its full meaning.[59]

Indeed, the fact that rivalrous conflicts among the disciples were already breaking out during Jesus's lifetime sheds special light on Peter's role. Inspired by the Father, Peter confessed Jesus in a unique fashion and Jesus gave him a unique mission: "Blessed are you, Simon Bar-Jona! For flesh and blood has not revealed this to you, but my Father who is in heaven. And I tell you, you are Peter, and on this rock I will build my church, and the powers of death shall not prevail against it" (Matt. 16:17–18). The death of Peter (see John 21:18–19) does not bring an end to the Church's need for a Petrine office of unity. As Markus Bockmuehl observes, "The principle of a continuation of the Petrine ministry *as such* seems clear in the memory of the man, beginning perhaps with classic 'Petrine primacy' texts such as Matthew 16:17–19; Luke 22:31–32; and John 21:15–17. All three texts imply a post-Easter continuation of Peter's task that seems intrinsically permanent and not tied to the identity of the one apostle."[60]

---

conceived of Peter as an authoritative link, perhaps *the* authoritative link, between Jesus on the one hand and the Matthean community on the other. . . . Also not impossible is the suggestion that Peter was thought of as holding some type of 'office' which others held after him. This would certainly go a long way towards explaining Matthew's interest in one who was, after all, long since dead" (651).

59. By contrast to my view that Jesus, according to the Gospels, anticipated the disciples' rivalry, Raymond E. Brown, SS, comments with regard to the Gospel of John that "the Jesus who sends the Paraclete never tells his followers what is to happen when believers who possess the Paraclete disagree with each other. The Johannine Epistles tell us what frequently happens: they break their *koinōnia* or communion with each other. If the Spirit is the highest and only authority and if each side appeals to him as support for its position, it is nigh impossible (particularly in a dualistic framework where all is either light or darkness) to make concessions and to work out compromises" (*Churches the Apostles Left Behind*, 121–22). According to Brown's historical reconstruction, the "Johannine community" existed for a time as a "Paraclete-guided community of people," but soon "it split up and went out of existence" (123). See also Brown's *Community of the Beloved Disciple*.

60. Bockmuehl, *Simon Peter*, 183. As an Anglican, Bockmuehl does not, of course, accept the papacy:

In his cantankerous dispute with Pope Stephen, Cyprian (d. 258) may be judged right to conclude that *all* bishops who confess the faith of Peter constitute the "rock" on which, according to Matt. 16, the church is founded (*Ep.* 26.1; cf. *Ep.* 74.17 of Firmilian to

Peter and his successors repeatedly fail, but not in such a way that the
"powers of death" negate the Church's mediation of divine revelation through
true teaching and holy sacraments. After predicting Peter's betrayal, Jesus
consoles him, "Simon, Simon, behold, Satan demanded to have you, that
he might sift you like wheat, but I have prayed for you that your faith may
not fail; and when you have turned again, strengthen your brethren" (Luke
22:31–32). It is Jesus's prayer, reaffirmed by the risen Lord in the Gospel of
John, that enables Peter, and the hierarchical priesthood beginning with the
Twelve, faithfully to serve the eucharistic unity of the new Israel gathered
around the Messiah.[61]

Conclusion: Revelation and Hierarchical Priesthood

The purpose of this chapter has been to inquire, in light of my previous emphasis on mission and the eucharistic liturgy, whether the hierarchical priesthood befits the mediation of divine revelation. Would the Church do better to
return to what Walter Rauschenbusch, rejecting the Jewish priesthoods, calls
"the ancient democracy of the Hebrew prophets and of post-exilic Judaism"?[62]

Cyprian). This is the appropriate challenge to a maximal papal arrogation of Peter's
ministry. Nevertheless, it is also the case that the remembered Peter's profile in the second
and subsequent centuries includes a recognition that his Petrine ministry was entrusted to
a continuing succession of ecclesial shepherds in various places of his activity (including
Antioch) but above all in Rome. This continues to make it permissible and appropriate
to speak of successors of Peter, even if half a millennium after the Reformation it remains the case that institutional trappings of authority and opulence ill become the early
church's memory of the Galilean fisherman whose way of discipleship neither sought
nor possessed power and opulence. (182)

Bockmuehl also carefully distinguishes between the "remembered Peter of the Gospels and
the Epistles" (ibid.) and the historical Peter—a far murkier figure—behind these diverse texts.
See also the various viewpoints found in Garuti, *Primacy of the Bishop of Rome*; Schatz, *Papal
Primacy*; Kasper, *Petrine Ministry*; Puglisi, *Petrine Ministry and the Unity of the Church*.

61. Commenting on Jesus's choice of twelve apostles from among his many disciples, and
on Jesus's further choice of three, N. T. Wright states:

The very existence of the twelve speaks, of course, of the reconstitution of Israel; Israel
had not had twelve visible tribes since the Assyrian invasion of 734 BC, and for Jesus
to give twelve followers a place of prominence, let alone to make comments about them
sitting on thrones judging the twelve tribes, indicates pretty clearly that he was thinking
in terms of the eschatological restoration of Israel. It is not so often noticed that, within
the twelve, there was a group of three—Peter, James and John—who functioned regularly as Jesus's closest personal aides. It is perhaps not accidental that this is a Davidic
symbol, echoing the three who were David's closest bodyguards. (*Jesus and the Victory
of God*, 299–300)

Wright makes it quite clear that Jesus ordered his community hierarchically.

62. Rauschenbusch, "*Christianity and the Social Crisis*," 85.

Without suggesting that Calvin and Rauschenbusch have identical ecclesiologies or views of ancient Israel, we can affirm that this would seem to be the position of Calvin. For Calvin, there was an original period in the Church's history when priestly rivalries did not exist. During this democratic period, presbyters and bishops were elected and accountable, and they did not claim authority other than as presiders whose role was to foster discussion and to implement the decisions of the meetings. After a few centuries of general harmony, the bishops of Rome undertook a devastating power-grab that gravely distorted the Church. The answer for Calvin is popular elections, meetings of boards of elders, and trust in the power of the gospel to unify believers. A similar story is told by Hobbes, although in his case it ends (and indeed begins) with the power of the civil sovereign, who, as it turns out, is crucially needed as an embodied unifying principle for Christians.

Nietzsche's *The Anti-Christ* develops a version of this story, now rooted in Israel's history along lines that Calvin would have abhorred. According to Nietzsche, the Jewish people were originally exemplary: "Their Yaweh was the expression of their consciousness of power."[63] The Jewish priesthood, however, perverted this concept of God, falsified Israel's history in the Bible, and turned the Jewish people into a despicable race. Predictably, "priestly" serves as perhaps Nietzsche's most negative adjective, and Nietzsche describes the Christian priest as "the most dangerous kind of parasite, the actual poison-spider of life."[64] For Nietzsche, the eucharistic liturgy could only be (on the priest's side) a pathetic instance of the will-to-power, and on the participants' side a grotesque instance of what Nietzsche finds to be Christianity's taking "the side of everything weak, base, ill-constituted."[65]

In the New Testament, we find a clear awareness of negative potentialities within priesthood. Rivalry can be seen to have been endemic to the Christian hierarchical priesthood from the outset. The twelve disciples, chosen by Jesus from a much larger group, struggle with one another in terms of privilege, ministry, and message—and such struggles continue in the early Church, according to Acts. During his earthly ministry, therefore, Jesus taught certain cross-centered ways of handling and limiting rivalry among his followers, above all through remembering him in the eucharistic liturgy and thereby being configured to his cruciform love. Indeed, Jesus appears to have formally established the ministry of the Twelve in the context of the Eucharist (the Last Supper)—a context that the Gospel of John explicates in terms of Jesus's

---

63. Nietzsche, *Anti-Christ*, 147.
64. Ibid., 162.
65. Ibid., 129.

humble washing of his disciples' feet.[66] Although whether the apostles should be called "priests" can be debated, they exemplify the hierarchical priesthood's commission to preach the gospel, celebrate the Eucharist, and guide the community of Jesus's followers.[67]

Given Peter's threefold denial of Jesus, Jesus's bestowal of unique authority upon Peter is also particularly instructive. We see this authority in the opening chapters of Acts. During the council at Jerusalem, it is Peter who gives the first speech, just as he gives the first speech in the upper room and at Pentecost. Yet how could Jesus, who preached humility and self-giving love, have willed not only a ministerial hierarchy among his disciples but also, within this hierarchy, a Petrine office, which elevates Peter among his brethren and therefore intensifies the danger of the pride that comes with power? We have seen that Jesus recognizes the dangers and seeks to alleviate them by various means. Why, then, does he choose this path for his eschatological community?[68]

We can gain some instruction on this point from Nietzsche. He presents Christianity as the enemy of the *Imperium Romanum* on the grounds that Christianity possesses "the instinct of *deadly hatred* towards everything that stands erect, that towers grandly up, that possesses duration, that promises life a future."[69] It would seem that hierarchical priesthood proves Nietzsche wrong, since it appears to "stand erect" and "towers grandly up."[70] But as Nietzsche recognized, Jesus's hierarchical priesthood is radically opposed to the *Imperium Romanum*. The hierarchical priesthood that Jesus institutes has the sharing

66. As Jesus says, "Do you know what I have done to you? You call me teacher and Lord; and you are right, for so I am. If I then, your Lord and Teacher, have washed your feet, you also ought to wash one another's feet" (John 13:12–14).

67. For an excellent discussion of this topic, see Torrell's *A Priestly People*.

68. Indebted to Albert Schweitzer and others, Dale C. Allison Jr. holds that Jesus himself erroneously taught the imminent (indeed immediate) "advent, after suffering and persecution, of a great judgment, and after that a supernatural utopia, the kingdom of God, inhabited by the dead come back to life, to enjoy a world forever rid of evil and wholly ruled by God" (*Historical Christ and the Theological Jesus*, 95; cf. Allison's *Constructing Jesus* for further elaboration). Following the approach of his teacher G. B. Caird, N. T. Wright has repeatedly addressed Allison's (and Schweitzer's) perspective by showing how Jesus fulfills the apocalyptic hopes of Israel and how the first Christians understand the Church within that (reconfigured) eschatology: see, for example, Wright, *Jesus and the Victory of God*, 202–9, 214–29. See also the helpful work—constructively critical of the positions of both Allison and Wright—of James D. G. Dunn in his *Christianity in the Making*, vol. 1, *Jesus Remembered*. Allison grants that the Gospel of John, at least, envisions the ongoing Church.

69. Nietzsche, *Anti-Christ*, 192.

70. See also the positive evaluation of privilege and hierarchy in the political philosophy of Aurel Kolnai, to whose work Graham McAleer drew my attention: Kolnai, *Privilege and Liberty*; Kolnai, *Ethics, Value and Reality*.

of eucharistic mercy as its mission, and it is sustained by Jesus's mercy. It is in this sense, reconfiguring power in terms of mercy, that Peter receives "the keys of the kingdom of heaven" (Matt. 16:19; cf. Isa. 22:22). Entrusted with "the ministry of reconciliation" (2 Cor. 5:18), the Church prevails against the powers of death by liturgically mediating the gospel to the world—thereby revealing not the power of humans to be in charge, but the cruciform power of the merciful One to whom "all authority in heaven and on earth has been given" (Matt. 28:18).

FOUR

Gospel

Yves Congar, who so deeply influenced the documents of the Second Vatican Council, observed that for patristic and medieval theologians "the Gospel is Jesus Christ. The Gospel is present when Christ is present and actively communicating his life."[1] Similarly, before his election as Pope Benedict XVI, Joseph Ratzinger remarked that "Jesus himself, the entirety of his acting, teaching, living, rising and remaining with us is the 'gospel.'"[2] It is this "entirety of his acting, teaching, living, rising and remaining with us" that is made present in the eucharistic liturgy (scriptural word and sacrament). Since "Christ is present and actively communicating his life," we can say with Paul, "I have been crucified with Christ; it is no longer I who live, but Christ who lives in me; and the life I now live in the flesh I life by faith in the Son of God, who loved me and gave himself for me" (Gal. 2:20).

1. Congar, *Tradition and Traditions*, 272. For Congar and the Council, see Yves Congar, *My Journal of the Council*.
2. Ratzinger, *Gospel, Catechesis, Catechism*, 51. For historical-critical background to "Christian insistence that there was only *one gospel*, proclamation of God's once-for-all provision of Jesus Christ" (25), see Stanton, *Jesus and Gospel*. From a somewhat different perspective, Christof Landmesser echoes Ratzinger's principle of unity: "The New Testament texts altogether make a claim that is connected throughout to a specific manner of speaking. The texts maintain that they are articulating a decisive claim concerning God's relation to humankind when they speak concretely about Jesus Christ. It is this claim of Jesus Christ that I have summarized . . . as the common reference point and unity-shaping element of the New Testament texts" ("Interpretative Unity of the New Testament," 176).

If the gospel is Jesus Christ, however, why does not Scripture's testimony to Jesus suffice for the mediation of divine revelation, especially after the end of the apostolic age? In reflecting upon this question, I first survey Scot McKnight's *The King Jesus Gospel*, which from a Protestant perspective shows the need for a "gospel culture" inclusive of the Church's sacraments and creedal confession.[3] Focusing on 1 Corinthians 15:1–5, McKnight examines ways in which the "gospel" involves more than simply the call to repent and believe in Jesus Christ. In McKnight's view, the early Church possessed an exemplary "gospel culture," as manifested by its creeds and by its practices of baptism and the Eucharist.[4] The early Church's "gospel culture," however, was inseparable from bishops who understood themselves to be successors of the apostles. Against various Christian heresies and schismatic movements, they enumerated the canonical books of Scripture and defined doctrines about God the Trinity, Christ, Mary, and so forth.

To draw out the significance of this doctrinal tradition with respect to the meaning of the gospel, I compare McKnight's approach with the interpretation of Paul's use of "gospel" offered by Thomas Aquinas in his commentaries on Romans and Galatians.[5] As we will see, Aquinas's theology of the

3. See McKnight, *King Jesus Gospel*. As he acknowledges, McKnight is heavily indebted to a similar discussion found in N. T. Wright, *What Saint Paul Really Said*, 39–62. See also Carson and Keller, "Gospel-Centered Ministry," 20–21:

> Not only does the gospel of Jesus Christ gather into itself all the trajectories of Scripture, but under the terms of the new covenant, all of Christian life and thought grow out of what Jesus has accomplished. This good news not only declares that God justifies sinners so that our status before him is secured but also that he regenerates us and establishes us in his saving kingdom. The gospel deals with more than the judicial, our standing before God, for it is the power of God that brings salvation (Rom. 1:18)—a comprehensive transformation. Everything is secured by Jesus's death and resurrection; everything is empowered by the Spirit, whom he bequeaths; everything unfolds as God himself has ordained this great salvation.

4. Similarly, arguing that 1 Corinthians 15:1–4 provides a summary of the "gospel" or "most basic Christian message," and that later arguments between Christians (from Nicea onward) often have failed to appreciate the shared core message, Ted A. Campbell proposes that Christians today need to recognize "a common Christian gospel in a broad ecumenical framework" (*Gospel in Christian Traditions*, 1–2). Campbell's emphasis on gospel unity, however, leads him to wonder about the value of doctrinal development, as when he deplores "the way in which elaborate definitions of unity have sometimes obscured rather than clarified the gospel message" and gives the example of debates over Chalcedonian Christology (122). James D. G. Dunn makes a similar charge, specifically with regard to what he calls "works of tradition" (*Jesus, Paul, and the Gospels*, 164), which he identifies as "episcopacy, for example, or an infallible papacy, believers' baptism, or biblical inerrancy" ("Gospel according to St. Paul," 143).

5. These two commentaries contain the central elements of Aquinas's theology of the Pauline "gospel," a topic that his other Pauline commentaries treat much more briefly. Aquinas's commentary on 1 Corinthians, unfortunately, is missing his discussion of 1 Corinthians 7:15–10:33 (this portion of text was filled in by an excerpt from the commentary of Peter of Tarantaise). As

"gospel" largely corresponds to the major emphases identified by McKnight, especially in holding that the gospel is Jesus Christ and that the gospel has to do with the whole of the history of salvation (rather than being simply about justification). Aquinas, however, shows more clearly how the "gospel" is inseparable from the doctrinal tradition of the Church—not least by explicitly bringing to bear the Church's Christological doctrines in his reading of the Pauline "gospel."

Scot McKnight on the Gospel

The Content of the Gospel

McKnight's book takes as its starting point the fact that for many Protestant evangelicals, the "gospel" describes God's offer of salvation that we accept by repenting of sin and confessing Jesus as Lord.[6] On this view, the gospel consists simply in justification by faith. McKnight affirms that hearing the gospel requires us to be born again by faith, and he contrasts this with sacramental Christian traditions that, he thinks, take for granted Church membership and thereby obscure the need for personal conversion in order to be a member of the Church. But he warns that evangelical Protestant traditions, concerned not to make the gospel into a message of works-righteousness, have trouble translating the call to faith into a path of robust discipleship.[7] The problem,

---

a result, we do not have Aquinas's commentary on 1 Corinthians 9:12–18, where Paul describes the right of preachers of the gospel to earn their living by means of this preaching and where Paul states, "If I preach the gospel, that gives me no ground for boasting. For necessity is laid upon me. Woe to me if I do not preach the gospel!" (1 Cor. 9:16).

6. As an example, McKnight points to Greg Gilbert's *What Is the Gospel?* For Gilbert, what Paul means by "the gospel" can be found by reading Romans 1–4 and noting the themes of God's sovereignty, human rebellion, the redemption won by the cross and resurrection of Christ, and the response of faith. I find largely the same account of the gospel in Chappell, "What Is the Gospel?," 115–16, 121, although Chappell later emphasizes that "salvation includes a renewed heart, empowered life, and transformed world" (134). See also Greear, *Gospel*, 5 (cf. 9–10); Stuhlmacher, "Theme," 23 (cf. Stuhlmacher, "Pauline Gospel," 154, 167, 169). Stuhlmacher criticizes the "new perspective" on Paul that deemphasizes (generally without, however, denying) the doctrine of justification: see Stuhlmacher, *Revisiting Paul's Doctrine of Justification*. See also D. Campbell, *Quest for Paul's Gospel*; N. T. Wright, *Justification*; Colijn, *Images of Salvation in the New Testament*.

7. See McKnight, *King Jesus Gospel*, 33. See also Thompson, *Pastoral Ministry according to Paul*, especially 15–19. McKnight argues that the "gospel" is often confused with the "plan of salvation," which he describes as follows: we recognize God's love, righteousness, and grace; we recognize that we are made in God's image but have rebelled against him, thereby standing under judgment; we hear the good news that Jesus Christ has reconciled us to God by his cross; and we embrace this good news by repentance and faith in the saving power of Jesus's death.

he argues, is that a focus on salvation (that is to say, simply on *decision* for Christ) has replaced the necessary focus on the gospel.[8]

To prepare us for his understanding of the "gospel," McKnight briefly explores the "Story of Israel/the Bible" in relation to the "Story of Jesus."[9] The story of Israel begins with the creation of the world as the cosmic temple, with Adam and Eve as the image of God, and then moves to their rebellion and their banishment from Eden, the choosing of Abraham, the choosing of the people Israel, their law and eventually their kings, and finally God's sending of his Son to accomplish what no mere human could do by redeeming us from sin and ruling the world (thereby fulfilling the vocation of Adam and of Israel) as its King, Messiah, and Lord. Jesus Christ establishes the kingdom of God; Jesus's Church is to bear witness to his victory and "to embody the kingdom as the people of God."[10] The second coming of Jesus Christ will consummate God's kingdom on earth through the establishment, not of a garden, but of a city: the "new Jerusalem."

In McKnight's view, the "gospel" is not this full story, but it makes sense only within the full story, since the story of Jesus belongs to the story of Israel. Jesus resolves not only the problem of personal sin but also, and more fundamentally, the problem of Israel's history and of human history. As Israel's King and Messiah, Jesus saves humans precisely by bringing Israel's history to its fulfillment, even though the full consummation awaits his second coming.

McKnight considers that the place in the New Testament that comes closest to offering a definition of the "gospel" is 1 Corinthians 15.[11] The key passage comes in 1 Corinthians 15:1–5:

> Now I would remind you, brethren, in what terms I preached to you the gospel, which you received, in which you stand, by which you are saved, if you hold it fast—unless you believed in vain. For I delivered to you as of first importance what I also received, that Christ died for our sins in accordance with the scriptures,

8. For a related discussion, see Max Turner's survey of various perspectives on the gift of the Spirit in Luke-Acts, "Spirit and Salvation in Luke Acts." Turner draws here upon Pao, *Acts and the Isaianic New Exodus*, as well as Dunn, *Baptism in the Holy Spirit*; Dunn, "Baptism in the Spirit." See also M. Turner, *Power from on High*.

9. McKnight, *King Jesus Gospel*, 34.

10. Ibid., 36. Compare Schreiner, *King in His Beauty*.

11. See also Oakes, *Infinity Dwindled to Infancy*, 64, where Oakes observes regarding 1 Corinthians 15:3–5: "This passage constitutes the essence of the gospel, and its one-sentence brevity determined the entire narrative shape of the four Gospels as we have them today." As Dunn comments, "The gospel according to Paul centers on the death and resurrection of Jesus and the consequent gift of the Holy Spirit to those who believe in this Christ and in God who acted through this Christ" ("Gospel according to St. Paul," 139; cf. 143–52). See also N. T. Wright, *What Saint Paul Really Said*, 60.

that he was buried, that he was raised on the third day in accordance with the scriptures, and that he appeared to Cephas, then to the twelve.

McKnight considers that this passage offers a road map to a "gospel culture."[12] Why so? In answer, he provides eight points of commentary on the passage. First, "gospel" here is a dynamic reality: Paul and the Corinthians are intimately connected by the gospel, so much so that when Paul says "I preached" a literal translation might be "I gospeled." The gospel that Paul "gospels" to the Corinthians works upon them: it is by this gospel that they are "saved." Second, the gospel is what Paul "received" and what the Corinthians "received." This gospel is traditional, then; it is not a mere personal teaching of Paul. Third, the content of the gospel is that Christ died, was buried, was raised, and appeared. The gospel or good news particularly announces these events. As McKnight says, "To gospel for Paul was to tell, announce, declare, and shout aloud the Story of Jesus Christ as the saving news of God."[13]

Fourth, the gospel resolves or brings to fulfillment the story of Israel.[14] In this regard McKnight points to Paul's repetition of the phrase "in accordance with the scriptures." Paul's letters are filled with citations of and allusions to Israel's Scriptures. This means that the gospel does not come from nowhere or merely offer a set of ideas; rather, the gospel has a backstory that is told in Israel's Scriptures. The gospel proclaims the fulfillment of God's covenantal promises to Israel. We can understand the content of the gospel—the four key events that happened to Jesus—only in light of his identity as Israel's Messiah and Lord.

Fifth, the gospel saves. Paul does not provide a systematic explanation of how Jesus's death reconciles us to God, but the gospel includes the reality that Jesus's death overcomes "our sins."[15] The story of Jesus cannot be told without recognition of sin as blocking us from God, and of Jesus's death as overcoming the impediment caused by sin. McKnight adds that Jesus identified fully with the human condition, died as our representative or substitute (standing in our place and receiving our punishment, including not only physical death but also spiritual death), and thereby reconciled us to God by bringing about

12. McKnight, *King Jesus Gospel*, 48.
13. Ibid., 50.
14. See also N. T. Wright, *What Saint Paul Really Said*, 48–49.
15. For historical-critical discussion, see McKnight, *Jesus and His Death*. For an instructive theology of atonement, see McKnight, *Community Called Atonement*. See also N. T. Wright's *Jesus and the Victory of God* and Dale C. Allison Jr.'s historiographically more cautious—and therefore theologically much leaner, reducing the Gospel portraits of Jesus largely to those texts that describe an eschatological prophet—*Constructing Jesus*.

the forgiveness of sins and leading us into God's presence.[16] Like many theologians, McKnight holds that appreciating what Jesus did for us on the cross requires a variety of approaches; no one theory of the cross's saving power will suffice. Citing Galatians 4:4–6 and 1 Corinthians 6:11, he observes that we should read "Christ died for our sins" with a variety of realities in view, including the sending of the Holy Spirit, our adoption as sons, and our justification and sanctification.

Sixth, although Paul mentions four events that happened to Jesus, the gospel has to do with Jesus's whole life, and also has to do with his second coming and the full consummation of the kingdom of God. The key point here is that the gospel is not solely about Jesus's redemptive death on the cross. Even the burial of Jesus is significant, because it shows that Jesus truly died and because it opens the possibility of Jesus's presence among the dead. Jesus's resurrection is crucial for "God's eschatological irruption into space and time" and for the new creation and final consummation of the entire creation.[17]

The final two points highlight Jesus's kingship and kingdom. The seventh point is that the center of the gospel is Jesus, the Messiah, Lord, and Son. He is the anointed King of Israel. He has conquered sin and death. The eighth point is that the gospel's goal is the complete glorification of God through his Son in the new creation, when everything will be subjected to God as it should have been from the beginning.[18] McKnight goes on to sum up his thesis about the meaning of "the gospel" in Paul, and he emphasizes three elements: salvific power, Jesus Christ as Messiah and Son, and the fulfillment of Israel's story (beginning at creation and being fully consummated only at the second coming of Jesus). As McKnight puts it, "The gospel for the apostle Paul is the salvation-unleashing Story of Jesus, Messiah-Lord-Son, that brings to completion the Story of Israel as found in the Scriptures of the Old Testament."[19]

16. In my view, substitution theories (as distinct from theories of satisfaction) go too far insofar as they imagine God pouring out his wrath upon Jesus. See my *Sacrifice and Community*, chap. 2. As James Dunn points out, "Paul never allowed room for any idea of Jesus's death propitiating an angry God" ("Gospel according to St. Paul," 142).

17. McKnight, *King Jesus Gospel*, 54.

18. For Wright's interpretation of the biblical portrait of the new creation, see N. T. Wright, *Surprised by Hope*. For my own interpretation, drawing upon Thomas Aquinas as representative of the broader Catholic tradition, see my *Jesus and the Demise of Death*.

19. McKnight, *King Jesus Gospel*, 61. Earlier he quotes N. T. Wright's summary: "'The gospel' itself, strictly speaking, is the narrative proclamation of King Jesus. . . . Or, to put it yet more compactly: Jesus, the crucified and risen Messiah, is Lord" (Wright, *What Saint Paul Really Said*, 45–46, quoted in McKnight, *King Jesus Gospel*, 58).

Gospel Culture

As an example of a "gospel culture," McKnight points to the early Christians, with their "rule of faith" and creedal confessions such as the Niceno-Constantinopolitan Creed. Quoting Ignatius of Antioch's confession of faith in Jesus Christ, he shows that this confession of faith closely reflects 1 Corinthians 15 and Romans 1. He finds the same thing in the rule of faith articulated by Irenaeus of Lyons, in Tertullian's presentation of the rule of faith in *Against Praxeas*, and in the questions asked of baptismal candidates in Hippolytus's *The Apostolic Tradition*. Turning to the Nicene Creed, McKnight highlights the clause that parallels 1 Corinthians 15: "For our sake he was crucified under Pontius Pilate; he suffered death and was buried. On the third day he rose again in accordance with the Scriptures; he ascended into heaven and is seated at the right hand of the Father. He will come again in glory to judge the living and the dead." Although McKnight is critical of important aspects of the early Church, he considers the earliest theologians and creeds to be generally effective in their "gospeling."[20] He also notes that baptism and the Eucharist (and the liturgical year) are central ways in which the Church shares in "the Story of Israel coming to completion in the saving Story of Jesus."[21]

McKnight assigns the blame for the shift from a "gospel culture" to a "salvation culture" in part to Augustine and in part to the Reformation.[22] He praises the Reformation for many things, including a valuable focus on the need for personal salvation. Even so, he considers that an unfortunate corollary of the Reformation was a shift to a "salvation culture." The Augsburg Confession of 1530, for example, is organized not according to the order of God the Father, God the Son, and God the Holy Spirit that one finds in the Niceno-Constantinopolitan Creed, but rather according to an order determined by what McKnight describes as "sections on *salvation and justification by faith*."[23] The Geneva Confession exhibits a similar emphasis, as does John Wesley's account of his Aldersgate experience. The result has been a

20. McKnight, *King Jesus Gospel*, 69. McKnight adds that, because the Church is not the kingdom, the early Church was nonetheless filled with problems, among them Constantinianism (from which flowed the crusades) and the development of a highly sacramental culture that eventually fostered a community of automatic members rather than real disciples.

21. Ibid., 158.

22. Ibid., 70.

23. Ibid., 71. For a more positive reading of the early Protestant confessions' relationship to the gospel, see T. Campbell, *Gospel in Christian Traditions*, 58–63. Campbell argues, however, that "in Evangelical Christian communities the redemptive meaning of Christ's work is very often pared down to the single element of Christ's death as a substitution for the death that humans owe for their complicity in sin," with the result that Christ's resurrection is neglected (71).

widespread "salvation culture" that understands the gospel as consisting in repentance and salvation through faith in Jesus Christ, who died for us.

McKnight concludes, "True gospeling that conforms to the apostolic gospel leads directly to who Jesus is."[24] He tests "true gospeling" by the "apostolic gospel" as found in Scripture, and he then assesses the degree to which the Church or churches have remained faithful to the apostolic gospel and true gospeling. But if Jesus's story fulfills the story of Israel, surely the New Testament witness to the Church as the "body of Christ" and the eschatological Israel cannot be reduced simply to the question of whether certain early post-apostolic Christians happened to get "true gospeling" right. Given the Pentecostal descent of the Holy Spirit upon the Church as the eschatological Israel, must not the content of "true gospeling" be assessed by the Church itself, as at the council of Jerusalem?

Thomas Aquinas on Paul's Gospel in Romans

Writing to a largely Protestant audience, McKnight remarks, "If we have any Protestant bones in our body, we want to know what they [the apostles] gospeled and how they gospeled, and we want our gospeling to be rooted in and conformed to their gospeling."[25] But how is it that we come to know what the apostles "gospeled and how they gospeled"?[26] Historical research has a place; so does individual reading of Scripture. But, as I have suggested above, much more is involved, as shown by Jesus's formation of his community of disciples headed by the Twelve, and by his charge to them to "do this in remembrance of me" (Luke 22:19) in the Eucharist. Namely, union

24. McKnight, *King Jesus Gospel*, 127.
25. Ibid., 115.
26. This question animates Joseph Ratzinger's foreword to his *Jesus of Nazareth*, xi–xxiv. Given the plethora of competing historical reconstructions of the figure of Jesus behind the Gospel narratives, Ratzinger observes that Jesus has "receded even further into the distance" despite the efforts of historians to draw us closer to him (xii). Ratzinger considers that the historical-critical method remains indispensable, but its limitations should be recognized, primarily the fact that it "has to leave the biblical word in the past. . . . It can glimpse points of contact with the present and it can try to apply the biblical word to the present; the one thing it cannot do is make it into something present *today*—that would be overstepping its bounds" (xvi). This is the cost of bracketing the question of God's activity, as does modern historiography—a high cost, since the gospel is the story of God's activity. Thus historical-critical scholarship cannot replace the people of God as interpreter of God's word. Ratzinger explains, "The People of God—the Church—is the living subject of Scripture; it is in the Church that the words of the Bible are always in the present. This also means, of course, that the People has to receive its very self from God, ultimately from the incarnate Christ; it has to let itself be ordered, guided, and led by him" (xxi).

with the "gospeling" of the apostles requires reading the apostolic gospel in light of the entirety of canonical Scripture and in light of the conciliar and creedal testimony of the Church that, as Joseph Ratzinger says, "listens to the word of God in common in the sacred liturgy."[27] This canonical and ecclesial mode of reading characterizes Thomas Aquinas's exegesis of the Pauline "gospel."[28]

The Gospel in Romans 1:1

In his Letter to the Romans, Paul mentions the word "gospel" (either in its noun or verb form, εὐαγγέλιον or εὐαγγελίζειν) numerous times, including in 1:1, 3, 9, 15, 16; 2:16; 10:15, 16; 11:28; 15:16, 19, 20; and 16:25.[29] Of these, the most important references come in Romans 1:1–3. In this passage, Paul begins by proclaiming himself to be "a servant of Jesus Christ, called to be an apostle, set apart for the gospel of God which he promised beforehand through his prophets in the holy scriptures, the gospel concerning his Son, who was descended from David according to the flesh" (Rom. 1:1–3). Aquinas treats separately each of the first three phrases: "a servant of Jesus Christ," "called to be an apostle," and "set apart for the gospel of God." It is the last phrase that is significant for our study. What does Aquinas make of Paul's claim to be "set apart for the gospel of God"?

Aquinas first observes that "gospel" means "good news." So far, so good; we can all understand that the message of salvation is "good news." But Aquinas takes this further by inquiring into what, in fact, constitutes the human good. What is ultimately the good for which humans were created? The gospel is good news, says Aquinas, because "it announces the news of man's union with God, which is man's good: 'It is good for me to cleave to God' (Ps. 73:28)."[30] What the gospel communicates or reveals is nothing less than the union of humans with God, the good for which God created humans.

---

27. See Ratzinger, "Sacred Scripture in the Life of the Church," 271. Regarding the medieval Church, Scot McKnight finds most offensive the "increasing centeredness of Marian themes," the centralization of power that produced such things as indulgences, and "a near automatic sacramentalization that impeded the message of personal response to the gospel" (*King Jesus Gospel*, 76). I do not think that McKnight understands Catholic theology of Mary, indulgences, and the sacraments, although there have obviously been abuses. See also McKnight's *Real Mary*, and my discussion of this book in my *Mary's Bodily Assumption*.

28. For the patristic background of Aquinas's Pauline commentaries, see Wilken, "Origen, Augustine, and Thomas."

29. For background to Paul's use of εὐαγγέλιον or εὐαγγελίζειν, see Stuhlmacher, "Pauline Gospel," especially 149.

30. Aquinas, *Commentary on the Letter of Saint Paul to the Romans*, no. 23, 9, accessed on the website of the Aquinas Center for Theological Renewal, Ave Maria University.

Aquinas then adds a further wrinkle: this union of humans with God, the union that makes the gospel "good news," is threefold.[31] First, the gospel reveals the union of God and man in Jesus Christ. Here Aquinas links Romans 1:1 with John 1:1, on the ground that it is the same gospel (in both Paul and John) that teaches that "the Word became flesh."[32] In a primary sense, therefore, the gospel or good news is the incarnation. Second, the gospel reveals the union of God and human beings that comes about by adoptive sonship. Here Aquinas links Romans 1:1 with Psalm 82:6, "I say, 'You are gods, sons of the Most High, all of you.'" In the Gospel of John, after quoting Psalm 82:6, Jesus argues that the meaning of this verse is that those to whom the word of God comes are "gods" (John 10:34–35). Aquinas draws the conclusion that the gospel is not only about Jesus Christ but also about his body, the Church, because God sends his Son into the world in order to adopt sons (and daughters) in the Son.

The third union is an extension of the first two. The gospel is not only about our adoptive sonship in our earthly life but also about the *consummation* of our adoptive sonship in eternal life. The gospel reveals the lordship of Jesus Christ, and therefore the gospel is intrinsically eschatological. In this regard Aquinas again links Romans 1:1 with the Gospel of John, this time with John 17:3, "And this is eternal life, that they know thee the only true God, and Jesus Christ whom thou hast sent." Aquinas also quotes Isaiah 52:7, which Paul quotes in Romans 10:15, "And how can men preach unless they are sent? As it is written, 'How beautiful are the feet of those who preach good

31. The three paragraphs that follow treat paragraph 24 of Aquinas's commentary.

32. In this regard, Richard Swinburne offers a keen insight that fits with and sheds light on what Aquinas is doing. Swinburne notes that

clearly some New Testament passages say or imply that Jesus Christ was God and had existed from all eternity: clearly the opening passage of St. John's Gospel for example carries this implication. Other New Testament passages do not seem to think of Christ in such exalted terms and seem to imply that his exalted status (possibly lower than that of God himself) was only his subsequently to the Resurrection. Romans 1:4 seems to have this lower Christology, when it speaks of Christ as "declared (ὁρισθέντος) to be the son of God with power, according to the spirit of holiness, by the resurrection of the dead." "Declared to be" might mean "recognized as" but is more naturally interpreted as "made." "Son of God" may mean simply a holy person, not necessarily divine. If we take St. John's Gospel and the Epistle to the Romans as two separate works written by two separate authors, the most plausible historical interpretation of the latter suggests that these authors had different views about the status of Christ. But if we think of them as having the same author, God, who also guided the Church to produce the creeds, the initially less natural interpretation of Romans must be the true one. . . . Saying this is quite compatible with claiming that St. Paul himself, at any rate while writing the Epistle to the Romans, had a lower Christology; if he did, he was inspired by God to write things whose meaning was a little different from what he supposed. (*Revelation*, 192–93)

news!'" Aquinas's citation of Isaiah 52:7 evokes the remainder of Isaiah's profoundly eschatological verse, which continues as follows: "who publishes peace, who brings good tidings of good, who publishes salvation, who says to Zion, 'Your God reigns.'" The full accomplishment of God's reign is what the gospel has in view.[33]

Having commented in this fashion on "gospel," Aquinas expands his lens in order to comment on "gospel of God" (still with respect to the phrase "set apart for the gospel of God"). The good news "of man's union with God" does not come from human beings; rather, God reveals the gospel, and so Paul calls it "the gospel of God." As a scriptural text in support of the view that the gospel is divine revelation, Aquinas employs Isaiah 21:10: "What I have heard from the LORD of hosts, the God of Israel, I announce to you." This verse completes an oracle in which the prophet receives the message, "Fallen, fallen is Babylon; and all the images of her gods he has shattered to the ground" (Isa. 21:9). The prophet delivers this message to Israel, which he describes as "my threshed and winnowed one" (Isa. 21:10).[34] Thus the context of the Isaianic passage quoted by Aquinas indicates that the gospel is eschatological good news of God's victory in Christ, proclaimed to God's "threshed and winnowed" people. Aquinas's point here is that the gospel comes from the living God of Israel, who brings about our union with God.

The Authority (and Reliability and Dignity) of the Gospel: Romans 1:2

Aquinas next turns to Romans 1:2, where Paul states that this gospel was "promised beforehand through [God's] prophets in the holy scriptures, the gospel concerning his Son, who was descended from David according to the flesh." The gospel, Aquinas reiterates, announces good things (our union with

---

33. By contrast, N. T. Wright imagines that Jesus's kingdom inauguration was forgotten by the later Church. He argues, "The Great Tradition has seriously and demonstrably distorted the gospels. Eager to explain who 'God' really was, the church highlighted Christology; wanting to show that Jesus was divine, it read the Gospels with that as the question; looking for Jesus's divinity, it ignored other central themes such as the kingdom of God. By the fourth century the church was not so eager to discover that God's kingdom had arrived and was to be implemented in Jesus's way, so it screened out that kingdom inauguration which lies at the heart of the Synoptic tradition" ("Response to Richard Hays," 63). Even more troublingly, Larry Hurtado supposes that the decline of eschatology was such that in the fourth century "imperial Christianity lost the earlier understanding of itself as the provisional witness to the Kingdom of God, and quickly imagined itself to be that Kingdom in its own structures and earthly prominence (which had in fact been established under Constantine by very familiar use of imperial force)" (*At the Origins of Christian Worship*, 115). I argue against this view in my *Jesus and the Demise of Death*, chap. 4.

34. For historical-critical background, see Childs, *Isaiah*, 153–54.

God) and does so by the authority of God. Aquinas interprets Romans 1:2 as being Paul's way of further explaining the authority that the gospel possesses.

The gospel has authority, first, because it was "promised beforehand through his prophets in the holy scriptures." Here Aquinas quotes Isaiah 48:5, "I declared them to you from of old, before they came to pass I announced them to you."[35] Isaiah 48 is especially relevant for the authority of the gospel. In this part of Isaiah's prophecy, God calls upon Israel to recognize that just as in the past he declared what he would do and then accomplished his promises, so now he will announce to Israel "new things, hidden things which you have not known" (Isa. 48:6).[36] These "new things" will bring about Israel's salvation and "everlasting joy" (Isa. 51:11), through the work of the suffering servant.[37]

For Aquinas, prophecies such as Isaiah 48:5 give an authoritative "antiquity" to the gospel. The gospel did not simply spring up with the proclamation that Jesus had risen from the dead; rather, God had prepared a people for the gospel over the course of centuries. As Aquinas notes, pagan opponents of the gospel derided it as something new.[38] Antiquity, however, is not the only evidence of the gospel's authority that Aquinas finds in Paul's statement that the gospel was "promised beforehand through his prophets in the holy scriptures" (Rom. 1:2). Aquinas also emphasizes that God made and fulfilled this promise. The gospel therefore has authority also because of its "firmitas," its reliability as

35. Aquinas, *Commentary on the Letter of Saint Paul to the Romans*, no. 26, 10. Following on the heels of Aquinas's quotation of Isaiah 21:10, this quotation of Isaiah 48:5 further indicates Aquinas's appreciation of the connections between Romans and Isaiah, connections that have been explored most recently in J. Ross Wagner's *Heralds of the Good News*.

36. See Childs, *Isaiah*, 372–79; Childs considers chap. 48 to illustrate well his "canonical approach."

37. For the connection of the suffering servant with Jesus, see *Summa theologiae* III, q. 46, a. 5, obj. 2; III, q. 47, a. 3. For exegetical and theological discussion, see especially Janowski and Stuhlmacher, *Suffering Servant*. See also the chapter on Aquinas in Childs, *Struggle to Understand Isaiah as Christian Scripture*, as well as Sawyer, *Fifth Gospel*.

38. See Wilken, *Christians as the Romans Saw Them*. As Wilken notes in the epilogue of his book:

Celsus believed that religion was inextricably bound to the unique customs of a people, to the laws of a nation. The ultimate legitimation of religious beliefs and practices did not rest on philosophical arguments about the nature of the gods but on ancient traditions that had been passed on from generation to generation. Age and custom were the final arbiters in religious matters. As the seer Teiresias says in Euripides's *Bacchae*, "The beliefs we have inherited, as old as time / cannot be overthrown by any argument." Because Christianity had no homeland and did not belong to one people or nation, its traditions, such as they were, could make no claim to antiquity. The one nation to which they could make any claim, Israel, the Christians themselves had repudiated. Hence there was no way that Christianity could make a claim on religious truth. The "old doctrine" was the "true doctrine." (201–2)

For Origen's response to Celsus's critique, see Martens, *Origen and Scripture*, 70–77.

rooted in God's faithful promises.[39] We know that the gospel is true because the gospel's author is God, and God does not lie. We know this not solely as a logical proposition about God's nature but also because of what God has done to show his faithfulness.[40]

In this respect Aquinas quotes Acts 13:32–33, which comes from a speech that Paul gave at Antioch of Pisidia.[41] In his speech (Acts 13:16–41), Paul begins by inviting the Israelites and the gentile God-fearers to recall that God chose the patriarchs of Israel, led the people of Israel out of Egyptian slavery, raised up David to be king, and promised a Davidic Messiah. Paul then proclaims that this Messiah is Jesus, who died on a cross, was raised from the dead, and appeared to many. The passage that Aquinas quotes is central to Paul's narrative of what McKnight terms the fulfillment of Israel's story in Jesus's story: "We bring you the good news that what God promised to the fathers, this he has fulfilled to us their children by raising Jesus" (Acts 13:32–33). The "firmitas" or reliability of the gospel is shown by God's faithfulness in fulfilling his promises to Israel.[42]

---

39. Aquinas, *Commentary on the Letter of Saint Paul to the Romans*, no. 26, 10.

40. For Plato's argument that God cannot lie and that God would not make things up as the poets do, see Plato, *Republic*, 381b–382c, 628–30. Plato is especially concerned with tales about the gods that present them as doing evil things and as causing evil. As Plato's Socrates says regarding human suffering, "But as to saying that God, who is good, becomes the cause of evil to anyone, we must contend in every way that neither should anyone assert this in his own city if it is to be well governed, nor anyone hear it, neither telling a story in meter or without meter, for neither would the saying of such things, if they are said, be holy, nor would they be profitable to us or concordant with themselves" (380b, 627). See also Wolterstorff, *Divine Discourse*, 206–7, 225–27.

41. Regarding Luke's rendering of Paul's sermon in Acts 13, Luke Timothy Johnson observes:
> We do not expect by this time a *précis* of Pauline theology, but recognize that in his speeches Luke stretches over the discourses of several speakers a single midrashic argument concerning the messianic movement and its crucified and raised founder. Paul's speech looks in equal parts like the discourses of Peter and the speech of Stephen. In fact, we are even somewhat startled at the conclusion of the speech with its Pauline coloration, until we recognize Luke's concern for *prosōpopoiia*. The one who speaks at the end about righteousness through faith in contrast to righteousness through the Law may not be Paul, but is, after all, not a bad simulacrum. (*Acts of the Apostles*, 237)

Johnson adds that "the speech is not really a report of what Paul said to the Jews at Antioch, but a reflection on the first mission by the apologetic historian Luke" (238–39). See also Porter, "Portrait of Paul in Acts."

42. See Hays, "Reading Scripture in Light of the Resurrection," 233: "The New Testament writers insist that we are to read Israel's story as a witness to the righteousness of God, climactically disclosed in Jesus Christ." Hays goes on to say that
> by vindicating the crucified Jesus, the resurrection marks the cross as "the decisive, apocalyptic event that makes sense of Israel's story." Furthermore, the New Testament's resurrection stories, no less than the Old Testament's narratives, continue to celebrate God's acts of saving power as proleptic signs of the ultimate triumph of God's righteousness (as, e.g., 1 Cor. 15:20–28 clearly indicates). In the time between Jesus's resurrection and

The first two reasons for the gospel's authority show the gospel's foundation in God's relationship to his people Israel. In the same vein, Aquinas gives a third reason, again based on Paul's statement that the gospel was "promised beforehand through his prophets in the holy scriptures." Namely, the gospel's authority derives not only from the God who promised but also from the prophets who, inspired by God, mediated this promise. Aquinas describes this as the "dignity" of the gospel's "ministers or witnesses."[43] These divinely dignified "ministers or witnesses" are the prophets to whom God gave some knowledge of the gospel. The antiquity of the gospel was shown by the fact that God "promised beforehand"; the reliability of the gospel by the fact that *God* promised. The fact that God promised "through his prophets" indicates how we come to hear the gospel. God gives the prophets the "dignity" of being "ministers or witnesses" of revelation.[44] Of course, there were also prophets whose prophecies were inspired by demons (supposed gods) such as Baal and who were thereby "prophets of demons."[45] The example that Aquinas gives comes from 1 Kings 18, where Elijah confronts and conquers the "four hundred and fifty prophets of Baal and the four hundred prophets of Asherah, who eat at Jezebel's table" (1 Kings 18:19). By contrast to these false prophets, true prophets received "dignity" from God because God granted them the honor of working through them. To underscore the extraordinary dignity granted to the true prophets, Aquinas cites Amos 3:7, which in the Vulgate reads "The Lord will not make a word [non faciet Dominus Deus verbum] without revealing his secret to his servants the prophets."[46]

---

parousia, therefore, the church lives under the sign of the cross while awaiting the consummation of God's promises. Thus the New Testament and the Old Testament are closely analogous in their eschatological orientation and in their posture of awaiting God's deliverance in the midst of suffering. (234–35)

Hays's position is quite similar to Aquinas's.

43. Aquinas, *Commentary on the Letter of Saint Paul to the Romans*, no. 26, 10.

44. As Corinne Patton remarks, Aquinas "posits a distinct type of inspiration and prophecy by which the biblical authors wrote, not shared by later interpreters. He does not address the inspiration of biblical authors apart from the question of prophetic knowledge, indicating that biblical authorship is a form of prophetic revelation. Prophetic knowledge of a revealed truth results from the inspiration of the prophet, an action of sanctifying grace that elevates the mind to receive the revealed truth" ("Canon and Tradition," 88). For further background see Gilby, "Biblical Inspiration"; Synave and Benoit, *Prophecy and Inspiration*.

45. Aquinas, *Commentary on the Letter of Saint Paul to the Romans*, no. 26, 10. For criticism of naming the pagan gods "demons," see Johnson, *Among the Gentiles*, 1–9. Aquinas is here following the perspective of the New Testament, which considers (as do I) that the characteristic activity of demons in the world consists in turning people away from the true God.

46. For historical-critical and canonical ways of construing the prophets' role, see Seitz, *Prophecy and Hermeneutics*. The Old Testament's distinctive contribution to Christian theology (and not solely its contribution as fulfilled by Jesus) is emphasized in a manner that accords with Aquinas's perspective by Seitz, *Character of Christian Scripture*, 90, 146–47.

With respect to the true prophets' "dignity," Aquinas also cites Peter's speech at Caesarea, as recorded in Acts 10.[47] In this speech, Peter first describes the words and deeds of Jesus and his crucifixion, resurrection, and appearances to the disciples. In the verse quoted by Aquinas, Peter identifies Jesus as the Messiah promised by the prophets: "To him all the prophets bear witness that every one who believes in him receives forgiveness of sins through his name" (Acts 10:43). By reference to Joel 2:28, "It shall come to pass afterward, that I will pour out my spirit on all flesh; your sons and daughters shall prophesy," Aquinas adds that all true prophets are such because the Holy Spirit inspires them. Aquinas refers to this verse in order to show that the source of prophetic dignity is the Holy Spirit. Given Peter's quotation of Joel 2:28 at Pentecost (Acts 2:17), we might also see here an appreciation of the unity of the testimony of Israel's prophets with the Spirit-filled testimony of the apostles.

According to Aquinas, there is a fourth way that Paul's statement in Romans 1:2 commends the gospel's authority. This fourth way consists in the fact that the prophets wrote down divine revelation "in the holy scriptures." God's promises, Aquinas observes, "were not merely spoken but recorded in writing."[48] God commands that this written record be made, as Aquinas notes by reference to Habakkuk 2:2, "And the LORD answered me, 'Write the vision; make it plain upon tablets, so he may run who reads it.'" Indebted to Augustine, Aquinas connects this fourth aspect of the gospel's authority with the historical time period in which the prophets began to write down their revelations.[49] God caused his words to the prophets to be written down at the time during which Rome began to emerge. The link between Rome and God's prophecies became apparent at the coming of Jesus Christ, who was born under Roman rule and died at the hands of the Romans. But more importantly, the connection between the Roman Empire and God's prophecies to Israel has to do with God's intention to draw together Jews and gentiles in the kingdom of God. Speaking to fellow Jews who did not believe him to be the Messiah, Jesus says in the verse that Aquinas quotes here, "You search the scriptures, because you think that in them you have eternal life; and it is they that bear witness to me" (John 5:39). The fact that the prophets wrote down God's promises "in the holy scriptures" enabled the gentiles, too, to search the Scriptures and to respond to Paul's evangelizing mission.

47. For historical-critical discussion of Peter's speech in Acts 10, emphasizing the "midrash-like concatenation of Psalm 107:20; Isaiah 52:7 (Nahum 2:1 LXX); Isaiah 61:1; Deuteronomy 21:22 and Hosea 6:2" (172), see Stuhlmacher, "Pauline Gospel," 171–72. See also Stanton, *Jesus of Nazareth in New Testament Preaching*, 67–85.

48. Aquinas, *Commentary on the Letter of Saint Paul to the Romans*, no. 26, 11.

49. See Augustine, *City of God* 18.27, 794.

The gospel, then, has authority because of its antiquity and reliability, and also because of the dignity of its prophets and the fact that under divine inspiration they wrote down the revelations they received for the sake of future generations. Aquinas next argues that the gospel has authority because of its content. Its content is Jesus Christ, the incarnate Son of God. Aquinas devotes significant attention to how Paul frames this content in Romans 1:3: "the gospel concerning his Son, who was descended from David according to the flesh."

Jesus Christ, the Content of the Gospel: Romans 1:3

For Aquinas, Romans 1:3 shows that the gospel is primarily the good news about the Son of God, eternally begotten of the Father.[50] This way of reading Romans 1 further exhibits Aquinas's commitment to reading the Pauline "gospel" in the context of the entirety of canonical Scripture and of the Church's councils and creeds. The eternal begetting, says Aquinas, "had been previously hidden."[51] In this regard Aquinas quotes the proverb in which the sage bemoans his lack of wisdom about God: "Who has ascended to heaven and come down? Who has gathered the wind in his fists? Who has wrapped up the waters in a garment? Who has established all the ends of the earth? What is his name, and what is his son's name? Surely you know!" (Prov. 30:4).[52] Taking the phrase "his son's name" as an anticipation of trinitarian doctrine, Aquinas suggests that Solomon seeks wisdom about God, including about the Son, but lacks this wisdom. Only the gospel fully reveals the Son of the Father. Thus, Aquinas notes that in the Gospel of Matthew, the Father testifies

50. Gordon D. Fee argues with regard to the Christology of Romans 1:2–3, "Although nothing is said explicitly here about the Son's being preexistent, and thus the eternal Son, this does find expression later in the letter in 8:3. On the basis of this later explicit statement, one may also recognize preexistence as presuppositional here" (*Pauline Christology*, 242). For discussion of "the gospel of God" and Jesus's preexistent sonship according to Paul, see also Byrne, *Romans*, 42–44.

51. Aquinas, *Commentary on the Letter of Saint Paul to the Romans*, no. 29, 11.

52. In his commentary on this text, Bruce K. Waltke offers the answer that God's name is YHWH, and that God's "son" signifies Israel. With regard to the latter, he explains, "In the Old Testament, the Lord brought Israel into existence and named his firstborn (cf. Exod. 4:22; Deut. 14:1; 32:5–6, 18–19; Isa. 43:6; 45:11; 63:16; 64:8 [7]; Jer. 3:4, 19; 31:20; Hosea 11:1)" (*Book of Proverbs*, 474). Writing from a Christian perspective, Waltke adds that

> in the New Testament Jesus Christ fulfills typical Israel, for a Gentile tyrant threatened his life at birth; he, too, returned from exile in Egypt, suffered in the wilderness, and taught on a mountain. Unlike Israel, he perfectly obeyed his Father (Matt. 2:15; Heb. 5:7–10). . . . He identifies himself as the Son of Man who comes on the clouds, the biblical symbol of divine transcendence. In Luke he is the incarnate Son of God by the virgin birth (Luke 1:29–33), and in John he is the eternal Son of God (John 17). As such he speaks with an immediate authority (cf. Matt. 7:28; 8:1–8; 12:8, 42; Heb. 3:3–6; Rev. 5:1–14), and through the Holy Spirit he guided his apostles into all truth (John 16:12–15). (ibid.)

to the Son at Jesus's baptism: "This is my beloved Son, with whom I am well pleased" (Matt. 3:17).[53]

Does this mean that the gospel is contained only in the New Testament, because only the New Testament contains the gospel's content, God's Son Jesus Christ? Aquinas argues that on the contrary, the whole of Scripture reveals divine wisdom, and the Son is "the Word and wisdom begotten."[54] In this regard he quotes Moses's exhortation to the people of Israel, "Keep them [the laws of the Torah] and do them; for that will be your wisdom and your understanding in the sight of the peoples, who, when they hear all these statutes, will say, 'Surely this great nation is a wise and understanding people'" (Deut. 4:6). The Torah reveals God's wisdom, and the gospel reveals the fullness of God's wisdom. This wisdom is found in the Son, who is "to those who are called, both Jews and Greeks, Christ the power of God and the wisdom of God," as Paul says in 1 Corinthians 1:24. It is this Christ, the wisdom of God, who is the content of the gospel.[55]

Aquinas thinks that the phrase "the gospel concerning his Son" (Rom. 1:3) signals the full divinity of the Son by means of the word "his." This may seem a real stretch. Indeed, Aquinas recognizes that there are various ways to understand what "Son" means in this context: one could think of Christ as God's adopted Son, or one could think of "Son" as the name that the Father assumes while on earth, or one could think of the Son as an exalted creature. But the Gospel of John, he observes, rules out such construals of God's Son. It seems to Aquinas that Paul's formulation, "his Son," also rules out the denial of the full divinity of the Son, even if less evidently than does the Gospel of John. This interpretation of the phrase "his Son" comes from Hilary of Poitiers, whom Aquinas cites here in defense of the view that the Son could not be "his Son" unless he were "his very own and natural" Son.[56] The Son of God ("his Son") can be such only if he fully shares his Father's nature.

Before turning from the topic of the gospel's content (the Son Jesus Christ), Aquinas raises a further question about why Paul mentions descent

53. On the name "Son" as a title for Jesus, see also Ratzinger, *Jesus of Nazareth: From the Baptism*, 335–45. Ratzinger argues that the title denotes the reality of Jesus's unique intimacy with the Father: "Jesus's prayer is the true origin of the term 'the Son'" (344).

54. Aquinas, *Commentary on the Letter of Saint Paul to the Romans*, no. 29, 11. For a similar orientation, focusing on the Wisdom literature, see Witherington, *Jesus the Sage*.

55. Rather similarly, Peter Stuhlmacher states, "The gospel confers the illuminating knowledge of the glory of Christ who—like wisdom in Old Testament and Jewish tradition—is the manifest and effective image of God to the world" ("Pauline Gospel," 154).

56. Aquinas, *Commentary on the Letter of Saint Paul to the Romans*, no. 33, 12. For the Fathers' way of discerning "patterns of scriptural co-naming of God and Christ" (156), see Anatolios, *Retrieving Nicaea*.

from David rather than descent from Abraham, to whom the promises were originally given. In Aquinas's view, the emphasis on David reflects the gospel's purpose with regard to the forgiveness of sin, because David (unlike Abraham) was a notable sinner. It also reflects Christ's kingship, something important to emphasize especially to the Romans, who imagined that they ruled the world. Lastly, Aquinas notes that Paul's proclamation of the gospel in Romans 1:2–3 excludes the central errors of the Manichaeans: their view that the God of the Old Testament differs from the Father, their view that the scriptures of Israel are wicked, and their view that Christ's body was an illusion.

In sum, from Paul's proclamation of "the gospel of God which he promised beforehand through his prophets in the holy scriptures, the gospel concerning his Son, who was descended from David according to the flesh" (Rom. 1:1–3), Aquinas draws the following three main conclusions about the "gospel." First, the gospel is about Jesus, who is the eternal Son, the Messiah of Israel, and the king of Jews and gentiles. Jesus is fully the Son of God and he is, at the same time, also fully human, of the royal family of David. Second, the gospel of Jesus Christ is the fulfillment of God's promises to Israel and indeed the fulfillment of the entirety of Israel's scriptures. The gospel's authority is confirmed by its antiquity and "firmitas," as well as by the dignity that God gave to Israel's prophets and by their inspired writings. Third, the gospel is good news because it is about our deification. The gospel proclaims the union of God and man in Jesus Christ, and it proclaims that in Jesus Christ we receive the forgiveness of sins and adoption as sons of God through the Holy Spirit, with the goal of attaining to eternal life in God.

Other References to "Gospel" in Romans

In Romans 1:9, Paul tells the Romans that he continually has them in prayer, as part of his ongoing service to God "in the gospel of his Son." Aquinas comments that the phrase "the gospel of his Son" is appropriate because the gospel is about Jesus Christ, was preached by Jesus Christ (see Luke 4:18), and was commanded by Jesus Christ to be preached by his apostles (see Mark 16:15).[57] When Paul twice mentions the gospel in Romans 1:15–16—"I am eager to preach the gospel to you also who are in Rome. For I am not ashamed of the gospel"—Aquinas emphasizes our reception of the gospel. We should be eager to hear this good news. Nonetheless, in Aquinas's interpretation of Paul, how we receive God's Word depends ultimately upon God's grace,

---

57. See Aquinas, *Commentary on the Letter of Saint Paul to the Romans*, no. 79, 29.

God's calling.[58] When in Romans 2:16 Paul says "according to my gospel," Aquinas comments that Paul is describing his preaching of the gospel, and "the preacher's industry achieves something."[59]

Aquinas again emphasizes God's grace in commenting on Romans 10:16, "But they have not all obeyed the gospel." Citing Jesus's words in John 6:45, Aquinas states that "the outwardly spoken word of the preacher is not sufficient to cause faith, unless a man's heart is attracted inwardly by the power of God speaking."[60] Yet this fact does not absolve from sin those who reject the gospel, because they do so by their free will.[61] Aquinas adds that it is God's grace that moves Paul to preach the gospel. Likewise, when Paul speaks of "the grace given me by God to be a minister of Christ Jesus to the Gentiles in the priestly service of the gospel of God, so that the offering of the Gentiles may be acceptable, sanctified by the Holy Spirit" (Rom. 15:15–16), Aquinas observes that the operation of God's grace configures Paul to the "service of the Gospel of God."[62] The gospel that Paul preaches was first preached by Jesus Christ, and we are moved to accept it by his Holy Spirit.[63]

Aquinas on Paul's "Gospel" in Galatians

Let me now turn to Aquinas's commentary on Galatians. In Galatians 1, Paul accuses the Galatians of abandoning the gospel, and Paul insists that the gospel that he preaches is without qualification the gospel of God:

> I am astonished that you are so quickly deserting him who called you in the grace of Christ and turning to a different gospel—not that there is another gospel, but there are some who trouble you and want to pervert the gospel of Christ. But even if we, or an angel from heaven, should preach to you a gospel contrary to that which we preached to you, let him be accursed. As we have said before, so now I say again, If any one is preaching to you a gospel contrary to that which you received, let him be accursed. . . . For I would have you know, brethren, that the gospel which was preached by me is not man's gospel. For I did not receive it from man, nor was I taught it, but it came through a revelation of Jesus Christ. (Gal. 1:6–9, 11–12)

58. See ibid., nos. 95–96, 34. For further discussion see my "Aquinas on Romans 8."

59. Aquinas, *Commentary on the Letter of Saint Paul to the Romans*, no. 223, 77.

60. Ibid., no. 842, 288. See also Cessario, *Christian Faith and the Theological Life*, 149–51; Sherwin, "Christ the Teacher," 188–90. Aquinas's position here is thoroughly Augustinian.

61. For background, although lacking an extensive discussion of implicit faith, see Osborne, "Unbelief and Sin."

62. See Aquinas, *Commentary on the Letter of Saint Paul to the Romans*, no. 1167, 403.

63. See ibid., no. 1223, 422. See also Emery, "Holy Spirit," 144–50.

How does Aquinas treat the issues that Paul raises here about the gospel? First, Aquinas argues that the "different gospel" to which the Galatians are turning is the Torah.[64] The Torah (or Old Law) is indeed good news, but the things that it explicitly proclaims have to do primarily with this world rather than with eternal life in intimate union with God. The goods of eternal life make the goods of this world look minuscule in comparison. For this reason, Aquinas states that the Old Law "is not completely perfect as is the gospel, because it does not announce the perfect and loftiest goods, but small and slight ones. But the New Law is perfectly and in the full sense a gospel, i.e., a good message, because it announces the greatest goods, namely, heavenly, spiritual, and eternal."[65] The gospel that Paul preaches is this perfect gospel, because it proclaims eternal goods in Christ Jesus.

It might seem, however, that if the Galatians' turning to certain practices of the Torah constituted an adherence to a "different gospel," then the New Testament diverges from the Old Testament, with the result that those who believe in the gospel can discard the scriptures of Israel. Aquinas responds that "it is another gospel according to the tradition of the deceivers."[66] Those who are deceiving the Galatians have destroyed the promise/fulfillment dynamic that unites the two testaments in the one gospel of Jesus Christ. By retaining the practices of the Torah as though Christ had not fulfilled them, those who are deceiving the Galatians have instituted the Torah as a separate gospel, a separate good news.[67] By contrast, says Aquinas, for Paul there is one gospel that differs in the goods that are promised but that does not differ at the deeper level of the realities that are proclaimed. The goods that are promised to Israel (land, peace, king, temple, and so forth) are figures of greater goods that are fully revealed in Christ Jesus and in the promises that he makes regarding the

64. See Witherington, *Grace in Galatia*, 83: "The Gospel of Moses, even though mediated by angels should not be received. In Paul's view it is no Gospel at all." By contrast, Aquinas holds that the Torah is good news (gospel), but imperfectly so.

65. Aquinas, *Commentary on Saint Paul's Epistle to the Galatians*, chap. 1, lect. 2, 12. Yves Congar argues in this regard:

St. Thomas Aquinas, who had a keen perception of the New Testament's originality as compared to the Old, worked into his theological synthesis a precise notion of the Gospel which can be extracted in a coherent form from many parts of his scriptural commentaries. He views it under two principal aspects: as a preaching or *doctrina* (with the great depth of meaning he gives to that word), and as a "new law" consisting principally (*principaliter*—the word is very strong, meaning "as its supreme governing principle") in the grace of the Holy Spirit, with all that this represents in the way of demands, and also of power, to bring about man's true relationship to God, his salvation and eternal life. (*Tradition and Traditions*, 273)

66. Aquinas, *Commentary on Saint Paul's Epistle to the Galatians*, chap. 1, lect. 2, 12.

67. See my *Christ's Fulfillment of Torah and Temple*, as well as my response to certain forms of contemporary Messianic Judaism in chap. 1 of my *Jewish-Christian Dialogue*.

kingdom of God. Aquinas explains, "Therefore it is another gospel if you consider the outward appearances; but as to the things that are contained and exist within, it is not another gospel."[68]

Commenting on Galatians 1:8, "Even if we, or an angel from heaven, should preach to you a gospel contrary to that which we preached to you, let him be accursed,"[69] Aquinas adds to his portrait of the kind of teaching that the gospel is. The gospel, he notes, was delivered to us directly by God himself; in this regard he quotes John 1:18; Hebrews 1:2; and Hebrews 2:3. The gospel has divine authority because it was preached by the Son Jesus Christ. No angel or human can preach a different gospel because "God's teaching would be against him."[70] For this reason, Paul in Galatians 1:8 is not simply asserting the superiority of his gospel as if it were a human teaching that depended on his own authority.

How can we know what exactly constitutes "a gospel contrary to that which we [Paul] preached to you" (Gal. 1:8)? Aquinas states that Paul's meaning is that we should not teach anything "completely alien [omnino alienum]" to the gospel—that is, anything that does not serve the gospel's "teaching and faith in Christ" or that cannot be found (either explicitly or implicitly) in the gospel.[71] What alien teachings does Aquinas have in view? He does not say directly, but instead he quotes 1 Thessalonians 3:10, where Paul says that he is "praying earnestly night and day" that he may see the Thessalonians "face to face and supply what is lacking in [their] faith." Whatever is "lacking" in the gospel but truly fosters the gospel can be supplied by preachers.

Discussing Paul's statement "The gospel which was preached by me is not man's gospel" (Gal. 1:11), Aquinas inquires into what it means for the gospel not to be "man's gospel."[72] Certainly the key point is that the source of the gospel is God. For a gospel not to be "man's gospel" also means that it is "not according to human nature out of tune with the divine rule or divine

---

68. Aquinas, *Commentary on Saint Paul's Epistle to the Galatians*, chap. 1, lect. 2, 12.

69. Drawing upon Martin Hengel and others, Peter Stuhlmacher argues that Galatians reflects the fact that

> after the Jerusalem Council, in Antioch and beyond, fundamental differences concerning the issue of law-observance surfaced between Paul, the emissaries of James, Peter, Barnabas, and the people at Antioch (cf. Gal. 2:11ff.). After the so-called Antiochian incident, in Galatia, Corinth, and Rome, as well as in Jerusalem and Antioch, the opponents of Paul appealed to Peter (and James) as the genuinely authoritative and true apostles and started a sort of countermission in the Pauline congregation. . . . These confrontations are reflected in all the letters of Paul that have come down to us. Paul was always compelled, pointedly and with his eyes on the focal points, to stand by his gospel. ("Theme," 17–18)

70. Aquinas, *Commentary on Saint Paul's Epistle to the Galatians*, chap. 1, lect. 2, 15.

71. Ibid., chap. 1, lect. 2, 16. For a classic treatment of this question (among others) see Augustine, *On Christian Doctrine*.

72. For historical-critical discussion, see Stuhlmacher, "Pauline Gospel," 152–53.

revelation."[73] The gospel is at odds with sinful human nature, which is filled with discord and contention rather than with the peace and reconciliation that characterize the gospel. In this regard Aquinas quotes 1 Corinthians 3:3, "For while there is jealousy and strife among you, are you not of the flesh, and behaving like ordinary men?" Not only, then, does Paul's rejection of the view that his gospel is "man's gospel" mean that the source of his gospel is God, but it also means that Paul's gospel teaches us to live in a new way rather than by following the sinful desires of fallen human nature.

Paul goes on to say that his authority to preach the gospel and his understanding of the gospel came solely "through a revelation of Jesus Christ" (Gal. 1:12).[74] While recognizing that Paul is claiming something unique to his own experience, Aquinas notes the ways in which Paul's claim teaches us about the gospel itself. Namely, Paul's statement "I did not receive it [the gospel] from man, nor was I taught it" (Gal. 1:12) should be applied to all preachers of the gospel. Paul's authority to preach the gospel comes from God rather than "purely" from man.[75] This is true for all vocations to preach the gospel. At the same time, Aquinas attends to the unique aspect of Paul's vocation, the fact that Paul received his understanding of the gospel "through a revelation of Jesus Christ." Aquinas asserts that Jesus "showed him everything clearly."[76] In support of the uniqueness of Paul's reception of the gospel, Aquinas refers to 2 Corinthians 12, where Paul describes being "caught up into Paradise"

73. Aquinas, *Commentary on Saint Paul's Epistle to the Galatians*, chap. 1, lect. 3, 19. The Latin reads, "secundum humanam naturam discordantem a regula seu revelatione divina."

74. Stuhlmacher points out that this claim seems to stand "in glaring contradiction to 1 Corinthians 15:1ff., where Paul himself describes the gospel as the tradition he received and passed on, a tradition common to him and to the apostles called before him (1 Cor. 15:11)" ("Pauline Gospel," 153). Stuhlmacher addresses this question extensively in "Pauline Gospel," 156–66. His basic conclusion is as follows: "As regards the relation of Paul's gospel to tradition, it seems to me to be of equally great importance that (1) Paul describes the gospel revealed to him as being itself a gift of salvation entrusted to him in order that he may preach it, that (2) in stating the gospel he expressly and willingly takes over old Jewish-Christian traditions of doctrine, and that (3) he continues to measure himself critically against those called to be apostles before him and compares himself with them" (157).

75. Aquinas, *Commentary on Saint Paul's Epistle to the Galatians*, chap. 1, lect. 3, 19. For further discussion see Becker, *Paul*, 77–81. In light of Galatians 1, Becker emphasizes, "The claim of apostleship presupposes, first, immediate dependence on God and Christ alone. The apostolic office does not come out of the church and also has no succession in the church, because that would do away with the immediate link between the person and God or Christ as sender. This unquestionable special position is matched by independence vis-à-vis the church" (80). Even though there are no apostles after the apostolic generation, however, there are successors of the apostles in the Church who are sent by God in a mediated, but nonetheless also "immediate," manner.

76. Aquinas, *Commentary on Saint Paul's Epistle to the Galatians*, chap. 1, lect. 3, 19. For an excellent contemporary way of putting this point, see Kirk, *Jesus Have I Loved, but Paul?*

(2 Cor. 12:3) and hearing "things that cannot be told, which man may not utter" (2 Cor. 12:4).[77] Aquinas also quotes Isaiah 50:4–5, where the prophet states, "The Lord GOD has given me the tongue of those who are taught. . . . The Lord GOD has opened my ear." The prophet Isaiah, then, stands as a precedent for Paul's reception of divine revelation, and Paul has mystical experiences that surpass even Isaiah's. Aquinas thinks that Paul's "conversion was perfect with respect to his understanding, because he was so instructed by Christ that there was no need to be instructed by the apostles."[78]

In Galatians 2:2, Paul recalls that after preaching the gospel for some years, he went up to Jerusalem with Barnabas and Titus. Paul states, "I laid before them (but privately before those who were of repute) the gospel which I preach among the Gentiles, lest somehow I should be running or had run in vain."[79] Does Paul here leave open the possibility that his gospel could have been in error or that he could have been in need of human confirmation? Citing Galatians 1:8, Aquinas denies that Paul is leaving open such possibilities in Galatians 2:2. Instead, he argues that because Paul "had not lived with Christ or been taught by the apostles," Paul had to be especially careful to demonstrate the unity of his gospel "with that of the other apostles."[80] In Aquinas's view, Paul never entertained doubt about "the truth of the gospel" (Gal. 2:5), which

---

77. For an increasingly influential contemporary reading of 2 Cor. 12:3–4, according to which Paul is fundamentally an "apocalyptic mystagogue" whose "experiences of heavenly travel" (35) are central, see Segal, *Paul the Convert*, 34–71. Segal reads all of Paul's letters through the lens of Paul's ecstatic ascension or journey; in his view, Paul's claims stand or fall depending on what we make of Second Temple Jewish mysticism, which as he notes is "strangely unfamiliar to modern Jewish and Christian religious sentiments" (61). For example, he argues, "First Enoch 37–71 contains the interesting narration of the transformation of Enoch into the son of man, but this might be a Christian addition to the text, since it agrees so completely with the transformation that Paul outlines" (ibid.). For scholarly background, see C. Newman, *Paul's Glory-Christology*; Kim, *Origin of Paul's Gospel*. I doubt, however, that Paul's theology should be read solely through the one element that Segal foregrounds. Nor is Paul's conversion experience simply another apocalyptic vision of a human figure on God's throne. See N. T. Wright, *Resurrection of the Son of God*, 378–98.

78. Aquinas, *Commentary on Saint Paul's Epistle to the Galatians*, chap. 1, lect. 4, 26.

79. For historical reconstruction of this event, see Becker, *Paul*, 87–94. Becker observes that "Paul describes this discussion and its outcome in his way in a long sentence. The Petrine apostolate is accepted as the norm. Peter unquestionably was the premier Easter witness, apostle, and original missionary (1 Cor. 15:5; Luke 24:34). Even if at the time of the Apostolic Council he had perhaps already turned over to James the leadership of the Jerusalem church (cf. the initial position of James in Gal. 2:9), he remained the symbolic head of post-Easter Jewish Christianity" (91). Similarly, Edith M. Humphrey observes that Paul "cares about the consonance of his message with theirs [the apostles'] and checks out the content of his gospel against their witness. For him, no less than those disturbing the churches, the principle of apostolic authority held—even though he had directly met Jesus on the road to Damascus" (*Scripture and Tradition*, 83).

80. Aquinas, *Commentary on Saint Paul's Epistle to the Galatians*, chap. 2, lect. 1, 35.

"teaches that neither circumcision nor uncircumcision profits anything, but faith."[81] Rather, Paul sought to show his unity with the leading apostles in order to reassure those to whom he had proclaimed the gospel, since some of those who had believed Paul's teaching now required reassurance that they need not practice the rites of the Torah. Paul even had to defend "the truth of the gospel" (Gal. 2:14) against Peter, who had been eating "with the Gentiles" until the "circumcision party" intimidated him (Gal. 2:12). Aquinas's theology of the gospel thus includes the aspect of justification by faith.[82]

Aquinas treats the gospel again in his comments on Galatians 3:8 and 4:13, but these comments are too brief to add anything to our study and we can pass over them. How, then, might we sum up the contributions made by Aquinas's treatment of the gospel in Galatians 1–2? Three contributions stand out. First, Aquinas reflects carefully on the relation of the gospel of Jesus Christ to the Torah. The gospel of Jesus Christ is not a "different gospel" from what is found in the Torah, even though the two promise different goods. This gospel requires the response of faith. Second, the gospel belongs not to Paul or to any human authority but rather is delivered directly by God through his Son Jesus Christ. It is neither "Paul's gospel" nor "man's gospel." In this regard Aquinas's reflections on why the gospel is opposed to the jealousy and strife of sinful human nature are particularly insightful. Third, even a unique personal revelation of the gospel, as Paul received from Jesus Christ on the road to Damascus, does not do away with the need to receive confirmation from the whole Church. The Church has a necessary role in the true proclamation of the gospel.

Conclusion: Revelation and the Gospel

Recall the eight points that McKnight makes about 1 Corinthians 15:1–5:

1. "gospel" is a dynamic reality;
2. the gospel must be received;
3. the basic content of the gospel is that Christ died, was buried, rose from the dead, and appeared to chosen witnesses;
4. the gospel brings to fulfillment the story of Israel;
5. the gospel saves us from our sins;
6. the gospel involves all that happened to Jesus and also includes his second coming and the final consummation of the kingdom of God;
7. the gospel's center is Jesus Christ, the Son of God;

81. Ibid., 39.
82. See also B. Marshall, "*Beatus vir.*"

8. and the gospel's goal is the glorification of God through his Son in the new creation.

Especially once we recognize that Christ's fulfillment of the story of Israel inaugurates his eschatological Church, and that the naming of Christ as "Son of God" cannot be separated from this Church's canonical and creedal determinations, McKnight's eight points fit well with what Aquinas says about Paul's use of "gospel" in Romans 1 and Galatians 1–2. Commenting on these passages from Paul, Aquinas focuses on Jesus Christ as the center of the gospel, the gospel as the fulfillment of Israel's story, God's commissioning of preachers of his gospel, and the gospel's goal of our deification, rooted in the union of God and man in Jesus Christ. Aquinas shows that although the scriptures of Israel and the New Testament promise different good things, they are not two gospels; rather, there is one gospel whose unity is apparent in the fulfillment of God's promises accomplished in and through the Messiah and his eschatological community.

What does this understanding of the gospel mean for what McKnight calls a "gospel culture" in the Church? Certainly the key element is the placement of Jesus Christ, the Son of God, at the heart of the Church's mission. For this reason, Aquinas's exegetical references to the patristic Church's teachings on the full divinity and full humanity of the Son are not eisegetical excursuses. Second, a "gospel culture" attends to the whole story of Israel/Church, from creation through the patriarchs and prophets, who show the "antiquity" of God's work, the wisdom by which he accomplishes his plan, and the "dignity" of participating in this saving economy. Third, the gospel is received from God and proclaimed by the incarnate Son of God. The divine authority, reliability, and inspired written form of the gospel (in Israel's scriptures) assure Paul that the content of his gospel cannot be false. Fourth, a "gospel culture" attends both to the forgiveness of sins and to our adoption as sons in the Son, all the way to our full sharing in the divine life in the everlasting kingdom of God. Fifth, Aquinas's point about Paul's seeking confirmation from Peter, John, and James suggests that the proper locus of a "gospel culture" is indeed the Church, with its liturgical and evangelizing mission to be the body of Christ. None of this takes away from justification by faith, but rather, as McKnight emphasizes, it puts justification by faith in its proper gospel context.

In short, at the center of a "gospel culture" stands Jesus Christ, who is Messiah, Son of God, and King. The gospel unites us in Christ's eschatological kingdom, which has been inaugurated but not yet fully consummated. Confessing the gospel in the context of our eucharistic "remembering" of Jesus, we share by the Holy Spirit in Jesus's self-offering to the Father. Even now, therefore, we bear witness (however imperfectly) to the truth that "Christ loved the church and gave himself up for her, that he might sanctify her, having cleansed her by the washing of water with the word, that he might present the church to himself in splendor, without spot or wrinkle or any such thing, that she might be holy and without blemish" (Eph. 5:25–27).

McKnight and Aquinas disagree, however, regarding whether the Church can be trusted to hand on the gospel faithfully. At issue is the truthfulness of the Church's tradition and doctrinal development, under the guidance of the Holy Spirit. In the next two chapters I argue that the gospel itself requires that the Church be able to hand on and interpret faithfully (if not nontumultu-ously) the content of the gospel. This handing on and interpretation goes by the names "tradition" and "development of doctrine."

FIVE

Tradition

In the course of its discussion of Tradition, having affirmed that Jesus Christ summed up divine revelation in himself, *Dei Verbum* observes that "God graciously arranged that the things he had once revealed for the salvation of all peoples should remain in their entirety, throughout the ages, and be transmitted to all generations."[1] According to *Dei Verbum*, Jesus Christ gave his apostles the mission of communicating the gospel to all humans. The apostles did so in two ways, through oral teaching and through sacred writings, both of which were guided by the Holy Spirit. They also appointed successors (bishops) who possess even today the mission of handing on the gospel in its fullness.[2] On this basis, *Dei Verbum* explains the nature of Tradition as follows: "Tradition transmits in its entirety the word of God which has been entrusted to the apostles by Christ the Lord and the Holy Spirit. It transmits it to the successors of the apostles so that, enlightened by the Spirit of truth, they may faithfully preserve, expound and spread it abroad by their preaching."[3]

---

1. See *Dei Verbum*, §7, 753.

2. Apostolic succession can be squared with much development of doctrine in specifying the role and duties of bishops (and of the bishop of Rome), without thereby supposing that a merely functional, rather than sacramental, succession existed in the earliest Church. For a proposal regarding the stages of this doctrinal development and the reasons for it, see J. Newman, *Essay on the Development of Christian Doctrine*, 148–65. For more recent historical reconstructions, see, for example, Rist, "Origin and Early Development of Episcopacy at Rome."

3. *Dei Verbum*, §9, 755. For discussion of *Dei Verbum*'s view of Tradition, which itself constitutes a development of earlier Catholic teaching on Tradition, see Dulles, "Revelation,

Tradition, then, is the Church's mode of transmitting "the word of God" that Christ and the Holy Spirit "entrusted to the apostles."[4] Tradition is the handing on of the salvific realities of the gospel, and as such Tradition can be found in the Church's "doctrine, life, and worship."[5] Tradition is the Church's faithful communication of the doctrines and practices of Christian faith across the generations. Tradition is closely connected to Scripture because the Church hands on the sacred writings as part of the faithful communication of divine revelation as summed up in and taught by Jesus Christ.

This view of Tradition, however, has been challenged on various fronts. While considering themselves to be the representatives of the Church's true Tradition, the sixteenth-century Reformers sought to rid the Church of a number of doctrines and practices that, in their view, were foreign to the gospel and were instead human inventions recognizable by their lack of accord with Scripture, such as papal supremacy, eucharistic sacrifice, merit, purgatory, various Marian doctrines, and so forth.[6] Along these lines, the

---

Scripture, and Tradition," 50–53; Viviano, "Normativity of Scripture and Tradition." See also Dulles, "Tradition."

4. In his chapter "Tradition and the Tacit," Andrew Louth emphasizes "an inarticulate living of the mystery, the tacit dimension, which is the heart of tradition, and from which theology must spring if it is to be faithful to the truth it is seeking to express" (*Discerning the Mystery*, 95).

5. *Dei Verbum*, §8, 754. Pelikan offers a helpful distinction between tradition as idol and as icon:

> Tradition becomes an idol, accordingly, when it makes the preservation and the repetition of the past an end in itself; it claims to have the transcendent reality and truth captive and encapsulated in that past, and it requires an idolatrous submission to the authority of tradition, since truth would not dare to appear outside it. . . . Tradition qualifies as an icon . . . when it does not present itself as coextensive with the truth it teaches, but does present itself as the way that we who are its heirs must follow if we are to go beyond it—to a universal truth that is available only in a particular embodiment. (*Vindication of Tradition*, 55–56)

Tradition mediates rather than encapsulates the divinely revealed realities of faith.

6. See Pelikan, *Christian Tradition*, 4:127–244; Oberman, "*Quo Vadis, Petre?*" As Pelikan puts it in *Vindication of Tradition*:

> The claim that the papacy had been divinely instituted and hence possessed supernatural authority was untenable, Luther and his colleagues charged, in the light of history, which showed that the institutions, the practices, and even the doctrines of the church had changed over centuries. "As it was in the beginning, is now, and ever shall be, world without end" applied to God and to the word of God, but not to the ever-mutable tradition of the church. Trained as many of them were in the critical methodology and "sacred philology" of Renaissance humanism, the Protestant Reformers helped to lay the foundations for historical research into the genesis and the evolution of cherished traditions that had come down from the Middle Ages and from the church fathers. By this research they exploded the assumption of a "consensus of the centuries," upon which the authority of tradition rested. What the Reformation of the sixteenth century had done in its historical critique of the papacy or the sacraments or the legends of the saints, the Enlightenment of the eighteenth century did to many other sacred traditions, including

eminent nineteenth-century Reformed theologian Herman Bavinck argues that "Scripture is the only adequate means of guarding against the corruption of the spoken word and of making it the possession of all human beings. . . . The brevity of life, the unreliability of memory, the craftiness of the human heart, and a host of other dangers that threaten the purity of transmission all make the inscripturation of the spoken word absolutely necessary if it is to be preserved and propagated."[7] He holds that only Scripture—and certainly not the Church's handing on of the gospel—is given infallibility by Christ and his Spirit. For Bavinck, therefore, "It is untenable to say that today we continue to receive Christian truth apart from Scripture. In the first century something like that was possible, but the streams of tradition and Scripture have long since converged, and the former has long been incorporated into the latter."[8]

---

some traditions that the mainstream of the Protestant Reformation had declared out of bounds for such destructive criticism. (4:44–45)

For emphasis on the Reformers' appreciation of their debt to tradition, see Hall, "Development of Doctrine." Colin Gunton argues that John Calvin was a "traditionalist" on the grounds that "he believed that the church had left the main road and that the Reformation was calling it back to its true course" (*Brief Theology of Revelation*, 83); and Timothy George argues that the Reformers greatly valued Tradition but not at the expense of Scripture: "Evangelicals can affirm the coinherence of sacred Scripture and sacred Tradition, but not their coequality" ("Evangelical Reflection on Scripture and Tradition," 34). See also the defense of *sola scriptura* by John Woodbridge in his "Role of 'Tradition'"; and the defense of Tradition from a Baptist perspective by D. H. Williams, *Retrieving the Tradition and Renewing Evangelicalism*, especially 69.

7. Bavinck, *Reformed Dogmatics*, 1:471. From a different theological perspective but with the same historical judgment, James Barr comments that "Protestantism was right to observe that Catholic traditions as they grew had failed to provide adequate safeguards against the possibility that the interpretative tradition might come to dominate the scripture and would thus distort its own meaning" (*Holy Scripture*, 29; cf. 31). Barr, however, goes on to add that the traditional "Catholic" and "Protestant" roles come to be reversed: the facts of scripture are once again obscured through the imposition of a tradition, but this time it is not a medieval Catholic tradition, it is a Protestant tradition, built upon the insights of the seventeenth century and anxious to maintain these insights *against* the evidence of the text of scripture or at least against the fact that quite different interpretations of the text are possible. . . . Biblical authority on Protestant terms (on Catholic or Orthodox terms it may be otherwise) exists only where one is free, on the ground of scripture, to question, to adjust, and if necessary to abandon the prevailing doctrinal traditions. (31; cf. 36–37 on the Reformation and historical criticism)

8. Bavinck, *Reformed Dogmatics*, 1:472. Bavinck argues further:
The church cannot perform this ministry of the word. It is nowhere promised infallibility. Always in Scripture the church is referred to the objective word, "to the teaching and to the testimony" [cf. Isa. 8:20]. Actually even Rome does not deny this. The church, i.e., the gathering of believers, is not infallible in the understanding of Rome, neither is the gathering of bishops, but only the pope. The declaration of papal infallibility is proof of the Reformation's thesis of the unreliability of tradition, the fallibility of the church, and even of the necessity of Scripture. For this declaration of infallibility implies that the truth of the revealed word is not or can not be preserved by the church as the gathering of believers, inasmuch as the church is still liable to error. The truth of the revealed word

More recently, the same problem has been posed from a Reformed perspective by Kevin Vanhoozer. Vanhoozer grants, of course, that the Holy Spirit has been at work in the Church and not solely in inspired Scripture. But he too warns against exaggerating the place, let alone the supposed infallibility, of the Church's mediation or "performance" of the Gospel.[9] In his view, the work of the Holy Spirit, as the work of the Lord of the covenant, risks being conflated with the work of the people of God if one supposes that the Church's doctrinal performance of the Gospel is always on key. The Spirit that works in the Church does so in order to point to Christ's glory, not to the Church's. When it comes to Jesus Christ, Vanhoozer suggests, our knowledge derives from Scripture. Guided by the Spirit, the Church strives to "perform" or actualize this knowledge. Vanhoozer therefore concludes, "The real theological issue at stake in the debate over the relative authority of Scripture and tradition (not that one has to take sides, only prioritize) is actually *Christology*. Are there postcanonical, Spirit-inspired or -illumined insights into the way of Jesus Christ that do not have the canonical testimony to Christ as their ultimate source and norm?"[10] To this question, I would answer no, so long as the interpretation of canonical testimony allows for typological reasoning and presumes the Church's interpretive authority.[11]

---

can be explained only in the light of the special assistance of the Holy Spirit of which, says Rome, the pope is the beneficiary. Rome and the Reformation agree, accordingly, that the revealed word can be preserved in its purity only by the institution of the apostolate, i.e., by inspiration. And the controversy between them pertains only to whether that apostolate has ceased or is continued in the person of the pope. (471)

For important clarifications and corrections of this view from a Catholic perspective, see Dulles, *Magisterium*, 64–72. See also the position of the Orthodox theologian Harkianakis, who (like Bavinck) rejects papal infallibility but who (like Dulles) affirms the infallibility of the Church: Harkianakis, *Infallibility of the Church*. For study of influential Catholic theologians who debated papal infallibility in the two centuries prior to the definition (with an eye to Vatican II's *Lumen Gentium*), see Costigan, *Consensus of the Church and Papal Infallibility*.

9. As Carl E. Braaten puts it from a Lutheran perspective, "The church is *simul iustus et peccator* until the rule of glory (*regnum gloriae*) because the eschatological righteousness it appropriates in faith reveals the sinful imperfections of its concrete life as a church. The eschatological power of the gospel relativizes all the structures of the church and of its tradition. Nothing in and of the church can be exempt from the criticism that emanates from the eschatological word of God in the Christ-happening" (*Mother Church*, 55).

10. Vanhoozer, *Drama of Doctrine*, 189; cf. Webster, "On Evangelical Ecclesiology."

11. Vanhoozer, however, likely would not agree to these conditions. His position seems similar to that of Oberman's "*Quo Vadis, Petre?*" Oberman holds that the position of Trent "implies not only that the *successio fidei* coincides with the *successio episcoporum*, but also an elevation of the authority of the Church above the authority of the canonized apostolic kerygma. Due to the restrictive localization of the *testimonium internum* of the Holy Spirit in the teaching office of the Church, Holy Scripture can only have a mute authority" ("*Quo Vadis, Petre?*," 286). My point is that much depends upon what authoritative Scripture says about the Church's authority, as well as upon what one makes of Scripture's own favorite interpretative

Catholic theology of Tradition has also been challenged in recent years by concerns that, having first emerged within classical Protestant liberalism, now dominate much of the Catholic theological academy.[12] Many contemporary Catholic theologians reject the Church's view of Tradition (and of Scripture for that matter). These theologians see *both* Scripture and Tradition principally as human constructions.[13] The result is that they no longer hear the gospel as a divinely authoritative word with doctrinal content that transcends the vicissitudes of history even while being embedded in particular times and places.[14] In the debates between some Catholic theologians and the Church's

---

modes (such as typological reasoning). For further discussion see Congar, *Tradition and Traditions*, especially 376–424. Commending Irenaeus's view of the relationship of Scripture and Tradition, Congar observes:

> We are not talking here, in Tradition, of *particular truths* not contained in the scriptural deposit or at least not in that which Scripture bears witness to. St. Irenaeus even says that there could be no truths which the apostles did not pass on in a public manner. No; we are talking here of the meaning of the whole. If we can find in "Tradition" particular truths which were not expressed in Scripture, this will doubtless be due to Tradition's own proper genius, by means of the "analogy of faith," in other words, thanks to the light that can be thrown on some particular question by the interrelation of various truths with one another, with their centre and with the end term of the whole investigation. This is peculiarly the case with the two Marian doctrines defined in the modern period, the Immaculate Conception and bodily Assumption of the Mother of God. (*Tradition and Traditions*, 391)

See also Hans Boersma's "On Baking Pumpkin Pie." For further discussion, including a defense of the role of typological reasoning in understanding the canonical testimony, see my *Mary's Bodily Assumption*.

12. For comment see Braaten, *Mother Church*, 72.

13. Nicholas Lash observes that

> if human experience is a constitutive element in revelation, then we are tempted to ask the question: Are we to conceive of revelation as a matter of man's understanding of himself and of his future, or as coming to him from "outside"? To put the question in this way, as a matter of mutually exclusive alternatives, is to confuse the issue. . . . Nevertheless, it is not easy to take with sufficient seriousness the function of human experience and self-understanding in the process of revelation, while at the same time safeguarding the God-given nature of that revelation. (*Change in Focus*, 13)

Even if the two ways of conceiving revelation are not *entirely* "mutually exclusive alternatives," the latter conception must for the Christian retain a strong priority at every stage.

14. In a different context, the biblical scholar Dale C. Allison Jr. advances a similar view: "Matthew amended Mark to advance a higher christology, and ideological tinkering must have gone on from the start. The questions all this raises are obvious" (*Historical Christ and the Theological Jesus*, 86). By contrast, consider Karl Barth's famous challenge to liberal Protestantism in the opening words of the preface to the first edition (reprinted in later editions) of his *Epistle to the Romans*, 1: "Paul, as a child of his age, addressed his contemporaries. It is, however, far more important that, as Prophet and Apostle of the Kingdom of God, he veritably speaks to all men of every age. The differences between then and now, there and here, no doubt require careful investigation and consideration. But the purpose of such investigation can only be to demonstrate that these differences are, in fact, purely trivial." For an effort to respond to liberal Judaism, while granting the truth of its critique of Scripture's historicity, see Kugel, *How to*

magisterium, a central issue has therefore been the doctrinal content and authority of Tradition, understood as the Church's ability to faithfully hand on the truth about Jesus Christ.

For this reason, the present chapter focuses not on classic works of the past century, such as Yves Congar's *Tradition and Traditions*, but on a more recent, and representative, contribution: Terrence Tilley's *Inventing Catholic Tradition*.[15] Tilley, who currently holds the Avery Cardinal Dulles Chair in Catholic Theology at Fordham University, sets forth a theology of "Catholic tradition" rooted in what he takes to be the necessity—in light of historical studies that in his view demonstrate frequent doctrinal invention and/or rupture—of the "abandonment of development as a credible theory of doctrinal change."[16] He envisions Catholic tradition as a continual re-invention of the

---

Read the Bible. His criticism of the canonical approach of Brevard Childs and others provides a window into his own solution, which I find intriguing but inadequate:

> Faced with the theological problems posed by modern biblical scholarship, canonical critics correctly insist that a text's original meaning is not necessarily its only meaning, indeed, that the original constituents of the Bible necessarily took on new meaning as soon as they began to be supplemented and edited and ultimately placed in a larger environment of texts, the biblical canon. But this apparently historical argument takes no account of what those texts actually meant at the time of their canonization. That is, canonical criticism draws the line at the canonical *text*. It does not seem to realize that the earliest "community of believers" canonized not only the text but their own peculiar way of reading and interpreting it. There was nothing optional about the latter: it *was* what the text meant. (679)

15. For a discussion of Tilley's book that makes clear how widely his views are shared, see the responses by Ann Riggs, Elizabeth A. Johnson, William L. Portier, and Roberto Goizueta in "Terrence W. Tilley's *Inventing Catholic Tradition*." Goizueta notes, "Tilley has given us what should rank as one of the most important scholarly treatments of this key theological concept since the publication of Yves Congar's magisterial *Tradition and Traditions*" (114), and he goes on to say, "Contemporary battles between conservatives and liberals are often, I would suggest, battles between two equally *modern* interpretations of tradition. Both sides presuppose an objectified, abstract, conceptual notion of tradition; one reifies tradition by constructing idols of the *tradita* while the other, mistakenly identifying the reification with the reality, rejects the *tradita* altogether" (ibid.). Goizueta, however, does not provide an example of a scholar who constructs "idols of the *tradita*." It seems to me that he is constructing a straw man here, since it is in fact "Congar's magisterial *Tradition and Traditions*" that now represents the "conservative" view. Of the four contributors to this symposium, Portier raises the most concerns; in particular, he urges that Tilley interact with the theologians and philosophers of the *nouvelle théologie*. But he concludes by emphasizing his "deep appreciation and admiration for Tilley's project as a whole and for his practice-oriented approach to tradition in this book. The intellectualist mainstream of Catholic theology in the United States badly needs a shot of Tilley, with his corrective emphasis on act over text, practice over belief" (111). My concern is that Tilley's oppositional framework of "practice over belief" deracinates the latter and thereby undermines the former.

16. Tilley, *Inventing Catholic Tradition*, 82. As Maurice Wiles puts it sardonically in response to Owen Chadwick's work on doctrinal development:

> I find little cause for surprise that his historical researches should not have given rise to much modern theological discussion of the question of doctrinal development. The

practice of Catholic faith, without enduring doctrinal truth. After surveying the argument of his book, I compare his position with some of the ways in which Scripture presents παράδοσις ("tradition"). I argue that the difference between Tradition and tradition—the latter being merely human and conveying no enduring doctrinal truth—is inscribed in Scripture itself.[17] The New Testament's various negative references to παράδοσις caution believers against

---

historical story is full of fascination. One reads and one admires; one admires not only the narrator of the story but also the characters within it; one admires the broad sweep of their intellectual convictions and the detailed subtlety of their individual reasonings. But it is like reading a debate about the movements of the planets before the invention of the telescope. The general problems with which they were concerned are real problems; but the particular problems to which they addressed themselves so vigorously are not ours; and, more emphatically still, the way in which they approached them cannot be ours. . . . The study of doctrinal development is a study of importance; but the debates of the eighteenth and nineteenth centuries must not be expected to throw any great light on the road we have to tread in pursuit of it at the present time. The most obvious of all divisions concerning the nature of doctrinal development in the life of the Church lies between those who consider all such development as has received the accredited sanction of the Church to be wholly true and those who believe it to include an element of error. (*Making of Christian Doctrine*, 1–2; cf. 11)

Wiles is right about this point of division, but he is wrong that the nineteenth-century debates are now theologically irrelevant, even for Protestants. For Wiles, the rejection of the absolute inerrancy of Scripture entails the rejection of an infallible Church (and thus of infallible dogma), but in making this argument he overlooks that one can hold to scriptural inerrancy without supposing that this inerrancy applies in every way (for example, to scientific and historical matters in every instance) and without denying a certain kind of real theological diversity in Scripture. For a better way forward, see Schenk, "*Officium Signa Temporum Perscrutandi.*"

17. See also the helpful discussion in Congar, *Tradition and Traditions*, 7–22. Regarding Paul's view of "tradition," for example, Congar observes that

Paul makes of the acts of transmission (παραδιδόναι) and reception (παραλαμβάνειν), or of conservation and holding (κατέχειν, κρατεῖν), the very structure or law of the régime of faith by which the communities were built up. The *content* of this "tradition" is seen to be composed of two groups of objects. On the one hand, there is the basic message of the faith, which must be received as a word *from God*. It is essentially centred on the death and resurrection of Christ. . . . Besides the central message of the faith, Paul "transmits" to the communities rules concerning their internal discipline or Christian behaviour ("parainesis"). . . . When dealing with St. Paul, we should not separate too sharply the "tradition" of the paschal faith from the "tradition" of apostolic rules of conduct. Both "build up" the community. Together they integrate the true religious relationship which the faithful must have with God in Christ. (9–10)

Congar goes on to argue that the practices are less binding than the doctrines:

However, the two categories of "tradition" are not entirely of equal standing: the events and doctrines *de Christo*, the objects of the kerygma, have an absolute and immutable character—they are "fundamental" (1 Cor. 3:10; Gal. 1:6ff.)—which is not possessed by those rules of conduct laid down by the apostles under the guidance of the Holy Spirit, and which we can see would be open to modification, or at least growth, according to the needs of the historical life of the Church. (11)

While agreeing with Congar regarding Paul's communication of "doctrines" that "have an absolute and immutable character," I would add that certain practices or "rules of conduct"

conceptions of "tradition" similar to Tilley's, whereas the New Testament's positive references to παράδοσις resonate broadly with *Dei Verbum*'s position on Tradition. As Edith Humphrey points out, for the New Testament "the idea of tradition includes an act of giving (*didōmi*) over (*para*), a gift that is given over (*paradosis*), and an implied reception of that gift."[18] If that gift is in fact at bottom a human invention, it is not the παράδοσις that the New Testament insists upon, and it falls under the condemnation of the New Testament.

Tradition as Faithful Re-inventing: Terrence Tilley's *Inventing Catholic Tradition*

In *Inventing Catholic Tradition*, Terrence Tilley argues for three major points that significantly affect how Catholics think about Tradition. These three points are the relativization of propositional truth, the view that Catholic tradition has no definite content or starting point, and the view that Catholic tradition evolves in a nonteleological fashion.[19] All three of these points are mistaken, in my view. My first task is therefore to survey Tilley's argument in some detail.

laid down by Paul also have that character. See also D. H. Williams, *Retrieving the Tradition and Renewing Evangelicalism*, 51–58.

18. Humphrey, *Scripture and Tradition*, 26.

19. For related perspectives on Catholic tradition, see also such works as Schillebeeckx, *Church*; Geffré, *Risk of Interpretation*; Boeve, *Interrupting Tradition*. See also George Tyrrell's 1898 essay "Sabatier on the Vitality of Dogmas," in comparison with the essays of Tyrrell's later period that we find in his *Through Scylla and Charybdis*, especially "Semper Eadem II," "'Theologism'—A Reply," "Revelation," "Mysteries," and "The Rights and Limits of Theology." On Tyrrell see Rafferty, "Tyrrell's History and Theology," especially 33. Special mention should be made here of John E. Thiel's *Senses of Tradition*, published in the same year as Tilley's book. Like Tilley, Thiel is indebted to the epistemological pragmatism of Wilfrid Sellars, who argues that (in Thiel's words) "what is called knowledge takes shape in an integrated network of revisable claims" and that "this meaningful whole is enmeshed in time and culture, ever aligning its interrelated claims for meaning to the circumstances in which knowledge—and faith—is practiced" (*Senses of Tradition*, 28–29). Thiel first engages what he calls the "literal sense of tradition"—namely, its communication of universally true expressions of the gospel in faith and practice. He points out that the seeming stability and universality of this literal sense is tied to the "continuing interpretation of divine revelation made and remade in every successive moment by the Christian community" (55). From this hermeneutical perspective, Thiel argues that there is room for further "senses" of tradition that allow for breaks and ruptures. Specifically, he proposes three further "senses" of tradition: "development-in-continuity" (represented in different ways by Johann Sebastian Drey, Johann Adam Möhler, John Henry Newman, and various reception theories); "dramatic development" (represented by John T. Noonan in *Church That Can and Cannot Change*, by some teachings of Vatican II, and by the lack of widespread contemporary reception of the Church's teachings on birth control and the ordination of women); and "incipient development" (represented by some cultural and theological changes instigated by feminist anthropology). In this way, Thiel joins together development-as-continuity with development-as-rupture, now under the one rubric of

Of the three points, the first is particularly crucial because it shapes the second and third in a determinative way. In order to understand Tilley's critique of propositional truth we should start with his broader account of truth. He thinks that it can no longer be held that truth arises from the adequation of the mind to being. Like Immanuel Kant and Ludwig Wittgenstein, Tilley considers that there are no "concepts of reality independent of our concepts," with the result that we cannot get below or behind our conceptual and narratival mental structure in order to know reality (being) in a deeper or more direct fashion.[20] He states that "at the beginning of the twenty-first century, foundational realism has been shown to be untenable, at least in any form strong enough to support a metaphysical system necessary to guarantee epistemic claims."[21] Although there have been philosophical realists who considered that our knowing apprehends being, for Tilley this is no longer an option that can be taken seriously.

If so, then are all knowledge claims merely mental constructs, so that no claim can be considered truer than any other claim? Indebted to Wilfrid Sellars, Tilley argues that one can be "radically constructivist" without thereby being "anti-realist."[22] Humans construct languages, from which follow linguistic acts that strive to advance particular claims. Our linguistic acts depend upon our constructed languages, and so our judgments do not directly apprehend reality. In describing the viewpoint of "anti-realists," Tilley observes that their position arises in reaction to realist and foundationalist theories: "Philosophers from Plato to the present have construed a foundational-realist theory of truth,

---

"tradition." He conceives of his position as balancing the principles of renewal and reception (through novelties and ruptures) with the principles of continuity and universality: prior to the eschaton we can have only historically partial views of the configuration of the Catholic tradition, rather than an "epic" or God's-eye view (cf. 14–15, 156–60, 193–95, 210–11). To my mind, Thiel's account of tradition, while more theologically nuanced than Tilley's, reduces in the end to Tilley's. For both, tradition is inevitably the site of contradictory breaks and ruptures, and for both the result is an antidogmatic view of the content of revelation, prior to the eschaton. For a response to Thiel on *Humanae Vitae* and "dramatic development," see Janet E. Smith, "*Sensus Fidelium* and *Humanae Vitae*."

20. Tilley, *Inventing Catholic Tradition*, 168. For further discussion see Tilley's *Wisdom of Religious Commitment* and his *Talking of God*. See also Tilley's "Toward a Practice-Based Theory of Tradition," which provides an essay-length version of his *Inventing Catholic Tradition*.

21. Tilley, *Inventing Catholic Tradition*, 168. Numerous scholars disagree with Tilley here, as do I. For recent arguments in favor of realism, see especially the work of Thomas Joseph White, OP, and Edward Feser. See also the following valuable studies: D. Hart, *The Experience of God*; Murphy, *God Is Not a Story*; D. Turner, *Faith, Reason and the Existence of God*; Markham, *Truth and the Reality of God*. For an influential position with affinities (despite a different conceptual vocabulary) to that of Tilley, see David Tracy's *Blessed Rage for Order*; cf. Thiel, *Senses of Tradition*, 198–203.

22. Tilley, *Inventing Catholic Tradition*, 156.

in which our knowledge is grounded in the 'fact' that our true claims mirror the world-as-it-is-in-itself (realism) and the 'fact' that the-way-the-world-is-in-itself is just what makes our claims true (foundationalism)."[23]

Tilley argues that there is room for a constructivist position that, even in rejecting foundationalism, still leaves room for a form of "realism." Namely, although we cannot measure our truth-claims by their adequation to the real, we can at least admit that when our truth-claims are borne out by empirical evidence, then this may well be the result of their actually being true. The real cannot ground our truth-claims because our truth-claims arise from our language rather than from contact with what is; but when our truth-claims are borne out empirically, this result may be taken as "an *effect* of our getting our claims right."[24] Again, this empirical evidence cannot be taken to ground our truth-claims because we obtain empirical evidence precisely through "our constructed concepts and practical investigations."[25] But when empirical or practical evidence shows us that a particular truth-claim is generally reliable, this result can confirm us in the view that our truth-claim (a mental construct) reflects reality. We can obtain this form of realism without accepting the foundationalist claim that we can have access to being in such a way that reality, as such, is what measures the truthfulness of our judgments. For Tilley, therefore, practice has priority both in how we arrive at truth-claims and in how we judge their truthfulness.[26]

It follows that truth-claims about the Triune God or Christ Jesus have their meaning within the Church's practice-generated languages. The truthfulness of such truth-claims can be judged, or appraised (to use Tilley's term), solely in terms of the empirical and practical results that will be perceptible in local

23. Ibid., 158.
24. Ibid., 160.
25. Ibid., 162.
26. Here I think of Gordon Kaufman's argument for provisionality of biblical and creedal conceptions of God on the grounds that "the only God we should worship today—the only God we can afford to worship—is the God who will further our humanization, the God who will help to make possible the creation of a universal and humane community" (*God, Mystery, Diversity*, 29). See also Hick, *Metaphor of God Incarnate*, 161. Friedrich Nietzsche also lends support to the disjunction of doctrine and practice: "It is false to the point of absurdity to see in a 'belief,' perchance the belief in redemption through Christ, the distinguishing characteristic of the Christian: only Christian *practice*, a life such as he who died on the Cross *lived*, is Christian. . . . Even today, *such* a life is possible, for *certain* men even necessary: genuine, primitive Christianity will be possible at all times. . . . *Not* a belief but a doing, above all a *not*-doing of many things, a different *being*" (*Anti-Christ*, 163; cf. 157–58). What Nietzsche means by the "life" that Christ lived is the opposite, of course, of what Christians have understood it to be, since it is rooted in serenely absolute self-will. For better approaches to the relationship between doctrine and practice, see Colin Gunton's *Brief Theology of Revelation*, 93–95; Merrigan, "Image of the Word," especially 27–47.

congregations of Christians.[27] These appraisals are endlessly changeable, and thus so are the truth-claims of any religious tradition, including the Catholic one. Tilley gives five "rules of thumb" or "adaptable standards" for the practice of appraising "religious claims."[28] Religious claims must (1) uncover something about "the world in which we live"; (2) they must fit with other recognized facts; (3) they must enable authenticity rather than self-deception; (4) they must enable fidelity to others and to the tradition (a fidelity that does not require repetition and that often requires rupture); and (5) they must "help create lives of truthfulness."[29] In short, although we cannot know God the Trinity or Jesus Christ in any direct way, we can make truth-claims about such referents and measure the truth of these claims by the results that they produce in us. The Catholic tradition's task is to seek increasingly to make truth-claims that "free a person and community to live in truthful ways."[30]

The Catholic tradition therefore should embrace the reality of ever-changing appraisals of its truth-claims, as one would expect in light of the ever-changing practices and contexts in which Christians live. Tilley observes, "What makes living religious traditions different from delusive or silly systems is that religious traditions' claims are subject to ongoing appraisal and modification."[31] We

27. For background see Schillebeeckx, *God the Future of Man*, especially chap. 6; see also Thiel's account of the contextuality, ambiguity, and obscurity that characterize the act of faith and his related account of the *sensus fidei* and *consensus fidelium* in Thiel, *Senses of Tradition*, chap. 5, especially 185–86.

28. Tilley, *Inventing Catholic Tradition*, 164.

29. Ibid., 164, 166. Compare here a list offered by Thomas H. Groome, which, despite serving a different purpose, bears notable similarities with Tilley's list:

> When it comes to interpreting Christian Story, it would surely help to have guidelines for making reliable interpretations and drawing out what is most life-giving. I will suggest five. In summary, Christian communities and persons should approach their scriptures and traditions: (1) as a great unfolding Story of the vital partnership between God and humankind; (2) bringing life to interpret Christian Story and Christian Story to interpret life; (3) expecting to encounter old and new spiritual wisdom; (4) being alert for distortions and forgotten legacies; and (5) always choosing *for life for all*." (*What Makes Us Catholic*, 19)

30. Tilley, *Inventing Catholic Tradition*, 166; see also Tyrrell, *Through Scylla and Charybdis*, 175 and elsewhere. It is unclear how Tilley knows what counts as suitable "results," human "authenticity," "truthful ways," and so forth. Abstracted from the instruction of the Word in the Spirit-filled Church, how can we know when we have found Christian authenticity? On this point see Guy Mansini, "Experience and Discourse"; Balthasar, *Moment of Christian Witness*.

31. Tilley, *Inventing Catholic Tradition*, 169. Applying this to the Catholic Church, Rosemary Radford Ruether and Eugene C. Bianchi argue that "Catholics must shake off the intellectual lethargy that, for too long, has allowed them to acquiesce in the view that the present church structure is divinely mandated for all time. They must begin to ask the hard questions about the relationship between historical realities and theological and ethical norms" (introduction to *A Democratic Catholic Church*, 7). Ruether and Bianchi seek to identify the Church's "basic message and ministry to society" and to ask "what kind of social ordering of human relationships best

cannot anticipate in advance the new practices and contexts that will cause our truth-claims to shift. But we can be assured that insofar as the claims generated by our practices/languages result in human authenticity, then we have spoken truly for that moment at least, and have spoken in a manner that reveals our sacramental ability to manifest "God's grandeur" in our lives.[32] We may need to speak in an entirely different way in the future, and that too would manifest God's grandeur insofar as our new ways of speaking foster human authenticity. We cannot know about God or Jesus directly, but we can measure our truth-claims by the communities that they foster. We can know something about ourselves, and if what we discover about ourselves reveals "authenticity," then we can judge from these results that our truth-claims about divine realities must be true at least for the moment, given the imperatives of our current practices and contexts.

Everything, then, boils down to the "authenticity" of believers in our local contexts and circumstances. Our truth-claims about God the Trinity, Jesus Christ, salvation, and so forth arise out of our practices/languages, and the truthfulness of these claims is appraised in terms of whether they foster authentic practices here and now. Truth-claims may purport to be about God, but since our practices and languages constitute our knowledge, they can be appraised for truthfulness only in terms of us. Since we are ever changing, the truth-claims of "Catholic tradition" are ever changing.[33]

Tilley accepts that "in one sense, our basic grammar is already defined in the *regula fidei*, the Creed."[34] But he makes clear that creedal statements are elastic insofar as "terminology can remain constant while the significance of terms changes, sometimes radically."[35] Given that the Church clearly defined the seven sacraments only in the medieval period, sacramental theology

---

approximates, even if always imperfectly, redemptive relationality" (13). See also the effort of Edward Schillebeeckx, OP, to reconceive Catholic ecclesiology on the basis of what he discovers to be "the heart of the gospel message" (*Church*, xiii). In addition to pressing for a democratic restructuring of the Catholic Church, Schillebeeckx proposes that Christian communities should no longer be divided by doctrinal differences: "All local and confessional churches are 'church' to the degree that they can affirm, encourage and further *communio*, communication, with other local churches" (197). See also the conclusion to Daniel Speed Thompson's *Language of Dissent*, 147–62, as well as Paul Lakeland's identification of the Church's "essentials" in his *Liberation of the Laity*, 260–62. For a better perspective, see Karl Barth, *The Church and the Churches*, 39–41.

32. Tilley, *Inventing Catholic Tradition*, 170.

33. For an exemplification of this viewpoint from the perspective of "critical theology," see Elisabeth Schüssler Fiorenza, "Discipleship of Equals." For background see Schillebeeckx, "New Critical Theory and Theological Hermeneutics"; see also, on the status of dogma within theologies founded upon and ordered to praxis, Lamb, "Political Theory and Enlightenment"; Portier, "Edward Schillebeeckx as Critical Theorist."

34. Tilley, *Inventing Catholic Tradition*, 12.

35. Ibid., 11.

appears to be particularly prone to such change. All theological claims, however, can be shown to conceal (whether more or less openly) a history of invention and rupture. Examples that Tilley gives include the inculturation of the concept of original sin and redemption, the variety of Christologies, and the subtleties of trinitarian theology. This is no less true in the Bible than in the history of the Church: "Believers' faith presumes that the Bible is in some sense *given* by God to humanity. Historical research seems to show that the Bible is *made* by human processes. Not only are books in the Bible composites of earlier traditions, but also evident inconsistencies can be found within and between its books."[36] Such inconsistencies profoundly mark Christian communities over time, and in fact such inconsistencies are present in all communities that possess traditions. As Tilley says, "A verbal token, translated from language to language and historical context to historical context, connected with different concepts to get its significance, and embodied in different cultures and practices, cannot simply 'mean the same thing.'"[37]

These reflections have already involved us in the other two main theses of Tilley's book. In his view, the Catholic tradition has no definite content and no definite starting point, and the Catholic tradition evolves in a nonteleological fashion. Again, this should be seen in light of his critique of propositional knowledge, as opposed to practical knowledge measured by the "authenticity" of believers. With regard to attempts to locate an essential doctrinal core that has been handed down in the Catholic tradition across the centuries, he observes that "even if there were clear verbal continuity in formulating 'essential' concepts and propositions of the tradition, there is great difficulty in determining the meanings of those concepts."[38] Along these lines, he suggests that the notion of a "deposit of faith" is profoundly misleading.[39] He explains, "The contexts in which that 'core' is expressed radically affect the expression; and if there is a 'deposit of faith' or other 'core' of a tradition, there can be

---

36. Ibid., 13–14. For a cautionary word, see Betz, "Glory(ing) in the Humility of the Word," 173. For a perspective in accord with Tilley's, see J. Collins's *Bible after Babel* and *Encounters with Biblical Theology*.

37. Tilley, *Inventing Catholic Tradition*, 34; cf. 27–28.

38. Ibid., 35.

39. Joseph Ratzinger agrees that simply to affirm that revelation was closed at the death of the last apostle is "far too simplistic," but he suggests that a middle ground is possible: "Revelation is indeed closed in terms of its material principle, but it is present, and remains present, in terms of its reality. Putting it another way: We are faced with a concept according to which revelation does indeed have its ἐφάπαξ, insofar as it took place in historical facts, but also has its constant 'today,' insofar as what once happened remains forever living and effective in the faith of the Church, and Christian faith never refers merely to what is past; rather, it refers equally to what is present and what is to come" ("Question of the Concept of Tradition," 86–87).

no direct access to that 'core.' All communicable expressions are necessarily contextualized expressions."[40]

If traditions are ever-changing, so that their propositional content is never stable, are traditions worth having? Tilley thinks that they are not only unavoidable but also worth having so long as they recognize themselves to be ever-changing constructions whose truthfulness is measured by whether they foster authentic practices. Failure to recognize their instability does not result in more stability. Tilley argues that instead it leads to efforts by authorities to impose their will by innovating under the guise of preserving a tradition. Such imposition, for Tilley, is an illegitimate form of "inventing" tradition. While changing a tradition is good and necessary, a bad "invention" is a change that is *deliberately* invented and imposed (as if it were no change at all) by sheer power. In Tilley's view, the main engine of such deliberate, cloaked "invention" in Catholic history has been the Roman magisterium, especially in the past half century.[41]

Tilley grants that in some sense Jesus can be said to inaugurate the Catholic tradition, but he emphasizes that Jesus himself belongs already within a tradition (Judaism). The Catholic tradition is "given" or "found," rather than made or invented, only in the sense that there is a givenness always present because we cannot make up a tradition from scratch: "Each construction

---

40. Tilley, *Inventing Catholic Tradition*, 35. The problems with "contextual" theologies are well articulated in Perišić, "Can Orthodox Theology Be Contextual?" For an approach that, while theologically much richer, has certain affinities with Tilley's, see D. Brown, *Tradition and Imagination*. Brown is right to see (with historical-critical scholars) "how deeply a developing tradition has helped shape the thinking of the biblical writers" (112). But having argued that the differences between the Gospels and tradition are "differences of degree rather than kind" (ibid.), Brown finds himself having to account for later doctrinal development at best in terms of "pressure . . . from various New Testament trajectories" (286) without being able to defend the normative status of the apostolic witness to Jesus Christ (see 111, 300). We can certainly grant both that there is inconsistency and diversity in Scripture, and that conceptual/imaginative reflection over time resulted in new ways of understanding events and narratives (doctrinal development or "evolving tradition" [300]), but this need not entail the denial of the existence of an intelligible "deposit" of revelation and thus also denial of a closed, uniquely inspired biblical canon. For further discussion of Brown's work, see Abraham, "Scripture, Tradition, and Revelation."

41. See Tilley, *Inventing Catholic Tradition*, 36–43, drawing upon various essays in Hobsbawm and Ranger, *Invention of Tradition*. Tilley's examples of such cloaked "inventions" range from the divergence of *Dignitatis Humanae* from nineteenth-century papal teachings about religious freedom, to the shifting of the altar in the celebration of the Eucharist (which, he argues, changed the Eucharist by obliterating its sacrificial symbolism), to the Congregation for the Doctrine of the Faith's rejection of inclusive-language translation (a rejection that Tilley finds particularly appalling, given that the Septuagint had also employed a relatively free translation style). See also Immanuel Kant's distinction between "ecclesiastical faith" and "pure religious faith," in *Religion within the Limits of Reason Alone*, 94–114.

arises out of previous practices and beliefs."[42] When certain "practitioners develop the belief that the originating events and people are the result of the creative presence and action of God," this belief can be affirmed, but only in a very limited sense: "That human constructs can also be divine creations is an affirmation that is at the heart of a tradition that relies on and produces an analogical imagination."[43] The point, however, is that the Catholic tradition involves no strong claim of a definite founding, let alone a divinely given revelation whose depths can be articulated doctrinally in an enduring manner.

For Tilley, therefore, it would be a mistake to suppose that doctrinal "development" is fueled by something other than ever-changing practices and contexts. The practice of handing on the Catholic tradition requires great flexibility with doctrinal propositions. On this view, the faithful practitioner of Christian tradition knows that "fidelity may require even abandoning traditional formulations," because "our fidelity is constituted not by a 'what' but by 'how.'"[44] To think of fidelity in terms of an essentialist "what," a cognitive core or deposit of faith, would be to miss the whole point. Rather, the historical practice of handing on the Catholic tradition has always involved profound doctrinal changes (ruptures and inventions) in order to meet the requirements of new practices and contexts, and thereby to foster authenticity among believers. This changing will not stop: we have no way of knowing what Catholics might believe in the future. As Tilley puts it, "We may sing a different tune than our forebears, and our successors will sing yet differently. . . . Faithfully transmitting our communal memory in fidelity to our past and our future is possible only in practice, only by engaging in the ongoing, ever-changing, and multilayered practice of *Inventing Catholic Tradition*."[45]

42. Tilley, *Inventing Catholic Tradition*, 173. Thus the constructions of "Christianity" will be highly diverse at all times and places, so that as Hegel puts it (in examining the issue of authority in Christianity), "Nothing has so many different meanings as the modern conception of what Christianity is, either in its essence, or in its particular doctrines and their importance or their relation to the whole" ("Positivity of the Christian Religion," 174).

43. Tilley, *Inventing Catholic Tradition*, 174. See Tracy, *Analogical Imagination*.

44. Tilley, *Inventing Catholic Tradition*, 185. Compare this to Francis Bacon's view of "heathen" religion as being peaceful because it "consisted rather in rites and ceremonies than in any constant belief" ("Of Unity in Religion," 67). See also Troeltsch, *Christian Faith*, 39, 41: "We feed on the tradition, but this tradition would be a dead thing were it not for the productivity of the one who receives life from it. . . . All these developments and transformations should not be viewed so much in terms of perfection, but rather in terms of a living adaptation to the present environment."

45. Tilley, *Inventing Catholic Tradition*, 186. For tradition as an action, see also the philosophical reflections of Jorge J. E. Gracia, *Old Wine in New Skins*. Gracia argues that "when Roman Catholics talk about beliefs as constituting a tradition, for example, they can be taken to be referring to the very actions of believing rather than to certain doctrines or to their textual formulation" (94). For an appreciation of this active sense of Tradition, without, however,

In other words, the continuity is in the practice, not in the doctrine. And the continuity of practice does not mean a continuity of practices, because practices change. What remains the same is quite simply "the practice of engaging in an act of judgment or appraisal that recognizes continuity."[46] Certainly a tradition has a history that is its givenness, but nothing in this history enables one to formulate a theory about the future development of the tradition. Tilley states that "it is not possible to devise a theory to predict future changes in *tradita* or to legitimate past changes."[47] When practices and contexts change, as they do continually and in an unpredictable way, a tradition must either change doctrinally or wither away, because practices are what generate doctrines. As we have seen, for Tilley the faithful practitioner of the tradition will be the one who works to "constantly invent the tradition."[48]

Tilley goes on to describe a set of five "rules of grammar" for the "Catholic intellectual tradition," rather than Catholic tradition per se (although on his view there seems to be little if any difference). These five rules include (1) an analogical and sacramental imagination, by which he means allowing for what appear to be conceptual contradictions; (2) the incarnation, as a sign

---

relativizing doctrinal truths or their creedal formulation (the content of Tradition), see Congar, *Tradition and Traditions*, 253 and elsewhere.

46. Tilley, *Inventing Catholic Tradition*, 121.

47. Ibid. For his part, Lewis Ayres agrees that no theory (or set of historical and logical arguments) can fully account for the actual course of doctrinal development, but Ayres insists that this does not mean that we can or should cease offering such theories: even if the course of doctrinal development eludes an easy explanation, neither is it irrational. See Ayres, *Nicaea and Its Legacy*; see also my discussion of doctrinal development and Ayres's approach in my chap. 6.

48. Tilley, *Inventing Catholic Tradition*, 121. By contrast, Congar's presentation of the relationship of identity and change allows for both, rather than assuming rupture and sheer invention:

"The faith which was once for all delivered to the saints" (Jude 3) is extended to a very great number of men, scattered through space and time, together with the apostolic doctrines and precepts. In this respect tradition is not in dependence on time: rather it triumphs over it, even, one might say, discounts it altogether. Tradition does not age, for to grow old is to change. It is the transmission through time, time which alters all things, of a deposit of faith; but, above and beyond the successive transmissions of this deposit, Christ the Incarnate Word, reigning as Lord above time, in giving the Church its very life, assures too the continuing identity of the truth possessed by the Church. "Jesus Christ is the same yesterday and today and for ever" (Heb. 13:8). We must go even further than this. Tradition is not the simple permanence of a structure, but a continual renewal and fertility *within* this given structure, which is guaranteed by a living and unchanging principle of identity [namely, Christ and the Holy Spirit]. (*Tradition and Traditions*, 264–65)

For Congar, Tradition is both "the transmission unchanged of a sacred deposit" and "the explanation which is made of this deposit, as a result of its being lived and defended, generation after generation, by the People of God. . . . What we receive in the twentieth century is always the 'faith which was once for all delivered to the saints' (Jude 3), but we cannot detach this deposit from the fellowship of the saints who have received it, preserved it and lived it from the time of the first 'saints' until our own times" (267–68).

of God's grace rather than as a logical problem, and universal hope; (3) radical inclusivity; (4) the worldliness and public character of the Church; and (5) the graciousness of the Creator God and the goodness of creation. When spelled out in light of Tilley's particular understanding of "incarnation," "church," and "God," these descriptive rules show themselves to be able to encompass widely divergent content.[49]

Tilley expresses attraction to John Henry Newman's view that the "idea of Christianity" unfolds historically without being identical to that historical unfolding. But for Newman, the "idea of Christianity" is not separable from a specific cognitive content, even if that content can always be unfolded more deeply.[50] By contrast, the (Schleiermachian) conclusion that Tilley draws from Newman is that "the faith, then, is not reducible to any one articulation of the [Christian] vision or any one way of practicing the faith. The faith is the faith, and the expressions are that by which we come to recognize and eventually to understand what it means to live in and live out that faith."[51] The creedal, dogmatic Christianity advocated by Newman, however, depends upon affirming that the content of Christian faith can be rightly expressed, even if not exhausted, by a particular "articulation of the vision." Newman does not separate faith and dogma in the way that Tilley does.[52] A similar problem arises when Tilley links his own approach with that of Avery Dulles's *Models of Revelation*. Dulles denies that revelation is either "the delivery of immutable divine propositions" *or* a subjective interior feeling or intuition.[53] Tilley claims to be doing the same, but the unique revelation of God to Israel (culminating in Jesus Christ) and the propositional truth of dogma are accepted by Dulles, in his nuanced fashion, while being profoundly relativized by Tilley.[54]

49. Tilley justifies limiting himself to these five rules on the grounds that to include further doctrinal principles would exclude works of Catholic intellectual tradition that happen not to mention these doctrines.

50. As Terrence Merrigan observes, "Newman was absolutely committed to the idea that the Christian religion contained truths that would not have been known had they not been disclosed by God in and through the life, death and resurrection of Jesus Christ" ("Revelation," 47; cf. 56–63). Merrigan adds that Newman also upheld "God's universal self-disclosure, at least as a sort of (ongoing) preparation for the reception of the Gospel" (47). These truths, expressed dogmatically (propositionally), can never, of course, exhaust the content of the revealed realities.

51. Tilley, *Inventing Catholic Tradition*, 112.

52. See, for example, J. Newman, "On the Introduction of Rationalistic Principles into Revealed Religion"; Newman, "Private Judgment"; Newman, "Contracted Views in Religion." For Newman's position on faith and dogma, see especially Merrigan, *Clear Heads and Holy Hearts*; Dulles, *Newman*; Walgrave, *Newman the Theologian*.

53. Tilley, *Inventing Catholic Tradition*, 171.

54. Thus Tilley asks how we can speak of an "original Christian 'interpretandum,'" given that Jesus's own claims (insofar as we can know them) and the New Testament's diverse interpretations of Jesus can be interpreted only within the developing and multifaceted streams

Tilley's account of the relationship of practices and doctrines is shaped by
various contemporary thinkers, including Robert Schreiter, Clifford Geertz,
Kathleen Boone, and James McClendon. A practice involves a shared vision
about the goal of the practice and its attainability, about the dispositions that
serve the attainment of this goal, and about the "grammar" or rules of the
practice that suggest what actions befit the practice. For Tilley, the Christian
vision involves understanding "human life as created, redeemed, and sustained
by the God present and revealed in and through Jesus the Christ."[55] In this
context, Tilley describes the Catholic tradition as a "set of enduring practices"
that build up the kingdom of God, in accord with the "grammar" contained
in "scripture, creeds, confessional statements, magisterial pronouncements,
catechisms."[56] But he emphasizes that doctrines are learned in and through
practices, in the particular context of local communities. Since there is no
universal language or universal experience, every doctrine must be continually
reinterpreted and adjusted at the level of the local congregation, in order to
meet the practical needs of specific believers. As an example, he states that
the universal "right to life" can be spelled out in many different ways, so that
"no appeal to the abstract claim is sufficient (and may not be necessary) to
adjudicate among competing concrete and practical uses of the claim."[57]

Since Tilley locates the significance of doctrinal truth-claims, such as those
found in Scripture and the Creeds, within competing and ever-changing local

---

of Second Temple Judaism(s). For Tilley, as for Troeltsch, an emphasis on praxis can obviate
these problems: "While I would not advocate keeping silent about doctrines, as the editors of
the *Apophthegmata* [*Patrum*] likely did, I would advocate not making them a litmus test for
sharing practices and forming communities of resistance and solidarity. Doctrines divide where
practices can unite" (*Disciples' Jesus*, 259). See also Tilley's point that "we cannot 'get back' to
an actual man, Jesus, and certainly not to his 'self-consciousness'—for all we have are records
of performances of the Jesus-movement" (57; cf. Lash, "Performing the Scriptures," 37–46).
Since Tilley considers that the Jesus-movement's practices do not merely serve as a resource
for Christology but in fact "*are* christology," he concludes that "Jesus" should be understood
as one

> who does not reveal truths but draws out from members of the movement insights that help
> them to see how to live truthfully; who graces the movement not by infusing its members
> with something from on high but by surfacing the divine creative grace in the movement
> and helping shape an ongoing movement of created, creative grace; who refuses to make
> the disciples into wholly dependent patients who respond to God's powerful Agent in
> passive acceptance but empowers them to become creative and graceful reconciling agents
> of the commonweal divine. (70)

See also Schillebeeckx, *Church*, 224.

55. Tilley, *Inventing Catholic Tradition*, 56.
56. Ibid., 58.
57. Ibid., 60. For a better account of the relationship of universal and particular in moral
discourse, see Novak, *Natural Law in Judaism*. See also Arkes, *Constitutional Illusions and
Anchoring Truths*.

practices and contexts, his articulation of "human life as created, redeemed, and sustained by the God present and revealed in and through Jesus the Christ" is supremely amorphous. Each of the terms in this phrase ("human life," "created," "redeemed," and so forth) has a variety of potential meanings that cannot be adjudicated by appeal to universal truth-claims. This situation befits the constant reimagining and remaking of doctrine that Tilley takes to belong to the practice of "tradition." Drawing upon Schreiter, Tilley sums up: "As with a language, so with a tradition; we really only have performances of the faith before us."[58] He uses the example of changes in the eucharistic liturgy (and in eucharistic piety) to argue that these performances/practices are ever-changing, with corresponding evidence that profound doctrinal instability is unavoidable and indeed desirable lest one think that "one set of theological words can be the necessary and sufficient expression of the presence of Christ."[59]

Tilley's critique of propositional truth is distilled in his six-point definition of "tradition as a set of practices."[60] The first point is that a proposition is intelligible only in terms of its practical use or application, and since this use often changes, so does the meaning of the proposition. The second, third, fourth, and sixth points reduce to the assertion that practices, which change regularly, shape and define the ever-changing meaning of propositions/doctrines. The fifth point is that there is no way to understand a "tradition" except in terms of practices, so that the "how" has priority over the "what."

Can Catholic "tradition" understood in this way develop? As we have seen, Tilley claims that Catholic tradition can develop if by that we mean that it can constantly recalibrate itself so as to promote "authenticity" among believers. For Tilley, this authenticity, and not any other content, is ultimately the meaning of the Catholic "tradition." This is not a teleological development, however, nor is it an unfolding of the doctrinal content of God's revelation. Instead it is a continual adjustment to the times so as to avoid withering and dying. This continual adjustment, Tilley makes clear, is not simply what he wishes would happen (although it certainly is that) but is in fact what has historically happened. Tilley rejects the idea of doctrinal progress not least on the grounds that it is arrogant: "The presumption that 'we' have made religious progress or become more religiously advanced (holier? wiser? more moral?) because 'we' have a more 'developed' notion of the papacy, the Eucharist, or religious liberty than our forebears cannot be sustained."[61] Of course, Catholic theories of development of doctrine have not generally claimed that

58. Tilley, *Inventing Catholic Tradition*, 65.
59. Ibid., 73n9. Of course no set of propositions can exhaustively describe realities of faith.
60. Ibid., 79.
61. Ibid., 81.

we are better Christians than our predecessors. But Tilley's point is probably directed toward those who agree with him that tradition is simply "a pattern of inculturation and contextual adaptation": such persons might be tempted to think that this contextual adaptation is ever-better. Tilley's commitment to tradition as an ever-changing adaptation cannot coexist with the claim that a particular adaptation, in a particular culture, expresses a *truer* doctrine (rather than a truer doctrine for that particular culture and context).[62]

But do doctrines have ontological referents, which can be more (or less) accurately expressed? Ontological reference is not possible, except for in the sense that one can measure one's truth-claim by the practical results (authenticity) that it fosters in believers. For Tilley, those who insist on ontological reference tend to become rigidly attached to an alleged "deposit of faith" with the result that they petrify Catholic "tradition" and make it "brittle and hegemonic," so that reactionary repression and narrowness result.[63] Instead, he says, we must learn "how to live the tradition."[64] To live the tradition is faithfully, and often radically, to change its doctrines and practices so as to meet contemporary needs. For Tilley, Catholic "tradition" is primarily this "how."[65]

62. Along similar lines, Troeltsch observes, "Allotment of truth to the different epochs of history and participation by individuals in the ultimate values of history belong to a realm that transcends history and lies beyond our knowledge. . . . A liberal and critical attitude toward history, which in its ups and downs sometimes approaches the ideal and sometimes departs from it, must free us from both skepticism and evolutionary progressivism" ("Faith and History," 143). Troeltsch's development on this point can be seen by comparing his "Rival Methods for the Study of Religion" (1916) with his "Christianity and the History of Religion" (1897). In the latter essay, Troeltsch takes an evolutionary view in which he seeks to identify a "religiosity" that gives "living embodiment to the central idea taking shape in the evolutionary process" ("Christianity and the History of Religion," 80), and he finds "in the Prophetic-Christian religion the high-point, or rather a new point of departure, in the history of religion" (84). In the former essay, Troeltsch concludes that "even an allegedly rationally-necessary scheme for the future is a palpably transparent illusion. The evolutionary goal is not, in fact, constructed from a scientifically established law of cause and effect, but every 'law' of cause and effect is itself derived from a sense for the uniqueness of the moment—however this sense may arise—and the facts are accordingly arranged in a sequence that makes the religious life (conceived more concretely or more abstractly) of the present, or even merely of the author, appear as the evolutionary goal that may be glimpsed at any point" ("Rival Methods for the Study of Religion," 76).

63. Tilley, *Inventing Catholic Tradition*, 85. The *nouvelle théologie* accused the neoscholastics of this, but Tilley here has in view the *nouvelle théologie* (or more specifically its followers today). For background see Mettepenningen, *Nouvelle Théologie*. See also Rowland, *Ratzinger's Faith*, especially 11–14.

64. Tilley, *Inventing Catholic Tradition*, 86. Cf. Troeltsch, *Christian Faith*, 45–46.

65. For Congar, by contrast, the source of Tradition is Jesus Christ, and Tradition exists because God wills for the revelation of Christ to be transmitted in the Church:

As witnesses to Christ and doctors of the new justice, the apostles *transmitted* the witness of a previous and sovereign master, greater than Moses. It is reasonable to suppose that they transmitted, from memory, not only the words of Jesus, with their simple and rhythmic

Παράδοσις and Catholic Tradition

Tilley does not quote from Scripture in his book. Given his account of con-stantly re-invented tradition, scriptural texts would hardly lead Tilley to change his position. In my view, however, Scripture's teachings about παράδοσις ("tradi-tion") are instructive for identifying the deficiencies of Tilley's account, despite its popularity among numerous Catholic theologians today. By examining a selection of the New Testament's positive and negative uses of παράδοσις, I inquire into whether a nondoctrinal "tradition" could be appropriate for the Church of Jesus Christ.[66] I find that the scriptural references to "tradition" not only rule out the validity of a nondoctrinal "tradition" but also shed light on the contours of the actual theology of Tradition that *Dei Verbum* teaches.

In the Gospels, the Pharisees accuse Jesus's disciples of transgressing "the tradition [παράδοσις] of the elders" by not washing their hands before eating (Matt. 15:2; cf. the parallel text in Mark 7:5–13).[67] Jesus responds forcefully to this charge. He accuses the Pharisees of obeying not God's word but their own constructions.[68] Turning their question against them, he asks, "And why

---

oral style, but even the very inflexions of his voice. . . . Progress in the understanding of the events and words which present revelation was achieved, however, in the Christian community, just as it occurred in Israel, and it was going on even while the apostles were still making their revelation. It, too, has been incorporated into the Christian message as it has been handed down to us. (*Tradition and Traditions*, 6)

Ratzinger similarly observes that "within the New Testament itself" we can see "the ecclesial process of interpreting what has been handed down" ("Question of the Concept of Tradition," 61).

66. For reasons of space, I do not include the multiple uses of the verb παραδίδωμι, which is often translated as "hand over," "deliver," "give over," or "commit," but which is in fact a verbal form of "tradition": see, for example, Luke 1:2; 10:22; Rom. 6:17; 1 Cor. 11:23; 15:3; Jude 3, and elsewhere. See Humphrey, *Scripture and Tradition*, 43.

67. See Davies and Allison, *Gospel according to Saint Matthew*, 2:520: "Because παράδοσις describes the Pharisaic tradition in Paul, in the gospels, and in Josephus, it was clearly a tech-nical term. It probably translates the Hebrew *massôret*. The tradition of the Pharisees had a controversial status before AD 70. The Sadducees repudiated it. So did those responsible for composing the Dead Sea Scrolls."

68. Thus Karl Barth wished to leave room for God's continual reformation of Christian doctrine on the grounds that the fallible Church must continually be united more closely to God's free and definitive revelation, God's radical inbreaking on behalf of sinners. Barth's position relativizes Church teaching with the goal of exalting divine revelation in Christ. See Barth, *Church Dogmatics*, I.1, 117–21, 248–75. Barth closely links Protestant liberalism and Roman Catholicism as instances of the idolatrous desire to make humans superior to the Word of God. He observes:

Though it puts tradition alongside the Bible, the Roman Catholic Church, too, has and reads and honours the Bible. But this is not the Bible in itself, the emancipated Bible, the Bible which confronts the Church as an authority. The fact that the Bible in its own concreteness is the Word of God, and that as such it is the supreme criterion of Church teaching, is not acknowledged here. What we have here is the Bible which belongs to

do you transgress the commandment of God [τὴν ἐντολὴν τοῦ θεοῦ] for the sake of your tradition?" (Matt. 15:3). Jesus takes the "commandment of God" to be God's own word, which Israel has received from God. In what does the "commandment of God" consist? Jesus gives as examples two commandments from the Torah: "Honor your father and your mother" (Exod. 20:12) and "For every one who curses his father or his mother shall be put to death" (Lev. 20:9). By contrast, the Pharisees' tradition is not supported by a commandment of God. Jesus summarizes the tradition quite negatively: "But you [Pharisees] say, 'If any one tells his father or his mother, "What you would have gained from me is given to God," he need not honor his father'" (Matt. 15:5). At issue is whether a son of impoverished parents is justified in giving to the temple the resources that otherwise could have nourished his parents. Jesus holds that the Pharisees' interpretation of the Torah in this regard undermines God's commandments in the Torah.[69]

---

the Church, which is understood aright and expounded aright and applied aright by its teaching office. This Bible is the Word of God by which all proclamation is to be measured. The *regula proxima fidei*, the nearest immediate plumbline of Catholic faith, is not, then, the verdict of the Bible but the verdict of the teaching office on the Bible. (257) Barth further explains the fallibility of Church dogma:
  Even and especially on Roman Catholic soil, if dogma is equated with God's Word, will it not have to be understood primarily as command in accordance with the usage of the Bible which was at least possible in the fathers of the first centuries too? . . . A command is what it is only in the act of the one who gives it and the one who obeys or disobeys it. One cannot give oneself a command in the way the Church gives itself Church dogmas. . . . The material and impersonal intrinsic truth ascribed to dogma, the contemplative objectivity which is the issue in Roman Catholic theology when it emphasises the sense of doctrinal proposition in the concept of dogma, this is for us the mark of a truth which is conditioned and limited not merely by the creatureliness of man but also by his sinfulness, a truth in comparison with which the truth of God in His revelation is quite different. By the very fact that as a proposition it can only be contemplated, that it is neutral and permits neutrality, that as a theory—and who can deny that Church dogma is this too?—it bears witness itself to where it belongs, namely, to the Church, its talk, its testimonies, its proclamation, its dialogue with itself—all this with great distinction, for it is not our intention to disparage Church dogma on this its proper level—and yet still to the Church and not the Word in which God addresses the Church. We do not understand and we can never understand how the truth that is put into the hands of the Church as Church dogma can be the truth of God. What we think we know as the truth of God's Word from the witness of Holy Scripture is a very different truth, a sovereign truth. (271–72)
My disagreement with Barth is rooted in Scripture's testimony to the Church and to its participation in Christ. Theocentricity does not require disclaiming the graced fidelity—with regard to the proclamation of the gospel and to the sacraments—of the Church's participation in Christ.
  69. As Humphrey comments:
  Jesus . . . declares that they have "put aside" the commandment of God, while elevating human commandments that originally were intended to *aid* in the keeping of the divine Torah. What the Pharisees call "the tradition of the elders" has been diminished in their hands and been rendered merely "the tradition of men," for the Pharisees are not

Even if the practice of temple offerings can be adapted in certain ways, according to Jesus it cannot be adapted in *this* way without contradicting the express content of the commandments. The revelation mediated by the Torah is not adaptable in a plastic manner; it has a content that must be respected. Put another way, the practical form taken in our lives by God's commandment to honor our father and mother will differ depending on our circumstances. But it will not differ so much as to suppose that God's commandment has no intelligibility outside the particular circumstances of those who obey it.

In short, Jesus suggests that the "tradition" of the Pharisees has here made of God's commandment a mere human construct, revisable by those who do not possess authority to revise it. As Jesus says, when we do not care for the material needs of our parents—despite the explicit meaning of God's commandments in Exodus 20:12 and Leviticus 20:9—our parents' poverty shows that we are failing to obey the laws that God has revealed. The revisable construct is not God's commandment but rather is the Pharisees' tradition by which they have sought to strengthen the temple's finances. Jesus warns them: "So for the sake of your tradition, you have made void the word of God. You hypocrites!" (Matt. 15:6–7). The "tradition" involved here is an interpretation of the Torah that contradicts God's own teachings in the Torah about what we owe in justice to our parents.

Jesus condemns their "tradition" not simply on his own authority but also by citing the authority of the prophet Isaiah. He quotes Isaiah 29:13 (in a version derived from, but not identical to, the Septuagint), "This people honors me with their lips, but their heart is far from me; in vain do they worship me, teaching as doctrines [διδασκαλίας] the precepts of men" (Matt. 15:8–9). In the RSV, Isaiah 29:13–14 reads,

---

maintaining a continuity between these traditions and the divine Word. Their problem is not tradition itself, but that they are using lesser traditions for the purpose of eluding the demands of the ongoing Tradition of God. Indeed, in speaking specifically about the oral traditions followed by the Pharisees (later to be encoded in the Mishnah), Jesus (to the surprise of some) does not challenge them in following these: "But woe to you Pharisees! For you tithe mint and rue and every herb, and neglect justice and the love of God; these you ought to have done, without neglecting the others" (Luke 11:42//Matt. 23:23). (*Scripture and Tradition*, 56)

Lest she give the impression that Jesus leaves these traditions intact, Humphrey adds that Jesus nonetheless implies "within this discourse that if the *inside* of a person is clean the outside will take care of itself (Luke 11:41//Matt. 23:26). This is an intimation of the new covenant that he would enact, so that the oral protective laws, called by the rabbis 'the hedge around the Law,' would no longer be necessary. When it becomes possible, by the Spirit and in the new creation, for the believer to have strength inwardly to keep the Law, then it will no longer be necessary to multiply instructions to prevent him or her from breaking it" (ibid.).

And the Lord said, "Because this people draw near with their mouth and honor me with their lips, while their hearts are far from me, and their fear of me is a commandment of men learned by rote; therefore, behold, I will again do marvelous things with this people, wonderful and marvelous; and the wisdom of their wise men shall perish, and the discernment of their discerning men shall be hid."

Does Isaiah 29, however, mean that new circumstances are leading God to *undo the truths* that Israel's "wise men" and "discerning men" have learned? Certainly the prophetic text points to a future act of God that will vindicate God's faithfulness to Israel, so that Israel will again "sanctify the Holy One of Jacob, and will stand in awe of the God of Israel" (Isa. 29:23). But Isaiah makes clear that the problem is not God's previous revelation, as if God were going to change it in a way that makes it no longer authoritative. Rather, the problem is that the "wise men" of the people no longer hear the word that God has given them. God aims not to show them that his word changes to meet the times but rather to instruct them about his word, which is not a "commandment of men" but rather is the word of the living God. God promises that when he accomplishes his plan for the restoration of Israel, his people "will stand in awe of the God of Israel. And those who err in spirit will come to understanding, and those who murmur will accept instruction" (Isa. 29:23–24).[70]

The point, then, is not to negate previous understandings but to awaken God's people to understanding. This awakening will take place when God does something that reveals him to be the living God, so that they no longer fear God only "by rote." Their fear of God should arise from the commandment of the living God rather than from "a commandment of men." They need to relearn how to hear God's word as God's, so that they respond to God interiorly, with awe and devotion, rather than treating God as though his commandment were merely commanded by human beings.

It should be clear that this is the very opposite of what Tilley advocates. Whereas Isaiah 29 speaks about *God* doing something that will show his people once again that God's word is the word of the living God who instructs them, Tilley treats the content of divine teaching as constructed by humans and radically changeable by humans. All Catholic tradition, for Tilley, is made or invented by humans (even that which is "given" is given simply in the sense of being made by earlier humans); and the same holds for the words of Scripture. When one treats the content of revelation as always in the process of being

70. In this regard Humphrey emphasizes that we must read Scripture as opening us to the living God, so that Scripture functions as an icon rather than a barrier or an "end in itself": see ibid., 60–62.

changed to fit new circumstances, then one is treating God's word simply as a human construction rather than as the word of the living God.[71]

The "tradition" that Jesus describes in Matthew 15 (and Mark 7) is a human construction that prevents the people of God from hearing and obeying the explicit content of God's word. If Catholic Tradition were what Tilley says it is—not a "what" but a "how," and a "how" that involves no enduring doctrinal and moral content (because the meaning of terms is always changing)—then it could not help but fall under the condemnation that Jesus directs toward what the Pharisees call "the tradition of the elders" (Matt. 15:2). A key aspect of this condemnation consists in Jesus's emphasis that "the commandment of God" has an actual truth-content that has been obscured by the Pharisees' tradition but that cannot be changed—namely, that we must care for our father and mother in need. It is also noteworthy that Jesus's distinction between a divine commandment and a human tradition could not cogently be made on Tilley's terms.

A second biblical perspective on tradition arises from Paul's use of the term παράδοσις. The Pauline letters contain various instances of the term, including Galatians 1:14; Colossians 2:8; 2 Thessalonians 2:15; 3:6; and 1 Corinthians 11:2.[72] In Galatians 1, Paul is speaking about the gospel that he preaches. This gospel, he emphasizes, "is not man's gospel. For I did not receive it from man, nor was I taught it, but it came through a revelation of Jesus Christ" (Gal. 1:11–12).[73] Here Paul certainly envisions revelation in terms of doctrinal and moral content, and he denies that this content comes from human making or

---

71. I grant, of course, the full human agency in the Spirit-guided expression of divine revelation. Humphrey observes that "the Scriptures themselves came out of traditions and then were interpreted, within Israel and within the Church, by tradition" (ibid., 64). See also Humphrey's discussion (138–49) of four instances of "modified tradition," including most notably the introduction of prayer to the Holy Spirit. She notes that these cases "are explicable by close attention to the intent and deeper meaning of the Scriptures, and by reference to the overall Christian story that finds its fulfillment in Jesus" (148).

72. Colossians and 2 Thessalonians are often considered to have been written by someone other than Paul and thus to reflect a somewhat later period of first-century Christianity.

73. K. K. Yeo insightfully remarks on this passage:
The word "received" (*parelabete*) has a technical meaning and refers to a body of tradition (1 Cor. 11:23; 15:1, 3; Phil. 4:9; 1 Thess. 2:13; 4:1). Paul did not simply create his gospel out of whole cloth, he received the gospel from the risen Lord and passed it to the Galatians as something he had received—as tradition. His reception of the gospel could be described as the *apokalypsis* (revelation) of God, so that any turning away from that gospel would be a rejection of God's call ([Gal.] 1:6) and a fall from grace ([Gal.] 1:6; 5:4). The word "tradition" does not mean human creation. As Paul had experienced it the apocalyptic intrusiveness of the Christ event was not a human creation. Similarly, the Torah, though received as a revelatory act from God through Moses, was in Paul's day guarded as sacred tradition and not as a human creation. (*Musing with Confucius and Paul*, 139)

inventing.[74] He testifies that he did not learn the gospel from merely human sources but received it while still a Pharisaic Jew, through a personal revelation of Jesus Christ, a revelation that was later confirmed by the apostles Peter and James when Paul visited them in Jerusalem. As a Pharisee, Paul persecuted the nascent Church and was "advanced in Judaism beyond many of my own age among my people, so extremely zealous was I for the traditions of my fathers" (Gal. 1:14). This use of "traditions" obviously refers to Pharisaic tradition, but since Paul is writing to gentile believers, it may also connote the entirety of the Mosaic law.[75] In referring to "the traditions of my fathers," therefore, Paul may have in view not only negative but also positive realities, even though he holds that salvation comes through Christ rather than through the law. Elsewhere he makes clear that the Jewish people (his "fathers") are the inheritors of divine revelation and God's elect people.

Colossians 2:8 contains a critique of "tradition" similar to the one that we found in Jesus's encounter with Pharisees, but this time the tradition to be avoided is that which stems from pagan culture (or from a mingling of pagan culture and Judaism). Paul warns the Colossians, "See to it that no one makes a prey of you by philosophy and empty deceit, according to human tradition, according to the elemental spirits of the universe, and not according to Christ"

This does not gainsay Ratzinger's point that "Tradition is, of its nature, always interpretation: it exists, not independently, but as explication, as interpretation 'according to the Scriptures.' That holds true even of the proclamation of Jesus Christ himself: that it appeared as fulfillment and thus as interpretation of something, though as authoritative interpretation, of course" ("Question of the Concept of Tradition," 65).

74. As Josef Pieper observes, therefore:

Where in the world has someone actually raised the claim to be conveying a message of divine provenance that affects the whole of reality and the core of human existence—a message, let it be noted, that, insofar as one wishes to have a share of it and take part in it at all, is to be accepted simply as something to be received? The answer that most readily comes to mind is that it is the tradition of Christian doctrine that raises precisely this claim. In fact, Christianity understands itself already by virtue of its mission as being called upon to preserve a divine message that had at one time been cast into history from falling into oblivion or from admixture with alien sources and to hand down that message as a holy tradition in an orderly "succession." ("Tradition," 277; cf. 270)

Pieper recognizes the complexity of this "handing down": "The *tradita* likewise call for unceasing attempts at interpretation and reformulation if they are actually to reach the current generation" (277; cf. 244–47).

75. See Witherington, *Grace in Galatia*, 104:

The phrase "the traditions of the fathers" has been taken by Dunn and others to refer to the oral *halakah* which was an extrapolation beyond the Mosaic Law though based on it, not a reference to the Mosaic Law itself. It would then be similar to the phrase found in Mark 7:5 "the tradition of the elders." It must, however, be remembered that Paul is writing in this letter primarily if not almost exclusively to Gentiles. The phrase "ancestral traditions" to them would have surely connoted the Mosaic Law, and perhaps also any oral extrapolations, but in any case would not have excluded the Law itself.

(Col. 2:8).[76] The wisdom of such human tradition is an illusion, an "empty deceit" that entraps those who accept it. The opposite of such human tradition is "Christ." For Paul, the term "Christ" here contains within it a plethora of doctrines and practices. Doctrinally speaking, Christ "is the head of all rule and authority" (Col. 2:10). Christ, although a man, possesses the fullness of divine life in a unique manner: "For in him the whole fulness of deity dwells bodily" (Col. 2:9). This doctrinal claim is certainly capable of being elaborated or developed in a number of ways, but there are also obviously ways in which one could interpret it that would evacuate it of the meaning that Paul gives it, for example, if one made the claim that the "whole fulness of deity" was not in fact embodied in Christ.[77]

Thus Colossians 2 sets up a doctrinal claim—"in him the whole fulness of deity dwells bodily"—against a merely "human tradition." The tradition that comes from God instructs us doctrinally about Christ. This instruction about Christ is related to, but distinct from, its extension in practices. With regard to the latter, Paul notes that "in him also you were circumcised with a circumcision made without hands, by putting off the body of flesh in the circumcision of Christ; and you were buried with him in baptism, in which you were also raised with him through faith in the working of God, who raised him from the dead" (Col. 2:11–12). For Colossians, therefore, the tradition that comes from God, as opposed to a merely "human tradition," teaches that baptism incorporates the believer into Christ in a manner parallel to the way in which circumcision incorporated the people of Israel. Faith in God's saving deeds and saving power is also mentioned as necessary for incorporation into Christ, as is Christ's resurrection from the dead (which presumes that Christ was raised from bodily death to a glorified bodily life, so that his

76. N. T. Wright comments, "'Human tradition,' a phrase picked up in 2:22, recalls the polemic of both Isaiah (29:13) and Jesus (Mark 7:5ff.) against the transformation of true, living religion into a set of ideas and rules handed on at a purely human level. This is not to deny that there is a proper use of 'tradition' within Christianity, when Christ himself works by his Spirit to bring his truth to a new generation through the witness of the church. What Paul has in mind is undoubtedly the traditions of the Rabbinic schools in which he had grown up" (*Epistles of Paul to the Colossians and to Philemon*, 101). Wright argues at length in favor of Pauline authorship of Colossians (21–34). For the opposite view, see M. MacDonald, *Colossians and Ephesians*, 6–15.

77. Rather than grounding Christology in Christ's words and deeds, Tilley argues that "christology always arises in disciples' imaginations. We start with Jesus as he is perceived and imagined on this earth. We start his story here even if we imagine or infer that it really began in heaven. If the 'binitarian' worship of Jesus is the community's recognizing in him the unique and profound agency of God in and through the movement God constituted as the Jesus-movement, and if this worship is quite early, then the pattern of christology charted above is also probably quite early" (*Disciples' Jesus*, 68). The references to "God" do little work in Tilley's formulation, since we can know only the products of the community's imagination.

body did not remain a corpse). Again, there are a variety of ways of developing this doctrinal content, but there are limits as well; one can easily imagine false developments. The divinely given alternative to the deceitful "human tradition" has doctrinal content that is not as malleable as Tilley's *Inventing Catholic Tradition* would have us suppose.[78]

In 2 Thessalonians we find two positive references to "tradition." The first reference is perhaps the most important for later Catholic Tradition. Paul states, "So then, brethren, stand firm and hold to the traditions which you were taught by us, either by word of mouth or by letter" (2 Thess. 2:15). It is evident first of all that these "traditions" have a strong doctrinal content (including doctrine about the practices appropriate to Christianity). Indeed, one of these doctrines has just been elucidated by Paul in this letter: the doctrine of Christ's second coming, which, says Paul, will be preceded by the coming of "the lawless one by the activity of Satan" (2 Thess. 2:9).[79] The coming of the antichrist, the "lawless one," reveals God's punishment for those who reject God and whom God condemns and abandons to their choice. Certainly there is room here for doctrinal elaboration, but again there will be a difference between abandoning Paul's claims about the antichrist and the second coming of Christ, on the one hand, and, on the other hand, developing them in accord with other testimony of Scripture. The content of the "traditions" delivered by Paul is deeply doctrinal—certainly (in Tilley's terms) a "what" and not just a "how." This extends to Paul's utter rejection of metaphysical dualism: the antichrist and the powers of evil cannot stand against Christ, but rather when

78. In *Disciples' Jesus*, Tilley argues that we should read such words as those found in Colossians 2 "as a score to be performed or a script to be enacted, rather than as a text to be read and interpreted" (76). Does not reading and interpretation, however, belong to performing and enacting any score or script? Tilley holds that the New Testament's central christological texts "do not first set patterns for belief, as some christologists seem to think, beliefs that Christians may accept, reject, modify, or develop. Rather, they set patterns for practice that Christians are to reenact to be part of the 'running performances' of discipleship—performances that take widely varying forms. Believing (having faith) is carried out by engaging in those practices, but beliefs are not the 'foundations' of practice, but shorthand guides abstracted from performance practice" (ibid.). It follows for Tilley that "christology is not to be rooted in systematic thought but in reconciling practice" (77). But the opposition here imagined between action/performance and intellectual endeavor is misleading. If intellectual work (including receptivity to Jesus's own words and deeds) does not ground practices/performances, then the latter are mere gestures, hardly human at all, to which almost any ideas can be correctly (but extrinsically) attached. Tilley's effort to suppress doctrines ends with practices that can have any meaning or no meaning. No wonder that Tilley cites with approval Wayne Meeks's suggestion that Jesus's first followers were fanatical mythologists: "We cannot ignore 'the exuberance of Jesus's followers that created in the first decades of the movement's existence, the wildest diversity of mythic portraits of Jesus'" (ibid., quoting Meeks, "Man from Heaven," 329).

79. On the "lawless one," see Johnson, *Writings of the New Testament*, 269.

the "lawless one" is revealed, "the Lord Jesus will slay him with the breath of his mouth and destroy him by his appearing and his coming" (2 Thess. 2:8).

It is also significant that Paul refers to two kinds of "traditions," both of which Paul communicates to the Thessalonians in accord with his mission as an apostle. These two kinds of traditions are those that Paul delivers "by word of mouth" and those that he delivers "by letter" (2 Thess. 2:15).[80] Looked at in this way, Tradition itself can be said to encompass Scripture, insofar as "the traditions which you were taught by us" include the teachings contained in Paul's letters (later recognized as Scripture). Second Thessalonians 2:15 can also appear to justify a distinction between scriptural traditions ("by letter") and nonscriptural traditions ("by word of mouth"), but we do not now possess a way of knowing what, if anything, the apostles taught orally that they did not teach in their writings. Even so, Paul's words demonstrate that there is an apostolic communication that belongs to the Church as a living subject and that in some way differs from Scripture, without denying the unity of divine revelation.[81] What Paul communicates "by word of mouth" is not, by his own testimony, anything less than the "gospel" (2 Thess. 2:14) and "the word of the Lord" (2 Thess. 3:1).[82]

---

80. See Fee, *First and Second Letters to the Thessalonians*. Fee's commentary employs Today's New International Version, which substitutes the word "teachings" for "traditions." Fee corrects this and comments, "The use of the word 'traditions' here, which has a long history in the Judaism in which Paul was raised, is his way of indicating that his teaching at the same time belongs to the much larger community of faith, of which they themselves have now become a part. Thus, by turning aside from his prior teaching, the Thessalonians have also turned aside from the common teaching of the early believers. But his concern at this point is with *his* teaching, which they are now disregarding" (305). Fee argues that "by letter" refers to the letter that we possess as 1 Thessalonians.

81. See Thiel, *Senses of Tradition*, 13–22, with discussion of the Council of Trent's "Decretum primum" (April 8, 1546) about the gospel proclaimed by Jesus Christ and handed on "in written books and in unwritten traditions which were received by the apostles from the mouth of Christ himself, or else have come down to us, handed on as it were from the apostles themselves at the inspiration of the Holy Spirit" ("Decretum primum," 663; cf. Ratzinger, "Question of the Concept of Tradition," 67–89). On the Church as a living subject (because constituted sacramentally as the body of Christ), in connection with the idea of "tradition," see Ratzinger, "Spiritual Basis and Ecclesial Identity of Theology," 52–55. Drawing upon Romans, Galatians, and 1 Corinthians, Ratzinger states that "according to Paul, the Church is in no wise a separate subject endowed with its own subsistence. The new subject is much rather 'Christ' himself, and the Church is nothing but the space of this new unitary subject, which is, therefore, much more than mere social interaction" (54). Turning to the Gospel of John, Ratzinger observes that "the Spirit effects a space of listening and remembering, a 'we,' which in the Johannine writings defines the Church as the locus of knowledge. Understanding can take place only within this 'we' constituted by participation in the origin" (55).

82. Ratzinger's comments are helpful for distinguishing between invention and interpretation:
What is true of the message of Christ, that it occurs in no other way but that of interpretation, is most certainly true of apostolic proclamation and still more so of the proclamation

In 2 Thessalonians, Paul also invokes "tradition" in order to delineate the boundaries of the Christian community. He states, "Now we command you, brethren, in the name of our Lord Jesus Christ, that you keep away from any brother who is living in idleness and not in accord with the tradition that you received from us" (2 Thess. 3:6). What is this "tradition"? Here it seems to be Paul's own personal example. When he was with the Thessalonians, he reminds them, he worked for his living rather than accepting food from others. Those who wish to live a Christian life cannot suppose that it is good to live in an unnecessary dependency upon the work of others. Paul urges that the Thessalonians find "in our [Paul's] conduct an example to imitate" (2 Thess. 3:9). Tradition as Paul conceives of it thus includes not only doctrines but also practices such as hard work. Yet here again we can perceive doctrinal stability: it would not be possible for Catholic Tradition, in its development, to substitute laziness for the hard work that Paul advocates. With regard to the lazy person, Paul commands that the community not associate with him, although Paul adds that they should "not look on him as an enemy, but warn him as a brother" (2 Thess. 3:15). He remains a "brother" in Christ even when, by turning away from "the tradition" that the Thessalonians "received" from Paul, he has consciously or unconsciously separated himself from the Christian community and its identifying practices.

A final place that Paul employs παράδοσις is in 1 Corinthians 11:2, where he tells the Corinthians, "I commend you because you remember me in everything and maintain the traditions even as I have delivered them to you."[83] These "traditions" surely include the practice of the Lord's Supper that he describes in 1 Corinthians 10–11. This practice requires the Corinthians not to eat food sacrificed to demons (1 Cor. 10:20–21) and to avoid eating the Lord's Supper

---

of the Church: as "tradition," it too ultimately has to remain interpretation "according to the Scriptures," to be aware of owing something to Scripture and being closely linked to Scripture. True, it too is not interpretation in the sense of mere exegetical interpretation, but in the spiritual authority of the Lord that is implemented in the whole of the Church's existence, in her faith, her life, and her worship. Yet it does remain, far more than the Christ-event that founded the Church, interpretation, linked with what has happened and what has been spoken. In this is expressed its connection with the concrete activity of God in this history and its historical uniqueness: the ἐφάπαξ, the "once only" aspect, which is just as essential to the reality of Christian revelation as the "forever." ("Question of the Concept of Tradition," 65)

83. Anthony C. Thiselton comments, "In his study of tradition and tradition terminology [K.] Wegenast argues that this epistle provides the first setting within which the notion of a received and transmitted doctrine and practice arose (esp. in relation to 11:23 and 15:3–5). This is plausible in the light of the Corinthian tendency to regard their own thought and practice as a unilateral affair (cf. 1:3; 14:36; and elsewhere)" (First Epistle to the Corinthians, 810–11). See also Wegenast, Das Verständnis der Tradition; Fitzmyer, First Corinthians, 408–9.

unworthily (1 Cor. 11:27–30). The Lord's Supper is not a practice that should privilege the wealthy, nor is it merely another meal. In Paul's account of this practice, we find significant doctrinal content about what the Lord's Supper is. Indeed, what the Lord's Supper is determines how we should practice it.[84] Paul explains, "The cup of blessing which we bless, is it not a participation in the blood of Christ? The bread which we break, is it not a participation in the body of Christ?" (1 Cor. 10:16). Because the cup and bread are a participation (κοινωνία) in Christ, our reception of the cup and bread truly unites us: "We who are many are one body, for we all partake of the one bread" (1 Cor. 10:17). Paul knows what the Lord's Supper is because of Jesus's own words and deeds. As Paul says, "For I received from the Lord what I also delivered to you, that the Lord Jesus on the night when he was betrayed took bread, and when he had given thanks, he broke it, and said, 'This is my body which is for you. Do this in remembrance of me.' In the same way also the cup, after supper, saying, 'This cup is the new covenant in my blood'" (1 Cor. 11:23–25). The "traditions" also include practices whose source is not directly attributed to Christ, including Paul's explanation in 1 Corinthians 11:3–16 about why women should not pray with their heads uncovered. In light of other biblical texts, the Church has judged that this practice has its meaning within a particular cultural context rather than being rooted in an enduring doctrine about women in relation to men, even if 1 Corinthians 11:3–16 does possess doctrinal import in other ways.[85]

At various points in his letters (and in those attributed to him) Paul summarizes the doctrinal content that he seeks to hand on to his congregations, and in this way too, Paul gives us a sense of what Tradition is. As we noted in the previous chapter, Paul says to the Corinthians, "Now I remind you, brethren, in what terms I preached to you the gospel, which you received, in which

84. From the opposite perspective, Tilley argues that practices determine the meaning of the Lord's Supper. Thus he argues that in the new context created by the turning of the altar after Vatican II, the doctrine of transubstantiation "may even acquire a new meaning hardly connected to the traditional sense, for example, that transubstantiation refers to the transformation of the worshiping assembly into the body of Christ in and through reception of the Eucharist. The point is that once the term *transubstantiation* is no longer connected with the ritual as traditionally performed, the meaning of the term becomes indeterminate" (*Inventing Catholic Tradition*, 71–72).

85. Indebted to Dale Martin, Aline Rousselle, and others, Anthony Thiselton points out that the Roman cultural context is crucial for understanding 1 Cor. 11:3–16. But he also draws upon Judith Gundry-Volf, Jerome Murphy-O'Connor, OP, Morna Hooker, and others to persuasively sketch the ongoing theological value of this passage. See Thiselton, *First Epistle to the Corinthians*, 800–809. See also Hays, *First Corinthians*, 181–91. Hays is particularly interested in how the Church might reinterpret 1 Cor. 11:3–16 in light of the full scope of Scripture and doctrinal tradition. See also the helpful discussion in Humphrey, *Scripture and Tradition*, 149–50.

you stand, by which you are saved, if you hold it fast—unless you believed in vain. For I delivered to you as of first importance what I also received" (1 Cor. 15:1–3). This gospel is not something that Paul made up but rather something that he received (in his case by means of God's revelation). The central content of this gospel is something that happened in Jerusalem—namely, Christ's death and resurrection.

Paul particularly wishes to underscore Christ's resurrection from the dead. Some of the Corinthians, by denying that there will be a resurrection of the dead, have instituted a rather radical change of doctrine. Paul lets them know that the handing on of divine revelation does not permit of such doctrinal malleability. As Paul says, "Now if Christ is preached as raised from the dead, how can some of you say that there is no resurrection of the dead? But if there is no resurrection of the dead, then Christ has not been raised; if Christ has not been raised, then our preaching is in vain and your faith is in vain" (1 Cor. 15:12–14).

Everything hinges, in other words, on the content of what Paul "delivered" to the Corinthians "as of first importance." If that content (the "what," in Tilley's phrase) is not true, then Paul's "preaching is in vain." Is it permissible to reinterpret the content of Christ's resurrection in such a way that it no longer matters whether the phrase refers to the dead Jesus being given life in the flesh again—and not just life but glorified life? Paul emphasizes that no reinterpretation of this kind will do: either the dead Jesus is now alive again in the flesh or Paul's entire mission is a blasphemous sham. Paul observes, "If Christ has not been raised, . . . we are even found to be misrepresenting God, because we testified of God that he raised Christ, whom he did not raise if it is true that the dead are not raised" (1 Cor. 15:15). It follows that the kind of malleability of doctrine that Tilley advocates in the name of "Catholic tradition" will not work in the case of Christ's resurrection.[86]

86. Affirming Christ's resurrection, Tilley argues at length against both skeptics and literalistic believers:

> The root problem is that people think of the resurrection as either a historical event or not a historical event. They think it one in a series of one damn thing after another—arrest, trial, crucifixion, resurrection. This thinking misleads them. The agents who arrested, tried, and crucified Jesus of Nazareth were human. The agent who raised him up was divine. If they're all "events," they're not of the same kind. The agents are as different as divine nature is different from human nature. . . . The question is not the event, but the agent. Were these events sustained by God or illusions in the minds of the witnesses? Could they be both? (Remember St. Joan)." (*Disciples' Jesus*, 272, 275)

Contrary to the opinion of Tilley, however, at the level of event we cannot exclude the question of what happened to Jesus's corpse. In raising the dead Jesus, God could not simply have left Jesus's corpse as a corpse. At this level, the events "sustained by God" must be something much more than "illusions in the minds of the witnesses." See also Haight, *Jesus, Symbol of God.*

Paul's statements elsewhere further confirm the doctrinal character of Tradition. Consider, for instance, his remark to the Romans that they should avoid "those who create dissensions and difficulties [σκάνδαλα], in opposition to the doctrine [διδαχή] which you have been taught" (Rom. 16:17). What is the "doctrine" that Paul has in view? It is "the gospel of God which he [God] promised beforehand through his prophets in the holy scriptures" (Rom. 1:1–2). The doctrine is God's revelation, God's word, not an invention of Paul's. Paul, of course, emphasizes certain things in his communication of this revelation, and Paul's formulations may bear clarification and development.[87] But this development would be false if it undermined his central teachings about Jesus Christ, grace, faith, and so forth. There is a real doctrinal content—a "what"—in Paul's "gospel and the preaching of Jesus Christ, according to the revelation of the mystery which was kept secret for long ages but is now disclosed and through the prophetic writings is made known to all nations" (Rom. 16:25–26). Again, the content of the gospel is not something that Paul or any merely human authority vouches for or invents. Some of the Corinthians imagine themselves to be followers of a particular apostle, but Paul rebukes them for thereby "behaving like ordinary men" (1 Cor. 3:3). The apostles, he explains, are merely servants of God who have received a mission to proclaim the truth of Jesus Christ crucified and risen: "So neither he who plants nor he who waters is anything, but only God who gives the growth" (1 Cor. 3:7).

In 2 Timothy, Paul's characteristic outlook with regard to tradition is extended to the successors of the apostles. In view of Timothy's pastoral office, Paul exhorts him, "Follow the pattern of the sound words which you have heard from me, in the faith and love which are in Christ Jesus; guard the truth that has been entrusted to you by the Holy Spirit who dwells within us" (2 Tim. 1:13–14). "Sound words" or "truth" obviously have doctrinal content—as well as practical import—that is not endlessly revisable. Likewise, Paul encourages Timothy to make provision for handing on this truth in the Church, just as the apostles handed on what they received from Jesus: "what you have heard from me before many witnesses[,] entrust to faithful men who will be able to teach others also" (2 Tim. 2:2). As D. H. Williams comments on 2 Timothy 1:13–14, for Paul "not only is there not a polarization between life in the Spirit and a concretized tradition, but both the content

---

87. Thus, in his *Essay on the Development of Christian Doctrine*, J. Newman states with respect to the history of a belief, "In time it enters upon strange territory; points of controversy alter their bearing; parties rise and fall around it; dangers and hopes appear in new relations; and old principles reappear under new forms. It changes with them in order to remain the same. In a higher world it is otherwise, but here below to live is to change, and to be perfect is to have changed often" (40). For discussion see McCarren, "Development of Doctrine," 121.

and the transmission of the Jesus tradition was superintended by the Holy Spirit."[88] The ecclesial transmission of a determinate content about Jesus and salvation is possible, according to 2 Timothy, because of "the Holy Spirit who dwells within us."

Conclusion: Revelation and Tradition

Let me return to *Dei Verbum*'s description of Tradition cited at the outset of this chapter: "Tradition transmits in its entirety the word of God which has been entrusted to the apostles by Christ the Lord and the Holy Spirit. It transmits it to the successors of the apostles so that, enlightened by the Spirit of truth, they may faithfully preserve, expound and spread it abroad by their preaching."[89] On this view, Tradition involves two aspects: an enduring doctrinal and moral content ("the word of God") and the mediation of divine revelation ("entrusted to the apostles by Christ the Lord and the Holy Spirit") rather than merely of human invention. Thus Jesus warns against displacing the "commandment of God" by means of a human "tradition" (Matt. 15:3), while Paul urges the Corinthians to "maintain the traditions even as I have delivered them to you" (1 Cor. 11:2). In the latter, positive meaning, "tradition" signifies divine revelation as handed on in the Church. Paul is engaged in just such a process of handing on, not least in his urgent reminder to the Corinthians: "I would remind you . . . in what terms I preached to you the gospel, which you received, in which you stand, by which you are saved. . . . For I delivered to you as of first importance what I also received" (1 Cor. 15:1–3).

What is at issue in Tradition, then, is the inbreaking of divine revelation, as opposed to "human tradition" or "philosophy and empty deceit" (Col. 2:8) that turn us away from God. This divine revelation includes the Torah (the "commandment of God") and the gospel, which are related to each other in Jesus, the Messiah of Israel. Jesus intends for his Church to proclaim the content of the gospel, of divine revelation. This proclamation will not always be well received: "They will lay their hands on you and persecute you, delivering you up to the synagogues and prisons, and you will be brought before kings and governors for my name's sake. This will be a time for you to bear testimony" (Luke 21:12–13).

As becomes clear when the risen Jesus opens his apostles' "minds to understand the scriptures" (Luke 24:45), the content of divine revelation cannot be

88. Williams, *Retrieving the Tradition and Renewing Evangelicalism*, 58.
89. *Dei Verbum*, §9, 755.

handed down, even in scriptural form, without being interpreted by the Church under the guidance of Christ and the Spirit. Tradition is necessary for the handing on of the content of divine revelation. In the Gospel of John—among the latest biblical texts—we find Jesus's promise to sustain this Tradition by the Holy Spirit (John 16:13).

Tilley agrees that tradition is necessary, but he eviscerates both it and divine revelation of the power to communicate enduring truth. As we have seen, Tilley advocates the kind of ever-changing human "tradition" that Jesus and Paul, in the New Testament, are at pains to reject. Tilley's inability adequately to identify God as the active and authoritative source of the gospel's doctrinal and moral teachings is one of the factors that produce his misreading of Catholic Tradition. He reduces Catholic Tradition to humanly constructed, timebound claims about the community and its ever-changing "authenticity," to the exclusion of divinely revealed truths about the Triune God, Jesus Christ, creation, the moral law, and so on.[90]

At various points in his book, however, Tilley argues that his account of tradition simply maps what has actually been the case in history. On this view, no matter what Scripture or Platonizing theologians might have to say about it in the abstract, Christianity in the concrete continually morphs into something quite different from its earlier incarnations. As an example, Tilley notes that in the *Syllabus of Errors* that accompanies Pope Pius IX's encyclical *Quanta Cura* (1864), Pius IX condemns as erroneous the proposition that "every man is free to embrace and profess that religion which, guided by the light of reason, he shall consider true." Tilley pairs this text with a passage from the Second Vatican Council's Declaration on Religious Freedom, *Dignitatis Humanae* (1965): "The human person has a right to religious freedom. . . . In matters religious no one is to be forced to act in a manner contrary to his own beliefs. Nor is anyone to be restrained from acting in accordance with his own beliefs, whether privately or publicly."[91] For Tilley, it is obvious that this pairing reveals a "patent contradiction."[92] He observes that this contradiction was embodied in the life of John Courtney Murray, who was silenced by the Church in 1955 for teaching what *Dignitatis Humanae*, under Murray's guidance, taught a decade later. Tilley concludes that, despite the efforts of a few tendentious and "tortuous accounts" that "have attempted to show an alleged continuity between these two statements," it remains the case that "no convincing theory of development has accounted for the 'course of development' that allows a

90. For further discussion of this problem, see also Elders, "Immutability of the Sense of Dogmas and Philosophical Theories."
91. See Tilley, *Inventing Catholic Tradition*, 116.
92. Ibid.

clear contradiction in 1965 of what the highest magisterial authority in the
Church taught in 1864."[93]

But why, given Tilley's concern for contextualized truth in other cases, is
Tilley so adamant that he has found an absolute contradiction ("reversals,
fractures") of previously definitive doctrine?[94] At the very least, he has not
shown that we obviously have a "patent contradiction" rather than, as Murray himself thought, a "development of doctrine." The development, indeed,
occurred through a rather "tortuous" process; but, after all, development is
not repetition or even (necessarily) a simple logical extension. Instead doctrinal development genuinely goes beyond earlier insights—for example, by
asking and answering new questions while retaining previous *definitive* doctrine on the subject and correcting *nondefinitive* teaching. To account for the
development, then, may well require complex reasoning! An adamant denial
of doctrinal development with respect to the duties of persons and the state
vis-à-vis divine revelation would require more than showing that the Church's
view of "religious freedom" changed rapidly in the mid-twentieth century. In
this light, let me now turn to a fuller treatment of the topic of development
of doctrine in the Church's mediation of divine revelation.

93. Ibid., 117.
94. Ibid., 119–20.

S I X

Development

In Jesus Christ, God "has made known to us in all wisdom and insight the mystery of his will, according to his purpose which he set forth in Christ as a plan for the fulness of time, to unite all things in him, things in heaven and things on earth" (Eph. 1:9–10). During his public ministry in Judea and Galilee, Jesus preached to large crowds and also taught his disciples privately. Those who heard him "were astonished at his teaching, for he taught them as one who had authority, and not as the scribes" (Mark 1:22). Jesus died for our sins and rose from the dead, and after his resurrection he spoke to his disciples and "opened their minds to understand the scriptures" (Luke 24:45).

It might seem, then, that there is no need for development of doctrine. After all, it would appear that Jesus had plenty of opportunity to teach everything that we need to know for salvation. If so, then the Church's task would be simply to hand on Jesus's teachings until his glorious return. Even Jesus's statement to his disciples, "I have yet many things to say to you, but you cannot bear them now," and his corresponding promise, "When the Spirit of truth comes, he will guide you into all the truth" (John 16:12–13), can be read as describing not a development of doctrine but instead further teachings about the future, since Jesus tells the disciples, "He [the Holy Spirit] will declare to you the things that are to come" (John 16:13).[1]

---

1. See Brown, *Gospel according to John*, 715–16. Brown's conclusion, however, is that "the declaration of the things to come consists in interpreting in relation to each coming generation the contemporary significance of what Jesus has said and done. The best Christian preparation for what is coming to pass is not an exact foreknowledge of the future but a deep understanding

In the writings that became the New Testament, however, we find ample evidence of development of doctrine. This is not only the case when the Gospel writers interpret their source material in diverse ways, or when Paul applies to a situation in one of his churches the teachings that he has received. The book of Acts shows the necessity of doctrinal development when it depicts the Church's process of discernment with respect to whether gentiles should observe the Mosaic law. The apostles and elders "gathered together" (Acts 15:6) to address this issue, and the Holy Spirit enabled the Church to make a judgment of truth—"it has seemed good to the Holy Spirit and to us" (Acts 15:28)—when faced with competing interpretations of divine revelation.

Over the centuries, doctrinal development has occurred with regard to the divinity of the Son and of the Holy Spirit, the humanity and divinity of Jesus Christ, the privileges of Mary, the efficacy of grace, the number and nature of the sacraments, and so on. The context of this development has often been one of intense disagreement and division. Yet due to the necessity of interpretation, we cannot have divine revelation without doctrinal development.[2] Even the canon of Scripture developed in the context of polemics between gnostic and Catholic Christians. The real alternative to doctrinal development is not the "pure gospel" but rather is doctrinal corruption.[3]

In this chapter, therefore, I examine divine revelation and development of doctrine by means of three steps. First, I explore what *Dei Verbum* says about

---

of what Jesus means for one's own time. . . . Verse 14 reinforces the impression that the Paraclete brings no new revelation because he receives from Jesus what he is to declare to the disciples" (716).

2. See, for example, Billings, *Word of God for the People of God*, 16–17, 47–53. As Billings remarks, "From a purely exegetical perspective, there are arguments for and against the Nicene tradition. But there is no neutral way to establish Nicene Christianity as the only way to read the biblical texts. . . . When interpreting passages such as Philippians 2:9–11, where Jesus Christ appears to receive adoration, all readers inhabit a Nicene or non-Nicene tradition of reading Scripture, whether they recognize it or not. All Christians, in fact, read the Bible from within particular traditions. The question is, what traditions are operative?" (49). Billings notes that he grew up in a Baptist church that understood itself to be "simply biblical" but that in fact "had a shared theology" and "doctrinal traditions" (ibid.).

3. John W. O'Malley, SJ, suggests that concern for doctrinal continuity is largely a Tridentine phenomenon:

> In reaction to the Reformers' accusation that the church had early on so completely broken with the Gospel that its subsequent history was a distortion of it, Catholic apologists rushed to assert the church's unbroken continuity with the apostolic era. Trent seconded this assertion. No previous council had ever so often and so explicitly insisted on its teaching's continuity with the authentic Christian past. Trent thus helped to develop the Catholic mind-set reluctant to admit change in the course of church history, a mind-set that more fully crystallized a little later with works like Cardinal Cesare Baronio's *Ecclesiastical Annals*. (*Trent*, 273–74)

In fact, however, this "mind-set" of insistence on "continuity with the authentic Christian past" is fully on display throughout the patristic and medieval periods, and for good reason.

the doctrinal development that occurs in the transmission of divine revelation, and I compare *Dei Verbum*'s remarks with John Henry Newman's seminal *An Essay on the Development of Christian Doctrine*.[4] Second, I present an example of how thinking about doctrinal development can fail theologically—namely, John T. Noonan's *A Church That Can and Cannot Change*. Given Noonan's notion of doctrinal development, any significant shift in the Church's teaching (such as Newman found in the transition from the pre-Nicene to the Nicene period) would be a rupture or corruption rather than a true development.[5] Third, I turn to recent scholarship on the Nicene period for two approaches to doctrinal development, by Lewis Ayres and Khaled Anatolios respectively. Their work on the enduring achievements of the Nicene period makes clear why the path followed by Noonan is inadequate, and they point the way forward to a better perspective.

Dei Verbum and John Henry Newman

Dei Verbum teaches that God, having revealed himself fully in Christ Jesus, ensured that "the things he had once revealed for the salvation of all peoples should remain in their entirety, throughout the ages, and be transmitted to all generations."[6] Christ taught his disciples by word and deed and bestowed the Holy Spirit, and the apostles "handed on, by the spoken word of their preaching, by the example they gave, by the institutions they established, what they themselves had received—whether from the lips of Christ, from his way of life and his works, or whether they had learned it at the prompting of the Holy Spirit."[7] Along with their oral teaching and their organization of the churches, certain apostles and other men of the apostolic period wrote the various texts that compose the New Testament. The apostles also appointed their successors by the laying on of hands. As *Dei Verbum* states, "In this way the Church, in her doctrine, life and worship, perpetuates

---

4. See Gerald H. McCarren's view that "the compability between Newman's *Essay* and the understanding of doctrinal development espoused by the Second Vatican Council is conspicuous" ("Development of Doctrine," 118).

5. Brian E. Daley, SJ, notes that Newman's mature approach to doctrinal development is similar to that of the seventeenth-century Catholic scholar Dionysius Petavius (Denys Pétau), who held that "many early Christian conceptions of God, Christ and human salvation were imprecise and even erroneous by later standards, and that a gradual development of orthodox doctrine, as it would eventually be normative for the whole Church, was only possible through the guidance of the Holy Spirit and the leadership of the Church's hierarchical *magisterium*" ("Church Fathers," 32–33).

6. *Dei Verbum*, §7, 753.

7. Ibid.

and transmits to every generation all that she herself is, and all that she believes."[8]

This integral transmission of the "single sacred deposit of the word of God" allows for development of doctrine.[9] The relationship of Scripture and Tradition is important in this regard, since both flow from the self-revealing God. *Dei Verbum* observes, "Sacred Scripture is the speech of God as it is put down in writing under the breath of the Holy Spirit. And Tradition transmits in its entirety the word of God which has been entrusted to the apostles by Christ the Lord and the Holy Spirit. It transmits it to the successors of the apostles so that, enlightened by the Spirit of truth, they may faithfully preserve, expound and spread it abroad by their preaching."[10] Tradition, then, includes a dynamic element, under the guidance of the Holy Spirit, that enables the bishops both to "preserve" and to "expound" the word of God in each generation. *Dei Verbum* explains that this dynamic element of Tradition enables the Church to canonize the books of Scripture, to understand and actualize Scripture more "thoroughly" (*penitius*), and to be led by the Holy Spirit "to the full truth."[11] Although divine revelation is fully given in Christ, "God, who spoke in the past, continues to converse with the spouse of his beloved Son."[12] As a result, doctrine develops in the Church. *Dei Verbum* states that apostolic Tradition "makes progress [*proficit*] in the Church, with the help of the Holy Spirit. There is a growth in insight into the realities and words that are being passed on."[13] This progress

8. Ibid., §8, 754.

9. Ibid., §10, 755.

10. Ibid., §9, 755. Gregory Baum contrasts revelation as "divine teaching" with revelation as "divine self-disclosure," but the two are clearly united both in Scripture (as is made particularly evident in Jesus Christ) and in *Dei Verbum*. See Baum, "Vatican II's Constitution on Revelation."

11. *Dei Verbum*, §8, 754–55. Thus Yves Congar cautions against supposing that "the literal text of the holy Scriptures, as such and by itself," is "sufficient to produce truth and salvation" (*Meaning of Tradition*, 95). Congar explains the necessity of reading Scripture in the Church (guided by Tradition) in an important passage:

> One of the greatest advantages of reading the holy Scriptures in the Church is the synthesis obtained. The more one studies the Fathers and learns about the liturgy, the more one admires their skill in putting the scriptural texts together, not from a merely literary point of view, as the exegetes do—which is very valuable in its own sphere—but going beyond the literal sense, sometimes even in a way that is quite disconcerting from an exegetical point of view, and relating these texts to the inner *reality* underlying the entire Scriptures, on a final analysis, the relationship of Covenant, the Christian mystery. The fact is that the Fathers and the liturgy are, above all, witnesses of the synthesis and meaning of Christian reality, which is also the supreme realm of tradition. (96–97)

12. *Dei Verbum*, §8, 755. For emphasis on this dialogic dimension, see C. Collins, *Word Made Love*.

13. *Dei Verbum*, §8, 754. For background and discussion, see Joseph Ratzinger's commentary on chap. 2 of *Dei Verbum*, "The Transmission of Divine Revelation." With regard to development

and growth occur due to the combination of study, intimate understanding of spiritual realities, and magisterial teaching.

The Church's growth in understanding will not cease until the eschaton, given the inexhaustible riches of God's word. None of this negates the fact that the Church, as we have seen, "perpetuates and transmits to every generation all that she herself is, and all that she believes." Under the guidance of the Holy Spirit, the development of doctrine does not undermine the unity of faith across the generations or introduce a new revelation. *Dei Verbum* remarks that the "most intimate truth which this revelation gives us about God and the salvation of man shines forth in Christ, who is himself both the mediator and the sum total of revelation."[14]

This portrait of the development of doctrine has numerous roots, but the most influential is John Henry Newman's *An Essay on the Development of*

---

of doctrine, Ratzinger explains, "The whole spiritual experience of the Church, its believing, praying and loving intercourse with the Lord and his word, causes our understanding of the original truth to grow and in the today of faith extracts anew from the yesterday of its historical origin what was meant for all time and yet can be understood only in the changing ages and in the particular way of each" (186). He goes on to describe the impact of an increased sense of the historical embeddedness of doctrine:

> The rejection of the suggestion to include again Vincent of Lérins's well-known text, more or less canonized by two councils, is again a step beyond Trent and Vatican I. . . . It is not that Vatican II is taking back what was intended in those quotations: the rejection of a modernistic evolutionism, an affirmation of the definitive character of the revelation of Christ and the apostolic tradition, to which the Church has nothing to add, but which is its yardstick. . . . This kind of new orientation simply expresses our deeper knowledge of the problem of historical understanding, which is no longer adequately expressed by the simple ideas of a given fact and its explanation, because the explanation, as the process of understanding, cannot be clearly separated from what is being understood. This interdependence of the two, which does not remove the ultimate basic difference between assimilation and what is assimilated, even if they can no longer be strictly isolated, is well expressed by the dialectic juxtaposition of the two clauses *Traditio proficit* and *crescit perceptio*. (187–88)

See also Lash, *Change in Focus*, 23, for the view that *Dei Verbum*'s affirmation of doctrinal development should be read in the context of the response to neo-scholasticism rather than as affirming an evolutionary or progressive view of the Church's growth in wisdom. From a Lutheran perspective, George Lindbeck criticizes this section of *Dei Verbum*: "Doctrinal development is not a matter of continuous and cumulative growth or explicitation of the Church's knowledge of revelation" ("Problem of Doctrinal Development," 66, quoted in Lash, *Change in Focus*, 28). But I think that doctrinal development does indeed involve progress in understanding, even though it is obvious that doctrinal development does not mean that particular doctrines, once formulated by the Church, are necessarily well understood in later centuries.

14. *Dei Verbum*, §2, 751. Lash considers that this description of Christ as "the sum total of revelation" indicates "how far the council had moved from that pre-conciliar scholastic theology which had assumed that revelation consisted in sets of propositions" (*Change in Focus*, 14).

Christian Doctrine, first published in 1845 at the time of his entrance into the Catholic Church.[15] Ian Ker warns against reading this work in an overly systematic fashion: Newman's central purpose is to evoke historical patterns rather than to offer logical proofs.[16] Newman argues first that, unless there is positive proof to the contrary, it is reasonable to assume that "the Christianity of the second, fourth, seventh, twelfth, sixteenth, and intermediate centuries is in its substance the very religion which Christ and His Apostles taught in the first," even if Christianity has also endured "modifications for good or for evil."[17] Citing the low-church Anglican theologian William Chillingworth (1602–1644) as a representative of the opposite view, Newman grants that "there are in fact certain apparent variations in its [historical Christianity's] teaching, which have to be explained," and he admits that scholars such as Chillingworth "have raised a real difficulty."[18] If historical Christianity does not teach a consistent message, then we cannot rely on the Church but instead must rely on our individual interpretation of Scripture to determine "what the revelation of God is, or rather if in fact there is, or has been, any revelation at all."[19] Newman does not think that he can *prove* that Christianity has taught a consistent message, but he does think that he can show historically the plausibility of this affirmation.

As an example of the difficulty, Newman takes up the doctrine of the Trinity. The pre-Nicene creeds do not explicitly affirm this doctrine, although they do mention the Father, Son, and Holy Spirit. When one turns to the greatest theologians of the pre-Nicene period—here Newman lists Ignatius of Antioch, Justin Martyr, Irenaeus, Hippolytus, Cyprian, Gregory Thaumaturgus, Dionysius of Alexandria, Methodius, Athenagoras, Clement, Tertullian, Origen, and Eusebius—the picture does not look good. Newman points out that in terms of their explicit statements, "St. Ignatius may be considered as a Patripassian, St. Justin arianizes, and St. Hippolytus is a Photinian"; while Tertullian speaks of a temporal generation of the Son, Origen subordinates the

---

15. I will quote from the revised edition, which Newman prepared in 1878. For the original edition, see Newman, *An Essay on the Development of Christian Doctrine* (1845).

16. Ker, foreword to Newman, *Essay on the Development of Christian Doctrine*, xxi. See also Newman, *Grammar of Assent*, chaps. 7–8, for the inadequacy of logical deduction in the formation and defense of Christian truth. For various assessments of and engagements with Newman's theory, see O. Chadwick, *From Bossuet to Newman*; Nichols, *From Newman to Congar*; Lash, *Newman on Development*.

17. Newman, *Essay on the Development of Christian Doctrine*, 5.

18. Ibid., 7, 9. Newman states, "I concede to the opponents of historical Christianity, that there are to be found, during the 1800 years through which it has lasted, certain apparent inconsistencies and alterations in its doctrine and its worship, such as irresistibly to attract the attention of all who inquire into it" (9).

19. Ibid., 9.

Son to the Father, and Eusebius favors semi-Arian views.[20] Justin even includes the angels in a doxology, as if the angels should be worshiped along with the Father, Son, and Holy Spirit. Nor do Hippolytus, Dionysius of Alexandria, Gregory Thaumaturgus, and Methodius fare much better; and Cyprian "does not treat of theology at all."[21] This leaves perhaps Clement, Irenaeus, and Athenagoras, or at least Newman does not comment on them. The point is simply that the pre-Nicene Church, as represented by its greatest theologians and bishops, hardly seems to affirm the doctrine of the Trinity. As Newman notes, even in the late fourth century Basil the Great had to exercise great caution when speaking on behalf of the divinity of the Holy Spirit.

Newman's conclusion is that, at least when interpreted in a strict manner, Vincent of Lérins's rule that "Christianity is what has been held always, everywhere, and by all," cannot suffice to delineate the content of Christian faith today.[22] By admitting this, Newman is not arguing that the doctrine of the Trinity represents a rupture with the pre-Nicene Church; rather, in light of Anglican efforts to invoke the Vincentian canon as the measure of sound doctrine, he is arguing that if we are wary of accepting any doctrine that historians cannot show to have been accepted by the earliest Church, then we will also have to be wary of accepting the doctrine of the Trinity.[23] The attempt to do without the Church, and to hold only that which the Bible explicitly teaches, does not work either, not least because the Bible does not present itself as a

20. Ibid., 17; cf. 135–36. As John Thiel remarks—in the course of arguing for a quite different view of doctrinal development—"Study of pre-Nicene Christianity . . . shows that subordinationism not only was prevalent in the early Christian centuries but also possessed, by virtue of its prevalence, a normativeness that only gradually—first in the third century and definitively in the fourth—came to be challenged by many as heterodox belief" (*Senses of Tradition*, 135). Thus in Thiel's view, an essentially settled, traditional, authoritative teaching of the pre-Nicene Church was reversed in the fourth century:

> As incipiently developing belief, the explicit claim for a nonsubordinationist christology entered the tradition as something striking, without precedence in the circulating scriptures that came to be regarded as the New Testament or in the earlier Christian writers accorded authority in the nascent Church. . . . The strength of Arian belief throughout the Christian world after Nicea makes it reasonable to conclude that the striking character of this incipient development would have been regarded as a scandalous betrayal of the true faith in other Christian communities decades, and perhaps even centuries, before the council was convened. (136)

21. Newman, *Essay on the Development of Christian Doctrine*, 17.
22. Ibid., 10; cf. 30. For helpful clarification of Vincent of Lérins's understanding of his rule (and of Newman on Vincent), see Guarino, *Vincent of Lérins*.
23. Brian Daley observes that "the classical Anglican position . . . often justified by the dictum of the fifth-century Gallic writer Vincent of Lérins that Apostolic doctrine can only be recognized in 'what has been held always, everywhere, and by all,' restricts normative Church dogma and practice to what can be demonstrated as common to all orthodox communities in Christian antiquity" ("Church Fathers," 37).

source to be interpreted without the Church.[24] The meaning of Scripture's words cannot be known without interpretation, which involves more than the mere repetition of Scripture's words.[25] A living ecclesial authority is necessary.

Newman's defense of doctrinal development rests in significant part upon his awareness that revelation is actively received and understood by human minds, a seemingly obvious point but one whose implications can be overlooked. He observes that "the highest and most wonderful truths, though communicated to the world once and for all by inspired teachers, could not be comprehended all at once by the recipients, but, as being received and transmitted by minds not inspired and through media which were human, have required only the longer time and deeper thought for their full elucidation."[26] He considers that the Protestant rejection of many Roman Catholic doctrines as corruptions and/or inventions fails to account for how ideas actually work.[27] It makes sense to suppose that when God reveals himself to us, the content of this revelation will require time to unfold or unpack. Different historical contexts will cause the same idea or ideas to be expressed differently, without thereby necessarily

24. See Newman, *Essay on the Development of Christian Doctrine*, 59. Newman adds: This moreover should be considered—that great questions exist in the subject-matter of which Scripture treats, which Scripture does not solve; questions too so real, so practical, that they must be answered, and, unless we suppose a new revelation, answered by means of the revelation which we have, that is, by development. Such is the question of the Canon of Scripture and its inspiration: that is, whether Christianity depends upon a written document as Judaism—if so, on what writings and how many—whether that document is self-interpreting, or requires a comment, and whether any authoritative comment or commentator is provided—whether the revelation and the document are commensurate, or the one outruns the other—all these questions surely find no solution on the surface of Scripture, nor indeed under the surface in the case of most men, however long and diligent might be their study of it. Nor were these difficulties settled by authority, as far as we know, at the commencement of the religion; yet surely it is quite conceivable that an Apostle might have dissipated them all in a few words, had Divine Wisdom thought fit. But in matter of fact the decision has been left to time, to the slow process of thought, to the influence of mind upon mind, the issues of controversy, and the growth of opinion. (60)

25. For example, Newman states: When it is declared that "the Word became flesh," three wide questions open upon us on the very announcement. What is meant by "the Word," what by "flesh," what by "became"? The answers to these involve a process of investigation, and are developments. Moreover, when they have been made, they will suggest a series of secondary questions; and thus at length a multitude of propositions is the result, which gather round the inspired sentence of which they come, giving it externally the form of a doctrine, and creating or deepening the idea of it in the mind. (ibid., 59; cf. 71 on the inexhaustible riches of Scripture)

In a different context, consider also the parallel injunction of Abraham Joshua Heschel, *Heavenly Torah*, 702.

26. Newman, *Essay on the Development of Christian Doctrine*, 29–30.

27. See ibid., 55–57. See also Newman, *Grammar of Assent*, 321.

losing consistency. As Newman says, "In time it [a great idea] enters upon strange territory; points of controversy alter their bearing; parties rise and fall around it; dangers and hopes appear in new relations; and old principles reappear under new forms."[28] Furthermore, since God's self-revelation does not attempt to resolve all conceptual problems before they arise in the Church, revelation anticipates the necessity of development and even of contentious development. For Newman, this implies that the Church must possess, under the Holy Spirit's guidance, an infallible charism to determine what are true developments: "A revelation is not given, if there be no authority to decide what it is that is given."[29]

Granted the necessity of the Church's charism for determining true doctrinal development, however, are there ways of defending the reasonableness of the Church's determinations? In this regard, Newman identifies seven "notes" that appear to characterize the doctrinal developments that the Church has approved and that would in fact be expected of development per se. These "notes" have to do with the coherence of the whole body of doctrine, not with establishing an easily traceable path for any particular doctrine.[30] The "notes" are preservation of type, continuity of principles, power of assimilation, logical sequence, anticipation of its future, conservative action upon its past, and chronic vigor. Development, rather than corruption, can generally be recognized by the fact that it nourishes unity, life, and vigor, although this should not be taken to imply that Newman relies solely on the analogy of a living organism. Newman also takes care not to reduce Christianity to "mere" ideas. Rather, as he says, "Christianity is dogmatical, devotional, practical all at once."[31] The central ideas of Christianity are known not merely notionally but really, insofar as the realities expressed by the ideas are personally encountered.[32]

---

28. Newman, *Essay on the Development of Christian Doctrine*, 40.
29. Ibid., 89; for discussion see Merrigan, "Revelation," 64–65. Newman continues:
> If Christianity be a social religion, as it certainly is, and if it be based on certain ideas acknowledged as divine, or a creed, (which shall here be assumed) and if these ideas have various aspects, and make distinct impressions on different minds, and issue in consequence in a multiplicity of developments, true, or false, or mixed, as has been shown, what power will suffice to meet and to do justice to these conflicting conditions, but a supreme authority ruling and reconciling individual judgments by a divine right and a recognized wisdom? . . . There can be no combination on the basis of truth without an organ of truth. (89–90)

See also the helpful observations of Thomas J. Norris in "Faith," 74–78; and, in the same volume, Sullivan, "Infallibility," 156–69, and Dulles, "Authority in the Church," 170–88.
30. For discussion of this point, see Walgrave, *Newman the Theologian*, 259–63.
31. Newman, *Essay on the Development of Christian Doctrine*, 36.
32. See Merrigan, "Newman on Faith in the Trinity," especially 102–11.

Guided by his seven "notes" for the characteristics that might be expected of true development, Newman treats a range of doctrinal debates in the Church's history. It is perhaps Newman's engagement with Church history that should most impress us, even if some details of his historical research no longer represent the most up-to-date scholarship.[33] His interest in actual Church history reflects his insistence upon a concrete ecclesiology. For Newman, it is indisputable on historical grounds that "the Roman Catholic communion of this day is the successor and representative of the Medieval Church, or that the Medieval Church is the legitimate heir of the Nicene; even allowing that it is a question whether a line cannot be drawn between the Nicene Church and the Church which preceded it."[34] Newman's reading of doctrinal development depends upon this sense of the living Church, and he is also aided by a theological appreciation of divine providence.[35] He observes that "there is the high antecedent probability that Providence would watch over His own work, and would direct and ratify those developments of doctrine which were inevitable."[36] He thinks it possible to show, with the benefit of hindsight, that each major development of doctrine is plausibly "an addition which illustrates, not obscures, corroborates, not corrects, the body of thought from which it proceeds."[37]

The method here is never one of logical proof, as though Newman were claiming to have identified an airtight model or set of rules by which doctrinal

33. See O. Chadwick, *From Bossuet to Newman*, 139. For his part, John Thiel considers that Newman's reading of history is shaped by his Platonism, which leads Newman to imagine an original, complete revelation: see Thiel, *Senses of Tradition*, 70. Thiel grants that "unlike a Platonist, though, Newman took the ancillary character of historicity seriously as a real, extended complement to the idea's essential wholeness. And unlike a Platonist, he saw temporality as productive, as a sphere in which God's revelation—given once and for all in the apostolic age—yet achieved a clarity that its earlier wholeness did not necessarily exhibit" (ibid.).

34. Newman, *Essay on the Development of Christian Doctrine*, 97; cf. 169. See Bouyer, *Newman*, 162, quoted in Pelikan, *Vindication of Tradition*, 25. In the latter book, Pelikan observes that Newman, in his early *The Arians of the Fourth Century*, gives a central place to the presence in the first centuries of an unwritten, normative apostolic tradition as a key source of trinitarian doctrine. See also Pelikan's helpful comments on Newman in his *Christian Tradition*, 5:265–79. Pelikan describes "the very development of 'development'" within Newman's thought; a major stimulus was that Newman, in the late 1830s and 1840s, "had been examining the role of tradition in the controversies between Arianism and the Nicene orthodoxy espoused by Athanasius, and had begun to see that on some troubling points the Arians appeared to have the argument from antiquity on their side; application of the Vincentian canon would not have led automatically to the orthodoxy of the Council of Nicea" (273–74).

35. See Merrigan, "'One Momentous Doctrine.'"

36. Newman, *Essay on the Development of Christian Doctrine*, 100. For discussion see McCarren, "Development of Doctrine," 123–24.

37. Newman, *Essay on the Development of Christian Doctrine*, 200.

development proceeds.[38] Rather, as in the *Grammar of Assent*, Newman arrives at certitude on the basis of cumulative probabilities. Since revelation is inseparable from interpretation, it is to be expected that God, having given a revelation, would ensure its development rather than corruption, so that each generation will be able to hear the gospel and share in its realities.[39] Scripture promises this ongoing presence of Christ and the Holy Spirit guiding the Church into all truth. In arguing that the actual developments that have occurred in the Church bear the marks of true development rather than corruption, Newman is fully aware that "the processes of reasoning, which legitimately lead to assent, to action, to certitude, are in fact too multiform, subtle, omnigenous, too implicit, to allow of being measured by rule."[40]

John T. Noonan and Development of Doctrine

Is Newman right, however, to insist that the Church's definitive interpretations of revelation consistently exhibit true development rather than corruption? Or has the Church's teaching included corruptions (false teaching) and ruptures, so that the Church has come to reject doctrines that were previously taught definitively?[41] If the Church has erred in its definitive doctrine, then Newman's teaching about development of doctrine would need to be entirely revised so as to account for doctrinal corruption, which Newman rules out as antagonistic to true development.[42] In this regard, the perspective of John T. Noonan's *The Church That Can and Cannot Change* is instructive.

38. For emphasis on this point, see McCarren, "Development of Doctrine," 128–29; Nichols, *From Newman to Congar*, 45; Dulles, *Newman*, 79. See also Ford, "Faithfulness to Type in Newman's *Essay on Development*," especially 36–39.
39. See Walgrave, *Newman the Theologian*, 246.
40. Newman, *Grammar of Assent*, 303.
41. The Church can teach doctrine definitively either through the "ordinary" or the "extraordinary" magisterium (or teaching office). See *Lumen Gentium*, §§24–25, 378–81. Most papal teaching belongs to the exercise of the "ordinary" magisterium. For a helpful discussion, see Welch, *Presence of Christ in the Church*, chaps. 1–3.
42. For such revision of Newman's principles, see, for instance, Küng, *The Church*. Emphasizing that "remaining in the truth is essentially a question of discipleship in the Spirit of Jesus Christ" (28)—a question of orthopraxis rather than of orthodoxy—Küng insists that the Church has erred frequently. As he puts it, "What happens in the event of error? First of all the answer must be that there is no need at all for panic. Error on the part of the Church's magisterium in serious definitions of faith or morals is in any case a fact—and we are still alive" (33). For his part, Charles Davis came to the same conclusions about the Church's teachings after Vatican II, and these conclusions caused him to renounce his priesthood and his Catholic faith: Davis, *Question of Conscience*. Other theologians of this period, like Küng, affirmed the occurrence of "error on the part of the Church's magisterium in serious definitions of faith or morals" but

Arguing that the Church's doctrine has indeed been marred by falsity and rupture, Noonan focuses specifically on the Church's teaching on slavery, usury, religious freedom, and the indissolubility of marriage. In the past century, he argues, the Church contradicted its previous teaching on these topics. In Noonan's view, this is not cause for alarm; rather, he emphasizes that we simply cannot know how (moral) doctrine will evolve. As he puts it, in a manner that imitates but goes beyond Newman, "The course of moral doctrine, like that of a great river, appears to follow no rule. Plunging over heights, striking boulders, creeping in almost motionless channels, it defies prediction, [and] can scarcely be the subject of science."[43]

Like many Catholic theologians today, Noonan holds that Newman's mistake was to think that doctrinal development does not include corruptions. Noonan does not deny Newman's achievement: Newman, he says, was the first to recognize "that Christian doctrine develops" without restricting this development "to a movement from the implicit to the explicit."[44] As Noonan observes, "Newman pointed to transformations of doctrine as tangible and organic, as many-sided and complex and real, as the passage from childhood to adulthood."[45] Indeed, the various ways in which Newman conceives of doctrinal development have stimulated "development of the idea of development"; and Newman cannot be accused of using "only the biological analogy."[46] The problem, however, is that when Newman "provided a checklist of the characteristics of true development, among them the requirement of not con-

---

did not leave the Church: see, for instance, Baum, *Credibility of the Church Today*; McBrien, *Do We Need the Church?*

43. Noonan, *Church That Can and Cannot Change*, 221; see also Noonan's "Development in Moral Doctrine." For discussion of Noonan's views, see Thiel, *Senses of Tradition*, 102–3; Dulles, "Development or Reversal?"; Sullivan, "Catholic Tradition and Traditions." Sullivan's essay is a response to Dulles's argument that Noonan has in fact identified cases in which "one can speak of development but not of the reversal of church doctrine" (Sullivan, "Catholic Tradition and Traditions," 118). Sullivan and Dulles agree, however, that Pope John Paul II's *Evangelium Vitae*, like the *Catechism of the Catholic Church* and the *Compendium of the Social Doctrine of the Church*, does not strictly define the institution of slavery as an intrinsic evil. Sullivan argues that nonetheless "the long-standing tradition that slavery was morally acceptable has been effectively reversed by the development of Catholic doctrine on the dignity of the human person" (122). This strikes me as correct insofar as there has certainly been a development, but the counter-tradition that viewed slavery as morally unacceptable needs to be given its due. For appreciative studies of Noonan's work, see Kaveny, "Listening for the Future in the Voices of the Past"; Reid, "Fundamental Freedom."

44. Noonan, *Church That Can and Cannot Change*, 3. Pelikan attends to others who published on development of doctrine before, or in the same year as, Newman: chief among these are Johann Sebastian Drey, Philip Schaff, and John Williamson Nevin. See Pelikan, *Christian Tradition*, 5:274–76.

45. Noonan, *Church That Can and Cannot Change*, 3.

46. Ibid., 226. See Lash, *Newman on Development*, 155.

tradicting a previous teaching," Newman did not fully appreciate—according to Noonan—that "a checklist is a mechanic's tool, useful for a quick overview" but "not to be slavishly followed."[47] In other words, Newman assumed that propositional contradiction would defeat true development, whereas for Noonan there are numerous contradictions, but "what is vital will survive; what is ephemeral will be discarded."[48]

With regard to moral doctrine, Noonan explains, "The test cannot be, Does Rule X contradict Rule Y?"[49] Such a test would lead to rejection of the Church (as in the case of Bishop Marcel Lefebvre at Vatican II), because such a test is too narrow for the Church's actual development. By rising from this propositional quagmire, Noonan thinks, one can find the right path, the path of love. As he emphasizes, "Newman's checklist is not the rule of faith. Qualifications, extensions, rejections create substantial difficulties."[50] The rule of faith depends not on a "checklist" that includes noncontradiction, but rather solely on "the teaching of the Lord Jesus" as found in Matthew 22.[51] When asked, what is the greatest commandment of the law?, Jesus answers by pointing not to propositional coherence or noncontradiction, but to the experiential coherence of love: "You shall love the Lord your God with all your heart, and with all your soul, and with all your mind. This is the great and first commandment. And a second is like it, You shall love your neighbor as yourself" (Matt. 22:37–39). Noonan explains that this teaching should be the true rule for measuring and understanding development of doctrine in the Church. He concludes, "Development proceeds directed by this rule. The love of God generates, reinforces, and seals the love of neighbor. What is required is found in the community's experience as it tests what is vital. On the surface, contradictions appear. At the deepest level, the course is clear."[52]

Noonan is aware, of course, that mere human experience cannot be the test, since "raw experience is chaos. Billions of events could count as human experience."[53] Rather, what is needed is empathy with the experience of others. This empathy flows from love. It is through empathy, love's knowledge, that Christian (moral) doctrine develops. Absent love's knowledge, Christian teachers "are not in a position to understand more."[54] But when opened to others' experience by empathy, Christian teachers "learn; their consciousness

47. Noonan, *Church That Can and Cannot Change*, 221.
48. Ibid.
49. Ibid.
50. Ibid., 222.
51. Ibid.
52. Ibid.
53. Ibid., 12.
54. Ibid., 13.

grows; the teaching they deliver is developed."[55] To expand our horizons or raise our consciousness through empathy with the experience of others is what allows us to develop Christian doctrine, rooted as it is not in mere ideas but in Jesus's commandment to love God and neighbor. When love marks the Christian community, the teachers in that community will be open to learn from the experience of all the members of the community. Noonan observes, "Certainly the experience of the Christian faithful counts—an experience that may not be captured in articulated rules but that underlies and influences development."[56]

On this view, the real contradiction would be to reject love and the experience of believers; other contradictions are superficial ones. Noonan argues that in Christian history, the wrong ideas have in fact led Christians to sin against love—for instance, by owning slaves. But empathetic attention to the experience of others has enabled the Christian community as a whole to overcome such wrong ideas and to develop its moral doctrine so as to be more attuned to the requisites of love. Noonan points out that Christians teach not only by words but by deeds. When the Church's leaders and saints do evil deeds (without knowing them to be evil), the Church engages in false teaching. In this sense, Noonan asserts that we do not need to debate the finer points of doctrinal history in order to show that the Church has engaged in false teaching. As an example, he points to the fact that the Church's leaders for generations castrated willing boys so as to enable them to sing more beautifully.

Noonan begins his book by noting that Newman recognized "the anomalies and novelties" of the Catholic Church's "transformations of doctrine" but did not extend this insight to moral doctrine.[57] In fact, when prompted by a

---

55. Ibid.

56. Ibid. See also Ormond Rush's *Eyes of Faith*. Noting that the Holy Spirit is the principle of the Church's reception of revelation, Rush spells this out in terms of the "sense of the faithful." He conceives of the sense of the faithful as a dialogue in the Spirit that produced authoritative Scripture and that now continues between believers, theologians, and the Church's magisterium. The Church's concept of the "sense of the faithful" is illustrated in *Lumen Gentium*, §12, 363:

> The holy People of God shares also in Christ's prophetic office: it spreads abroad a living witness to him, especially by a life of faith and love and by offering to God a sacrifice of praise, the fruit of lips praising his name (cf. Heb. 13:15). The whole body of the faithful who have an anointing that comes from the holy one (cf. 1 John 2:20 and 27) cannot err in matters of belief. This characteristic is shown in the supernatural appreciation of the faith [*sensus fidei*] of the whole people, when, "from the bishops to the last of the faithful" they manifest a universal consent in matters of faith and morals. By this appreciation of the faith, aroused and sustained by the Spirit of truth, the People of God, guided by the sacred teaching authority [*magisterium*] , and obeying it, receives not the mere word of men, but truly the word of God (cf. 1 Thess. 2:13), the faith once for all delivered to the saints (cf. Jude 3). The People unfailingly adheres to this faith, penetrates it more deeply with right judgment, and applies it more fully in daily life.

57. Noonan, *Church That Can and Cannot Change*, 3.

correspondent in 1863, Newman refused to hold that slavery is intrinsically evil on the grounds that Saint Paul did not hold it so. By contrast, for Pope John Paul II in *Veritatis Splendor* the inviolability and dignity of the human person clearly preclude slavery. In his discussion of slavery ("the elephant in the room"), Noonan focuses "on what appears to be true of slaveholding in every context: the right of the owner to determine the identity, education, and vocation of the slave and to possess the fruit of the slave's body. Acts exercising these kinds of domination were once accepted by the Church as without sin. They are no longer."[58]

Noonan acknowledges, of course, the biblical critique of slavery:

- God refuses to allow his chosen people to make slaves out of their fellow Israelites (Exod. 21; Neh. 5).

- Jesus teaches, "So whatever you wish that men would do to you, do so to them; for this is the law and the prophets" (Matt. 7:12).

- Paul calls himself a "slave of Christ Jesus" (Rom. 1:1) and identifies all Christians as Christ's slaves (1 Cor. 7:22; cf. Luke 1 on Mary).

- Paul states that "there is neither Jew nor Greek, there is neither slave nor free, there is neither male nor female; for you are all one in Christ Jesus" (Gal. 3:28).

- Paul urges Philemon to receive Onesimus "no longer as a slave but more than a slave, as a beloved brother, especially to me but how much more to you, both in the flesh and in the Lord" (Philem. 16).[59]

58. Ibid., 6. See also the Reformed theologian Kevin J. Vanhoozer's emphasis that not everything the church says and does can automatically claim to be the work of the Spirit; nor does every church doctrine mediate the presence of God. Simply to equate the church with the Spirit's work is to blur the distinction between the covenant Lord and his covenant people, a blurring that also risks falling prey to an overemphasis on "immanence." God is indeed present, yet not in a way that we can simply take for granted; the church is *simul justus et peccator*. We must resist the presumption of coincidence (e.g., the church says = God says; the church does = God does) here too. (*Drama of Doctrine*, 188) Vanhoozer is right to refuse "simply to equate the church with the Spirit's work." Nonetheless, the Church's sacraments and definitive teachings are indeed governed by the Holy Spirit, as taught in *Lumen Gentium*, §§4, 39, 352, 396.

59. As Noonan remarks of the Letter to Philemon, "It is impossible to read these lines and to think of Useful [= "Onesimus"] as a nothing, deprived of humanity. He is identified with his father in Christ. He is to be loved as Paul himself is loved. . . . Could enslavement in its essentials survive if Paul's letter presented the paradigm? Paul sees freedom for one man only; he doesn't tell Philemon, 'You must free all your slaves.' Could slavery survive the commandment to love one's neighbor as oneself? The New Testament did not confront the institution with the commandment" (*Church That Can and Cannot Change*, 34–35).

- Revelation 18:13 casts scorn on those merchants who weep for their cargoes of Babylon's goods, including "slaves, that is, human souls."[60]

Yet Scripture also accepts and seemingly sanctions slavery, as in Colossians 3:22 and Ephesians 6:5. As a result, Noonan points out, the Fathers and medievals almost without exception considered slavery a permissible evil.

To give a sense of the situation, Noonan tells the story of Pope Gregory the Great discovering Anglo boys being sold in the slave market in Rome. Pope Gregory responds by seeking the conversion of Britain, not the liberty of the enslaved boys. Indeed, Pope Gregory himself purchased some of the English boys and designated them for "servitude to Almighty God" (whether this meant a monastic life is unclear).[61] When slaves were escaping their masters by claiming asylum in churches, Pope Gregory wrote a letter urging that these slaves be returned to their masters. The point is that Pope Gregory accepted slavery as a matter of course.

Noonan does not deny that there were exceptions. Gregory of Nyssa, for example, preached a fiery sermon against slavery. Thomas Aquinas, while holding slavery to be a permissible evil, nonetheless rejected Aristotle's way of grounding human slavery in the notion of "natural slaves" (the basis for theories of permanent slavery).[62] Anselm of Canterbury presided over a Church council in London that banned the slave trade. Likewise, a number of Baroque theologians—including the Dominicans Thomas de Vio (Cardinal Cajetan), Bartolomé de Las Casas, and Tomás Mercado—condemned slavery and the slave trade when they witnessed its expansion during the conquest of the Americas.[63] The same condemnation of the African slave trade came from

60. For a highly critical discussion of the New Testament's approaches to slaves and slavery, see Harrill, *Slaves in the New Testament*. Harrill concludes that nineteenth-century American "proslavery spokesmen were holding the more defensible position from the perspective of historical criticism" (192). The complexity of the topic in the New Testament—even Harrill, whose goal is to undermine "Bible-based" sexual ethics in the contemporary Church, claims only that the proslavery position is "more defensible"—helps to explain the Church's development of doctrine. The Pauline household codes can be read in an "apophatic" mode where they function to place all fallen economic orders within the framework of love (both masters and slaves must act with love) without approving fallen economic orders. In such a reading, Paul's instruction to Philemon must receive the determinative place: "So if you consider me your partner, receive him as you would receive me" (Philem. 17). For discussion see N. T. Wright, *Epistles of Paul to the Colossians and to Philemon*, 169–70, 187.

61. Noonan, *Church That Can and Cannot Change*, 38.

62. See Boersma, "'This Is the Day Which the Lord Has Made'"; Capizzi, "Children of God"; Franks, "Aquinas's Use of Aristotle on the Virtue of Justice." Noonan comments rather unfairly on Gregory of Nyssa in *Church That Can and Cannot Change*, 41. Noonan is even more critical of Aquinas (56–58).

63. See Noonan, *Church That Can and Cannot Change*, 70–77, 80. Cajetan argued that "on a human being, so long as he is held in slavery, personal violence is continually inflicted"

numerous popes. But the popes often supported slavery in various other ways, even in the nineteenth century.[64] Most twentieth-century theologians up until Vatican II, along with the 1917 Code of Canon Law, continued to maintain that slavery does not violate natural law.

The history that Noonan relates regarding slavery is a sad one. The extent of historical complicity of the Catholic Church with the various forms of slavery is deeply deplorable.[65] Yet Noonan himself acknowledges that not only Scripture but also many theological and magisterial texts contain significant criticisms of slavery. Slavery was consistently seen as an evil, even if generally as an unavoidable evil. Furthermore, theological and magisterial criticisms of slavery increase in depth and extent over the course of Church history. Despite the widespread acceptance of slavery as a constituent element of fallen society, therefore, the presence of a simultaneous and growing critique should be important for assessing what development of doctrine means in the case of slavery. It is this tradition of critique that finds voice in the nineteenth-century papal magisterium and that is amplified by the Second Vatican Council's *Gaudium et Spes*.[66]

Can one say of the Church's contemporary rejection of slavery, as Newman says of a true development, that it "is an addition which illustrates, not obscures, corroborates, not corrects, the body of thought from which it proceeds"?[67] The rejection of slavery certainly corrects much previous Catholic practice and also corrects some instructions given by popes and curial officials over the centuries. Yet we may still conclude that the rejection of slavery involved a true development of doctrine that "illustrates" and "corroborates" the long-standing and profound concerns about slavery

---

(quoted in ibid., 72); Las Casas confessed the sin of having taken part in enabling the slave trade, which he attacked vigorously. But neither Cajetan nor Las Casas was an abolitionist, and most Baroque moralists, including Alfonsus de Liguori, supported slavery.

64. Noonan shows the support given to slavery by Pope Paul III in *Sublimis Deus* (1537) and by the catechism of the Council of Trent, and he argues that Pope Leo XIII grossly exaggerated earlier popes' efforts to combat slavery. For the beginnings of the shift, Noonan points to Pope Gregory XVI's *In supreme Apostolatus fastigio* (1839) and especially Pope Leo XIII's *In plurimus* (1888) and *Catholicae Ecclesiae* (1890). See Noonan, *Church That Can and Cannot Change*, 105–14.

65. Noonan lists the saints and religious orders that owned slaves, but he exaggerates the shock that would come to these Christians from learning that they had sinned by being complicit in this system, which the Church never presented as a moral good. To learn that we have sinned in ways that we were unaware of is not an unexpected experience for Christians.

66. See Noonan, *Church That Can and Cannot Change*, 119–21. For the view that *Gaudium et Spes* and the *Catechism of the Catholic Church* do not condemn slavery per se, but nonetheless make clear that slavery must be condemned as a violation of human dignity, see Sullivan, "Catholic Tradition and Traditions," 122.

67. Newman, *Essay on the Development of Christian Doctrine*, 200.

that we find in Scripture, in the theological tradition, and in the teaching of many popes.[68]

Noonan recognizes that the gospel challenged the traditional view of slavery. He observes, "That the gospel as preached by Paul opened Christian communities to slaves is incontestable. They who were stateless, ancestorless, personless were recognized as equal souls. There was opened for them a life that would transcend the life they lived."[69] But he remains unwilling to give much place to the biblical, theological, and magisterial antecedents to the Church's twentieth-century condemnation of slavery. To my mind, however, this position would also make it difficult for him to consider Nicene trinitarian doctrine as a real development of pre-Nicene theology.[70] If Newman's account of Nicene faith is correct, then for a doctrinal development (rather than doctrinal rupture or contradiction) to occur, it is not necessary that there be a large amount of prior teaching in the developed doctrine's favor. Instead, it is simply necessary that the doctrine, as developed, does not contradict a definitively taught prior doctrine.

Noonan rightly points out that slavery constitutes an attack on human personhood. No human would want to be a slave even if treated well, let alone when treated poorly. Yet Noonan assumes that the presence of prior contradictory teaching and practice means that doctrinal development in Newman's sense cannot have occurred. Guided by this assumption, Noonan undervalues the fact that Scripture and the theological tradition viewed slavery in negative terms (even when accepting it). He mistakenly assumes that the acceptance of slavery by many popes, and the intervention of some popes and curial officials in favor of slavery, stands as definitive Church teaching. He thereby neglects the indications of true doctrinal development present in the positions taken by nineteenth-century popes against the slave trade and slavery. Thus his claim that "John Paul discovered slavery to be

68. In his chapter on slaves and ex-slaves who became Christian saints, Noonan is somewhat surprised that this elevation of former slaves did not (at least at the time) call the institution into question. See *Church That Can and Cannot Change*, 45. Even in late medieval Europe, supposedly Christian societies accepted slavery. However, Noonan describes a "transformation" between 900 and 1100, due in part to Christian values, "from societies built on slave labor to societies where serfs had replaced the slaves" (52). As Noonan observes, "By the thirteenth century slavery had disappeared in England and France" (53).

69. Ibid., 33.

70. On this point see Thiel, *Senses of Tradition*, 136–39. Arguing for breaks within tradition (what he calls "incipient development"), which are then covered up by later tradition, Thiel states, "Although his earlier strategy of commending the sense and not the letter of the *homoousion* formula conceded its novelty as an expression, Athanasius now insisted on the place of the formula in tradition to such a degree that he attributed the alarm at its reception to the pretense of ignorance on the part of those who questioned its authority" (138).

intrinsically evil"[71] is misleading insofar as "discovered" signals an absence of true development of doctrine.

I have focused on slavery because it is Noonan's most extensive case study. His discussion of religious freedom, by contrast, is surprisingly short. He briefly mentions the view of Lactantius (AD 240–320) that one cannot compel religious practice, but he focuses on Augustine's and Aquinas's acceptance of religious persecution. In the twelfth century, he notes, Christians began to employ the death penalty against heretics and the Inquisition became commonplace.[72] Although Noonan mentions Erasmus's opposition to religious persecution, he points out that Erasmus's great contemporaries Thomas More and Bartolomé de Las Casas disagreed with him. Noonan comments briefly upon three nineteenth-century encyclicals that condemned freedom of conscience and worship: *Mirari vos* (1832), *Quanta cura* (1863), and *Immortale Dei* (1885).

But again, Noonan makes his case too woodenly with respect to development of doctrine. He certainly demonstrates the sad truth that religious persecution, like slavery, was widely accepted and practiced by Catholics. He shows that the Church's magisterium taught explicitly in the nineteenth century against religious freedom, albeit in the context of the Enlightenment understanding of "religion" and of "freedom." But he does not make a real effort—perhaps because he thinks the conclusion is obvious[73]—to show that

71. Ibid., 5.
72. Noonan describes what happened:
The Inquisition did not involve mass murder on the scale of Nazi or Communist atrocities. It was reasonably selective. It sometimes led to the deaths of persons whose positions, by the criteria of the day, were formally heretical. Sometimes it led to the execution of the actually innocent. Always it put terror at the service of truth. Always it assured unity of faith by suppressing those who challenged the Church. . . . Luther could have had little doubt as to his destiny if he had been captured and sent to Leo. With this mighty salvo [Leo X's 1520 bull *Exsurge Domine*], the wars of religion were begun. Among the condemned propositions was number 33: "To burn heretics is contrary to the will of the Spirit." (ibid., 152)
Pope John Paul II, in *Adveniente millennio tertio* (1994), no. 36, repented on behalf of the Church's members for the view "that an authentic witness to the truth could include suppressing the opinion of others."
73. This is the view of Terrence W. Tilley, as we have seen. Tilley states:
No convincing theory of development has accounted for the "course of development" that allows a clear contradiction in 1965 of what the highest magisterial authority in the Church taught in 1864. Some tortuous accounts have attempted to show an alleged continuity between these two statements. However, as J. Robert Dionne put it, "there can be no doubt whatever that the Council reversed the position of Pius IX and his successors," that the teaching of *Dignitatis Humanae* is "not continuous" with the earlier doctrine, and that arguments in favor of continuity are, at best, "tendentious." (*Inventing Catholic Tradition*, 117)

Dignitatis Humanae must necessarily be a break or rupture in the Church's teaching, rather than a development of doctrine (in Newman's sense). In fact, Noonan does not pay sustained exegetical attention either to *Dignitatis Humanae* or to the nineteenth-century papal encyclicals, on the assumption that their meaning is evident. Without a richer account of the nineteenth-century debate about "religion" and "freedom," along with further analysis of how to determine when a doctrinal truth has been taught definitively, there is no way for Noonan to be able to offer an informed judgment about whether or not true doctrinal development—in the sense of real corroboration and deepening of earlier teaching, allowing for a simultaneous critique of errors—is actually present in the text of *Dignitatis Humanae*.[74] He assumes that because

---

Tilley's summary of Dionne's position, however, is misleading. According to Dionne's more nuanced reading of *Dignitatis Humanae*:

> That a human being in religious matters especially has the duty to seek the truth and to adhere to it once it is found; that a human being has an objective duty to inform his or her conscience honestly and responsibly; that he or she has the objective duty to follow even an erroneous conscience, and that the assent of faith may not be forced: These answers to Questions (A), (B), (C), and (D) respectively were fully shared by the Fathers of Vatican II and the Popes who preceded them. As a result of drawing the logical conclusions from these shared values, the Council Fathers, conscious of the problem of continuity, developed the distinctive contribution of *Dignitatis humanae*. Continuity with the Popes from Pius IX onward was further enhanced by a unanimously negative answer to Question (F): For the Council Fathers as for the previous ordinary papal magisterium, a human being does not have an objective right to worship God in a way other than the way God is worshiped in the Roman Church and those other local Christian churches in union with it. . . . But there is a sense in which the Council Fathers reversed the teaching of the ordinary papal magisterium, for the distinctive contribution of *Dignitatis humanae* amounts to an affirmative answer to Question (E): Does a human being in the present economy of salvation have the *objective* right to worship God in the manner in which a responsible use of intellect indicates he or she should? If the official documents of the papal magisterium from Pius IX up to and including Pius XII held to variations of the old thesis/hypothesis model (though unusually without its explicit label), in which religious freedom in the sense of Question (E) is officially meaningless, then the Council in affirmatively answering in its own way that same question asserts that the Question is *not* meaningless but a fundamental human right. (*Papacy and the Church*, 193)

74. Martin Rhonheimer holds that the nineteenth-century papal "equating of religious freedom with indifferentism . . . was undone with the Second Vatican Council. With it, what the popes of the nineteenth century rejected as heretical still is heresy: religious indifferentism. But religious freedom as a civil right is no longer affected by this verdict" ("Benedict XVI's 'Hermeneutic of Reform' and Religious Freedom," 1052). Rhonheimer cites Pope Benedict XVI's Christmas message delivered to the Roman Curia on December 22, 2005, in which Pope Benedict argues (with *Dignitatis Humanae* in mind) that "in this interplay on different levels between continuity and discontinuity lies the nature of true reform." Rhonheimer shows that for Pope Benedict, *Dignitatis Humanae*'s affirmation of the right of religious freedom "implies the abrogation of the earlier claim of the so-called 'rights of truth' to political and legal guarantees, and the renunciation of state repression of religious error. However one views the question, the conclusion is unavoidable: precisely this teaching of the Second Vatican Council is what

there are divergent notes in prior teaching and practice, there can be no true development of doctrine in *Dignitatis Humanae*.

When Noonan focuses at the end of his book on development of doctrine, he frames the issue in terms of those who fear the Church admitting error and those who understand that change (and error) are part of all life, including the Church's.[75] His opponents, he thinks, resist admitting change (in the sense of correcting earlier, false Church teaching) for natural psychological reasons. He states, "The deepest resistance to change may arise at the vital core of the resister. Life certainties are being disturbed. The resister has staked his or her salvation on the truth of certain religious propositions and on the impossibility of error in any one of them. It is unbearable that any of these propositions should fall into doubt, desuetude, or repudiation."[76] He pictures these resisters as closing their eyes to all evidence, no matter how strong, of a change or rejection of past Church teaching. They close their eyes, embracing "a contented assumption that all morals are beyond alteration," because they fear that if they admit one such rupture, then the certitude of all Church doctrine will fail.[77] As a solution to this psychological dilemma, Noonan proposes that "resisters" should evaluate other doctrines and measure the grounds for

Pius IX condemned in his encyclical *Quanta Cura*" (ibid., 1032; cf. 1042). Rhonheimer continues, "Pope Benedict concluded his exemplification of the 'hermeneutic of reform' with the doctrine of religious freedom with a concise statement: 'The Second Vatican Council, with its new definition of the relations between the Church's faith and certain basic elements of modern thought, reelaborated or corrected some decisions made in the past'" (1032). Rhonheimer explains further, "The magisterium of the Church in the field of social teaching also contains, together with immutable principles founded on the doctrine of the faith, a mass of implementations that are often, in hindsight, rather dubious. What is involved here is not a type of 'teaching' similar to Catholic teaching in matters of faith and morals, where the Church interprets the natural law in an obligatory manner—as in the cases of questions concerning contraception, abortion, euthanasia, and other moral norms in the field of bioethics" (1045). In its social teaching, the Church applies the natural law to concrete situations using historically conditioned conceptions of the state that do not have "the privilege of resting on the apostolic Tradition or of being a constitutive element of the *depositum fidei*" (1046). I find Rhonheimer's general approach on this topic to accord well with that of Pope Benedict XVI. See also F. Sullivan, "Catholic Tradition and Traditions," 126; Dulles, "Development or Reversal?," 60; Ratzinger, "On the Status of the Church and Theology Today," 379–82. For recent discussion of *Dignitatis Humanae*, see also Hittinger, "Declaration on Religious Freedom"; Pink, "Interpretation of *Dignitatis Humanae*."

75. See, for a similar framing of the issue, Powell, *Papal Infallibility*. My point is not to deny that change and error are part of the Church's life, but rather to argue that the Church is preserved by the Holy Spirit from certain kinds of error in the salvific communication of divine revelation (in accord with Jesus's promises).

76. Noonan, *Church That Can and Cannot Change*, 195. For a response to this kind of argumentation based on the alleged psychological repressions of one's opponents, see C. S. Lewis, "'Bulverism,'" 271–77.

77. Noonan, *Church That Can and Cannot Change*, 194.

their certitude; it may be that the ruptures in certain doctrines do not affect the truth of other doctrines.

According to Noonan, the main thing that "resisters" must come to understand is that the Church has not only changed but also erred. All institutions err, including trustworthy institutions. Noonan grants that the Church possesses, within strict limits, the charism of "infallibility."[78] If this is so, however, then it seems that the "resisters" need only hold that prior teachings, insofar as they were contradicted at Vatican II, were not taught definitively. In such a case there could in fact be no doctrinal rupture or contradiction in Newman's sense; there would simply be a development of doctrine. In short, Noonan should have reflected more on what kind of continuity is required for a true doctrinal development.[79]

78. See ibid., 195. Noonan also sets forth, without comment, the standard way of speaking about the Church's communication of divine revelation, a way that precludes doctrinal contradiction: "The Church cannot change. In the Church's care is what is the deposit of faith—a core of revealed truth that no extrinsic force has power to enlarge or diminish. The deposit is secure in the Church's treasury. The Church proclaims what is necessary for salvation. God's requirements are stable. The revelation that was made in the person of Jesus Christ was complete and final" (6–7).

79. Joseph A. Komonchak warns that "Pope Benedict's view [of Vatican II] has been oversimplified into a contrast between a hermeneutic of discontinuity and one of continuity and interpreted as a rejection of any approach that would speak of the council as a difference-making event in any sense other than spiritual" ("Interpreting the Council and Its Consequences," 166; see also for the same point Komonchak's "Benedict XVI and the Interpretation of Vatican II"). With respect to "rupture," Komonchak expresses concern that some of Joseph Ratzinger / Pope Benedict XVI's comments about the interpretation of Vatican II

> could suggest that historic events are not to be expected, at least none that suggest rupture or break, that is, discontinuity. The Church, he claims, is a single historical subject, and its journey is one of continuous progress toward deeper understanding of the faith; it is not marked by fractures or breaks, or by leaps either. This theological claim is one that not only historians but many theologians, too, will find very puzzling. Their first question will be about the relationship between the Church so described and the actual communities of believers who have constituted the Church in the past and constitute it today. They will wonder, for example, whether it was all progress when the Church ceased to be persecuted and became established; whether the Church did not change significantly when the Roman Empire collapsed; whether the Gregorian Reform did not represent a break from the Church of the ninth and tenth centuries; whether the necessities of polemic did not narrow the Church's theological vision in the second Christian millennium; whether modern circumstances did not require the Church to look differently at the questions of Church and State and religious freedom. ("Interpreting the Council and Its Consequences," 167)

But Ratzinger (and Newman) are well aware of these historical shifts, and, indeed, both Ratzinger and Newman advert often to very similar lists. Pope Benedict XVI allows for "discontinuity," but Pope Benedict XVI does not allow for discontinuity understood as "rupture." See also my "Pastoral Perspectives on the Church in the Modern World," where I argue that *Gaudium et Spes* exhibits notable doctrinal development but not discontinuity in the sense of rupture. Komonchak himself is willing to say that when one approaches Vatican II "doctrinally,

For Noonan, development (or change) occurs by means of three factors: listening to revelation; human experience and empirical investigation; and the intellectual, moral, and social progress of humanity. The ways in which revelation can be understood depend partly upon the cultural situation of the recipients. Thus Noonan speaks of analogy, balance, logic, and experience as ways in which development occurs. While agreeing that all these are involved, I observe that Noonan does not devote sufficient attention to what it means for the Church to be able to define a doctrinal truth in an enduring fashion, given that our experience and cultural contexts are always changing. Without examining this question in detail, it is not really possible to speak either of development or of rupture. This is so because unless enduring doctrinal truth exists, there could only be changing historical expressions that accord with particular cultural contexts.[80] What Noonan needs is a richer account of the nature of doctrine and doctrinal development. This brings us back to Newman—and to Newman's favorite test case, the period of the definition of Nicene orthodoxy.

---

there is clear continuity" ("Benedict XVI and the Interpretation of Vatican II," 107). Yet the opening chapter of the volume in which Komonchak's essay appears insists upon discontinuity as radical rupture:

> Traditional theories of essentially continuous doctrinal development will have to be rethought—and rethought in such a way as to render them capable of accounting for radically discontinuous change in doctrinal matters central to the church's very self-understanding. . . . The understandable reluctance of their nervous predecessors notwithstanding, what is not in doubt is the urgent need for contemporary Catholic theologians to accept the fact that doctrinal rupture or radically discontinuous change has in the past been an unquestionable reality in the life of the church. (Oakley, "History and the Return of the Repressed," 49)

80. For further background consider Garrigou-Lagrange, "La nouvelle théologie où va-t-elle?," recently translated by Suzanne M. Rini as "Where Is the New Theology Leading Us?" After quoting Henri Bouillard's statement that "since spirit evolves, an unchanging truth can only maintain itself by virtue of a simultaneous and correlative evolution of all ideas, each proportionate to the others" (Bouillard, *Conversion et grace chez S. Thomas d'Aquin*, 219), Garrigou-Lagrange remarks:

> An unchangeable relationship can only be conceived of as such if there is something unchangeable in the two terms that it unites. Otherwise, for all intents and purposes, it is like saying that the waves of the sea can be stapled together. Of course, the two ideas that are united in an unchangeable affirmation are sometimes at first confused and then later distinguished one from the other, such as the ideas of nature, of person, substance, accident, transubstantiation, the Real Presence, sin, original sin, grace, etc. But if these are not fundamentally unchangeable, how then will the affirmation which unites them by the verb "to be" be unchangeable? ("Where Is the New Theology Leading Us?," 64)

Historical context for Garrigou-Lagrange's essay is provided by Jürgen Mettepenningen, "Truth, Orthodoxy and the *Nouvelle Théologie*," and Nichols, "Thomism and the Nouvelle Théologie." Nichols argues that Thomism is a central and crucial exponent of the Church's "classical ontological theology" but that Marie-Michel Labourdette and especially Garrigou-Lagrange made the mistake of refusing to accept other modes of doing theology.

Development of Doctrine in the Nicene Period: Lewis Ayres and Khaled Anatolios

Recall that *Dei Verbum* states that "the Church, in her doctrine, life and worship, perpetuates and transmits to every generation all that she herself is, and all that she believes."[81] The Church receives revelation fully from God in Christ Jesus, and God ensures through the Holy Spirit that "the things he had once revealed for the salvation of all peoples should remain in their entirety, throughout the ages, and be transmitted to all generations."[82] At the same time, this handing on of revelation is not simply a static event, in which the Church's understanding of revelation never changes. Rather, says *Dei Verbum*, "The Tradition that comes from the apostles makes progress in the Church, with the help of the Holy Spirit. There is growth in insight into the realities and words that are being passed on."[83] *Dei Verbum*'s position, as I suggested, is also John Henry Newman's. But what if, as Noonan suggests with regard to moral doctrine, there is a flat contradiction rather than a progression or "growth in insight"?

In considering this question further, let me turn here to the approaches to doctrinal development taken by two contemporary Catholic scholars of Nicene trinitarian doctrine, Lewis Ayres and Khaled Anatolios. Their approaches will help us to avoid the mistake of assuming that every apparent propositional contradiction means that a doctrinal development in Newman's sense cannot have occurred. They also underscore Newman's point that we cannot *prove* that the doctrinal determinations of the Church conform to Scripture and Tradition, although we can identify the characteristic notes of a true development.

Lewis Ayres: History and Dogma

Lewis Ayres begins with the observation that Arius, whose determined advocacy of the view that the Son is a uniquely exalted creature set in motion the fourth-century debates, "has increasingly been seen as a representative of a wider tradition that seems to have been part of the mainstream of Christian thought—and probably within the bounds of what might be considered the boundaries of pre-Nicene orthodoxy."[84] Newman, as we saw, recognized the

---

81. *Dei Verbum*, §8, 754.

82. Ibid., §7, 753.

83. Ibid., §8, 754. As this development occurs, some traditions, not definitively taught, are shown not to belong to the faith. As Francis Sullivan puts it, "Some long-standing traditions in the church were not authentic expressions of the Word of God as handed down in the teaching, life, and worship of the church but were really human traditions" ("Catholic Tradition and Traditions," 130).

84. Ayres, *Nicaea and Its Legacy*, 425; cf. 11–15.

extent to which pre-Nicene theologians depicted the Son and Holy Spirit as not fully divine in the Nicene sense. The key problem, therefore, consists in accounting for how prior teaching is corrected in some respects while holding that the Church's handing on of revelation has truly developed rather than corrupted.

In nineteenth- and early-twentieth-century theories of doctrinal development, Ayres sees two main paths. The first path is to present development in terms of the growth of a living organism—for example, from acorn to tree. On this view, ideas develop like organisms, gradually unfolding their full potential of meaning. Ayres attributes this position to Newman and the Tübingen school, although, as we have seen, Newman's seven "notes" are broader than the organic analogy.[85]

According to Ayres, the second path was developed by Baroque scholastic theologians and, in the early twentieth century, was influentially set forth by Francisco Márin-Sola (whom Ayres does not identify by name).[86] Márin-Sola argued for a demonstrable progress of development. As Ayres describes this path, "The earliest deposit of Christian faith was seen as the foundation for the developed faith of later centuries, broader propositional content being slowly deduced from logical principles."[87] Citing Nicholas Lash's *Change in Focus: A Study in Doctrinal Change and Continuity*, Ayres observes that both the organic and the logical-deductive path falter under historical study; doctrinal development in the concrete cannot be shown to work always either along the lines of the predictable growth of an organism or of the logical deduction of implicit propositions from explicit ones.[88]

85. See Walgrave's *Newman the Theologian* on this point. Ayres's (or Nicholas Lash's) view of two paths, one "organic" and the other "logical," is misleading.

86. See Márin-Sola, *L'Évolution homogène du dogme catholique*. Jan Walgrave, OP, criticizes the work of the Baroque scholastics who influenced Márin-Sola: "To Suarez and Lugo it is already self-evident that the truth, revealed by God and assented to by faith, is no more than a system of propositions. ... 'Logicism' in conceiving the development of doctrine and rationalism in evaluating the part and requirements of rational argument in the analysis of faith are two offshoots of the same propositional conception of the nature of revelation" (*Unfolding Revelation*, 151–52). In scholastic terminology, the key distinction is between formal/explicit and virtual/implicit revelation. See also the excellent chapters by Aidan Nichols, OP, on Ambrose Gardeil and the neoscholastics in his *From Newman to Congar*, 155–94. As Nichols shows, for theologians such as Marcolinus Maria Tuyaerts, OP, and Charles Boyer, SJ—representative of "those who held to the position that *both* the connexion of subsequent doctrine with the apostolic deposit *and* the historical genesis of such doctrine must be thought of as essentially logical in character"—Márin-Sola's position was "not rational enough" (182–83).

87. Ayres, *Nicaea and Its Legacy*, 426. Ayres adds, "In liberal Protestant contexts development could of course much more easily be seen as a basic story of departure from an original kernel or the carrying of that kernel through history with various accretions" (ibid.).

88. See Lash, *Change in Focus*, 144–54. As Lash asks, "Are we reduced to saying that the authors of the new testament said or believed A, the fathers B, the medievals C, ourselves D, and that this is all that can be said about it?" (150; cf. 25). In dialogue with theologians such

Nonetheless, Ayres is clear that theologians cannot renounce the task of showing the unity and continuity of the Church's handing on of revelation. This would merely give in to historicism, and, as a de facto result, it would force believers to rely upon one of the two paths noted above rather than seeking a better way.[89] Ayres finds a better path in the work of Henri de Lubac. In an essay published in 1948 under the title "Bulletin de théologie fondamentale: Le problème du développement du dogme," de Lubac challenges the neoscholastic emphasis on doctrinal development as logical deduction from revealed propositions.[90] While complimenting Márin-Sola for granting that there is a "vital" or "affective" (rather than merely logical) impulse in doctrinal development, de Lubac warns against the "reduction of the fact of development to the mechanism of theological conclusions" and the "reduction of the problem of development to a problem of pure human logic."[91] He emphasizes that the

as Edward Schillebeeckx, OP, Bernard Lonergan, SJ, Maurice Bénevot, Avery Dulles, SJ, and Gregory Baum, all of whom were writing on this topic in the late 1960s, Lash expresses sympathy with Baum's proposal that doctrinal development occurs as the Church in each age "re-focuses" the gospel in light of new problems. The question, however, is to what extent "the articles of the creed, and solemnly defined dogmatic definitions may be said to be transculturally invariant, at least in the sense that no christian 'structure' would be complete which omitted any of them from its list of 'elements'" (154). Lash finds that new creeds will be necessary but should not be taken to exclude the classical creeds. Although this position is more moderate than some, it exaggerates the inability of doctrinal formulations to transcend their cultural and historical context. See also Jossua, "Immutabilité, progrès ou structurations multiples."

89. See Ayres, *Nicaea and Its Legacy*, 426.

90. See also Louis Charlier's *Essai sur le problème théologique*, 27. Describing Charlier's critique of neoscholastic accounts of doctrinal development, Boersma observes that for neoscholastic theologians

    theology had become a science originating in rational principles and leading to logical conclusions. In Thomas's Aristotelian philosophy, it had been possible to know something either by directly apprehending it—when the principles (*principia*) and the thing (*res*) were identical—or by apprehending the effects of the causes (or the conclusions of the principles), in which case one only had virtual knowledge (*science virtuelle*). In this Aristotelian approach, therefore, theological conclusions were "virtually" contained in the absolute, immutable, and eternal principles [the articles of faith], and one could deduce these conclusions by way of "rigorous demonstration." (*Nouvelle Théologie and Sacramental Ontology*, 213)

See also the concerns raised in White, "Precarity of Wisdom," 95–97. Robin Darling Young charges Henri de Lubac, too, with ahistorical rationalism (rooted in misplaced nostalgia). Young's viewpoint, however, is a good example of the "perspectivalism" that negates the truth-bearing capacity of dogmatic propositions. See Young, "Soldier of the Great War," 142–43; cf. 163. Young seems to take for granted that the "Church" (one, holy, catholic, apostolic) has never existed except in the imagination of naïve believers.

91. de Lubac, "Problem of the Development of Dogma," 253, 258; cf. 270. Even more than Márin-Sola, however, de Lubac's main opponent in this 1948 essay is Charles Boyer, as Aidan Nichols shows in his *From Newman to Congar*, 206–11.

revelation of God in Jesus Christ is received as a whole mystery known by the light of faith.[92] It is thus received, he thinks (problematically in my view, given the necessity of propositions in human cognition), in a prepropositional state—that is, as the mystery of God's action, a mystery that the light of faith enables us to receive as a whole and that goes far beyond human words and deductions. Ayres summarizes what he learns from de Lubac: "'Revelation' is the action of God in Christ: all subsequent reflection on that action is already abstraction from what is necessarily in essence mystery. Such abstraction may well be necessary, and the Spirit-led development of that abstraction also essential, but we can only consider the idea of development in light of awareness of the mystery at its core."[93] Divine revelation, as an inexhaustible mystery known in faith, does not give its truth to those who approach it as if it were like any merely human communication. On this point, Ayres and Newman would surely agree.

92. See de Lubac, "Problem of the Development of Dogma," 264–67, 273–75. As Nichols points out, the major source for de Lubac's essay was an unpublished essay of Pierre Rousselot, SJ, called "Petite théorie du développement du dogme" that was published by de Lubac in 1965. From Rousselot, de Lubac takes the insight that revelation is the whole mystery of Jesus Christ as personally known by the apostles. The propositional and conceptual specification of this revelation takes place under the impulse (in de Lubac's words) "of the action of the mystery. This is the exigency of the dogma of the unity of Christ, a religious exigency, perceived religiously, which has forced the intelligence to discoveries that it now uses in its elaboration of the dogma. This elaboration can therefore well assume a logical form: it is nonetheless a demonstration after the fact; an effect much more than a cause or even than a means of invention or of inventory of the dogmatic truth expressed as a conclusion" ("Problem of the Development of Dogma," 266–67). For discussion see Nichols, *From Newman to Congar*, 196–204.

93. Ayres, *Nicaea and Its Legacy*, 427. De Lubac comments that
> under its form of action and under its form of revelation, as reality and as the object of faith, this unique and total Thing carries one and the same name in Scripture and in Christian Tradition: it is *mystery*. It is already a first abstraction, therefore, to separate completely the gift and the revelation of the gift, the redemptive action and the knowledge of redemption, the mystery as act and the mystery as proposed to faith. It is a second abstraction to separate from this total revelation or this "Whole of Dogma" certain particular truths, enunciated in separate propositions, which will concern respectively the Trinity, the incarnate Word, baptism, grace, and so on. Legitimate and necessary abstractions, we repeat—for the mind can only preserve the total truth by actively exercising itself on it and according to its own laws—but on condition that we be aware of it and that we not fail to understand the concrete "Whole" whose contents we will never exhaust. ("Problem of the Development of Dogma," 274–75)

Although de Lubac speaks of these "particular truths, enunciated in separate propositions," as "legitimate and necessary abstractions," it seems to me that in describing propositions of faith as the fruit of a second stage of abstraction, he does not give sufficient place either to Jesus Christ's own propositional teaching about his actions (for example, his teaching at the Last Supper about his coming death) or to the point that the action of God in Christ, even if we can only receive it as a "Whole" and thus as mystery, cannot be thought without language and thus cannot be possessed apart from language (propositions).

In Ayres's view, however, "Virtually all modern theories of doctrinal de-velopment . . . assume success in such a theory involves providing a way in which the paths of continuity in doctrine can be traced and understood by the human observer."[94] Here I would emphasize that while Newman clearly was interested in understanding "the paths of continuity in doctrine," his seven "notes" provide us with a quite broad vantage point (much like his illative sense) for appreciating concrete historical developments.[95] I think that New-man would partly agree with Ayres's statement that "Christians working with a theology of the Triune God's maintenance and guidance of the Church . . . should no more expect to be able to trace the paths of that continuity with certainty than we expect to be able to locate the history of grace in the Church with certainty."[96] Newman would add that "certainty" in tracing doctrinal development allows for the place of antecedent probabilities and fittingness. As a historian of the Nicene period, Ayres has a large stake in insisting that we cannot *prove* that Nicene theology faithfully develops the content of divine revelation. Rather than placing this burden upon historians' shoulders, Ayres suggests that in faith we must trust the Church to be "able to judge the ap-propriate structure of a faith resulting from development."[97] Here Ayres and Newman are in full accord.

While combating rationalism on the one hand, on the other hand Ayres equally insists that theologians "must attempt to narrate the continuity of their core beliefs with those of the apostles."[98] Ayres has in view "scriptural

---

94. Ayres, *Nicaea and Its Legacy*, 427.
95. On the "illative sense," see Newman, *Grammar of Assent*, chap. 9.
96. Ayres, *Nicaea and Its Legacy*, 427.
97. Ibid.
98. Ibid. Walgrave expresses the concern that de Lubac's understanding of revelation leaves too little room for propositional knowledge, especially as communicated by Jesus Christ and his apostles. In his evaluative summary of de Lubac's position, Walgrave states that for de Lubac,

> under the impact of God's reality upon the mind through the illuminating grace of faith, man apprehends His revelation as a whole, and development of doctrine is a gradual translation of that global apprehension into forms of human language. Once more, this is a valuable insight; but it must be corrected by the essential complementary view that in the post-apostolic Church the global apprehension, although effected by an inner light, is, on the level of conscious knowledge, mediated by a message that comes from without; so that in relation to the conscious life of faith the object of that apprehension is ruled by the scriptural word and the dogma of the primitive Church. The basic and essential pattern of what in faith presents itself to the believing mind after the manner of explicit knowledge is determined by the dogmatic content of the primitive message. It must be stressed that if the development of doctrine is rather an analysis and description of something present to the mind in its wholeness, the essential condition of its being convertible into explicit human knowledge is its being presented to man in the form of a message. It is the proper characteristic of faith that it is both a real apprehension, or a mysterious contact with a supernatural concrete whole, brought about in man by a divine

texts that speak of Christ's guarantee that the Church will be maintained in truth through the presence of the Spirit and because the Church is the body of Christ, being led in the Spirit to share in the relationship of God, Word, and Spirit."[99] He also argues that "pro-Nicene theology offers a more coherent reading of the plain sense of Scripture," and he explores what this "plain sense" is and how Scripture should function in the Church.[100] Nicea can be defended as a development of doctrine. Even so, Newman's opponents (and, I would add, Newman himself) were right to think that "if doctrine develops thus, perhaps only the Church's possession of an inspired teaching office can guide the truly historically attentive Christian."[101] Historians cannot prove that Nicene dogma is exegetically foolproof.

The role of propositional truth in revelation and the development of doctrine is not taken up directly by Ayres. In a rather undifferentiated manner, he approves de Lubac's "arguing against Catholic accounts of development that focused on ensuring continuity in propositional content" and holds that the original revelation was prepropositional.[102] But Ayres's equal emphasis that

---

light, and an assent to a verbal proposition reaching man from without and enabling him to grasp it in a human way and to assimilate and use it in his conscious life. The inner divine contact and the outer message are two essential aspects, neither separable nor confused, of the one theandric reality of revelation and faith. (*Unfolding Revelation*, 341)
I agree with Walgrave's concerns here, but he needs to specify more clearly what he means by the "inner divine contact": Does it have a cognitive element, as seems required by real illumination? For elucidation of this point, see Merrigan, *Clear Heads and Holy Hearts*, 82–102, especially 85–90.

99. Ayres, *Nicaea and Its Legacy*, 427–28.
100. Ibid., 428.
101. Ibid., 429.
102. Ibid., 427. For a perspective similar to de Lubac's, allowing, however, for the distinct perspectives on propositional truth held by the Jesuits and Dominicans of the day, see also Chenu, *Une école de théologie*, 129–50. Here is the place also to mention Gerard Loughlin's recent proposal, from which I demur, that de Lubac, Chenu, and the other major figures of the *nouvelle théologie* were merely repeating the insights of Modernists such as Alfred Loisy and George Tyrrell, just as Garrigou-Lagrange thought (although for Loughlin this is high praise). For Loughlin, "Eternal and absolute truths are known in the *recognition* of a community, and this is not to look inward, to some supposed psychological resource, to 'one's ultimately ineffable subjective experience,' nor upward, to some plane of reality just out of sight. It is to look *between*, to the relationships that constitute the *communitas* of the community, the commonality of shared agreement and disagreement, of dispute in conversation, and of reconciliation in worship. Thus the invariant affirmation is always finally elusive" ("*Nouvelle Théologie*," 49–50). I think Loughlin's view of truth as being located in "the *communitas* of the community" and in "the commonality of shared agreement and disagreement" (a "commonality" that supposedly leads to "reconciliation in worship") reduces to the claim that the Church cannot teach real knowledge of divine revelation. For an analysis of Alfred Loisy and George Tyrrell on doctrinal development (or the lack thereof) that distinguishes the Modernists from the *nouvelle théologie*, see Nichols, *From Newman to Congar*, 71–135. For a view similar to Loughlin's, see Carroll, "Philosophical Foundations of Catholic Modernism."

Christians "must attempt to narrate the continuity of their core beliefs with those of the apostles" tells in favor of enduring propositional truths ("core beliefs") and their role in the apostolic and ecclesial communication of revelation. No doubt like de Lubac, Ayres is less concerned with the status of propositional truth in revelation and development of doctrine than he is with ensuring that theories of doctrinal development avoid claiming an implausible demonstrative rigor.

Khaled Anatolios: Performing Trinitarian Doctrine

Addressing many of the same issues, Khaled Anatolios argues that we will be able to properly appreciate Nicene trinitarian doctrine only if we enter into the very "logic whereby trinitarian doctrine developed," and so today "we must creatively re-perform the acts of understanding and interpretation that led to those statements," especially with regard to the divine transcendence and the primacy of Christ.[103] Anatolios begins by sketching three influential contemporary ways of approaching trinitarian doctrine. The first way assumes that trinitarian doctrine is about us, rather than about God. Trinitarian doctrine, on this view, speaks very helpful words, but these words are fundamentally about us rather than about God (even if we can apply them to God at least in a metaphorical way). On this view, the "immanent Trinity" constitutes an impenetrable mystery, and so a trinitarian doctrine shows its strength or weakness in terms of whether it is liberative and nourishing for our life in this world.[104]

The second way argues that trinitarian doctrine does indeed express God's immanent reality, because God's self-revelation in Christ and the Spirit coincides *directly* with God's immanent reality.[105] The major problem here is that this position "seems to strictly conflate God's eternal trinitarian being with the economic features acquired by the Trinity in God's work of salvation."[106] The third way is the search for a created analogy for the Trinity; indebted to Richard of St. Victor, many contemporary theologians consider the most appropriate analogy to be the communion of human persons as, for example, in

103. Anatolios, *Retrieving Nicaea*, 1. See also Anatolios's "Canonization of Scripture," 15–27.

104. See, for example, the observation of Bernard J. Cooke, SJ, in 1969 that "a Christian today shares the contemporary impatience with knowledge that has no relevance for life" (Cooke, *Beyond Trinity*, 28).

105. The second way can lead back to the first: see LaCugna, *God for Us*; Rahner, *Trinity*. Yves Congar, OP, responds to Rahner's trinitarian axiom ("the immanent Trinity is the economic Trinity, and vice versa") in his *I Believe in the Holy Spirit*, 3:11–17.

106. Anatolios, *Retrieving Nicaea*, 4. See B. Marshall, "Unity of the Triune God"; Emery, "*Theologia* and *Dispensatio*."

a family (father, mother, child).[107] Anatolios warns that it would be a mistake if this focus on analogies was also considered to be the major focus of the fourth- and fifth-century theologians. He observes, "When the meaning of trinitarian doctrine is located principally in some particular creaturely analogue, it becomes separable from other aspects of the Christian mystery. Instead of trinitarian meaning being embedded in the whole nexus of Christian faith, it tends to be reduced to the features of the analogue itself."[108]

Anatolios recognizes that propositional clarification was central to the task of those involved in the development of trinitarian doctrine, and that we must inquire into the intelligibility of the fathers' teachings. But we must undertake this inquiry in the right way. The goal of the inquiry should be to "*perform* the meaning of trinitarian doctrine by learning to refer to the trinitarian being of God through the entirety of Christian existence."[109] For this reason, Anatolios emphasizes that the fathers sought conceptual clarification not for its own sake but because our salvation and the integrity of our worship depend upon it. Their conceptual work retained a profound awareness of divine mystery. According to Anatolios (and here I would nuance his position, while agreeing with his critique of rationalism), they were not claiming to speak about the Trinity "in the manner of a direct cognitive correspondence between propositions and their referents."[110] Instead they sought to prescribe "'authoritative rules of discourse, attitude, and action' that ensure the success of the act of referring to the Triune God."[111] The development of trinitarian doctrine thus

107. See Scola, "Nuptial Mystery."
108. Anatolios, *Retrieving Nicaea*, 6.
109. Ibid., 8. For theological use of "performance"—which need not elevate practice over theory, since theoretical reflection certainly belongs to Christian "performance"—see especially Hans Urs von Balthasar's *Theo-Drama*, vol. 1, *Prologomena*. See also such works as Lash, "Performing the Scriptures"; F. Young, *Art of Performance*, especially 160–7; Fodor and Hauerwas, "Performing Faith"; Vanhoozer, *Drama of Doctrine*, chap. 5. Vanhoozer eloquently observes, "The Spirit is the active presence of Christ, enabling and empowering performances that participate in the prior performance of the Word made flesh. It follows that ecclesial performances are authentically Christian only to the extent that they embody and exemplify a properly *dominical* spirit" (*Drama of Doctrine*, 182).
110. Anatolios, *Retrieving Nicaea*, 8. Direct cognitive correspondence between human propositions and God is possible analogously. See Long, *Analogia Entis*.
111. Anatolios, *Retrieving Nicaea*, 8. The interior quotation is from Lindbeck, *Nature of Doctrine*, 18. To my mind, the phrase "authoritative rules of discourse, attitude, and action" does not quite convey what the Nicene fathers were doing. The full passage in Lindbeck reads:

> It has become customary in a considerable body of anthropological, sociological, and philosophical literature . . . to emphasize neither the cognitive nor the experiential-expressive aspects of religion; rather, emphasis is placed on those respects in which religions resemble languages together with their correlative forms of life and thus are similar to cultures (insofar as these are understood semiotically as reality and value systems—that is, as idioms for the construing of reality and the living of life). The function of church

involved "a syntax that enfolded the entirety of Christian existence"—that is to say, "a global interpretation and performance of the whole of Christian existence."[112] This latter insight is surely right.

Anatolios also suggests that we think about trinitarian doctrine via Jean-Luc Marion's phenomenological notion of a "saturated phenomenon," one whose reality exceeds our cognitive grasp because it involves an overwhelming "excess of presencing."[113] Christian existence is "saturated" in this sense by the Triune God. The development of doctrine that occurred in the Nicene period was fueled by this saturation. On this basis, Anatolios makes clear that we learn the meaning of a doctrine by entering into the exigencies, broader than but including conceptual reasoning, that led Christians to this doctrinal development. Christian doctrine develops not merely as a set of ideas, in an abstract vacuum, but within a way of life saturated by trinitarian presence.[114]

---

doctrines that becomes most prominent in this perspective is their use, not as expressive symbols or as truth claims, but as communally authoritative rules of discourse, attitude, and action. This general way of conceptualizing religion will be called in what follows a "cultural-linguistic" approach, and the implied view of church doctrine will be referred to as a "regulative" or "rule" theory. (17–18)

Lindbeck contrasts his "cultural-linguistic" position with two other ways of conceiving of Christian doctrine: cognitive-propositionalist, and experiential-expressivist. He states, "For a propositionalist, if a doctrine is once true, it is always true, and if it is once false, it is always false" (16). Given Lindbeck's overly broad definition of a "propositionalist," I am a propositionalist—and, more importantly, so are the Church fathers. The fathers would surely affirm that "if a doctrine is once true, it is always true," insofar as a doctrine truly expresses a divinely revealed reality. As Geoffrey Wainwright suggests, Lindbeck's "cultural-linguistic" framework can be squared with "doctrinal realism" ("Ecumenical Dimensions of Lindbeck's 'Nature of Doctrine,'" 121), but this requires some work, especially with regard to the status of propositional truth. See also O'Neill, "Rule Theory of Doctrine and Propositional Truth"; Emery, "Thomas Aquinas, Postliberal?"; B. Marshall, "*The Nature of Doctrine* after 25 Years"; Murphy, *God Is Not a Story*.

112. Anatolios, *Retrieving Nicaea*, 8–9. On the mode of scriptural exegesis that undergirds Athanasius's trinitarian reasoning, see ibid., 108–22. See also Ayres, "'There's Fire in That Rain,'" 618:

Christians became the scriptural community that they did[,] not merely by choosing books and marking distinctions between those books and others, but also by choosing to *use and read* those books in a certain way, by means of certain reading practices. . . . Some examples of such practices include: careful attention to whose voice a given section of text should be understood to represent; close attention to patterns of word use and expression within the text of scripture (or in a particular scriptural author or text); close comparison of phrases and titles taken to be parallel and mutually illuminating; close attention to common tropes used by an author; etymological analysis of names; explanations of possible meanings of terms by the use of contemporary scientific and philosophical material.

113. Anatolios, *Retrieving Nicaea*, 10. See Marion, *In Excess*.

114. This emphasis on the whole way of life, rather than upon concepts isolated from this fuller picture, invites clarification regarding the status of propositions in theological discourse. As Anthony C. Sciglitano Jr. points out, the work of the key representatives of the *nouvelle théologie*

For his theory of development of doctrine, Anatolios relies especially upon the French Catholic philosopher Gabriel Marcel's *Reflection and Mystery*, which was written shortly after de Lubac's essay on doctrinal development.[115] Marcel terms the typical way in which we think about our experience "primary reflection," and he holds that propositional faith-commitments belong to this level. Anatolios notes, "Breaks will arise in this flow of experience because the ever-newness and strangeness of God will always challenge our closed, narrowly constructed coherences, and also because the comprehensive scope of Christian faith, as a global interpretation of reality, will always confront competing interpretations."[116] These experiential breaks should produce a

---

systematically elevates symbol (*Vorstellung*) over concept (*Begriff*). This does not mean that they turn to an irrationalist form of theology, but rather that human reason needs to be regulated by the symbolic world of Scripture and Christian worship, within which a deeper reason is disclosed that can heal and perfect distorted or inadequate human reason. This divine reason, however, cannot be reduced to human propositions and univocal statements; rather, it presents itself in the paradoxical joinings of spirit and matter, meaning and expression that can disclose a reality that transcends human rationality, yet does not destroy it. Indeed, only insofar as these paradoxical forms guide reason, can reason itself find its true vocation. Put otherwise, symbolic paradox reveals divine mystery. ("Pope Benedict XVI's *Jesus of Nazareth*," 174–75)

This insistence on the inadequacy of "human propositions and univocal statements" is, on the one hand, nothing new: not only the fathers but also Thomas Aquinas and indeed almost the whole Christian theological tradition would certainly agree. The question, on the other hand, is whether the appropriate response is to elevate "symbol (*Vorstellung*) over concept (*Begriff*)." The fathers' intense conceptual work militates, in my view, against the favoring of "symbol." The notion of "symbol" does not serve theology better than does the notion of conceptual judgments of truth, once one recognizes that the latter, too, allow for surplus of meaning. On symbolic mediation and Jesus as a symbol, from diverse perspectives due to their different starting points, see Rahner, "Theology of the Symbol"; Dulles, *Models of Revelation*, 131–54; Haight, *Jesus, Symbol of God*, 8–9.

115. See Marcel, *Mystery of Being*, vol. 1, *Reflection and Mystery*. The two volumes of *The Mystery of Being* were delivered as the Gifford Lectures in 1949–1950. See also the use of Marcel's work on mystery in Weinandy, *Does God Suffer?*, 30–32. Marcel receives positive attention in Daniélou's programmatic "Les orientations présentes de la pensée religieuse."

116. Anatolios, *Retrieving Nicaea*, 35. As Anatolios goes on to show, however, figures such as Athanasius, Gregory of Nyssa, and Augustine do not in fact offer "closed, narrowly constructed coherences." In light of twentieth-century critiques of the role of propositional truth in Christian doctrine, care needs to be taken here so that Anatolios's intended meaning does not become obscured. In this regard, see, for example, Lieven Boeve's "Orthodoxy, History and Theology." Boeve's project of "recontextualisation" can initially sound similar to Marcel's project, a fact that underscores the crucial role of the affirmation of enduring propositional truth about the realities of salvation. Boeve observes that "contextual novelty puts pressure on historically conditioned expressions of faith and their theological understanding, and drives towards a recontextualisation. Contextual sensitivities and thought patterns start shifting; older forms of tradition lose their familiarity and plausibility; and effects of alienation often arise" (194). The result for Boeve is a radical emphasis on the historical particularity of Christian claims, so that one cannot speak (as Edward Schillebeeckx does in his notion of "consecutive fusions of

creative "reintegration" or "reunification" through what Marcel calls "second-ary reflection."[117] This reunification, of course, does not enable us to grasp the transcendent mystery of faith, but it can and should provide a deeper

---

horizons," or as Hans Küng does in his view of "paradigm shifts" [192]) about "a substance of faith, which, although not available in itself, is the same in all horizons" (193), or about Jesus Christ, historically reconstructed, as the center of theology. Boeve argues that one cannot separate "identity" and "rupture" in theology, because theology "only exists as contextual theology, and the development of tradition as the ongoing process of recontextualisation" (193). For Boeve, in the conceptual expressions of Christian faith, there is nothing enduring that transcends the particularity of the present moment and present context. This goes well beyond Marcel's notion of experiential breaks, but—by exaggerating the difficulty of apprehending past truth-claims today and thereby undermining "mystery" from the opposite direction from that of "closed, narrowly constructed coherences"—it shows the significance of the debate over propositional judgments of truth. See also Boeve's *Interrupting Tradition*, where he argues, in a linguistic-Schleiermachian key, that Christian faith should be understood as an "*open narrative*," one that "has learned to perceive itself as respectful, particular witness to radical otherness (constitutive of the otherness of the concrete other) and that is capable of developing a praxis of the open narrative (implying sensitivity towards the other, witness to the other, self- and world-criticism)"; and where he proposes that Jesus himself, in the Gospels, reveals "what it means to exist in/as an open narrative" inasmuch as he appears as "*God's interrupter*, interrupting closed narratives on behalf of God" (110, 119; cf. 127, 134, 141). In the context of the late-nineteenth- and early-twentieth-century Catholic Modernist movement (and thus in dialogue with Protestant liberalism as well), see the defense of propositional judgments of truth offered by Ambrose Gardeil, OP, *Le Donné révélé et la théologie*.

117. Anatolios, *Retrieving Nicaea*, 35; for a similar view see Pieper, "Tradition," 288, 290. Advocating a more radical sense of "reintegration," Schillebeeckx argues in his *God the Future of Man*—a collection of essays written in the midst of his postconciliar theological shift—that given the hermeneutical circle involved in divine revelation, doctrinal development

> is most profoundly a question of the identity of faith *in* the reintegration itself of faith and not a question of an "unchangeable element of faith," as though this could ever be isolated. The christology of the Bible (the biblical *interpretation* of Jesus of Nazareth) and the christology of Chalcedon (the interpretation in faith of the biblical interpretation and thus a reinterpretation) clearly bear witness to two different social contexts and worlds of thought, yet they also bear witness at the same time to the one, imperishable faith in Jesus, the Christ, our Lord. What does the word say to *us* in the Bible? It says the same thing, but it says it in a contemporary interpretation. (11)

He goes on to explain that "there are no formulae of faith which are, as formulae, endur-ingly valid, capable of transmitting the living faith to men of all ages. Is this relativism? Not at all. It is what is meant by the identity of the faith with itself *in history*. . . . Is there, then, no precise content of faith? Of course there is. But there is no explicitly fixed *representation* of truth—which is not the same thing" (40). What, then, is this "precise content of faith"? He states, "The real content of human knowing and believing is the ever present *mystery* of promise—the mystery which is not uttered, which is everywhere reaching towards expression but in itself is never thought. . . . The thing which is of itself indefinable—the mystery of promise which gives itself in history—ensures the identity of the faith *in* the Church's successive interpretations of the faith" (41). On this view, in the propositional act of faith we do not attain intellectually to any knowledge (judgment of truth) but rather grasp apophatically at a "mystery of promise." This seems quite far from the apostle Paul's joy, marked by an act of propositional judgment, in "the redemption which is in Christ Jesus, whom God put forward as an expiation by his blood, to be received by faith" (Rom. 3:24–25).

penetration into the mystery. Development of doctrine, then, is what happens when our faith commitments are challenged in some way and we respond with "secondary reflection."

Marcel's "reintegration" is different from logical deduction or from the unfolding of an idea because "secondary reflection" engages the whole of our Christian life rather than merely engaging one idea or set of ideas. From this perspective, Anatolios explains that doctrinal "continuity is not merely static adherence to a set of propositions but also a dramatic and sometimes tumultuous process of continually retrieving the truth of the saving relationship with God in Christ"—although Anatolios here should also underline the truth-bearing capacity of doctrinal propositions.[118] As he observes, doctrinal development has to do with "reconstructing coherence,"[119] with "coherence" here involving the whole of Christian life, rather than simply moving logically or organically from one idea to the next. Propositionalist theories of the development of doctrine make the mistake of locating doctrinal development on the level of primary reflection rather than secondary reflection. In the case of trinitarian doctrine specifically, the Church's response to Arius's ideas led not to a mere logical or organic addition of another idea (the Trinity) to Christian life, but to "reconceiving the entirety of Christian faith" in order faithfully to uphold the truth of salvation.[120] All the elements of Christian faith and life

118. Anatolios, *Retrieving Nicaea*, 35. As N. T. Wright puts it (seeking to draw attention to the "whole story" of Israel and Jesus Christ), "Simply putting a checkmark beside all twenty-nine (or however many) true doctrines is not good enough" ("Reading Paul, Thinking Scripture," 65). Discussing the *nouvelle théologie*'s opposition to propositionalism, Brian Daley, SJ, asks rhetorically:

> Can language about God ever be understood with the same analytical clarity, the same literal assurance of reference, which common sense normally attaches to scientific statements about worldly experience? Is the whole of theology, as the organized articulation of the church's faith, to be understood as making the same kind of epistemological claim on the believer as the central core of dogma, summed up in creeds and conciliar definitions? Are our concepts of God always, necessarily, not only analogical but symbolic—not only proportioned to human understanding, but also invitations to worship and contemplation? ("*Nouvelle Théologie* and the Patristic Revival," 381)

Certainly our concepts of God are "proportioned to human understanding" and are "invitations to worship and contemplation," and certainly language about God is analogical in a way that "scientific statements about worldly experience" are not. Daley concludes that "the *nouvelle théologie* was really about the rediscovery of sacramental modes of thought, through renewed contact with Christian authors who thought and read scripture in sacramental as well as literal terms" (382). For the rich mingling of figurative/sacramental and demonstrative argumentation in Aquinas's *Summa theologiae*, see Nichols, "St. Thomas Aquinas on the Passion of Christ."
119. Anatolios, *Retrieving Nicaea*, 35.
120. Ibid. Not every century, of course, is as epoch-making as the fourth century. Nor do contemporary Christians need to reenter into the "secondary reflection" of every epoch-making controversy to the degree that Anatolios proposes (otherwise Christian faith would become

were touched by and involved in the fourth- and fifth-century debates. Anatolios therefore prescribes "a reinvolvement in the secondary reflection that brought about the formulation of trinitarian doctrine," so as to discern the breaks in experience that occasioned such a profound, dynamic reintegration.[121]

We have traveled quite far from Noonan's assurance that if one sees any element of apparent contradiction, one can be sure that one has found a doctrinal rupture. In fact, if Noonan had devoted more time to reflecting upon the theories of development of doctrine, including Newman's, he might not have found it necessary to frame his case studies in the way that he did. At least, he might have emphasized that a good bit of erroneous but nondefinitive teaching does not preclude true doctrinal development in Newman's sense. He might have also recognized the weakness of a woodenly propositional approach to particular instances of doctrinal development.

I agree with Ayres and Anatolios that the development of Christian doctrine is much more than a process by which propositional truths are added to a list of propositional truths, even if logical progression is discernible in much doctrinal development (for instance, in the affirmations of Chalcedon and of Constantinople II). Doctrinal continuity often involves experiential "breaks"—though not ruptures with past definitive doctrine—and "reintegration."[122] For his part,

---

existentially impossible), but Anatolios's point that the fourth-century debates must not be reduced to logical diagrams is true and helpful.

121. Ibid. Again, this position is different from Lieven Boeve's claim that "continuity thus takes shape in rupture" (Boeve, *Interrupting Tradition*, 142), both because of Marcel's and Anatolios's metaphysical commitments and because their understanding of "breaks" differs from Boeve's account of "rupture" (in part due to their view of sin, which contrasts with Boeve's argument that our fundamental problem is "closed narratives" or totalizing metanarratives [143; cf. 167]).

122. Very much along these lines, see Benedict XVI, "Proper Hermeneutic for the Second Vatican Council," ix–xv, which contrasts the "hermeneutic of discontinuity and rupture" with the "hermeneutic of reform." For his part, Nicholas Lash proposes that "four factors" make for "doctrinal continuity in the process of tradition" (*Change in Focus*, 175). His four factors are "the unchanging reference of christian doctrine to certain historical events; the pattern of the church's liturgical worship; the fact that the church has always been a structured community; and, fourthly, that there has been a continuity of christian meanings which was to be looked for, not so much in what has been *said* in the church at different periods, but rather in the concern or intention which had given rise to successive doctrinal statements" (175–76). But this separation of "what has been *said*" (or "successive doctrinal statements") from "the concern or intention," and his preference for the latter, risks relativizing the Church's propositional judgments of truth, unless Lash's "what has been *said*" means simply to refer to instances such as the subordinationist teachings of the ante-Nicene fathers (some of them bishops). Lash wishes to hold that the New Testament is authoritative in its witness to Christ and that "there are moments in the history of christian tradition when the church confesses its faith with peculiar decisiveness, confidence and clarity, and that the affirmations thus made remain—in different ways, and in varying degrees—normative for subsequent belief and exploration" (181). See also Maurice Wiles, *Making of Christian Doctrine*, chaps. 2–5.

Newman points out that tests or notes "for ascertaining the correctness of developments in general may be drawn out . . . but they are insufficient for the guidance of individuals in the case of so large and complicated a problem as Christianity, though they may aid our inquiries and support our conclusions in particular points."[123] As Newman goes on to say, such notes "are instruments rather than warrants of right decisions," and "they rather serve as answers to objections brought against the actual decisions of authority, than are proofs of the correctness of those decisions."[124] In Newman's view, this is why the Church requires a magisterium guided by the Holy Spirit: otherwise, on the basis of reason alone, it would not be possible to follow the course of true doctrinal development.

Thus we can affirm not only mystery but also "breaks" and reintegration, without holding that the Church has undergone corruption or rupture with respect to its definitive interpretations of the gospel. The Church is not a merely human institution but rather is the Body of Christ enabled by Jesus to mediate divine revelation under the guidance of the Holy Spirit. The Spirit ensures that the Church faithfully "perpetuates and transmits to every generation all that she herself is, all that she believes."[125]

123. Newman, *Essay on the Development of Christian Doctrine*, 78.
124. Ibid.
125. *Die Verbum*, §8, 754. See also Paul VI's encyclical *Mysterium Fidei* (September 3, 1965), especially §10. The Congregation for the Doctrine of the Faith's *Mysterium Ecclesiae* (June 24, 1973) affirms that "the meaning of pronouncements of faith depends partly upon the expressive power of the language used at a certain point in time and in particular circumstances" and that "it sometimes happens that some dogmatic truth is first expressed incompletely (but not falsely), and at a later date, when considered in a broader context of faith or human knowledge, it receives a fuller and more perfect expression," but *Mysterium Ecclesiae* also adds that "the meaning of dogmatic formulas . . . remains ever true and constant in the Church, even when it is expressed with greater clarity or more developed," so that it is false to say that "dogmatic formulas (or some category of them) cannot signify truth in a determinate way, but can only offer changeable approximations to it, which to a certain extent distort or alter it" (§5). See also the International Theological Commission's *The Interpretation of Dogma* (1989). The issue is nicely put by John Thiel: "As much as the flux and particularities of historicity may be acknowledged within scripture and tradition themselves, and thus within their interpretation, theology that remains within the assumptions of the Church affirms the inspired truth of God's revelation and therefore cannot accept the terms of historicist interpretation entirely as they might be set by the other disciplines" (*Senses of Tradition*, 74). Thiel therefore advocates a "retrospective conception of tradition" that "always makes the actual present moment its standpoint and from this human perspective looks back to the Christian past for a continuity that cannot be surveyed across a finished past but is instead glimpsed continually in and as tradition's development" (83; cf. especially 92–95). In my view, however, we should not deny that there is something "finished" about past doctrinal determinations. To do this is not to freeze every aspect of the doctrine (as if we had a fully "God-eye" view: cf. 91), but simply to affirm a definitive doctrine's enduring truth.

Conclusion: Revelation and Doctrinal Development

At the outset of this chapter, I outlined what *Dei Verbum* teaches about the transmission of divine revelation and about the doctrinal development that takes place in sacred Tradition. The Council's approach bears the imprint of John Henry Newman: on the one hand, the Council emphasizes continuity in the content of divine revelation as handed on by the apostles through Scripture and Tradition; on the other hand, it insists upon the presence of real growth and development of understanding, so that the first Christians are not imagined to have known all that there is to know about the Christian mystery.[126] The second section of the chapter examined John Noonan's *A Church That Can and Cannot Change*. Concentrating upon moral doctrine, Noonan reviews three areas where the Church's teaching has changed (a fourth area, marriage and divorce, is in his view currently changing). On the basis of his three case studies, Noonan suggests that Newman's exclusion of corruption/contradiction from doctrinal development was a mistake.[127]

In my view, Noonan provides us with an example of how not to evaluate doctrinal development. His case studies certainly demonstrate that the Church once condoned and even approved actions and ideas that the Church no longer condones or approves.[128] But his case studies do not demonstrate

126. For an approach to doctrinal development that, with respect to the path of a doctrine before its definitive formulation, goes further than *Dei Verbum*'s more cautious wording, see Congar, "Church History as a Branch of Theology."

127. See Noonan, *Church That Can and Cannot Change*, 221; cf. the more forceful statement of this same point found in Oakley, "History and the Return of the Repressed," 49, cited above (Oakley's article appears in a book that he coedited and dedicated to Noonan, and Oakley praises Noonan's book on p. 32). According to Oakley, when one compares the Councils of Constance and of Basel, on the one hand, with the First and Second Vatican Councils, on the other, one finds a radical rupture in definitive Church teaching about the locus of ecclesial authority (moderate conciliarism versus papal infallibility). Oakley's argument hinges upon the status of the Council of Constance's decree of April 1415, *Haec sancta synodus*, and thus involves other issues including the validity of the Council at that date, its emergency powers, and the relationship of *Haec sancta synodus* to the Council's later actions, including the November 1417 election of Pope Martin V. To my mind, this period of three rival claimants to the papacy is too murky to justify Oakley's historical assurance that *Haec sancta synodus* stands as definitive Catholic dogma. For a further claim of doctrinal rupture, see the comparison by Edward Schillebeeckx, OP, of two conciliar texts, one from the 1442 Council of Florence-Ferrara and one from the Second Vatican Council, on the issue of whether anyone can be saved outside the Catholic Church. See Schillebeeckx, *Church*, xvii. For a contrasting view, see Dulles, "Who Can Be Saved?" See also Lash's *Change in Focus*, 174–75, where Lash takes up the problem of Pope Boniface VIII's strong papal claims in his bull *Unam Sanctam*. Responding to Schillebeeckx's project, Aidan Nichols urges that "the fundamental hermeneutical vantage point to be occupied by the Catholic theologian—whether in his reading of Scripture, or in his evaluation of the human condition—must be that represented by the Church's tradition itself" (*From Newman to Congar*, 276).

128. See also, along these lines, Lacey, "Leo's Church and Our Own."

the presence of a doctrinal rupture rather than a true development. In this regard, much rests on how to determine when the Church has articulated a definitive doctrine, since only in such cases could a true contradiction or rupture occur. As Newman makes clear, the Church's magisterium, under the guidance of the Holy Spirit, makes this determination; no "notes" or rules for doctrinal development can decide it in advance, although neither will the Church's doctrinal development be without historically perceivable warrants.

The third section of the chapter examined these issues in light of contemporary scholarship on doctrinal development in the Nicene period.[129] Ayres's main concern is that the historian of doctrine not be expected to prove that a true development has occurred. Doctrinal development in the Church's understanding of divine revelation involves the whole mystery of Christ. It follows that the truth of Nicene trinitarian doctrine is not something that we can prove by using the most up-to-date historical-critical methods. For his part, Anatolios likewise warns against approaching Nicene theology as mere logicians, as though the topic of the Trinity were separable from the full scope of Christian existence. He argues for an account of development of doctrine that recognizes our need to reintegrate our faith commitments within new frameworks brought about by new questions. This position is close to Newman's view that the articulation of Christian doctrine is often a tumultuous process in which the contending positions each have a claim to plausibility. Out of this tumultuous process new insights arise

---

129. On the developmental process, see also Wiles, *Making of Christian Doctrine*, 142–46, even though Wiles thinks of "development" as a sociological event that of necessity includes erroneous teaching. For Wiles, "True continuity with the age of the Fathers is to be sought not so much in the repetition of their doctrinal conclusions or even in the building upon them, but rather in the continuation of their doctrinal aims" (173). By limiting continuity to this volitional or subjective dimension, Wiles seeks to avoid cognitively "objectifying" doctrines and instead to adhere strictly to a set of "permanent aims of Christian doctrine" (180). He denies that he thereby falls into a purely subjective understanding of doctrine, but I think that in fact he does. Charles Journet quotes a passage from Garrigou-Lagrange's *Le sens commun* that makes the central point: "Far from *subjecting itself* to these concepts, Revelation *makes use* of them. . . . Before making use of these concepts and these terms, Christ, through the Church, has judged them, and approved them in a wholly divine light, which is not measured by time but by unchanging eternity. These concepts, plainly inadequate, could always be made more precise, but never given up" (Garrigou-Lagrange, *Le sens commun*, 189, quoted in Journet, *What Is Dogma?*, 89–90). See also the First Vatican Council's Dogmatic Constitution on the Catholic Faith, *Dei Filius*, chap. 4, 809: "For the doctrine of the faith which God has revealed is put forward not as some philosophical discovery capable of being perfected by human intelligence, but as a divine deposit committed to the spouse of Christ to be faithfully protected and infallibly promulgated. Hence, too, that meaning of the sacred dogmas is ever to be maintained which has once been declared by holy mother church, and there must never be any abandonment of this sense under the pretext or in the name of a more profound understanding."

that enrich the whole of Christian life and shed new light on the whole of divine revelation.[130]

Ayres's and Anatolios's criticisms of propositionalist views of doctrinal development should be paired with an equally strong affirmation of the truth of the Church's doctrinal propositions (which Ayres and Anatolios fully embrace).[131] Here we can benefit from Romanus Cessario's *Christian Faith and the Theological Life*. Cessario treats the object of faith in a threefold manner: First Truth, truth-bearing statements, and the supernatural light of faith. Strictly speaking, the object of faith is God alone, First Truth. Truth-bearing statements "acquire their dignity and importance within the Christian religion precisely because of faith's formal object, that is, because they express God's Truth within the context of the Church's life and mission."[132] But can finite and culturally embedded concepts express, in an enduring fashion, inexhaustible divine mysteries?

130. Schillebeeckx takes this in a different, anthropocentric direction in the last chapter of his *God the Future of Man*, where he argues that "Christian commitment to the world by concern for man will therefore be the exegesis or hermeneutics of the new concept of God, in which God is really shown to be the 'wholly New One.' . . . Hermeneutics consisting of the very practice of Christian life are therefore the *basis* for the concrete exegesis of ancient, biblical or magisterial texts" (184).

131. With regard to Vatican II, Hermann J. Pottmeyer comments that "'progressive' interpretations have occasionally forgotten that the Council retracted nothing in the dogmas of Trent and Vatican I" ("New Phase in the Reception of Vatican II," 40). Pottmeyer adds, however, that Vatican II "did indeed relativize these dogmas in the sense that it no longer regarded their formulations as the absolutely final stage of development in the understanding of the faith, but instead located them within the whole tradition of faith" (ibid.). Even so, Pottmeyer cautions against "the hermeneutical misunderstanding summed up in the slogan: Beyond the Council out of fidelity to the Council! . . . The hermeneutical misunderstanding of which I am speaking finds expression in the attempt to separate the 'spirit' of the Council from its letter and then leave the letter behind" (41–42).

132. Cessario, *Christian Faith and the Theological Life*, 61–62. Cessario rejects the view that "doctrines serve as noninformative and nondiscursive symbols of inner feelings, attitudes, or existential orientations" (63). As Charles Journet states, "The object of faith is both the statement [or proposition] so far as this touches reality and reality so far as this is shown in the statement. It is both the statement to which faith assents and reality that becomes open to it by this assent, toward which it tends, and in which it terminates" (*What Is Dogma?*, 19). For his part, Nicholas Lash points out, "It is fashionable nowadays sharply to contrast faith conceived as an intellectual assent to propositions with a view of faith as 'personal adhesion,' patterned on the analogy of personal relationships between human beings. But however inadequate the former conception may be, it cannot simply be replaced by the latter. 'Le Coeur a ses raisons que la raison ne connait pas.' But he would be a foolish man who allowed his life to be so dictated by his heart that his head was quite unable to assent to any propositions concerning whom he loved and why" (*Change of Focus*, 17). See also Aidan Nichols's remark that "[Ambrose] Gardeil's contribution to the understanding of the development of doctrine lies in his sane and generous view of propositional truth—its importance and its dignity" (*From Newman to Congar*, 175).

In response to this issue, Cessario reflects upon the emergence in the medieval period of the notion of the "article of faith." He emphasizes that the medieval theologians were not thereby "confining God to the limits of created words," but instead "their concern in associating divine truth with truth-bearing statements was to show that human language can serve as an instrument for raising the creature to God."[133] As Cessario further explains, "Under the guidance of the Holy Spirit, the Church uses the articles of faith to conceptualize the biblical revelation, so that divine truth remains centered in the historical reality that marks its appearance on earth and at the same time is liberated from the confines that any particular culture or time would otherwise impose on it."[134] To accept the articles of faith requires "surrender to a God who both exists as Truth and speaks the Truth" and "begets an even greater love of the revealed truth."[135] Conceived along these lines, the act of faith is not a mere matter of learning about propositions. Rather, through the mediation of "the conceptual content of the proposition (*enuntiabile*)," faith's judgment "lays hold of the very realities that the articles express and mediate."[136]

By taking this sapiential path, however, have we ascended beyond the historical messiness of Church teaching?[137] The rootedness of Church teaching in historical controversies is well known. The question is whether these historical controversies produced propositional judgments of truth that are normative for later Christians.[138] If not, then history's significance for Chris-

---

133. Cessario, *Christian Faith and the Theological Life*, 63.

134. Ibid., 64. For a fuller analysis of the "articles of faith," see 64–76. For a historical overview of "dogma," with a critique of the neoscholastic period for separating the "articles of faith" from the doxological context of the Apostles' Creed, see Lash, *Change of Focus*, 46–57. Lash associates the shift to "system" with the rise of rationalism, but it seems to me that Lash's understanding of the "symbolic"—which he terms "man's attempt to articulate his understanding of the mystery of his future in God" (52)—raises the specter of rationalism much more than does the medieval and neoscholastic view of doctrine.

135. Cessario, *Christian Faith and the Theological Life*, 74.

136. Ibid. It follows that faith "possesses the complexifying and proposition-transcending character of all human judgment-acts," although the propositions (or articles of faith) never simply fall away: "The propositional terms are the real medium of existential assent: judgment always says both '*this* is' and 'this *is*'" (75–76).

137. For further elucidation of what I mean by "sapiential," see White, "Precarity of Wisdom," 102–9. See also Ashley, "Transition to Historical Mindedness"; Lamb, "Eschatology of St. Thomas Aquinas."

138. This question should be addressed to positions such as that of Joseph A. Komonchak, who blurs the issue in his "Local Realization of the Church." He comments:

It is easy enough to say, as did Pope Paul VI, that there are "many secondary elements" in the Church's message, which may change, and an "essential content, a living substance, which cannot be modified or ignored." But the real problem is in knowing how to separate that substance from culturally conditioned elements. Traditional Catholicism bears the marks of the long history through which it has transformed Western culture and been

tian faith would be denigrated, even negated, rather than elevated.[139] Nicea is important precisely because faith involves true propositional confession, and not otherwise. To affirm the development of doctrine thus requires a particular understanding of doctrine, well expressed by the Reformed theologian T. F. Torrance, to whom I will give the last word. As Torrance rightly says, in the early Church "faith was not regarded . . . as some form of non-cognitive or non-conceptual relation to God, but was held to involve acts of recognition, apprehension and conception, of a very basic intuitive kind, in the responsible assent of the mind to truth inherent in God's self-revelation to mankind."[140]

---

itself transformed in the process. There is not now, nor has there ever been, a Catholicism that represents some pure, transcultural quintessence of Christianity. Catholicism is what Catholicism has become through its history. (89)

With proper qualifications, this would be true; but to claim simply that "Catholicism is what Catholicism has become through its history" is to side with historicism. For a fully historicized view of theology, see Giuseppe Ruggieri, "Faith and History," 97–98.

139. See the emphasis on historical study in A. N. Williams, "Future of the Past." As Williams points out, "If once the danger lay in a woodenly authoritarian appeal to the Christian theological past, in our time the danger lies rather in a more or less complete relativization of its significance, in some instances amounting to vehement denial that it might have any contemporary import" (358). Williams suggests that we can avoid doctrinal relativism—a concern that she thinks was fairly raised by Labourdette—by "discerning between legitimate diversity and antithetical divergence, and between dogma and theologoumena, along with the recognition that the area designated by 'dogma' will always and necessarily be much smaller than that describable as legitimate theologoumena" (359). In her vision of theological diversity, however, Williams does not have room for the neoscholastics, whom she considers to have been involved in a mere "theology of repetition" (357). For his part, Schillebeeckx denies that relativizing the truth-bearing potential of each period of Church history (including the biblical periods) means "that these historical and socio-cultural mediations are worthless for faith or to be neglected. On the contrary, they have a very positive function, for all their relativity, since they are the only possible vehicles for the meaning of the offer of revelation to which an answer is given in faith, precisely because the gospel, which is not bound to one culture, can nevertheless be seen and found *in* the special features of particular, culturally limited structures of understanding (only there and precisely there)" (*Church*, 37). Schillebeeckx's claim is undermined, however, by his apophatic view of the propositional content of "the gospel" (other than its eschatological pointing to a God who is coming).

140. T. F. Torrance, *Trinitarian Faith*, 20, quoted in Nichols, *From Newman to Congar*, 277. Nichols emphasizes that "while, in divine revelation, images are of the greatest importance as carriers of meaning . . . there must also be judgement—and hence doctrinal determinations—concerning the significance of what these images connote. It is this objective evangelical truth, expressed in a body of doctrine, which bonds the Church to the 'creative source of its being in the Gospel,' and structures its life and mission in accordance with the 'pattern of divine truth' embodied in Christ" (*From Newman to Congar*, 277–78; the interior quotations come from Torrance, *Trinitarian Faith*, 31). By contrast, N. T. Wright accepts the "Christian 'rule of faith'" but warns against "hemming one another in through ever more carefully worded dogmatic statements which reflect ever narrower definitions within particular traditions" (*Last Word*, 136). Wright's view of dogmatic statements is clearly propositionalist.

SEVEN

Inspiration

Dei Verbum proclaims the uniqueness of Scripture as the inspired word of God: "Sacred Scripture is the speech of God as it is put down in writing under the breath of the Holy Spirit."[1] But what does it mean for human words to be the word of God, and thus to be uniquely inspired to mediate divine revelation? It would be impossible to exhaust this topic, which has so many dimensions.[2] Given my focus on the mediation of divine revelation, the present chapter engages one aspect of biblical inspiration—namely, the relationship of divine inspiration to the truth of the historical narratives of Scripture. I begin with certain assumptions: biblical authors/redactors and biblical texts are inspired by the Holy Spirit within the covenantal people of God, biblical texts often bear the imprint of many authors and redactors writing some time after the events they describe, and the whole of Scripture is inspired to teach what God willed to make known for the sake of our salvation.

---

1. *Dei Verbum*, §9, 755. See also the *Catechism of the Catholic Church*, §§ 102, 104: "Through all the words of Sacred Scripture, God speaks only one single Word, his one Utterance in whom he expresses himself completely. . . . In Sacred Scripture, the Church constantly finds her nourishment and her strength, for she welcomes it not as a human word, 'but as what it really is, the word of God' [1 Thess. 2:13]."

2. For a range of approaches, see my "Inspiration of Scripture." Some portions of the present chapter are drawn from this earlier essay. Regarding the doctrine of inspiration, I agree with the position sketched by John Webster in his *Holy Scripture*, which I discussed in chap. 2 above, as well as with the similar account (indebted to Webster) found in Billings, *Word of God for the People of God*, 90–94.

On this basis, I first examine what Scripture itself says about its historical truth and how Scripture conceives of the nature of history. I then survey the approaches of Origen and Augustine to Scripture's historical truth and to the nature of history. My aim is to highlight the need for a more "critical" understanding of history, one that allows for God's providential guidance of every aspect of the biblical texts and thus allows for typological resonances. In this light, historical-critical doubts about the historicity of this or that person or event become less pressing, because a typologically rich text retains its historical character under God's providence. My final section, indebted to the biblical scholar Denis Farkasfalvy, seeks to bring together the strengths of Origen's and Augustine's approaches in light of historical-critical scholarship.

Scripture, History, and Divine Providence

Did all the persons and events found in Scripture's historical narratives actually exist or happen?[3] Scripture itself does not often raise this question explicitly, but there are important exceptions to this general rule. The Gospel of John, for example, testifies to the truthfulness of its author: "We know that his testimony is true" (John 21:24). Even more powerfully, Paul states

---

3. The importance of this question is not sufficiently appreciated by Hans Frei, *Eclipse of Biblical Narrative*; for a particularly helpful discussion of Frei's approach, see Wolterstorff, *Divine Discourse*, 230–36. By Scripture's "historical narratives," I have in mind all biblical texts that purport to narrate things that happened in the past and that do so without clear indications that historical description is not intended. Thus, I accept the contention of Iain Provan, V. Philips Long, and Tremper Longman III that "the 'Genesis project' is a project in history writing" (*Biblical History of Israel*, 111). They grant that many passages of the Torah, including passages in the Torah's historical narratives such as the stories about Joseph, are not primarily concerned with history, and they also recognize that "no explicit extrabiblical attestation is given to the patriarchs or the events mentioned in the biblical texts" (113). But they argue that the portrait of the patriarchs accords with what we know of the time period from other ancient documents, not least by attributing to the patriarchs behaviors (such as marrying a half-sister) that were objectionable in later periods. For their part, John Barton and Julia Bowden point out that the names Abraham, Isaac, Jacob, Moses, Aaron, Hophni, and Phineas were common in the historical contexts in which they appear in Scripture, whereas such names are not found in later periods: see Barton and Bowden, *Original Story*, 127–28. Barton and Bowden conclude, "What emerges from the points made above about 'archaic' features of the patriarchal narratives is that there is a great deal in the stories no one in later times could have invented" (131). Yet Barton and Bowden also remind us of "how little we can really be sure of where the early history of Israel is concerned" (ibid.). See also the evidence regarding Israel's unique worship of YHWH, in Tryggve N. D. Mettinger, *No Graven Image?*; Grabbe, "'Many Nations Will Be Joined to Yhwh.'" For further perspectives on the Old Testament's historical narratives, see, for example, Halpern, *First Historians*; Schniedewind, *How the Bible Became a Book*; Hoffmeier, *Israel in Egypt*; Shinan and Zakovitch, *From Gods to God*. On the New Testament, see, for example, Bauckham, *Jesus and the Eyewitnesses*; Dunn, "Let John Be John."

that "if Christ has not been raised, then our preaching is in vain and your faith is in vain. We are even found to be misrepresenting God, because we testified of God that he raised Christ" (1 Cor. 15:14–15). In writing to the Corinthians, Paul takes with the greatest possible seriousness the accuracy of his claim that Jesus Christ was raised from the dead on the third day; if it did not happen, then Paul's entire ministry, by his own account, has been a blasphemous and useless lie.[4]

Compared to Paul's concern for the historical accuracy of his proclamation of Christ's resurrection, his interest in the historical accuracy of his description of Old Testament events seems much less. When Paul describes the exodus of the Israelites from Egypt, for instance, he states that "they drank from the supernatural Rock which followed them, and the Rock was Christ" (1 Cor. 10:4). Exodus 17 and Numbers 20 both describe this rock as a stationary rock that Moses strikes and from which water miraculously pours forth. According to Exodus, the rock was located "at Horeb" (Exod. 17:6) and Moses named the place "Massah" and "Meribah" (Exod. 17:7). According to Numbers 20, the rock was located in Kadesh, in the wilderness of Zin. By saying that the rock "followed them," Paul shows less concern for historical actuality than he does with respect to Jesus's resurrection. This is true even if Paul has typological reasoning in mind (as he certainly does) that enables him to conceive of this rock as moving from place to place.[5]

A similar pattern can be observed in Jesus's teachings. For example, Jesus frequently presents Moses as the author of the Torah. Thus Jesus tells the healed leper to "offer the gift that Moses commanded" (Matt. 8:4) and states, "For your hardness of heart Moses allowed you to divorce your wives, but from the beginning it was not so" (Matt. 19:8). Jesus calls Exodus "the book of Moses" (Mark 12:26). Jesus compares his future crucifixion to Moses's mounting upon a pole an image of a snake (which Moses did at God's command, so that those bitten by snakes could look at the image and be cured): "And as Moses lifted up the serpent in the wilderness, so must the Son of man be lifted up, that whoever believes in him may have eternal life" (John 3:14–15; cf. Num. 21:8–9). If there was not a historical Moses who, while dwelling in the wilderness at a certain point in history, lifted up an image of a serpent, would Jesus's comparison fall to the ground? Or is Jesus simply making a comparison that is grounded in an earlier story familiar to his hearers but

4. For discussion see N. T. Wright, *Resurrection of the Son of God*, 277–374.

5. For further discussion see my "Readings on the Rock," which includes detailed discussions of the positions of Richard B. Hays, Peter Enns, and Peter Leithart. Paul's understanding of the rock has parallels in other Second Temple Jewish literature, including the *Targum Onqelos*, the Tosefta (*Sukkah* 3.11), and the *Book of Biblical Antiquities*.

that does not require that the historical Moses actually did this thing at some point in the past? In the gospels, Jesus does not say.

Scripture, then, sometimes insists on the accuracy of its historical narratives, as in the cases of John 21:24 and 1 Corinthians 15:14–15. More often, however, historical accuracy is either presumed, not worried about, or handled rather loosely. As Richard B. Hays puts it with regard to historical-critical exegetical methodology, "Let us not deceive ourselves about this: Paul would flunk our introductory exegesis course. . . . Paul provides us with a model of hermeneutical freedom."[6] This does not mean that Scripture lacks historical accuracy; it simply means that Scripture generally treats this issue differently than modern historians.[7]

By contrast, Scripture quite often insists upon a second kind of historical claim, foreign to modern historians—namely, the reality of God's providential governance of history.[8] The book of Acts, for instance, describes the apostles as praising God by saying, "Sovereign Lord, who didst make the heaven and the earth and the sea and everything in them" (Acts 4:24). The apostles proclaim that in Jerusalem "there were gathered together against thy holy servant Jesus, who thou didst anoint, both Herod and Pontius Pilate, with the Gentiles and the peoples of Israel, to do whatever thy hand and thy plan had predestined to take place" (Acts 4:27–28).[9] Jesus in the Gospel of Matthew makes a similarly all-encompassing claim about divine providence. He observes, "Are not two sparrows sold for a penny? And not one of them will fall to the ground without your Father's will. But even the hairs of your head are all numbered" (Matt. 10:29–30).[10] God permits our sinfulness without

---

6. Hays, *Echoes of Scripture in the Letters of Paul*, 181, 186.

7. With regard to the Hebrew Scriptures/Old Testament, Meir Sternberg notes that while the biblical narrative is obviously historical—Sternberg points to the historical claims implicit in "how often customs are elucidated, ancient names and current sayings traced back to their origins, monuments and fiats assigned a concrete reason as well as a slot in history, persons and places and pedigrees specified beyond immediate needs, written records like the Book of Yashar or the royal annals explicitly invoked" (*Poetics of Biblical Narrative*, 31)—nonetheless the narrators proceed upon different lines than do modern historians: "Anonymity in ancient narrative validates supernatural powers of narration; and in Israelite culture, which not only institutionalized prophecy but invested its writings with canonical authority, the narrator's claim to omniscience dovetails rather than conflicts with his claim to historicity" (33). See also Wolterstorff, *Divine Discourse*, chap. 14, where Wolterstorff builds constructively but critically upon Sternberg's insights in order to present the "illocutionary stance" of the evangelists, which allows at times for "going beyond and even against the available chronicle" (259).

8. For further discussion see my *Participatory Biblical Exegesis*. See also my "Linear and Participatory History in Augustine's *City of God*." For issues raised by God's providential governance of history, see my *Predestination*.

9. On this topic see especially Squires, *Plan of God in Luke-Acts*.

10. For historical-critical discussion, see Davies and Allison, *Gospel according to Saint Matthew*, 2:208.

thereby having his plan of salvation frustrated. Paul makes this clear in many places—for instance, when he proclaims that "where sin increased, grace abounded all the more, so that, as sin reigned in death, grace also might reign through righteousness to eternal life through Jesus Christ our Lord" (Rom. 5:20–21).

Scripture displays this providential and active involvement of God in history by drawing typological connections between events, connections of a kind that are hardly possible for secular historiography to admit.[11] In the New Testament, Jesus appears as a new Isaac, a new Joshua, a new Moses, a new David.[12] Mary's Magnificat in Luke 1 echoes Hannah's song of praise and also compares with the rejoicing of other barren women of Israel. An angel of the Lord tells the father of John the Baptist that John will be a new Elijah (see Luke 1:16–17). Likewise, an angel of the Lord tells Mary that Jesus will receive from God "the throne of his father David, and he will reign over the house of Jacob for ever; and of his kingdom there will be no end" (Luke 1:32–33).[13] In the Gospel of John, Jesus presents his body as the new temple, the source from which the Holy Spirit flows to enliven God's people (John 7:37–39).[14] The Letter to the Hebrews, which depicts Christ as a new Joshua and a new Melchizedek, argues that the whole Torah has a typological meaning revealed in Christ and the Church (see Heb. 10:1). Paul observes that the experiences of the Israelites on the exodus were types or symbols that "were written down for our instruction, upon whom the end of the ages has come" (1 Cor. 10:11). The book of Revelation employs a vast array of types in depicting the course of history and its consummation. The Old Testament too contains much typology; Joshua, for example, is presented as the new Moses in Joshua 1–5. The presence of typology in Scripture's historical narratives shows that Scripture's view of history is quite different from views that make human history autonomous from God. Of course, the presence of typology does not in itself demonstrate a lack of concern for historical

11. In his apostolic exhortation *Verbum Domini* (2010), Pope Benedict XVI brings out the significance of typology: "From apostolic times and in her living Tradition, the Church has stressed the unity of God's plan in the two Testaments through the use of typology; this procedure is in no way arbitrary, but is intrinsic to the events related in the sacred text and thus involves the whole of Scripture" (§41).

12. See, for example, Huizenga, *New Isaac*; Ounsworth, *Joshua Typology in the New Testament*; Strauss, *Davidic Messiah in Luke-Acts*; Hoskins, *That Scripture Might Be Fulfilled*; Le Donne, *Historiographical Jesus*. For the assumption that these typological connections are mere invention, see Goulder, *Type and History in Acts*, 205.

13. See J. Green, *Gospel of Luke*, 88–89.

14. For discussion see Hoskins, *Jesus as the Fulfillment*.

actuality or accuracy. But when compared to modern (secular) historiography, it does show a different understanding of how historical narrative can communicate truth.[15]

Origen and Augustine: The Twofold Meaning of History

In the patristic period, two fathers in particular stand out for their approaches to Scripture's twofold account of history (outward events and typological connections): Origen and Augustine.[16] Origen devoted his life to commenting on the books of Scripture, and he also provides a theology of Scripture in his *On First Principles*. Augustine's *City of God* develops a profound biblical theology of history. Both Origen and Augustine employ typological interpretation, and both take seriously the question of the historical accuracy of biblical passages. They probe deeply into the purposes of divine revelation and into the role that inspired Scripture plays in communicating this historical revelation. I will suggest that a contemporary theology of revelation, history, and inspiration should adopt elements from both of their perspectives.

Origen

Origen is best known for his appreciation of typology in history.[17] He considers that we should take Paul as our teacher for how to read the Torah. Frequently, Paul emphasizes the typological meaning (as in 1 Cor. 10). Origen remarks, "Do you see how much Paul's teaching differs from the literal meaning? What

15. On typology in the Old Testament and intertestamental literature, see especially Kugel, *How to Read the Bible*. On New Testament and patristic typology, see especially Daniélou, "Symbolism and History"; Daniélou, *From Shadows to Reality*. Whereas Daniélou differentiates typology sharply from allegory, Henri de Lubac, SJ, rejects this sharp distinction: see de Lubac, "'Typologie' et 'allégorisme.'" See also Ayres, "'There's Fire in That Rain.'"

16. For instructive use of Origen in showing that certain passages of the Old Testament should be taken metaphorically, see Swinburne, *Revelation*, 188–91; for his discussion of Origen and Augustine, see ibid., 202–5. As Swinburne states, "The human authors grasped much of God's nature and purposes. But where they misunderstood that, what they wrote down had sufficient truth to it that, in a larger context, it came to have a sense which it would not have on its own, in which it was altogether true" (197; cf. 201).

17. For background see de Lubac, *History and Spirit*; Daniélou, *Origen*, 139–73; Martens, *Origen and Scripture*; Torjesen, *Hermeneutical Procedure and Theological Method in Origen's Exegesis*. On Origen's use of allegory (treated by the above works as well), see also Martens, "Origen against History?"; Boyarin, "Origen as Theorist of Allegory"; Dawson, *Allegorical Readers and Cultural Revision in Ancient Alexandria*. For the view that both Origen and Augustine make the mistake of reifying the biblical text—substituting "for the Biblical conception of word and spirit the notion of a sacred letter that has only marginal justification in the Bible itself"—see Vawter, *Biblical Inspiration*, 28.

the Jews supposed to be a crossing of the sea, Paul calls a baptism; what they supposed to be a cloud, Paul asserts is the Holy Spirit. . . . And again, the manna which the Jews supposed to be food for the stomach and the satiation of the appetite, Paul calls 'spiritual food.'"[18] Origen does not reject the historical reference of these texts from Exodus, but he asserts that the much more important meaning is the meaning that is conveyed by typology. Likewise, the primary meaning of the ten plagues is a typological one, because history's primary meaning has to do with our spiritual renewal. Origen proposes along these lines that "Moses, who comes to Egypt and brings the rod with which he punishes and strikes Egypt with the ten plagues, is the Law of God which was given to this world that it might reprove and correct it with the ten plagues, that is the ten commandments which are contained in the Decalogue."[19] Moses's rod itself, read as a type, has the power truly to subjugate and conquer Egypt because it "is the cross of Christ by which this world is conquered and the 'ruler of this world' with the principalities and the powers are led in triumph."[20]

Similarly, when Origen arrives at Exodus 20, where God amplifies his condemnation of idolatry by explaining, "I the LORD your God am a jealous God, visiting the iniquity of the fathers upon the children to the third and the fourth generation of those who hate me" (Exod. 20:5), Origen comments that this passage has been mocked by the gnostics as proof of an evil God and also seems to conflict with later words of God, such as Ezekiel 18:20, "The son shall not suffer for the iniquity of the father, nor the father suffer for the iniquity of the son; the righteousness of the righteous shall be upon himself, and the wickedness of the wicked shall be upon himself." In response, Origen observes, "We have often said already that not everything in divine Scripture is said to the outer man, but many things are said to the inner man."[21] Reading Exodus 20:5 as an instruction to the inner man, Origen holds that the "third and fourth generation" indicates those whom we embroil in our sin (whom we thereby make into children of the devil), since we hardly ever sin alone but instead lure others to help us sin and to sin with us. God punishes both us and those whom we have enticed to help us sin; in this sense God punishes both the "fathers" and the "children" involved in the same sin. Origen is perfectly aware, of course, that this is not the meaning that the "outer man" would garner from this text. Following Paul, however, he aims to read the Torah primarily for the meaning of history that has to do with divine providence and our ordering to eternal life, the interior meaning of history.

18. Origen, *Homilies on Exodus*, Homily 5, 276.
19. Ibid., Homily 4, 267.
20. Ibid.
21. Ibid., Homily 8, 329.

Origen takes the same approach to the historical narratives of Israel's wars of conquest and extermination of the people of the land. For example, Joshua 8 presents God as commanding Joshua to lead Israel into battle against Ai and to slaughter every citizen of Ai, leaving only the cattle alive.[22] In Joshua 8:24–26, we read:

> When Israel had finished slaughtering all the inhabitants of Ai in the open wilderness where they pursued them, and all of them to the very last had fallen by the edge of the sword, all Israel returned to Ai, and smote it with the edge of the sword. And all who fell that day, both men and women, were twelve thousand, all the people of Ai. For Joshua did not draw back his hand, with which he stretched out the javelin, until he had utterly destroyed all the inhabitants of Ai.

This kind of warfare, which was certainly practiced in the ancient Near East, requires the slaughter of defenseless noncombatants, including all the women and children of the city. Spiritually, the slaughtering of children could hardly have been good for Israelite soldiers, let alone for the children themselves, and so why did God command it? Origen reads the narrative as rich in the typological meaning of history, which he considers to be the sole meaning intended by the Holy Spirit as author. As he says, "If in this manner we understand what is written, perhaps the reading will seem worthy of the pen of the Holy Spirit."[23] He justifies this interpretive approach by reference to Paul's insistence that the Torah "was written for our sake" (1 Cor. 9:10).

Regarding passages such as Joshua 8, Origen points out that the gnostics Marcion, Valentinus, and Basilides "refuse to understand these things in a manner worthy of the Holy Spirit": they read historical passages such as this one as evidence that the God of Israel is evil.[24] By contrast, says Origen, a Christian interpreter "understands that all these things are mysteries of the kingdom of heaven" whose meaning is that "Jesus Christ wars against opposing powers and casts out of their cities, that is, out of our souls, those who used to occupy them."[25] To read these passages as though the Holy Spirit, as author, intended us to receive the outward historical meaning rather than the inward historical meaning would lead us into a grave misconception of God. Origen observes that his approach ensures that such passages "will also appear more devout and more merciful, when he [Joshua] is said to have so

22. For contemporary reflection see, for example, Cowles et al., *Show Them No Mercy*.
23. Origen, *Homilies on Joshua*, Homily 8, 91.
24. Ibid., Homily 12, 123. On Marcion, Valentius, and Basilides, see Grant, *Heresy and Criticism*; Thomassen, *Spiritual Seed*; Brakke, *Gnostics*.
25. Origen, *Homilies on Joshua*, Homily 13, 125. On Origen's christological reading of Joshua, see also de Lubac, *History and Spirit*, 214–15.

subverted and devastated individual cities that 'nothing that breathed was left in them, neither any who might be saved nor any who might escape' [Josh. 8:22]."[26]

In this vein, Origen prays that all his own sins will be utterly destroyed in the same way that Joshua (Jesus) utterly conquers at God's command. Origen explains that "at first, the work of the Word of God is to pluck up evil habits, the thorns and thistles of vices, because as long as those roots fill the occupied land, it cannot receive the good and holy seed."[27] Once God has utterly destroyed these enemies through the power of Jesus/Joshua, so that none of them is left alive or breathing, then we are truly filled with the Spirit of Jesus Christ. This is how to understand the historical-typological meaning of Joshua 11:11, "And they put to the sword all who were in it, utterly destroying them; there was none left that breathed, and he burned Hazor with fire."[28] The meaning is typological, but in Origen's providential understanding of history, it is fully a historical meaning.

In book 4 of Origen's *On First Principles*, he reflects more systematically upon how to interpret Scripture in light of the two dimensions of history—namely, the outward events and their inner dynamism. The writings of the prophets, he considers, make manifest to all readers their divine origin.[29] All the writings of Scripture are inspired by God, even though "our weakness cannot discern in every sentence the hidden splendour of its teachings."[30] He comments that those who read with strict historical literalness, rather than attending to the inner dimension of history, end up by denying that Jesus was the Messiah on the grounds that the wolf has not in fact lain down with the lamb (see Isa. 11). Likewise, such readers can err by taking as literal fact the descriptions of God as jealous, as changeable, and as creating evil (see Exod. 20:5; 1 Sam. 15:11; 18:10; Isa. 45:7). He warns that "even the simpler of those who claim to belong to the Church, while believing indeed that there is none greater than the Creator, in which they are right, yet believe such things about him as would not be believed of the most savage and unjust of men."[31] A simple reading of the historical narrative cannot do justice to its divine authorship, which penetrates to the providential ordering of history

26. Origen, *Homilies on Joshua*, Homily 13, 127.
27. Ibid., 128.
28. See ibid., Homily 15, 143.
29. Origen, *On First Principles*, book 4, chap. 1, 265 (Greek text).
30. Ibid., 267 (Greek text). Origen adds, "For if it had been the hackneyed methods of demonstration used among men and preserved in books that had convinced mankind, our faith might reasonably have been supposed to rest in the wisdom of men and not in the power of God" [cf. 1 Cor. 2:5] (ibid.).
31. Ibid., book 4, chap. 2, 271 (Greek text).

and which never (despite outward appearances) asserts anything contrary to the truth and glory of God.

Given the interpretive mistakes that result from failing to understand the "spiritual sense" and reading instead "according to the bare letter," Origen attempts to set forth certain principles for scriptural interpretation for the benefit of all who believe, with Origen, "that the sacred books are not the works of men, but that they were composed and have come down to us as a result of the inspiration of the Holy Spirit by the will of the Father of the universe through Jesus Christ."[32] Origen argues that there are three ways that Scripture teaches, and he compares these ways to the human body, soul, and spirit: from more evident and more outward to less evident and more inward. He thinks that some passages of Scripture have only a spiritual meaning, in accord with history's interior providential dynamism. Of the two meanings present in historical narrative, the spiritual meaning is the more important, although the "bodily" meaning is helpful too. Origen urges that we follow Paul's interpretive example and seek primarily the "heavenly sanctuary" and "the good things to come" rather than the "copy and shadow," to use the image given by Hebrews 8:5 and 10:1 and by Colossians 2:17. The events of the Old Testament, in God's providence, have a profound typological dimension that we must learn to appreciate. God's purpose in inspiring Scripture by the Holy Spirit was to teach us about heavenly realities and about the transcendent goal of human life. God placed these truths, often in a hidden manner, within narratives about the visible creation, about human deeds (often including wars), and about a system of law, all of which are instructive outwardly and point inwardly toward their fulfillment.[33]

Lest we be entirely absorbed by the laws and the historical narrative, God ensured that they contain enough intellectual "stumbling-blocks" to stimulate us to look through them toward the divine realities they prefigure and prophesy.[34] Indeed, Origen is willing to suppose that some parts of Scripture's historical narrative were introduced so as to illumine the spiritual meaning of history, but lack a basis in actual historical events.[35] As Origen remarks, "Sometimes a few words are inserted which in the bodily sense are not true, and at other times a greater number."[36] Some of the laws too are not instructive in the "bodily"

32. Ibid., 272 (Greek text).
33. See ibid., 285 (Greek text).
34. Ibid. (Greek text).
35. Origen states that "wherever in the narrative the accomplishment of some particular deeds, which had been previously recorded for the sake of their more mystical meanings, did not correspond with the sequence of the intellectual truths, the scripture wove into the story something which did not happen, occasionally something which could not happen, and occasionally something which might have happened but in fact did not" (ibid., 286 [Greek text]).
36. Ibid.

sense but instead were inserted under the inspiration of the Holy Spirit for their spiritual meaning. This principle holds even for the New Testament: "For the history even of these is not everywhere pure, events being woven together in the bodily sense without having actually happened; nor do the law and commandments contained therein entirely declare what is reasonable."[37] He gives some examples of what he means. In the Old Testament, for instance, between the first and second "day" there could have been no evening and morning because the sun, moon, and stars were not yet created (see Gen. 1:5–13); likewise, God could hardly have been "walking in the garden in the cool of the day" (Gen. 3:8). Origen considers irrational the Torah's commandment not to eat vultures, since no one would want to do so. God's commandment to the people of Jerusalem in Jeremiah 17:21—"Take heed for the sake of your lives, and do not bear a burden on the sabbath day"—strikes Origen as impossible to obey literally. With respect to the New Testament, Origen gives the example of Matthew 4:8, "The devil took him [Jesus] to a very high mountain, and showed him all the kingdoms of the world." As Origen remarks, there is no mountain from which a human being could see "all the kingdoms of the world." Again, when Jesus commands the apostles to "carry no purse, no bag, no sandals; and salute no one on the road" (Luke 10:4), Origen notes that we should not take this literally, since Jesus would have been irrational had he forbidden the apostles to greet anyone on the road. The point is that those who read the laws and historical narratives of Scripture solely for historical accuracy, misread them and neglect the divine stimulus to pursue the spiritual meaning that is at the heart of history.

Does Origen's approach to biblical history leave us with no basis for confidently believing that (for example) Christ rose bodily from the dead? Origen recognizes the problem and responds to it. He remarks that some readers may suspect him of "saying that because some of the history did not happen, therefore none of it happened; and because a certain law is irrational or impossible when taken literally, therefore no laws ought to be kept to the letter; or that the records of the Saviour's life are not true in a physical sense."[38] Against this possible misreading, Origen states that he believes that most events recorded in Scripture actually happened, including events pertaining to Abraham, Isaac, Jacob, Solomon, and others. He cites the Ten Commandments and the moral teaching of Jesus and Paul as obvious examples of commandments that should be obeyed to the letter. Yet he insists that "the exact reader will hesitate in regard to some passages, finding himself unable to decide without considerable

---

37. Ibid., 287 (Greek text).
38. Ibid., book 4, chap. 3, 294 (Greek text).

investigation whether a particular incident, believed to be history, actually
happened or not, and whether the literal meaning of a particular law is to be
observed or not."[39] When we find ourselves in this situation, what should we
do? Origen recommends that we undertake a careful investigation of Scripture
to see whether we find similar passages elsewhere that might provide insight
into the historical or literal value of the passage in question. We also should
try to "grasp the entire meaning" of the passage so as to separate out what
has only a spiritual meaning.

Origen adds that in these efforts we should be inspired by Paul's statement that "he is not a real Jew who is one outwardly, nor is true circumcision
something external and physical. He is a Jew who is one inwardly, and real
circumcision is a matter of the heart, spiritual and not literal" (Rom. 2:28–29).
In the same way, a skilled reader of Scripture will not hesitate to seek in biblical history a spiritual meaning that leads us toward our eschatological goal.
In biblical prophecies regarding the city of Jerusalem, for example, we should
look primarily toward the eschatological and heavenly new Jerusalem, rather
than to an earthly city in Judea. Likewise, Egypt and Babylon often have
a typological role in prophecies, and it would be a mistake to focus on the
earthly Egypt and Babylon (or Tyre and Sidon, for that matter). Furthermore,
all the things that happened to the Israelites in Egypt and during the exodus,
and all the laws about the tabernacle, have a spiritual meaning. The skilled
reader, aided by God, will find this providential and eschatological meaning
of history, whereas an unskilled reader will find only the outward meaning
of history.[40] But even the skilled reader will not be able to exhaust Scripture's
meaning. Like Paul, we should cry in wonder, "O the depth of the riches and
wisdom and knowledge of God! How unsearchable are his judgments and
how inscrutable his ways!" (Rom. 11:33).

Augustine

How does Augustine's approach compare with Origen's?[41] Augustine fully
agrees that biblical history has two dimensions, one expressing the outward

39. Ibid., 296 (Greek).
40. See ibid., 306 (Greek).
41. To my knowledge, Augustine does not refer to Origen's view of Scripture. Peter Martens
notes that Diodore of Tarsus (died 394) and Theodore of Mopsuestia (ca. 350–428), contemporaries of Augustine, strongly criticized Origen on the issue of history, and that Origen also
received criticism on this issue from Methodius of Olympus, Eustathius of Antioch, Epiphanius
of Salamis, Theophilus of Alexandria, and Jerome. See Martens, "Origen against History?,"
636–41. In the early fourth century Pamphilus (joined by Eusebius of Caesarea) defended Origen
on this issue: see Pamphilus, *Apology for Origen*. In the section of Pamphilus's *Apology* still

events and one expressing the interior providential/eschatological dynamism of history. Augustine insists, however, that the historical narratives of Scripture always speak with historical accuracy about actual persons and events. So far as I can tell, the closest that Augustine comes to Origen's view that Scripture contains some historical errors is when Augustine holds that both the Septuagint version and Jerome's version (based on the Hebrew) of the Old Testament are inspired and true, even when they contradict each other.[42] Yet Augustine does insist that particular passages should be read figuratively if otherwise they would injure charity.

Among the many texts of Augustine that could be cited, I will briefly discuss relevant portions of Augustine's *On Christian Doctrine* and *City of God*.[43] In *On Christian Doctrine*, Augustine provides a detailed analysis of "signs" and argues that charity is the rule for rightly interpreting scriptural signs: no interpretation is a true one that does not build up charity. In book 3, he asks how we should interpret Scripture's ambiguous words or signs. He warns both against interpreting figurative signs literally, as he considers some of the Jewish people to have done, and against interpreting literal signs figuratively. Signs can be literal only if they correspond with the truth of faith and nourish love of God and neighbor. Thus, for difficult passages that involve God's vengefulness or the Israelites' desire to slay their enemies, the true interpretation involves the overcoming of the reign of cupidity. Since nothing opposed to charity can be the true meaning of Scripture, it follows that if a biblical passage seems to justify vice, then it has only a figurative sense. Augustine is open to a biblical passage having more than one meaning and having meanings that were known to the Holy Spirit but not to the original author. When faced with ambiguous passages, he urges us to compare them with similar biblical passages and, if the ambiguity persists, to be cautious about determining a definite meaning.

---

extant, however, Pamphilus does not cite the texts in Origen that troubled his detractors but instead focuses on texts where Origen affirms his belief in the historical actuality of biblical persons and events.

42. See Augustine, *City of God* 18.43–44, 821–23. For Augustine's use of the Vulgate, see La Bonnadière, "Did Augustine Use Jerome's Vulgate?"; for Jerome's use of the Septuagint, see M. Williams, *Monk and the Book*. For recent examination of the Septuagint's status, see Müller, *First Bible of the Church*; Hengel and Deines, *Septuagint as Christian Scripture*; Wagner, "Septuagint and the 'Search for the Christian Bible'"; Wooden, "Role of 'the Septuagint.'" See also such studies as Chapman, *Law and the Prophets*; Barr, *Holy Scripture*, 23–29, 49–61. The issue of translation is explored at some length in Griffiths, *Song of Songs*, xxiii–xxxiv. See especially his account on xxx of the discussion of two kinds of authenticity/authority—that of the original texts in the original languages, and that of the Vulgate—in Pope Pius XII's encyclical *Divino Afflante Spiritu*, §21.

43. For further discussion see my "Scriptural and Sacramental Signs."

In *City of God*, Augustine envisions the whole of human history under the rubric of the formation of two cities, the city of God and the city of man. The former consists of all those who love God above creatures; the latter consists of all those who love creatures above God. Beginning in book 15, Augustine offers a detailed analysis of biblical history that gives us a better appreciation for his understanding of the two aspects of history in the biblical narratives. He begins with Cain and Abel, since here the divide between the two cities becomes clear: Cain embodies the earthly city and Abel the heavenly one. Scripture presents the line of the heavenly city as descending not from Abel, of course, but from Seth via Noah to Abraham and his descendents.

Augustine finds both outward and interior meanings in the biblical history of Cain. On the one hand, Augustine thinks that Cain's slaying of Abel, Cain's banishment, and Cain's later city-building activities actually happened in the course of human history. On the other hand, he also thinks that Cain and Abel's history has an interior meaning—namely, as typologically or allegorically symbolizing Christ's Passion and those who killed Christ in their envy. This interior meaning could not have been apparent to Cain and Abel, but it is the primary meaning that God intends in his providence. Given the primacy of this typological or interior meaning, however, Augustine fears that the actual occurrence of these things in history could be obscured or denied. He defends Scripture's portrait of Cain's life, "in case it may seem incredible that a city should have been built by one man at a time when there were apparently only four men in existence on earth."[44] To those for whom it seems incredible, Augustine responds that not all human beings are mentioned by Scripture, but only those who fit with Scripture's purpose of tracing the development of the heavenly city. Thus there were in fact more than four men on earth when Cain "built a city, and called the name of the city after the name of his son, Enoch" (Gen. 4:17). Similarly, faced with texts that indicate that for generations humans enjoyed life spans of close to a thousand years, Augustine defends the view that early humans lived longer and were bigger. He argues that righteousness declined because the "sons of God" (Gen. 6:2), whom he interprets as members of the city of God, married "daughters of men" who belonged to the city of man, with the result that the next generation was wicked.

Augustine combines his defense of the view that the biblical narrative consistently records things that actually happened with an equal or even greater

---

44. Augustine, *City of God* 15.8, 607. For further discussion of Augustine's defense of the historicity of Cain's founding of a city (and other such details), see also O'Daly, *Augustine's "City of God,"* 164–81. See also C. W. Freeman, "Figure and History," 319–29.

emphasis on the interior providential meaning of biblical history. He finds in Enoch's assumption into heaven (Gen. 5:24) a symbol of our future resurrection. He deems Noah's ark to be "a symbol of the City of God on pilgrimage in this world."[45] The ark's dimensions symbolize the human body of Christ, the ark's door symbolizes the wound in Christ's side from which flowed sacramental blood and water, and the ark's beams symbolize the strength and stability of the saints' holiness. These typological or allegorical meanings are not definitive, but they serve to illumine the interior meaning of history under God's providence. Others, Augustine observes, will identify different symbolic meanings. All interpreters, however, should agree that the flood narrative is not solely "a reliable historical record without any allegorical meaning, or, conversely, that those events are unhistorical, and the language purely symbolical."[46]

Retaining both dimensions of history is crucial for Augustine. He interprets the tower of Babel as an actually existing city (Babylon) that symbolizes the sin of pride.[47] He also addresses how, after the flood, animal species came to dwell on remote islands. Regarding Genesis 22, the near-sacrifice of Isaac, he notes that the ram provided by God symbolizes Jesus Christ. He explains Abraham's second wife Keturah, with whom Abraham has at least six children, as symbolizing "the carnal people who suppose themselves to belong to the new covenant."[48] As Augustine sums up his view of biblical history: "Historical events, these, but events with prophetic meaning! Events

45. Augustine, *City of God* 15.26, 643.

46. Ibid., 15.27, 645. See C. W. Freeman, "Figure and History," 319–29.

47. Richard Swinburne does the same, but with a different view of the historical claims of the Genesis text. Thus Swinburne observes:

> Did the Yahwist (the compiler of the J-strand of the first five books of the Old Testament), or even the compiler of the Book of Genesis, see himself as producing a book saying that Genesis 11:1–9 (the story of the Tower of Babel) was literally true? I am inclined to think that the Yahwist made no sharp division between historical and metaphorical accounts of the human condition. He thought that the divisions among men, symbolized by the divisions of language, were caused by humans exalting themselves above their status (possibly symbolized by towers which the Babylonians built) and so he incorporated into his book an account of roughly how this came about. But, I suspect, he never asked himself the question of just how rough "roughly" was. . . . My reason for this suspicion is that while the compiler sets his various sections including this one in somewhat of a historical sequence (suggesting a concern with literal history), he makes no attempt to make the separate stories fit together: Genesis 11:1 assumes that the human race is living together in one place whereas the previous chapter . . . had given an account of how the descendants of Noah had given rise to various different races living in different places. (*Revelation*, 173–74)

Swinburne's view strikes me as likely.

48. Augustine, *City of God* 16.34, 696.

on earth, but directed from heaven! The actions of men, but the operation of God!"[49]

Not surprisingly, then, Augustine also sees Christ and the Church as symbolized by the events of Jacob's life, events that truly took place in history. Jacob's dream about the ladder between heaven and earth receives its full meaning in the incarnation (see John 1:51). When Jacob receives a blessing and a limp after wrestling with the mysterious stranger (Gen. 32), Augustine notes that Jacob is blessed in his descendents who believe in Christ and crippled in those who do not. When Jacob on his deathbed blesses Judah, this is a prophecy of Christ. Regarding Moses and the exodus from Egyptian slavery, Augustine emphasizes the christological symbolism of the paschal lamb. The change from the old covenant to the new is symbolized by Samuel taking over from Eli and David from Saul. The song of Hannah, Samuel's mother, prefigures the Church's fruitfulness by grace, just as Solomon's building of the temple and reign of peace prefigure Christ.

In sum, the words and deeds recorded in the historical narrative of the Old Testament all have a twofold purpose—namely, to set forth what happened and to place it within its providential context. Both meanings are equally "historical," since history has both an outward and an inward dimension. As I noted, Augustine's insistence upon the historical accuracy of the biblical narratives does not lead him to deny that the Holy Spirit inspired the places where the Hebrew version and the Septuagint translation differ on historical matters.[50] He considers these differences to be a way in which the Holy Spirit guides readers "to rise above the level of mere historical fact and to search for meanings which the historical record itself was intended to convey."[51] As a general rule, however, Augustine's privileging of the interior meaning of history does not reduce his commitment to the view that the events described in Scripture actually happened in history.

Building upon Origen and Augustine

How can Origen's and Augustine's approaches help us to understand Scripture's inspired mediation of historical revelation. First and foremost, the exclusion of the providential sense of history from modern biblical historiography has had disastrous effects. Without this interior sense of history, Scripture can witness to discrete events but cannot witness to a whole divine plan moving

49. Ibid., 16.37, 701.
50. See ibid., 18.43, 821. Jerome disagreed with Augustine on this.
51. Ibid., 18.44, 823.

from creation to the consummation of all things. The loss of the providential course of history robs history of its central truth. The resulting logic makes it impossible to read Scripture as Scripture. It becomes a mere collection of widely diverse ancient texts.[52]

This result is unconsciously exemplified by David Carr, a Christian interpreter, in his recent introductory textbook, *An Introduction to the Old Testament: Sacred Texts and Imperial Contexts of the Hebrew Bible*. At the outset of this textbook, Carr first observes that even though "for many, the experience of reading the Bible in historical context is much like finally getting to see a movie in color that beforehand had only been available in black and white," it does not follow "that the meaning of the Bible can or should be limited to the settings in which it was originally composed."[53] Not only might some readers still enjoy the drama "in black and white" but also the meaning of the Bible changes with each generation as it is reinterpreted in new settings. These historically discrete meanings, however, do not bear any necessary dramatic relationship to each other. Carr makes this especially clear when he writes, "To pursue this historical approach, we will *not* read the Bible from beginning to end. Instead, we will look at biblical texts in relationship to the different historical contexts that they addressed. This means that rather than starting with the creation stories of Genesis 1–3, this book starts with remnants of Israel's earliest oral traditions."[54] Whatever the result of this approach might be, this is certainly not a study of the Bible as "Bible."

Carr's approach shows that when one rejects the Bible's twofold understanding of history, one reads the biblical texts in a quite different way from that envisioned by the Church's Bible. The Bible becomes a collection of ancient documents whose historical value rests on often problematic reconstructions of what actually happened in the history that lies behind the narratives. Carr urges that this situation is beneficial even for those who read the Bible as a sacred text, because "where once the Bible might have seemed a monolithic,

---

52. See the cautionary remark by Ignace de la Potterie, SJ, that under the rubrics now obtaining in the critical study of history,

> Christian "truth" would be nothing more than a series of past events that are studied under their phenomenal aspect and in their succession. Christian truth would be the prisoner of the horizontal world of history; truth-as-revelation would cease to exist, and we would be in danger of slipping into historicism. Christian truth, of course, is located *also* on the level of history, since divine revelation is realized in deeds and words that are the very stuff of human life. But to the horizontal dimension of historical truth Christian truth adds a new, vertical dimension that is essential to it. This dimension does not fall within the realm of scientific history. Truth can be described as the presence and self-manifestation of mystery at the very heart of historical events. ("History and Truth," 99)

53. Carr, *Introduction to the Old Testament*, 19.
54. Ibid., 19–20.

ancient set of rules, it becomes a rich variety of perspectives that have stood the test of time."[55] He supposes that believers embrace the Bible simply because it embodies a "set of rules" and "a lesson book for life."[56] Having shorn the Bible of its own awareness of the providential/eschatological dimension of history and reduced it to an ethical manual, he imagines that he is offering a challenging academic course similar to "a good course in history or English literature" and that he has shown how "academic study of the Bible is quite a different thing from study of the Bible in Sunday school or even high school religion classes in parochial schools."[57] He shows no signs of realizing that he has stripped the biblical text of the one thing that makes it most intellectually and spiritually challenging.

Even a scholar as complex and self-critical as Dale Allison, whose historical expertise is the New Testament, can fall into this reductive view of history. Allison argues that given the labor specific to the historiographical task, historical research should be separated as much as possible from theology. As he puts it, "The status and function of a canonical text within the church are not the same as the status and function of that text within the academy. As a historian, I am all for tearing up the surface of the Gospels and doing the messy work of excavating them for history. As a churchgoer, however, I believe that the Gospels should be preached and interpreted as they stand, as canonical literature."[58] Allison also argues that historians must take into account the possibility that human history is much more spiritually or supernaturally charged than secular historiography generally supposes. For Allison, a miracle story cannot be ruled out as unhistorical, even though neither can it be ruled in as historical.[59] He also warns against "reducing the mental world to the physical world."[60] He makes clear that theologians cannot wait for historians to reach conclusions before undertaking theological reading of the Jesus of the

55. Ibid., 21.
56. Ibid.
57. Ibid.
58. Allison, *Historical Christ and the Theological Jesus*, 43; cf. 44.
59. See ibid., 49, 74. Regarding the resurrection of Jesus, Allison treats at length, and very sympathetically, the view that Jesus's friends could have experienced hallucinatory visions of Jesus after Jesus's death and could on this basis have understood Jesus to be "resurrected." Allison holds that the historical likelihood is that the tomb of Jesus was empty. He considers that this empty tomb could have been caused by many reasons other than bodily resurrection. See his *Resurrecting Jesus*, 364–75. I was mistaken in my book *Jesus and the Demise of Death*, in which I devoted a paragraph to Allison's position on Jesus's resurrection, to reduce his position to his sympathetic treatment of the hallucinatory-vision hypothesis. If I have now understood him correctly, Allison does not think there is sufficient evidence to argue on the basis of historical probability either that Jesus was, or that he was not, resurrected bodily.
60. Allison, *Historical Christ and the Theological Jesus*, 79.

Gospels: "Truly assured results are few and the academic conflicts are many, and theologians must take great care when they seek to build upon the ground of modern criticism. Foundations can shift."[61] Demonstrating his own theological erudition, Allison knowledgeably cites Origen's position (and Gregory of Nyssa's) regarding the lack of historical actuality of certain biblically narrated events, such as those that have to do with God's commanding violence.[62]

Problems with respect to Allison's understanding of the historical task appear, however, in his dismissiveness of the Gospel of John as a historical witness to Jesus Christ. After criticizing "defensive, tendentious, unhistorical exegesis conducted on behalf of traditional christology"—for example, Thomas Aquinas's question in the *Summa theologiae* about why Jesus prayed, a traditional question rooted in the mystery of Jesus's two natures—Allison suggests that the source of the problem is not so much hellenizing Church fathers but the Gospel of John itself.[63] He observes:

> Is it in truth theologically inconsequential that John's Gospel, "the major battle-field in the New Testament during the Arian controversy," is today little used as a source for the historical Jesus? Does it matter that the long discourses in John, which contain the New Testament's highest christology, have been, beginning with Strauss, recognized by many scholars to come not from Jesus himself but to be instead Christian meditations from the end of the first century? Is it not a serious defect when Pope Benedict XVI, in his book on Jesus, allows the image of Jesus in John's Gospel to dominate his *historical* reconstruction? Do not the words "Jesus Christ" change or lose at least some of their meaning when one ceases to imagine him composing the so-called high-priestly prayer (John 17) or saying, "I am the way, the truth, and the life" (John 14:6)?[64]

61. Ibid.; cf. 38–39, 55–59. See also Allison, *Constructing Jesus*, 435–62.
62. See Allison, *Historical Christ and the Theological Jesus*, 34–35.
63. Ibid., 85.
64. Ibid., 85–86. The interior quotation is from Hanson, *Search for the Christian Doctrine of God*, 834. Allison finds in the Gospel of John a precedent for gutting Jesus's own (mistaken) eschatology:

> We are not, however, without any backing from tradition when we promote—for ourselves, not for Jesus—a less than literal interpretation of apocalyptic eschatology. John's Gospel gives us canonical precedent for this sort of hermeneutical move. While the book retains the concept of a "last day," it nonetheless represents a fundamental rethinking of Christian existence. It replaces the eschatological speech of Matthew 24–25; Mark 13; and Luke 21 with the intimate words of encouragement at the Last Supper (John 13–17), which mostly omits apocalyptic expectations. Written when the delay of the parousia could be felt (cf. 2 Peter 3:1–10), the Gospel prudently focuses not on Jesus coming on the clouds of heaven in the future but on the Spirit coming to believers in the present. It emphasizes not that the dead will someday rise (although it does not deny that) but rather that the living can even now enjoy eternal life. It teaches not the impending defeat of evil in a cosmic judgment but the routing of the devil at Jesus's crucifixion. It is almost as though

One might respond to these questions by arguing that John's Gospel deserves more credit as a historical source. That is the approach of (for instance) Richard Bauckham's *The Testimony of the Beloved Disciple*.[65] Bauckham presents historical arguments about such topics as the Gospel of John's awareness of Jesus's context and whether Jesus could have said or done certain things attributed to him in the Gospel of John. For my part, I would urge Allison to consider that identifying the Gospel of John as "Christian meditations from the end of the first century" does not require dismissing the historicity of the Gospel of John. After all, if Jesus is historically unique as the incarnate Son, then these "Christian meditations" may be precisely what is needed to provide a rounded historical portrait of Jesus.[66]

Given his perspective on the Gospel of John, Allison assumes that Jesus did not know his identity as the divine Son: "Those who subscribe to Nicea should be anxious, for the historical Jesus did not think of himself what they think of him. . . . Traditional, orthodox christologies have assumed that Jesus was fully aware of his own godhead and spoke accordingly, whereas modern criticism has, in the judgment of many of us, exterminated this possibility."[67] But how can historical research show us what it means to "know" one's identity as Son, let alone what Jesus thought of himself or what Jesus knew of the

---

the Evangelist systematically set out to translate the literal into the figurative, sought to reinterpret, in terms of present religious experience, the apocalyptic mythology he found in the Jesus tradition. Even here, however, we must candidly acknowledge a hitch. The Gospel, at least in its canonical form, seems to deny what it is doing. It takes for granted, indeed asserts, that its thoughts are the thoughts of Jesus, and that its reinterpretation is really no reinterpretation at all. (*Historical Christ and the Theological Jesus*, 99–100)

65. See Bauckham, *Testimony of the Beloved Disciple*. See also D. Smith, "John."

66. Thus Allison's criticism of Joseph Ratzinger for employing the Gospel of John in chaps. 8 and 10 of volume 1 of his *Jesus of Nazareth* could benefit from Ratzinger's argument that the "deeper value" of biblical words is penetrated over time by the community under the guidance of the Holy Spirit. Ratzinger remarks in this regard, "At this point we get a glimmer, even on the historical level, of what inspiration means: The author does not speak as a private, self-contained subject. He speaks in a living community, that is to say, in a living historical movement not created by him, nor even by the collective, but which is led forward by a greater power that is at work" (*Jesus of Nazareth: From the Baptism*, xx). Within the set of four Gospels, this point should be applied especially to the Fourth Gospel. See, for example, Dunn, "John's Gospel and the Oral Gospel Tradition," 183–85. See also Balthasar, *Glory of the Lord*, 7:152–59, 374–85.

67. Allison, *Historical Christ and the Theological Jesus*, 89. Allison adds, "As for those who reject or radically reinterpret Nicea and Chalcedon, a historical Jesus who placed himself at the center of a mythological end-time scenario is not likely to be regarded with affection. For such an individual conceived himself to be extraordinary and indeed unique, in a category of his own" (ibid.). If such a Jesus was wrong about his role in the end-time scenario—and Allison suggests that Jesus was wrong (96–98)—then his exalted self-conception would be deeply disturbing. Allison recognizes this but attempts to shrug it off by arguing that a "domesticated" Jesus would be "no Jesus at all" (90).

Father? For Allison, the answer consists in certain passages from the Synoptic Gospels that attribute limitations to Jesus's knowledge by comparison with the Father's knowledge. But this answer simply assumes that Jesus's statements in the Gospel of John about his knowledge are incommensurable with Jesus's statements on this topic in the Synoptic Gospels. Allison considers that the classical theological ways of squaring such statements have "all but liquidated" Jesus's humanity, "making him a historically impossible figure."[68] However, classical notions of Jesus's beatific knowledge hardly need have the result that Allison fears, since beatific knowledge is utterly nonconceptual and therefore would be more like mystical or suprarational experience of the divine presence.[69]

In my view, then, a more "critical" understanding of history is needed, in which the interior dimension of history provides the basis for thinking about God acting in and through history, and thus for apprehending the full dimensions of the *historical* testimony to Jesus Christ. As we have seen, Origen and Augustine agree in this regard, but they disagree about whether there are passages in Scripture's historical narratives that recount persons and events that did not actually exist or happen. Certainly, Augustine is willing to countenance historical contradiction between the Septuagint and the Hebrew text of Scripture (the Old Testament) on the grounds that both are inspired by the Holy Spirit. When writing against the Manichaeans' absurd views on natural science, furthermore, he observes that ignorance and error in natural science "becomes an obstacle if he [a Christian] thinks his view of nature belongs to the very form of orthodox doctrine, and dares obstinately to affirm something he does not understand."[70] But when faced with biblical texts that record unlikely events, such as human life spans reaching almost a thousand years, Augustine consistently defends the view that they actually happened. Origen, by contrast, is willing to suppose that some events recorded in Scripture's historical narratives did not actually happen but instead have "only" an inner or spiritual meaning—such meanings, of course, being central to the way in which Scripture's historical narratives mediate revelation.

Is Origen right about the characteristics of inspired Scripture, through which God truthfully reveals himself and our destiny? Or is Augustine right? In answering this question, we should reflect upon which answer would move us further down the slippery slope that leads to denying the historical actuality of the living God's relationship with his people Israel. One problem

68. Ibid., 82.
69. See especially Maritain, *On the Grace and Humanity of Jesus*; Mansini, "Understanding St. Thomas."
70. Augustine, *Confessions* 5.5.9, 77.

with affirming that everything happened as recorded in Scripture's historical narratives is that this view can push believers very quickly down the slippery slope; thus, evidence that camels were domesticated in the ancient Near East well after the most likely date on which Abraham's servant "took ten of his master's camels and departed" (Gen. 24:10) could, if found to be irrefutable, destroy someone's faith.[71]

Could God have chosen to govern the historical narratives of Israel's Scripture in such a way that some persons or events recorded therein had from the outset a typological meaning but (at least in certain respects) not historical actuality? In the process of the construction of Israel's Scripture, could God have willed that Jesus Christ and the Church fulfill some typological but not historically actual person or event (or details about certain persons or events)?[72] Historical research does not provide sufficient evidence to conclude with certitude about the actuality of specific Old Testament persons and events, but historical research does suggest the likelihood that historical actuality is not present in every case, or at least that the Old Testament's historical narratives take considerable historical liberties in their presentation of persons and events.

The biblical scholar Michael Fishbane, for example, paints a complex portrait of the development of Scripture's historical narratives. He argues that "the tendency to draw excessively determinate distinctions between scribes and authors is rooted in excessively determinate notions of what the authoritative

71. In graduate school, I had a professor who had just such an experience during his own graduate-school days.

72. For a similar set of questions (and for insightful answers), see Betz, "Glory(ing) in the Humility of the Word." Regarding the doctrine of inerrancy, Betz asks:

> Does it mean, for example, that Scripture is a divine dictation, which could be said to override the sensibilities of Scripture's human authors, rendering them incapable of the slightest historical error? Or does it mean that the intentions of the Holy Spirit with regard to faith, morals and all that is necessary for our salvation are infallibly executed in and through the freedom of the authors he inspired, which honors not only human freedom but also the genius of the Holy Spirit, who is able to accomplish his will in and through the freedom of those he inspires? Does it mean inerrant at the level of the letter, so that we must suppose God to have commanded Abraham to sacrifice Isaac and to have killed the firstborn of Egypt, et cetera, or does it mean inerrant sometimes with regard to the letter, as in the report that Jesus was born in Bethlehem of Judea in the days of Herod (Matt. 2:1), and at other times inerrant at the level of its figurative meaning or content, of which the external letter is a mere vehicle? (ibid., 169–70n104)

Betz goes on to note that "a literalist conception of inerrancy, which reduces the inerrancy of Scripture to its letter," has the "effect of stripping Scripture of its mystery, flattening its many dimensions, and reducing it to a series of propositional statements and historical claims" (173n112). By contrast, John H. Sailhamer argues that, at least according to Hans Frei's understanding of precritical biblical interpretation, "for there to be figuration, the events of both Testaments must be real. Only in that way can a real (historical) connection exist between the two events" (*Meaning of the Pentateuch*, 91).

status of the *traditum* meant in ancient Israel."[73] In ancient Israel, a traditional version of the biblical text, handed on by scribes, could be altered by scribes. Fishbane finds instances in which "theological corrections are not motivated by grammatical or verbal ambiguity but by a perceived theological dissonance between the wording of the received *traditum* and the religious values and sensibilities of the reader or tradent."[74] Consider also Brevard Childs's commentary on Exodus 1–2, which describes the persecution of the Israelites and the birth of Moses. Childs suggests that "the primary element in the history of tradition was the birth legend which was secondarily expanded to include the broad threat to the people."[75] Regarding the command to kill the firstborn males, he argues that this is not "a late interpolation into an older slavery-in-Egypt tradition," but he also points to unresolved difficulties such as "the fact that there are no other references in the Old Testament to the genocide tradition (except Ps. 105:25)" and the fact that "the later stories in Exodus seem to contradict the picture of Israel's slave conditions as an exercise in genocide."[76] For his part, David Carr accepts that the early Israelites told stories about the patriarchs, but he holds that "those stories changed radically over the centuries of oral and then oral-written tradition, and there are numerous elements in them that point specifically to later periods in Israel's history."[77]

73. Fishbane, *Biblical Interpretation in Ancient Israel*, 87. See also Schniedewind, *How the Bible Became a Book*, where he notes regarding the Old Testament that "for the *authors* of the Bible, *authorship* seems unimportant" (11)—although I would add that divine authorship was in some cases, such as the Decalogue, thought to be very important. Presupposing that only human authors and redactors were involved, Schniedewind states, "The meaning of the Bible depends more on when the Bible was written than on who wrote it" (ibid.).

74. Fishbane, *Biblical Interpretation in Ancient Israel*, 81. See also Bernard M. Levinson's *Deuteronomy and the Hermeneutics of Legal Innovation*, which emphasizes—departing in certain ways from the perspectives of both "canonical criticism" and "inner biblical exegesis"—

> the extent to which [inner-biblical] exegesis may make itself independent of the source text, challenging and even attempting to reverse or abrogate its substantive content, all the while under the hermeneutical mantle of consistency with or dependency upon its source. Exegesis is thus often radically transformative: new religious, intellectual, or cultural insights are granted sanction and legitimacy by being presented as if they derived from authoritative texts that neither contain nor anticipate those insights. . . . Deuteronomy's reuse of its textual patrimony was creative, active, revisionist, and tendentious. It functioned as a means for cultural transformation. Comparable is the work of the Chronicler during the Judaean restoration. The Chronicler programmatically rewrote the Deuteronomistic History and presented the distinctive religious and political innovations of the Persian period, such as the idea of the citizen-Temple state, as if they represented the familiar norms of the preexilic Judaean monarchy. (15–17)

75. Childs, *Book of Exodus*, 10. See also the issues raised in Childs's *Myth and Reality*. Childs argues that the authors who wrote the Old Testament texts altered "the form of myth so as to be able to use it" (*Myth and Reality*, 7).

76. Childs, *Book of Exodus*, 11.

77. Carr, *Introduction to the Old Testament*, 47.

He also accepts that some kind of exodus from Egypt occurred but not as extensive as the one portrayed in the book of Exodus.

If so, were the scribes and redactors lying, untruthful, and/or uninspired by the Holy Spirit, or is this simply what we should expect given the characteristic elements of the ancient genre of history?[78] In responding to such questions, we should insist that the sacred writers were inspired and were not liars, while also insisting that they freely employed the historical genres of their day.

Regarding specific scriptural persons and events, we can generally allow theological and historical-critical discernment to take its course. In most instances, historical minimalism shows itself to be unable to account for the evidence and to be inflated and ideological in its claims.[79] At the same time, the effort to stabilize the slippery slope of historical doubt by compiling a list of scriptural persons and events that *must* have existed/occurred in this or that way should also largely be resisted. In most cases what we should say about a specific person or event is best worked out through a theological-historical dialogue rooted in faith's engagement with the particular narratives and the available historical evidence. This approach avoids the perplexities caused by making blanket statements that do not attend to the specifics of each case.

In the case of a central event such as Jesus's resurrection, the whole New Testament attests to it, and it is a central element of the gospel. Much historical research has supported its plausibility and shown that on historical grounds it cannot be disproved. A theological-historical dialogue here warrants the firm embrace of the historical truth of Jesus's resurrection—without thereby cutting off further historical research into this event. Regarding other events, there may be less clarity either theologically or historically, and the Church has the task of discerning how various scriptural persons and events belong to the mystery of the gospel proclaimed by the Church for the salvation of

78. In his *Summa theologiae*, II-II, q. 110, a. 3, Thomas Aquinas asks whether every lie is a sin. The first objection suggests that the evangelists lied by offering different accounts of historical events. In answer, Aquinas argues that one must focus on the intended meaning of the evangelists. He adds, "It is unlawful to hold that any false assertion is contained either in the Gospel or in any canonical Scripture, or that the writers thereof have told untruths, because faith would be deprived of its certitude which is based on the authority of Holy Writ. That the words of certain people are variously reported in the Gospel and other sacred writings does not constitute a lie." The key issue for Aquinas is what would constitute a lie for the biblical authors. They would have to intend to lie rather than simply be following the rules of their genres and cultural-literary traditions. See Thomas Aquinas, *Summa theologiae*, II-II, q. 110, a. 3, ad 1. For discussion of this problem, see also Swinburne, *Revelation*, 165–70.

79. See, for example, William G. Dever's *What Did the Biblical Writers Know?*, which responds in detail to the perspective of historically minimalist works such as Philip R. Davies's *In Search of "Ancient Israel"* and Niels P. Lemche's *Israelites in History and Tradition*. See also Evans, *Historical Christ and the Jesus of Faith*.

the world. The theological-historical dialogue can assist the Church's ongoing discernment—not a historically minimalist or theologically antisupernatural dialogue, but a real and mutual conversation, faith seeking understanding.

We can gain instruction in these matters from the teaching office of the Church, which over the past century and a half has highlighted the unity and truth of Scripture. Pope Leo XIII in his encyclical *Providentissimus Deus* (1893) teaches that we should not imagine that inspiration and truth are lacking from any portion of Scripture: "It is absolutely wrong and forbidden, either to narrow inspiration to certain parts only of holy Scripture, or to admit that the sacred writer has erred."[80] In *Spiritus Paraclitus* (1920), Pope Benedict XV warns against the view of those who accept that every word of Scripture is divinely inspired but who "claim that the effect of inspiration—namely absolute truth and immunity from error—is to be restricted to that primary or religious element," so that the religious core would be free from error but the historical narratives of Scripture could contain error.[81] What does "error" mean here? In *Divino Afflante Spiritu* (1943), Pope Pius XII confirms the teaching of Leo XIII that "there is no error whatsoever if the sacred writer, speaking of things of the physical order, 'went by what sensibly appeared' as the Angelic Doctor says, speaking either 'in figurative language, or in terms which were commonly used at the time, and which in many instances are in daily use at this day, even among the most eminent men of science.'"[82] Pius XII clearly has in mind here the charge that Scripture teaches scientific error, and he goes on to quote from Augustine's *On the Literal Meaning of Genesis* to the effect that the Holy Spirit did not intend in Genesis to teach the truths of natural science. This does not mean, however, that we should divide Scripture into a fallible human sense and an infallible, inward divine sense, as Pius XII observes in *Humani Generis* (1950). Again, we cannot approach Scripture as though only *parts* of it were possessed of truth and divine inspiration; Scripture is not a mere amalgam of disparate texts.

These encyclicals should be interpreted in light of the Dogmatic Constitution *Dei Verbum*.[83] *Dei Verbum* again affirms the inspiration of the whole of Scripture. The Holy Spirit's inspiration ensures the Gospels' "historicity" (*historicitatem*), their faithful teaching of "what Jesus, the Son of God, while

---

80. Leo XIII, *Providentissimus Deus* (1893), no. 21. For historical surveys of the background of *Providentissimus Deus* and the other key magisterial texts (including *Dei Verbum*), see Atkinson, "The Interpenetration of Inspiration and Inerrancy," 205–24; Burtchaell, *Catholic Theories of Biblical Inspiration since 1810.*

81. Benedict XV, *Spiritus Paraclitus* (1920), no. 19; cf. no. 22.

82. Pius XII, *Divino Afflante Spiritu* (1943), no. 3.

83. See the approach taken by Pablo T. Gadenz, "Magisterial Teaching on the Inspiration and Truth of Scripture."

he lived among men, really did and taught for their eternal salvation."[84] The entirety of the Old and New Testament was written under the inspiration of the Holy Spirit.[85] *Dei Verbum* regards the authors of Scripture, as well as the biblical text, as inspired by God. Since God operates as a transcendent rather than a competitive cause, God authors Scripture in a way that allows for and requires the full operation of the human authors. God chose the human authors, acted "in them and by them," and ensured that they wrote "whatever he wanted written, and no more," so that Scripture is entirely God's word.[86] Like the action of grace, God's inspiration of the human authors involved their intelligent and free "full use of their powers and faculties" in writing the texts of Scripture; they were "true authors" rather than mere transmitters.[87] God expressed his meaning through human words and literary genres/conventions, which we must understand in light of the cultural context of the human authors. Scripture expresses the words of God in human words that are "in every way like human language," fully human—just as the Word incarnate took on full humanity.[88]

Moreover, *Dei Verbum* also teaches that where the human author, in recounting, explaining, or foretelling the economy of salvation, intended to affirm something, this affirmation is also affirmed by the Holy Spirit, so that "the books of Scripture, firmly, faithfully and without error, teach that truth which God, for the sake of our salvation, wished to see confided to the sacred Scriptures."[89] The divine authorship of all Scripture requires that we cannot apprehend the meaning of Scripture solely by seeking the human authors'

84. *Dei Verbum*, §19, 761.
85. See ibid., §§11, 14, 20.
86. Ibid., §11, 756–57; cf. §24.
87. Ibid., §11, 756–57.
88. Ibid., §13, 758. See Enns, *Inspiration and Incarnation*.
89. *Dei Verbum*, §11, 757. The Latin text reads, "*Cum ergo omne id, quod auctores inspirati seu hagiographi asserunt, retineri debeat assertum a Spiritu sancto, inde scripturae libri veritatem, quam Deus nostrae salutis causa litteris sacris consignari voluit, firmiter, fideliter et sine errore docere profitendi sunt.*" For discussion of what this affirmation by the Holy Spirit entails, see Ward, *Religion and Revelation*, 212. Although Ward's views of Scripture and theology differ from my own, I agree with his remark that "the Christian need have little hesitation in affirming that Scripture is inerrant, not in every minute factual detail, but in all those truths which God intends to be present therein to lead us to salvation" (ibid.). Ward observes, "Biblical revelation does seem to involve propositions, and yet it does not seem to be a matter of inserting clear propositions into human minds; the process is much more mysterious than that" (213). But when Ward turns to describing this mysterious process, he reduces revelation simply to "the shaping by God of human thoughts and feelings so as to challenge, guide, and motivate the lives of those who seek to worship God and relate their lives to God" (215; cf. 231). He also sets up unnecessary disjunctions: "Revealed propositions in the biblical tradition are typically historical (not timeless truths), existential (not neutral descriptions), morally demanding (not factually informative), and covenantal (not universal)" (226).

meaning. Rather, in order to appreciate the unified meaning of the whole Scripture, we must take "into account the Tradition of the entire Church and the analogy of faith."[90] Because of the divine authorship of Scripture, the ultimate interpreter of Scripture is the Church, which carries forward, in the Holy Spirit, the apostolic mission of teaching the people of God.[91]

Does *Dei Verbum* allow for the presence in Scripture's historical narratives of persons or events that did not exist or happen, at least in the manner recorded? It certainly does not allow for a rejection of the Gospels' historicity. As noted above, the Gospels teach "what Jesus, the Son of God, while he lived among men, really did and taught for their eternal salvation." *Dei Verbum* also makes clear that Scripture contains nothing that God did not wish it to contain, and Scripture contains the whole truth that God wished it to contain. But Scripture contains this truth in a fully human manner, in a way that accords fully with the modes of writing and cultural forms of expression that flourished during the times in which the biblical texts were composed. This seems to give room for the kind of limitations in historical writing that Origen perceived.[92] It also gives room for cultural forms of expression, even at times regarding

90. *Dei Verbum*, §12, 758. For further discussion see Pope Benedict XVI, *Verbum Domini*, §39. Pope Benedict comments that,

> viewed in purely historical or literary terms, of course, the Bible is not a single book, but a collection of literary texts composed over the course of a thousand years or more, and its individual books are not easily seen to possess an interior unity; instead, we see clear inconsistencies between them. This was already the case with the Bible of Israel, which we Christians call the Old Testament. It is all the more so when, as Christians, we relate the New Testament and its writings as a kind of hermeneutical key to Israel's Bible, thus interpreting the latter as a path to Christ.

91. Pope Benedict XVI suggests an analogy: "As the Word of God became flesh by the power of the Holy Spirit in the womb of the Virgin Mary, so sacred Scripture is born from the womb of the Church by the power of the same Spirit" (*Verbum Domini*, §19). See also de la Potterie, "Interpretation of Holy Scripture," 220–66.

92. See also Pope John Paul II's April 23, 1993, *Address on the Pontifical Biblical Commission's "The Interpretation of the Bible in the Church."* In this address, he urges that the biblical texts be understood "in their historical, cultural context," and he criticizes the view that "since God is the absolute Being, each of his words has an absolute value, independent of all the conditions of human language" (§8). On the contrary, in expressing himself in human language, God accepts its limitations, including historical and cultural ones. God can do this while maintaining the truth of his biblical word because "the God of the Bible is not an absolute Being who, crushing everything he touches, would suppress all differences and nuances" (§8). It is not "error" for biblical texts to reflect the historical and cultural limitations of the genres available at the times in which the biblical texts were written. Thus Pope John Paul gladly cites Pope Pius XII's statement in *Divino Afflante Spiritu*, "Just as the substantial Word of God became like men in every respect except sin, so too the words of God, expressed in human languages, became like human language in every respect except error" (§6). Pope John Paul also observes that the exegete needs faith in order to perceive God's word and thus to perceive the true nature and meaning of the Scriptures.

God, whose meaning must be understood in light of the entirety of Scripture's witness.[93] Even so, theologians need to challenge the theology of history at work in contemporary biblical scholarship, which excises from what counts as "historical" the providential dimension of history, thereby cutting God off from history and undoing, for the purpose of understanding the historical dimension of the biblical narratives, the Bible's own understanding of history.

Whither the Doctrine of Biblical Inspiration?

My focus thus far has been on what the affirmation that the Holy Spirit inspires Scripture means for the historical narratives found within Scripture. I have suggested that the approaches set forth by Origen and Augustine offer a basic template for addressing this question today. Origen rightly allows that Scripture's historical narratives may contain persons or events that did not actually happen or exist and whose meaning is therefore typological. To say that the meaning of some passages may be solely typological is not thereby to do away with the value of outward history;[94] rather, it is simply to recall that typology belongs to the heart of history.[95] The purpose of both history and Scripture is

---

93. Pope Benedict XVI states in this regard:

God chose a people and patiently worked to guide and educate them. Revelation is suited to the cultural and moral level of distant times and thus describes facts and customs, such as cheating and trickery, and acts of violence and massacre, without explicitly denouncing the immorality of such things. This can be explained by the historical context, yet it can cause the modern reader to be taken aback, especially if he or she fails to take account of the many "dark" deeds carried out down the centuries, and also in our own day. In the Old Testament, the preaching of the prophets vigorously challenged every kind of injustice and violence, whether collective or individual, and thus became God's way of training his people in preparation for the Gospel. So it would be a mistake to neglect those passages of Scripture that strike us as problematic. Rather, we should be aware that the correct interpretation of these passages requires a degree of expertise, acquired through a training that interprets the texts in their historical-literary context and within the Christian perspective which has as its ultimate hermeneutical key "the Gospel and the new commandment of Jesus Christ brought about in the paschal mystery." (*Verbum Domini*, §42; the interior quotation is from the Synod of Bishops' *Propositio* 29)

See also, on the inspiration of Scripture, *Verbum Domini*, §19.

94. See Martens, "Origen against History?," 645–50. Against the critique advanced by R. P. C. Hanson, Martens observes both that Origen fully accepted "that history was the field of God's direct self-disclosure" (650) and that Origen's view of history was more expansive than that of Hanson, since "Origen was willing to associate revelation, and thus significance, with far more than 'events'" (ibid.). Martens also cites Jean Daniélou's collection of "passages where Origen asserts the historicity of biblical narratives" (653n32): see Daniélou, *Origen*, 139–99. For Hanson's critique of Origen, see Hanson, *Allegory and Event*.

95. See also Richard Bauckham's reflections on the place of symbolism/typology within the Gospel of John's historiography, in Bauckham, *Testimony of the Beloved Disciple*, chap. 4.

to guide us to eternal life, and so the providential dynamism of God's plan for our salvation is a fully historical dynamism. The unity and meaning of history are unintelligible without this dimension, which requires faith.

Origen and Augustine agree that Jesus Christ reveals this interior meaning of history in its fullness, so that all history should be read in light of Jesus Christ, as Augustine paradigmatically reads it in *City of God*. That Jesus was born of the Virgin Mary, ministered in Israel as the Messiah, established his Church by gathering his twelve disciples, suffered and died on the cross, and was raised bodily from the dead and manifested to the apostles are historical events that Origen and Augustine agree most certainly happened. For Augustine, all other events should be interpreted in accord with the charity revealed in Christ Jesus: the inspiration of Scripture means that every passage of Scripture has the love of God and neighbor as its true (even if hidden) goal and meaning. Lest Origen push us too far toward not valuing the outward history of Israel, Augustine reminds us of its importance (a point with which Origen would agree). For Origen, God's purpose in permitting some passages of Scripture's historical narratives to have solely typological meaning was to ensure that we would not make the mistake of resting simply in the outward meaning of history. Like Augustine, Origen envisions the goal of reading Scripture to be human transformation.

When Thomas Aquinas addresses the question of whether the spiritual senses of Scripture can be the basis of *sacra doctrina*, he answers that "all the senses are founded on one—the literal—from which alone can any argument be drawn, and not from those intended in allegory."[96] He adds that "nothing necessary to faith is contained under the spiritual sense which is not elsewhere put forward by the Scripture in its literal sense."[97] The literal sense, of course, includes typological connections such as Jesus as the new Adam, and so Aquinas is not simply speaking about facts presented in historical narratives.[98] Like Augustine, Aquinas warns against ascribing "to the Scriptures statements that are proved evidently to be false," in this case with respect to natural science.[99] We should affirm the historicity of the Gospels, while at the same time, due to the complexity of biblical genres (a complexity whose extent was not known to Aquinas or Augustine), we should remain cautious

---

Again, we should recall that the presence of typology—as, for example, in the birth narratives of Jesus—does not mean that historical actuality need be denied. See Joseph Ratzinger (Pope Benedict XVI), *Jesus of Nazareth: The Infancy Narratives*.

96. Aquinas, *Summa theologiae* I, q. 1, a. 10, ad 1.

97. Ibid.

98. For important patristic background, see Ayres, "'There's Fire in That Rain.'"

99. Thomas Aquinas, *On the Power of God*, q. 4, a. 1, ad 5.

about claiming that Scripture's historical narratives recount only events and persons that occurred or existed as described in Scripture.

Along these lines, the Cistercian biblical scholar and theologian Denis Farkasfalvy has made helpful contributions. In his view, the Church fathers' understanding of inspiration has two aspects: first, the charism of the inspired author whose mind is illumined to understand the realities about which he writes (and whose writings therefore require that the interpreter be enlightened by faith); second, "the structure of the inspired text in which the literal sense veils and reveals a deeper sense of doctrinal, moral, and eschatological dimensions."[100] The first aspect expresses the principle of mediation in God's revelation to his people: God reveals himself through the inspired words and deeds of chosen persons. Farkasfalvy suggests that the doctrine of inspiration may be equally applicable "to collectivities of concrete historical human beings, who, in the same process by which the Church came about, played their role of leadership and mediation under the guidance of the Holy Spirit, bringing the memory of prophetic and apostolic preaching into written forms in the way God wanted these to be recorded in his Church's sacred books."[101] From this perspective, Scripture is both a record of God's history with his people and a prime exemplar (in its composition and development) of that historical encounter.[102] Within that history, moreover, Scripture functions to advance God's history with his people, as Scripture mediates "(analogously) inspired encounters with God within the Church, by both communities and individual believers."[103]

Farkasfalvy identifies a quasisacramental "presence of a spiritual fullness in the biblical text, a capability to reveal not only truths but ultimately the One who said 'I am the Truth.'"[104] Inspiration ensures that in Scripture we encounter not simply data whose truth is guaranteed by the Holy Spirit, but the

---

100. Farkasfalvy, "How to Renew the Theology of Biblical Inspiration?," 231. For a fuller exposition of his theology of Scripture, see his *Inspiration and Interpretation*.

101. Farkasfalvy, "How to Renew the Theology of Biblical Inspiration?," 249. On the problem of pseudepigraphy, see Swinburne, *Revelation*, 170–73; Meade, *Pseudepigraphy and Canon*. On inspiration as applicable to collectivities, see Rahner, *Inspiration in the Bible*, a work that Farkasfalvy appropriates critically. For related investigations, see Alonso Schökel, *Inspired Word*; Ratzinger, *God's Word*.

102. Farkasfalvy explains, "Jesus and his apostles spoke and acted 'in fulfillment of the Scriptures,' the prophetic word accumulated, distilled, and redacted into sacred literature through the special history that prepared the coming of the Incarnate Word. By their ministry, Jesus and his apostles enlightened the believers about the inspired character of the written records of Israel's salvation history. In this sense the Christian canonicity of the Old Testament, although ultimately also 'prophetic' (that is, based on the tradition of Israel), is 'apostolic' (that is, its guarantee and credibility are received from their apostolic attestation)" ("How to Renew the Theology of Biblical Inspiration?," 251–52).

103. Ibid., 249.

104. Ibid.

inexhaustibly rich tripersonal God who cannot be known simply by knowing historical facts. This vision of inspiration is trinitarian: the Father authors the biblical drama, the Son is its central protagonist, and the Holy Spirit guides the biblical authors and readers to a personal encounter in faith with the realities of the drama, which the letter of the text can only partially reveal.

Farkasfalvy defends the inspiration of all the words of Scripture, but he emphasizes that divine "authorship" must be understood analogously.[105] God providentially ensures that the biblical books, as a whole and in their parts, are his word, and in this sense God makes no errors. But God does allow the human authors, as must be expected from truly human writing, to make errors, to lack eloquence, and so forth—deficiencies that God certainly does not possess but that God condescends to employ. With these human deficiencies in view, Farkasfalvy repeats that inerrancy should be understood as ensuring that "each part of the Bible offers a path to Christ who is that Truth that God offered mankind for the sake of salvation."[106] He adds that inspiration and inerrancy ensure not superhuman propositional accuracy but rather our access, through each and every part of Scripture, to the divine realities that constitute our salvation: "This fullness of meaning or 'spiritual sense' that the Church Fathers affirmed to be accessible through each and every part of Scripture is not a collection of propositions in one-to-one correspondence with the individual grammatical units of the biblical text, but the ultimate sense of the whole, in which the unity, sacredness, relevance, and sanctifying force of the Bible lies."[107] We have this access to God's inspired and inerrant word when we read it in faith, in the same Spirit in which it was written.

This dimension becomes especially apparent when one draws in another crucial element of Farkasfalvy's proposal, what he calls "the Eucharistic provenance of the Christian Bible."[108] Farkasfalvy, indebted to the work of the Lutheran biblical scholar Oscar Cullmann, argues that the letters of Paul contain

105. Farkasfalvy criticizes *Dei Verbum* for failing to include "the focal issue of Rahner's book on inspiration, the distinction between 'author' and 'originator,'" with the result that "the question of God's transcendental authorship—and thus the fact that human and divine roles in inspiration can both be called 'authorship' only in an analogous sense—receives no attention" (Ibid., 237). In a footnote, Farkasfalvy credits Luis Alonso Schökel, SJ, along with Alonso Schökel's student and translator Francis Martin, with rethinking the concept "Deus auctor scripturarum." Farkasfalvy also warns with regard to §11 of *Dei Verbum*, "One does not see how to avoid a false conclusion that in the process of divine inspiration, the human being's consciousness sets limits to the divine meaning. . . . In fact, there is much content in the biblical text of which the human author, according to his historically limited perspective, remains partially or fully unaware" (239).

106. Ibid., 252; cf. 244–46, where he discusses the debate over inerrancy during the drafting of *Dei Verbum*.

107. Ibid., 253.

108. Farkasfalvy, *Inspiration and Interpretation*, 63 (title of chap. 4).

an array of indications that they were meant to be read within the eucharistic celebrations of the earliest Christian communities.[109] In Farkasfalvy's view, the Passion Narratives of the Gospels also suggest this liturgical connection, as do stories such as Jesus's multiplication of the loaves and feeding of the thousands in the wilderness. The narratives of Jesus's itinerant preaching also foster liturgical reading, because they center upon him arriving, encountering the needs of human beings for healing and teaching, and meeting those needs.[110] In the Gospel of Matthew, for instance, Jesus consistently manifests "himself as the one who is coming."[111] In the Gospel of John, Jesus's coming is revealed fully to be the coming of the Word, the Son of the Father. Farkasfalvy observes that "his coming is in a transcendental sense a descent, so that in the explicitly Eucharistic text about the bread of life this coming is said to be 'coming down from heaven.'"[112] Farkasfalvy also highlights the liturgical character of the book of Revelation and its emphasis on Christ as the one who is coming.[113] As Scott Hahn puts it, "If biblical inspiration consists of the Spirit conveying the Word of God through fallible human instruments, the liturgical celebration is where the Spirit continues to bear the Word into the world through a canonized series of human gestures and utterances."[114]

Conclusion: Revelation and Biblical Inspiration

The biblical scholar Brant Pitre observes that a "climate of historical skepticism . . . has characterized a great deal of modern biblical scholarship."[115] This skeptical climate in part preceded the rise of historical research into the ancient

109. See Cullmann, *Early Christian Worship*. See also Heil, "Paul and the Believers of Western Asia." Heil argues that in the Letters to Philemon, Colossians, and Ephesians, "Paul enables and facilitates believers to join him in his ongoing worship of thanksgiving, prayer, and praise to God for this grace. Delivered as an oral performance within a liturgical assembly, each letter functions as an epistolary ritual of worship. Each begins and ends with liturgical greetings of divine grace that function as ritual speech-acts, acts which do what they say, communicating a renewed experience of the grace of God aimed at extending the worship of believers into their everyday lives" ("Paul and the Believers of Western Asia," 90).

110. As Farkasfalvy says, of course, "The claim we make about the 'Eucharistic cradle' of the synoptic tradition *per se* need not be applied in a rigid way to every single passage" (*Inspiration and Interpretation*, 75).

111. Ibid., 77.

112. Ibid., 78.

113. Here he refers to Feuillet, *Apocalypse*, 85, where Feuillet urges that the liturgical aspects of the book of Revelation be appreciated without exaggerating them.

114. Hahn, "For the Sake of Our Salvation," 41. For Hahn's position, which favors the view that Scripture's historical narratives do not contain persons or events that did not actually happen or exist, see his *Letter and Spirit*, especially 165–67.

115. Pitre, "Mystery of God's Word," 59.

Near East and the biblical texts, and in part arose from this historical research, whose roots date to the Renaissance.[116] The teachings of the magisterium, not least the papal encyclicals that sought to combat views that truncated Scripture's inspiration and truth, rightly insist upon Scripture's ability as a unified whole to faithfully mediate divine revelation. Scripture cannot be divided into "inerrant" and "errant" parts, or "inspired" and "uninspired" parts. Scripture is a whole, and the whole of it, including every single part, mediates divine revelation truthfully.

At the same time, as I have noted, there is no reason to contest every claim by biblical scholars and historians of the ancient Near East that the historical narratives of Scripture contain a person or event that did not exist or happen in the way that Scripture records. This would distort the uniqueness of inspired Scripture from a different direction.[117] It would rest Scripture's mediation of divine revelation upon an utter transcendence of the genre and cultural context of historical narrative in the time periods during which the biblical texts were written, and it would place Christians at odds with the labor of historians to locate the biblical texts in historical context. Furthermore, counting as "historical" only what can be empirically known of the outward events would leave unopposed the central problem, which is the rejection of the providential (typological) dimension of history. The inspired Scripture teaches us that the truth about history is finally knowable only through the One who, by his Pasch, has revealed God's eschatological plan of love: "Weep not; lo, the Lion of the tribe of Judah, the Root of David, has conquered, so that he can open the scroll and its seven seals" (Rev. 5:5).[118]

116. See, for example, Popkin, *History of Scepticism*; Rummel, *Humanist-Scholastic Debate in the Renaissance and Reformation*, especially chap. 5: "Biblical Scholarship: Humanistic Innovators and Scholastic Defenders of Tradition"; Jenkins and Preston, *Biblical Scholarship and the Church*; Scholder, *Birth of Modern Critical Theology*; Legaspi, *Death of Scripture and the Rise of Biblical Studies*; Morrow, "French Apocalyptic Messianism."

117. Thus Douglas Farrow argues in detail that "a strict view of inerrancy has no solid base of support in Scripture and that it is not called for by careful reflection on other lines of evidence. . . . We must let the Bible establish its own character, determining both our commitment to its truthfulness and our openness to irregularities in the text" (*Word of Truth*, 133). Along similar lines, see I. Marshall, *Biblical Inspiration*.

118. For further discussion see Mangina, *Revelation*, 84–91.

EIGHT

Philosophy

Quoting John Chrysostom, *Dei Verbum* remarks that "in sacred Scripture, without prejudice to God's truth and holiness, the marvellous 'condescension' of eternal wisdom is plain to be seen 'that we may come to know the ineffable loving-kindness of God and see for ourselves how far he has gone in adapting his language with thoughtful concern for our nature.'"[1] This "condescension" or adaptation of God's "language" to the language of the biblical writers included the biblical use of Hellenistic philosophical language and insights, not least what Richard Bauckham calls "Hellenistic true-god-language."[2] Nonetheless, many contemporary biblical scholars view with suspicion the contributions of Hellenistic philosophical culture. In the view of N. T. Wright, for example, "Western orthodoxy . . . has had for too long an overly lofty and detached view of God. It has always tended to approach the christological question by assuming this view of God and then by fitting Jesus into it."[3] As Wright explains:

1. *Dei Verbum*, §13, 758, citing John Chrysostom, *In Gen.* 3, 8 (hom. 17, 1 [*PG* 53:134]).
2. Bauckham, *Jesus and the God of Israel*, 246. He identifies similar language about the true God in Philo, Josephus, the *Sibylline Oracles*, the *Pseudo-Orpheus*, and the *Apocalypse of Abraham*. For further discussion of Philo, see Soskice, "Athens and Jerusalem, Alexandria and Edessa," as well as Weinandy's *Does God Suffer?*, 74–82. See also Boyarin, "Gospel of the *Memra*."
3. N. T. Wright, *Challenge of Jesus*, 123; see also Wright, "Response to Richard Hays," and in the same volume Wright's "Whence and Whither Historical Jesus Studies?" Wright's concerns in certain respects parallel the Reformers' appropriation of the humanist critique of scholasticism, as well as Karl Barth's warnings against Plato and Aristotle. See also, along similar anti-Hellenistic lines, Rauschenbusch, *"Christianity and the Social Crisis"*; Newbigin,

> My proposal is not that we know what the word *god* means and manage some-
> how to fit Jesus into that. Instead, I suggest that we think historically about a
> young Jew possessed of a desperately risky, indeed apparently crazy, vocation,
> riding into Jerusalem in tears, denouncing the Temple and dying on a Roman
> cross—and that we somehow allow our meaning for the word *god* to be recen-
> tered around that point.[4]

Certainly Jesus fulfills God's promises and manifests himself to be Emmanuel
("God with us") by riding into Jerusalem, denouncing the Temple, dying on a
cross, and rising from the dead. When we know Jesus, we know the goodness,
love, and humility of God in a far greater way than is otherwise possible; in
the Spirit, we know the Son of the Father.[5] Yet the New Testament's "meaning
for the word *god*" belongs to an ongoing scriptural reflection about Israel's
God that exhibits, by the Second Temple period, the significant presence of
Hellenistic philosophical insights. Indeed, the New Testament's Christologies
are appreciative of "lofty" descriptions of the Creator God, such as immortal,
invisible, eternal, and immutable.

The New Testament's appropriation of Hellenistic philosophical culture
to illumine the attributes of the Creator God of Israel can be seen in many
places, including 1 Timothy's praise of God as "the King of ages, immortal,
invisible, the only God" (1 Tim. 1:17) and as "the blessed and only Sovereign, the King of kings and Lord of lords, who alone has immortality and
dwells in unapproachable light" (1 Tim. 6:15–16). Discussing the typological
portrait of Melchizedek in Hebrews 7:3, "He is without father or mother
or genealogy, and has neither beginning of days nor end of life, but resem-
bling the Son of God he continues a priest for ever," Bauckham observes that
its language reflects the fact that for philosophically sophisticated Greeks,
true deity means being "unbegotten or ungenerated (*agennētos*)—having no

---

Open Secret, 24–26; Moltmann, *Trinity and the Kingdom*. Robert W. Jenson's position is more
metaphysically complex than Moltmann's, but he too builds upon a strong sense of "the old
dissonance between the metaphysical principles of the Greeks and the storytelling of the gospel" (*Systematic Theology*, 1:112). For alternative views, see, for example, Weinandy, *Does God
Suffer?*; Soskice, "Athens and Jerusalem, Alexandria and Edessa"; Allen, "Exodus 3 after the
Hellenization Thesis"; Hart, *The Beauty of the Infinite*, 160–66.

The present chapter includes material that appeared in an earlier version in my "God and
Greek Philosophy in Contemporary Biblical Scholarship." Kavin Rowe published a response to
my article, in which he argued that my position amounts to the view that Plato spoke "Chris-
tianese"—which I certainly do not think—and to an endorsement of numerous deleterious
separations. See Rowe, "God, Greek Philosophy, and the Bible."

4. N. T. Wright, *Challenge of Jesus*, 123–24.

5. See, for example, Joseph Ratzinger's interpretation of Jesus's temptations, in Ratzinger,
Jesus of Nazareth: From the Baptism, chap. 2.

parents—and unoriginated (*agenētos*)—having no other kind of origin—as well as being imperishable forever."⁶ Bauckham grants, of course, that "terms which for non-Jewish writers defined *a* true deity, for Jewish writers define *the one and only* true deity."⁷

Indeed, as Hans Urs von Balthasar remarks, "The 'syncretism' of the Bible is a fact denied by no one. It begins in the Old Testament, where the last books to be written not only speak in a generally Hellenistic style (Maccabees), but in Stoic and (neo-) Platonic ways (Wisdom and, even, Ecclesiasticus). Philosophical 'logos' enters into the service of Jewish thinking about God."⁸ But does this mean that Hellenistic philosophers had some true insights about "true deity" (in Bauckham's phrase), so that what Balthasar terms "philosophical 'logos'" had a real truth to offer "Jewish thinking about God," despite the philosophers' failure to know the living God fully or worship him properly?

Thomas Aquinas observes with regard to these philosophers, "Human reason is very deficient in things concerning God. A sign of this is that philosophers in their researches by natural investigation into human affairs, have fallen into many errors, and have disagreed among themselves."⁹ In addition to worshiping multiple gods and being unaware of the communion of the Trinity, the election of Israel, and the incarnation and paschal mystery of Christ, Hellenistic philosophers held to such beliefs as (in the words

---

6. See Bauckham, *Jesus and the God of Israel*, 246, citing Neyrey, "'Without Beginning of Days or End of Life.'" Admittedly, Bauckham eschews Hellenistic philosophical categories—preferring "personal identity" over ontological descriptions of "divine nature"—in his "God Crucified," in *Jesus and the God of Israel*, 1–59.

7. Bauckham, *Jesus and the God of Israel*, 248. Ben Witherington III notes that this Hellenistic influence was certainly not as significant as the Jewish influence on the New Testament's language about God, but even here we should be careful not to introduce an implicit dichotomy between "Hellenistic" and "Jewish": "All the writers of the New Testament are monotheists deeply indebted to Jewish monotheism and not indebted, or very little indebted, to Platonic or other sorts of Greek speculations about God. Christianity is a sectarian development of early Judaism, not a syncretistic combination of Judaism with some other extant forms of Semitic or Greco-Roman religion. Of course, the Judaism that Christianity grew out of was to some degree Hellenized, and this too is reflected in the New Testament (e.g., Luke-Acts and Hebrews)" (*Indelible Image*, 2:382). See also Troels Engberg-Pedersen's efforts to connect Paul's anthropology and ethics with that of the Stoics in *Paul and the Stoics* and, much more controversially in my view, *Cosmology and the Self in the Apostle Paul*. See also the essays collected in Engberg-Pedersen, *Paul in His Hellenistic Context*; Rasimus, Engberg-Pedersen, and Dunderberg, *Stoicism in Early Christianity*; and Engberg-Pedersen, *Paul beyond the Judaism/Hellenism Divide*. In the same vein, see Abraham J. Malherbe's collection of essays *Paul and the Popular Philosophers*, which focuses on moral instruction and which pays particular attention to the Cynics. Malherbe observes that Paul "remains *Paulus christianus*, but without that making him any the less *Paulus hellenisticus*" (9).

8. Balthasar, *Glory of the Lord*, 4:243.

9. Aquinas, *Summa theologiae*, II-II, q. 2, a. 4.

of Jaroslav Pelikan) "the transmigration of souls, the materiality of the divine nature, the coexistence and coeternity of matter, and 'the *ananke* of *heimarmene*.'"[10] Not for nothing does Paul argue that although the gentiles claimed "to be wise, they became fools" (Rom. 1:22).[11] Taking aim at their pride, Paul at Corinth chose "to know nothing" among the Corinthians "except Jesus Christ and him crucified" rather than adopting "lofty words or wisdom" (1 Cor. 2:1–2).[12]

Is there a way then, to affirm the New Testament's critique of pagan idolatry without denying that certain Hellenistic philosophical insights are in fact true, even if only partially so, about the living God of Israel—that is to say, to affirm that certain Hellenistic insights, despite their limitations, succeed in referring to the same *reality* as do Scripture's various statements about God?[13]

10. Pelikan, *Christianity and Classical Culture*, 194.

11. Luke Timothy Johnson criticizes Paul for "totally [adopting] the Hellenistic Jewish view of Gentile religion" and for consistently showing "the same deep disdain for anything specifically Gentile in character" (*Among the Gentiles*, 4). Johnson links his approach to the positive outlook of many Renaissance humanist scholars toward Greco-Roman religion. These Renaissance views contrasted with the view of many early Protestant scholars that patristic Christians, under the influence of Greco-Roman religious practices, had corrupted "the simplicity of the Gospels" (11). Although Johnson supposes that his approach will enable Christians "to assess the ways in which they truly are different and must agree to remain different" (283), however, understanding the Christian difference requires, in my view, the biblical critique of pagan idolatry. After all, it remains the case that, as John Henry Newman says, "the precepts of a religion certainly may be absolutely immoral; a religion which simply commanded us to lie, or to have a community of wives, would *ipso facto* forfeit all claim to a divine origin. Jupiter and Neptune, as represented in the classical mythology, are evil spirits, and nothing can make them otherwise" (*Grammar of Assent*, 419). Along lines similar to Johnson's, see John M. G. Barclay's "decision to capitalize the word 'God' in all contexts, whether in reference to the God of Jews or the God/Gods of Gentiles," rather than to "succumb to the Jewish and Christian presumption that only their Deity is truly 'God,' while the rest are merely 'gods' (or worse)" (*Jews in the Mediterranean Diaspora*, 15). For a defense of Roman *religio* (against Augustine), see Ando, *Matter of the Gods*; in the same vein, relativizing belief in favor of practice, see North, "Pagan Ritual and Monotheism."

12. Arguing that from the outset Jerusalem rejected Athens, Charles Freeman's sadly misinformed *Closing of the Western Mind* suggests that "Christianity, under the influential banner of Paul's denunciation of Greek philosophy, began to create the barrier between science—and rational thought in general—and religion that appears to be unique to Christianity" (5–6). Freeman's book is representative of a broad swath of recent popular studies attacking Christianity.

13. I cannot here address A. N. Williams's view that the New Testament's own language is itself frequently incompatible with trinitarian theology: see Williams, "Does 'God' Exist?" As Williams summarizes the problem:

> Inasmuch as predicating *action* of some entity called "God" suggests that "God" is a subject, and indeed a subject capable of agency, use of the word "God" violates a fundamental principle of Christian theology. At one level, there is nothing new in this assertion, no novelty in stipulating that "God" designates divine nature subsisting in the Father, the Son and the Spirit and nothing else. Yet despite the clarity of the tradition

Without supposing that the Hellenistic philosophers were proto-Christians and without conjuring a purely natural rationality untainted by the fall, I think that the answer to this question must be yes. In Scripture, we find a "mutual enrichment" between biblical and Greek thought.[14] To make this case, I begin by setting forth the largely critical views of Hellenistic philosophy found in two excellent recent works of biblical scholarship, by Daniel Kirk and Kavin Rowe, respectively. In light of the concerns of Kirk and Rowe, I offer a threefold scriptural argument in favor of the insightfulness of Hellenistic philosophy even with reference to the living God. First, I argue on the basis of Acts 17 and 19 that at least some pagans, according to Acts, possessed some true, even if partial and inadequate, insights about God. Second, I compare Wisdom of Solomon, which belongs to Catholic and Orthodox Scripture and which significantly influenced the New Testament writings, with Paul's Letter

---

on this point, Christians have continued to use the word "God," most problematically as the subject of verbs denoting personal agency which have a definite direct object, and this usage creates and fosters the impression, either that anhypostatic divine nature itself is somehow capable of agency, or that divine actions pertain neither to the Father, nor to the Son, nor to the Spirit, but to a fourth divine hypostasis named "God." (476–77) Gilles Emery, OP, treats this problem in his *Trinity*, 47–50.

14. Pope Benedict XVI, "Regensburg Lecture," 136. He argues for a "profound harmony between what is Greek in the best sense of the word and the Biblical understanding of faith in God" (134–35). He goes on to sketch the history of calls "for a dehellenization of Christianity" (139). This history is incisively traced in Dale B. Martin's "Paul and the Judaism/Hellenism Dichotomy," beginning with Ferdinand Christian Baur (or W. M. L. de Wette) and ending with Alan Segal. Martin concludes that "here at the end of the twentieth century, the Hellenism/Judaism dualism, developed with such different meanings in nineteenth-century Germany, may be doing different business, but it is still in business" (58). See also the analysis of Adolf von Harnack's Hellenization thesis, rooted in philosophical idealism and a negative view of dogma, in W. Rowe, "Adolf von Harnack and the Concept of Hellenization." For a condensed version of the account of Hellenization offered in von Harnack's massive *History of Dogma*, see von Harnack, *What Is Christianity?*; see also von Harnack, *History of Dogma*, 1:43–50. For the influence of Baur, J. G. Droysen, Wilhelm Bousset, and Rudolf Bultmann, see also Meeks, "Judaism, Hellenism, and the Birth of Christianity," 18–20. As Meeks notes, those who (rightly) reacted to this portrait "chose the opposite pole. *Real* Christianity, they urged, was thoroughly *Jewish*, not Hellenistic at all or Hellenized only in its outer forms or later corruptions. . . . Until quite recently most students of early Christianity continued to imagine a cultural chasm between Judaism and Hellenism, but the map of the country on either side of the chasm became more and more complicated" (21, 23). The element of anti-Catholic polemic in Baur is noted by Martin, "Paul and the Judaism/Hellenism Dichotomy," 34. See also Schweitzer, *Paul and His Interpreters*, regarding which Martin observes that "for Schweitzer, the Jewish and the Greek represent 'two different worlds of thought,' and that both could have existed side by side in Paul is unthinkable" ("Paul and the Judaism/Hellenism Dichotomy," 36). The same split (in this case between Jewish and Hellenistic/gentile Christians) is found in Bultmann's *Theology of the New Testament*. For a recent Harnackian approach to trinitarian theology, seeing it as the fruit of Hellenistic (Middle Platonic) philosophy, see Hillar, *From Logos to Trinity*. For the opposite emphasis, see Boyarin, *Jewish Gospels*.

to the Romans on the topic of the gentiles' knowledge of God's "invisible nature, namely, his eternal power and deity" (Rom. 1:20).[15] Third, in light of widespread belief in a bodily God, including within Israel and within pagan cultures, I suggest that the doctrine of Israel's God developed in Scripture in a manner that required, and continues to require, certain salutary insights found in Hellenistic philosophy.[16] These insights were appropriated and enhanced by patristic and medieval theologians, East and West, and remain a valuable part of the inheritance of the Church.[17]

God and Greek Philosophy: Setting the Stage

In this section I engage portions of two recent works of biblical scholarship, Daniel Kirk's *Unlocking Romans* and Kavin Rowe's *World Upside*

15. For further discussion, including a plea for Protestantism to reopen the Old Testament canon so as not to exclude the most significant Second Temple Jewish writings, see Hengel and Deines, *Septuagint as Christian Scripture*, especially 105–27. On the significance of the Wisdom of Solomon for the New Testament writings, see Witherington, *Jesus the Sage*. James Barr accurately points out that

> scholarship is likely to be much affected by the canonical or non-canonical status of the books used as evidence. Wisdom provides a uniquely important link in terms of natural theology between the Hebrew books and Paul. Where Wisdom counts as a fully canonical book, this linkage is fully displayed "within the Bible." Its obviousness is much greater, and the awareness of it within the religious community to which the scholars belong is much more natural and more profound. Where Wisdom is taken to belong "only" to the Apocrypha, consciousness of it and its ideas within the religious community is very low. (*Biblical Faith and Natural Theology*, 78; cf. Barr's *Holy Scripture*, 40–45)

See also the historical research of Armin Lange, "From Literature to Scripture." I cannot agree with Benjamin D. Sommer's account of "trans-canonical unity" that "severely damages the notion of scripture's unity" ("Unity and Plurality in Jewish Canons," 109).

16. Troels Engberg-Pedersen notes that in the late first century BC a significant philosophical debate was ongoing about whether divinity should be conceived in a material way. He states that Wisdom of Solomon

> starts out describing its main theme, Lady Wisdom herself, in terms that derive from the Stoic doctrine of the πνεῦμα. Gradually, however, more Platonizing terms begin to creep in. And eventually it is (almost) explicitly stated that this is because a Stoicizing account cannot do justice to the character of God that this Jewish writer favors. This suggests . . . that one point of contention of the Platonists vis-à-vis the Stoics was the Stoic material conception of God. Or to put it in more positive terms, the Platonists were after some form of "transcendence" in the picture of God that they did not find clearly enough in Stoicism. ("Setting the Scene," 11)

17. For the fathers' (critical) use of Hellenistic philosophical insights about God, see especially Pelikan's marvelous *Christianity and Classical Culture*. See also Pelikan, *Christian Tradition*, vol. 1; Wilken, *Remembering the Christian Past*, 38; Wilken, *Spirit of Early Christian Thought*; Radde-Gallwitz, *Basil of Caesarea, Gregory of Nyssa*. The necessary role of the fathers in contemporary biblical interpretation and theology is defended by Joseph Ratzinger, "Formal Principles of Catholicism," 133–52.

Down.[18] My thesis is that a proper reception of divine revelation should not focus on a rivalry or absolute incommensurability between the biblical worldview and Hellenistic philosophical culture with respect to discourse about God. Certainly Israel's God is not Plato's or Aristotle's god, but nonetheless some Hellenistic insights about the divine successfully refer to the real, living God of Israel.

Daniel Kirk: Biblical Particularists versus Philosophical Universalists

In *Unlocking Romans*, Daniel Kirk distinguishes strongly between biblical "particularists" and what might be termed philosophical universalists. The latter do not pay sufficient attention to God's actions in history as narrated in Scripture; instead, they presuppose certain philosophical attributes of God and then impose those attributes upon the God of the biblical narrative.[19] As an example, Kirk points to a theologian whose vocal criticisms of Aristotle's role in theology might make him seem fully a biblical "particularist": Martin Luther. Reading Romans 1:17, "For in it [the gospel] the righteousness of God is revealed through faith for faith," Luther assumes that the "righteousness of God" is God's attribute of holiness. Humans lack holiness and therefore need to receive this attribute from God; God imputes his attribute of holiness to sinful humans. Regarding Luther's view of God's attribute of "righteousness" or holiness, Kirk observes that "the echoes of Plato are important here."[20]

18. Many other biblical scholars hold similar views, so my intention is not to single out Kirk and Rowe. Another influential example is Douglas A. Campbell's *Deliverance of God*. By means of an elaborate reconstruction of a supposed opponent of Paul to whom Campbell gives the name "the Teacher," Campbell argues that Paul is not speaking in his own voice in the key passages of Romans 1. Campbell's negative views about Greek metaphysics are clear. For example, he writes, "The presence of two fundamentally incompatible epistemologies, one philosophical and rationalist and the other historical, revelatory, and personal—is apparent especially when 1:19–20 and 2:14–15 are juxtaposed with 2:17–20 and 3:10–19, although the tension is present whenever Scripture is cited in relation to a point originally established by 1:18–32" (399; cf. 204).

19. Larry W. Hurtado comments in this regard, "The NT writers took the common Greek noun for 'god,' *theos*, and with the addition of the definite article sought to indicate that they were referring to a very particular deity, not to some general notion of divinity of that time" (*God in New Testament Theology*, 6). A quick skim of Plato's *Timaeus* (for example) shows, however, that the Greeks too used the definite article.

20. Kirk, *Unlocking Romans*, 3. Compare Charles B. Cousar's similar concern:
   Classic theology has had the tendency to begin with a general definition of the attribute and then in applying it to God to lift it to an infinite level. *Power* implies such things as might, strength, control, domination, and authority. God's power, then, means infinite might, sovereignty, omnipotence, supreme majesty, and superiority over all things. The impression conveyed is of a dominant deity, with ultimate control, and unlimited capacity to do whatever is wished and whose power is manifested in extraordinary events, in amazing stories of success, in tales that always have happy endings. Paul, on the other

Bemoaning the dominance of "Plato's god of ideal form and perfect moral goodness" and "Aristotle's unmoved mover" in traditional Christian discourse about God, Kirk cites Augustine and Anselm as prime examples of Christian theologians who too often define God without direct reference to the biblical narrative.[21] The Westminster Shorter Catechism comes in for the same critique. It defines God as "a spirit; infinite, eternal, and unchangeable in his being, wisdom, power, holiness, justice, goodness and truth."[22] Kirk contrasts these answers to "What is God?" with the biblical concern for "Who is God?" or "Which God?" For Kirk, universal attributes cannot properly identify Israel's God because "God's identity is inseparable from a particular people and from certain actions performed on behalf of that people."[23] To imagine that one could know God through universal attributes would be to fail to know the God who reveals himself historically, "in limiting and particular actions."[24]

Kirk is no doubt aware of the biblical passages that describe God in terms of attributes. Jesus teaches that "no one is good but God alone" (Luke 18:19). He urges his followers, "Be perfect, as your heavenly Father is perfect" (Matt. 5:48). He proclaims that "God is spirit" (John 4:24). First Timothy too praises God in a manner that evokes the attributes that Kirk critiques: "To the King of ages, immortal, invisible, the only God, be honor and glory for ever and ever" (1 Tim. 1:17). Paul remarks that "ever since the creation of the world his [God's] invisible nature, namely, his eternal power and deity, has been clearly perceived in the things that have been made" (Rom. 1:20). James observes that "God cannot be tempted with evil and he himself tempts no one" (James 1:13), and he adds, "Every good endowment and every perfect gift is from above, coming down from the Father of lights with whom there is no

---

hand, talks of the power of God in terms of weakness, failure, a scandalizing death by crucifixion. In language not only the opposite of but in fact the contradiction of much western theology, God's power is expressed in a particular event of unsuccessful and even distasteful dimensions. (*A Theology of the Cross*, 46)

Would Paul indeed reject the view of God as possessed of "infinite might, sovereignty, omnipotence, supreme majesty, and superiority over all things"? And where does Cousar find in "classic theology" the view that God's power is always manifested "in amazing stories of success, in tales that always have happy endings"? Paul states of Jesus that "he was crucified in weakness, but lives by the power of God" (2 Cor. 13:4); and Paul assures us that nothing can thwart "God's purpose of election" (Rom. 9:11) and that "if God is for us, who is against us?" (Rom. 8:31).

21. Kirk, *Unlocking Romans*, 1.

22. Ibid., 1–2; see Westminster Shorter Catechism, Q/A 4.

23. Kirk, *Unlocking Romans*, 2. I agree that God's identity is inseparable from his activity among the people of Israel, but I think that it was nonetheless possible for non-Israelites to refer, in certain limited ways, to the living God.

24. Ibid.

variation or shadow due to change" (James 1:17). When 1 John tells us that "God is love" (1 John 4:16), this corresponds with Jesus's teaching that God's goodness is infinitely greater than ours: "What father among you, if his son asks for a fish, will instead of a fish give him a serpent; or if he asks for an egg, will give him a scorpion? If you then, who are evil, know how to give good gifts to your children, how much more will the heavenly Father give the Holy Spirit to those who ask him!" (Luke 11:11–13).

In the Bible, of course, these attributes are never separated from God's acts in history. The Psalms bear witness to this unity of the divine attributes and God's creative and salvific actions. Consider Psalm 147, where the psalmist describes God as Redeemer and Creator, and then proceeds to apply the attributes of power and understanding to God: "The LORD builds up Jerusalem; he gathers the outcasts of Israel. He heals the brokenhearted, and binds up their wounds. He determines the number of the stars, he gives to all of them their names. Great is our LORD, and abundant in power; his understanding is beyond measure" (Ps. 147:2–5). Similarly, Psalm 145 proclaims God's goodness and righteousness in light of God's creative and redemptive actions. The psalmist states, "On the glorious splendor of thy majesty, and on thy wondrous works, I will meditate. Men shall proclaim the might of thy terrible acts, and I will declare thy greatness. They shall pour forth the fame of thy abundant goodness, and shall sing aloud of thy righteousness" (Ps. 145:5–7).[25]

Is it right, then, to blame the Westminster Shorter Catechism for stating that God is "a spirit; infinite, eternal, and unchangeable in his being, wisdom, power, holiness, justice, goodness and truth"? Kirk suggests that historical revelation and metaphysical discourse are at odds: "Is the righteousness revealed in Paul's gospel a divine ethical quality? Or is it God's saving activity in faithful adherence to his covenants with Israel?"[26] But I would propose that God's righteousness may well be both a "divine ethical quality" and "God's saving activity." Why should these two be mutually exclusive? Kirk holds that "the specific identity of God as the God of Israel entails a recognition that the standards of judging God's actions (i.e., for determining whether or not God is righteous) are themselves determined by the Scriptures of Israel."[27] But Jesus himself, when describing God's goodness

25. In his *Biblical Faith and Natural Theology*, James Barr identifies three other psalms as particularly instructive regarding "natural theology": Psalms 19, 104, and 119. See Barr, *Biblical Faith and Natural Theology*, 81–90.

26. Kirk, *Unlocking Romans*, 6.

27. Ibid., 7. I note also that "saving" and "faithful" are themselves words that cannot *simply* be defined in terms of what God has done in history, since what is salvific for humans and what

in Luke 11, appeals not to the Scriptures of Israel but to the example of a human father who gives his son a fish rather than a serpent and an egg rather than a scorpion. Certainly this example is by no means opposed to the Scriptures of Israel, but why would one need to say that such "standards" of goodness are "determined" narratively by Israel's Scriptures alone?[28] Could they not also be determined by our recognition of the created order in which serpents and scorpions do not appease our hunger but instead hurt us? The point is that universal attributes of God need not be opposed to faithful description of "the God of particulars, the God whose righteousness is tied to a particular story in which God has promised to act in a particular way and to bless a particular people."[29] God's righteousness is enacted and revealed in this particular history of the blessing of his particular people, but the "standards for judging God's actions" are not solely determined by the story. They are also determined by our recognition of certain ethical qualities that belong to goodness. A god who would give us a scorpion to eat would not be the good God.

This point does not undermine the truth that "God has tied his character to the blessing of his faithful people."[30] God's characteristic righteousness is manifested in his accomplishment of his eschatological promises for the salvation of his people. One can agree that when Paul speaks of "the righteousness of God" (Rom. 1:17) he has in view God's eschatological restoration of Israel through the resurrection of Jesus. That God's "righteousness" is God's historical action in Christ Jesus, however, does not mean that God's righteousness is not also an attribute. Hellenistic philosophical depictions of the divine in terms of spirit, beauty, goodness, love, and eternity are true insights into God, despite the fact that these insights were entangled with false conceptions as well.[31] These insights aided biblical authors in describing the Creator God who acted in Israel and in Christ Jesus.

---

fidelity involves are not *simply* defined by divine action, given their reference to the world that God has created. For the basic problem here, see Plato's *Euthyphro*.

28. On this point see especially Murphy, *God Is Not a Story*.

29. Kirk, *Unlocking Romans*, 8.

30. Ibid., 11.

31. It might also be worth pointing out that Hellenistic "popular" religion, in which context Hellenistic philosophical culture operated, also employed particular stories (rather than universal attributes) in order to understand its gods. See Burkert, *Greek Religion*, 182–83. See also Hans Urs von Balthasar's discussion of Homer in his *Glory of the Lord*, 4:43–77, as well as his exploration of Plato on 166–215. For protomonotheistic or monotheistic (generally in an expanded sense) developments in pagan religion and philosophy, both before and after the rise of Christianity, see Peter Van Nuffelen, "Pagan Monotheism as a Religious Phenomenon," 16–33, and Frede, "Case for Pagan Monotheism," as well as the essays collected in Mitchell and Van Nuffelen, *Monotheism between Pagans and Christians*.

Kavin Rowe: Rival Narratives

Kavin Rowe's *World Upside Down* seeks to correct the view that Luke-Acts, written by a gentile convert, is sycophantic toward the Roman Empire. As Rowe ably demonstrates, Acts portrays the significant disruption of Roman culture that resulted from the new understanding of God and the new way of life proclaimed by Paul and the other apostles.[32] For Rowe, the world is a place of competing narratives, which shape our way of life and are in turn shaped (and made intelligible) by our way of life: "Our way of reading the world is always and necessarily bound up with the lives we are living," because "practices shape our sight."[33] To speak of a "moral or metaphysical order" is to identify *our perception of* such an order—that is to say, the narrative that frames our lives—or, as Rowe puts it, "that underwrites the reality in which it makes sense to do these things [particular cultic practices]."[34] Christians "construe reality" on the basis of faith in the crucified and risen Jesus; to be a "Christian" is "to wager one's total perception on the insiders' reading of those who follow the Jesus who was dead."[35] There is no "independent order" outside of the competing narrative construals of reality.[36] Truth therefore has a "practical contour or shape" because it is tested and revealed in our practices, our "entire pattern of life."[37] The book of Acts, Rowe concludes, offers a way

---

32. For background see Clark, *Christianity and Roman Society*; Wilken, *Christians as the Romans Saw Them*. Commenting on the place of Judaism within the Roman Empire, Clark observes:

> Judaism was a special case, both because of its monotheism and because it is an ethnic as well as a religious category. Jewish monotheism, that is, belief that there is one and only one god, was not compatible with traditional religion or with "divine honours" for emperors, and the customs derived from Jewish scripture marked Jews as different from others. . . . But there were also positive responses to Judaism. Romans who were interested in philosophy respected Jews for their monotheism, their refusal to make images of their god, and their adherence to their ancient law. Jews offered sacrifice, even if it was only to one god and at one temple, for as long as the Temple stood, and they were willing to offer sacrifice for the well-being of the emperor. (*Christianity and Roman Society*, 6)

33. C. Rowe, *World Upside Down*, 151.

34. Ibid., 145.

35. Ibid., 156.

36. Ibid., 160. For a philosophical response to philosophical claims of this kind, see especially MacIntyre, *Dependent Rational Animals*, including his preface in which he notes, "I was in error in supposing an ethics independent of biology to be possible," in part because "no account of the goods, rules and virtues that are definitive of our moral life can be adequate that does not explain—or at least point us towards an explanation—how that form of life is possible for beings who are biologically constituted as we are, by providing us with an account of our development towards and into that form of life" (x). See also MacIntyre, *First Principles*.

37. C. Rowe, *World Upside Down*, 161. It is evident that our practices influence the way we see the world, but, nonetheless, this view of truth is inadequate to the full scope of our knowing (and inadequate, I hope to show, to the New Testament authors' own philosophical contexts

of knowing that is "irreducibly particular."[38] It follows that "to affirm that God has 'created heaven and earth' is, in Luke's narrative, simultaneously to name the entire complex of pagan religiousness as idolatry and, thus, to assign to such religiousness the character of ignorance."[39]

Rowe notes that this does not mean that pagan culture, including pagan philosophy, possesses no "goods"; on the contrary, Luke anticipates the presence of such goods.[40] They are goods, however, that are in need of salvation. As Rowe points out, not every "individual facet of pagan existence is directly affected by the Christian theological critique. At the very least, there remains, in Peter Brown's terms, the 'neutral technology of life.'"[41] But the radical reconfiguration of God's identity around creation and resurrection nonetheless makes clear that "the difference between Christianity and paganism is deeper and more comprehensive than our modern linguistic habits tend to reveal."[42] Before inquiring into how this affects theological reception of Hellenistic philosophical insights, I wish to raise some questions regarding Rowe's way of phrasing the difference.

The key issue is whether those who differ significantly in their theological narratives can share any true insights about the living God. What is required

---

and presuppositions). For the linguistic and metaphysical issues involved, including how language functions and refers ontologically to realities, see Kripke, *Naming and Necessity*; Kripke, *Reference and Existence*. See also Hart, *Experience of God*; te Velde, *Aquinas on God*, 95–102.

38. C. Rowe, *World Upside Down*, 176.

39. Ibid., 50. Janet Martin Soskice highlights the importance of Philo in these discussions. Because Philo accepts the biblical revelation of *creatio ex nihilo*, she argues, he understands God in a much different way than does the Hellenistic philosophical culture upon which he draws heavily. In this light she states that "the divine titles with which we are concerned, such as 'incomprehensible,' 'simple,' 'uncontainable,' 'eternal' and 'One,' are treated throughout by Philo, not as divine 'attributes' as we might have them, but as divine 'names,' and his interest in naming God is driven by his Jewish piety" ("Athens and Jerusalem, Alexandria and Edessa," 152). The result is that "Philo is overwhelmed by the ultimacy—and the intimacy—of the God of Israel. Aristotle's god in not intimate or provident, and has no knowledge of particulars. Philo's God, as Creator, knows every thing in particular and is a God of Providence" (160). In short, although Hellenistic philosophers could identify certain truths about God, such as "God is One and Prime Mover," Hellenistic philosophers lacked knowledge of "who God is for us," (159) and their God was neither sufficiently transcendent nor sufficiently "for us." Yet the deep insufficiency of Hellenistic philosophical knowledge of God does not mean that Hellenistic philosophers utterly failed to arrive at truths about God that New Testament authors could presuppose and employ within a quite different theological framework. Insofar as some Greek philosophical concepts were and are true (even if insufficient), their truth makes possible their appropriation (as philosophical concepts) in other theologies. My point should be understood as a call for nuance rather than as a denial of the Christian (and Jewish) difference. See also MacIntyre, *God, Philosophy, Universities*.

40. C. Rowe, *World Upside Down*, 171.

41. Ibid., 51.

42. Ibid.

for successful reference to the living God? Gregory of Nazianzus suggests that some shared knowledge about the living God is possible through reflection on the work of bees, whose complex honeycombs make clear that they have a Maker: "Bees devise honeycombs which hold together with hexagonal, matching cavities, made elaborately firm by a partition and by the subtlety of alternate straight lines and angles, in hives too dark for them to see the structure of the comb."[43] For his part, Rowe weds the truth of statements about "God" fully to the narrative in which they are embedded.[44] As he sees it, Luke's purpose in Acts 17:21–31 involves "subsuming Graeco-Roman religio-philosophical knowledge into the biblical story."[45] He contrasts Acts with the perspective of the Jewish thinker Aristobulus, who, like Acts 17:28, engages with Aratus's *Phaenomena*.[46] Aristobulus supposes that certain truths about

43. Gregory of Nazianzus, *On God and Christ*, 56 (Oration 28, no. 25). See also F. Norris, "Of Thorns and Roses"; Beeley, *Gregory of Nazianzus*, 72–80.

44. In a 2002 article, Rowe demonstrates sensitivity to the kind of problem that I am raising. Following Brevard Childs, Rowe argues, "The biblical text is not inert but instead exerts a pressure ('coercion') upon its interpreters and asserts itself within theological reflection and discourse such that there is (or can be) a profound continuity, grounded in the subject matter itself, between the biblical text and traditional Christian exegesis and theological formulation" ("Biblical Pressure and Trinitarian Hermeneutics," 308). Rowe should extend this insight to philosophical reflection, so as to make clearer (against the Kantian assumptions that remain operative in Wittgenstein) that the realities that manifest themselves in the world exert pressure upon linguistic construals of reality.

45. C. Rowe, *World Upside Down*, 36–37. Does this "biblical story" include the Wisdom of Solomon? James E. Bowley and John C. Reeves make the case that "'the Bible' is not and furthermore never was," since "there are many diverse 'canons' endorsed by contemporary faith communities (ranging from five to eighty or more books) from a variety of textual families. Just as there are only Bibles, so also there are only canons" ("Rethinking the Concept of 'Bible,'" 4, 8). Although I think this overstates matters, and although I do not agree with their claim regarding Second Temple literature that we should "consider the bulk of this material, both biblical and non-biblical, as a single culturally variegated literary continuum which juxtaposes a number of alternative or parallel ways of recounting a particular story or tradition" (8), nonetheless Rowe's appeal to "the biblical story" would benefit from taking up this question.

46. For background see especially Barclay, *Jews in the Mediterranean Diaspora*, 150–58. Only five fragments from Aristobulus's work survive. Barclay notes, "The cultural claim, which appears in four of the five fragments, is the assertion that the Jewish 'school of thought' is both prior and superior to any Greek philosophy. . . . It is Aristobulus's boast that Moses's text, the basis of the Jewish way of life, is the well from which the greatest Greek philosophers drew, though they were unable to preserve the purity of the original source" (150). Aristobulus emphasizes that (in Barclay's words) "to use Greek names for the Deity is to introduce an 'impurity' and 'impiety' from which Jews alone, with their nameless God, are exempt" (152). Thus when quoting the proem of Aratus's *Phaenomena*—the same Stoic work quoted by Paul in Acts 17:28—Aristobulus changes the word "Zeus" to "God," while accepting "Aratus' conception of the God *in* nature" (153). Aristobulus also highlights God's power and sovereignty, often, however, in impersonal terms. See also Barclay's discussion of the *Letter of Aristeas* in 138–50, as well as the conclusions that he draws in 429–34. The complexity of the situation is well expressed by Barclay's summary of Philo's two-sided position:

the divine attained by Hellenistic philosophers accord with the revelation of the God of Israel, whereas (in Rowe's view) Acts 17:28 quotes Aratus in order "to criticize the basic theological error in pagan idolatry, namely, that because human beings are the 'offspring' of divinity, they can image God in their form."[47] The conflict between Hellenistic philosophical culture and Acts's "rival conceptual scheme" means for Rowe that Hellenistic philosophical statements about divinity do not, for Acts, contain true insights.[48]

Put another way, when incorporated into the Christian story, Hellenistic philosophical insights are no longer philosophical, since they have been transformed. Rowe observes that "Luke takes the terms of pagan discourse but in so doing strips them of their philosophical or theological content by transforming them into terms that, in Luke's view, simultaneously criticize pagan philosophy and point toward the truth of Paul's preaching."[49] Thus there are no elements of Hellenistic "natural theology" that can be taken as true in themselves by Christian authors. Rowe uses the terms "alters," "subverts," and "subsumes" to speak of Hellenistic philosophical insights within Acts's narrative. He holds that "the pagan philosophical phrases have *sensu stricto* ceased propounding pagan philosophy. No longer do they speak the thoughts of a system whose intellectual basis exists outside of Luke's story."[50] Acts, says Rowe, "allows pagan philosophy to speak truth not on its terms

---

Philo occasionally acknowledges that others have a correct conception of God (*Virt* 65; *Spec Leg* 2.165), yet he refuses to accept the validity of their cult. In the latter passage he credits to all, Greek and barbarian, recognition of the supreme, invisible "father of Gods and men," yet he immediately convicts all non-Jews of honouring "created Gods" (*Spec Leg* 2.165–66). If only Jews can correct this error, only the Jewish temple can be regarded as sacred to the One God. Both Philo (*Spec Leg* 1.67) and Josephus (*C Ap* 2.193) affirm that there is only "one temple for the One God"; were that defiled, Philo argues, there would be left no trace of the reverence paid to the one true God (*Legatio* 347). For all his capacity for abstraction, Philo cannot regard what goes on elsewhere as proper worship. (430–31)

In short, it is quite possible, and fully consistent, to accept as true a Hellenistic philosophical insight about divinity but to continue to charge that same philosophy (and culture) with grave idolatry.

47. C. Rowe, *World Upside Down*, 38. Aristobulus himself criticizes pagan impiety. See also such works as J. Collins, "Cult and Culture." Collins's view that the Wisdom of Solomon's "natural theology" is "not fully compatible with biblical ideas of revelation and election" (40) strikes me as doubtful, not least because Wisdom of Solomon contains a powerful critique of idolatry and a lengthy recitation of God's saving work among the people of Israel. See also Collins's "Biblical Precedent for Natural Theology," as well as a work cited by Collins, Erich Gruen's *Heritage and Hellenism*.

48. C. Rowe, *World Upside Down*, 40. In this regard Rowe cites MacIntyre, *Whose Justice? Which Rationality?*, and Karl Barth's *Church Dogmatics*, II/1.

49. C. Rowe, *World Upside Down*, 201–2 (endnote 179 to p. 40).

50. Ibid., 40.

but on Luke's."[51] When Luke quotes Hellenistic philosophical insights within the Christian hermeneutical framework, "Luke renders hermeneutically ineffective the original intellectual structures that determined philosophically the meaning of the pagan phrases."[52]

By no means do I wish to contest everything that Rowe is saying here. Hellenistic philosophical culture was deeply implicated in pagan idolatry. The efforts of Greek and Roman philosophers to rise from contingent things to eternal realities contained many errors. Lacking "christological specification" and the "transcendence of the Creator God," Greek and Roman philosophers did not get the identity of "God" right, with profound consequences for their way of life.[53] As Rowe observes, "Even a complex notion of idolatry and the recognition of goods within pagan life do not render the basic difference commensurable: between the affirmation and the denial of the break between God and the world there can be no rapprochement."[54]

Nonetheless, I disagree with Rowe's view that the best Hellenistic philosophical insights, when embedded in the Christian narrative, are no longer "philosophical" because they have been separated from the "original intellectual structures that determined philosophically the meaning of the pagan phrases." To my mind, Rowe unduly limits the ability of pagan philosophical phrases to refer successfully to the living God.[55]

It may be helpful here to ask to what degree the "original intellectual structures" determine the philosophical meaning of Hellenistic insights about divinity. In Plato's philosophy, for example, there is a significant degree of indeterminacy, of admission that Socrates (or Diotima, or Timaeus) does not know quite what he (or she) is talking about.[56] Plato's dialogues often gesture toward realities that Plato admits are too difficult for him to apprehend. Socrates's Diotima may be right that all of us humans "long to make the good our own" and thus also long for immortal union with the eternal "good," but she leaves unresolved many issues pertaining to the nature of the good.[57] This is equally true of Socrates's discussion of the form of the good in the *Republic*, where Socrates argues that the good is "the cause of knowledge" and is the transcendent source of the "existence and essence" of all objects

51. Ibid.
52. Ibid.
53. Ibid., 24, 36. See Hadot, *Philosophy as a Way of Life*; Hadot, *What Is Ancient Philosophy?*; John M. Cooper, *Pursuits of Wisdom*.
54. C. Rowe, *World Upside Down*, 50.
55. For further background see Kenney, *Mystical Monotheism*, 1–56.
56. For discussion see Zuckert, *Plato's Philosophers*, 860–61; Matthews, "Epistemology and Metaphysics of Socrates."
57. Plato, *Symposium* 205a, 557; see also 207a, 559. See also Armstrong, "After the Ascent."

of knowledge.[58] Timaeus holds that "the father and maker of all this universe is past finding out, and even if we found him, to tell of him to all men would be impossible."[59] Yet Timaeus reasons that it is at least true to say that the creator (or demiurge) "was good, and the good can never have any jealousy of anything. And being free from jealousy, he desired that all things should be as like himself as they could be."[60] Since Plato seems aware of the indeterminacy of his positions, their meaning is arguably fluid enough to offer at least some limited truths that in fact refer to the living God of Israel, without imagining that Plato knew the good Creator God.[61]

Regarding the best "pagan phrases," in short, one need not suppose that their meaning is determined, in a strict sense, by their "original intellectual structures." Consider Diotima's remark that beauty (the good) exists "of itself and by itself in an eternal oneness, while every lovely thing partakes of it in such sort that, however much the parts may wax and wane, it will be neither more nor less, but still the same inviolable whole."[62] This doctrine of the participation of all finite things in eternal beauty (or goodness) may pertain, in its "original intellectual structures," to a doctrine of divine ideas or forms that even Plato himself may have later discounted.[63] Yet beyond its "original intellectual structures," Diotima's understanding of beauty also evidences a profound reflection upon reality. The structures of existence, rather than pri-

58. Plato, *Republic* 508e–509b, 774.

59. Plato, *Timaeus* 28c, 1161–62.

60. Plato, *Timaeus* 29e, 1162. For further discussion of Plato's *Timaeus*, whose creator or "demiurge" is certainly not equivalent to the Creator God of Israel, see Sarah Broadie's *Nature and Divinity in Plato's Timaeus*, as well as Zuckert's superb survey in *Plato's Philosophers*, chap. 6. See also Kenney's observation regarding *Timaeus*:

> There has been a tendency for modern readers to slip anachronistically into a theistic approach to these passages based in particular upon the notion of the craftsman's goodness. Since the maker desired to make things good like himself, then he might seem to be the real beneficent source of the order and goodness within "becoming." Hence, he might be identified with the paradigm. This exegetical inference is unwarranted. The notion of goodness involved is based on the craftsman image; it has a strong component of teleology and utility. . . . In saying this I do not wish to suggest that this imagery is quite antithetical to any suggestion of divine beneficence in cosmic production, only that the concept of goodness involved does not include this notion and so offers no foundation for identifying the demiurge, the beneficent craftsman of the world who makes it like unto himself, with the paradigm of order. (*Mystical Monotheism*, 17–18; cf. Zuckert, *Plato's Philosophers*, 468–69)

61. Although of course Plato might have possessed implicit faith, and God might have made himself known to the ancient Greeks in some way through "seeds of the Word": on this point see Pieper, "Tradition," 257–66, 280–85.

62. Plato, *Symposium* 211b, 562. On participation in the one, see, for example, *Parmenides* 165e–166b, 955–56.

63. For discussion see Harte, "Plato's Metaphysics." See also Fine, *On Ideas*.

marily the philosopher's "intellectual structures," may be determinative here for the philosophical meaning of Diotima's vision, even if in Plato's presentation the meaning remains not fully worked out (and/or falsely worked out in certain important respects).

Similarly, one thinks of Aristotle's analysis of change and motion in this world, an analysis that leads him to the conclusion that there must be eternal Act, sheer To Be, who "is indivisible and without parts and has no magnitude at all."[64] Why suppose that Aristotle's positions here are "determined philosophically" by their "intellectual structures," rather than by the structure of existence? Although Aristotle gets many things wrong about God (as, for example, when he tries to understand how eternal Act could think about other things[65]), why should we rule out the *philosophical* character of Aristotle's insight into Pure Act when later Christian theologians employ it to help articulate what Scripture means by "the King of ages, immortal, invisible, the only God" (1 Tim. 1:17)?[66] It seems to me better to affirm, on the one hand, that Hellenistic philosophers were caught up in grave idolatry, but to assert, on the other hand, that some Hellenistic judgments about divinity are true (in a limited way). This is the position taken by the Church fathers, and it is my view as well.

To sum up: Rowe's goal is to show, in Acts, the "incommensurability between the life-shape of Christianity in the Graeco-Roman world and the larger pattern of pagan religiousness."[67] Christian faith and practice differ radically from "pagan religiousness." Rowe and I agree on that point, and thus I admire his larger project in *World Upside Down*. But I wish Rowe would agree that Acts appropriates some true Hellenistic philosophical insights about God, even though the pagans themselves understood these true insights—for example, that divinity is not material and is "good"—from within the idolatrous context

64. Aristotle, *Physics* 9.182.

65. See Aristotle, *Metaphysics* 12.209.

66. Indeed, in another important recent essay, "For Future Generations," Rowe states, "The need to speak in the language of doctrine is not due primarily to the metaphysical predilections of the Greek world but rather arises out of a dynamic that is internal to the biblical text itself"—to which he adds in a footnote, "The point here is not to deny the importance of Greek metaphysics for the outworking of Christian doctrine but instead to make a critical move against earlier accounts of the relationship between doctrine and Scripture that would see the former as Greek philosophical distortions of the latter (see, e.g., Adolf Harnack, *Das Wesen des Christentums* [Gütersloh: Gütersloher Verlaghaus, 1999])" (189).

67. C. Rowe, *World Upside Down*, 50. Stanley K. Stowers is nonetheless right, as far as I can tell, that "the network of practices that Paul conceived as assemblies of Christ had structural similarities to the Hellenistic philosophies because both organized themselves by similar practices and goals" ("Does Pauline Christianity Resemble a Hellenistic Philosophy?," 95).

of the worship of multiple gods.[68] One need not suppose that any Hellenistic philosopher possessed a proper understanding of God in order to allow for what Augustine and other fathers called "plundering the Egyptians." Some bits of treasure were real even if they were not properly employed (or adequately understood) in idolatrous "Egypt"; some Hellenistic philosophical insights about θεός, despite being mingled with grave error, were and are true.[69]

Paul in Athens and Ephesus

Hans Urs von Balthasar provides us with a thought experiment for better appreciating Paul's situation, according to Acts 17, at the Areopagus in Athens. Balthasar asks us to imagine what the response today, in a cosmopolitan Western city, would be to Paul's speech at the Areopagus of Athens. The high point of this speech is clearly its culmination, the proclamation that God has raised Jesus from the dead. Indeed, it is this claim that generates the arguments that Paul has on that day at the Areopagus. The Athenians who are gathered for philosophical discourse at the Areopagus—identified as "Epicurean and

68. Again, I am not here expressing a syncretistic view, as though it would be right to worship Plato's "θεός" or Aristotle's "Pure Act," or as though these philosophers were proto-Christians. To identify true insights about God in Hellenistic philosophy does not thereby unite Christian worshipers with pagan worshipers; as Barclay points out, Philo of Alexandria strongly underscored this fact. This point can be extended into interreligious dialogue, so as to make clear that the affirmation that Jews, Muslims, and Christians worship the one God does not necessitate syncretism. In his essay "A Common Word for a Common Future," Miroslav Volf emphasizes that the areas of agreement about God do not render otiose the areas of disagreement: "To have the dual command of love in common does *not* equate with being amalgamated into one and the same religion. Even if there is significant agreement on love of God and neighbor, many differences remain—differences that are not accidental to faith but that have historically defined them [Judaism, Christianity, and Islam]. Some of these differences concern their basic understandings of God, love, and neighbor" (21).

69. Kenney makes the point that what is sometimes called "classical theism" in fact "was not classical, for it was never clearly or fully articulated in philosophical theology prior to the late third or fourth century AD. Neither was it an indigenous product of the Greco-Roman tradition" (*Mystical Monotheism*, 43). The fathers and medievals knew that their doctrine of God "was not classical," even as they drew on numerous true Hellenistic insights—including ones found in Scripture—in formulating their teachings about God. This debt need not produce what John Webster, with analytic philosophical theists in view, calls "an abstract concept of *deitas*, a preconception of divinity that is not generated from or corrected by God's evangelical self-enactment and self-communication but emerges out of the need for a perfect being as a causal explanation of features of the contingent world" ("Perfection and Participation," 381). But it does require allowing that Hellenistic philosophical reflection generated some insights that are true about the living God, even though these insights were mingled with grave error. Insofar as they were true, these insights did in fact serve the scriptural mediation of God's self-communication. There is no need to deem these insights nonphilosophical when they appear in Scripture (or in later theology). See also Thomas Joseph White's helpful introduction.

Stoic philosophers" (Acts 17:18)—challenge Paul only when he proclaims Jesus's resurrection.

Thus we read of their response to his lengthy speech, "Now when they heard of the resurrection of the dead, some mocked; but others said, 'We will hear you again about this'" (Acts 17:32). What they want him to explain further is the resurrection of Jesus. They do not ask him to defend his claim that "the God who made the world and everything in it, being Lord of heaven and earth, does not live in shrines made by man, nor is he served by human hands, as though he needed anything, since he himself gives to all men life and breath and everything" (Acts 17:24–25). This claim might seem controversial, since it undermines the idea of many gods. Paul makes clear that there is one God who "made the world and everything in it" and who "gives to all men life and breath and everything."[70] Paul leaves no room for other gods in charge of various realms; all things come from the one God, who transcends the world as its Creator. The philosophers gathered at the Areopagus do not quibble with this claim, nor with Paul's further, related claim that "we ought not to think that the Deity is like gold, or silver, or stone, a representation by the art and imagination of man" (Acts 17:29). Instead they quibble only with his concluding assertion that God raised Jesus from the dead.

Balthasar comments on Paul's speech: "Today his opponents would not wait till he began to speak of the resurrection of Christ, when the old sages of Athens shook their heads, but would object at the very beginning of the speech, where Paul sought to connect the Gospel with the fact of natural religion."[71] Most intellectuals today would hardly bother to argue with Paul's claim about Jesus's resurrection, since their worldview accounts both for religious enthusiasm and for absurd events (such as something coming from nothing). Rather, they would take offense at the notion that there is a God by whom Jesus could be resurrected. They would halt Paul's discourse at the very outset, when he remarks, "I perceive that in every way you are very religious" (Acts 17:22).

---

70. As Hurtado points out:

    In all the NT texts, the "God" affirmed is the deity proclaimed in the writings that constitute what came to be the Christian OT. This deity is the sole creator of all things, the supreme heavenly ruler of the cosmos for whom no cult-image is appropriate (or at least not the usual kind) and to whom alone among the other deities of the religious environment cultic worship is to be offered. In the NT texts, "God" is the God of Abraham, Isaac, and Jacob, the deity who gave the Torah through Moses, the God of ancient Israel, and in relation to whom Jesus's own significance and status is presented. This deity is at once both transcendent and distinguishable from all of creation and even from other putatively divine beings and yet is also revealed through the biblical prophets and, most fully, in Jesus. (*God in New Testament Theology*, 98)

71. Balthasar, *God Question and Modern Man*, 62.

For Paul, of course, Athens is a place of disgusting idolatry. Paul tells the assembled crowd that as he passed through the city he saw many objects of worship, the best one being the altar explicitly devoted to "an unknown god." Paul's point, obviously, is not that this altar merits particular praise but rather that they have not known the true God. Thus we read that "while Paul was waiting for them [Silas and Timothy] at Athens, his spirit was provoked within him as he saw that the city was full of idols" (Acts 17:16). When he preaches the risen Jesus, some among his audience even suppose that he is simply proclaiming yet another god (Acts 17:18), which interests them but does not bother them.

Despite Paul's dismay at Athenian idolatry, he tells the crowd at the Areopagus that God providentially arranged the world so that all nations "should seek God, in the hope that they might feel after him and find him" (Acts 17:27). God would not have arranged things so that nations might "seek God" and even "find him" if such activities were not somehow possible. To make his point, Paul quotes excerpts from two pagan writers: "'In him we live and move and have our being'" and "'For we are indeed his offspring'" (Acts 17:28). I interpret Paul (or Acts) here to be saying that these writers articulated some truth, but only a partial truth. Paul concludes with a note of judgment, "Being then God's offspring, we ought not to think that the Deity is like gold, or silver, or stone, a representation by the art and imagination of man" (Acts 17:29). Yet Paul in Acts emphasizes God's mercy toward the past idolatry of those who now have faith in Jesus Christ. Paul tells the Athenians, "The times of ignorance God overlooked, but now he commands all men everywhere to repent, because he has fixed a day on which he will judge the world in righteousness by a man whom he has appointed, and of this he has given assurance to all men by raising him from the dead" (Acts 17:30–31).[72]

Paul's speech to the Athenians in Acts reflects the situation prevailing among first-century pagan intellectuals. Their receptiveness to Paul's account of the one God should be taken seriously. Other pagans, however, were much less amenable to Paul's teaching that "the God who made the world and everything in it, being Lord of heaven and earth, does not live in shrines made by man, nor is he served by human hands, as though he needed anything, since he himself gives to all men life and breath and everything" (Acts 17:24–25). Thus, in Acts 19, we find that Paul has to flee from the city of Ephesus when his teachings put the city into an uproar. Demetrius, employed in making shrines

---

72. Similarly, according to Acts, Peter announces God's forgiveness to the Jewish people. In his speech at Solomon's portico in the temple in Jerusalem, Peter says, "And now, brethren, I know that you acted in ignorance, as did also your rulers" (Acts 3:17). Peter calls upon them to repent and receive Jesus crucified and risen, just as Paul urges the Athenians to do the same.

of Artemis, accuses Paul of misleading "a considerable company of people, saying that gods made with hands are not gods" (Acts 19:26). The Athenian philosophers had been unperturbed by this claim, but Demetrius is incensed by it. He recognizes with fury that if Paul's words gain a hearing—not Paul's words about Jesus's resurrection but his words about the transcendent God—then "the temple of the great goddess Artemis may count for nothing . . . she may even be deposed from her magnificence, she whom all Asia and the world worship" (Acts 19:27).

In the ensuing riot, the clerk of the city of Ephesus is compelled to reaffirm the worship of Artemis in a manner that contrasts strikingly with the friendly reception that Paul's ideas about God received at the Areopagus: "Men of Ephesus, what man is there who does not know that the city of the Ephesians is temple keeper of the great Artemis, and of the sacred stone that fell from the sky? Seeing then that these things cannot be contradicted, you ought to be quiet and do nothing rash" (Acts 19:35–36). Yet even this response indicates that Paul's message about God, if not necessarily his message about Jesus, already has some purchase among the educated elite in Ephesus. The clerk of Ephesus steps in to oppose the lynch mob and thereby risks his own authority and life, which suggests that he may well have had some sympathy with Paul's views.

Wisdom of Solomon and Romans: Knowing God from Created Things

As is well known, Romans 1 bears the influence of Wisdom of Solomon, written by a Hellenistic Jew in the second or first century BC.[73] According to David

---

73. Douglas Campbell remarks, "That the Wisdom of Solomon is playing some role in the early arguments of Romans, and especially in 1:18–32, is widely acknowledged. But the full extent of this intertextual relationship is seldom appreciated. It is strikingly extensive" (*Deliverance of God*, 360). Campbell goes on to demonstrate this in some detail, and he also argues, as we have seen, that the "relationship is at times mischievous, and even subversive" (362). For the view that Paul is using Wisdom of Solomon to frame views with which Paul disagrees, see also Schmithals, *Der Römerbrief*. James Barr helpfully observes in this regard that

> Romans 1–2 may contain, or seem to contain, elements that are absent from the other genuine Pauline letters. . . . I think one would have to judge with Schmithals that this material is very largely taken over from Jewish polemics or missionary preaching toward the Gentiles. But, if so, why might Paul have used it here? I think one might be able to explain it as follows: the plan of Romans, in this respect, is to compare the status of Jews and Gentiles in relation to God's justice. Both, according to Paul, are under the wrath of God for their failings. For the Jews, it is easy enough to explain: they had the Law of Moses, but did not obey it. But what about the Gentiles? This was more complicated. They had known that which was knowable of God but failed to honour him accordingly

Winston, Wisdom of Solomon aims to show that Israel's "way of life, rooted in the worship of the One true God, is of an incomparably higher order than that of their pagan neighbors, whose idolatrous polytheism has sunk them into the mire of immorality."[74]

Like Paul in Romans 1, Wisdom of Solomon states that those who did not know the one Creator (Israel's God) were "foolish" because "they were unable from the good things that are seen to know him who exists" (Wis. 13:1). Had they used their reason properly, they would have known "him who is"—as the Septuagint translates God's name in Exodus 3:14—from the good things that we can perceive around us. Since the good things of this world do not produce their own being or nature, a "craftsman" must have made them (13:1). No finite thing, even "the circle of the stars" (13:2), can be the cause of everything else while itself being uncaused. The finite power and beauty of the good things of this world bear witness to the transcendent power and beauty of God the Creator. The Hellenistic philosophers devoted their lives to studying these "good things," and so they were blameworthy for failing "to find sooner the Lord of these things" (Wis. 13:9).[75]

Wisdom of Solomon, however, is willing to make some allowances for the mistakes of the philosophers, because at least they were seeking the truth: "Yet these men are little to be blamed, for perhaps they go astray while seeking God and desiring to find him. For as they live among his works they keep searching, and they trust in what they see, because the things that are seen

---

and devoted the veneration proper to him to images of humans or, worse, of animals. (*Biblical Faith and Natural Theology*, 54–55)

See also Campbell, *Deliverance of God*, 359. On Romans's debt to Wisdom of Solomon, see also Barr, *Biblical Faith and Natural Theology*, 61–80.

74. Winston, *Wisdom of Solomon*, 63. See also Reese, *Hellenistic Influence on the Book of Wisdom*; Perdue, *Wisdom and Creation*. Perdue observes that in Wisdom of Solomon 13–15, "the teacher digresses from his syncrisis of contrasts to engage in a polemic against pagan religion. . . . In the polemic against nature worship (13:1–9), the teacher argues against the deification of nature, which results from the failure of humans, even philosophers, to differentiate between the creator and the works by which he should be known" (*Wisdom and Creation*, 313). James Barr rightly argues *both* that "the real source from which Christian natural theology sprang is Hebraic" and that "much of the New Testament, and especially of the letters, is much more Greek in its terms, its conceptuality, and its thinking than main trends of modern biblical theology have tended to allow" (*Biblical Faith and Natural Theology*, 56).

75. For further discussion see J. Collins, *Jewish Wisdom in the Hellenistic Age*, 231. Collins draws a line from Wisdom of Solomon to the *prima pars* of Thomas Aquinas's *Summa theologiae* (232). See also Marcus, "Divine Names and Attributes in Hellenistic Jewish Literature." Barr observes that "no one thinks that the New Testament is primarily and essentially a document of natural theology. But that structures held in common with Greek thought are common features of Jewish and of Christian intellectual life within the Hellenistic world has simply to be accepted. . . . It was Jewish religion that made attractive the (eclectic) integration of certain Greek ideas and concepts" (*Biblical Faith and Natural Theology*, 76).

are beautiful" (Wis. 13:6–7). They were seeking God, and they recognized the beauty of finite things. They may have gone astray in their reasoning, but at least they were seeking and desiring God. But Wisdom of Solomon does not make too many allowances, since "not even they are to be excused; for if they had the power to know so much that they could investigate the world, how did they fail to find sooner the Lord of these things?" (Wis. 13:8–9).

According to Wisdom of Solomon, the greater failure belongs to those who actually worshiped finite things as gods. The philosophers who practiced pagan worship without believing that finite things were God should certainly not be excused, but they are less blameworthy and pitiful than are the people who actually worshiped the images of the gods. Such people supposed that the gods dwelt in the images or even that the images were the gods.[76] Discussing the worshipers of images (rather than the philosophically minded pagans), Wisdom of Solomon catalogues the vices that flow from the worship of images:

> Afterward it was not enough for them to err about the knowledge of God, but they live in great strife due to ignorance, and they call such great evils peace. For whether they kill children in their initiations, or celebrate secret mysteries, or hold frenzied revels with strange customs, they no longer keep either their lives or their marriages pure, but they either treacherously kill one another, or grieve one another by adultery, and all is a raging riot of blood and murder, theft and deceit, corruption, faithlessness, tumult, perjury, confusion over what is good, forgetfulness of favors, pollution of souls, sex perversion, disorder in marriage, adultery, and debauchery. For the worship of idols not to be named is the beginning and cause and end of every evil. (Wis. 14:22–27)

Many of these vices involve the actual religious practice of idolaters—their bloody "initiations," their "secret mysteries," and their "frenzied revels." Other vices flow from their religious practice, which distorts all aspects of their lives. According to Wisdom of Solomon, their lives are marked by murder, theft, lying, sexual perversion, and so forth. Therefore God will punish them "on two counts: because they thought wickedly of God in devoting themselves to idols, and because in deceit they swore unrighteously through contempt for holiness" (Wis. 14:30). Their idolatrous worship produced a life marked by lack of holiness.

Romans 1 has numerous affinities with these passages from Wisdom of Solomon 13–14.[77] After proclaiming the gospel to be "the power of God for

76. For discussion of this point in ancient Mesopotamia, see Kugel, *God of Old*, 82–85.
77. The extent of Paul's direct knowledge of Wisdom of Solomon is, of course, unknown. Philip S. Alexander urges scholars not

salvation to every one who has faith" (Rom. 1:16), Paul seeks to show that all humans need the salvation offered by God through faith in Jesus Christ. The gentiles, he argues, find themselves under God's wrath and in need of salvation because they have worshiped idols and fallen headlong into all sorts of vicious habits.[78] They cannot be excused by ignorance, for they knew God but refused to worship him; as Paul states, "God gave them up in the lusts of their hearts to impurity, to the dishonoring of their bodies among themselves, because they exchanged the truth about God for a lie and worshiped and served the creature rather than the Creator, who is blessed for ever" (Rom. 1:24–25). Wisdom of Solomon, we recall, distinguishes the philosophers from the worshipers of images, although both are blameworthy. By contrast, Paul lumps all gentiles together.

Paul makes clear that the basic problem of rebellion affects all humans. He remarks, "You have no excuse, O man, whoever you are, when you judge another; for in passing judgment upon him you condemn yourself, because you, the judge, are doing the very same things" (Rom. 2:1). Not only the gentiles but also the Jews fall under condemnation: "All men, both Jews and Greeks, are under the power of sin" (Rom. 3:9). He draws support for this claim from various psalms and also from Isaiah 59, which depicts God as finding that the world does not contain a single righteous man or woman.

Paul's condemnation of the gentiles is rooted in the claim that they knew God, or at least that they were culpable for not knowing God. Just as Wisdom of Solomon teaches that "from the greatness and beauty of created things comes a corresponding perception of their Creator" (Wis. 13:5), Paul teaches that "what can be known about God is plain to them, because God has shown it to them. Ever since the creation of the world his invisible nature, namely, his eternal power and deity, has been clearly perceived in the things that have been made" (Rom. 1:19–20). However, as we noted, Paul differs from Wisdom of Solomon in that the latter distinguishes between the philosophers and

---

to ask how he [Paul] may have fused Judaism and Hellenism (as if these were clearly different entities) to make something new (Gentile Christianity), or whether he should be considered more Hellenistic than Jewish (or vice versa). Instead we should focus on how Paul, a Hellenized Diaspora Jew, would have been able to make sense of the Jewish culture of Jerusalem and Judea when he encountered it as a young man, on how he took the teaching of a Palestinian Jewish sect and "translated" it for the benefit of Greeks outside Palestine, on what cultural resources those Greeks had at hand to make sense of his message. ("Hellenism and Hellenization as Problematic Historiographical Categories," 80)

78. As Stowers observes, "Paul's basic teaching began with the call to turn from idols to a true God and included the idea that worship of the false gods entailed bondage to passions and desire (1 Thess. 1:10, cf. 4:1–5; Rom. 1:18–32). Turning to the true God meant a dramatic reorientation and mastery of passions and desire, but also a continuing struggle for self-mastery" ("Does Pauline Christianity Resemble a Hellenistic Philosophy?," 92).

those who worship images. For Wisdom of Solomon, "all people who were ignorant of God were foolish by nature" (Wis. 13:1), but the worshipers of images were much more ignorant and foolish than others. Paul goes further and argues that certain people actually knew the truth about God and suppressed this truth. Such people began by knowing God's "eternal power and deity" through "the things that have been made," but they refused to worship God. Their minds therefore "became futile" (Rom. 1:21) so that they could no longer think clearly. They claimed "to be wise," but in fact they were fools (Rom. 1:22), as demonstrated by their worship of creatures.

The somewhat positive note about the (still blameworthy) philosophers that we observed in Wisdom of Solomon is thus not present in the same way in Romans. Paul does not give credit to a set of people who, even if they went astray, did so "while seeking God and desiring to find him" (Wis. 13:6). Paul does not distinguish such people from those "who give the name 'gods' to the works of men's hands" (Wis. 13:10). For Paul, all the gentiles "became fools" by sharing in idolatrous worship when they should have known better. Lest we exaggerate the difference between Paul and Wisdom of Solomon, however, we should underscore that the latter says that "not even they [the philosophers] are to be excused" (Wis. 13:8). Furthermore, from a different angle it may be Paul, not the author of Wisdom of Solomon, who is more positive about the possibility of philosophical knowledge about God. After all, Paul insists that the gentiles have suppressed the truth about God: Paul thinks that they "knew God" and that "what can be known about God is plain to them" (Rom. 1:19, 21). By contrast, the author of Wisdom of Solomon seems to think that the intelligent gentiles *should* have known God—because "from the greatness and beauty of created things comes a corresponding perception of their Creator" (Wis. 13:5)—but nonetheless that even the wisest gentiles were at best quite slow in finding the one Creator God.[79]

79. Again, neither Paul nor Wisdom of Solomon has a positive view of gentile knowledge of God, given that the gentiles worshiped idols and lacked wisdom. For further discussion see Grabbe, *Wisdom of Solomon*, 57–61. Arguing that this negative view of the gentiles exaggerated the actual state of things, Barr notes that Paul

> seems to talk as if all Greeks or Gentiles are complete idolaters, totally sunk in idolatry, which was hardly true and could hardly have fitted with his own experience on his journeys in the Hellenistic world; and not only this, he seems to extend this by infinite logical consequence to suggest that all of them were full of wickedness, envy, murder, disobedience to parents, and the like, and that they all not only did these things but commended others when they did so. There are therefore some substantial gaps, to put it mildly, between the Hellenistic-Jewish anti-idolatrous rhetoric that Paul inherited and applied, and the realities of life in the Greco-Roman world. (*Biblical Faith and Natural Theology*, 73–74)

In this regard, I agree with Rowe's emphasis that the difference between worshiping the true God and failing to worship the true God makes all the difference. Barr himself goes on to

Whatever their disagreements, Paul and the author of Wisdom of Solomon are agreed in considering, for reasons *pertaining to* their critique of pagan idolatry, that the one God who created all things (the God of Israel) can be known on the basis of "the things that have been made" (Rom. 1:20).[80] N. T. Wright states, "Paul clearly does believe that when humans look at creation they are aware, at some level, of the power and divinity of the creator," so that there is a "divine self-revelation in creation."[81] In Romans and Acts, Paul condemns the idolatry of the pagans (including the pagan intellectuals), recognizes that some truth about the living God is available to the pagans through reason, and proclaims to them the forgiveness available through faith in Christ Jesus. Acts contrasts Paul's dismay when he found that Athens "was full of idols" (Acts 17:16) with Paul's assurance that God providentially arranged that the gentiles "should seek God, in the hope that they might feel after him and find him" (Acts 17:27).[82] A similar contrast is present in Romans, which teaches that the gentiles knew truths about the living God, but that these truths about God have been overwhelmed by rebellion, idolatry, and impurity. This combination of deplorable pagan idolatry and true pagan insights into God fits with the viewpoint of Wisdom of Solomon and should shape our perspective as well.

---

observe, in a somewhat different context, that "no one is trying to show that Jewish religion and Stoic philosophy, taken as wholes, are the same thing" (76).

80. With reference to Acts 17 and Romans 1, as well as to John 1, Henry Chadwick remarks, "Here already we are meeting the tension between the concept of a natural or general revelation of God to all men endowed with reason (and presumably apparent especially in men whose rational powers are most highly developed) and a unique act of God in a chosen person, in the Word made flesh. The particularity of the Incarnation is the way by which the universality of God's creative providence is known and understood. Conversely, God's universal care for his creatures makes intelligible and reasonable the particular care manifest in redemption" (*Early Christian Thought and the Classical Tradition*, 4). Chadwick's use of "tension" in the first sentence quoted above is belied, I think, by the mutually illuminative relationship that he sketches in the latter two sentences.

81. N. T. Wright, *Letter to the Romans*, 432. Wright, however, bemoans the fact that Romans 1:19–21 has "had to bear the weight of debates about 'natural theology'" (ibid.). From a contemporary Reformed perspective, Paul Helm argues that "Paul endorses a view of natural revelation of more modest proportions, what we shall call *minimal natural revelation*: although God does manifest himself in nature this manifestation is uniformly rejected by man due to their perversity. And only through accepting God's special revelation can this view be accepted" (*Divine Revelation*, 30).

82. Barr, overlooking the implications of Acts 17:16 in my view, holds that "Acts 17 says nothing about idolatry leading to foul immorality, and on the contrary speaks of God's overlooking of past idolatry" (*Biblical Faith and Natural Theology*, 70). He adds that Acts 17 "shares something of the universalist spirit of Wisdom, while Paul in Romans is much more fixed upon the diversity of the two classes of Jews and Gentiles. Again, Wisdom includes the theme of people 'seeking God and desiring to find him,' somewhat reminiscent of the groping and seeking to find him mentioned in the Areopagus speech (Wis. 13:6)" (ibid.).

The Development of the Biblical Doctrine of God

The issues we have been raising about the biblical God and Hellenistic philosophical culture have a wide bearing. As Peter Enns and many others have noted, God, in providentially guiding the formation of the scriptural texts, allowed the human authors to portray God's nature in seemingly contradictory ways.[83] There are texts that speak about God "walking in the garden in the cool of the day" (Gen. 3:8) and about God's "mighty arm" and "right hand" (Ps. 89:13); there are also texts that describe God as saying, "Then I thought I would pour out my wrath upon them and spend my anger against them in the midst of the land of Egypt" (Ezek. 20:8), and, "I gave them statutes that were not good and ordinances by which they could not have life; and I defiled them through their very gifts in making them offer by fire all their first-born, that I might horrify them; I did it that they might know that I am the Lord" (Ezek. 20:25–26). By contrast, there are texts that proclaim about God, "Heaven and the highest heaven cannot contain thee; how much less this house which I have built" (1 Kings 8:27); that have God emphasize, "I have no pleasure in the death of any one, says the Lord GOD; so turn, and live" (Ezek. 18:32); and that insist that "God did not make death, and he does not delight in the death of the living" (Wis. 1:13). Similarly, there are texts that teach that "God is spirit" (John 4:24); that "no one is good but God alone" (Mark 10:18); and that "God is love, and he who abides in love abides in God, and God abides in him" (1 John 4:16).

The unification of these portraits of God is made more difficult by the fact that the God described in the Torah, and indeed in most or even all of the Old Testament, can seem to be a bodily God.[84] It is a scholarly commonplace that before the Babylonian exile, the people of Israel thought of YHWH as bodily. Benjamin Sommer offers an extensive selection of texts to support the view that Israel worshiped a bodily God throughout the entire biblical period.[85] In his creative engagement with these texts, Sommer proposes that rather than being limited to one body, "God's bodies are unlimited. A God who can be in various *asherot* and *maṣṣebot* and in heaven at the same time is embodied

---

83. For discussion see Enns, *Inspiration and Incarnation*, 97–111. See also Swinburne, *Revelation*, 180–84.

84. For his part, Aristobulus, like Philo, holds that such texts about Israel's God must be interpreted in accord with what befits the Creator and thus must be interpreted allegorically or metaphorically. See Barclay, *Jews in the Mediterranean Diaspora*, 154–55.

85. See Sommer, *Bodies of God and the World of Ancient Israel*; cf. Neusner, *Incarnation of God*.

but in no way constrained."[86] Sommer's theology of divine bodiliness and fluidity builds upon the portraits of the early worship of YHWH that have been provided by contemporary historians of the ancient Near East, including Mark Smith and William Dever.[87]

Does the development of Israelite monotheism rule out a bodily God, as, for example, through the repudiation of the gods in Isaiah 41:29, "Behold, they are all a delusion; their works are nothing; their molten images are empty wind"? Scholars debate whether Israel moved from monolatry to monotheism in the Second Temple period.[88] For his part, Sommer holds that Israel's religion is consistently a "monotheistic" monolatry.[89] According to Sommer,

86. Sommer, *Bodies of God and the World of Ancient Israel*, 142. Sommer holds that "Yhwh's fluidity does not render Yhwh something akin to a polytheistic deity, even though . . . the gods of ancient Near Eastern polytheism were fluid. Rather, the perception of divinity we have explored here reflects Yhwh's freedom, even as it expresses Yhwh's grace—more specifically Yhwh's desire to become accessible to humanity. This conception renders God an unfathomable being, but nevertheless one with whom we can enter into dialogue" (143). The key to "fluidity" is that Yhwh is not constrained by one body, but the question remains as to the fundamental finitude and becoming of this "God." Metaphysically, one cannot see how a finite being like this, no matter how many bodies he might have, can be the source of being who sustains all beings. This God could not rightly claim, "I am the first and I am the last" (Isa. 44:6).

87. Patrick Miller speculates that the name YHWH may have begun as another name for El, the Canaanite god who was considered father of humans and of the heavenly hosts. Earliest worship of YHWH depicted him as Israel's divine warrior, righteous judge, and king. He was creator, father, everlasting, wise, merciful, and faithful. He was characterized by steadfast love (*ḥesed*), holiness, and jealousy (the demand to be worshiped alone). At least by the time of Elijah, YHWH has a conflictual relationship with the other deities. See Miller, *Religion of Ancient Israel*. See also Mettinger, *No Graven Image?*, 195. Mettinger explains that "Israelite aniconism has a West Semitic pedigree. It is West Semitic cultic tradition that provides the religio-historical background to the Israelite phenomenon" (197).

88. Barclay underscores

the Jewish critique of the worship of many, or "created," Gods. Gentile polytheism was not simply an intellectual error (the false belief that there was more than one God); it was also an insult to the true God that worship should be offered to what were, at most, his agents and subordinates (Philo, *Conf* 168–73). In this regard, Jews could adopt a stance of philosophical purism (cf. Josephus's *purissima pietas*, *C Ap* 2.82), insisting on the unity, singleness and uniqueness of the Divine. Such could be expressed with varying degrees of sophistication, ranging from the simple slogan of the *Shema'* to Philo's philosophical expositions of the Monad. Although Jews stood here on common ground with most philosophers, it was of immense importance that this stance enabled them to reject both Graeco-Roman mythology and the practice of Graeco-Roman cult, both of which were irreducibly polytheistic. (*Jews in the Mediterranean Diaspora*, 431–32)

For polytheism in Israel, see M. Smith, *Early History of God*; M. Smith, *Origins of Biblical Monotheism*; Dever, *Did God Have a Wife?*

89. Sommer, *Bodies of God and the World of Ancient Israel*, 147. For the view that during the Babylonian exile, as witnessed by Deutero-Isaiah (Isa. 41:1–5, 21–29; 43:8–13; 44:6–8) and by the Deuteronomists (Deut. 4:35, 39; 2 Sam. 7:22; 1 Kings 8:60), Israel moved from monolatry to monotheism, see Albertz, "Does an Exclusive Veneration of God." Albertz argues that

Israel's religion counts as monotheism not because it denies the existence of other gods but because "Yhwh's will is never frustrated by forces of nature, by matter, or by other gods. Only in one area can Yhwh be thwarted: by human free will."[90] From a different angle, Nathan MacDonald argues that the term "monotheism" is simply not helpful.[91] Warning that the seventeenth-century concept of "monotheism" replaced the living God who covenantally elects Israel with an abstract, metaphysical, universalized deity, MacDonald argues that not only Deuteronomy but also Second Isaiah and other biblical texts commonly cited in favor of monotheism are not "monotheistic" in the abstract, metaphysical sense. These texts instead require Israel to praise and proclaim God as the one Savior and Lord, and to obey and love him as such.[92] This view fits with Sommer's insistence that the Hebrew Bible's "religious ideals demand that the Israelites render to Yhwh exclusive loyalty."[93]

From a broadly similar perspective, but with a somewhat different set of issues in mind, the biblical scholar Jon Levenson affirms metaphysical dualism on the grounds that otherwise one would "trivialize creation by denying

---

monotheism, when not joined to state power, militates against violence in ways that monolatry does not.

90. Sommer, *Bodies of God and the World of Ancient Israel*, 171.

91. See Nathan MacDonald, *Deuteronomy and the Meaning of 'Monotheism.'* For MacDonald, the danger of "monotheism" consists in its tendency to portray Israel as a progenitor of the deist Enlightenment. As an example MacDonald points to Sigmund Freud's proposal that the pure monotheistic tenets espoused by "the Egyptian Moses were too much for the Jewish people, and they killed him. The imperfections of the Law were introduced by the Midianite Moses, who worshipped the volcanic deity, YHWH, and the pure worship of the Aten was suppressed" (20). See Freud's *Moses and Monotheism*, 1–137. For an especially negative view of monotheism, in particular its sharp "distinction between true and false" (Assmann, *Price of Monotheism*, 118), see Assmann's *Moses the Egyptian* and his more recent *The Price of Monotheism*. For another critique of the term "monotheism" (but also of Assmann's project), see Markschies, "Price of Monotheism." Assmann "defends" Judaism's version of monotheism as at least somewhat better than Christianity's and Islam's: see *Price of Monotheism*, 119. See also Marilynne Robinson, "The Fate of Ideas," 113–19; as well as my *Betrayal of Charity*, chap. 1: "Is Charity Violent?"

92. See Nathan MacDonald, *Deuteronomy and the Meaning of 'Monotheism,'* 221. For Julius Wellhausen and Abraham Kuenen, the concept of "monotheism," credited to the prophets, served to undermine the particularistic aspects of the Old Testament. MacDonald finds unfortunate antiparticularist views of "monotheism" also at work in the leading Old Testament scholars from the twentieth century, notably William Albright (who argues that Mosaic Yahwism is monotheistic), Yehezkel Kaufmann (who emphasizes Israel's intuition of God's sovereignty), and Robert Gnuse (who proposes an evolutionary movement toward a transcendent, universal, and ethical God).

93. Sommer, *Bodies of God and the World of Ancient Israel*, 159. Cf. Kugel, *How to Read the Bible*, 685. Nicole Belayche notes that in the pagan world, "the term *heis theos,* 'alone/unique,' signifies that the divinity was alone of its type, unmatched (*praestans* in Apuleius's words), capable of achieving the impossible, but not one god as such. It is the equivalent of a relative superlative form, like *hypsistos,* designed to affirm the unequalled characteristics of the god celebrated" ("*Deus deum . . . summorum maximus,*" 166).

the creator a worthy opponent."[94] He challenges the view that God creates from nothing and sustains everything in being: "This notion of the God who sustains all things, though derived from some common biblical affirmations, is difficult to reconcile with the old mythological image of the divine warrior at combat with the inimical forces."[95] It also does not fit the emphasis on God's "maintenance of boundaries" found in other biblical texts.[96] If God were a sovereign Creator *ex nihilo*, then God could not truly be at war with anything, since everything would be in God's hands. The important point for us to note here consists in the fact that Levenson's dualist doctrine of God derives from, and attempts to make sense of, numerous biblical texts about God/YHWH that suggest that Israel's God is one among other gods.

Another eminent biblical scholar, James Kugel, also highlights biblical texts that cut against the grain of what Bauckham terms "Hellenistic true-god-language." In the early books of Scripture, Kugel finds a vibrant spiritual world in which humans regularly encounter God/YHWH, because this God is localized and bodily. By contrast, later depictions of encounter with God are highly spiritual or mystical, rooted in prayer and yearning for an absent, distant, awe-inspiring God. Early descriptions of encounter with God/YHWH, Kugel notes, involve direct engagement with what at first appears to be an angel (or a man) and then turns out to be God. In the flaming bush, for example, Moses finds first "the angel of the Lord" (Exod. 3:2) and then YHWH. In these early descriptions of human encounter with God, "the spiritual is not something tidy and distinct, another order of being. Instead, it is perfectly capable of intruding into everyday reality, as if part of this world."[97]

Regarding the absent, distant God, Kugel singles out Wisdom of Solomon for his sharpest criticism. In Kugel's view, Wisdom of Solomon makes God aloof and deracinates the active God who showed up in the burning bush to care for his enslaved people. The author of Wisdom of Solomon, Kugel states, "did not like the idea of depicting God as actively intervening in the

94. Jon D. Levenson, *Creation and the Persistence of Evil*, preface to the 1994 edition, xxv. On God and the gods, see also Levenson, *Sinai and Zion*, 56–70, 137–38. Levenson holds that Israelite "monotheism" is monolatry. He finds that "texts like Jeremiah 10:2–10 are the closest to genuine monotheism, the belief in the reality of only one deity," and he concludes that "although no other religion has been discovered with the same 'monotheism,' almost all the elements of Israel's belief in the oneness/uniqueness of YHWH show convincing parallels in the Gentile world" (*Sinai and Zion*, 68). For a response to Levenson's *Creation and the Persistence of Evil*, see my *Scripture and Metaphysics*, chap. 2.

95. Levenson, *Creation and the Persistence of Evil*, xxv. For demonstration of the coherence of the metaphysically simple God with the images of God's warfare against forces of evil, see Hart, *Doors of the Sea*.

96. Levenson, *Creation and the Persistence of Evil*, xxv.

97. Kugel, *God of Old*, 36.

affairs of men, either by Himself or through some angel. Instead this author liked to think that it was an entity called *Wisdom* that actually did things on earth, while God remained in heaven."[98] Kugel notes that Israel found a way of relating to this distant, aloof God—namely, through the regularity of Torah observance. The cost, however, was divine spontaneity, presence, and freedom to act in history: "A certain paradox was built into the cosmic God and his service. Huge, remote, and utterly alone, he had unlimited power. But precisely for that reason, he was also more predictable—even, in a way, more controllable."[99]

One might argue that Kugel fails to do justice to the God of Jeremiah, Isaiah, or Job. Their God is transcendent but not "predictable" or "controllable." Likewise, Paul praises not an aloof God but "the Father of mercies and God of all comfort, who comforts us in all our affliction, so that we may be able to comfort those who are in any affliction, with the comfort with which we ourselves are comforted by God" (2 Cor. 1:3–4). One might further remark that the God of Sommer and Levenson would be finite, a mere being among beings, profoundly limited and creaturely in every way. But the point is that their accounts of God/YHWH, whether one agrees with them or not, do indeed derive from certain scriptural narratives.[100]

Given such interpretations of Israel's narratives about God, would things be clearer if we focused solely on the New Testament? Recently, the Catholic theologian Stephen Webb has argued that the invisibility of God does not entail nonbodiliness. Responding to the traditional view of the immateriality of the divine Word, Webb relies in particular upon Colossians 1:15–16, "He is the image of the invisible God, the first-born of all creation; for in him all things were created, in heaven and on earth, visible and invisible, whether thrones or dominions or principalities or authorities—all things were created through him and for him."[101] In Webb's view, Paul cannot here mean to signal the Father's (immaterial) begetting of the immaterial Son, since if this were

98. Ibid., 21; cf. 61.
99. Ibid., 198.
100. To these instances, one might add Neil B. MacDonald's assumption that an eternal God could not act freely in time, since an eternal God could never really enter time (a misunderstanding of what "time" and "eternity" are and how they relate): "It will be a minimal requirement of any theory descriptive of this [Old Testament] trajectory that it presupposes a *God acting in the same time frame as the people Israel*; not a God who as it were acts from eternity. The exodus narrative is quite clear that God speaks to Israel and Moses in particular *then and there*; the narrative-agent that is God is not speaking from eternity" (*Metaphysics and the God of Israel*, xiv).
101. See Webb, *Jesus Christ, Eternal God*, 206. Webb, like Neil MacDonald, is significantly indebted to Karl Barth, even though he goes further than Barth. For a survey of and critical response to Webb's book, see Phillip Cary's review, "Material God."

so, then the Son could not be "first-born" among creatures.[102] For Webb, the solution is that "the body of Jesus is a perfect fit for God."[103] From eternity, the Triune God has *chosen to be matter* in order to choose us as his family, "so that we too can progress eternally into the divine substance without losing our identities."[104] For theism shaped by Platonic influences, says Webb, materiality is inevitably imperfect by comparison to immateriality. But if the bodily Son does not relate eternally to the (bodily) Father, this would mean that behind Jesus's materiality stands an immaterial life to which we still have no real access, because we know only the bodily Jesus.[105] It would follow that "there are . . . two opposed spaces—an immaterial space occupied by God and a material place occupied by us."[106] In making this case, Webb thinks he is following the scriptural narrative as summed up in Jesus Christ.[107]

In light of all this, the simple claim that I wish to advance is that Hellenistic philosophical culture, as it shows itself in Second Temple Jewish writings and in the New Testament, is necessary if we are to avoid construing the biblical God univocally as a limited entity among entities. To read the biblical God aright, we must grant some true insights about the living God to the pagan philosophers, even while denying that these truths, partial and mingled with error as they were, enabled the pagan philosophers properly to know the living

102. Webb is aware that the Arians employed Col. 1:15 to show that the Son is not God, since they held that "God is unbegotten, uncreated, and ungenerated" (*Jesus Christ, Eternal God*, 207).

103. Ibid., 292.

104. Ibid.

105. But see the discussion of Nestorianism (in its various forms across the centuries) found in Oakes, *Infinity Dwindled to Infancy*.

106. Webb, *Jesus Christ, Eternal God*, 292.

107. Given the nature of material amalgamations, had the Word already been bodily, he could hardly have *become* human flesh without ceasing to be the kind of matter that he previously was. Had God always chosen to be the heavenly flesh of Jesus Christ, then he could not have *become* incarnate of Mary (see John 1:14). On this point see Edward Oakes's presentation of the views of the Lutheran pietist theologian Johanna Petersen (1644–1724), in *Infinity Dwindled to Infancy*, 275–78. Petersen, who is not cited by Webb, built upon the Lutheran rejection of the distinction between the Logos *asarkos* and the Logos *ensarkos*. Whereas Calvin accepted this traditional distinction, Petersen holds to "the preexistence of the heavenly God-*humanity* of Jesus Christ" and considers it "significant that in his letter to the Philippians Paul makes the subject of the preexistence *Christ Jesus*" (275). Along lines that would also apply to Webb, Oakes concludes that "if she is right that the solution to the problem of the real presence is to be found in the preexistent heavenly flesh of Christ, then she is caught in a dilemma: either she has made matter eternal with God (thus denying creation *ex nihilo*), or she has lapsed into Arianism (by making the heavenly Christ a creature, however exalted). Either Christ's flesh, however 'heavenly,' must preexist the universe (thereby making matter somehow coterminous with God's eternity), or else Christ's preexistence must be a part of creation" (276). A material God would, of course, be temporal (even if everlastingly so), since God's unique eternity depends upon his simplicity.

God. God's self-revelation invited and benefited from certain true insights of Hellenistic philosophical culture. In short, divine revelation made fruitful use of the historical and cultural context (cf. *Dei Verbum* §12) of the biblical authors and redactors.

Conclusion: Revelation and Hellenistic Philosophy

The biblical scholar Dale Martin remarks that "the American neo-orthodox inclination to portray Paul's thought as fundamentally Jewish rather than Greek reflects American pietistic concerns about revelation and culture. Hellenism comes to represent natural theology, whereas Judaism represents revelation."[108] Martin is right about this tendency, even if he need not have restricted it to Americans. Although "natural theology" arose within Hellenistic philosophical culture, it cannot be separated from "Judaism" (or creation theology) in the Second Temple period. True Hellenistic philosophical insights inform the New Testament, not only in Romans and Acts but also in the "Hellenistic true-god-language" found throughout the New Testament.

Even so, is it possible to apply a Hellenistic philosophical insight (such as divine eternity) to the Creator God of Israel without radically transforming this insight? In one sense, the answer is obviously no. YHWH, the Creator God of Israel, reveals himself in history and enters into covenant with his people, culminating in the sending of the Messiah Jesus, the incarnate Son of the Father. This God is not "eternal" in the same way that the Hellenistic philosophers conceived of divine eternity. In another sense, however, the self-revelation of the living God did in fact make use of certain Hellenistic philosophical insights about "God," such as divine eternity, in a manner that affirmed the truth (however partial and limited) of these insights. Hellenistic philosophical culture aided Paul in his efforts to proclaim "the God who made the world and everything in it" (Acts 17:24). As we have seen, Paul in Acts and

---

108. D. Martin, "Paul and the Judaism/Hellenism Dichotomy," 52. Martin continues: Note also how these post-war American assumptions are both like and unlike their nineteenth-century precursors. The Hellenic/Jewish dualism is retained, along with some of the significances of the different sides. Thus both earlier and later scholars identify individualism with Hellenism. But whereas that was a saving aspect for nineteenth-century Germans, for whom individualism was a valued commodity of both the Enlightenment and Romanticism, it was a problem by the middle of the twentieth century, when it could be made to symbolize the fractured, atomized, anonymous state of modernity with its loss of communities. And whereas individualism in conjunction with universalism represented truth to Kantian and Hegelian liberals, the same combination represented for American scholars, nurtured in pietism and evangelicalism, the loss of revelation or Christianity's claim to special access to truth. (ibid.)

Romans is threading a needle: insisting on the one hand that the gentiles were and are idolaters, while granting on the other hand that they had some true insights into the living God whom nonetheless they did not properly know.

It is difficult to retain the balance that Paul attains. But for God's revelation to be rightly estimated we need to retain this balance, one that helps us to appreciate the development of the doctrine of God both within Scripture and in the patristic period as well. It is a balance that takes full account of God's pedagogy, and that has been eloquently restated by Pope Benedict XVI in his Regensburg Lecture: "Despite the bitter conflict with those Hellenistic rulers who sought to accommodate it forcibly to the customs and idolatrous cult of the Greeks, Biblical faith, in the Hellenistic period, encountered the best of Greek thought at a deep level, resulting in a mutual enrichment evident especially in the later wisdom literature."[109] Only if we preserve this scriptural balance can we understand the role of Hellenistic philosophical culture in the formation of Christian doctrine—that is to say, in the Church's mediation of divine revelation.

109. Benedict XVI, "Regensburg Lecture," 136.

Conclusion

In a recent essay, John Webster distances his own Reformed ecclesiology, which he roots in "a deep sense of the perfection of Christ, that is the utter uniqueness, integrity and sufficiency of the Word made flesh," from "those styles of Christian historiography . . . which regard the history of the church as simply one long decline from apostolic purity. Such a reading of the Christian past is a denial of *credo in Spiritum Sanctum*."[1] Webster is right to bemoan those

---

1. Webster, "Purity and Plenitude," 60–61; cf. Billings, *Word of God for the People of God*, 133. See also Webster's gentle but acute critique of Rowan Williams's emphasis on (in Webster's words) "the indeterminacy of Scripture in the life of the church, in that Scripture keeps certain questions alive rather than offering definitive solutions" (Webster, "Rowan Williams on Scripture," 121). Webster argues that in responding to Williams's emphasis on indeterminacy,

> appeal might be made to the divine promise that accompanies Scripture and its reading: Holy Scripture will be part of God's gift of truth to the church. That gift is certainly a gift in time, not a moment of sheer transparency. However, it cannot be deferred to the eschaton: the church may *expect* God to use its uses of Scripture and so to complete the prophetic work begun in the authors themselves. The church is authorized to confess that Scripture is *Holy Scripture*. "Holy Scripture" does not, of course, mean that Scripture is a closed bit of textual territory that affords us a "total perspective" on everything, but it does mean that Scripture is sanctified and therefore guarded by God, that truthful speech is not just an eschatological possibility but rather a calling and task that the church can fulfill as it trusts the divine promise. Is there a threat of false consciousness in all this? Of course. But the safeguard is not historical or hermeneutical indeterminacy; rather, it is an operative doctrine of the superintendence of the Holy Spirit, who guides the church into the truth. (ibid.)

With reference to Williams's theology (but along lines that could be extended to many other contemporary theologies), Webster also rightly raises concerns about "the slenderness of Jesus's agency in the history of his reception in the church's sign-making and discipleship. He does not seem to be the agent of the distribution of his benefits; it is as if his energy is dispersed into the process of human 'making sense' of Jesus" (122). Webster's excellent points can all be applied to the Church's mediation of divine revelation.

approaches that read "the history of the church as simply one long decline from apostolic purity." This is particularly the case when it comes to the mediation of divine revelation. At issue is whether the Church's mediation of divine revelation has in fact been "one long decline from apostolic purity," if indeed (from a purely historical perspective) one can speak of a period of "apostolic purity" at all.[2]

Against ecclesiastical fall narratives, I have argued in this book that the Church truthfully mediates God's revelation to us, due to the efficacious missions of the Son and the Holy Spirit.[3] This mediation of the gospel, which takes place in God's missional people through the liturgy, priesthood, and Tradition, does not compete with or undercut Scripture's truthful mediation of divine revelation. Indeed, the one supports and is implied by the other; otherwise Paul could hardly hope that Timothy would be able truly to "guard" what had been "entrusted" to him (1 Tim. 6:20).[4] Timothy's "care for God's church" (1 Tim. 3:5) belongs within the Holy Spirit's work of guiding Israel and the Church in the writing and transmission of the Scriptures. The Holy Spirit's inspiration of Scripture and the Holy Spirit's guidance of the people of God are inextricably bound together.[5] This is the point of John Henry Newman's

2. For further critical discussion of ecclesiastical fall narratives (or *Verfallsgeschichte*), see O'Collins, *Rethinking Fundamental Theology*, 264–67. See also the diverse perspectives of Dunn, *Unity and Diversity in the New Testament*; Hahn, *Theologie des Neuen Testaments*; and Matera, *New Testament Theology*, especially 428.

3. Regarding the Orthodox Church, I note with the Second Vatican Council's Decree on Ecumenism, *Unitatis Redintegratio*, that the Patriarchal Churches of the East, "although separated from us, yet possess true sacraments, above all—and by apostolic succession—the priesthood and the Eucharist, whereby they are still joined to us in closest intimacy. Therefore some worship in common [*communicatio in sacris*], given suitable circumstances and the approval of Church authority, is not merely possible but is encouraged" (*Unitatis Redintegratio*, §15, 465). *Unitatis Redintegratio* recognizes that between the churches of the Reformation and the Catholic Church "there are very weighty differences not only of a historical, sociological, psychological and cultural character, but especially in the interpretation of revealed truth" (468). One of the main purposes of the Second Vatican Council, in my view, was to overcome such differences wherever possible from the Catholic side. See also Pope John Paul II's encyclical *Ut Unum Sint* (1995). For recent ecumenical investigations, see DeVille, *Orthodoxy and the Roman Papacy*; Hütter, "Christian Unity and the Papal Office" (among his final Lutheran writings); Noll and Nystrom, *Is the Reformation Over?*; Payton, *Getting the Reformation Wrong*.

4. After showing that Basil the Great understood Scripture and Tradition as a hermeneutic circle, and that Basil assumed the Church of his day to be in accord with both, Darren Sarisky argues that the doctrinal corruption of the Church forced the Reformers to choose between Scripture and Tradition, and understandably they chose Scripture. But in my view, once it becomes a choice between the two, the affirmation of any faithful mediation of divine revelation is in deep trouble. See Sarisky, *Scriptural Interpretation*, 224–25.

5. See in this regard Neil B. MacDonald's discussion of "modernity's legacy in bequeathing among other things a thoroughly historical understanding of the literary formation of the Bible," in *Metaphysics and the God of Israel*, xi.

story of the man who began with the "dogma . . . that a priesthood was a corruption of the simplicity of the Gospel" and who moved by logical stages to the rejection of *all* mediation ("the true and only revelation of God to man is that which is written on the heart"), until finally rejecting belief in God as an unnecessary encumbrance of the human spirit.[6]

Leo Tolstoy's *The Kingdom of God Is within You* provides a representative instance of how ecclesiastical fall narratives cut off Jesus Christ from both ecclesial and scriptural mediation. Tolstoy holds that the greatest event ever to occur in human history is that Jesus Christ came preaching "inward perfection, truth, and love," from which should have flowed the end of war and the reign of truth and love, the kingdom of God.[7] According to Tolstoy, no religious laws or institutions are necessary to produce inward perfection; thus, Jesus set aside all Jewish and Roman laws and institutions. Jesus's followers, however, imagined that miraculous and mystical elements were needed to support Jesus's claims, and so they added these false elements. Indeed, some of his followers misunderstood Jesus so badly as to propose that gentile converts should be circumcised and follow Jewish law. The apostles successfully countered this misunderstanding, but in doing so they made a fatal error, even worse than their addition of the miraculous to Jesus's ministry: they claimed the authority of the Holy Spirit, God himself, for their teachings ("it has seemed good to the Holy Spirit and to us" [Acts 16:28]).

According to Tolstoy, this delusional claim set the course for the Church's rapid decline. To back up the claim that God was speaking through the Church, early Christians concocted the story of the descent of the Holy Spirit at Pentecost and pretended that the apostles themselves had performed miracles. All too quickly, Jesus's teaching of inward perfection faded into the background, as the Church, compelled by the logic of its claim to be speaking for God, asserted increasingly complex and unbelievable dogmas. Tolstoy observes, "Thus it was from the earliest times, and so it went on, constantly increasing, till it reached in our day the logical climax of the dogmas of transubstantiation and the infallibility of the Pope, or of the bishops, or of Scripture, and of requiring a blind faith rendered incomprehensible and utterly meaningless."[8] This blind faith does not even have God as its object, since the place of God has now been taken by the pope, bishops, Scripture, and so forth.

By the time of Constantine, then, "faith" merely meant believing in whatever the Church demanded. But surely, says Tolstoy, giving voice to an imagined

---

6. Newman, *Grammar of Assent*, 246.
7. Tolstoy, *Kingdom of God Is within You*, 40.
8. Ibid., 43.

interlocutor, "the Church is holy; the Church was founded by Christ. God could not leave men to interpret his teaching at random—therefore he founded the Church."[9] Rejecting such views, Tolstoy emphasizes that Jesus's simple teaching of love and truth, of inward perfection, did not need to be mediated by a Church. Jesus did not found the Church, and the Church is not holy. Indeed, Tolstoy points out, "In the Gospels there is a warning against the Church, as it is an external authority, a warning most clear and obvious in the passage where it is said that Christ's followers should 'call no man master.'"[10]

Tolstoy notes that the word "church" appears only twice in the Gospels, "once in the sense of an assembly of men to decide a dispute, the other time in connection with the obscure utterance about a stone—Peter, and the gates of hell."[11] These two passages are the sole basis for the whole edifice of an infallible Church filled with sacraments and miracles. In Tolstoy's view, if Christ had wanted to found a Church, he would have done so in a way that proved its validity; the fact that he did not do so is shown by all the different Christian communities that each claim to be Christ's "Church." For Tolstoy, therefore, the Church arose not from Christ but from disputes among the early Christians that led to each group claiming divine authority. The truth about the "one Church," which does not exist, is that it is a charade by which one group of power mongers excludes others who do not believe in certain teachings of which Jesus himself would have known nothing. Tolstoy concludes that "the churches as churches, as bodies, which assert their own infallibility, are institutions opposed to Christianity."[12] By contrast to the "Church," which "represents pride, violence, self-assertion, stagnation, and death," real Christianity represents "meekness, penitence, humility, progress, and life."[13]

What about reformers in the churches who do what they can to weed out excesses? The problem with such reformers, says Tolstoy, is their failure to recognize that the Church has always been a principle not of unity but of division. Since Christ's simple teaching of love and truth does not need human mediation, the Church's (or churches') prideful efforts to impose such mediation have led solely to "wars, battles, inquisitions, massacres of St. Bartholomew, and so on."[14] Tolstoy does not deny that there have been some good Chris-

9. Ibid.
10. Ibid.
11. Ibid.
12. Ibid., 51.
13. Ibid.
14. Ibid. See in this regard Grant Kaplan's insightful comments on Gotthold Lessing's classic work of Enlightenment drama, *Nathan the Wise*. Kaplan notes:

> There are many reasons to applaud Lessing's play. He attacks religiously based violence and hatred, reminds us that faith without works is dead (James 2:17), and exposes the

tians, such as Francis of Assisi, but he makes clear that they were good despite, rather than because of, the Church's ministrations.

Tolstoy makes clear that the ecclesiastical fall of Christianity necessarily distorts the writings that became the New Testament. This is a logical position, and one held as well—from quite a different perspective—by John Howard Yoder, who blames Constantine for the Church's fall but who traces this fall ultimately back to the Old Testament.[15] In Yoder's view, it was Ezra and Nehemiah who reintroduced violent nationalism and reversed the prophet Jeremiah's insistence that the people of Israel should be nonviolent sojourners among the nations.

No less a theologian than Jonathan Edwards exonerates Constantine, whom Edwards sees as heroically overturning pagan idolatry and as channeling the resources of the Roman Empire toward God's holy people on earth. However, continues Edwards, shortly after the conversion of the Irish and the Scots, the Antichrist came into the ascendant, not to be seriously challenged for a thousand years until the rise of the sixteenth-century Reformers. Edwards observes, "The true church in this space was for many hundred years in a state of great obscurity; like the woman in the wilderness, she was almost hid from sight and observation."[16] Essentially what happened is that pagan idolatry, having been put down by Constantine, rose again in the teachings of the Roman Catholic Church.

According to Edwards, "The rise of Antichrist was gradual. The christian church corrupted itself in many things presently after Constantine's time;

---

superficiality of most confessional discord. Despite these laudatory elements, one can still ask whether Lessing too hastily discards historical revelation with the bathwater of religious intolerance. Through the parable of the ring, he brackets the veracity of historical revelation: whether the ring has power becomes irrelevant from Lessing's standpoint; likewise, whether Moses received the tablets from God or came up with the commandments on his own no longer matters. Lessing ignores the question of whether Jesus's words are divinely revealed by focusing on the obedience of his followers. For Lessing, Christianity is only true to the extent that the community of believers embodies its message. One can applaud Lessing's desire to hold believers accountable, but the question still remains whether God *reveals* anything that humanity could not attain on its own. Lessing "solves" the problem of historical revelation by bracketing it. *Nathan the Wise* shifts the *telos* of religion from metaphysical to ethical concerns. That Christianity teaches an Incarnation or that Islam teaches Muhammad is God's final prophet makes no difference. Lessing determines orthodoxy by appealing to orthopraxy, but in such a manner that orthodoxy becomes a means to an end. (*Answering the Enlightenment*, 21–22)

Defending Lessing's parable of the ring, Lieven Boeve argues that its point is to shift religious truth away from propositional claims to "a deeply rooted element of our affection for God, of our complete abandonment to God" (*Interrupting Tradition*, 174).

15. See, for example, Yoder, *For the Nations*; Yoder, *Jewish-Christian Schism Revisited*. I respond to Yoder in my *Ezra and Nehemiah*. See also Marilynne Robinson, "The Fate of Ideas."

16. Edwards, "History of the Work of Redemption," 1:595.

growing more and more superstitious in its worship, and by degrees bringing in many ceremonies into the worship of God, till at length they brought in the worship of saints, and set up images in their churches."[17] This growing idolatry was assisted by, and reflected in, the power-mongering of the priests and bishops, especially the bishop of Rome. The bishop of Rome first "claimed the power of universal bishop over the whole christian church; wherein he was opposed for a while, but afterwards was confirmed in it by the civil power of the emperor in the year six hundred and six. After that he claimed the power of a temporal prince, and so was wont to carry two swords, to signify that both the temporal and the spiritual sword was his."[18] Finally the bishop of Rome showed himself to be literally the Antichrist, by claiming "the very same power that Christ would have done, if he was present on earth reigning on his throne; or the same power that belongs to God, and was used to be called *God on earth*; to be submitted to by all the princes of christendom."[19]

Among Catholics too, versions of the ecclesiastical fall narrative have become popular in recent decades. To take one influential example, Edward Schillebeeckx argues that a "Neoplatonic-hierarchical conception of the church" emerged sometime after AD 500 and beginning in "the eleventh century led to an intensive centralization of ecclesiastical power in Rome."[20] Although things were already quite bad in the medieval period, it was the Council of Trent that proved decisive in instantiating juridically this "Neoplatonic-hierarchical conception of the church."[21] Once this was done, the Holy Spirit became the prerogative of the hierarchy of the Church, which asserted its allegedly Spirit-given power to dominate the laity.

As in other accounts of the Church's fall, a key bogeyman is papal infallibility. Schillebeeckx states that "in this view the Pope becomes the 'representative of Christ' in this world, just as the governors were the representatives of the Roman emperor in distant places. So the gift of the Holy Spirit was reduced to obedience at a lower level, that of the believers, to what was said or decided at the top of the hierarchy. This picture of the church completely excluded believers from the level on which decisions were made."[22] According

17. Ibid. Regarding the date of Antichrist's ascendance, Edwards notes that "it is certain that the twelve hundred and sixty days, or years, which are so often in Scripture mentioned as the time of the continuance of Antichrist's reign, did not commence before the year of Christ four hundred and seventy-nine; because if they did, they would have ended, and Antichrist would have fallen before now" (ibid.).

18. Ibid.

19. Ibid.

20. Schillebeeckx, *Church*, 198.

21. Ibid.

22. Ibid., 199.

to Schillebeeckx, the power-mongering of the pope deprived lay Catholics, especially women, of any sense that they had received the gift of the Holy Spirit. Schillebeeckx concludes that after the Council of Trent, the Church completed its tragic collapse: rather than being served by pastors, the laity became simply "the objects of the priestly, hierarchical and male proclamation and pastorate."[23]

This ecclesiastical fall narrative can easily be extended back into biblical times, which were hardly free of human power-mongering. April DeConick argues that Jeremiah and Ezekiel, who were prophets and priests in the seventh century BC, undertook a brutal crusade against worship of "the Queen of Heaven, the goddess whom the Jerusalemite women loved so much that they baked her special ritual cakes."[24] Likewise, Garry Wills's book *Why Priests?* contains a chapter titled "Killer Priests," in which he explains that Jesus, a "radical Jewish prophet" who spoke out against "the Jewish ruling structures of his time," was killed by the Jewish priests whom he vociferously opposed: "For years the Pharisees, Sadducees, and Scribes stalked Jesus, discredited him, threatened and harassed him from Galilee to Jerusalem. But when it came time to close in for the kill, they turned the dirty work over to the priests."[25] If Jesus was not a priest, and if the Jewish priests were his eager killers, then how did Christianity come to possess a ministerial priesthood? Wills explains that at first, during "the Jesus generation," there was no priesthood.[26] No priest took charge at the communal meals in which the community remembered Jesus. Later there came to be "Servants, Elders, Overseers," but still no priests, since leadership at this time was still purely administrative rather than Spirit-given or cultic.[27] The emergence of priestly "Holy Men" came about, says Wills, due to the Letter to the Hebrews, which served as the basis for a deadly theology of the cross, eucharistic sacrifice, and transubstantiation that secured the status of priests and has long kept "Catholics at a remove from other Christians—and at a remove from the Jesus of the Gospels, who was a biting critic of the priests of his day."[28]

23. Ibid.
24. DeConick, *Holy Misogyny*; for essentially the same argument, made in much more detail, see Dever, *Did God Have a Wife?*
25. Wills, *Why Priests?*, 71, 80. As he mentions, in his youth Wills spent five years in a Jesuit seminary.
26. Ibid., 7.
27. Ibid., 8.
28. Ibid., 3. As Wills goes on to say, claiming the authority of Augustine for his position, "Jesus directly achieves this harmonization of mankind with himself. One does nothing but disrupt this harmony by interjecting superfluous intermediaries between Jesus and his body of believers. When these 'representatives' of Jesus to us, and of us to Jesus, take the feudal forms

Why was the Letter to the Hebrews so deleterious? Standing as a "striking anomaly" among the New Testament writings, Hebrews combines "idiosyncratic, indeed, eccentric, logic (exemplified in the treatment of Melchizedek and Jesus as priest) and sophisticated language."[29] Until the fourth century, Wills suggests, Hebrews—even when respected—was kept safely out of the biblical canon. The bottom line for Wills is that Hebrews judaizes Christianity in a terribly unfortunate way by presenting "Jesus as *both* the sacrificing priest and the victim being sacrificed. This is a bold concession to Jewish thought. Early Christians had abolished the priesthood. The Letter restores it—in a new light, but one that underlines the basic dignity of the priesthood in all its forms."[30] Even though for Wills the Letter to the Hebrews makes clear that only Jesus and no other Christian can be a priest, and even though Wills thinks that Hebrews makes no connections with the Eucharist (not even at 13:10), Hebrews' convoluted logic and rhetorical leaps succeeded historically in connecting Jesus's cross with sacrifice and priesthood. The result was that "as the priesthood developed—along with the concept of the Eucharist as less a meal than a sacrifice—the community was reduced from participation to spectatorship, and parallels with Jewish Temple procedures were adopted from the Letter to Hebrews."[31] The roots of nearly two millennia of ecclesiastical fall, therefore, are to be found both in the Church's history and in Scripture, particularly in Hebrews' reversal of Jesus's alleged antipathy toward Jewish priests and cultic worship.

Wills writes as a Catholic, albeit as one who does "not believe in popes and priests and sacraments."[32] Writing in defense of atheism, the scientist Richard Dawkins makes similar points about Scripture and the Church. He grants that "from a moral point of view, Jesus is a huge improvement over the cruel ogre of the Old Testament."[33] But Dawkins considers that the New Testament corrupted the portrait of Jesus by presenting him as the victimized Son of a bloodthirsty Father. Having surveyed many of the instances in which Israel's priests and leaders slaughtered people recklessly in the name of YHWH, Dawkins comments, "So far, so vindictive: par for the Old Testament course. New Testament theology adds a new injustice, topped off by a new sadomasochism whose viciousness even the Old Testament barely exceeds."[34]

---

of hierarchy and monarchy, of priests and papacy, they affront the camaraderie of Jesus with his brothers" (200).

29. Ibid., 120.
30. Ibid., 133.
31. Ibid., 248.
32. Ibid., 256. See also Wills's *Why I Am a Catholic* and *Papal Sin*.
33. Dawkins, *God Delusion*, 250.
34. Ibid., 251.

In Dawkins's view, the Father killed his Son so as to atone for a sin supposedly committed by a man, Adam, who never existed. Dawkins does not limit this sacrifice-theology to Hebrews but finds it throughout the New Testament.

How can we respond to these ecclesiastical fall narratives, not least in their antiscriptural forms? We might begin by observing with John Webster that in Scripture (and the Church) we "hear, not God's own voice in unmediated force and power to persuade, but God's voice as it has been heard and then repeated by other creatures. Because it takes human form, the divine Word may be held in dishonour."[35] Webster goes on to urge us not to be dismayed that God did not provide us with "revelatory immediacy."[36] But can Christians truly be undismayed by the actual history of the human mediation of divine revelation? For example, given that there have been many bad popes (and even a period when three rivals each claimed to be pope), can anyone hold that the Church, in its definitive teaching, has continued to be "the pillar and bulwark of the truth"? Tolstoy's point is that if humans have been involved, and humans certainly have, then it is all too likely that they (we) have botched things thoroughly. It seems plausible that the Church's claim to mediate divine revelation faithfully over the centuries, in Scripture and in Tradition, cannot stand up to scrutiny.[37]

In response to such concerns, the present book has defended the fidelity of the mediation of divine revelation with the goal of showing its fittingness and plausibility. I began with the missions of the Son and Holy Spirit in the world, our missions in Jesus Christ, and the mission of evangelization. As

---

35. Webster, "Domain of the Word," 9. Webster goes on to say that "the heart of the difficulty we face in attending to Scripture is not the conceivability of revelation's taking creaturely form but our antipathy to it. Lost creatures (and the not-so-lost in the church) make Scripture's humanity a ground for despising its embassy" (12).

36. Ibid., 9.

37. Thus Alister McGrath's emphasis on Protestantism's adaptability strikes me as having, as its downside, the undermining of the mediation of divine revelation. While recognizing Martin Luther's certitude about his own teachings and John Calvin's view of the clarity of Scripture, McGrath holds that

> the capacity to adapt is the birthright of Protestantism. The contrast with both Catholicism and Orthodoxy could not be greater at this point. Although both consider the wooden repetition of yesterday's certainties to be inadequate, preferring to work with the idea of a "living tradition" that is capable of at least a degree of development, both equally emphasize the fixity of their doctrinal and institutional forms. . . . From its outset, Protestantism stated its identity in terms of a method rather than its outcome—a means by which ideas would be generated and governed, not a specific set of ideas resulting from its application. The Protestant principle of grounding matters of doctrine and ethics in the Bible and subjecting these to constant review immediately generated controversy. (*Christianity's Dangerous Idea*, 466–67)

Scot McKnight says, Scripture "is designed to create missional people."[38] The Creator God whose supreme generosity manifests itself in the extraordinary outpouring of creatures also manifests his supreme generosity—indeed manifests it in a manner so humble and loving that it should move us to wonder and awe—by becoming one of us without ceasing to be the divine Son, by sharing in our history, by bearing our sinful alienation in his redemptive death, and by restoring us to communion with our divine Father. Through the incarnate Son, we receive the outpouring of the Holy Spirit. The purpose is communion, friendship, and love, an everlasting sharing in the trinitarian communion that begins even now in the eschatological community of the eucharistic Church, the mystical body of Christ.

McKnight rightly emphasizes "the *ecclesial* shape of the kingdom and the atoning work of Jesus."[39] But has not this ecclesial body failed, given that humans have warred and sinned since Christ rose from the dead, just as humans warred and sinned prior to his resurrection? In fact, the Gospels tell us that Jesus instructed his disciples to expect such troubles to continue until the

38. McKnight, *Community Called Atonement*, 147. The "nexus between soteriology and ecclesiology" is, as Frank Matera observes, described in various ways in the New Testament writings:

> For example, the Synoptic tradition presents the church as a community of disciples because it begins with Jesus's proclamation of the kingdom of God. The Pauline tradition portrays the church as a sanctified community, the body of Christ, and the temple of God because it begins with Christ's redemptive death and resurrection. The Johannine tradition portrays the church as a community of disciples who enjoy the communion of the Father and the Son because it begins with the incarnation. For all of these traditions the church is the outcome of God's salvific work in Christ. Those who have been redeemed live in a sanctified community as they wait for the coming of their Lord. (*New Testament Theology*, 448)

39. McKnight, *Community Called Atonement*, 14. Arguing that the New Testament contains such a diversity of ecclesiologies that the "Church" is best understood as a combination of the strengths of the various Protestant, Catholic, and Orthodox churches, Raymond E. Brown, SS, proposes that no Church can claim that Scripture validates its distinctive ecclesiology. For Brown, "a frank study of NT ecclesiologies should convince every Christian community that it is neglecting part of the NT witness" (*Churches the Apostles Left Behind*, 149). I agree with Brown that there is a relatively wide range of ecclesiological emphases in the New Testament, but I do not think that the diversity of New Testament ecclesiologies rules out an intelligible visible unity of the Church across time and space. In addition to eccentric views such as his claim that the mystical body imagery of Colossians/Ephesians "remains abstract and impersonal," Brown's book contains some excellent pastoral insights, such as his reminder (in connection with the Gospel of John) that "in addition to providing doctrine and pastoral care, liturgy and sacraments, and a supportive sense of belonging to a caring community, a church must bring people into some personal contact with Jesus so that they can experience in their own way what made people follow him in the first place. . . . That Christ willed or founded the church may be adequate theology for some; but an abstraction, focused on the past, will not be enough to keep others loyal to a church unless they encounter Jesus there" (96–97; see also his account of the ecclesiology of Vatican II and its reception, on 73–74).

judgment. Yet in the eucharistic liturgy, Jesus Christ enfolds us—sinners—into his love. Insofar as we partake in love, which manifests itself in spiritual and material almsgiving, our eucharistic communion transforms the world and points toward the world's eschatological re-creation. In this regard, as Séamus Tuohy puts it, the eucharistic liturgy is not "simply the *re*-presentation of the sacrificial death of Jesus Christ; it is not only the participation in the real and active presence of the risen Christ in the Church . . . but it is also the *pre*-presentation of the *parousia*, an anticipatory presence of the future coming of the kingdom of God, a foretaste of the fullness of joy promised by Christ."[40]

As we have seen, many ecclesiastical fall narratives blame priests and their hunger for power. Priests, as the leaders of the Church, are always a convenient scapegoat for the community's sins. It would be naïve to imagine a priesthood composed of fallen human beings in which desire for power and other human desires are always virtuously ordered to the common good. Jesus knew this well, not least through his experience with the twelve disciples whom he gathered for the mission of inaugurating the eschatological Church. Indeed, the tendency to blame the priests reduces in fact to blaming Jesus, and it misses the fact that the priestly ministry—including the Petrine ministry—provides a principle of unity-in-diversity and, so often, an example of extraordinary self-giving love.

The narratives of ecclesiastical fall relieve their adherents of the need to suppose that what the Church teaches today is in fact the same true gospel that the apostles proclaimed. Indeed, it has now become commonplace to encounter historical narratives in which Jesus appears as a Jewish apocalyptic fanatic, Paul as a Hellenistic-mystical fanatic, and the Church fathers as power-mongering inventors of doctrines that fostered their self-serving interest in a hierarchical Church.[41] As we saw, Terrence Tilley rejoices in such continual re-invention, and John T. Noonan argues that ruptures are an important way of freeing

---

40. Tuohy, "Communion in the Supper of the Lamb," 165.

41. For one such approach, see Paula Fredriksen's *Sin*. Fredriksen's opening two sentences prepare us for her perspective: "Jesus of Nazareth announced the good news that God was about to redeem the world. Some 350 years later, the church taught that the far greater part of humanity was eternally condemned" (1). See also Kerr, "If Jesus Knew He Was God, How Did It Work?" For a representative popularization, see Selina O'Grady's *And Man Created God*. O'Grady teaches that

> Paul had in fact depoliticized his king. His Christ is a purely spiritual figure, as Geza Vermes and many other New Testament scholars have pointed out. The Jewish Messiah was a king who, with God's help, would come to liberate an oppressed Israel, sweep the Romans from power, encourage the return of the Jews from the Diaspora and preside over a world without evil. The Jews' Messiah was part spiritual, part political saviour. Paul's Messiah owed more to Isis and the other mystery deities for whom death and resurrection played a crucial role. Christ was a cosmic saviour only, concerned with another world, not this one. He promised a better life not on earth, but in Heaven. (350)

contemporary Catholics from earlier false doctrines. In my view, however, Christians should be loath to grant that the Holy Spirit has not ensured the fidelity of the Church's doctrinal development. Indeed, Christians are generally agreed about the truthfulness of the doctrinal developments of the first few centuries. For persons who deny that the Holy Spirit has ever guided the Church (or, for that matter, that the Holy Spirit has ever existed), it makes sense to reject a consistent Tradition or doctrinal development. But it does not make sense for Christians to do so, especially once one recognizes that doctrine develops in ways that reflect historical vitality rather than a strictly logical unfolding.

The way in which the Holy Spirit works in the human mediation of divine revelation is also at issue in biblical inspiration and in the appropriation of Hellenistic philosophical insights within Scripture. Again we find a real historical vitality and breadth: the human mediation of divine revelation makes of Scripture a two-Testament book that is profoundly shaped by human historical modes of writing and thinking, and that is strengthened and clarified even with regard to the nature of God by pagan philosophical insights. We find in Scripture an articulation of divine revelation that appreciates typological patterns and that emphasizes the presence of God's active providence in overseeing the human mediation of divine revelation. As John Webster observes, "Setting Scripture in the realm of providence excludes from the beginning the secularization of the history from which the biblical texts emerge."[42] Those who lack belief in God's providence will hardly be able to trust the typological patterns of history that we find in Scripture, whereas those formed by the liturgy and by belief in God's providence would hardly be able to trust a narrative mediation of divine revelation that lacked such typological patterns. Integrating faith and reason, we can discern the fittingness of the historical developments that characterize Scripture and can seek to respond to our contemporary culture's "anxiety that [the prophets and apostles'] ministry and message may mislead" (in Webster's words).[43]

For this task, of course, everything depends upon the missions of the Son and Spirit. But as we have seen, even many who think that the divine missions are real also think that the Church has failed to be faithful in its mediation of divine revelation. Some extend this arrogance backward into Old Testament times and argue that Jesus is basically the only bright spot intervening between the dominance of Jewish institutions and the dominance of hierarchical Christian institutions. The constant pattern in all of this is that wherever human mediation is found we can be sure that there will be a strong critique

42. Webster, "Domain of the Word," 14.
43. Ibid., 30.

of this human mediation—whether this means blaming priests or assuming that the normal modes of ancient historical writing poison Scripture's ability to communicate God's word. Given our experience of human weakness and sinfulness, it is natural to suppose that real human mediation cannot be other than detrimental to the priority, transcendence, and purity of divine revelation.[44] As Edith Humphrey notes, many people tacitly "assume that tradition is simply the *human* guarding of what may have been a divine revelation, and we know that humans can be mistaken about what they have seen and heard."[45]

But as Humphrey goes on to emphasize, Jesus Christ willed that his gospel be mediated by weak human beings. According to the Gospel of Luke, for example, Jesus commissioned seventy of his followers to go out and proclaim the gospel of the kingdom of God, and he told them, "He who hears you hears me, and he who rejects you rejects me, and he who rejects me rejects him who sent me" (Luke 10:16). In fact, as Humphrey says, "Despite the tendency of human failure, *persons* are commissioned to communicate the *person* Jesus, who communicates God the Father—our faith is, from beginning to end, personal. It is not simply a body of teaching material that can be deposited in a book."[46] This befits the Lord who literally gives himself into the hands of sinners and who sends his Holy Spirit upon the very disciples who betrayed him.[47] This equally befits the God who makes covenant with his people Israel and who remains always faithful to his covenants.

44. Edith Humphrey comments:
After all, the world can hardly be blamed for dismissing the words of weak and fallible human beings who may or may not accurately represent Jesus, either in word or in deed. On top of that, ordinary humans hardly possess the life, the glory, or the stature of that One true Human Being who is also God. Frequently, and with reason, we lament the weakness of the Church and speak with compassion about those who *think* that they have rejected Christianity, when all along they have been offended by God's people and so received a compromised version of the Way. (*Scripture and Tradition*, 92–93)
45. Ibid., 93. She adds, "The idea of tradition confers some sort of authority upon the one passing on the tradition; we are skeptical in this day and age of authority structures, especially when that involves leaders in history whom we can neither control nor interrogate" (ibid.).
46. Ibid. See also Humphrey's discussion of mediation on 122–31. Humphrey concludes that everywhere, then, there is an interplay between God's action and human action, a kind of tension between the sovereign actions of the Lord, who comes and calls and shines, and the responsiveness of the Church. Within the Christian body too there is an interplay between the apostles and those who hear their words; there is both a corporate nature to be discerned in the Church, and a personal responsibility for each member to be responsive to the apostolic tradition. . . . Mediation and the immediate presence of God do not cancel each out, nor are they at war. Each of us has a role to play, but all is of God himself. Our integrity as the Church depends on each bearing his or her own burden, but all of us bearing the burdens of others. (129–30)
47. Humphrey notes in this regard, "The Father has 'given over' the Son into the hands of humanity; the Son has 'traditioned' the Holy Spirit to us" (ibid., 134).

According to the Gospel of Matthew, the risen Jesus tells his disciples, "I am with you always, to the close of the age" (Matt. 28:20). The fact that Jesus has gone "to the Father" does not mean that he abandons his people or stops speaking to us.[48] Thus Jesus tells us in the Gospel of John, "I have yet many things to say to you, but you cannot bear them now. When the Spirit of truth comes, he will guide you into all the truth; for he will not speak on his own authority, but whatever he hears he will speak" (John 16:12–13). Along these same lines, in the book of Acts, Paul exhorts the elders of Ephesus, "Take heed to yourselves and to all the flock, in which the Holy Spirit has made you guardians, to feed the church of the Lord which he obtained with his own blood" (Acts 20:28).

What would such care for "the church of the Lord" look like? Paul obviously has no illusions that the course of the Church in Ephesus will be smooth, or, as we might put it, that the human mediation of divine revelation will be untroubled. On the contrary, Paul goes on to say, "I know that after my departure fierce wolves will come in among you, not sparing the flock; and from among your own selves will arise men speaking perverse things, to draw away the disciples after them" (Acts 29:29–30).[49] We must not treat our baptismal incorporation into Christ's holy Church as an excuse for presumption. Drawing upon Origen's *Homilies on Ezekiel*, Hans Urs von Balthasar observes that "the gravest, the most momentous guilt is to be found in Jerusalem, in the members of the Church. And the more pharisaically proud they are of their ecclesiastical purity and *gnosis*, the guiltier they are."[50] Somewhat similarly, Moses says in Deuteronomy, "Beware lest you say in your heart, 'My power and the might of my hand have gotten me this wealth.' You shall remember the LORD your God, for it is he who gives you power to get wealth; that he may confirm his covenant which he swore to your fathers, as at this day" (Deut. 8:17–18).

In light of warnings such as these, it is clear that the human mediation of divine revelation cannot be a merely human work. It can succeed, and has succeeded, only by the power of the exalted Christ and the Holy Spirit. Thus Balthasar adds that "it is true that the Church 'has' the Holy Spirit, but that does not mean that the Church as a whole—and each of her members—does not have to pray constantly for the presence of the Spirit."[51] The risen Christ breathes the Holy Spirit upon his apostles (John 20:22) so that the Church

48. See Farrow, *Ascension Theology*.

49. The force of this warning does not depend upon whether it should be attributed to Paul or to the author of Luke-Acts.

50. See Balthasar, "*Casta Meretrix*," 257.

51. Ibid., 261. On the *sancta ecclesia* and the *communio sanctorum*, see F. Martin, "Holiness of the Church."

"might be holy and without blemish" (Eph. 5:27). Of course there have been and will be many blemishes in the Church on earth, necessitating continual repentance and renewal, but these blemishes do not prevent the truthful mediation of the apostolic teaching and sacramental ministry. Otherwise the apostolic community would indeed have been left "desolate" (John 14:18). In this sense the Church is truly Christ's body, already filled powerfully with the Holy Spirit, though at the same time still urgently in need of and eagerly awaiting eschatological completion through Christ's second coming.[52]

It follows that, as the Reformed theologian Gabriel Fackre observes (though he would not agree with all of my conclusions), "The individual believer cannot overleap the centuries to make simple contact with the purity of biblical times. The church plays a crucial role in any interpretation of Scripture, both descriptively and normatively."[53] Believers who try to "overleap the centuries to make simple contact with the purity of biblical times" have fallen into overly negative views of the Church's mediation of divine revelation. For what Fackre terms the Church's "crucial role" to be sustained, neither the Church nor Scripture need be perfect in the sense of being free from any marks of the many limited (and limiting) persons and cultures that have, humanly speaking, constituted both the Church and the biblical texts. Even in the uniquely Spirit-filled period of the apostles, many indications of the Church's limitations were

52. As Thomas Aquinas states, "To be *a glorious Church not having spot or wrinkle* is the ultimate end to which we are brought by the Passion of Christ. Hence this will be in heaven, and not on earth, in which *if we say we have no sin, we deceive ourselves*, as is written (1 Jo. i. 8)" (*Summa theologiae* III, q. 8, a. 3, ad 2).

53. Fackre, *Doctrine of Revelation*, 193. Fackre goes on to say:

> The church is the Body of Christ. The community brought to be at Pentecost was born and lives by the Spirit of the Son. This people, then and now, is inextricably related to Jesus Christ as a Body to its Head. Epistemologically stated, the Word enfleshed is inseparable from the Word communicated to us. As such, a continuity exists between Incarnation and its ecclesial derivatives, apostolic inspiration and post-apostolic illumination. . . . The disputed point . . . is not *whether* there is a continuity along the line of Christ, Bible and church—Incarnation, inspiration and illumination—but, as Rahner says, *how* that linkage is understood and *who* constitutes the hermeneutical community. (194)

Fackre follows Karl Barth in adopting a "dialectical" or eschatological view of the Church's knowledge: "Yes, the Word discloses itself unfailingly in the Church. No, not inerrantly so. Yes, Christ is epistemically present in the church. No, not unbrokenly so. . . . The radical singularity and primacy of the Word incarnate do not permit of fusion with subsequent chapters in the narrative of revelation" (195–96). No magisterial office, Fackre emphasizes, can possess Jesus's authority or displace the priesthood of the whole people of God; nor should biblical inspiration be thought to be on a level with ecclesial illumination, since Scripture always stands above the Church. In my view, there certainly is "discontinuity as well as continuity between Christ and the church" and between the Church and the Word, but this needs to be combined with recognition of the efficacy of the Church's mediation of divine revelation under the guidance of the exalted Christ and his Spirit.

present, such as the contention between Peter and Paul. Thus it is correct to
say, with Balthasar, that "the Spirit is both in and above order in the Church;
right from the beginning (ever since the election of the Twelve and their being
given *exousia*) there has been a certain tension between official ministerial
order and community charisms. . . . The Spirit's testimony and the Church's
testimony are not simply identical, nor are they of equal rank."[54] The Spirit
of Christ guides and teaches the Church, but not everything that the Church
says and does—either in its ministerial order or in its community charisms—is
of the Spirit. The key, however, is that the exalted Son Jesus Christ, who with
the Father sends the "Spirit of truth" (John 15:26) upon his apostolic community, ensures that this Church, when definitively expositing (missionally and
liturgically) the scriptural content of divine revelation, does not lead astray
Christ's flock by corrupting the apostolic teaching and sacramental ministry.

We have faith, then, that Christ and the Spirit are faithful in their ongoing
work of teaching and sanctifying "the elect lady and her children" (2 John 1).
This faith enables us, in the words of the evangelical scholar Bryan Litfin, to
"begin to understand something of the grandeur of the community to which
we belong—what the Apostles' Creed calls the 'communion of saints.' . . . It
should give us a sense that we are not alone, that we are part of something
grand and magnificent, that we must fight the good fight in our generation
like those who went before us."[55] There is not merely romanticism but also
real truth in John Henry Newman's remark that "the Visible Church was, at
least to her children, the light of the world, as conspicuous as the sun in the
heavens; and the Creed was written on her forehead, and proclaimed through
her voice."[56] To be caught up in the salutary teaching and sacramental life of
the Church, encountering Jesus Christ in the midst of his friends, brings us
joy. With the Psalmist, therefore, let us joyfully proclaim, "How precious is
thy steadfast love, O God! The children of men take refuge in the shadow of
thy wings. They feast on the abundance of thy house, and thou givest them
drink from the river of thy delights. For with thee is the fountain of life; in
thy light do we see light" (Ps. 36:7–9; cf. Ps. 8).

---

54. Balthasar, *Theo-Logic*, 3:248–49. Balthasar points out that "the Spirit is also in and above
the community charisms; he is 'in' them insofar as he genuinely bestows them upon individuals for their use, giving them the spiritual qualities necessary; he is 'above' them insofar as no
member of the Body of Christ can stubbornly insist on his own charisma and try to wield it
against the comprehensive ecclesial order of the Body" (248).

55. Litfin, *Getting to Know the Church Fathers*, 29.

56. Newman, *Grammar of Assent*, 378.

Bibliography

Abraham, William J. *Canon and Criterion in Christian Theology: From the Fathers to Feminism*. Oxford: Oxford University Press, 1998.

———. *Crossing the Threshold of Divine Revelation*. Grand Rapids: Eerdmans, 2006.

———. *The Divine Inspiration of Scripture*. Oxford: Oxford University Press, 1981.

———. "Scripture, Tradition, and Revelation: An Appreciative Critique of David Brown." In *Theology, Aesthetics, and Culture: Responses to the Work of David Brown*, edited by Robert MacSwain and Taylor Worley, 13–28. Oxford: Oxford University Press, 2012.

Ad Gentes. In Flannery, *Conciliar and Post Conciliar Documents*, 813–56.

Alberigo, Giuseppe, Jean-Pierre Jossua, and Joseph A. Komonchak, eds. *The Reception of Vatican II*. Translated by Matthew J. O'Connell. Washington, DC: Catholic University of America Press, 1987.

Albertz, Rainer. "Does an Exclusive Veneration of God Necessarily Have to Be Violent? Israel's Stony Way to Monotheism and Some Theological Consequences." In Becking, *Orthodoxy, Liberalism, and Adaptation*, 35–51.

Alexander, Philip S. "Hellenism and Hellenization as Problematic Historiographical Categories." In Engberg-Pedersen, *Paul beyond the Judaism/Hellenism Divide*, 63–80.

Allen, Michael. "Exodus 3 after the Hellenization Thesis." *Journal of Theological Interpretation* 3 (2009): 179–96.

Allert, Craig D. *A High View of Scripture? The Authority of the Bible and the Formation of the New Testament Canon*. Grand Rapids: Baker Academic, 2007.

Allison, Dale C., Jr. *Constructing Jesus: Memory, Imagination, and History*. Grand Rapids: Baker Academic, 2010.

———. *The Historical Christ and the Theological Jesus*. Grand Rapids: Eerdmans, 2009.

———. *Resurrecting Jesus: The Earliest Christian Tradition and Its Interpreters*. London: T&T Clark, 2005.

Alonso Schökel, Luis, SJ. *The Inspired Word*. Translated by Francis Martin. New York: Herder, 1967.

Anatolios, Khaled. "The Canonization of Scripture in the Context of Trinitarian Doctrine." In *The Oxford Handbook of the Trinity*, edited by Gilles Emery, OP, and Matthew Levering, 15–27. Oxford: Oxford University Press, 2011.

———. *Retrieving Nicaea: The Development and Meaning of Trinitarian Doctrine*. Grand Rapids: Baker Academic, 2011.

Ando, Clifford. *The Matter of the Gods: Religion and the Roman Empire*. Berkeley: University of California Press, 2008.

Anizor, Uche. *Kings and Priests: Scripture's Theological Account of Its Readers*. Eugene, OR: Pickwick, 2014.

Aristotle. *Metaphysics*. Translated by Hippocrates G. Apostle. Grinnell, IA: The Peripatetic Press, 1979.

———. *Physics*. Translated by Hippocrates G. Apostle. Grinnell, IA: The Peripatetic Press, 1980.

Arkes, Hadley. *Constitutional Illusions and Anchoring Truths: The Touchstone of the Natural Law*. Cambridge: Cambridge University Press, 2010.

Armstrong, John M. "After the Ascent: Plato on Becoming Like God." *Oxford Studies in Ancient Philosophy* 26 (2004): 171–83.

Ashley, Benedict, OP. "Transition to Historical Mindedness." In *The Ashley Reader: Redeeming Reason*, edited by Benedict Ashley, OP, 13–25. Naples, FL: Sapientia Press, 2006.

Ashton, John. *Understanding the Fourth Gospel*. 2nd ed. Oxford: Oxford University Press, 2007.

Assmann, Jan. *Moses the Egyptian: The Memory of Egypt in Western Monotheism*. Cambridge, MA: Harvard University Press, 1997.

———. *The Price of Monotheism*. Translated by Robert Savage. Stanford, CA: Stanford University Press, 2010.

Astell, Ann W. "'Exilic' Identities, the Samaritans, and the 'Satan' of John." In *Sacrifice, Scripture, and Substitution: Readings in Ancient Judaism and Christianity*, edited by Ann W. Astell and Sandor Goodhart, 397–408. Notre Dame, IN: University of Notre Dame Press, 2011.

Atkinson, Joseph C. "The Interpenetration of Inspiration and Inerrancy as a Hermeneutic for Catholic Exegesis." *Letter & Spirit* 6 (2010): 191–224.

Augustine. *City of God*. Translated by Henry Bettenson. New York: Penguin, 1984.

———. *Confessions*. Translated by Henry Chadwick. Oxford: Oxford University Press, 1991.

———. *On Christian Doctrine*. Translated by D. W. Robertson Jr. New York: Macmillan, 1958.

————. *The Trinity*. Edited by John E. Rotelle, OSA. Translated by Edmund Hill, OP. Brooklyn, NY: New City Press, 1991.

Ayres, Lewis. *Augustine and the Trinity*. Cambridge: Cambridge University Press, 2010.

————. *Nicaea and Its Legacy: An Approach to Fourth-Century Trinitarian Theology*. Oxford: Oxford University Press, 2004.

————. "'There's Fire in That Rain': On Reading the Letter and Reading Allegorically." *Modern Theology* 28 (2012): 616–34.

Ayres, Lewis, and Stephen E. Fowl. "(Mis)reading the Face of God: The Interpretation of the Bible in the Church." *Theological Studies* 60 (1999): 513–28.

Bacon, Francis. "Of Unity in Religion." In Francis Bacon, *The Essays*, edited by John Pitcher, 67–71. New York: Penguin, 1985.

Balthasar, Hans Urs von. "*Casta Meretrix*." In *Explorations in Theology*. Vol. 2, *Spouse of the Word*, translated by John Saward, 193–288. San Francisco: Ignatius Press, 1991.

————. *The Glory of the Lord: A Theological Aesthetics*. Vol. 1, *Seeing the Form*. Edited by Joseph Fessio, SJ, and John Riches. Translated by Erasmo Leiva-Merikakis. San Francisco: Ignatius Press, 1982.

————. *The Glory of the Lord: A Theological Aesthetics*. Vol. 4, *The Realm of Metaphysics in Antiquity*. Edited by John Riches. Translated by Brian McNeil, CRV, Andrew Louth, John Saward, Rowan Williams, and Oliver Davies. San Francisco: Ignatius Press, 1989.

————. *The Glory of the Lord: A Theological Aesthetics*. Vol. 6, *Theology: The Old Covenant*. Edited by John Riches. Translated by Erasmo Leiva-Merikakis and Brian McNeil, CRV. San Francisco: Ignatius Press, 1991.

————. *The Glory of the Lord: A Theological Aesthetics*. Vol. 7, *Theology: The New Covenant*. Edited by John Riches. Translated by Brian McNeil, CRV. San Francisco: Ignatius Press, 1989.

————. *The God Question and Modern Man*. Translated by Hilda Graef. New York: Seabury Press, 1967.

————. *The Moment of Christian Witness*. Translated by Richard Beckley. San Francisco: Ignatius Press, 1994.

————. *Theo-Drama: Theological Dramatic Theory*. Vol. 1, *Prolegomena*. Translated by Graham Harrison. San Francisco: Ignatius Press, 1988.

————. *Theo-Drama: Theological Dramatic Theory*. Vol. 3, *The Dramatis Personae: The Person in Christ*. Translated by Graham Harrison. San Francisco: Ignatius Press, 1992.

————. *Theo-Logic: Theological Logical Theory*. Vol. 3, *The Spirit of Truth*. Translated by Graham Harrison. San Francisco: Ignatius Press, 2005.

Barclay, John M. G. *Jews in the Mediterranean Diaspora: From Alexander to Trajan (323 BCE–117 CE)*. Edinburgh: T&T Clark, 1996.

Barr, James. *Biblical Faith and Natural Theology*. Oxford: Oxford University Press, 1993.

————. *Holy Scripture: Canon, Authority, Criticism.* Oxford: Oxford University Press, 1983.

Barth, Karl. *The Church and the Churches.* Grand Rapids: Eerdmans, 2005.

————. *Church Dogmatics* I.1, *The Doctrine of the Word of God.* 2nd ed. Translated by G. W. Bromiley. Edinburgh: T&T Clark, 1975.

————. *Church Dogmatics* III.2, *The Doctrine of Creation.* Translated by H. Knight, G. W. Bromiley, J. K. S. Reid, and R. H. Fuller. Edinburgh: T&T Clark, 1960.

————. *The Epistle to the Romans.* 6th ed. Translated by Edwyn C. Hoskyns. Oxford: Oxford University Press, 1933.

————. *Evangelical Theology: An Introduction.* Translated by Grover Foley. Grand Rapids: Eerdmans, 1963.

————. *The Theology of John Calvin.* Translated by Geoffrey W. Bromiley. Grand Rapids: Eerdmans, 1995.

Bartholomew, Craig G., and Michael W. Goheen. *The Drama of Scripture: Finding Our Place in the Biblical Story.* Grand Rapids: Baker Academic, 2004.

Barton, John, and Julia Bowden. *The Original Story: God, Israel, and the World.* Grand Rapids: Eerdmans, 2004.

Bauckham, Richard. *Bible and Mission: Christian Witness in a Postmodern World.* Grand Rapids: Baker Academic, 2003.

————. *Jesus and the Eyewitnesses: The Gospels as Eyewitness Testimony.* Grand Rapids: Eerdmans, 2006.

————. *Jesus and the God of Israel: "God Crucified" and Other Studies on the New Testament's Christology of Divine Identity.* Grand Rapids: Eerdmans, 2009.

————. *The Testimony of the Beloved Disciple: Narrative, History, and Theology in the Gospel of John.* Grand Rapids: Baker Academic, 2007.

Baum, Gregory. *The Credibility of the Church Today: A Reply to Charles Davis.* New York: Herder & Herder, 1968.

————. "Vatican II's Constitution on Revelation: History and Interpretation." *Theological Studies* 28 (1967): 51–75.

Bavinck, Herman. *Our Reasonable Faith.* Grand Rapids: Eerdmans, 1956.

————. *Reformed Dogmatics.* Vol. 1, *Prolegomena.* Edited by John Bolt. Translated by John Vriend. Grand Rapids: Baker Academic, 2003.

Bea, Augustin, SJ. *De Inspiratione Scripturae Sacrae.* Rome: Pontificio Instituto Biblico, 1930.

Becker, Jürgen. *Paul: Apostle to the Gentiles.* Translated by O. C. Dean Jr. Louisville: Westminster John Knox, 1993.

Becking, Bob, ed. *Orthodoxy, Liberalism, and Adaptation: Essays on Ways of Worldmaking in Times of Change from Biblical, Historical and Systematic Perspectives.* Leiden: Brill, 2011.

Beeley, Christopher A. *Gregory of Nazianzus on the Trinity and the Knowledge of God: In Your Light We Shall See Light.* Oxford: Oxford University Press, 2008.

Belayche, Nicole. "*Deus deum . . . summorum maximus* (Apuleius): Ritual Expressions of Distinction in the Divine World in the Imperial Period." In Mitchell and Van Nuffelen, *One God*, 141–66.

Belcher, Kimberly Hope. *Efficacious Engagement: Sacramental Participation in the Trinitarian Mystery*. Collegeville, MN: Liturgical Press, 2011.

Bellandi, Andrea. *Fede cristiana come "Stare e comprendere": La giustificazione dei fondamenti della fede in Joseph Ratzinger*. Rome: Editrice Pontifica Università Gregoriana, 1996.

Bellini, Peter J. *Participation: Epistemology and Mission Theology*. Lexington: Emeth Press, 2010.

Benedict XV, Pope. *Spiritus Paraclitus*. 1920.

Benedict XVI, Pope. "A Proper Hermeneutic for the Second Vatican Council." In Lamb and Levering, *Vatican II: Renewal*, ix–xv.

———. "The Regensburg Lecture." In James V. Schall, SJ, *The Regensburg Lecture*, 130–48. South Bend, IN: St. Augustine's Press, 2007.

———. *Verbum Domini*. 2010.

Berkouwer, G. C. *Holy Scripture*. Grand Rapids: Eerdmans, 1975.

Betti, Umberto. *Diario del concilio, 11 ottobre 1962–Natale 1978*. Bologna: EDB, 2003.

———. *La dottrina del Concilio Vaticano II sulla trasmissione della rivelazione*. Rome: Antonianum, 1985.

Betz, John R. "Glory(ing) in the Humility of the Word: The Kenotic Form of Revelation in J. G. Hamann." *Letter & Spirit* 6 (2010): 141–79.

Bevans, Steven B., SVD, and Roger P. Schroeder, SVD. *Constants in Context: A Theology of Mission for Today*. Maryknoll, NY: Orbis Books, 2004.

Bianchi, Enzo. "The Centrality of the Word of God." In Alberigo, Jossua, and Komonchak, *Reception of Vatican II*, 115–36.

Billings, J. Todd. *Calvin, Participation, and the Gift: The Activity of Believers in Union with Christ*. Oxford: Oxford University Press, 2007.

———. *The Word of God for the People of God: An Entryway to the Theological Interpretation of Scripture*. Grand Rapids: Eerdmans, 2010.

Billot, Ludovicus (Louis), SJ. *De Inspiratione Sacrae Scripturae Theologica Disquisitio*. 2nd ed. Rome: Ex Typographia Iuvenum Opficium a S. Joseph, 1906.

Bird, Michael F. *Are You the One Who Is to Come? The Historical Jesus and the Messianic Question*. Grand Rapids: Baker Academic, 2009.

Blenkinsopp, Joseph. *Ezra-Nehemiah: A Commentary*. Philadelphia: Westminster, 1988.

———. *Judaism: The First Phase; The Place of Ezra and Nehemiah in the Origins of Judaism*. Grand Rapids: Eerdmans, 2009.

Bockmuehl, Markus. "Is There a New Testament Doctrine of the Church?" In Bockmuehl and Torrance, *Scripture's Doctrine and Theology's Bible*, 29–44.

———. *Seeing the Word: Refocusing New Testament Study*. Grand Rapids: Baker Academic, 2006.

————. *Simon Peter in Scripture and Memory: The New Testament Apostle in the Early Church*. Grand Rapids: Baker Academic, 2012.

Bockmuehl, Markus, and Alan J. Torrance, eds. *Scripture's Doctrine and Theology's Bible: How the New Testament Shapes Christian Dogmatics*. Grand Rapids: Baker Academic, 2008.

Boersma, Hans. *Nouvelle Théologie and Sacramental Ontology: A Return to Mystery*. Oxford: Oxford University Press, 2009.

————. "On Baking Pumpkin Pie: Kevin Vanhoozer and Yves Congar on Tradition." *Calvin Theological Journal* 42 (2007): 237–55.

————. "'This Is the Day Which the Lord Has Made': Scripture, Manumission, and the Heavenly Future in Saint Gregory of Nyssa." *Modern Theology* 28 (2012): 657–72.

Boeve, Lieven. *Interrupting Tradition: An Essay on Christian Faith in a Postmodern Context*. Louvain: Peeters, 2003.

————. "Orthodoxy, History and Theology: Recontextualisation and Its Descriptive and Programmatic Features." In Becking, *Orthodoxy, Liberalism, and Adaptation*, 185–204.

Boguslawski, Steven, OP, and Robert Fastiggi, eds. *Called to Holiness and Communion: Vatican II on the Church*. Scranton, PA: University of Scranton Press, 2009.

Boland, Vivian, OP, and Thomas McCarthy, OP, eds. *The Word Is Flesh and Blood: The Eucharist and Sacred Scripture*. Dublin: Dominican Publications, 2012.

Bouillard, Henri, SJ. *Conversion et grace chez S. Thomas d'Aquin: Étude historique*. Paris: Aubier, 1944.

Bouyer, Louis. *Liturgical Piety*. Notre Dame, IN: University of Notre Dame Press, 1978.

————. *Newman: His Life and Spirituality*. Translated by J. Lewis May. New York: Meridian Books, 1960.

Bowley, James E., and John C. Reeves. "Rethinking the Concept of 'Bible': Some Theses and Proposals." *Henoch* 25 (2003): 3–18.

Boyarin, Daniel. "The Gospel of the *Memra*: Jewish Binitarianism and the Prologue to John." *Harvard Theological Review* 94 (2001): 243–84.

————. *The Jewish Gospels: The Story of the Jewish Christ*. New York: The New Press, 2012.

————. "Origen as Theorist of Allegory: Alexandrian Contexts." In *The Cambridge Companion to Allegory*, edited by Rita Copeland and Peter Struck, 39–54. Cambridge: Cambridge University Press, 2010.

Braaten, Carl E. *Mother Church: Ecclesiology and Ecumenism*. Minneapolis: Fortress, 1998.

————. "The Problem of Authority in the Church." In *The Catholicity of the Reformation*, edited by Carl E. Braaten and Robert W. Jenson, 53–66. Grand Rapids: Eerdmans, 1996.

Bradshaw, Paul F. *Eucharistic Origins*. Oxford: Oxford University Press, 2004.

Brakke, David. *The Gnostics: Myth, Ritual, and Diversity in Early Christianity*. Cambridge, MA: Harvard University Press, 2010.

Broadie, Sarah. *Nature and Divinity in Plato's Timaeus*. Cambridge: Cambridge University Press, 2012.

Brock, Brian. *Singing the Ethos of God: On the Place of Christian Ethics of Scripture*. Grand Rapids: Eerdmans, 2007.

Brown, David. *Tradition and Imagination: Revelation and Change*. New York: Oxford University Press, 1999.

Brown, Raymond E., SS. *The Churches the Apostles Left Behind*. New York: Paulist Press, 1984.

———. *The Community of the Beloved Disciple*. New York: Paulist Press, 1979.

———. *The Gospel according to John, XIII–XXI*. Garden City, NY: Doubleday, 1970.

———. *Priest and Bishop: Biblical Reflections*. New York: Paulist Press, 1970.

Brown, Raymond E., SS, and John P. Meier. *Antioch and Rome: New Testament Cradles of Catholic Christianity*. New York: Paulist Press, 1983.

Brueggemann, Walter. *Theology of the Old Testament: Testimony, Dispute, Advocacy*. Minneapolis: Fortress, 1997.

Bryan, Steven M. *Jesus and Israel's Traditions of Judgement and Restoration*. Cambridge: Cambridge University Press, 2002.

Bultmann, Rudolf. *Theology of the New Testament*. 2 vols. Translated by Kendrick Grobel. London: SCM, 1952–1955.

Burkert, Walter. *Greek Religion*. Cambridge, MA: Harvard University Press, 1985.

Burtchaell, James Tunstead, CSC. *Catholic Theories of Biblical Inspiration since 1810: A Review and Critique*. Cambridge: Cambridge University Press, 1969.

Butler, Jon. *Awash in a Sea of Faith: Christianizing the American People*. Cambridge, MA: Harvard University Press, 1990.

Byrne, Brendan, SJ. *Romans*. Collegeville, MN: Liturgical Press, 1996.

Byrskog, Samuel. "A 'Truer' History: Reflections on Richard Bauckham, *Jesus and the Eyewitnesses: The Gospels as Eyewitness Testimony*." *Nova et Vetera* 6 (2008): 483–89.

Calvin, John. *Institutes of the Christian Religion*. Translated by Henry Beveridge. Grand Rapids: Eerdmans, 1989.

Campbell, Douglas A. *The Deliverance of God: An Apocalyptic Rereading of Justification in Paul*. Grand Rapids: Eerdmans, 2009.

———. *The Quest for Paul's Gospel: A Suggested Strategy*. New York: T&T Clark, 2005.

Campbell, Ted A. *The Gospel in Christian Traditions*. Oxford: Oxford University Press, 2009.

Canty, Aaron. "Bonaventurian Resonances in Benedict XVI's Theology of Revelation." *Nova et Vetera* 5 (2007): 249–66.

Capizzi, Joseph E. "The Children of God: Natural Slavery in the Thought of Aquinas and Vitoria." *Theological Studies* 63 (2002): 31–52.

Carmichael, Calum M. *The Laws of Deuteronomy*. Ithaca, NY: Cornell University Press, 1974.

Carr, David M. *An Introduction to the Old Testament: Sacred Texts and Imperial Contexts of the Hebrew Bible*. Oxford: Wiley-Blackwell, 2010.

Carroll, Anthony J. "The Philosophical Foundations of Catholic Modernism." In Rafferty, *George Tyrrell and Catholic Modernism*, 38–55.

Carson, D. A., and Timothy Keller, eds. *The Gospel as Center: Renewing Our Faith and Reforming Our Ministry Practices*. Wheaton: Crossway, 2012.

———. "Gospel-Centered Ministry." In Carson and Keller, *Gospel as Center*, 11–21.

Cary, Phillip. "Material God." *First Things* 223 (May 2012): 63–65.

Catechism of the Catholic Church. 2nd ed. Vatican City: Libreria Editrice Vaticana, 1997.

Cessario, Romanus, OP. "Aquinas on Christian Salvation." In Weinandy, Keating, and Yocum, *Aquinas on Doctrine*, 117–37.

———. *Christian Faith and the Theological Life*. Washington, DC: Catholic University of America Press, 1996.

Chadwick, Henry. *Early Christian Thought and the Classical Tradition: Studies in Justin, Clement, and Origen*. Oxford: Oxford University Press, 1966.

Chadwick, Owen. *From Bossuet to Newman*. 2nd ed. Cambridge: Cambridge University Press, 1987.

Chan, Simon. *Liturgical Theology: The Church as Worshiping Community*. Downers Grove, IL: InterVarsity, 2006.

Chapman, Stephen B. *The Law and the Prophets: A Study in Old Testament Canon Formation*. Tübingen: Mohr Siebeck, 2000.

Chapp, Larry. "Revelation." In Oakes and Moss, *Cambridge Companion to Hans Urs von Balthasar*, 11–23.

Chappell, Bryan. "What Is the Gospel?" In Carson and Keller, *Gospel as Center*, 115–34.

Charlier, Louis. *Essai sur le problème théologique*. Thuillies: Ramgal, 1938.

Chenu, Marie-Dominique, OP. *Une école de théologie: Le Saulchoir*. Paris: Cerf, 1985.

Childs, Brevard S. *The Book of Exodus: A Critical, Theological Commentary*. Louisville: The Westminster Press, 1974.

———. *Isaiah: A Commentary*. Louisville: Westminster John Knox, 2001.

———. *Myth and Reality in the Old Testament*. 2nd ed. London: SCM, 1962.

———. *The Struggle to Understand Isaiah as Christian Scripture*. Grand Rapids: Eerdmans, 2004.

Chung-Kim, Esther. *Inventing Authority: The Use of the Church Fathers in Reformation Debates over the Eucharist*. Waco: Baylor University Press, 2011.

Clark, Gillian. *Christianity and Roman Society*. Cambridge: Cambridge University Press, 2004.

Clarke, W. Norris, SJ. "Is a Natural Theology Still Viable Today?" In Clarke, *Explorations in Metaphysics: Being—God—Person*, 150–82. Notre Dame, IN: University of Notre Dame Press, 1994.

Colijn, Brenda B. *Images of Salvation in the New Testament*. Downers Grove, IL: IVP Academic, 2010.

Collins, Christopher S., SJ. *The Word Made Love: The Dialogical Theology of Joseph Ratzinger / Benedict XVI*. Collegeville, MN: Liturgical Press, 2013.

Collins, John J. *The Bible after Babel: Historical Criticism in a Postmodern Age*. Grand Rapids: Eerdmans, 2005.

———. "The Biblical Precedent for Natural Theology." *Journal of the American Academy of Religion* 45, no. 1, supplement (1977): 35–67.

———. "Cult and Culture: The Limits of Hellenization in Judea." In *Hellenism in the Land of Israel*, edited by John J. Collins and Gregory E. Sterling, 38–61. Notre Dame, IN: University of Notre Dame Press, 2001.

———. *Encounters with Biblical Theology*. Minneapolis: Fortress, 2005.

———. *Jewish Wisdom in the Hellenistic Age*. Louisville: Westminster John Knox, 1997.

Colson, Charles, and Richard John Neuhaus, eds. *Your Word Is Truth: A Project of Evangelicals and Catholics Together*. Grand Rapids: Eerdmans, 2002.

Congar, Yves, OP. "Church History as a Branch of Theology." *Concilium* 7 (1970): 85–96.

———. "The Different Priesthoods: Christian, Jewish and Pagan." In Yves Congar, OP, *A Gospel Priesthood*, translated by P. J. Hepburne-Scott, 74–89. New York: Herder and Herder, 1967.

———. *I Believe in the Holy Spirit*. Vol. 3. Translated by David Smith. New York: Herder & Herder, 1983.

———. *Lay People in the Church: A Study for a Theology of the Laity*. Rev. ed. Translated by Donald Attwater. London: Geoffrey Chapman, 1985.

———. *The Meaning of Tradition*. Translated by A. N. Woodrow. San Francisco: Ignatius Press, 2004.

———. *My Journal of the Council*. Edited by Denis Minns. Translated by Mary John Ronayne and Mary Cecily Boulding. Collegeville, MN: Liturgical Press, 2012.

———. *Tradition and Traditions: An Historical and Theological Essay*. Translated by Michael Naseby and Thomas Rainborough. New York: Macmillan, 1967.

Congregation for the Doctrine of the Faith. *Mysterium Ecclesiae*. June 24, 1973. www.Vatican.va.

Cooke, Bernard J., SJ. *Beyond Trinity*. Milwaukee: Marquette University Press, 1969.

Cooper, John M. *Pursuits of Wisdom: Six Ways of Life in Ancient Philosophy from Socrates to Plotinus*. Princeton: Princeton University Press, 2012.

Costigan, Richard F., SJ. *The Consensus of the Church and Papal Infallibility: A Study in the Background of Vatican I*. Washington, DC: Catholic University of America Press, 2005.

Council of Trent. "Decretum primum: recipiuntur libri sacri et traditiones apostolorum" (April 8, 1546). In *Decrees of the Ecumenical Councils*. Vol. 2, *Trent to*

Vatican II, edited by Normon P. Tanner, SJ, 663–64. Washington, DC: Georgetown University Press, 1990.

Cousar, Charles B. *A Theology of the Cross: The Death of Jesus in the Pauline Letters.* Minneapolis: Fortress, 1990.

Cowles, C. S., et al. *Show Them No Mercy: Four Views on God and Canaanite Genocide.* Grand Rapids: Zondervan, 2003.

Crisp, Oliver D., and Michael C. Rea, eds. *Analytic Theology: New Essays in the Philosophy of Theology.* Oxford: Oxford University Press, 2009.

Crisp, Thomas M. "On Believing That the Scriptures Are Divinely Inspired." In Crisp and Rea, *Analytic Theology*, 187–213.

Cullmann, Oscar. *Christ and Time: The Primitive Christian Conception of Time and History.* Rev. ed. Translated by Floyd V. Filson. Louisville: Westminster John Knox, 1964.

———. *Early Christian Worship.* London: SCM, 1953.

Daley, Brian E., SJ. "The Church Fathers." In Ker and Merrigan, *Cambridge Companion to John Henry Newman*, 29–46.

———. "'In Many and Various Ways': Towards a Theology of Theological Exegesis." *Modern Theology* 28 (2012): 597–615.

———. "Knowing God in History and in the Church: *Dei Verbum* and 'Nouvelle Théologie.'" In Flynn and Murray, *Ressourcement*, 333–51.

———. "The *Nouvelle Théologie* and the Patristic Revival: Sources, Symbols and the Science of Theology." *International Journal of Systematic Theology* 7 (2005): 362–82.

Dalferth, Ingolf U. "Die Mitte ist außen: Anmerkungen zum Wirklichkeitsbezug evangelischer Schriftauslegung." In *Jesus Christus als die Mitte der Schrift: Studien zur Hermeneutik des Evangeliums*, edited by Christof Landmesser et al., 173–98. Berlin: de Gruyter, 1997.

Daniélou, Jean, SJ. *From Shadows to Reality: Studies in the Biblical Typology of the Fathers.* Translated by Dom Wulstan Hibberd, OSB. London: Burns & Oates, 1960.

———. "Les orientations présentes de la pensée religieuse." *Études* 249 (1946): 5–21.

———. *Origen.* Translated by W. Mitchell. New York: Sheed and Ward, 1955.

———. "Symbolism and History." In Jean Daniélou, *The Lord of History: Reflections on the Inner Meaning of History*, translated by Nigel Abercrombie, 130–46. Chicago: Henry Regnery, 1958.

Dauphinais, Michael, Barry David, and Matthew Levering, eds. *Aquinas the Augustinian.* Washington, DC: Catholic University of America Press, 2007.

Dauphinais, Michael, and Matthew Levering. *Holy People, Holy Land: A Theological Introduction to the Bible.* Grand Rapids: Brazos, 2005.

———, eds. *Reading John with St. Thomas Aquinas: Theological Exegesis and Speculative Theology.* Washington, DC: Catholic University of America Press, 2005.

Davies, Philip R. *In Search of "Ancient Israel."* Sheffield: Journal for the Study of the Old Testament, 1992.

Davies, W. D., and Dale C. Allison Jr. *The Gospel according to Saint Matthew*. Vol. 2, *Commentary on Matthew VIII–XVIII*. Edinburgh: T&T Clark, 1991.

Davis, Charles. *A Question of Conscience*. New York: Harper & Row, 1967.

Dawkins, Richard. *The God Delusion*. Boston: Houghton Mifflin, 2006.

Dawson, David. *Allegorical Readers and Cultural Revision in Ancient Alexandria*. Berkeley: University of California Press, 1992.

DeConick, April D. *Holy Misogyny: Why the Sex and Gender Conflicts in the Early Church Still Matter*. London: Continuum, 2011.

Dei Filius. In *Decrees of the Ecumenical Councils*. Vol. 2, *Trent to Vatican II*, edited by Norman P. Tanner, SJ, 804–9. Washington, DC: Georgetown University Press, 1990.

Dei Verbum. In Flannery, *Conciliar and Post Conciliar Documents*, 750–65.

De la Potterie, Ignace, SJ. "History and Truth." In *Problems and Perspectives of Fundamental Theology*, edited by René Latourelle and Gerald O'Collins, translated by Matthew J. O'Connell, 87–104. New York: Paulist Press, 1982.

———. "Interpretation of Holy Scripture in the Spirit in Which It Was Written." In *Vatican II: Assessment and Perspectives*. Vol. 1, edited by René Latourelle, 220–66. New York: Paulist Press, 1988.

De Lubac, Henri, SJ. *Carnets du concile*. 2 vols. Edited by Loïc Figoureux. Paris: Cerf, 2007.

———. *Catholicism: A Study of Dogma in Relation to the Corporate Destiny of Mankind*. London: Burns, Oates and Washbourne, 1950.

———. *History and Spirit: The Understanding of Scripture according to Origen*. Translated by Anne Englund Nash and Juvenal Merriell. San Francisco: Ignatius Press, 2007.

———. "The Problem of the Development of Dogma." In Henri de Lubac, *Theology in History*, translated by Anne Englund Nash, 248–80. San Francisco: Ignatius Press, 1996.

———. "'Typologie' et 'allégorisme.'" *Recherches de science religieuse* 34 (1947): 180–226.

Dever, William G. *Did God Have a Wife? Archaeology and Folk Religion in Ancient Israel*. Grand Rapids: Eerdmans, 2005.

———. *What Did the Biblical Writers Know and When Did They Know It? What Archaeology Can Tell Us about the Reality of Ancient Israel*. Grand Rapids: Eerdmans, 2001.

DeVille, Adam A. J. *Orthodoxy and the Roman Papacy: "Ut Unum Sint" and the Prospects of East-West Unity*. Notre Dame, IN: University of Notre Dame Press, 2011.

Dickens, W. T. "Balthasar's Biblical Hermeneutics." In Oakes and Moss, *Cambridge Companion to Hans Urs von Balthasar*, 175–86.

———. *Hans Urs von Balthasar's Theological Aesthetics: A Model for Post-Critical Biblical Interpretation*. Notre Dame, IN: University of Notre Dame Press, 2003.

Dionne, J. Robert, SM. *The Papacy and the Church: A Study of Praxis and Reception in Ecumenical Perspective*. New York: Philosophical Library, 1987.

Dix, Gregory. *The Jew and the Greek: A Study in the Primitive Church*. Westminster: Dacre Press, 1953.

Downing, F. Gerald. *Has Christianity a Revelation?* Philadelphia: Westminster Press, 1964.

Dulles, Avery, SJ. "Authority in the Church." In Ker and Merrigan, *Cambridge Companion to John Henry Newman*, 170–88.

———. "Development or Reversal?" *First Things* (October 2005): 53–61.

———. *Magisterium: Teacher and Guardian of the Faith*. Naples, FL: Sapientia Press, 2007.

———. *Models of Revelation*. 2nd ed. Maryknoll, NY: Orbis Books, 1992.

———. *Newman*. London: Continuum, 2002.

———. "Revelation, Scripture, and Tradition." In Colson and Neuhaus, *Your Word Is Truth*, 35–58.

———. *Revelation Theology: A History*. New York: Herder & Herder, 1969.

———. "Tradition: Authentic and Unauthentic." *Communio* 28 (2001): 377–85.

———. "Who Can Be Saved?" In Avery Dulles, *Church and Society: The Laurence J. McGinley Lectures, 1988–2007*, 522–34. New York: Fordham University Press, 2008.

Dunn, James D. G. *Baptism in the Holy Spirit: A Re-Examination of the New Testament Teaching on the Gift of the Spirit in Relation to Pentecostalism Today*. London: SCM, 1970.

———. "Baptism in the Spirit: A Response to Pentecostal Scholarship on Luke-Acts." *Journal of Pentecostal Theology* 3 (1993): 3–27.

———. *Christianity in the Making*. Vol. 1, *Jesus Remembered*. Grand Rapids: Eerdmans, 2003.

———. *Christianity in the Making*. Vol. 2, *Beginning from Jerusalem*. Grand Rapids: Eerdmans, 2009.

———. *Did the First Christians Worship Jesus? The New Testament Evidence*. Louisville: Westminster John Knox, 2010.

———. "The Gospel according to St. Paul." In *The Blackwell Companion to Paul*, edited by Stephen Westerholm, 139–53. Oxford: Blackwell, 2011.

———. *Jesus, Paul, and the Gospels*. Grand Rapids: Eerdmans, 2011.

———. "John's Gospel and the Oral Gospel Tradition." In *The Fourth Gospel in First-Century Media Culture*, edited by Anthony Le Donne and Tom Thatcher, 157–85. London: T&T Clark, 2011.

———. "Let John Be John: A Gospel for Its Time." In *The Gospel and the Gospels*, edited by Peter Stuhlmacher, 293–322. Grand Rapids: Eerdmans, 1991.

———. *The Oral Gospel Tradition*. Grand Rapids: Eerdmans, 2013.

———. *Unity and Diversity in the New Testament*. 2nd ed. London: SCM, 1990.

Edwards, Jonathan. "A History of the Work of Redemption, Containing the Outlines of a Body of Divinity, Including a View of Church History, in a Method Entirely New." In *The Works of Jonathan Edwards*, 1:532–619. Peabody, MA: Hendrickson, 1998.

Elders, Leo, SVD. "The Immutability of the Sense of Dogmas and Philosophical Theories." In *Faith and Reason: The Notre Dame Symposium 1999*, edited by Timothy L. Smith, 21–35. South Bend, IN: St. Augustine's Press, 2001.

Emery, Gilles, OP. "The Holy Spirit in Aquinas's Commentary on Romans." In Levering and Dauphinais, *Reading Romans with St. Thomas Aquinas*, 127–62.

———. "Missions invisibles et missions visibles: Le Christ et son Esprit." *Revue Thomiste* 106 (2006): 51–99.

———. "*Theologia* and *Dispensatio*: The Centrality of the Divine Missions in St. Thomas's Trinitarian Theology." *The Thomist* 74 (2010): 515–61.

———. "Thomas Aquinas, Postliberal? George Lindbeck's Reading of St. Thomas." Translated by Matthew Levering. In *Trinity, Church, and the Human Person: Thomistic Essays*, 263–90. Naples, FL: Sapientia Press, 2007.

———. "Trinitarian Theology as Spiritual Exercise in Augustine and Aquinas." In Dauphinais, David, and Levering, *Aquinas the Augustinian*, 1–40.

———. *The Trinity: An Introduction to Catholic Doctrine on the Trinity*. Translated by Matthew Levering. Washington, DC: Catholic University of America Press, 2011.

Engberg-Pedersen, Troels. *Cosmology and the Self in the Apostle Paul: The Material Spirit*. Oxford: Oxford University Press, 2010.

———. *Paul and the Stoics*. Louisville: Westminster John Knox, 2000.

———, ed. *Paul beyond the Judaism/Hellenism Divide*. Louisville: Westminster John Knox, 2001.

———, ed. *Paul in His Hellenistic Context*. Minneapolis: Fortress, 1994.

———. "Setting the Scene: Stoicism and Platonism in the Transitional Period in Ancient Philosophy." In *Stoicism in Early Christianity*, edited by Tuomas Rasimus, Troels Engberg-Pedersen, and Ismo Dunderberg, 1–14. Grand Rapids: Baker Academic, 2010.

Enns, Peter. *The Evolution of Adam: What the Bible Does and Doesn't Say about Human Origins*. Grand Rapids: Brazos, 2012.

———. *Inspiration and Incarnation: Evangelicals and the Problem of the Old Testament*. Grand Rapids: Baker Academic, 2005.

Erasmus, Desiderius. *The Praise of Folly*. Translated by Clarence H. Miller. New Haven: Yale University Press, 1979.

Evans, C. Stephen. *The Historical Christ and the Jesus of Faith: The Incarnational Narrative as History*. Oxford: Oxford University Press, 1996.

Evdokimov, Paul. *Orthodoxy*. Translated by Jeremy Hummerstone and Callan Slipper. Hyde Park, NY: New City Press, 2011.

Fackre, Gabriel. *The Doctrine of Revelation: A Narrative Interpretation*. Grand Rapids: Eerdmans, 1997.

Fagerberg, David W. "The Cost of Understanding Schmemann in the West." *St. Vladimir's Theological Quarterly* 53 (2009): 179–207.

Farkasfalvy, Denis, OCist. "How to Renew the Theology of Biblical Inspiration?" *Nova et Vetera* 4 (2006): 231–54.

———. "Inspiration and Interpretation." In Lamb and Levering, *Vatican II: Renewal*, 77–100.

———. *Inspiration and Interpretation: A Theological Interpretation to Sacred Scripture*. Washington, DC: Catholic University of America Press, 2010.

Farrow, Douglas. *Ascension and Ecclesia: On the Significance of the Doctrine of the Ascension for Ecclesiology and Christian Cosmology*. Grand Rapids: Eerdmans, 1999.

———. *Ascension Theology*. London: T&T Clark, 2011.

———. *The Word of Truth and Disputes about Words*. Winona Lake, IN: Eisenbrauns, 1987.

Fee, Gordon D. *The First and Second Letters to the Thessalonians*. Grand Rapids: Eerdmans, 2009.

———. *Pauline Christology: An Exegetical-Theological Study*. Peabody, MA: Hendrickson, 2007.

Feuillet, André. *The Apocalypse*. New York: Alba House, 1965.

Fine, Gail. *On Ideas: Aristotle's Criticism of Plato's Theory of Forms*. Oxford: Clarendon, 1993.

Fiorenza, Elisabeth Schüssler. "A Discipleship of Equals: Ekklesial Democracy and Patriarchy in Biblical Perspective." In *A Democratic Catholic Church: The Reconstruction of Roman Catholicism*, edited by Eugene C. Bianchi and Rosemary Radford Ruether, 17–33. New York: Crossroad, 1993.

Fisch, Thomas. "Schmemann's Theological Contribution to the Liturgical Renewal of the Churches." In *Schmemann, Liturgy and Tradition: Theological Reflections of Alexander Schmemann*, edited by Thomas Fisch, 1–10. Crestwood, NY: St. Vladimir's Seminary Press, 1990.

Fishbane, Michael. *Biblical Interpretation in Ancient Israel*. Oxford: Oxford University Press, 1985.

Fisher, Anthony, OP. "Catholic Moral Tradition." Unpublished lecture.

Fitzmyer, Joseph A., SJ. *First Corinthians: A New Translation with Introduction and Commentary*. New Haven: Yale University Press, 2008.

———. *The Gospel according to Luke*. 2 vols. Garden City, NY: Doubleday, 1981/1985.

Flannery, Austin, OP, ed. *The Conciliar and Post Conciliar Documents*. Vol. 1 of *Vatican Council II*. Northport, NY: Costello, 1996.

Flynn, Gabriel, and Paul D. Murray, eds. *Ressourcement: A Movement for Renewal in Twentieth-Century Catholic Theology*. Oxford: Oxford University Press, 2012.

Fodor, James, and Stanley Hauerwas. "Performing Faith: The Peaceable Rhetoric of God's Church." In Stanley Hauerwas, *Performing the Faith: Bonhoeffer and the Practice of Nonviolence*, 75–109. Grand Rapids: Brazos, 2004.

Ford, John T., CSC. "Faithfulness to Type in Newman's *Essay on Development*." In *Newman Today*, edited by Stanley L. Jaki, 17–48. San Francisco: Ignatius Press, 1989.

Franks, Christopher A. "Aquinas's Use of Aristotle on the Virtue of Justice." Unpublished essay.

Frede, Michael. "The Case for Pagan Monotheism in Greek and Graeco-Roman Antiquity." In Mitchell and Van Nuffelen, *One God*, 53–81.

Fredriksen, Paula. *Sin: The Early History of an Idea*. Princeton: Princeton University Press, 2012.

Freeman, Charles. *The Closing of the Western Mind: The Rise of Faith and the Fall of Reason*. New York: Alfred A. Knopf, 2003.

Freeman, Curtis W. "Figure and History: A Contemporary Reassessment of Augustine's Hermeneutic." In *Augustine: Presbyter Factus Sum*, edited by Joseph T. Lienhard, SJ, Earl C. Muller, SJ, and Roland J. Teske, SJ, 219–29. New York: Peter Lang, 1993.

Frei, Hans. *The Eclipse of Biblical Narrative: A Study in Eighteenth and Nineteenth Century Hermeneutics*. New Haven: Yale University Press, 1974.

Freud, Sigmund. *Moses and Monotheism: Three Essays*. In *The Standard Edition of the Complete Psychological Works of Sigmund Freud*. Vol. 23. Edited by J. Strachey. New York: W. W. Norton, 1976.

Friedman, Richard Elliott. *Who Wrote the Bible?* 2nd ed. New York: HarperCollins, 1997.

Gadenz, Pablo T. "Magisterial Teaching on the Inspiration and Truth of Scripture: Precedents and Prospects." *Letter & Spirit* 6 (2010): 67–91.

Gardeil, Ambrose, OP. *Le Donné révélé et la théologie*. Paris: Cerf, 1932.

Garrigou-Lagrange, Réginald, OP. "La nouvelle théologie où va-t-elle?" *Angelicum* 23 (1946): 126–46.

———. *Le sens commun, la philosophie de l'être et les formules dogmatiques*. Paris: Beauchesne, 1909.

———. "Where Is the New Theology Leading Us?" Translated by Suzanne M. Rini. *Josephinum Journal of Theology* 18 (2011): 63–78.

Garuti, Andriano, OFM. *Primacy of the Bishop of Rome and the Ecumenical Dialogue*. Translated by Michael Miller. San Francisco: Ignatius Press, 2004.

Gathercole, Simon J. *The Pre-existent Son: Recovering the Christologies of Matthew, Mark, and Luke*. Grand Rapids: Eerdmans, 2006.

Geffré, Claude. *The Risk of Interpretation: On Being Faithful to the Christian Tradition in a Non-Christian Age*. Translated by D. Smith. New York: Paulist Press, 1987.

George, Timothy. "An Evangelical Reflection on Scripture and Tradition." In Colson and Neuhaus, *Your Word Is Truth*, 9–34.

Gilbert, Greg. *What Is the Gospel?* Wheaton: Crossway, 2010.

Gilby, Thomas, OP. "Biblical Inspiration." Appendix 13 of Thomas Aquinas, *Summa theologiae*. Vol. 1, *Christian Theology (Ia. 1)*, translated by Thomas Gilby, OP, 142–46. Cambridge: Cambridge University Press, 2006.

Gioia, Luigi, OSB. *The Theological Epistemology of Augustine's "De Trinitate."* Oxford: Oxford University Press, 2008.

Girard, René. *I See Satan Fall Like Lightning*. Translated by James G. Williams. Maryknoll, NY: Orbis Books, 2001.

Gordon, Bruce. *Calvin*. New Haven: Yale University Press, 2011.

Goris, Harm. "Theology and Theory of the Word in Aquinas: Understanding Augustine by Innovating Aristotle." In Dauphinais, David, and Levering, *Aquinas the Augustinian*, 62–78.

Goulder, Michael D. *Type and History in Acts*. London: SPCK, 1964.

Grabbe, Lester L. "'Many Nations Will Be Joined to Yhwh in That Day': The Question of Yhwh outside Judah." In *Religious Diversity in Ancient Israel and Judah*, edited by Francesca Stavrakopoulou and John Barton, 175–87. London: T&T Clark, 2010.

———. *Wisdom of Solomon*. London: T&T Clark International, 2003.

Gracia, Jorge J. E. *Old Wine in New Skins: The Role of Tradition in Communication, Knowledge, and Group Identity*. Milwaukee: Marquette University Press, 2003.

Granados, José, Carlos Granados, and Luis Sánchez-Navarro, eds. *Opening Up the Scriptures: Joseph Ratzinger and the Foundations of Biblical Interpretation*. Grand Rapids: Eerdmans, 2008.

Grant, Robert M. *Heresy and Criticism: The Search for Authenticity in Early Christian Literature*. Louisville: Westminster John Knox, 1993.

Greear, J. D. *Gospel: Recovering the Power That Made Christianity Revolutionary*. Nashville: B&H, 2011.

Green, Joel B. *The Gospel of Luke*. Grand Rapids: Eerdmans, 1997.

Gregory XVI, Pope. *In supremo Apostolatus fastigio*. 1839. www.Vatican.va.

Gregory of Nazianzus. *On God and Christ: The Five Theological Orations and Two Letters to Cledonius*. Translated by Lionel Wickham. Crestwood, NY: St. Vladimir's Seminary Press, 2002.

Griffiths, Paul J. *Song of Songs*. Grand Rapids: Brazos, 2011.

Groome, Thomas H. *What Makes Us Catholic: Eight Gifts for Life*. New York: Harper Collins, 2002.

Gruen, Erich. *Heritage and Hellenism: The Reinvention of Jewish Tradition*. Berkeley: University of California Press, 1998.

Guarino, Thomas G. *Vincent of Lérins and the Development of Christian Doctrine*. Grand Rapids: Baker Academic, 2013.

Gunton, Colin E. *A Brief Theology of Revelation*. London: T&T Clark, 1995.

Hadot, Pierre. *Philosophy as a Way of Life*. Edited by Arnold I. Davidson. Translated by Michael Chase. Oxford: Blackwell, 1995.

———. *What Is Ancient Philosophy?* Translated by Michael Chase. Cambridge, MA: Harvard University Press, 2002.

Hahn, Ferdinand. *Theologie des Neuen Testaments*. 2 vols. Tübingen: Mohr Siebeck, 2002.

Hahn, Scott W. "For the Sake of Our Salvation: The Truth and Humility of God's Word." *Letter & Spirit* 6 (2010): 21–45.

———. *Letter and Spirit: From Written Text to Living Word in the Liturgy.* New York: Doubleday, 2005.

Haight, Roger, SJ. *Jesus: Symbol of God.* Maryknoll, NY: Orbis Books, 1999.

Halbertal, Moshe. *On Sacrifice.* Princeton: Princeton University Press, 2012.

Hall, H. Ashley. "The Development of Doctrine: A Lutheran Examination." *Pro Ecclesia* 16 (2007): 256–77.

Halpern, Baruch. *The First Historians: The Hebrew Bible and History.* University Park: Pennsylvania State University Press, 1996.

Hanson, R. P. C. *Allegory and Event: A Study of the Sources and Significance of Origen's Interpretation of Scripture.* Richmond, VA: John Knox, 1959.

———. *The Search for the Christian Doctrine of God: The Arian Controversy.* Edinburgh: T&T Clark, 1988.

Harkianakis, Stylianos. *The Infallibility of the Church in Orthodox Theology.* Redfern, Australia: St. Andrew's Orthodox Press, 2008.

Harper, Brad, and Paul Louis Metzger. *Exploring Ecclesiology: An Evangelical Ecclesiology.* Grand Rapids: Brazos, 2009.

Harrill, J. Albert. *Slaves in the New Testament: Literary, Social, and Moral Dimensions.* Minneapolis: Fortress, 2006.

Harrison, Brian W. "Restricted Inerrancy and the 'Hermeneutic of Discontinuity.'" *Letter & Spirit* 6 (2010): 225–46.

Harrison, Nonna Verna. *God's Many-Splendored Image: Theological Anthropology for Christian Formation.* Grand Rapids: Baker Academic, 2010.

Harrison, Ross. *Hobbes, Locke, and Confusion's Masterpiece: An Examination of Seventeenth-Century Political Philosophy.* Cambridge: Cambridge University Press, 2003.

Hart, David Bentley. *The Beauty of the Infinite: The Aesthetics of Christian Truth.* Grand Rapids: Eerdmans, 2003.

———. *The Doors of the Sea: Where Was God in the Tsunami?* Grand Rapids: Eerdmans, 2005.

———. *The Experience of God: Being, Consciousness, Bliss.* New Haven: Yale University Press, 2013.

Hart, Trevor. "Revelation." In *The Cambridge Companion to Karl Barth*, edited by John Webster, 37–56. Cambridge: Cambridge University Press, 2000.

Harte, Varity. "Plato's Metaphysics." In *The Oxford Handbook to Plato*, edited by Gail Fine, 191–216. Oxford: Oxford University Press, 2008.

Harvey, Van A. *The Historian and the Believer.* Philadelphia: Westminster, 1966.

Hatch, Nathan O. *The Democratization of American Christianity.* New Haven: Yale University Press, 1991.

Haught, John F. *The Revelation of God in History.* Wilmington, DE: Michael Glazier, 1988.

Hays, Richard B. *Echoes of Scripture in the Letters of Paul*. New Haven: Yale University Press, 1989.

———. *First Corinthians*. Louisville: Westminster John Knox, 1997.

———. "Reading Scripture in Light of the Resurrection." In *The Art of Reading Scripture*, edited by Ellen F. Davis and Richard B. Hays, 216–33. Grand Rapids: Eerdmans, 2003.

———. "What Is 'Real Participation in Christ'? A Dialogue with E. P. Sanders on Pauline Soteriology." In *Redefining First-Century Jewish and Christian Identities: Essays in Honor of Ed Parish Sanders*, edited by Fabian E. Udoh et al., 336–51. Notre Dame, IN: University of Notre Dame Press, 2008.

Healy, Mary. *The Gospel of Mark*. Grand Rapids: Baker Academic, 2008.

Healy, Nicholas J. *The Eschatology of Hans Urs von Balthasar: Being as Communion*. Oxford: Oxford University Press, 2005.

Healy, Nicholas J., and David L. Schindler. "For the Life of the World: Hans Urs von Balthasar on the Church as Eucharist." In Oakes and Moss, *Cambridge Companion to Hans Urs von Balthasar*, 51–63.

Hegel, G. W. F. *Lectures on the Philosophy of Religion*. Berkeley: University of California Press, 1988.

———. "The Positivity of the Christian Religion." Translated by T. M. Knox. In *On Christianity: Early Theological Writings*, 67–181. New York: Harper & Brothers, 1961.

Heil, John Paul. "Paul and the Believers of Western Asia." In *The Blackwell Companion to Paul*, edited by Stephen Westerholm, 79–82. Oxford: Blackwell, 2011.

Heim, Maximilian Heinrich. *Joseph Ratzinger: Life in the Church and Living Theology: Fundamentals of Ecclesiology with Reference to "Lumen Gentium."* Translated by Michael J. Miller. San Francisco: Ignatius Press, 2007.

Helm, Paul. *The Divine Revelation: The Basic Issues*. Vancouver: Regent College Publishing, 1982.

Helmer, Christine, and Christof Landmesser, eds. *One Scripture or Many? Canon from Biblical, Theological, and Philosophical Perspectives*. Oxford: Oxford University Press, 2004.

Hengel, Martin. *Acts and the History of Earliest Christianity*. Translated by John Bowden. Philadelphia: Fortress, 1980.

———. *The Johannine Question*. Translated by John Bowden. London: SCM, 1989.

———. *Saint Peter: The Underestimated Apostle*. Translated by Thomas H. Trapp. Grand Rapids: Eerdmans, 2010.

Hengel, Martin, and Roland Deines. *The Septuagint as Christian Scripture: Its Prehistory, and the Problem of Its Canon*. Translated by Mark E. Biddle. Grand Rapids: Baker Academic, 2002.

Heschel, Abraham Joshua. *Heavenly Torah: As Refracted through the Generations*. Edited and translated by Gordon Tucker and Leonard Levin. New York: Continuum, 2005.

————. *The Sabbath*. New York: Farrar, Straus and Giroux, 1951.

Hick, John. *The Metaphor of God Incarnate*. London: SCM, 1993.

Hillar, Marian. *From Logos to Trinity: The Evolution of Religious Beliefs from Pythagoras to Tertullian*. Cambridge: Cambridge University Press, 2012.

Hittinger, F. Russell. "The Declaration on Religious Freedom, *Dignitatis Humanae*." In Lamb and Levering, *Vatican II: Renewal*, 359–82.

Hobbes, Thomas. *Leviathan*. Edited by Edwin Curley. Indianapolis: Hackett, 1994.

Hobsbawm, Eric, and Terence Ranger, eds. *The Invention of Tradition*. Cambridge: Cambridge University Press, 1983.

Hoffmeier, James K. *Israel in Egypt: The Evidence for the Authenticity of the Exodus Tradition*. Oxford: Oxford University Press, 1996.

Holmes, Stephen. "Christology, Scripture, Divine Action and Hermeneutics." In *Christology and Scripture: Interdisciplinary Studies*, edited by Andrew T. Lincoln and Angus Paddison, 156–70. London: T&T Clark, 2007.

Höpfl, H., and B. Gut. *Introductio Generalis in Sacram Scripturam*. Rome: Arnado, 1950.

Hoskins, Paul M. *Jesus as the Fulfillment of the Temple in the Gospel of John*. Eugene, OR: Wipf and Stock, 2006.

————. *That Scripture Might Be Fulfilled: Typology and the Death of Christ*. Maitland, FL: Xulon Press, 2009.

Huizenga, Leroy A. *The New Isaac: Tradition and Intertextuality in the Gospel of Matthew*. Leiden: Brill, 2009.

Humphrey, Edith M. *Scripture and Tradition: What the Bible Really Says*. Grand Rapids: Baker Academic, 2013.

Hurtado, Larry W. *At the Origins of Christian Worship: The Context and Character of Earliest Christian Devotion*. Grand Rapids: Eerdmans, 1999.

————. *God in New Testament Theology*. Nashville: Abingdon, 2010.

————. *Lord Jesus Christ: Devotion to Jesus in Earliest Christianity*. Grand Rapids: Eerdmans, 2003.

Husbands, Mark, and Daniel J. Treier, eds. *The Community of the Word: Toward an Evangelical Ecclesiology*. Downers Grove, IL: IVP Academic, 2005.

Hütter, Reinhard. "Christian Unity and the Papal Office: On the Encyclical *Ut Unum Sint / That They May Be One*." In Reinhard Hütter, *Bound to Be Free: Evangelical Catholic Engagements in Ecclesiology, Ethics, and Ecumenism*, 185–93. Grand Rapids: Eerdmans, 2003.

Hütter, Reinhard, and Matthew Levering, eds. *Ressourcement Thomism: Sacred Doctrine, the Sacraments, and the Moral Life: Essays in Honor of Romanus Cessario, OP*. Washington, DC: Catholic University of America Press, 2010.

International Theological Commission. *The Interpretation of Dogma*. 1989. www .Vatican.va.

Janowski, Bernd, and Peter Stuhlmacher, eds. *The Suffering Servant: Isaiah 53 in Jewish and Christian Sources*. Translated by Daniel P. Bailey. Grand Rapids: Eerdmans, 2004.

Jeanrond, Werner. *Text and Interpretation as Categories of Theological Thinking*. Dublin: Gill and Macmillan, 1988.

Jenkins, Allan K., and Patrick Preston. *Biblical Scholarship and the Church: A Sixteenth-Century Crisis of Authority*. Aldershot: Ashgate, 2007.

Jenson, Robert W. *Canon and Creed*. Louisville: Westminster John Knox, 2010.

———. *Systematic Theology*. Vol. 1, *The Triune God*. Oxford: Oxford University Press, 1997.

John Paul II, Pope. *Address on the Pontifical Biblical Commission's "The Interpretation of the Bible in the Church."* April 23, 1993. www.Vatican.va.

———. *Adveniente millennio tertio*. 1994. www.Vatican.va.

———. *Novo Millennio Ineunte*. Translated by the Vatican. Boston: Pauline Books & Media, 2001.

———. *Redemptoris Missio*. In *The Encyclicals of John Paul II*, edited by J. Michael Miller, CSB, 436–96. Huntington, IN: Our Sunday Visitor, 2001.

———. *Ut Unum Sint*. In *The Encyclicals of John Paul II*, edited by J. Michael Miller, CSB, 782–831. Huntington, IN: Our Sunday Visitor, 2001.

Johnson, Luke Timothy. *The Acts of the Apostles*. Collegeville, MN: Liturgical Press, 1992.

———. *Among the Gentiles: Greco-Roman Religion and Christianity*. New Haven: Yale University Press, 2009.

———. *The Writings of the New Testament: An Interpretation*. Philadelphia: Fortress Press, 1986.

Jossua, Jean-Pierre, OP. "Immutabilité, progrès ou structurations multiples des doctrines chrétiennes?" *Revue des sciences philosophiques et théologiques* 52 (1968): 173–200.

Journet, Charles. *L'Église du Verbe Incarné: Essai de théologie speculative; Sa structure interne et son unité catholique (première partie)*. Saint-Maurice: Éditions Saint-Augustin, 1999.

———. *What Is Dogma?* Translated by Mark Pontifex, OSB. San Francisco: Ignatius Press, 2011.

Jüngel, Eberhard. "The Church as Sacrament?" In Eberhard Jüngel, *Theological Essays*, translated by J. B. Webster, 1:191–213. Edinburgh: T&T Clark, 1989.

Kadavil, Mathai. *The World as Sacrament: Sacramentality of Creation from the Perspectives of Leonardo Boff, Alexander Schmemann and Saint Ephrem*. Leuven: Peeters, 2005.

Kant, Immanuel. *Religion within the Limits of Reason Alone*. Translated by Theodore M. Greene and Hoyt H. Hudson. New York: Harper & Row, 1960.

Kaplan, Grant. *Answering the Enlightenment: The Catholic Recovery of Historical Revelation*. New York: Crossroad, 2006.

————, ed. and trans. *Faithfully Seeking Understanding: Selected Writings of Johannes Kuhn*. Washington, DC: Catholic University of America Press, 2009.

Kasper, Walter, ed. *The Petrine Ministry: Catholics and Orthodox in Dialogue*. Translated by the staff of the Pontifical Council for Promoting Christian Unity. New York: Paulist Press, 2006.

Kaufman, Gordon. *God, Mystery, Diversity: Christian Theology in a Pluralistic World*. Minneapolis: Fortress, 1996.

Kaveny, M. Cathleen. "Listening for the Future in the Voices of the Past: John T. Noonan, Jr., on Love and Power in Human History." *Journal of Law and Religion* 11 (1994–1995): 203–27.

Kemp, Kenneth W. "Science, Theology, and Monogenesis." *American Catholic Philosophical Quarterly* 85 (2011): 217–36.

Kenney, John Peter. *Mystical Monotheism: A Study in Ancient Platonic Theology*. Providence: Brown University Press, 1991.

Ker, Ian. Foreword to *An Essay on the Development of Christian Doctrine*, by John Henry Newman, xvii–xxvii. Notre Dame, IN: University of Notre Dame Press, 1989.

Ker, Ian, and Terrence Merrigan, eds. *The Cambridge Companion to John Henry Newman*. Cambridge: Cambridge University Press, 2009.

Kereszty, Roch, OCist. "The Eucharist and Mission in the Theology of Hans Urs von Balthasar." In Schindler, *Love Alone Is Credible*, 3–15.

Kerr, Fergus, OP. "If Jesus Knew He Was God, How Did It Work?" In *The Pope and Jesus of Nazareth: Christ, Scripture and the Church*, edited by Adrian Pabst and Angus Paddison, 50–67. London: SCM, 2009.

Kilby, Karen. *Balthasar: A (Very) Critical Introduction*. Grand Rapids: Eerdmans, 2012.

Kim, Seyoon. *The Origin of Paul's Gospel*. 2nd ed. Grand Rapids: Eerdmans, 1984.

Kimball, Dan. *The Emerging Church: Vintage Christianity for New Generations*. Grand Rapids: Zondervan, 2003.

King, Ross. *Machiavelli: Philosopher of Power*. New York: HarperCollins, 2007.

Kirk, J. R. Daniel. *Jesus Have I Loved, but Paul? A Narrative Approach to the Problem of Pauline Christianity*. Grand Rapids: Baker Academic, 2011.

————. *Unlocking Romans: Resurrection and the Justification of God*. Grand Rapids: Eerdmans, 2008.

Klawans, Jonathan. *Purity, Sacrifice, and the Temple: Symbolism and Supersessionism in the Study of Ancient Judaism*. Oxford: Oxford University Press, 2006.

Koenig, John. *The Feast of the World's Redemption: Eucharistic Origins and Christian Mission*. Harrisburg, PA: Trinity Press International, 2000.

Kolnai, Aurel. *Ethics, Value and Reality*. New Brunswick, NJ: Transaction, 2008.

————. *Privilege and Liberty, and Other Essays in Political Philosophy*. Edited by Daniel J. Mahoney. Lanham, MD: Lexington Books, 1999.

Komonchak, Joseph A. "Benedict XVI and the Interpretation of Vatican II." In Lacey and Oakley, *Crisis of Authority*, 93–110.

———. "Interpreting the Council and Its Consequences: Concluding Reflections." In *After Vatican II: Trajectories and Hermeneutics*, edited by James L. Heft, SM, and John O'Malley, SJ, 164–72. Grand Rapids: Eerdmans, 2012.

———. "The Local Realization of the Church." In Alberigo, Jossua, and Komonchak, *Reception of Vatican II*, 77–90.

Köstenberger, Andreas J., and Peter T. O'Brien. *Salvation to the Ends of the Earth: A Biblical Theology of Mission*. Downers Grove, IL: IVP Academic, 2001.

Kripke, Saul A. *Naming and Necessity*. Oxford: Blackwell, 1991.

———. *Reference and Existence: The John Locke Lectures*. Oxford: Oxford University Press, 2013.

Kugel, James L. *The God of Old: Inside the Lost World of the Bible*. New York: Free Press, 2003.

———. *How to Read the Bible: A Guide to Scripture, Then and Now*. New York: Free Press, 2007.

Küng, Hans. *The Church—Maintained in Truth: A Theological Meditation*. Translated by Edward Quinn. New York: Seabury, 1980.

Kuntz, J. Kenneth. *The Self-Revelation of God*. Philadelphia: Westminster, 1967.

La Bonnadière, Anne-Marie. "Did Augustine Use Jerome's Vulgate?" In *Augustine and the Bible*, edited and translated by Pamela Bright, 42–51. Notre Dame, IN: University of Notre Dame Press, 1999.

Lacey, Michael J. "Leo's Church and Our Own." In Lacey and Oakley, *Crisis of Authority*, 57–92.

Lacey, Michael J., and Francis Oakley, eds. *The Crisis of Authority in Catholic Modernity*. Oxford: Oxford University Press, 2011.

Lackey, Jennifer. *Learning from Words: Testimony as a Source of Knowledge*. Oxford: Oxford University Press, 2008.

LaCugna, Catherine Mowry. *God for Us: The Trinity and Christian Life*. New York: HarperCollins, 1993.

Lakeland, Paul. *The Liberation of the Laity: In Search of an Accountable Church*. New York: Continuum, 2003.

Lamb, Matthew L. "The Eschatology of St. Thomas Aquinas." In Matthew Lamb, *Eternity, Time, and the Life of Wisdom*, 55–72. Naples, FL: Sapientia Press, 2007.

———. "Political Theory and Enlightenment: Toward a Reconstruction of Dogma as Socially Critical." In Matthew Lamb, *Solidarity with Victims: Toward a Theology of Social Transformation*, 100–115. New York: Crossroad, 1982.

Lamb, Matthew L., and Matthew Levering, eds. *Vatican II: Renewal within Tradition*. Oxford: Oxford University Press, 2008.

Landmesser, Christof. "Interpretative Unity of the New Testament." Translated by Christine Helmer. In Helmer and Landmesser, *One Scripture or Many?*, 159–85.

Lange, Armin. "From Literature to Scripture: The Unity and Plurality of the Hebrew Scriptures in Light of the Qumran Library." In Helmer and Landmesser, *One Scripture or Many?*, 51–107.

Lash, Nicholas. *Change in Focus: A Study of Doctrinal Change and Continuity.* London: Sheed and Ward, 1973.

———. *Newman on Development: The Search for an Explanation in History.* Shepherdstown, WV: Patmos Press, 1975.

———. "Performing the Scriptures." In Nicholas Lash, *Theology on the Way to Emmaus,* 37–46. London: SCM, 1986.

Latourelle, René, SJ. *Theology of Revelation.* Staten Island, NY: Alba House, 1966.

Law, David. *Inspiration.* London: Continuum, 2001.

Le Donne, Anthony. *The Historiographical Jesus: Memory, Typology, and the Son of David.* Waco: Baylor University Press, 2009.

Legaspi, Michael C. *The Death of Scripture and the Rise of Biblical Studies.* Oxford: Oxford University Press, 2010.

Leithart, Peter J. *1 & 2 Kings.* Grand Rapids: Brazos, 2006.

———. *Deep Exegesis: The Mystery of Reading Scripture.* Waco: Baylor University Press, 2009.

———. *The Priesthood of the Plebs: A Theology of Baptism.* Eugene, OR: Wipf and Stock, 2003.

Lemche, Niels P. *The Israelites in History and Tradition.* Louisville: Westminster John Knox, 1998.

Leo X, Pope. *Exsurge Domine.* 1520.

Leo XIII, Pope. *Catholicae Ecclesiae.* 1890.

———. *In plurimus.* 1888.

———. *Providentissimus Deus.* 1893.

Léon-Dufour, Xavier, SJ. *Sharing the Eucharistic Bread: The Witness of the New Testament.* Translated by Matthew J. O'Connell. New York: Paulist Press, 1987.

Levenson, Jon D. *Creation and the Persistence of Evil: The Jewish Drama of Divine Omnipotence.* Princeton: Princeton University Press, 1994.

———. *Sinai and Zion: An Entry into the Jewish Bible.* San Francisco: Harper & Row, 1985.

Levering, Matthew. "Aquinas on Romans 8: Predestination in Context." In Levering and Dauphinais, *Reading Romans with St. Thomas Aquinas,* 196–215.

———. *The Betrayal of Charity: The Sins That Sabotage Divine Love.* Waco: Baylor University Press, 2011.

———. *Christ and the Catholic Priesthood: Ecclesial Hierarchy and the Pattern of the Trinity.* Chicago: Hillenbrand Books, 2010.

———. *Christ's Fulfillment of Torah and Temple: Salvation according to Thomas Aquinas.* Notre Dame, IN: University of Notre Dame Press, 2002.

———. "Christ, the Trinity, and Predestination: McCormack and Aquinas." In *Trinity and Election in Contemporary Theology,* edited by Michael T. Dempsey, 244–73. Grand Rapids: Eerdmans, 2011.

———. *Ezra and Nehemiah.* Grand Rapids: Brazos, 2007.

———. "God and Greek Philosophy in Contemporary Biblical Scholarship." *Journal of Theological Interpretation* 4 (2010): 169–85.

———. "The Inspiration of Scripture: A *Status Quaestionis*." *Letter & Spirit* 6 (2010): 281–314.

———. *Jesus and the Demise of Death: Resurrection, the Afterlife, and the Fate of Christians*. Waco: Baylor University Press, 2012.

———. *Jewish-Christian Dialogue and the Life of Wisdom: Engagements with the Theology of David Novak*. London: Continuum, 2010.

———. "Linear and Participatory History in Augustine's *City of God*." *Journal of Theological Interpretation* 5 (2011): 175–96.

———. *Mary's Bodily Assumption*. Notre Dame, IN: University of Notre Dame Press, forthcoming.

———. *Participatory Biblical Exegesis: A Theology of Biblical Interpretation*. Notre Dame, IN: University of Notre Dame Press, 2008.

———. "Pastoral Perspectives on the Church in the Modern World." In Lamb and Levering, *Vatican II: Renewal*, 165–83.

———. *Predestination: Biblical and Theological Paths*. Oxford: Oxford University Press, 2011.

———. "Readings on the Rock: Typological Exegesis in Contemporary Scholarship." *Modern Theology* 28 (2012): 707–31.

———. *Sacrifice and Community: Jewish Offering and Christian Eucharist*. Oxford: Blackwell, 2005.

———. "Scriptural and Sacramental Signs: Augustine's *Answer to Faustus*." *Letter & Spirit* 7 (2011): 91–118.

———. *Scripture and Metaphysics: Aquinas and the Renewal of Trinitarian Theology*. Oxford: Blackwell, 2004.

Levering, Matthew, and Michael Dauphinais, eds. *Reading Romans with St. Thomas Aquinas*. Washington, DC: Catholic University of America Press, 2012.

Levinson, Bernard M. *Deuteronomy and the Hermeneutics of Legal Innovation*. Oxford: Oxford University Press, 1997.

Lewis, C. S. "'Bulverism'; or, The Foundation of 20th Century Thought." In C. S. Lewis, *God in the Dock: Essays on Theology and Ethics*, edited by Walter Hooper, 271–77. Grand Rapids: Eerdmans, 1970.

Lindbeck, George A. *The Nature of Doctrine: Religion and Theology in a Postliberal Age*. Philadelphia: Westminster, 1984.

———. "The Problem of Doctrinal Development and Contemporary Protestant Theology." *Concilium* 1 (1967): 64–72.

Litfin, Bryan M. *Getting to Know the Church Fathers: An Evangelical Introduction*. Grand Rapids: Brazos, 2007.

Long, Steven A. *Analogia Entis: On the Analogy of Being, Metaphysics, and the Act of Faith*. Notre Dame, IN: University of Notre Dame Press, 2011.

Loughlin, Gerard. "*Nouvelle Théologie*: A Return to Modernism?" In Flynn and Murray, *Ressourcement*, 36–50.

Louth, Andrew. *Discerning the Mystery: An Essay on the Nature of Theology*. Oxford: Oxford University Press, 1983.

Lumen Gentium. In Flannery, *Conciliar and Post Conciliar Documents*, 350–426.

MacDonald, Margaret Y. *Colossians and Ephesians*. Collegeville, MN: Liturgical Press, 2000.

MacDonald, Nathan. *Deuteronomy and the Meaning of "Monotheism."* Tübingen: Mohr Siebeck, 2003.

MacDonald, Neil B. *Metaphysics and the God of Israel: Systematic Theology of the Old and New Testaments*. Grand Rapids: Baker Academic, 2006.

MacIntyre, Alasdair. *Dependent Rational Animals: Why Human Beings Need the Virtues*. Chicago: Open Court, 1999.

———. *First Principles, Final Ends and Contemporary Philosophical Issues*. Milwaukee: Marquette University Press, 1990.

———. *God, Philosophy, Universities: A Selective History of the Catholic Philosophical Tradition*. Lanham, MD: Rowman & Littlefield, 2009.

———. *Whose Justice? Which Rationality?* Notre Dame, IN: University of Notre Dame Press, 1988.

MacKinnon, Donald. "Some Reflections on Hans Urs von Balthasar's Christology with Special Reference to Theodramatik II/2 and III." In *The Analogy of Beauty: Essays for Hans Urs von Balthasar at Eighty*, edited by John Riches, 164–79. Edinburgh: T&T Clark, 1986.

Maier, Jean-Louis. *Les Missions divines selon saint Augustin*. Fribourg: Éditions Universitaires Fribourg Suisse, 1960.

Malherbe, Abraham J. *Paul and the Popular Philosophers*. Minneapolis: Fortress, 1989.

Mangina, Joseph L. *Revelation*. Grand Rapids: Brazos, 2010.

Mansini, Guy, OSB. "Can Humility and Obedience Be Trinitarian Realities?" In *Thomas Aquinas and Karl Barth: An Unofficial Protestant-Catholic Dialogue*, edited by Bruce L. McCormack and Thomas Joseph White, OP, 71–98. Grand Rapids: Eerdmans, 2013.

———. "Experience and Discourse, Revelation and Dogma in Catholic Modernism." Unpublished essay.

———. "Understanding St. Thomas on Christ's Immediate Knowledge of God." *The Thomist* 59 (1995): 91–124.

Marcel, Gabriel. *The Mystery of Being*. Vol. 1, *Reflection and Mystery*. Translated by G. S. Fraser. London: Harvill, 1950.

Marcus, Ralph. "Divine Names and Attributes in Hellenistic Jewish Literature." *Proceedings of the American Academy for Jewish Research* 3 (1931–1932): 43–120.

Márin-Sola, Francisco, OP. *L'Évolution homogène du dogme catholique*. 2 vols. Paris: Librairie Victor LeCoffre, 1924.

Marion, Jean-Luc. *In Excess: Studies of Saturated Phenomena*. Translated by R. Horner and V. Berraud. New York: Fordham University Press, 2004.

Maritain, Jacques. *On the Grace and Humanity of Jesus*. Translated by Joseph W. Evans. New York: Herder and Herder, 1969.

Markham, Ian S. *Truth and the Reality of God: An Essay in Natural Theology*. Edinburgh: T&T Clark, 1998.

Markschies, Christoph. "The Price of Monotheism: Some New Observations on a Current Debate about Late Antiquity." In Mitchell and Van Nuffelen, *One God*, 100–111.

Marshall, Bruce D. "Aquinas the Augustinian? On the Uses of Augustine in Aquinas's Trinitarian Theology." In Dauphinais, David, and Levering, *Aquinas the Augustinian*, 41–61.

———. "*Beatus vir*: Aquinas, Romans 4, and the Role of 'Reckoning' in Justification." In Levering and Dauphinais, *Reading Romans with St. Thomas Aquinas*, 216–37.

———. "*The Nature of Doctrine* after 25 Years." In George Lindbeck, *The Nature of Doctrine: Religion and Theology in a Postliberal Age: 25th Anniversary Edition*, vii–xxvii. Louisville: Westminster John Knox, 2009.

———. "The Unity of the Triune God: Reviving an Ancient Question." *The Thomist* 74 (2010): 1–32.

———. "What Does the Spirit Have to Do?" In Dauphinais and Levering, *Reading John with St. Thomas Aquinas*, 62–77.

Marshall, I. Howard. *Biblical Inspiration*. Grand Rapids: Eerdmans, 1982.

Martens, Peter W. "Origen against History? Reconsidering the Critique of Allegory." *Modern Theology* 28 (2012): 635–56.

———. *Origen and Scripture: The Contours of the Exegetical Life*. New York: Oxford University Press, 2012.

Martin, Dale B. "Paul and the Judaism/Hellenism Dichotomy: Toward a Social History of the Question." In Engberg-Pedersen, *Paul beyond the Judaism/Hellenism Divide*, 29–61.

Martin, Francis. "The Holiness of the Church: *Communio Sanctorum* and the Splendor of Truth." In *Sacred Scripture*, 157–77.

———. "Joseph Ratzinger, Benedict XVI, on Biblical Interpretation: Two Leading Principles." *Nova et Vetera* 5 (2007): 285–313.

———. "Literary Theory, Philosophy of History, and Exegesis." In *Sacred Scripture*, 21–41.

———. "Reading Scripture in the Catholic Tradition." In Colson and Neuhaus, *Your Word Is Truth*, 147–68.

———. "Revelation and Its Transmission." In Lamb and Levering, *Vatican II: Renewal*, 55–75.

———. *Sacred Scripture: The Disclosure of the Word*. Naples, FL: Sapientia Press, 2006.

———. "Some Aspects of Biblical Studies since Vatican II: The Contribution and Challenge of *Dei Verbum*." In *Sacred Scripture*, 227–47.

Martin, Ralph. *Will Many Be Saved? What Vatican II Actually Teaches and Its Implications for the New Evangelization*. Grand Rapids: Eerdmans, 2012.

Martinich, A. P. "The Bible and Protestantism in *Leviathan*." In *The Cambridge Companion to Hobbes's* Leviathan, edited by Patricia Springborg, 375–91. Cambridge: Cambridge University Press, 2007.

———. *The Two Gods of Leviathan*. Cambridge: Cambridge University Press, 1992.

Matera, Frank J. "The Jesus of Testimony: A Convergence of History and Theology." *Nova et Vetera* 6 (2008): 491–99.

———. *New Testament Ethics: The Legacies of Jesus and Paul*. Louisville: Westminster John Knox, 1996.

———. *New Testament Theology: Exploring Diversity and Unity*. Louisville: Westminster John Knox, 2007.

Matthews, Gareth B. "The Epistemology and Metaphysics of Socrates." In *The Oxford Handbook of Plato*, edited by Gail Fine, 114–38. Oxford: Oxford University Press, 2008.

McBrien, Richard P. *Do We Need the Church?* New York: Harper & Row, 1969.

McCall, Thomas. "On Understanding Scripture as the Word of God." In Crisp and Rea, *Analytic Theology*, 171–86.

McCarren, Gerald H. "Development of Doctrine." In Ker and Merrigan, *Cambridge Companion to John Henry Newman*, 118–36.

McCormack, Bruce L. "The Being of Holy Scripture Is in Its Becoming: Karl Barth in Conversation with American Evangelical Criticism." In *Evangelicals and Scripture: Tradition, Authority, and Hermeneutics*, edited by Vincent Bacote, Laura C. Miguelez, and Dennis E. Okholm, 55–75. Downers Grove, IL: InterVarsity, 2004.

McDonough, Sean M. *Christ as Creator: Origins of a New Testament Doctrine*. Oxford: Oxford University Press, 2009.

McGrath, Alister. *Christianity's Dangerous Idea: The Protestant Revolution—A History from the Sixteenth Century to the Twenty-First*. New York: HarperCollins, 2007.

McIntosh, Mark A. "Christology." In Oakes and Moss, *Cambridge Companion to Hans Urs von Balthasar*, 24–36. Cambridge: Cambridge University Press, 2004.

McKnight, Scot. *A Community Called Atonement*. Nashville: Abingdon, 2007.

———. *Jesus and His Death: Historiography, the Historical Jesus, and Atonement Theory*. Waco: Baylor University Press, 2005.

———. *The King Jesus Gospel: The Original Good News Revisited*. Grand Rapids: Zondervan, 2011.

———. *The Real Mary: Why Evangelical Christians Can Embrace the Mother of Jesus*. Brewster, MA: Paraclete, 2007.

Meade, David G. *Pseudepigraphy and Canon*. Grand Rapids: Eerdmans, 1987.

Meeks, Wayne A. "Judaism, Hellenism, and the Birth of Christianity." In Engberg-Pedersen, *Paul beyond the Judaism/Hellenism Divide*, 17–27.

———. "The Man from Heaven in Paul's Letter to the Philippians." In *The Future of Early Christianity: Essays in Honor of Helmut Koester*, edited by Birger A. Pearson et al., 329–36. Minneapolis: Fortress, 1991.

Merrigan, Terrence. *Clear Heads and Holy Hearts: The Religious and Theological Ideal of John Henry Newman*. Leuven: Peeters, 1991.

———. "The Image of the Word: Faith and Imagination in John Henry Newman and John Hick." In *Newman and the Word*, edited by Terrence Merrigan and Ian T. Ker, 5–47. Leuven: Peeters, 2000.

———. "Newman on Faith in the Trinity." In *Newman and Faith*, edited by Ian Ker and Terrence Merrigan, 93–116. Leuven: Peeters, 2004.

———. "'One Momentous Doctrine Which Enters into My Reasoning': The Unitive Function of Newman's Doctrine of Providence." *Downside Review* 108 (1990): 254–81.

———. "Revelation." In Ker and Merrigan, *Cambridge Companion to John Henry Newman*, 47–72.

Mettepenningen, Jürgen. *Nouvelle Théologie—New Theology: Inheritor of Modernism, Precursor of Vatican II*. London: T&T Clark, 2010.

———. "Truth, Orthodoxy and the *Nouvelle Théologie*: Truth as Issue in a 'Second Modernist Crisis' (1946–1950)." In Becking, *Orthodoxy, Liberalism, and Adaptation*, 149–82.

Mettinger, Tryggve N. D. *No Graven Image? Israelite Aniconism in Its Ancient Near Eastern Context*. Stockholm: Almqvist & Wiksell, 1995.

Meyendorff, John. *Catholicity and the Church*. Crestwood, NY: St. Vladimir's Seminary Press, 1983.

Middleton, Richard. *The Liberating Image: The Imago Dei in Genesis 1*. Grand Rapids: Brazos, 2005.

Miller, Patrick D. *The Religion of Ancient Israel*. Louisville: Westminster John Knox, 2000.

Mills, William C. *Church, World, and Kingdom: The Eucharistic Foundation of Alexander Schmemann's Pastoral Theology*. Chicago: Hillenbrand Books, 2013.

Mitchell, Stephen, and Peter Van Nuffelen, eds. *Monotheism between Pagans and Christians in Late Antiquity*. Leuven: Peeters, 2010.

———, eds. *One God: Pagan Monotheism in the Roman Empire*. Cambridge: Cambridge University Press, 2010.

Moberly, R. W. L. "Genesis 12:1–3: A Key to Interpreting the Old Testament?" In R. W. L. Moberly, *The Theology of the Book of Genesis*, 141–61. Cambridge: Cambridge University Press, 2009.

Moloney, Francis, SDB. "The Gospel of John as Scripture." *Catholic Biblical Quarterly* 67 (2005): 454–68.

Moltmann, Jürgen. *The Trinity and the Kingdom*. San Francisco: Harper, 1991.

Mongrain, Kevin. *The Systematic Thought of Hans Urs von Balthasar: An Irenaean Retrieval*. New York: Crossroad, 2002.

Montague, George T., SM. *First and Second Timothy, Titus*. Grand Rapids: Baker Academic, 2008.

Moran, Gabriel. *Theology of Revelation*. New York: Herder & Herder, 1966.

Morris, Leon. *The Gospel according to John*. Rev. ed. Grand Rapids: Eerdmans, 1995.

Morrow, Jeffrey L. "French Apocalyptic Messianism: Isaac La Peyrère and Political Biblical Criticism in the Seventeenth Century." *Toronto Journal of Theology* 27 (2011): 203–14.

Müller, Mogens. *The First Bible of the Church: A Plea for the Septuagint*. Sheffield: Sheffield Academic Press, 1996.

Murphy, Francesca Aran. *God Is Not a Story: Realism Revisited*. Oxford: Oxford University Press, 2007.

Nabert, Jean. *Le désir de Dieu*. Paris: Aubier-Montaigne, 1966.

Nasuti, Harry Peter. *Tradition History and the Psalms of Asaph*. Atlanta: Society of Biblical Literature, 1988.

Neusner, Jacob. *The Incarnation of God: The Character of Divinity in Formative Judaism*. Philadelphia: Fortress, 1988.

Newbigin, Lesslie. *One Body, One Gospel, One World*. London: International Missionary Council, 1958.

———. *The Open Secret: An Introduction to the Theology of Mission*. Rev. ed. Grand Rapids: Eerdmans, 1995.

———. *Trinitarian Doctrine for Today's Mission*. Carlisle, England: Paternoster, 1998.

Newman, Carey C. *Paul's Glory-Christology: Tradition and Rhetoric*. Leiden: Brill, 1992.

Newman, Elizabeth. *Untamed Hospitality: Welcoming God and Other Strangers*. Grand Rapids: Brazos, 2007.

Newman, John Henry. "Contracted Views in Religion." In John Henry Newman, *Parochial and Plain Sermons*, 545–51. San Francisco: Ignatius Press, 1987.

———. *An Essay in Aid of a Grammar of Assent*. Westminster, MD: Christian Classics, 1973.

———. *An Essay on the Development of Christian Doctrine*. Notre Dame, IN: University of Notre Dame Press, 1989.

———. *An Essay on the Development of Christian Doctrine*. Edited by J. M. Cameron. Harmondsworth: Pelican Books, 1974.

———. "On the Introduction of Rationalistic Principles into Revealed Religion." In *Essays Critical and Historical*, 1:30–101. New York: Longmans, Green, and Co., 1897.

———. "Private Judgment." In *Essays Critical and Historical*, 2:336–74. New York: Longmans, Green, and Co., 1895.

Neyrey, Jerome H. "'Without Beginning of Days or End of Life' (Heb. 7:3): Topos for a True Deity." *Catholic Biblical Quarterly* 53 (1991): 439–55.

Nichols, Aidan, OP. *From Newman to Congar: The Idea of Doctrinal Development from the Victorians to the Second Vatican Council*. Edinburgh: T&T Clark, 1990.

———. *No Bloodless Myth: A Guide through Balthasar's Dramatics*. Washington, DC: Catholic University of America Press, 2000.

———. "St. Thomas Aquinas on the Passion of Christ: A Reading of *Summa theologiae* IIIa, q. 46." *Scottish Journal of Theology* 43 (1990): 447–59.

———. "Thomism and the Nouvelle Théologie." *The Thomist* 64 (2000): 1–19.

———. *The Thought of Pope Benedict XVI: An Introduction to the Theology of Joseph Ratzinger*. 2nd ed. London: Burns & Oates, 2007.

Niebuhr, H. Richard. *The Meaning of Revelation*. New York: Macmillan, 1946.

Nietzsche, Friedrich. *Twilight of the Idols and The Anti-Christ*. Translated by R. J. Hollingdale. London: Penguin, 1990.

Noll, Mark A., and Carolyn Nystrom. *Is the Reformation Over? An Evangelical Assessment of Contemporary Roman Catholicism*. Grand Rapids: Baker Academic, 2005.

Noonan, John T., Jr. *A Church That Can and Cannot Change: The Development of Catholic Moral Teaching*. Notre Dame, IN: University of Notre Dame Press, 2005.

———. *Contraception: A History of Its Treatment by the Catholic Theologians and Canonists*. Enlarged ed. Cambridge, MA: Harvard University Press, 1986.

———. "Development in Moral Doctrine." *Theological Studies* 54 (1993): 662–77.

———. *The Scholastic Understanding of Usury*. Cambridge, MA: Harvard University Press, 1957.

Norris, Frederick W. "Of Thorns and Roses: The Logic of Belief in Gregory Nazianzen." *Church History* 53 (1984): 455–64.

Norris, Thomas J. "Faith." In Ker and Merrigan, *Cambridge Companion to John Henry Newman*, 73–97.

North, John. "Pagan Ritual and Monotheism." In Mitchell and Van Nuffelen, *One God*, 34–52.

Nostra Aetate. In Flannery, *Conciliar and Post Conciliar Documents*, 738–42.

Novak, David. *Natural Law in Judaism*. Cambridge: Cambridge University Press, 1998.

Oakes, Edward T., SJ. *Infinity Dwindled to Infancy: A Catholic and Evangelical Christology*. Grand Rapids: Eerdmans, 2011.

Oakes, Edward T., SJ, and David Moss, eds. *The Cambridge Companion to Hans Urs von Balthasar*. Cambridge: Cambridge University Press, 2004.

Oakley, Francis. "History and the Return of the Repressed in Catholic Modernity: The Dilemma Posed by Constance." In Lacey and Oakley, *Crisis of Authority*, 29–56.

Oberman, Heiko A. "Calvin's Legacy: Its Greatness and Limitations." In *Two Reformations*, 116–68.

———. "Toward the Recovery of the Historical Calvin." In *Two Reformations*, 97–105.

———. *The Two Reformations: The Journey from the Last Days to the New World*. Edited by Donald Weinstein. New Haven: Yale University Press, 2003.

———. "*Quo Vadis, Petre?* Tradition from Irenaeus to *Humani Generis*." In *The Dawn of the Reformation: Essays in Late Medieval and Early Reformation Thought*, 269–96. Grand Rapids: Eerdmans, 1992.

O'Collins, Gerald, SJ. *Fundamental Theology*. New York: Paulist Press, 1981.

———. *Rethinking Fundamental Theology: Toward a New Fundamental Theology*. Oxford: Oxford University Press, 2011.

———. *Retrieving Fundamental Theology*. New York: Paulist Press, 1993.

———. *Theology and Revelation*. Notre Dame, IN: Fides, 1968.

O'Daly, Gerald. *Augustine's "City of God": A Reader's Guide*. Oxford: Oxford University Press, 1999.

O'Grady, Selina. *And Man Created God: A History of the World at the Time of Jesus*. New York: St. Martin's, 2012.

O'Malley, John W., SJ. *Trent: What Happened at the Council*. Cambridge, MA: Harvard University Press, 2013.

———. *What Happened at Vatican II*. Cambridge, MA: Harvard University Press, 2008.

O'Neill, Colman, OP. "The Rule Theory of Doctrine and Propositional Truth." *The Thomist* 49 (1985): 417–42.

———. *Sacramental Realism: A General Theory of the Sacraments*. Chicago: Midwest Theological Forum, 1998.

Origen. *Homilies on Exodus*. In *Homilies on Genesis and Exodus*, translated by Ronald E. Heine, 227–387. Washington, DC: Catholic University of America Press, 1982.

———. *Homilies on Joshua*. Edited by Cynthia White. Translated by Barbara J. Bruce. Washington, DC: Catholic University of America Press, 2002.

———. *On First Principles*. Translated by G. W. Butterworth. Gloucester, MA: Peter Smith, 1973.

Osborne, Thomas M., Jr. "Unbelief and Sin in Thomas Aquinas and the Thomistic Tradition." *Nova et Vetera* 8 (2010): 613–26.

Ounsworth, Richard, OP. *Joshua Typology in the New Testament*. Tübingen: Mohr Siebeck, 2012.

Pamphilus. *Apology for Origen with the Letter of Rufinus on the Falsification of the Books of Origen*. Translated by Thomas P. Scheck. Washington, DC: Catholic University of America Press, 2010.

Pannenberg, Wolfhart, et al. *Revelation as History*. Translated by Edward Quinn. New York: Macmillan, 1968.

Pao, David W. *Acts and the Isaianic New Exodus*. Grand Rapids: Baker Academic, 2002.

Patton, Corinne. "Canon and Tradition: The Limits of the Old Testament in Scholastic Discussion." In *Theological Exegesis: Essays in Honor of Brevard S. Childs*, edited by Christopher Seitz and Kathryn Greene-McCreight, 75–95. Grand Rapids: Eerdmans, 1999.

Paul III, Pope. *Sublimis Deus*. 1537.

Paul VI, Pope. *Mysterium Fidei*. September 3, 1965.

Payton, James R., Jr. *Getting the Reformation Wrong: Correcting Some Misunderstandings*. Downers Grove, IL: IVP Academic, 2010.

Pelikan, Jaroslav. *Christianity and Classical Culture: The Metamorphosis of Natural Theology in the Christian Encounter with Hellenism*. New Haven: Yale University Press, 1993.

—. *The Christian Tradition: A History of the Development of Doctrine*. Vol. 1, *The Emergence of the Catholic Tradition (100–600)*. Chicago: University of Chicago Press, 1971.

—. *The Christian Tradition: A History of the Development of Doctrine*. Vol. 4, *Reformation of Church and Dogma (1300–1700)*. Chicago: University of Chicago Press, 1984.

—. *The Christian Tradition: A History of the Development of Doctrine*. Vol. 5, *Christian Doctrine and Modern Culture (Since 1700)*. Chicago: University of Chicago Press, 1989.

—. *The Vindication of Tradition*. New Haven: Yale University Press, 1984.

Perdue, Leo G. *Wisdom and Creation: The Theology of Wisdom Literature*. Nashville: Abingdon, 1994.

Perišić, Vladan. "Can Orthodox Theology Be Contextual?" *St. Vladimir's Theological Quarterly* 56 (2012): 399–413.

Perrin, Nicholas. *Jesus the Temple*. Grand Rapids: Baker Academic, 2010.

Perrin, Nicholas, and Richard B. Hays, eds. *Jesus, Paul and the People of God: A Theological Dialogue with N. T. Wright*. Downers Grove, IL: IVP Academic, 2011.

Philips, Gérard. *Carnets conciliaires de Mgr. Gérard Philips, Secrétaire adjoint de la Commission doctrinale*. Edited by Karim Schelkens. Leuven: Peeters, 2006.

Pieper, Josef. "Tradition: Its Sense and Aspiration." In Josef Pieper, *For the Love of Wisdom: Essays on the Nature of Philosophy*, edited by Berthold Wald, translated by Roger Wasserman, 233–94. San Francisco: Ignatius Press, 2006.

Pinckaers, Servais, OP. "Ethics and the Image of God." Translated by Mary Thomas Noble, OP. In Servais Pinckaers, OP, *The Pinckaers Reader: Renewing Thomistic Moral Theology*, edited by John Berkman and Craig Steven Titus, 130–43. Washington, DC: Catholic University of America Press, 2005.

Pink, Thomas. "The Interpretation of *Dignitatis Humanae*: A Reply to Martin Rhonheimer." *Nova et Vetera* 11 (2013): 77–121.

Pitre, Brant. "The Mystery of God's Word: Inspiration, Inerrancy, and the Interpretation of Scripture." *Letter & Spirit* 6 (2010): 47–66.

Pius XII, Pope. *Divino Afflante Spiritu*. 1943.

Plantinga, Alvin. *Warranted Christian Belief*. Oxford: Oxford University Press, 2000.

Plato. *The Collected Dialogues of Plato*. Edited by Edith Hamilton and Huntington Cairns. Princeton: Princeton University Press, 1961.

—. *Parmenides*. Translated by Michael Joyce and F. M. Cornford. In *Collected Dialogues*, 921–56.

—. *Republic*. Translated by Paul Shorey. In *Collected Dialogues*, 576–844.

—. *Symposium*. Translated by Michael Joyce. In *Collected Dialogues*, 527–74.

————. *Timaeus*. Translated by Benjamin Jowett. In *Collected Dialogues*, 1153–1211.

Plested, Marcus. *Orthodox Readings of Aquinas*. Oxford: Oxford University Press, 2012.

Popkin, Richard. *The History of Scepticism: From Savonarola to Bayle*. Revised and expanded ed. Oxford: Oxford University Press, 2003.

Porter, Stanley E. "The Portrait of Paul in Acts." In *The Blackwell Companion to Paul*, edited by Stephen Westerholm, 124–38. Oxford: Blackwell, 2011.

Portier, William L. "Edward Schillebeeckx as Critical Theorist: The Impact of Neo-Marxist Social Thought on His Recent Theology." *The Thomist* 48 (1984): 341–67.

Pottmeyer, Hermann J. "A New Phase in the Reception of Vatican II: Twenty Years of Interpretation of the Council." In Alberigo, Jossua, and Komonchak, *Reception of Vatican II*, 27–43.

Powell, Mark E. *Papal Infallibility: A Protestant Evaluation of an Ecumenical Issue*. Grand Rapids: Eerdmans, 2009.

Provan, Iain, V. Phillips Long, and Tremper Longman III. *A Biblical History of Israel*. Louisville: Westminster John Knox, 2003.

Puglisi, James, ed. *Petrine Ministry and the Unity of the Church*. Collegeville, MN: Liturgical Press, 1999.

Radde-Gallwitz, Andrew. *Basil of Caesarea, Gregory of Nyssa, and the Transformation of Divine Simplicity*. Oxford: Oxford University Press, 2009.

Rafferty, Oliver P., ed. *George Tyrrell and Catholic Modernism*. Dublin: Four Courts Press, 2010.

————. "Tyrrell's History and Theology: A Preliminary Survey." In *George Tyrrell and Catholic Modernism*, 21–37.

Rahner, Karl, SJ. *Inspiration in the Bible*. Translated by C. H. Henkey. New York: Herder, 1961.

————. "The Theology of the Symbol." In Karl Rahner, *Theological Investigations*, 4:221–52. London: Darton, Longman, and Todd, 1974.

————. *The Trinity*. Translated by Joseph Donceel. New York: Crossroad, 1998.

Rahner, Karl, SJ, and Joseph Ratzinger. *Revelation and Tradition*. New York: Herder and Herder, 1966.

Rasimus, Tuomas, Troels Engberg-Pedersen, and Ismo Dunderberg, eds. *Stoicism in Early Christianity*. Grand Rapids: Baker Academic, 2010.

Ratzinger, Joseph. "Biblical Interpretation in Conflict: On the Foundations and the Itinerary of Exegesis Today." In Granados, Granados, and Sánchez-Navarro, *Opening Up the Scriptures*, 1–29.

————. "Dogmatic Constitution on Divine Revelation: Origin and Background." Translated by William Glen-Doepel. In *Commentary on the Documents of Vatican II*, edited by Herbert Vorgrimler, 3:155–98. New York: Crossroad, 1989.

————. "Formal Principles of Catholicism." In *Principles of Catholic Theology*, 85–190.

————. *God's Word: Scripture—Tradition—Office*. Edited by Peter Hünermann and Thomas Söding. Translated by Henry Taylor. San Francisco: Ignatius Press, 2008.

————. *Gospel, Catechesis, Catechism: Sidelights on the Catechism of the Catholic Church*. San Francisco: Ignatius Press, 1997.

————. *Jesus of Nazareth: From the Baptism in the Jordan to the Transfiguration*. Translated by Adrian J. Walker. New York: Doubleday, 2007.

————. *Jesus of Nazareth: The Infancy Narratives*. Translated by Philip J. Whitmore. New York: Doubleday, 2012.

————. "The Key Question in the Catholic-Protestant Dispute: Tradition and *Successio Apostolica*." In *Principles of Catholic Theology*, 239–84.

————. *Offenbarungsverständnis und Geschichtstheologie Bonaventuras und Bonaventura-Studien*. Vol. 2 of *Gesammelte Schriften*. Edited by Gerhard Ludwig Müller. Freiburg: Herder, 2009.

————. "On the Status of the Church and Theology Today." In *Principles of Catholic Theology*, 367–93.

————. Preface to *Commentary on the Documents of Vatican II*, edited by Herbert Vorgrimler, 3:167–69. New York: Crossroad, 1989.

————. "Primacy, Episcopacy, and *Successio Apostolica*." In *God's Word*, 13–39.

————. *Principles of Catholic Theology: Building Stones for a Fundamental Theology*. Translated by Mary Frances McCarthy, SND. San Francisco: Ignatius Press, 1987.

————. "The Question of the Concept of Tradition: A Provisional Response." In *God's Word*, 41–89.

————. "Sacred Scripture in the Life of the Church." In *Commentary on the Documents of Vatican II*, edited by Herbert Vorgrimler, 3:262–72. New York: Crossroad, 1989.

————. *The Spirit of the Liturgy*. Translated by John Saward. San Francisco: Ignatius Press, 2000.

————. "The Spiritual Basis and Ecclesial Identity of Theology." In Joseph Ratzinger, *The Nature and Mission of Theology: Essays to Orient Theology in Today's Debates*, translated by Adrian Walker, 45–72. San Francisco: Ignatius Press, 1995.

————. *Theological Highlights of Vatican II*. Translated by Henry Traub, SJ, Gerard C. Thormann, and Werner Barzel. New York: Paulist Press, 1966.

————. *The Theology of History in St. Bonaventure*. Translated by Zachary Hayes, OFM. Chicago: Franciscan Herald Press, 1971.

————. "The Transmission of Divine Revelation." In *Commentary on the Documents of Vatican II*, edited by Herbert Vorgrimler, 3:181–98. New York: Crossroad, 1989.

Rauschenbusch, Walter. *"Christianity and the Social Crisis" in the 21st Century*. Edited by Paul Raushenbush. New York: HarperCollins, 2007.

Reese, J. M. *Hellenistic Influence on the Book of Wisdom and Its Consequences*. Rome: Biblical Institute Press, 1970.

Reid, Charles J., Jr. "The Fundamental Freedom: Judge John T. Noonan Jr.'s Historiography of Religious Liberty." *Marquette Law Review* 83 (1999): 367–433.

Reno, R. R. "Rahner the Restorationist." *First Things* 233 (May 2013): 45–51.

Rhonheimer, Martin. "Benedict XVI's 'Hermeneutic of Reform' and Religious Freedom." *Nova et Vetera* 9 (2011): 1029–54.

Richard of St. Victor. *On the Trinity* 6.14. In *Trinity and Creation: A Selection of Works of Hugh, Richard and Adam of St. Victor*, edited by Boyd Taylor Coolman and Dale M. Coulter, 333–34. Hyde Park, NY: New City Press, 2011.

Riches, John. "The Biblical Basis of Glory." In *The Beauty of Christ: An Introduction to the Theology of Hans Urs von Balthasar*, edited by Bede McGregor, OP, and Thomas Norris, 56–72. Edinburgh: T&T Clark, 1994.

Ricoeur, Paul. "Toward a Hermeneutic of the Idea of Revelation." In Paul Ricoeur, *Essays on Biblical Interpretation*, edited by Lewis S. Mudge, 73–118. Philadelphia: Fortress, 1980.

Riggs, Ann, Elizabeth A. Johnson, William L. Portier, and Roberto Goizueta. "Terrence W. Tilley's *Inventing Catholic Tradition*: Four Perspectives." *Horizons* 28 (2001): 105–19.

Rist, John M. "The Origin and Early Development of Episcopacy at Rome." In *What Is Truth? From the Academy to the Vatican*, 201–32. Cambridge: Cambridge University Press, 2008.

Robinson, Marilynne. "The Fate of Ideas: Moses." In *When I Was a Child I Read Books*, 95–124. New York: Farrar, Straus and Giroux, 2012.

Rombs, Ronnie. "Augustine on Christ." In *T & T Clark Companion to Augustine and Modern Theology*, edited by C. C. Pecknold and Tarmo Toom, 36–53. London: T&T Clark, 2013.

Rosenzweig, Franz. *The Star of Redemption.* Translated by Barbara E. Galli. Madison: University of Wisconsin Press, 2005.

Rousselot, Pierre, SJ. "Petite théorie du développement du dogme." *Recherches de science religieuse* 53 (1965): 355–90.

Rowe, C. Kavin. "Biblical Pressure and Trinitarian Hermeneutics." *Pro Ecclesia* 11 (2002): 295–312.

———. *Early Narrative Christology: The Lord in the Gospel of Luke.* New York: Walter de Gruyter, 2006.

———. "For Future Generations: Worshipping Jesus and the Integration of the Theological Disciplines." *Pro Ecclesia* 17 (2008): 186–209.

———. "God, Greek Philosophy, and the Bible: A Response to Matthew Levering." *Journal of Theological Interpretation* 5 (2011): 69–80.

———. *World Upside Down: Reading Acts in the Graeco-Roman Age.* Oxford: Oxford University Press, 2009.

Rowe, William V. "Adolf von Harnack and the Concept of Hellenization." In *Hellenization Revisited: Shaping a Christian Response within the Greco-Roman World*, edited by Wendy E. Helleman, 69–98. Lanham, MD: University Press of America, 1994.

Rowland, Tracey. *Ratzinger's Faith: The Theology of Pope Benedict XVI.* Oxford: Oxford University Press, 2008.

Ruether, Rosemary Radford, and Eugene C. Bianchi. Introduction to *A Democratic Catholic Church: The Reconstruction of Roman Catholicism*, edited by Eugene C. Bianchi and Rosemary Radford Ruether, 7–13. New York: Crossroad, 1993.

Ruggieri, Giuseppe. "Faith and History." In Alberigo, Jossua, and Komonchak, *Reception of Vatican II*, 91–114.

Rummel, Erika. *The Humanist-Scholastic Debate in the Renaissance and Reformation*. Cambridge, MA: Harvard University Press, 1995.

Rush, Ormond. *The Eyes of Faith: The Sense of the Faithful and the Church's Reception of Revelation*. Washington, DC: Catholic University of America Press, 2009.

Sailhamer, John H. *The Meaning of the Pentateuch: Revelation, Composition and Interpretation*. Downers Grove, IL: IVP Academic, 2009.

Sarisky, Darren. *Scriptural Interpretation: A Theological Exploration*. Oxford: Wiley-Blackwell, 2013.

Saward, John. "*L'Église a ravi son coeur*: Charles Journet and the Theologians of *Ressourcement* on the Personality of the Church." In Flynn and Murray, *Ressourcement*, 125–37.

Sawyer, John F. A. *The Fifth Gospel: Isaiah in the History of Christianity*. Cambridge: Cambridge University Press, 1996.

Schatz, Klaus, SJ. *Papal Primacy: From Its Origins to the Present*. Translated by John A. Otto and Linda M. Maloney. Collegeville, MN: Liturgical Press, 1996.

Scheffczyk, Leo. "Sacred Scripture: God's Word and the Church's Word." *Communio* 28 (2001): 26–41.

Schenk, Richard, OP. "*Officium Signa Temporum Perscrutandi*: New Encounters of Gospel and Culture in the Context of the New Evangelization." In *Called to Holiness and Communion: Vatican II on the Church*, edited by Steven Boguslawski, OP, and Robert Fastiggi, 69–105. Scranton, PA: University of Scranton Press, 2009.

————. "What Does the Trinity 'Add' to the Reality of the Covenants?" In Schindler, *Love Alone Is Credible*, 105–12.

Schillebeeckx, Edward, OP. *Church: The Human Story of God*. Translated by John Bowden. New York: Crossroad, 1993.

————. *God the Future of Man*. Translated by N. D. Smith. New York: Sheed and Ward, 1968.

————. "The New Critical Theory and Theological Hermeneutics." In Edward Schillebeeckx, *The Understanding of Faith: Interpretation and Criticism*, translated by N. D. Smith, 124–55. New York: Sheed and Ward, 1974.

————. *Revelation and Theology*. 2 vols. Translated by N. D. Smith. New York: Sheed and Ward, 1967.

————. *The Understanding of Faith: Interpretation and Criticism*. Translated by N. D. Smith. New York: Sheed and Ward, 1974.

Schindler, David L., ed. *Love Alone Is Credible: Hans Urs von Balthasar as Interpreter of the Catholic Tradition*. Grand Rapids: Eerdmans, 2008.

Schley, Donald G. *Shiloh: A Biblical City in Tradition and History*. Sheffield: Sheffield Academic Press, 1989.

Schmemann, Alexander. *For the Life of the World: Sacraments and Orthodoxy*. 2nd ed. Crestwood, NY: St. Vladimir's Seminary Press, 1973.

———. *Introduction to Liturgical Theology*. Translated by Asheleigh E. Moorehouse. Crestwood, NY: St. Vladimir's Seminary Press, 2003.

———. "The Liturgical Revival and the Orthodox Church." In *Liturgy and Tradition*, 101–14.

———. "Liturgy and Eschatology." In *Liturgy and Tradition*, 89–100.

———. "Liturgy and Theology." In *Liturgy and Tradition*, 49–68.

———. *Liturgy and Tradition: Theological Reflections of Alexander Schmemann*. Edited by Thomas Fisch. Crestwood, NY: St. Vladimir's Seminary Press, 1990.

———. *O Death, Where Is Thy Sting?* Crestwood, NY: St. Vladimir's Seminary Press, 2003.

———. "Symbols and Symbolism in the Byzantine Liturgy: Liturgical Symbols and Their Theological Interpretation." In *Liturgy and Tradition*, 115–28.

———. "Theology and Eucharist." In *Liturgy and Tradition*, 69–88.

Schmithals, Walter. *Der Römerbrief*. Gütersloh: Gerd Mohn, 1988.

Schnackenburg, Rudolf. *God's Rule and Kingdom*. Translated by John Murray. Edinburgh: Nelson, 1963.

Schniedewind, William M. *How the Bible Became a Book*. Cambridge: Cambridge University Press, 2004.

Scholder, Klaus. *The Birth of Modern Critical Theology: Origins and Problems of Biblical Criticism in the Seventeenth Century*. Translated by John Bowden. London: SCM, 1990.

Schönborn, Christoph. *God Sent His Son: A Contemporary Christology*. Translated by Henry Taylor. San Francisco: Ignatius Press, 2010.

Schreiner, Thomas R. *The King in His Beauty: A Biblical Theology of the Old and New Testaments*. Grand Rapids: Baker Academic, 2013.

Schwager, Raymund, SJ. *Jesus of Nazareth: How He Understood His Life*. Translated by James G. Williams. New York: Crossroad, 1998.

Schweitzer, Albert. *Paul and His Interpreters: A Critical History*. London: Black, 1912.

Sciglitano, Anthony C., Jr. "Pope Benedict XVI's *Jesus of Nazareth*: Agape and Logos." *Pro Ecclesia* 17 (2008): 159–85.

Scola, Angelo. "The Nuptial Mystery: A Perspective for Systematic Theology?" *Communio* 30 (2003): 209–34.

Segal, Alan F. *Paul the Convert: The Apostolate and Apostasy of Saul the Pharisee*. New Haven: Yale University Press, 1990.

Seitz, Christopher R. "Accordance: The Scriptures of Israel as Eyewitness." *Nova et Vetera* 6 (2008): 513–22.

———. *The Character of Christian Scripture: The Significance of a Two-Testament Bible*. Grand Rapids: Baker Academic, 2011.

————. *Prophecy and Hermeneutics: Toward a New Introduction to the Prophets.* Grand Rapids: Baker Academic, 2007.

Senior, Donald, CP. "The Gospels and the Eucharist." In *The Word Is Flesh and Blood: The Eucharist and Sacred Scripture,* edited by Vivian Boland, OP, and Thomas McCarthy, OP, 76–87. Dublin: Dominican Publications, 2012.

Sherwin, Michael, OP. "Christ the Teacher in St. Thomas's *Commentary on the Gospel of John.*" In Dauphinais and Levering, *Reading John with St. Thomas Aquinas,* 173–93.

Shinan, Avigdor, and Yair Zakovitch. *From Gods to God: How the Bible Debunked, Suppressed, or Changed Ancient Myths and Legends.* Translated by Valerie Zakovitch. Philadelphia: Jewish Publication Society, 2012.

Smith, D. Moody. "John: A Source for Jesus Research?" In *John, Jesus and History.* Vol. 1, *Critical Appraisals of Critical Views,* edited by Paul N. Anderson, Felix Just, SJ, and Tom Thatcher, 165–78. Leiden: Brill, 2007.

————. "When Did the Gospels Become Scripture?" *Journal of Biblical Literature* 119 (2000): 3–20.

Smith, James K. A. *The Fall of Interpretation: Philosophical Foundations for a Creational Hermeneutic.* Downers Grove, IL: InterVarsity, 2000.

Smith, Janet E. "The *Sensus Fidelium* and *Humanae Vitae.*" In Boguslawski and Fastiggi, *Called to Holiness and Communion,* 291–319.

Smith, Mark S. *The Early History of God: Yahweh and the Other Deities in Ancient Israel.* 2nd ed. Grand Rapids: Eerdmans, 2002.

————. *The Origins of Biblical Monotheism: Israel's Polytheistic Background and the Ugaritic Texts.* Oxford: Oxford University Press, 2001.

Smith, W. Cantwell. *What Is Scripture? A Comparative Approach.* London: SCM, 1993.

Sokolowski, Robert. *Eucharistic Presence: A Study in the Theology of Disclosure.* Washington, DC: Catholic University of America Press, 1994.

Sommer, Benjamin D. *The Bodies of God and the World of Ancient Israel.* Cambridge: Cambridge University Press, 2009.

————. "Unity and Plurality in Jewish Canons: The Case of the Oral and Written Torahs." In Helmer and Landmesser, *One Scripture or Many?,* 108–50.

Soskice, Janet Martin. "Athens and Jerusalem, Alexandria and Edessa: Is There a Metaphysics of Scripture?" *International Journal of Systematic Theology* 8 (2006): 149–62.

Sparks, Kenton L. *God's Word in Human Words: An Evangelical Appropriation of Critical Biblical Scholarship.* Grand Rapids: Baker Academic, 2008.

Springborg, Patricia. "Thomas Hobbes and Cardinal Bellarmine: *Leviathan* and the 'Ghost of the Roman Empire.'" *History of Political Thought* 16 (1995): 503–31.

Squires, John T. *The Plan of God in Luke-Acts.* Cambridge: Cambridge University Press, 1993.

Staniloae, Dumitru. *The Experience of God.* Edited and translated by Ioan Ionita and Robert Barringer. Brookline, MA: Holy Cross Orthodox Press, 1994.

Stanton, Graham N. *Jesus and Gospel*. Cambridge: Cambridge University Press, 2004.

———. *Jesus of Nazareth in New Testament Preaching*. Cambridge: Cambridge University Press, 1974.

Sternberg, Meir. *The Poetics of Biblical Narrative: Ideological Literature and the Drama of Reading*. Bloomington: Indiana University Press, 1985.

Stowers, Stanley K. "Does Pauline Christianity Resemble a Hellenistic Philosophy?" In Engberg-Pedersen, *Paul beyond the Judaism/Hellenism Divide*, 81–102.

Strauss, Mark L. *The Davidic Messiah in Luke-Acts: The Promise and Its Fulfillment in Lukan Christology*. Sheffield: Sheffield Academic Press, 1995.

Stuhlmacher, Peter, ed. *The Gospel and the Gospels*. Grand Rapids: Eerdmans, 1991.

———. "The Pauline Gospel." Translated by John Vriend. In *Gospel and the Gospels*, 149–72.

———. *Revisiting Paul's Doctrine of Justification: A Challenge to the New Perspective*. Translated by Daniel P. Bailey. Downers Grove, IL: InterVarsity, 2001.

———. "The Theme: The Gospel and the Gospels." Translated by John Vriend. In *Gospel and the Gospels*, 1–25.

Sullivan, Francis A., SJ. "Catholic Tradition and Traditions." In Lacey and Oakley, *Crisis of Authority*, 113–33.

———. "Infallibility." In Ker and Merrigan, *Cambridge Companion to John Henry Newman*, 156–69.

Surin, Kenneth. *The Turnings of Darkness and Light*. Cambridge: Cambridge University Press, 1989.

Swinburne, Richard. *Revelation: From Metaphor to Analogy*. Oxford: Oxford University Press, 1992.

Synave, Paul, OP, and Pierre Benoit, OP. *Prophecy and Inspiration: A Commentary on the Summa Theologica II–II, Questions 171–178*. Translated by Avery Dulles, SJ, and Thomas L. Sheridan, SJ. New York: Desclée, 1961.

Te Velde, Rudi A. *Aquinas on God: The "Divine Science" of the Summa theologiae*. London: Ashgate, 2006.

Thiel, John E. *Senses of Tradition: Continuity and Development in Catholic Faith*. Oxford: Oxford University Press, 2000.

Thiemann, Ronald F. *Revelation and Theology: The Gospel as Narrated Promise*. Notre Dame, IN: University of Notre Dame Press, 1985.

Thiselton, Anthony C. *The First Epistle to the Corinthians: A Commentary on the Greek Text*. Grand Rapids: Eerdmans, 2000.

Thomas Aquinas. *Commentary on Saint Paul's Epistle to the Galatians*. Translated by F. R. Larcher, OP. Albany, NY: Magi Books, 1966.

———. *Commentary on the Letter of Saint Paul to the Romans*. Edited by Jeremy Holmes and John Mortensen. Translated by Fabian Larcher, OP. Lander, WY: The Aquinas Institute for the Study of Sacred Doctrine, 2012.

————. *On the Power of God* (*Quaestiones disputatae de potentia Dei*). Translated by the English Dominican Fathers. Eugene, OR: Wipf and Stock, 2004.

————. *Summa theologiae*. Translated by the Fathers of the English Dominican Province. Westminster, MD: Christian Classics, 1981.

Thomassen, Einar. *The Spiritual Seed: The Church of the "Valentinians."* Leiden: Brill, 2006.

Thompson, Daniel Speed. *The Language of Dissent: Edward Schillebeeckx on the Crisis of Authority in the Catholic Church*. Notre Dame, IN: University of Notre Dame Press, 2003.

Thompson, James W. *Pastoral Ministry according to Paul: A Biblical Vision*. Grand Rapids: Baker Academic, 2006.

Tilley, Terrence W. *The Disciples' Jesus: Christology as Reconciling Practice*. Maryknoll, NY: Orbis Books, 2008.

————. *Inventing Catholic Tradition*. Maryknoll, NY: Orbis Books, 2000.

————. *Talking of God: An Introduction to Philosophical Analysis of Religious Language*. Mahwah, NJ: Paulist Press, 1978.

————. "Toward a Practice-Based Theory of Tradition." In *Tradition and Tradition Theories: An International Discussion*, edited by Torsten Larbig and Siegfried Wiedenhofer, 247–80. Berlin: LIT Verlag, 2006.

————. *The Wisdom of Religious Commitment*. Washington, DC: Georgetown University Press, 1995.

Tolstoy, Leo. *The Kingdom of God Is within You: Christianity Not as a Mystic Religion but as a New Theory of Life*. Translated by Constance Garnett. Rockville, MD: Wildside Press, 2006.

Torjesen, Karen Jo. *Hermeneutical Procedure and Theological Method in Origen's Exegesis*. Berlin: Walter de Gruyter, 1986.

Torrance, T. F. *The Trinitarian Faith: The Evangelical Theology of the Ancient Catholic Church*. Edinburgh: T&T Clark, 1988.

Torrell, Jean-Pierre, OP. *A Priestly People: Baptismal Priesthood and Priestly Ministry*. New York: Paulist Press, 2013.

Tracy, David. *The Analogical Imagination*. New York: Crossroad, 1981.

————. *Blessed Rage for Order: The New Pluralism in Theology*. New York: Seabury, 1975.

Troeltsch, Ernst. *The Christian Faith: Based on Lectures Delivered at the University of Heidelberg in 1912 and 1913*. Edited by Gertrud von le Fort. Translated by Garrett E. Paul. Minneapolis: Fortress, 1991.

————. "Christianity and the History of Religion." In *Religion in History*, 77–86.

————. "Faith and History." In *Religion in History*, 134–45.

————. *Religion in History*. Translated by James Luther Adams and Walter F. Bense. Minneapolis: Fortress, 1991.

————. "Rival Methods for the Study of Religion." In *Religion in History*, 73–76.

Tuohy, Séamus, OP. "Communion in the Supper of the Lamb." In Boland and Mc-Carthy, *Word Is Flesh and Blood*, 164–74.

Turner, Denys. *Faith, Reason and the Existence of God*. Cambridge: Cambridge University Press, 2004.

Turner, Max. *Power from on High: The Spirit in Israel's Restoration and Witness in Luke-Acts*. Sheffield: Sheffield Academic Press, 1996.

———. "The Spirit and Salvation in Luke Acts." In *The Holy Spirit and Christian Origins: Essays in Honor of James D. G. Dunn*, edited by Graham N. Stanton, Bruce W. Longenecker, and Stephen C. Barton, 103–16. Grand Rapids: Eerdmans, 2004.

Tyrrell, George. "Sabatier on the Vitality of Dogmas." In George Tyrrell, *The Faith of the Millions: A Selection of Past Essays*, 115–35. London: Longmans, Green, and Co., 1904.

———. *Through Scylla and Charybdis; or, The Old Theology and the New*. London: Longmans, Green, and Co., 1907.

Unitatis Redintegratio. In Flannery, *Conciliar and Post Conciliar Documents*, 452–70.

Ursinus, Zacharius. "Ursine's Hortatory Oration to the Study of Divinity, Together with the Manifold Use of Catechisme." In *The Summe of the Christian Religion, Delivered by Zacharius Ursinus . . . First Englished by D. Henry Parry*, 1–13. London, 1645.

Van der Toorn, Karel, ed. *The Image and the Book: Iconic Cult, Aniconism, and the Rise of Book Religion in Israel and the Ancient Near East*. Leuven: Peeters, 1997.

———. *Scribal Culture and the Making of the Hebrew Bible*. Cambridge, MA: Harvard University Press, 2007.

Vanhoozer, Kevin J. *The Drama of Doctrine: A Canonical-Linguistic Approach to Christian Theology*. Louisville: Westminster John Knox, 2005.

———. "A Person of the Book? Barth on Biblical Authority and Interpretation." In *Karl Barth and Evangelical Theology: Convergences and Divergences*, edited by Sung Wook Chung, 26–59. Grand Rapids: Baker Academic, 2006.

Vanhoye, Albert, SJ. "The Reception in the Church of the Dogmatic Constitution 'Dei Verbum.'" Translated by Sean Maher. In Granados, Granados, and Sánchez-Navarro, *Opening Up the Scriptures*, 104–25.

Van Nuffelen, Peter. "Pagan Monotheism as a Religious Phenomenon." In Mitchell and Van Nuffelen, *One God*, 1–33.

Vawter, Bruce. *Biblical Inspiration*. Philadelphia: Westminster, 1972.

Verhey, Allen. *Remembering Jesus: Christian Community, Scripture, and the Moral Life*. Grand Rapids: Eerdmans, 2005.

Vicedom, Georg F. *The Mission of God: An Introduction to a Theology of Mission*. Edited by Gilbert A. Thiele and Dennis Hilgendorf. St. Louis: Concordia, 1965.

Viviano, Benedict Thomas, OP. "The Normativity of Scripture and Tradition in Recent Catholic Theology." In Bockmuehl and Torrance, *Scripture's Doctrine and Theology's Bible*, 125–40.

Volf, Miroslav. *After Our Likeness: The Church as the Image of the Trinity*. Grand Rapids: Eerdmans, 1998.

―――. "A Common Word for a Common Future." In *A Common Word: Muslims and Christians on Loving God and Neighbor*, edited by Miroslav Volf, Ghazi bin Muhammad, and Melissa Yarrington, 18–27. Grand Rapids: Eerdmans, 2010.

Von Harnack, Adolf. *The History of Dogma*. 7 vols. Translated by Neil Buchanan. London: Williams & Norgate, 1894–1899.

―――. *Das Wesen des Christentums*. Gütersloh: Gütersloher Verlaghaus, 1999.

―――. *What Is Christianity?* Translated by Thomas Bailey Saunders. New York: Harper & Row, 1957.

Wagner, J. Ross. *Heralds of the Good News: Isaiah and Paul in Concert in the Letter to the Romans*. Leiden: Brill, 2003.

―――. "The Septuagint and the 'Search for the Christian Bible.'" In Bockmuehl and Torrance, *Scripture's Doctrine and Theology's Bible*, 17–28.

Wainwright, Geoffrey. "Ecumenical Dimensions of Lindbeck's 'Nature of Doctrine.'" *Modern Theology* 4 (1988): 121–32.

―――. *Lesslie Newbigin: A Theological Life*. New York: Oxford University Press, 2000.

―――. "A Remedy for Relativisim: The Cosmic, Historical, and Eschatological Dimensions of the Liturgy according to the Theologian Joseph Ratzinger." *Nova et Vetera* 5 (2007): 403–29.

Walatka, Todd. "Theological Exegesis: Hans Urs von Balthasar and the Figure of Moses." *Pro Ecclesia* 19 (2010): 300–317.

Waldstein, Michael. "The Mission of Jesus and the Disciples in John." *Communio* 17 (1990): 311–33.

Walgrave, Jan Hendrik, OP. *Newman the Theologian: The Nature of Belief and Doctrine as Exemplified in His Life and Works*. New York: Sheed and Ward, 1960.

―――. *Unfolding Revelation: The Nature of Doctrinal Development*. Philadelphia: Westminster, 1972.

Waltke, Bruce K. *The Book of Proverbs: Chapters 15–31*. Grand Rapids: Eerdmans, 2005.

Wannenwetsch, Bernd. *Political Worship*. Translated by Margaret Kohl. Oxford: Oxford University Press, 2004.

Ward, Keith. *Religion and Revelation: A Theology of Revelation in the World's Religions*. Oxford: Oxford University Press, 1994.

Watson, Francis. *Gospel Writing: A Canonical Perspective*. Grand Rapids: Eerdmans, 2013.

Webb, Stephen H. *Jesus Christ, Eternal God: Heavenly Flesh and the Metaphysics of Matter*. Oxford: Oxford University Press, 2012.

Webster, John. "Biblical Reasoning." In *Domain of the Word*, 115–32.

―――. *Confessing God: Essays in Christian Dogmatics II*. London: T&T Clark, 2005.

———. "The Dogmatic Location of the Canon." In *Word and Church: Essays in Christian Dogmatics*, 9–46. Edinburgh: T&T Clark, 2001.

———. "The Domain of the Word." In *Domain of the Word*, 3–31.

———. *The Domain of the Word: Scripture and Theological Reason*. London: T&T Clark, 2012.

———. "God and Conscience." In *Word and Church*, 233–62.

———. "Hermeneutics in Modern Theology: Some Doctrinal Reflections." In *Word and Church*, 47–86.

———. *Holiness*. Grand Rapids: Eerdmans, 2003.

———. *Holy Scripture: A Dogmatic Sketch*. Cambridge: Cambridge University Press, 2003.

———. "Illumination." In *Domain of the Word*, 50–64.

———. "On Evangelical Ecclesiology." In *Confessing God*, 153–93.

———. "On the Clarity of Holy Scripture." In *Confessing God*, 33–68.

———. "Perfection and Participation." In White, *Analogy of Being*, 379–94.

———. "Purity and Plenitude: Evangelical Reflections on Congar's *Tradition and Traditions*." In *Yves Congar: Theologian of the Church*, edited by Gabriel Flynn, 43–65. Leuven: Peeters, 2005.

———. "Rowan Williams on Scripture." In Bockmuehl and Torrance, *Scripture's Doctrine and Theology's Bible*, 105–23.

———. "The Self-Organizing Power of the Gospel of Christ: Episcopacy and Community Formation." In *Word and Church*, 191–210.

———. "Theological Theology." In *Confessing God*, 11–31.

———. "Theology and the Peace of the Church." In *Domain of the Word*, 150–70.

———. *Word and Church: Essays in Christian Dogmatics*. Edinburgh: T&T Clark, 2001.

Wegenast, K. *Das Verständnis der Tradition bei Paulus und in den Deuteropaulinen*. Neukirchen: Neukirchener, 1962.

Weinandy, Thomas G., OFM Cap. "Aquinas: God *IS* Man: The Marvel of the Incarnation." In Weinandy, Keating, and Yocum, *Aquinas on Doctrine: A Critical Introduction*, 67–89.

———. *Does God Change? The Word's Becoming in the Incarnation*. Still River, MA: St. Bede's Publications, 1985.

———. *Does God Suffer?* Notre Dame, IN: University of Notre Dame Press, 2000.

———. "The Human Acts of Christ and the Acts That Are the Sacraments." In Hütter and Levering, *Ressourcement Thomism*, 150–68.

Weinandy, Thomas G., OFM Cap., Daniel A. Keating, and John P. Yocum, eds. *Aquinas on Doctrine: A Critical Introduction*. London: T&T Clark, 2004.

Welch, Lawrence J. *The Presence of Christ in the Church: Explorations in Theology*. Ave Maria, FL: Sapientia Press, 2012.

344 *Bibliography*

Wenz, Armin. *Das Wort Gottes—Gericht und Rettung: Untersuchungen zur Autorität der Heiligen Schrift in Bekenntnis und Lehre der Kirche*. Göttingen: Vandenhoeck und Ruprecht, 1996.

White, Thomas Joseph, OP, ed. *The Analogy of Being: Invention of the Antichrist or the Wisdom of God?* Grand Rapids: Eerdmans, 2011.

———. "The Crucified Lord: Thomistic Reflections on the Communication of Idioms and the Theology of the Cross." In *Thomas Aquinas and Karl Barth: An Unofficial Protestant-Catholic Dialogue*, edited by Bruce L. McCormack and Thomas Joseph White, OP, 157–89. Grand Rapids: Eerdmans, 2013.

———. "Intra-trinitarian Obedience and Nicene-Chalcedonian Christology." *Nova et Vetera* 6 (2008): 377–402.

———. "Introduction: The *Analogia Entis* Controversy and Its Contemporary Significance." In White, *Analogy of Being*, 1–31.

———. "Kenoticism and the Divinity of Christ Crucified." *The Thomist* 75 (2011): 1–41.

———. "The Precarity of Wisdom: Modern Dominican Theology, Perspectivalism, and the Tasks of Reconstruction." In Hütter and Levering, *Ressourcement Thomism*, 92–123.

———. "Toward a Post-secular, Post-conciliar Thomistic Philosophy: *Wisdom in the Face of Modernity* and the Challenge of Contemporary Natural Theology." *Nova et Vetera* 10 (2012): 521–30.

Wicks, Jared, SJ. "*Dei Verbum* Developing: Vatican II's Revelation Doctrine, 1963–1964." In *The Convergence of Theology: A Festschrift Honoring Gerald O'Collins, SJ*, edited by Daniel Kendall, SJ, and Stephen T. Davis, 109–25. New York: Paulist Press, 2001.

———. "*Dei Verbum* under Revision, March–April 1964: Contributions of Charles Moeller and Other Belgian Theologians." In *The Belgian Contribution to the Second Vatican Council*, edited by Doris Donnelly et al., 460–94. Leuven: Peeters, 2008.

———. "Six Texts by Prof. Joseph Ratzinger as *Peritus* before and during Vatican Council II." *Gregorianum* 89 (2008): 233–311.

———. "Vatican II on Revelation—From behind the Scenes." *Theological Studies* 71 (2010): 637–50.

Wiles, Maurice. *The Making of Christian Doctrine: A Study in the Principles of Early Doctrinal Development*. Cambridge: Cambridge University Press, 1967.

Wilken, Robert Louis. *The Christians as the Romans Saw Them*. 2nd ed. New Haven: Yale University Press, 2003.

———. "Origen, Augustine, and Thomas: Interpreters of the Letter to the Romans." In Levering and Dauphinais, *Reading Romans with St. Thomas Aquinas*, 288–301.

———. *Remembering the Christian Past*. Grand Rapids: Eerdmans, 1995.

———. *The Spirit of Early Christian Thought: Seeking the Face of God*. New Haven: Yale University Press, 2003.

Williams, A. N. "Does 'God' Exist?" *Scottish Journal of Theology* 58 (2005): 468–84.

———. "The Future of the Past: The Contemporary Significance of the *Nouvelle Théologie*." *International Journal of Systematic Theology* 7 (2005): 347–61.

Williams, D. H. *Retrieving the Tradition and Renewing Evangelicalism: A Primer for Suspicious Protestants*. Grand Rapids: Eerdmans, 1999.

Williams, Megan Hale. *The Monk and the Book: Jerome and the Making of Christian Scholarship*. Chicago: University of Chicago Press, 2006.

Williams, Rowan. "Trinity and Revelation." In *On Christian Theology*, 131–47. Oxford: Blackwell, 2000.

Wills, Gary. *Papal Sin: Structures of Deceit*. New York: Image, 2001.

———. *Why I Am a Catholic*. New York: Mariner, 2003.

———. *Why Priests? A Failed Tradition*. New York: Penguin, 2013.

Winston, David. *The Wisdom of Solomon*. New York: Doubleday, 1979.

Wisse, Maartin. *Trinitarian Theology beyond Participation: Augustine's "De Trinitate" and Contemporary Theology*. London: T&T Clark, 2011.

Witherington, Ben, III. *Grace in Galatia: A Commentary on Paul's Letter to the Galatians*. Grand Rapids: Eerdmans, 1998.

———. *The Indelible Image: The Theological and Ethical Thought World of the New Testament*. Vol. 2, *The Collective Witness*. Downers Grove, IL: IVP Academic, 2010.

———. *Jesus the Sage: The Pilgrimage of Wisdom*. Minneapolis: Fortress Press, 1994.

Wolterstorff, Nicholas. *Divine Discourse: Philosophical Reflections on the Claim That God Speaks*. Cambridge: Cambridge University Press, 1995.

Woodbridge, John. "The Role of 'Tradition' in the Life and Thought of Twentieth-Century Evangelicals." In Colson and Neuhaus, *Your Word Is Truth*, 103–46.

Wooden, R. Glenn. "The Role of 'the Septuagint' in the Formation of the Biblical Canon." In *Exploring the Origins of the Bible: Canon Formation in Historical, Literary, and Theological Perspective*, edited by Craig A. Evans and Emanuel Tov, 129–46. Grand Rapids: Baker Academic, 2008.

Work, Telford. *Living and Active: Scripture in the Economy of Salvation*. Grand Rapids: Eerdmans, 2002.

Wright, Christopher J. H. *The Mission of God: Unlocking the Bible's Grand Narrative*. Downers Grove, IL: IVP Academic, 2006.

Wright, N. T. *The Challenge of Jesus: Rediscovering Who Jesus Was and Is*. Downers Grove, IL: InterVarsity Press, 1999.

———. *The Epistles of Paul to the Colossians and to Philemon: An Introduction and Commentary*. Grand Rapids: Eerdmans, 1986.

———. *Jesus and the Victory of God*. Minneapolis: Fortress, 1996.

———. *Justification: God's Plan and Paul's Vision*. Downers Grove, IL: IVP Academic, 2009.

———. *The Last Word: Beyond the Bible Wars to a New Understanding of the Authority of Scripture*. New York: HarperCollins, 2005.

——. *The Letter to the Romans: Introduction, Commentary, and Reflections.* In *The New Interpreter's Bible.* Vol. 10, *Acts, Romans, 1 Corinthians.* Nashville: Abingdon, 2002.

——. *The New Testament and the People of God.* Minneapolis: Fortress, 1992.

——. "Reading Paul, Thinking Scripture." In Bockmuehl and Torrance, *Scripture's Doctrine and Theology's Bible,* 59–71.

——. "Response to Richard Hays." In Perrin and Hays, *Jesus, Paul and the People of God,* 62–65.

——. *The Resurrection of the Son of God.* Minneapolis: Fortress, 2003.

——. *Surprised by Hope: Rethinking Heaven, the Resurrection, and the Mission of the Church.* New York: HarperCollins, 2008.

——. *What Saint Paul Really Said: Was Paul of Tarsus the Real Founder of Christianity?* Grand Rapids: Eerdmans, 1997.

——. "Whence and Whither Historical Jesus Studies in the Life of the Church?" In Perrin and Hays, *Jesus, Paul and the People of God,* 115–58.

Wright, William M., IV. "A 'New Synthesis': Joseph Ratzinger's *Jesus of Nazareth.*" *Nova et Vetera* 7 (2009): 35–66.

——. "Pre-Gospel Traditions and Post-critical Interpretation in Benedict XVI's *Jesus of Nazareth*: Volume 2." *Nova et Vetera* 10 (2012): 1015–27.

Yannoulatos, Anastasios. *Mission in Christ's Way: An Orthodox Understanding of Mission.* Brookline, MA: Holy Cross Orthodox Press, 2010.

Yeo, K. K. *Musing with Confucius and Paul: Toward a Chinese Christian Theology.* Cambridge: James Clarke & Co., 2008.

Yoder, John Howard. *For the Nations: Essays Public and Evangelical.* Grand Rapids: Eerdmans, 1997.

——. *The Jewish-Christian Schism Revisited.* Edited by Michael G. Cartwright and Peter Ochs. Grand Rapids: Eerdmans, 2003.

Young, Frances. *The Art of Performance: Towards a Theology of Holy Scripture.* London: Darton, Longman and Todd, 1993.

Young, Robin Darling. "A Soldier of the Great War: Henri de Lubac and the Patristic Sources for a Premodern Theology." In *After Vatican II: Trajectories and Hermeneutics,* edited by James L. Heft, SM, and John O'Malley, SJ, 134–63. Grand Rapids: Eerdmans, 2012.

Zuckert, Catherine H. *Plato's Philosophers: The Coherence of the Dialogues.* Chicago: University of Chicago Press, 2009.

Subject Index

Name Index

Aaron, 70, 72–73, 218n3
Abel, 18n60, 230
Abihu, 70
Abraham, 50n49, 52, 82, 116, 130, 218n3, 227, 230–31, 238, 269n70
Abraham, William, 20n66, 63, 152n40
Adam, 18n60, 116, 293
Albertz, Rainer, 278n89
Albright, William, 279n92
Alexander, Philip S., 273n77
Allen, Michael, 252n3
Allert, Craig D., 66n31
Allison, Dale C., Jr., 106n58, 110n68, 117n15, 143n14, 159n67, 220n10, 234–37
Alonso Schökel, Luis, 246n101, 247n105
Anatolios, Khaled, 30, 129n56, 177, 198, 204–11, 213–14
Ando, Clifford, 254n11
Anizor, Uche, 87n2, 88n2
Anselm of Canterbury, 190
Apollos, 106n57
Apuleius, 279n93
Aquinas, Thomas. See Thomas Aquinas
Aratus, 263–64
Aristobulus, 263–64, 277n84
Aristotle, 190, 251n3, 257–58, 267, 268n68
Arius, 198, 209
Arkes, Hadley, 156n57
Armstrong, John M., 265n57
Ashley, Benedict, 215n137
Ashton, John, 74n59
Assmann, Jan, 279n91
Astell, Ann W., 89n8

Athanasius, 184n34, 192n70, 206n112, 207n116
Athenagoras, 180–81
Atkinson, Joseph, 241n80
Augustine, 4, 25n84, 30–31, 39–40, 83n95, 93, 119, 127, 133n71, 193, 207n116, 218, 222, 228–32, 237, 241, 244–45, 254n11, 268, 291n28
Ayres, Lewis, 30, 38n9, 60n4, 62n13, 154n47, 177, 198–204, 206n112, 210, 213–14, 222n15, 245n98

Bacon, Francis, 95n34, 153n44
Balthasar, Hans Urs von, 4, 5n9, 28, 37, 43–49, 55–56, 149n30, 205n109, 236n66, 253, 260n31, 268–69, 298, 300
Barclay, John M. G., 254n11, 263n46, 268n68, 277n84, 278n88
Barnabas, 105, 133n69, 135
Baronio, Cardinal Cesare, 176n3
Barr, James, 59n2, 141n7, 229n42, 256n15, 259n25, 271n73, 272n74, 275n79, 276n82
Barth, Karl, 10, 20n68, 22n75, 25, 32n94, 62, 68n43, 95n33, 143n14, 150n31, 159n68, 251n3, 264n48, 281n101, 299n53
Bartholomew, Craig G., 51n54
Bartimaeus, 99–100
Barton, John, 218n3
Basilides, 224
Basil the Great, 181, 286n4
Bauckham, Richard, 2n6, 49n47, 74n59, 103n52, 218n3, 236, 244n95, 251–53
Baum, Gregory, 178n10, 186n42, 200n88
Baur, Ferdinand Christian, 255n14

355